THE WORLD IN MARCH 1939

SURVEY OF INTERNATIONAL AFFAIRS
1939–1946

The World in March 1939

EDITED BY

ARNOLD TOYNBEE

Director of Studies in the Royal Institute of International Affairs
Research Professor of International History
in the University of London
(Both on the Sir Daniel Stevenson Foundation)

AND

FRANK T. ASHTON-GWATKIN

'And the king shall do according to his will; and he
shall exalt himself, and magnify himself above every
god, and shall speak marvellous things against the
God of gods, and shall prosper till the indignation
be accomplished: for that that is determined shall
be done.' *Dan.* xi. 36

Issued under the auspices of the Royal Institute
of International Affairs

OXFORD UNIVERSITY PRESS

LONDON   NEW YORK   TORONTO

1952

Oxford University Press, Amen House, London E.C.4
GLASGOW NEW YORK TORONTO MELBOURNE WELLINGTON
BOMBAY CALCUTTA MADRAS CAPE TOWN
Geoffrey Cumberlege, Publisher to the University

PRINTED IN GREAT BRITAIN
AT THE UNIVERSITY PRESS, OXFORD
BY CHARLES BATEY, PRINTER TO THE UNIVERSITY

καὶ στρατηγεῖσθ᾽ ὑπ᾽ ἐκείνου, βεβούλευσθε δ᾽ οὐδὲν αὐτοὶ
συμφέρον περὶ τοῦ πολέμου, οὐδὲ πρὸ τῶν πραγμάτων
προορᾶτ᾽ οὐδέν, πρὶν ἂν ἢ γεγενημένον ἢ γιγνόμενόν τι
πύθησθε. ταῦτα δ᾽ ἴσως πρότερον μὲν ἐνῆν· νῦν δ᾽ ἐπ᾽ αὐτὴν ἥκει
τὴν ἀκμήν, ὥστ᾽ οὐκέτ᾽ ἐγχωρεῖ. δοκεῖ δέ μοι θεῶν τις, ὦ ἄνδρες
Ἀθηναῖοι, τοῖς γιγνομένοις ὑπὲρ τῆς πόλεως αἰσχυνόμενος τὴν
φιλοπραγμοσύνην ταύτην ἐμβαλεῖν Φιλίππῳ. εἰ γὰρ ἔχων ἃ
κατέστραπται καὶ προείληφεν ἡσυχίαν ἔχειν ἤθελε καὶ μηδὲν
ἔπραττεν ἔτι, ἀποχρῆν ἐνίοις ὑμῶν ἄν μοι δοκεῖ, ἐξ ὧν
αἰσχύνην καὶ ἀνανδρίαν καὶ πάντα τὰ αἴσχιστ᾽ ὠφληκότες ἂν
ἦμεν δημοσίᾳ· νῦν δ᾽ ἐπιχειρῶν ἀεί τινι καὶ τοῦ πλείονος
ὀρεγόμενος ἴσως ἂν ἐκκαλέσαιθ᾽ ὑμᾶς, εἴπερ μὴ παντάπασιν
ἀπεγνώκατε.

DEMOSTHENES, *First Philippic*, 41–2

You take your marching orders from him; you have never
made an adequate plan of campaign for yourselves; you do
not foresee any event—until you learn that something has
already happened or is actually happening. Hitherto perhaps
you have been able to get away with this; now things have
reached a major crisis and it is no longer possible. It seems
to me, Athenians, as if one of the gods, from shame at the
policy of our city, has put this aggressive appetite into Philip.
For if he wished to remain quiet in possession of what he has
already seized and snatched, and made no further move,
I think some of you would be satisfied with a state of affairs
which would have earned us as a people the reproach of shame,
cowardice, and utter disgrace. Now, by always attempting
something new and grasping after more, he may perhaps
provoke even you, if in fact you have not abdicated all moral
purpose.

THE PLAN OF THE BOOK

THIS book is an attempt to sketch, as an introduction to the history of the war of 1939–45 in the *Survey of International Affairs* series, the broad outlines and salient features of the international landscape that presented itself in March 1939 to the alert eyes of the aggressor Powers.

That date has been chosen for the present *tour du monde* because the German occupation of Bohemia and Moravia on the night of 14 March 1939 was, from many points of view, the true beginning of a Second World War that was formally begun by the German invasion of Poland on 1 September following. March 1939 marks a turning-point in history which offers an instructive field of vision to the student of international affairs who pauses here to look round him. Yet, even from this vantage point, it would be misleading to look round without also looking before and after; for, in a longer perspective, the choice of any precise date to mark the outbreak of war is an arbitrary distortion of the truth, though it may be a necessary convenience. The truth is that the world slid into the Second World War by degrees, and that this lamentable process was drawn out over a span of more than ten years. A creeping agony that, in the end, was to affect the whole world really began with Japan's opening of hostilities in Manchuria on 18 September 1931, and it was consummated only by Japan's attack on Pearl Harbour on 7 December 1941; for a war in which six out of the seven Great Powers of the day were already belligerents by this latter date did not become a world war in the full sense until it had likewise engulfed the United States of America.

The survey of the world in March 1939 that is attempted in this volume is divided, as will be seen, into three parts of unequal length. The international situation, as it stood at that date, is looked at first from a political and then from an economic angle of vision (Parts I and II), while the brief concluding section (Part III) sums up the unstable and already tottering balance of power and the ideological controversy in which it found expression.

The political survey (Part I) is subdivided on geographical lines drawn from the standpoint of the aggressor Powers. The first subdivision covers the world Powers whose interests and possessions were so widely distributed that they came within both Germany's and Japan's field of aggression. Great Britain, the United States, and the Soviet Union were indeed all eventually forced into war by the aggressors; and, when the moment came, all but one of the other Dominions of the British Crown decided to share Great Britain's fortunes, while a number of the Latin American members of the Pan American Union showed a corresponding sense of solidarity with the United States. In March 1939, however, none of these countries was yet in the front line; and, even after a war which had been aflame for eight years in the Far East took light in Europe as well, the two fields of international conflict did not merge with one another until the United States became a belligerent. In the international arena in March 1939, there were still two separate vortexes of international tension and conflict—one created by Japan and one created by Germany—and in this volume these are dealt with separately in two different subdivisions. Within each of these subdivisions, the countries, or groups of countries, in danger of being attacked are surveyed in an ascending order of their peril— starting with those at the outer limits of the regional aggressor's range of action, going on to those that found themselves within point-blank range of his batteries (psychological, diplomatic, and military), and concluding, in either subdivision, with a picture of the aggressor Power itself.

The economic survey (Part II) is focused on the Great Powers, and it has been found possible here to draw a broad picture without subdividing the map of the world in such detail as in the political panorama. This method seems capable of giving both a clearer and a more stereoscopic view than would a single reconnaissance, political and economic, country by country.

ARNOLD TOYNBEE

March 1951

Authorization has been obtained for all major quotations, and full reference to the book, the author, and the publisher has been given in each case in a footnote under the first mention of the work.

CONTENTS

PART I

A POLITICAL SURVEY

A. THE WORLD POWERS

CONTENTS
Part II

COMPARATIVE STRENGTH OF THE GREAT POWERS
By H. C. HILLMANN

CONTENTS

PART III

THE BALANCE OF POWER

MAPS

ABBREVIATIONS
USED IN CITING REFERENCES IN FOOTNOTES

Beloff, i, ii

Max Beloff: *The Foreign Policy of Soviet Russia 1929–1941*, 2 vols. (London, Oxford University Press for Royal Institute of International Affairs, 1947–9).

Birmingham Bureau: Memorandum no. 12

Birmingham Bureau of Research on Russian Economic Conditions: *Results of the Second Five-Year Plan and the Project of the Third Five-Year Plan*, Memorandum no. 12, July 1939.

Bonnet: *De Washington*

Georges Bonnet: *De Washington au Quai d'Orsay* (*Défense de la paix*, vol. i: Geneva, Bourquin, Éditions du Cheval Ailé, 1946).

Churchill: *Second World War*, i, ii, iii

Winston S. Churchill: *The Second World War*. Vol. i: *The Gathering Storm*; vol. ii: *Their Finest Hour*; vol. iii: *The Grand Alliance* (London, Cassell, 1948–50; Boston, Houghton Mifflin, 1948–50).

Ciano: *Diario (1937–8)*

Galeazzo Ciano: *1937–1938 Diario* (Bologna, Cappelli, 1948).

Ciano: *Diario (1939–43)*

Galeazzo Ciano: *Diario 1939 (–1943)*, 2 vols, 4th ed. (Milan, Rizzoli, 1947); *Ciano's Diary 1939–1943*, ed. Malcolm Muggeridge (London, Heinemann, 1947).

Ciano: *Europa*; Eng. version

L'Europa verso la catastrofe: 184 colloqui verbalizzati da Galeazzo Ciano (Milan, Mondadori, 1948); *Ciano's Diplomatic Papers*, ed. Malcolm Muggeridge, trans. Stuart Hood (London, Odhams Press, 1948).

Cmd. 6106

Great Britain, Foreign Office: *Documents concerning German-Polish Relations and the Outbreak of Hostilities between Great Britain and Germany on September 3, 1939*, Cmd. 6106 (London, H.M.S.O., 1939).

Cruttwell: *Peaceful Change*

C. R. M. F. Cruttwell: *A History of Peaceful Change in the Modern World* (London, Oxford University Press for Royal Institute of International Affairs, 1937).

D.Brit.F.P., 3rd series, i, ii, iii

Documents on British Foreign Policy 1919–1939, ed. E. L. Woodward and Rohan Butler. Third Series. Vols. i and ii: 1938; vol. iii: 1938–9 (London, H.M.S.O., 1949–50).

D.Ger.F.P., series D, i, ii.

Documents on German Foreign Policy, 1918–1945, from the Archives of the German Foreign Ministry, published jointly by the British Foreign Office and the U.S. Department of State. Series D (1937–45). Vol. i: *From Neurath to Ribbentrop (September 1937–September 1938)*; vol. ii: *Germany and Czechoslovakia (1937–1938)* (Washington, U.S.G.P.O. and London, H.M.S.O., 1949).

Documents . . . from the Archives of the German Ministry of Foreign Affairs, publ. by the U.S.S.R.

Ministry of Foreign Affairs of the U.S.S.R.: *Documents and Materials relating to the Eve of the Second World War from the Archives of the German Ministry of Foreign Affairs; vol. i, November 1937–1938* (Moscow, Foreign Languages Publishing House, 1948).

Documents (R.I.I.A.)

Documents on International Affairs for 1928–38, 13 vols.; for 1939–46, in progress (London, Oxford University Press for Royal Institute of International Affairs, 1929–).

Documents secrets (Eristov)

Documents secrets du Ministère des Affaires Étrangères d'Allemagne. Trans. from the Russian by Madeleine and Michel Eristov. Vol. i: *Turquie*; vol. ii: *Hongrie*; vol. iii: *Espagne* (Paris, Éditions Paul Dupont, 1946–7).

Dokumente der Deutschen Politik	*Dokumente der Deutschen Politik 1933–1939* initiated by the Deutsche Hochschule für Politik and continued by the Deutsches Auslandswissenschaftliches Institut. 7 vols. (Berlin, Junker and Dünnhaupt, 1935–40).
Donosti: *Mussolini*	Mario Donosti, pseud.: *Mussolini e l'Europa* (Rome, Edizioni Leonardo, 1945).
Feiling: *Chamberlain*	Keith Feiling: *The Life of Neville Chamberlain* (London, Macmillan, 1947).
Gafencu: *Derniers Jours*	Grigore Gafencu: *Les Derniers Jours de l'Europe: un voyage diplomatique en 1939*. Revised ed. (Paris, Egloff, 1947); *The Last Days of Europe*, trans. Fletcher Allen (London, Muller, 1947).
Gooch and Temperley	*British Documents on the Origins of the War 1898–1914*, ed. G. P. Gooch and Harold Temperley. 13 vols. (London, H.M.S.O., 1926–38).
H.P.C.	*A History of the Peace Conference of Paris*, ed. H. W. V. Temperley. 6 vols. (London, Oxford University Press for British Institute of International Affairs, 1920–4).
Hitler: *Speeches* (Baynes)	*The Speeches of Adolf Hitler, April 1922–August 1939*, trans. and ed. N. H. Baynes, 2 vols. (London, Oxford University Press for Royal Institute of International Affairs, 1942).
I.M.T. Nuremberg	*Trial of the Major War Criminals before the International Military Tribunal, Nuremberg, 1945–1946*. Proceedings and documents in evidence. 42 vols. (Nuremberg, International Military Tribunal, 1947–9).
Livre jaune français	France, Ministère des Affaires Étrangères: *Le Livre jaune français. Documents diplomatiques 1938–1939. Pièces relatives aux événements et aux négociations qui ont précédé l'ouverture des hostilités entre l'Allemagne d'une part, la Pologne, la Grande-Bretagne et la France d'autre part* (Paris, Imprimerie Nationale, 1939).
Macmillan Report	Great Britain, Treasury: *Committee on Finance and Industry: Report*, Cmd. 3897 (London, H.M.S.O., 1931).
Mein Kampf; tr. Murphy	Adolf Hitler: *Mein Kampf*, 2 vols. in 1, 305th–306th ed. (Munich, NSDAP, 1938); *Mein Kampf*, trans. James Murphy, 2 vols. in 1 (London, Hurst & Blackett, 1939).
Nazi-Soviet Relations	U.S. Department of State: *Nazi-Soviet Relations 1939–1941: Documents from the Archives of the German Foreign Office*, ed. R. J. Sontag and J. S. Beddie. Dept. of State Publication 3023 (Washington, U.S.G.P.O., 1948).
N.C.A.	*Nazi Conspiracy and Aggression*. (A collection of documentary evidence and guide materials prepared by the American and British prosecuting staffs for . . . the International Military Tribunal at Nürnberg.) 8 vols. with 'Opinion and Judgement' and Supplements A and B (Washington, U.S.G.P.O., 1946–7).
Polish White Book	Poland, Ministry for Foreign Affairs: *Official Documents concerning Polish-Soviet Relations 1933–1939* (Polish White Book). [Translated and] published by Authority of the Polish Government (London, Hutchinson, [1940]).
Spanish Government	U.S. Department of State: *The Spanish Government and the Axis: Documents*, Dept. of State Publication 2483 (Washington, U.S.G.P.O., 1946).
Toynbee: *Study*	Arnold J. Toynbee: *A Study of History*, vols. i–iii, 2nd ed. (London, Oxford University Press for Royal Institute of International Affairs, 1935), vols. iv–vi (London, Oxford University Press for Royal Institute of International Affairs, 1939).

NOTE

British Parliamentary Debates (Hansard) are cited in the form suggested in the bound volumes of the Official Reports, preceded by the date (if not given above in the text) and followed by the column number, e.g.

(for the House of Commons)
  28 September 1938, H.C.Deb. 5th ser., vol. 339, col. 12;

(for the House of Lords)
  16 March 1938, H.L.Deb. 5th ser., vol. 108, coll. 182–3.

PART I

A POLITICAL SURVEY

A. THE WORLD POWERS

(i) The Western Hemisphere
By Arnold Toynbee

(a) THE ATTITUDE OF THE AMERICAN PUBLIC TOWARDS FOREIGN AFFAIRS DURING THE INTER-WAR YEARS

ON 15 March 1939 the least imminently threatened region of the world was the Western Hemisphere, and one of the least apprehensive countries within that region was the United States. At the same time, the relative security which the United States then still possessed in fact was much less substantial than the majority of her citizens imagined it to be—as was borne in upon Americans in the mass when, in the summer of 1940, they suddenly found themselves confronting a Third Reich with all the resources of continental Europe at her command, and with no European Power, save Great Britain alone, still standing in the fighting line between a triumphant Germany and an unprepared America.

In the spring of 1939, however, it had not yet become apparent to the American people that, in geopolitical terms, as a result of recent and fast accelerating advances in the conquest of space and time by human technique, the Atlantic was now rapidly shrinking to the former dimensions of the English Channel, and the Straits of Dakar, between the westward bulge of Africa and the eastward bulge of Brazil, to those of the Straits of Dover. American feeling and policy were then still governed by past facts which had already become partly or wholly irrelevant to the international situation in which the United States was now actually placed.

Perhaps the most powerful of these influences from the past was the fact that over 9 per cent. of the living generation of white inhabitants of the United States,[1] and the ancestors of all of them no longer ago, at the earliest, than ten or twelve generations back, had, at some particular moment, deliberately pulled up their roots from ancestral ground in Europe and had crossed the Atlantic in order to start, on the American side of it, a new life free from the unhappy elements in their European heritage. This epoch-making new departure in their personal family back-

---

[1] In 1940 the total population of the United States numbered 131,669,275 persons, of whom 11,419,138 were foreign-born.

ground was an experience, or tradition, that was common to all Americans of whatever local European origin and whatever the date at which they or their forebears had landed on American shores. The magnet which had drawn them had been the hope of finding a 'promised land', insulated by Ocean Stream from the wilderness of Europe from which they had managed to break their way out; and, in general, their original expectations had been more than fully realized. As it had been opened up, stage by stage, from coast to coast, the North American continent had proved to be stocked with natural resources beyond the dreams of the first settlers and early pioneers, and at the same time the young American nation had seemed to be succeeding in its political aim of tapping, developing, and enjoying this new-found wealth undisturbed by the power politics of the Old World. The achievement of independence from Great Britain, the subsequent disappearance of French and Spanish rule from the Americas, and the steady rise in the strength of the United States to a level at which it could deal on equal terms with the greatest Powers in Europe, had apparently been successive stages in realizing Washington's ideal of avoiding European entanglements. This history had made Americans more conscious of national well-being and privilege than of national power and responsibility, and they had been correspondingly exasperated to find, through becoming involved in the First World War, that the mastery of their peculiarly favourable situation, to which they felt themselves to have earned a right, was not, after all, secure.[1]

Under the spur of this exasperation, the first American reaction had been vehemently to reject the suggestion that their involvement in the First World War might be the consequence of any deep change in the secular flow of world history; and they had therefore been unwilling to take this unwelcome experience as evidence of an enduring fact that it was beyond their power to conjure away or as the presentation of a standing challenge that must be met by some radical change in long-term policy. The lead in favour of such a change which President Wilson had given in promoting the establishment of a League of Nations had been repudiated by his countrymen when they refused to make the United States a member of a new international institution that was so largely American in inspira-

---

[1] This American state of mind, between the years 1914 and 1939, was comprehensible to contemporary English observers who had themselves inherited an expectation of continuing to enjoy a privileged position of insular security bequeathed to them by ancestors who had emigrated from continental Europe. During the thirty-five years that had elapsed between the outbreak of war in 1914 and the time of writing of the present chapter, the English themselves had been finding it difficult enough to adjust themselves to the loss of their former relative immunity from the changes to which the continental peoples were exposed. Yet the psychological difficulty for most English people was not so great as it was for all Americans. Except for a few descendants of seventeenth-century Huguenot refugees, the English in 1951 were not the offspring of people who had come from the Continent in recent times with the deliberate intention of shaking themselves free from continental troubles.

tion. Few of them realized at the time that, in taking this decision, they were not severing the new entangling tentacles that Europe had un-expectedly cast round them since 1914, but, on the contrary, were con-demning their country to play a leading part in a second and more terrible general war hardly more than twenty years later.

This did not strike many Americans at the time as a serious possibility, while on the other hand many of them had made up their minds to believe that their participation in the general war from which they had just emerged had been gratuitous, inexpedient, and uncalled-for, and had only been brought about by causes that—if they were the true and sole causes—were unquestionably public scandals. Among the causes can-vassed in the forum of American public opinion during the inter-war years,[1] the obvious repercussions of German militarism in an ever more closely interwoven world did not figure prominently—partly, no doubt, because Germany, as the defeated party, was temporarily out of the pic-ture, and partly also, perhaps, because to have admitted such a cause as that would have been to give away the very case that a majority of the American people were eager to make. The alleged causes that were given prominence by Americans who held these views were the misguided idealism of President Wilson; the arts of European (meaning Allied, and mainly British) diplomacy, which in the United States was traditionally supposed to be always more than a match for American wits; and the unpatriotic self-seeking of American manufacturers and bankers, who had speculatively supplied and financed the Allies, and had then lobbied the Administration into war in order to save their private fortunes by securing victory for their debtors. The conclusion from this reconstruction of the story of the involvement of the United States was that the American people had been manœuvred into the First World War; that this had been an avoidable disaster; and that measures could and should be taken to prevent this deplorable piece of history from ever repeating itself.

This American resolve was strengthened by American disillusionment over the post-war policy of the European victors. These would not re-nounce the terms of the secret treaties which, without the assent or, indeed, the official knowledge of the United States, they had made with one another during the war, for dividing the spoils of victory; they would not disarm; and, last but not least, they would not repay their debts to the United States Treasury (though they did repay their debts to private American financiers).

This debate in the United States on recent history and future policy in the sphere of foreign affairs had begun soon after the close of hostilities and

[1] See the *Survey of International Affairs, 1938* (London, Oxford University Press for Royal Insti-tute of International Affairs, 1941), i. 575–80. (Hereafter this series will be referred to as *Survey* for [year].)

had at once precipitated a bitter conflict in the arena of American domestic politics. The translation into these domestic terms of an international issue which was proved by the sequel to be really one of life and death for the United States shows how little the experience of the First World War had shaken the American people's traditional sense of being secure against external dangers, or curbed their traditional tendency—which followed from this—to deal with foreign affairs, if at all, as mere points in the old and intricate game of politics on the home front. The personal quarrel between a Democratic President Wilson and the Republican majority in the Congress of the day, which was the immediate occasion of the Senate's refusal to ratify the Peace Treaty of Versailles, including the Covenant of the League of Nations, masked a secular antagonism between the President and the Senate, springing from the absence of provisions for co-ordinating the powers assigned to them respectively in the Constitution; and in 1939 this constitutional mechanism of 'check and balance', longer-lived than individual lives and independent of personal idiosyncrasies, was one of the principal considerations in the attitude of the Senate of that day towards their dealings with President Franklin D. Roosevelt over legislation designed to safeguard the interests of the United States in regard to the undeclared war then already being waged between Japan and China and the threatened war between Nazi Germany and Great Britain and France.[1] In 1939 Congress was determined to safeguard the United States, as far as this could be done by legislation at Washington, from being involved in war again, though, subject to this prior and overriding aim, they were in agreement with the President in not wanting to take action that might have the incidental effect of weighting the scales in favour of an aggressor to the detriment of his victims. But these purposes in the minds of senators were cut across and confused by an anxiety not to enact anything—even in pursuit of these purposes—that would increase the President's prerogative by enlarging the field of his freedom to act on his own discretion.[2]

Another point at which foreign affairs impinged on domestic politics was the sentimental interest taken by certain groups of 'hyphenated' Americans—retrospectively and from a comfortable distance off—in the fortunes of their countries or communities of origin, for some of these groups happened to command blocks of votes which counted for much in the nice calculations of American party politics. They did not go to the length of advocating any active intervention on the part of the United States on behalf of the European countries whose cause they championed, for that was not practical politics and was indeed in many cases contrary to their own inclinations as partially acclimatized Americans; but they

[1] See *Survey* for 1938, i. 642–50.
[2] This will be further dealt with in later volumes of the *Survey* for 1939–46.

did effectively further their former countries' cause by campaigning against any suggestion for intervention on behalf of these countries' European enemies, in the telling role of watch-dogs jealously on guard over the traditional American policy of non-intervention in European affairs. It is true that both the Irish-American and the German-American lobby, which had been in the forefront during the First World War, had lost some of their former influence: the Irish-Americans because the wind had been taken out of their sails by the emergence of an Eire which appeared to the American public in general to be a substantial realization of legitimate Irish national aspirations; the German-Americans partly because the passage of another quarter of a century had carried the process of their assimilation a long way forward, and partly because the recent and small but vociferous Nazi-minded minority among them had defeated its own aims by the truculence of its propaganda. On the other hand, a section of the Jewish-Americans were already beginning to take over from the Irish-Americans the role, seldom vacant in the American political circus, of principal blackener of the British lion's face.

During the increasingly critical last ten years before the outbreak of the Second World War, the domestic affairs of the United States cut across her foreign policy in yet a third way: the 'break on Wall Street' in the autumn of 1929[1] plunged the American people into an economic crisis at home which preoccupied millions of individual citizens with acute personal distresses and anxieties, and, before the depression itself had begun to lift, the measures introduced by the Roosevelt Administration for combating it—amounting, as these did, to a minor social revolution comparable to those through which some of the Western European countries had been passing during the preceding quarter of a century—became a subject of bitter domestic political controversy under the name of 'the New Deal'.[2] This absorption of the people of the United States in contentious domestic issues at a time when momentous events, involving their destiny, were taking place in the arena of international affairs, seems less surprising when we recall the similar absorption of the French people in their far more dangerously exposed geographical and political position, during the crucial years 1936–9, in the battle for and against the domestic programme of the Front Populaire.[3] Another point of American domestic politics that was having an effect in the international field by March 1939 was the expectation that the Roosevelt Administration would come to an end in 1940, and that its successor—whether that were a weak Democratic régime or a Republican one—would steer a new course in its foreign policy.[4]

[1] See *Survey* for 1931, pp. 43–4 and 199–200.
[2] See *Survey* for 1933, pp. 16–35.   [3] See below, pp. 171–8.
[4] It is interesting to note that Ciano, when he tried on 12 August 1939 to postpone the war, argued with prescience that the outbreak of war would mean a third term for Roosevelt. (See *Trial of the Major War Criminals before the International Military Tribunal, Nuremberg, 1945–1946:*

The American attitude to foreign affairs during the inter-war years, as it has been described so far, might perhaps nevertheless seem selfish, superficial, and even frivolous if we failed to take account of the influence of other considerations which were morally more admirable, even though politically no more practical, in the long run, than those that we have reviewed so far. The American people, like the British, were capable of combining a hard-headed egotism with a sincere idealism in a mixture of motives which, in the eyes of mystified foreign observers, seemed as if it must be naïve if it really was not hypocritical. The motives—intended to be 'hard-boiled'—actuating the realist wing of the isolationist movement might not have made so much headway as they did if they had not been able to translate themselves into action without being compelled to come out completely into the open. An opportunity for operating unavowed was provided for them by a genuinely idealistic climate of opinion that had been created by the pacifist movement in general, and, within it, not only by the liberal free-thinking wing (which was small in numbers, though influential out of proportion to them), but by the aggregate weight of the, on the whole, conservative-minded churches. Among these, again, the pacifist element in the ultra-conservative Catholic Church was especially noticeable, and it was conspicuously active during the years 1939–41.

An underlying serious-mindedness was revealed in the statesmanlike action which was being quietly and unobtrusively taken in the United States to acquire more knowledge of international affairs, to get on good terms with the Latin American republics, and latterly to rearm.

During the inter-war period, no other nation took such copious and sustained measures to make and keep itself closely and accurately acquainted with what was going on in the world outside its own frontiers. The American people were now putting themselves through a course of international studies, not only in university departments, special research institutions, and widely ramifying organizations for popular discussion and information at home, but by foreign travel on the grand scale (until the slump began in 1929) and, not least, by the posting, at key-points abroad, of newspaper and radio reporters—including some of signal ability —with a wide and attentive public of readers and listeners at home.[1]

This effective though undesigned intellectual preparation for possible

documents in evidence (Nuremberg, International Military Tribunal, 1947–9) xxix. 49 (1871–PS); translation in *Nazi Conspiracy and Aggression* (Washington, U.S.G.P.O., 1946–8) iv. 514–15. [Hereafter these two collections of documents will be referred to as *I.M.T. Nuremberg* and *N.C.A.*].) Fifteen months later it was Hitler who brought up the same consideration (after the event) against the Italians, when he reproached Mussolini for not having postponed his Greek adventure until after the American elections (see Hitler's undated letter to Mussolini, probably of early November 1940, *I.M.T. Nuremberg*, xxxii. 94–5 (2762–PS); *N.C.A.* v. 410).

[1] The effect of this twenty-five-years-long national course of voluntary self-education was borne in upon the present writer, who was present at both the Paris Peace Conferences, by the difference which he observed between the United States Delegation of 1946 and that of 1919.

future action on a world-wide field was contemporary with a notable new departure, within the narrower limits of the Western Hemisphere, in the policy of the United States towards her sister republics there.

(b) THE CHANGE IN THE LATIN AMERICAN POLICY OF THE UNITED STATES

The Monroe Doctrine had been a warning issued by the United States to European Powers that she would resist any future attacks on their part upon the integrity and independence of the republics of Latin America. It was a unilateral act of the United States, taken, without previous consultation of the beneficiaries, in the interests of the United States herself; it was not a collective arrangement between all the independent states of the Western Hemisphere either for their joint security against European Powers or for their several security against one another. The conflicts between Latin American countries over disputed territory, which were in full swing when the Doctrine was enunciated at Washington on 2 December 1823, had continued intermittently throughout the 116 years between that date and the spring of 1939. The latest and not least deadly of them had been the war of 1932–5 between Paraguay and Bolivia for possession of the Gran Chaco.[1] More pertinent still, the Doctrine did not guarantee any Latin American republic against aggression on the part of the United States. The first clash of arms between the Mexican Government and secessionist United States settlers in the Mexican state of Texas had occurred in 1826, less than three years after the date of President Monroe's pronouncement, and the eventual war of 1846 between Mexico and the United States had resulted in the conquest and annexation by the United States of a larger and richer slice of Latin American territory than any that had changed hands among the Latin American countries themselves on any occasion between the time of the establishment of their independence and the eve of the Second World War. Indeed, the Monroe Doctrine actually gave the United States an opening for intervention that might be indistinguishable from aggression in the eyes of a Latin American country that was the object of it; for it might be argued—and on some occasions was argued—in the United States that the Administration at Washington could not fairly require other Powers to abstain from intervening in Latin American countries for the safeguarding of their own interests unless the United States herself undertook the responsibility of intervening there, when she judged this necessary, in the capacity of an international policeman, to maintain order or to restore it. Accordingly the phase of conquest, which had ended in 1846 and had been solely at the

---

[1] See *Survey* for 1930, pp. 421–36; *Survey* for 1933, pp. 393–438; and *Survey* for 1936, pp. 837–72.

expense of Mexico,[1] had been followed by a phase of intervention which, at one time or another, affected not only Mexico but many of the isthmian and insular republics as well. The prevalent policy of the United States towards her Latin American neighbours during the years 1893 to 1927 had been stigmatized, by critics of it in the United States, as 'dollar diplomacy', because, not unnaturally, the private interests that were the occasions of political and military interventions by the United States in Caribbean countries were much more often the interests of American citizens than those of subjects of European Powers.[2]

The new departure, in the Latin American policy of the United States, was the deliberate abandonment, in and after 1927, of dollar diplomacy, backed by intervention, in favour of a new 'policy of the good neighbour'. The inauguration, prosecution, and rapid success of this good neighbour policy, culminating, on the eve of 15 March 1939, in the Lima Conference of 9–27 December 1938, have been recorded elsewhere in this series.[3] The extent of the change in the atmosphere of United States–Latin American relations that was produced by this new departure in so short a time was remarkable, and, for this, great credit was due to the people of the United States as well as to the Administration. The resolute abandonment of armed intervention, and even of diplomatic pressure, on behalf of the private interests of United States citizens in Latin American countries compelled United States business undertakings to resign themselves in some cases[4] to severe losses of invested capital and disappointing curtailments of future profits. Some of the acts of Latin American governments from which United States business interests thus suffered were brusque, arbitrary and, in United States opinion, unjust. Nevertheless, the United States Government found themselves able to pursue their good neighbour policy at this price without encountering any serious opposition on the home front. This was noteworthy in a country in which political power was in the hands of a business community that was accustomed to lobbying at Washington. And this substantial evidence of national good faith no doubt largely accounts for the speed and the cordiality of the response which the new departure in United States policy

[1] The United States might perhaps be held in some sense to have made up for her aggression at Mexico's expense between 1826 and 1846 by having liberated Cuba from Spanish rule, and thereby called a new Latin American republic into existence, in 1902. The merit thus acquired by the United States in Latin American estimation was, however, to some extent offset when, in 1913, she proceeded to call another new Latin American republic into existence by liberating Panama, not from Spain, but from the existing Latin American republic of Colombia.

[2] See *Survey* for 1925, vol. ii, part IV (i–iii); *Survey* for 1927, pp. 400–21; *Survey* for 1930, p. 376; *Survey* for 1933, part III (i–iii). Also Charles P. Howland: *Survey of American Foreign Relations*, 1928, section 1 (New Haven, Yale University Press, 1928).

[3] See *Survey* for 1927, part IV; *Survey* for 1930, part V (i); *Survey* for 1933, pp. 318 seqq.; *Survey* for 1936, pp. 806, 808; *Survey* for 1938, i. 658–89.

[4] See *Survey* for 1936, pp. 808–9.

evoked on the Latin American side. Argentina, who had suffered little
from dollar diplomacy but who fancied herself as the premier state in
Latin America, might not be mollified; in the eyes of Argentine nationalists
the fundamental offence of the United States was the irremediable one of
her disparity in power and bulk, which dwarfed Argentina as well as
Panama and cast the tip of the long shadow of the North American giant
over the Rio de la Plata. Most other Latin American countries, however,
including Mexico, who had the sorest memories to get over, were by this
time convinced that the new professions of the United States towards them
were sincere and that it was to their own advantage to grasp the powerful
hand that was now being held out to them.

(c) The German Challenge to American Hegemony over Latin America

In initiating the good neighbour policy the United States was mainly
actuated by idealism and enlightened self-interest. The deliberate practice of power politics was widely felt to be un-American, and the ill will
that dollar diplomacy had aroused in Latin American hearts was recognized as being prejudicial to United States interests on a broad view, even
though the victims of this past policy might have had no prospect of
translating their resentment into any effective action. Some time after the
change of United States policy and consequent change of psychological
climate had begun to make themselves felt, a new motive for concord
and co-operation had presented itself to the United States and to the
Latin American countries alike when, in 1933, Germany had taken the
same political turning as Italy before her;[1] and, when subsequently, in
1936, these two totalitarian Powers had joined forces in the Berlin–Rome
Axis,[2] a new shadow—this time of coming aggression from Europe—had
been cast over South America below the bulge of Brazil: a menace to
which Latin America had not been seriously exposed since the date, now
more than a hundred years past, when, to the satisfaction and relief of
the United States, Great Britain had headed off the Powers of the Holy
Alliance from their half-formed design of restoring, by armed intervention
of their own, the Spanish Government's authority over the insurgent
colonists in the Spanish Empire of the Indies.

In the spring of 1939, Nazi Germany held a number of strong cards in
her hands for playing one day—should opportunity arise—a power game
with the United States for the stakes of hegemony over Latin America.

The first of these cards, which Germany was already playing, was
economic. Whereas the surplus products of the tropical and semi-tropical
Latin American countries round the Caribbean were mostly comple-

---

[1] See *Survey* for 1933, pp. 111–34.   [2] See *Survey* for 1936, part III (vii).

mentary to those of the United States,[1] those of the temperate and semi-temperate countries south of the bulge of Brazil were mostly supplementary to similar home products of the United States,[2] and could therefore find no adequate markets there. They had, however, a natural market in the leading industrial countries of Western Europe. British and German ports were no more distant from those of Brazil and Argentina than were the ports of the United States; and British and German industrial production was not balanced, as was that of the United States, by a home production of foodstuffs more than sufficient to cover the home demand, while it was itself far more than sufficient to cover the home demand for manufactures. There was thus a favourable opening for an extensive exchange of British and German manufactures against South American foodstuffs and other primary products; and since the first claim to supply the United Kingdom market for foodstuffs was possessed by the British Dominions—a sentimental consideration which had been translated into fiscal terms in the Ottawa Agreements of 1932[3]—Germany had an intrinsic advantage over Great Britain, as well as over the United States, in the competition for trade with Latin America, apart from the immediate temporary successes that she scored, in Latin America as in Eastern Europe, by the Nazi technique of bilateral trading between governments on a basis of barter.

Yet neither this technical device nor her freedom from a prior obligation to offer a market for foodstuffs produced elsewhere than in South America sufficiently accounts for Germany's success, in the inter-war years, in forging ahead of Great Britain in the South American trade. One important, and wholly legitimate, cause of Germany's commercial prowess was the readiness of German business men to settle down in South American cities (and this not only in the capitals of the republics), to marry South American wives, to build up businesses of their own, and to throw themselves into the life of the country of their adoption. By contrast, British business men in South America were, with rare exceptions, no more than temporary and perhaps somewhat exigent and disdainful sojourners. In this respect, at least, there was no reason why the British should not have done as well as their German competitors. The figures given in the next paragraph, which show that, by the end of the inter-war period, Germany

[1] The mineral oil of Venezuela, which ranked high in importance among Caribbean exports, was, of course, supplementary, not complementary, to the oil of the United States. But the approaching exhaustion of United States oil reserves, together with the vast and increasing consumption of oil and oil products in the United States, gave the Venezuelan oilfields an assured place in the economy of the United States.

[2] An obvious exception was the coffee of Brazil, but the Brazilians with their coffee were less fortunately placed than the Venezuelans with their oil. While the demand of the United States for oil was apparently unlimited, the amount of coffee that the people of the United States could drink was not an expandable quantity, and the Brazilians therefore had to look for other markets as well for their great coffee crop.

[3] See *Survey* for 1932, pp. 27–34.

was selling more to the Latin American countries than Great Britain was, while at the same time she was buying less from them, are another indication that, in this field at this time, the British were behind the Germans in enterprise and vigour.

Though trade between Germany and Latin America had been brought to a standstill during the First World War by the British blockade, by 1938 Germany was supplying 16·2 per cent. of Latin American imports, as compared with 33·9 per cent. supplied in that year by the United States and 11·7 per cent. by the United Kingdom. In the same year, Germany was taking 10·5 per cent. of Latin American exports, as compared with 30·2 per cent. going to the United States and 16·8 per cent. going to the United Kingdom. In Brazil and Chile, where the success of her trade drive was greatest, Germany ousted the United States in 1936 from the position, held by the latter Power in those two countries since the First World War, of being the chief market for their exports. These figures show that, by the eve of the Second World War, the position of supremacy in the external trade of Latin America, which the United States had captured from Great Britain as a consequence of the First World War, was being decidedly challenged by Germany. In spite of the inherent advantage accruing to the United States from the vastness of the scale of all her economic activities, she was being handicapped in her economic competition with Germany in Latin America by a conflict, which in Germany was not nearly so acute, between the interest of the home producer of primary products in preserving the home market for himself and the interest of the producer of manufactures in enabling Latin America to pay in primary products for the manufactures that he wished to sell to her.

A second card held by Germany was the important German element in the populations of Argentina, Brazil, and Chile—a card that was reinforced after the forging of the Berlin–Rome Axis and its expansion into a Berlin–Rome–Tokyo triangle, in so far as these partnerships for aggression took practical effect in Latin America, through the presence of a much more numerous Italian element in the population of the first two of the same three Latin American countries and of a by no means negligible Japanese element in Brazil, as well as in several of the Latin American countries with Pacific seaboards. These 'hyphenated' Latin Americans no doubt figured prominently in Axis plans to make the flag follow trade, but just as the quick success achieved by the German technique of commercial penetration soon began to cancel itself out, in Latin America as well as in Eastern Europe, by as quickly revealing to the other party the disadvantages in store for him in the second chapter of the story, so likewise the German technique of political penetration tended to defeat itself in Latin America, as well as in the United States, through its very aggresssiveness.

Though most Latin American republics, for most of the time since their first achievement of independence, had not been democratically governed except on paper, their political genius was, in its own way, as alien as that of the United States from the totalitarianism of a Nazi Germany or a Fascist Italy. An undisciplined pre-constitutional individualism, not a regimented post-constitutional collectivism, was the mainspring of their political life, and its historical affinities were with the contemporary Anarchism of Spain, the nineteenth-century Bonapartism of France, the sixteenth-century turbulence of their own Conquistadores, and the medieval feuds between factions, foaming over into intermittent dictator-ships, in the city-states of Northern and Central Italy. The gulf that divided a home-grown Latin American dictatorship from the Fascist-Nazi political formation of a single-party phalanx drilled by a leader was illuminated by the collision in Brazil in May 1938 between President Getulio Vargas and the Integralistas.[1] This abortive Brazilian totalitarian movement was suspected of having been fomented by Brazilian Germans under instructions from Berlin. It is true that in Latin America—where German immigrants could comport themselves as a separate and superior race more easily than they could in the United States—some naturalized Germans were Nazi-minded. A majority, however, of those who took pains to preserve their *Deutschtum* by maintaining separate German schools and associations were loyal citizens of the Latin American country of their adoption. Another large section—strongly represented among Catholic German immigrants who did not find themselves divided from their Latin American fellow citizens by any religious barriers—was amenable to assimilation; and this was also the state of mind of the vast majority of the Italian immigrants, who did not find it difficult to exchange one romance language for another, while in matters of religion they were either simple Catholics or sophisticated free thinkers of the French school also affected by native Latin American intellectuals.

(d) The Geopolitical Position of South America

Thus, though the Axis Powers held strong cards in Latin America, and had been playing them with some success, there were indications, in 1939, that they might be beginning to defeat themselves—and this in their economic as well as in their political game. Such set-backs, however, might be more than retrieved by *coups de main*. In Germany itself in 1933, Hitler had gained his ends by a sudden naked resort to the necessary quantum of force at a stage when the tide of feeling in his favour was already ebbing from its high watermark.[2] For this reason, considerations

---

[1] See *Survey* for 1938, i. 672.
[2] See *Survey* for 1933, pp. 139–52, and *Survey* for 1938, vol. i, part II (ii).

of armaments and strategy could not be left out of account in Latin America any more than they could in Europe, and from the geopolitical standpoint South America, from 'the bulge' southwards, was the Achilles' heel of the Western Hemisphere and therefore of the United States.

On a map drawn on Mercator's projection and looked at with a landsman's eyes, the Western Hemisphere might appear to be an *alter orbis*, united in itself and sundered from the rest of the world. A different geographical analysis would have been given in 1939 by the pilot of an aeroplane or indeed in 1500 by the pilot of one of those Portuguese caravels that accidentally discovered South America by running into the eastward bulge of Brazil in the act of trying to round the westward bulge of Africa en route for India. To instructed eyes, the Isthmus of Panama was neither a wasp-waist nor even an umbilical cord, but a mere curiosity of political geography giving a misleading appearance of unity to a couple of large islands—one lying off the West African extremity and the other off the North-East Asian extremity of the sole continent in the world, and each island having at least as close a connexion with its opposite corner of the continent as it had with the other American island across the Caribbean.

It has already been mentioned that, by sea, the south-eastern coast of South America, below the bulge of Brazil, was as near to the ports of Great Britain and Germany as to those of the United States. By 1939, this commercial shipping route between South America and Western Europe had been duplicated by a commercial air route via Dakar; where civil aviation had blazed a trail, a military command of the air might follow; and the Germans were already preparing the way for the next move beyond that by enterprisingly opening up and successfully operating commercial air routes in Latin America itself. At the same time, North America was linked with Asia by steamship routes that—following a shorter circle than the path of the Spanish galleons that had made the first transit of the Pacific from Acapulco, on the west coast of Mexico, to Manila, in the Philippines—ran from San Francisco and Vancouver to Yokohama and Shanghai. The Second World War was soon to reinforce this sea-route, by 'ties, which, though light as air, are as strong as links of iron',[1] along a chain of new airfields, skirting the eastern foot of the Rocky Mountains, from the continental United States across British Columbia into Alaska, and on beyond over Siberia into the heart of the Soviet Union. At the time of writing, in 1951, this process of air-welding the island of North America on to the continent of the Old World seemed in prospect of being carried much farther. When the air over the North Pole had been conquered for aviation, as it was to be, North America would find itself in immediate contact with the Eurasian side of the continent not only at the point where Alaska almost touched Siberia, but from there eastwards all

[1] Edmund Burke: *Speech on Conciliation with America*, 1775.

the way round to where the east coast of Greenland confronted the North Cape, along an almost 3,000-miles-long air-frontier on which the northernmost territories belonging to the United States, Canada, and Denmark would march with those of the Soviet Union.[1]

Though at the time of writing these geopolitical consequences of the accelerating progress in technique were being eagerly and widely canvassed in the United States, in 1939 they would probably have been dismissed by an overwhelming majority of Americans as fantastic dreams of demented German theorists, with no basis in sober fact. In these circumstances, the President of the United States had the task of persuading his countrymen to accept, and act on, grim truths that were already apparent to himself and to his responsible naval and military advisers.

(e) THE UNITED STATES PROGRAMME FOR THE DEFENCE OF THE WESTERN HEMISPHERE

In an address delivered to Congress on 4 January 1939, President Roosevelt prepared the way for the naval, military, and 'civil' air estimates —additional to the impressively large defence programme already on the stocks—that he was to present to Congress in his forthcoming message of 12 January.

All about us [he said] rage undeclared wars—military and economic. All about us grow more deadly armaments—military and economic. All about us are threats of new aggression—military and economic.

Storms from abroad directly challenge three institutions indispensable to Americans, now as always. The first is religion. It is the source of the other two—democracy and international good faith. . . .

We know what might happen to us of the United States if the new philosophies of force were to encompass the other continents and invade our own. We, no more than other nations, can afford to be surrounded by the enemies of our faith and our humanity. Fortunate it is, therefore, that in this Western Hemisphere we have, under a common ideal of democratic government, a rich diversity of resources and of peoples functioning together in mutual respect and peace. . . .

We have learned that effective timing of defense, and the distant points from which attacks may be launched, are completely different from what they were twenty years ago.

[1] Since the date in the sixteenth century of the Christian Era when Spaniards pushing westwards met Portuguese pushing eastwards in the longitudes of Melanesia, the Philippines, and Japan, the habitable and traversable portion of the earth's surface had been shaped like a broad body-belt running continuously round the tropical and temperate zones but not covering either pole. With the air-conquest of the North Pole, this traversable area would assume the very different shape of a tea-cosy, drawn down over the North Pole but leaving the South Pole still out in the cold. Whether this 'annihilation of the North Pole' would be a blessing or a curse to the previously sundered peoples whom it would convert into immediate neighbours was a question that would be answered by their response to this new political challenge from applied science, whatever the response was destined to be.

We have learned that survival cannot be guaranteed by arming after the attack begins—for there is new range and speed to offense.

We have learned that, long before any overt military aet, aggression begins with preliminaries of propaganda, subsidized penetration, the loosening of ties of good will, the stirring of prejudice, and the incitement to disunion. . . .

The mere fact that we rightly decline to intervene with arms to prevent acts of aggression does not mean that we must act as if there were no aggression at all. Words may be futile, but war is not the only means of commanding a decent respect for the opinions of man-kind. There are many methods short of war, but stronger and more effective than mere words, of bringing home to aggressor governments the aggregate sentiments of our own people.

At the very least, we can and should avoid any action, or any lack of action, which will encourage, assist, or build up an aggressor. We have learned that when we deliberately try to legislate neutrality, our neutrality laws may operate unevenly and unfairly—may actually give aid to an aggressor and deny it to the victim. The instinct of self-preservation should warn us that we ought not to let that happen any more.

And we have learned something else—the old, old lesson that probability of attack is mightily decreased by the assurance of an ever ready defense. . . . First we must have armed forces and defenses strong enough to ward off sudden attack against strategic positions and key facilities essential to ensure sustained resistance and ultimate victory. Secondly, we must have the organization and location of those key facilities so that they may be immediately utilized and rapidly expanded to meet all needs without danger of serious interruption by enemy attack.[1]

The President's reading of the international situation was to be endorsed by Congress in the following months in action that was more eloquent than the words in which individual Congressmen might have denied that the situation was as he described it. Though recalcitrant to the President's wishes in the matter of neutrality legislation,[2] they voted these and subsequent armaments estimates without any appreciable hesitation or opposition to the President's thesis that the area to be defended, if required, by United States arms embraced the whole of the Western Hemisphere and not merely such part of it as was United States territory. In this matter, Congress only parted company with the President and his professional advisers on the question where the outer limits of the area to be defended were to be drawn.

The inclusion of Canada seemed so much a matter of course that the personal guarantee given to her, on Canadian soil, by President Roosevelt on 18 April 1938 had caused no stir in the United States.[3] Though Canada was not a member of the Pan American Organization, a place there was

---

[1] *The Public Papers and Addresses of Franklin D. Roosevelt . . . 1939 volume: War—and Neutrality* (London, Macmillan, 1941), p. 1.

[2] See *Survey* for 1938, i. 649–51; the subject will also be dealt with in a later volume of the *Survey* for 1939–46.   [3] See *Survey* for 1938, i. 634–5.

being kept warm for her; and, though she was not a republic, she was recognized in the United States as being a fully self-governing country that was closer to the United States, in institutions, language, and blood, as well as in the literal geographical sense, than any Latin American country. Moreover, the terms of the Monroe Doctrine already committed the United States to opposing by force of arms any change in Canada's political situation except the formal change from Dominion status to juridical independence. Difference of opinion declared itself at Washington not over the northward extension of the defence area of the United States overland to include Canada but over the extent to which the area should be pushed out westwards into the Pacific and eastwards into the Atlantic in order to meet the new conditions of diplomacy and war to which the President had referred in the passage above quoted.

The shrinking from trans-oceanic entanglements which had always been, and still remained, the governing factor in United States feeling and policy towards Europe was not operative to anything like the same degree when it was a question of Eastern Asia. It was from the European, not the Asiatic, shores of the Old World that the forebears of the living generation of United States citizens[1] had embarked in the hope of leaving their political troubles behind them; and, though the roundness of the world had been translated into the practical terms of circumnavigation 400 years since, it had not yet made sufficient impact upon the American imagination to bring home to it the truth that Eastern Asia and Europe were merely different names for the opposite edges of the same dangerous continent. Hence, across the Pacific, the United States on successive occasions had almost asked for the trouble that, across the Atlantic, she was so anxious to avoid. In 1853 she had aroused Japan from a two and a half centuries-long slumber by sending Admiral Perry to knock at her door; and in 1898 she had light-heartedly seized the Philippine Islands, under Japan's nose, as an incidental consequence of a war, fought on the orthodox principles of United States foreign policy, to complete the extinction of Spanish sovereignty in Latin America.

The Philippines were due to attain complete independence by 4 July 1946,[2] and in 1939 the United States was moving steadily towards this goal, while the Filipinos were beginning to hang back. This inversion of the usual situation as between a colonial Power and its subjects was due, on the Filipinos' side, to a tardy realization that the nominal boon of independence might in fact bring down upon them economic adversity and a political subjection much harsher than any that they had experienced either at American or at Spanish hands. On the American side, the motive of jettisoning, betimes, a distant possession which they might find them-

---

[1] Save for a very small, and politically quite impotent, minority of Chinese and Japanese origin.   [2] See *Survey* for 1938, i. 624–5.

selves unable to defend in the event of war with Japan does not seem to have played any part.[1] The main motives were a political idealism which made Americans ill at ease in the 'imperialist' role associated in American minds with unregenerate Europeans, and a hard-headed determination of the American growers of sugar and other Filipino products to push the Philippines out of the cosy interior of the United States customs fence into the bleak outer world.[2]

There remained the question of what exact defence commitments the United States should undertake in the Pacific; and on this point, as early as 1939, the United States navy revealed a policy, and will, of its own which might have forewarned the Japanese navy of the stupendous naval operations, across the whole breadth of the Pacific, that their American antagonists were to carry out with triumphant success in the coming war of 1941–5. While the United States sugar interests were eager to put the Philippine sugar plantations outside the United States tariff wall, the United States was no less eager to make sure that, in war as in peace, she should be able to keep herself supplied with Manila fibre from the Philippines and with rubber, tin, antimony, chromium, manganese, and tungsten from Netherlands India and British Malaya—a region which was of much greater importance than Latin America for the economy of the United States. In 1939 the United States navy was already on the move to provide itself with greatly extended facilities in the Pacific on a number of stepping-stone islands, and the navy came into collision with Congress over its plans for fortifying the Island of Guam besides improving naval facilities there.[3] Guam was a United States possession surrounded by the ex-German-owned islands that had been under Japanese mandate since the peace settlement after the First World War, and it was notorious that Japan had long since been fortifying these islands in contravention of the terms both of her mandate and of Article 19 of the Five-Power Washington Treaty of 6 February 1922.[4] The lapse of that treaty since 31 December 1936[5] had now set the United States free to retort to the action which Japan had taken in breach of her international engagements; but, though the Americans disliked the Japanese, detested their aggression against China, and were ashamed of the profits made by United States exporters from the business of being the principal suppliers of materials to feed the Japanese war machine,[6] the immense forbearance towards Japan, of which they had given proof in December 1937 under the sharp test of the Panay

---

[1] See below, p. 103.   [2] See below, pp. 100–1.
[3] See *Survey* for 1938, i. 625–6.   [4] See *Survey* for 1920–3, Appendix V (1–3).
[5] See *Survey* for 1936, p. 110.
[6] In 1938 the supply of American aeroplanes to Japan had been stopped by the Administration at Washington through an exercise of secret pressure on the manufacturers—a move which was supported by public opinion when it was made known to the public in January 1939. There had not, however, been any cessation of the supply of other key materials, such as oil and scrap iron.

incident,[1] now showed itself again. As far as Guam was concerned, the navy was compelled to postpone the execution of its fortifications plans by the manifest unwillingness of Congress to consider a project which, in the view of a majority of Senators and Representatives who had public opinion behind them, was provocative towards Japan and inconsistent with a United States policy of rearmament in defence of isolation.[2]

(f) The Attitude of the United States towards Great Britain and France

If this opposition was aroused by a proposal to fortify an American-owned island across the Pacific, it is not surprising that far greater storms should have blown up over the question of what the policy of the United States should be towards an island across the Atlantic that was anchored far nearer to the dangerous continent than either Guam or the Philippines, and for which the United States had no legal or moral responsibility.

Though Great Britain could not, and did not, claim any right to look for political support for herself from the United States, there was a widespread and persistent belief in the latter country that if ever she ventured out of the seclusion of her own Western Hemisphere she was in peril of being made use of, unawares, by an adroit British diplomacy to pull British chestnuts out of the fire, help to preserve the British Empire, or otherwise minister to British interests. The conception of the United States in this role was most distasteful to American minds, and this bogy was made play with by American isolationists to keep their public to heel. The possible dilemma between provokingly serving British interests and perilously neglecting American interests was sharply presented at a moment when the formidable progress made by Germany and her Italian and Japanese partners in aggression, in a world ever more closely interwoven by the contemporary progress of applied science, was causing the United States grave concern about her own security and was at the same time imperilling Great Britain's position to a far higher degree. Was the Atlantic still a wide enough moat to protect the Americas even if the whole of the Old World, with all its industrial, military, naval, and air resources, were to fall under the control of the triangle of totalitarian Powers? Or was it impossible for the United States to defend herself effectively against attack from the east except by setting her first line of defence at the English Channel, or even at the Maginot Line, and making it her business to ensure that Great Britain and France should remain independent and democratic? Or were the two Western European Powers, in combination, capable of defending themselves and their pacific European neighbours by their own exertions, and thereby incidentally providing, willy-nilly, for

[1] See *Survey* for 1937, i. 278, 312–17.   [2] See *Survey* for 1938, i. 626.

the security of the United States without its being necessary for her to take any action at all of her own?

'Is England worth fighting for?'[1] The very formulation of this question was irritating to American minds in 1939, when the traditional dislike of isolationists for European entanglements, and of idealists for 'British Imperialism', was reinforced by disapprobation and contempt for the policy of appeasing aggressors at the expense of China, Ethiopia, Czecho-slovakia, and the Spanish Republic that was being pursued at the time by the Chamberlain and Daladier Governments. American condemnation of the Anglo-French diplomatic capitulation at Munich was sincere,[2] with however ill a grace it might appear, in British and French eyes, to come from that side of the Atlantic. To most American minds it did not occur, at the time, that the refusal of the United States in 1920 to become a party to the Covenant of the League of Nations was the greatest single cause of French and British weakness in face of the resurgent Germany of the 1930s. They did not realize that, by holding aloof, the United States had crippled the Western European democracies' ability to stand up to aggression in two distinct ways: not only by the withholding of the American support that would have weighted the scales against aggression so decisively as to rule out all thought of it, but by embarrassing Great Britain and France, in any attempt that they might think of making to resist the aggressors without American aid, through the uncertainty as to whether a neutral United States would tolerate their using to the full, against the common enemy, the naval blockade, which was the best weapon in their ill-stocked armoury. This last-mentioned embarrassment was, indeed, eventually removed by United States legislation prohibiting the entry of American shipping into a war area.[3] Yet, even so, the very legislation on which Congress was insisting for the safeguarding of United States neutrality might operate in favour of an aggressor—as President Roosevelt pointed out in the address above quoted and on other occasions.[4] If, for Great Britain and France in American eyes, resistance to aggression was an over-riding duty to which a supposed national interest in appeasement ought not to have been given precedence, how could it be maintained— a French or British rejoinder to American criticism might have inquired —that the same duty was not incumbent on the United States and not paramount over her own supposed interest in isolation? The same moral law must surely hold good for the same genus Homo in both hemispheres; and, if propinquity singled out France and Great Britain as Powers that should take the first brunt of a collision with Germany in defence of

[1] This was the title of an article by Elmer Davis in *The New Republic* of 15 February 1939. Compare 'The Americans and the New Pacific' by Eliot Janeway in *Asia*, February 1939.

[2] See *Survey* for 1938, i. 600–6.

[3] This will be dealt with in a later volume of the *Survey* for 1939–46.

[4] See the footnote to the Preface to the *Survey* for 1936.

Czechoslovakia, the same principle of selection would have drafted the United States for being the first to come to the rescue of China against Japan. To British minds in 1939 it seemed unreasonable that citizens of an inactive United States should criticize the passivity of Great Britain *vis-à-vis* Japan over the question of the Open Door in China at a time when, in Europe, Great Britain had to reckon with the prospect of Germany's making war at any moment.

Moreover, if the batteries of American criticism were to be concentrated on the French and British governing class, in an accusation that these oligarchies had been 'selling Czechoslovakia down the river', and thereby jeopardizing their own countries' independence and soiling their own honour, for the sake of precariously preserving the wealth, privileges, and amenities of their class for a few years or months longer, it might be retorted that the way of life that they were indeed desperately anxious to preserve was that which was called by the good names of democracy, individualism, and freedom of enterprise in the United States as well as in Western Europe, and by the bad names of demoplutocracy and capitalism in Italy, Germany, and the Soviet Union in reference to the European democracies and the United States without distinction. The governing class of the United States had never dreamed of being called on, in its own case, to sacrifice amenities which it condemned its French and British counterparts for ransoming at the dishonourable price of throwing a small democratic country to the wolves. Considerations such as these inspired in British minds a resentment against American criticism which did nothing to allay the deep distrust instilled into American minds by Chamberlain's policy. As Americans saw it, the British were now committing that betrayal of the cause of collective security which they had accused the Americans of committing in the past. In the light of British action when it came to the test, those past British reproaches against American isolationism now began to seem hypocritical. In some American minds, a suspicion was arising that what the British had really deplored was perhaps not the refusal of the United States to support the League of Nations—towards which Great Britain herself was also indifferent, as it now would appear—but the refusal of the United States to make it her business to serve British interests.

It will be seen that there were manifold occasions for mutual misunderstanding and exasperation between the United States and the Western European democracies on which Hitler might count on the eve of his coup of 15 March 1939.

(ii) The British Commonwealth
By Arnold Toynbee

(a) THE STRATEGIC POSITION OF THE COMMONWEALTH

The British Commonwealth interlocked with the Western Hemisphere at two points, since Canada and the Caribbean territories dependent on the United Kingdom were both situated within the American geographical area, though they were neither of them included in the political *entente* of states members of the Pan American Organization. The two links were both important; for in 1939 Canada was the second strongest of the states members of the Commonwealth, while the British possessions in the Caribbean lay in strategic positions athwart the Atlantic approaches from the Old World to the Panama Canal. Like the countries of the Pan American Organization, those of the British Commonwealth were not on all fours with one another in the degree of their exposure to the danger of attack by Germany, but this general resemblance in the geopolitical disposition of these two groups of states was less striking than two differences, both of which were to the Commonwealth's disadvantage. In the first place, the Commonwealth was echelonned in much greater depth, extending, as it did, from the American outer fringe of Germany's field of fire to a forward position within point-blank range of Germany's now rapidly multiplying weapons of offence. In the second place, the member of the Commonwealth that found itself in this most dangerously exposed position was the United Kingdom—the leading member, whose fortunes would be fateful for those of all her dependencies and partners—whereas, in the Western Hemisphere, the United States was somewhat farther withdrawn from the German danger-point than either Brazil or Canada. In fact, Canada, which was one of the two least sheltered countries of the Western Hemisphere, was the most sheltered country of the Commonwealth, considering that the United Kingdom lay between her and Germany, while the titanically powerful United States stood shoulder to shoulder with her on the Pacific as well as on the Atlantic front.

This contrast in relative degree of insecurity between the British Commonwealth and the Western Hemisphere in 1939 was accentuated by an even sharper contrast between the weakness of the Commonwealth's strategic position at this date and the strength of it as recently as half-a-century back. During the hundred years running from the victory of the British navy at Trafalgar in 1805, Great Britain had possessed a decisive superiority in naval power over any conceivable combination of continental European naval Powers, while since 1814 till the close of the nineteenth century she had not had to contemplate the prospect of facing a continent united under the military hegemony of a single aggressive Power. Since the four or five mutually jealous Powers of nineteenth-century continental Europe were the only Great Powers, besides Great Britain herself, in the world of that age, the ring of sea-power with which Great Britain had by then encircled Europe and its Middle Eastern appendages, from the North Sea and North Atlantic through the Mediterranean to the Indian Ocean, had provided virtually complete security not only for Great Britain herself but for all parts of the British Empire all over the world. This enviable state of affairs had, however, been the product of an accidental combination of fortunate circumstances that could not be expected to last, and, by the turn of the nineteenth and twentieth centuries, the temporary security of the British Empire was already being seriously impaired in several ways.

In the first place, the progress of modern technique and its application to armaments had brought into action two new weapons, the submarine and the aeroplane, which to some extent offset Great Britain's two advantages of insularity and superiority in surface naval craft in any trial of strength between her and a continental Power. The menace of the submarine to Great Britain had been demonstrated in the First World War; the Second World War was to demonstrate the menace from the air.

In the second place, the menace of a continent forcibly united for the purpose of aggression—a nightmare which had been temporarily banished by the overthrow of Napoleon—had returned with the rise of the German Reich. In the First World War, Germany had demonstrated her strength by requiring the united efforts of the rest of the world to prevent her from achieving her ambition of world conquest. In 1939, under a régime which made the Prussian tradition appear almost humane by contrast, Germany was still more demonically bent upon a fresh career of aggression.

In the third place, the Continent—whether destined to remain the seat of more Powers than one or to be overshadowed by a single Power of superlative strength—was no longer the only place in the world, apart from the British Isles, in which Great Powers were to be found. Partly thanks to the protection automatically afforded during the nineteenth century by British sea-power, as a by-product of the safeguarding of British interests, to all the world outside the Continent against all potential aggressors except the British Empire itself, the United States and Japan had each attained the stature of a Great Power before the nineteenth century was over, and this emergence of two new Great Powers outside the ring of British sea-power round continental Europe had taken the nineteenth-century defences of the British Empire in the rear.

The first response of British policy to this new challenge had been to make sure of the friendship of both these two rising Oceanic Powers, and in 1939 this was still British policy towards the United States. Any

prospect of a genuine and lasting friendship between the British Commonwealth and Japan had, however, been ruled out, first by a growing sense of
apprehension and hostility towards Japan in the United States and in the
British Dominions with seaboards on the Pacific—a consideration which
had had a decisive effect on the outcome of the Washington Naval Conference of 1921–2[1]—and secondly by the career of aggression at China's
expense on which Japan had embarked in 1931[2] and which she was still
pursuing with all her might in 1939.[3] A Japan who was thus flagrantly
breaking her solemn pledges under the Covenant of the League of Nations
could not be given official countenance by the members of the British
Commonwealth—for all of whom the League Covenant and the Kellogg
Pact continued to be the declared bases of public policy and the personal
ideal of an appreciable proportion of their citizen-bodies.

It is true that, after Japan, in 1931, had justified all the worst fore-
bodings about her intentions, Australian public opinion and governmental
policy all but boxed the compass by veering round from their almost
militant attitude of the early 1920s to something very like a mood of
appeasement. One explanation of this apparent paradox is to be found in
the sense of relief experienced in Australia—in some quarters at any rate
—when the Japanese tiger made its long-dreaded spring in a direction
opposite to that in which Australia lay. Australian hopes of averting a
Japanese assault upon Australia by taking care not to hinder Japan from
sating her appetite on China were not only unedifying but short-sighted.
For, in their present mood, the masters of Japan might be expected at any
time to follow up their continental adventure if successful, or to try to
screen its failure if unsuccessful, by further adventures in other directions.
The Japanese navy was known to be jealous of the scope for action which
the army had been enjoying since 1931, and was no doubt already thirsting
for worlds of its own to conquer.

It might have seemed that this danger from the new power of Japan was
more than offset by the weight, in the anti-Japanese scale, of the greater
new power of the United States. At this time, however, the policy of the
United States was a highly uncertain, and therefore somewhat embarrassing, factor in the policy of any other Power that had to take American
policy into account. For, as has been noted above,[4] American feelings
were torn between a detestation of Japanese aggression and a determination not to be involved in war and not to pick British chestnuts out of the
fire—even if this fire were to be kindled by Japanese arson.

The opening of a third breach in the nineteenth-century security of the
British Empire was foreshadowed, in the circumstances of 1939, by the
existence, outside the ring of British sea-power round Europe, of overseas

---

[1] See *Survey* for 1920–3, pp. 452–5, 484–99.   [2] See *Survey* for 1931, pp. 430, 438.
[3] See below, pp. 119–20.   [4] See above, pp. 17–19.

empires belonging to half a dozen countries on the Atlantic seaboard of continental Europe.

Throughout the century of her maritime supremacy, Great Britain— chastened by the painful experiences of the dead set against her that had been made by all the other Powers in 1778–83 to redress a balance that had inclined inordinately in her favour twenty years before—had studiously refrained from pushing her recaptured advantage so far as to make her fortunate position invidious. Accordingly, in the peace settlement after the Napoleonic Wars, she had returned to their previous owners a number of colonial territories which she had conquered, during those wars, either from France herself or from states temporarily incorporated in, or subordinated to, the French Empire; and thereafter she had not attempted to obstruct the participation of France, Belgium, Germany, Portugal, Italy, and Spain, side by side with herself, in the partition of Africa. In the circumstances of the nineteenth century, such overseas possessions of continental European states were indeed hostages to British sea-power rather than menaces to British security. Their significance might change, however, if the continental countries owning them were once again to fall under the influence, ascendancy, or domination of some single aggressive continental Power; for these non-British overseas empires, if brought together under a single control for aggressive purposes, would offer, in the aggregate, as promising a basis for the achievement of world dominion as the British Empire itself.

Netherlands India and the Belgian Congo, for instance, were the equals of British Malaya as sources of key products.[1] Indeed, in 1939, the Belgian Congo already held that primacy in the production of radio-active materials that was to enhance her importance when the problem of splitting the atom had been solved. Moreover, in all three principal colonial areas of the world of the day—South-East Asia (both insular and continental), Tropical Africa, and the Caribbean—the possessions of the continental European colonial Powers jostled the British Empire at close quarters, and included strategic positions not inferior to those which British sea-power had at its disposal. Gibraltar was now confronted by the roomier Spanish Zone of Morocco; Malta by the better-placed Italian island of Pantellaria and the more commodious French African naval base at Bizerta;[2] Great Britain's ally Egypt by the Italian possessions in Libya and East Africa; Aden by the French port of Jibuti; British Malaya by Dutch Sumatra and Java; the once mainly British-controlled International Settlement at Shanghai by the still French-administered French Settlement there;[3]

[1] For the economic importance of British Malaya and Netherlands India see below, pp. 88–94.

[2] Permission to use French naval facilities at Bizerta was sought by, and begrudged to, the British navy during the trial of strength between the League of Nations and Italy in 1935–6 (see *Survey* for 1935, ii. 259–70).

[3] See *Survey* for 1926, pp. 362–72.

Durban by the Portuguese port of Lourenço Marques; Freetown by the French naval and air base at Dakar. The West Indies included French and Dutch, as well as British, islands. At the north-eastern approaches to North America, the overseas territories of a Danish commonwealth[1] in the Faroes and in Iceland and Greenland outflanked the British Isles and offered stepping-stones between the European continent and Labrador. At the north-western approaches to the Soviet Union, the perennially ice-free channel, skirting the Norwegian province of Finmark and connecting the port of Murmansk with the British Empire and the rest of the world, was now flanked by Norwegian territory on both sides, since Spitsbergen had come under the Norwegian flag in virtue of a multilateral treaty concluded in 1920.[2] The Nazi rulers of Germany were no doubt thinking in these terms while they were laying their plans to get their western and northern continental neighbours into their power.

It will be seen that the change for the worse in the strategic position of the British Commonwealth was far-reaching. In the situation as it had stood in the nineteenth century, the United Kingdom was like a shepherdess who, by skill or luck, had managed to corral all the wolves formerly infesting her sheep-run in one pen with a single entrance. So long as she stood on guard, sufficiently well armed, at the point of egress—and this was just where geography had obligingly placed her—she was in a position to ensure, single-handed, the safety of the whole of her flock, however much it might increase and multiply, and however widely it might range over distant vale or mountain. In 1939, the United Kingdom was still virtually single-handed; for the still non-self-governing overseas territories dependent on her naturally continued to look to her for their defence, while the self-governing Dominions, though now constitutionally responsible for securing their own safety, had hardly yet begun to shake off a century-old habit of taking it for granted that they were, and would be, perfectly defended by the Royal Navy. The contributions that each of the Dominions was making towards its own defence and towards that of the Commonwealth as a whole were still far, in 1939, from being proportionate to the ratio of their wealth and population at the time as compared with the resources of the United Kingdom. Meanwhile, however, the task of defending the Commonwealth had become one that would have taxed its total united resources. Inside the continental European wolf-pen, the largest and grimmest of the corralled wolves was once more showing signs

---

[1] Though the recently coined British term 'Commonwealth of Nations' was not officially used to describe the dominions of the Danish Crown, the constitutional relation between Iceland and Denmark at this date was not very different from that between the overseas Dominions of the British Commonwealth and the United Kingdom. See below, p. 157.

[2] See below, p. 158, note 2. For text of treaty see Great Britain, Foreign Office: *Treaty regulating the Status of Spitsbergen and conferring the Sovereignty on Norway . . . Paris, February 9, 1920,* Cmd. 2092 (London, H.M.S.O., 1924).

of dominating the rest of the pack, with an eye to rushing the exit in a combined surprise attack; this German wolf was also clawing down the walls of the pen towards the south-east and the south; and out in the open the shepherdess, glancing nervously over her shoulder, could now see the shapes of two large creatures looming above the Oceanic horizon—one of which had shown itself a wolf by pulling down a stray sheep without a shepherd, while the other, though apparently amicable, was very large in bulk and very erratic in its movements. The predatoriness of Japan, the fate of China, and the 'Anglo-Saxon attitudes' of the United States were so many additional anxieties for the United Kingdom.

Under these conditions, the still almost single-handed Western European warden of the British Commonwealth could not hope any longer to be able effectively to perform her task at need unless she could continue to put forth her strength at three widely separated points at once. On the defence of what theatre should the United Kingdom concentrate?

Should she husband her forces at home, against the possibility that Germany might attack her, across the Straits of Dover, with the war potential of a whole continent united by force or fraud once again, as in Napoleon's day, under the command of a single war-lord? Since the United Kingdom herself was still the unrelieved guardian of the whole Empire and Commonwealth, she could hardly neglect her own defence at home without jeopardizing that of her dependants and partners all over the world. But could she neglect the defence of the Middle East either? Though, from Germany, the Middle East could be reached literally over-land by no other route than via the Soviet Union, there were two points at which the waters demarcating 'Asia' and 'Africa' from 'Europe' could be jumped. One of these narrows—far narrower than the Straits of Dover— was the Black Sea Straits, and these had never been known to stop, or even check, an invader. The Bosporus at Constantinople was no greater a barrier than the Hudson at New York, and many of the Second Rome's inhabitants slept nightly in 'Asia' and worked daily in 'Europe' without thinking more about it than their American contemporaries who com-muted between the Jersey Side and Manhattan. The other narrow point was the waist of the Mediterranean between Sicily and North Africa; and though this stretch of water, in contrast to the Bosporus and Dardanelles, was appreciably wider than the English Channel and very much wider, even at its narrowest point, than the Dover Straits, it was easier than these —as imminent events were to prove—for German land forces to cross in the political and strategic circumstances of the day. Though the piece of Africa lying nearest to Sicily, Tunisia, was in French and not in Italian hands, Italy was mistress of Pantellaria—an island lying full in the fair-way, in a more commanding strategic position than Malta—and, more important still, she held a broad landing-stage on the African mainland in

Libya, to which Sicily was a stepping-stone and from which both French North Africa and Egypt could be attacked by an expeditionary force equipped and led by the German partner in the Italo-German Axis.[1]

If German forces—taking either the short roundabout step across the Black Sea Straits or the longer direct leap across the Central Mediterranean—were to reach the Nile Valley, the Suez Canal, or the South Persian oilfields, they would not only hamstring the British navy by depriving it of its main source of fuel; they would also sever the tail of the British Empire from its body and its head. To the over-sanguine eyes of German professors of geopolitics, it looked in 1939 as though the British lion had degenerated into a chimera. Though the lion's head might still glower sullenly across the North Sea and the Channel at a continent once again in process of political unification under the hegemony of the Third Reich, had not the lion's herculean body suffered a woeful metamorphosis into the scraggy shape of a Maltese goat, and his swingeing tail into the elongated caudal appendage of a Chinese dragon, trailing limply round the indented southern coasts of Asia all the way from Suez to Hongkong? Surely this senile chimera (*Mischwesen*, as the German might have thought of it) would fall an easy prey to the good German sword, especially if Germany were to succeed in inveigling her Japanese junior partner into performing the congenial operation of cutting off the decrepit monster's no longer defensible tail?[2]

This German optimism about the prospects of successfully attacking the British Empire was perhaps partly matched by a certain complacency about the prospects of defence in the minds of the professional advisers of the Government of the United Kingdom. While they had resigned themselves to the prospect of temporarily losing Hongkong in the event of a Japanese attack, they had laid their plans for standing fast at Singapore. Apparently they had not foreseen that the impetus of the Japanese onset would carry the Japanese navy to the Andaman Islands and the Japanese army into Manipur. Still more remote, perhaps, from their minds in 1939 was the vision of a German garrison in the Channel Islands. Nevertheless, British professional anticipations were to prove less wide of the mark than German; for, even after France had fallen and Japan had opened fire, the temporary losses of British territory were to be amazingly small. The German siege-guns trained from Spanish territory upon Gibraltar[3] were

---

[1] See also below, pp. 128–9.

[2] The writer's guess, in making the first draft of this passage in 1947, that these geopolitical calculations had exhilarated aggressive German minds during the years when Hitler and his fellow conspirators were secretly planning a Second World War, was subsequently vindicated by the publication of Ribbentrop's memorandum of 12 January 1938 in *Documents on German Foreign Policy, 1918–1945, from the Archives of the German Foreign Ministry*, publ. jointly by the British Foreign Office and the U.S. Department of State (Washington, U.S.G.P.O., and London, H.M.S.O., 1949), series D, i. 163–4. (This collection will hereafter be referred to as *D.Ger.F.P.*, series D.)   [3] See *Survey* for 1938, i. 355–6.

never to go off; Malta was neither to be bombed nor to be starved into surrender; no German or Italian soldier was to set eyes on the Nile, or Japanese soldier on the Brahmaputra, except as a prisoner of war; the overrunning of British Somaliland by an Italian force was to be swiftly avenged by a British conquest of all Italian possessions in Africa to the last square metre; and the British Isles, British India, Australia, and New Zealand, as well as British West Africa, the Union of South Africa, and the Dominion of Canada, were to remain uninvaded.

Such mercies might seem little short of miraculous; yet the general strategic and political lesson of the Second World War for the British Commonwealth and Empire was to be a very grave one. The course of the war was to make it as plain as a pikestaff that, in the geopolitical circumstances of the twentieth century, it had become quite impossible to defend the whole Commonwealth by the unaided efforts of the Commonwealth itself, and *a fortiori* impossible by those of the United Kingdom alone.[1] Though in 1939–45, as in 1914–18, the Dominions were to disappoint German expectations by rallying vigorously to the support of the United Kingdom—this time with the exception of Eire, but once again not of South Africa—it is virtually certain that something nearer five-sixths than one-sixth of the British Empire would have been successfully overrun by the converging hosts of its assailants if a stream of supplies had not eventually begun to flow from the United States. It is also quite certain that— for all the gallantry and endurance shown by a 'forgotten' British army under the almost intolerable conditions of jungle-warfare in the tropics— Australia and New Zealand could not have been successfully defended, nor Burma, Malaya, and the insular dependencies of the United Kingdom, Australia, and New Zealand in the Pacific successfully reconquered, if the lion's share of the burden of responsibility for winning the war in the Pacific had not been taken upon the titanic shoulders of the United States. Even when allowance has been made for the fact that the combination of aggressor Powers against which the British Empire had to fight in the Second World War happened to be the one, out of all the alternative possibilities, to which the Empire was most vulnerable, the moral of this experience was that the Empire could not hope to survive, except within a framework of alliance or collective security sufficiently effective to be, for the future, not only invincible in the event of war but unchallengeable by even the hardiest would-be aggressor.[2] The most that could be said was

---

[1] This point of British weakness had been spied by Hitler at least as early as 5 November 1937, when he held a conference with his military commanders: see minutes of the meeting (Hossbach Memorandum) dated 10 November 1937: *I.M.T. Nuremberg*, xxv. 407–8 (386–PS); trans. in *D.Ger.F.P.*, series D, i. 33; *Documents on International Affairs 1939–46* (London, Oxford University Press for Royal Institute of International Affairs, 1951) [referred to hereafter as *Documents* (R.I.I.A.)], i. 19–20; cf. *N.C.A.* iii. 299–300.

[2] At the time of writing the British Empire's sheet anchor was a defensive alliance of Western

that, in this, the states members of the British Commonwealth found themselves in the same boat as every other state in the world with the possible two exceptions of the United States and the Soviet Union, and that, while the effect of the Second World War was to diminish the strength of the United Kingdom, it was simultaneously to increase that of Canada and Australia, two hitherto mainly agricultural countries in both of which the Second World War gave a powerful impetus to the process of industrialization.

(b) The Attitudes and Policies of Individual Members of the Commonwealth

These untoward changes in the nineteenth-century situation presented problems not only to the Commonwealth as a whole but to each of its self-governing states members. In 1939 there were six already fully self-governing member states: Canada, South Africa, New Zealand, Australia, Eire, and the United Kingdom (to cite them in an ascending order of insecurity). There were also two Oriental countries—India and Burma—which had been promised eventual Dominion status and were both already on the road towards that goal, though they had not yet reached it.[1] In each of these eight countries, the play of local politics under the pressure of alarming international events gave rise to attitudes and policies that were to become factors in the making of international history.

On one, not uncontested, constitutional theory, the British Commonwealth was in international law a political unity in virtue of the allegiance owed by all British subjects to a common Crown, and on this view all parts of the Commonwealth would find themselves juridically at war with any state with which the King was at war—either through having had war declared on him by the Government of such state, or through having declared war, himself, in execution of the constitutionally given advice of Ministers in any one of his fully self-governing Dominions. In practice, the United Kingdom alone was likely—on account both of her predominant position in the Commonwealth and of her exposed position in the world—to bring belligerency upon her partners, and the practical question was what line each of these partners would take if this situation were to arise again as it had arisen in 1914. They might go beyond the constitutional obligation incumbent on them on the theory of the indivisibility of the Crown by throwing themselves into an active participation in the war at the United Kingdom's side; or they might confine themselves to a 'passive belligerency'; or, if unwilling to incur the risk of enemy reprisals by

countries under the aegis of the United States, which had been improvised as a substitute for the world-wide system of collective security which the United Nations Organization had been intended to provide.   [1] See below, pp. 65 seqq. and 72–6.

shouldering the obligations (such as interning enemy aliens and impound-
ing enemy vessels and other assets within their jurisdiction) that even
passive belligerency would impose, they might advance a doctrine of the
divisibility of the Crown; maintain that they could not be placed in a
state of war through any act not done either by or to themselves; and
proclaim their neutrality at the price of incurring the alternative risk of
breaking their existing link with their fellow members of the Commonwealth if these fellow members were to treat such action as being tantamount to a repudiation of the bond, whatever this might be held to be, by
which members of the Commonwealth were associated with one another.

While the juridical obligations common to all members of the Commonwealth were thus disputable, and their possible consequences obscure,
each fully self-governing state member had also to wrestle with its own
special problems. Each case was a highly individual one, since these
eight countries, linked though they were by a common political allegiance,
were very diverse in location, history, culture, religion, and race. While
the United Kingdom and Eire were old European communities, and India
and Burma still older Asiatic communities, the other four were products
of relatively recent European settlements overseas. While the United
Kingdom was a predominantly Protestant country, Eire was no less predominantly Catholic, Canada half Catholic and Australia one-quarter
Catholic, and India and Burma overwhelmingly non-Christian. Burma
was predominantly Hinayanian Buddhist, and British India, though she
contained almost the whole of the vast Hindu population of the world
apart from the Balinese in Netherlands India, was also the home of so
numerous a Muslim minority as to make British India, in point of numbers,
the leading Muslim, as well as the leading Hindu, country in the world.
The Union of South Africa—where the white settlers of European origin
were outnumbered by the black settlers of Tropical African origin in the
proportion of approximately five to two,[1] with the whole of the rest of
Black Africa pressing down upon the Union's northern frontier and feeding the labour force in the mines on which the Union's prosperity depended
—was at grips with a race problem that made that of the United States
seem child's-play by comparison.

There were also wide differences—very pertinent to the political situation in 1939—in the historic circumstances in which different communities
in the Commonwealth had originally come into political association with
the Kingdom of England, and in the present attitude of these communities to these *faits accomplis*. Scotland had entered into political union of
her own free will and on a footing of equality which had eventually

[1] When the 1936 census was taken White South Africans totalled 2,003,857, Bantus 6,596,689
and others (unspecified) 989,352. The Bantus were still later arrivals than the Teutons. The
previous inhabitants—Hottentots and Bushmen—were neither black nor white but yellow.

extended to the once wild Gaelic-speaking Highlanders as well as to the sedately respectable English-speaking Lowlanders; and there had likewise been some freedom in the negotiation, though not much equality in the effects, of the treaties in virtue of which the surviving Indian-administered Indian states had entered into a relation of clientship with the British Government in India. The conquest of the Maoris by the British invaders of New Zealand had left no sinister legacy of either political rancour or inter-racial tension, though in 1939 the hard-fought Anglo-Maori wars were not yet a hundred years old. The contemporary and far more formidable Anglo-Sikh wars had had an almost equally auspicious sequel. On the other hand, the political and psychological effects of other British conquests, both modern and ancient, were in 1939 still actively in operation. The conquest of the two South African Dutch Republics in 1902, of the Kingdom of Upper Burma in 1885, and of the then wild tribes of Ireland between the twelfth and the seventeenth century had not yet been either forgotten or forgiven by the descendants of the victims of these acts of English aggression. In Bengal and in the subsequently acquired provinces of the British-administered lion's share of India, a similar temper had begun to declare itself, by delayed action, at about the turn of the nineteenth and twentieth centuries, with the coming to manhood of a generation which no longer had any living knowledge, even by hearsay from its parents, of the anarchy that had afflicted India from the death of the Emperor Awrangzīb to the completion of the establishment of the British Raj. Indian Muslims whose forebears had been thankful to be saved by a British ascendancy from a Hindu *revanche* were in 1939 more conscious of the fact that the British Raj had been preceded by a Muslim one, while Hindus whose forebears had been saved by the same British ascendancy from the fate of being liberated from Muslim rule by their Marattha co-religionists were in 1939 more conscious of the possibility that the broken-down Muslim Raj might have been succeeded by a Hindu one if the British had not then importunately intervened. As for the French Canadians, they did not bear the grudge that the Dutch South Africans bore against their British conquerors, and they recognized and appreciated the liberality shown by the Government of the United Kingdom on the morrow of the conquest, when it had guaranteed them the free practice of their Catholic religion and their French law.[1] Yet though the French Canadians had enjoyed self-government, on a footing of perfect equality with their English-speaking fellow countrymen, since the middle of the nineteenth century,[2] a gulf remained fixed between the two Canadian

[1] The Quebec Act passed by the British Parliament in 1774 provided for the use of French civil law, and guaranteed freedom of worship for the Roman Catholic Church which had been promised in the Treaty of Paris of 10 February 1763.

[2] Responsible self-government was recommended in the Durham Report, drawn up in 1838, and was achieved during Lord Elgin's Governorship (1847–54).

communities, and in 1939 the French Canadians, like the Dutch South Africans, the Southern Irish, the Burmans, and the Indians, still betrayed their descent from a conquered people in a characteristically morbid concentration on their own parish pump politics and an apparent unawareness of the world-shaking events of the day in which their parochial fortunes were at stake.

Such self-centredness was indeed characteristic in some measure of most members of the Commonwealth at this time for divers reasons. While in the ex-conquered communities it was a psychological consequence of the experience of having been originally brought into the Commonwealth by force, in the states members that had been brought into existence at a recent date by settlement from Europe there also came into play the fascination—noticeable likewise in the United States and in the 'ABC' republics of temperate South America—which a new country is apt to exercise upon the pioneers who are opening it up. English-speaking shared with French-speaking Canadians, and English-speaking with Dutch-speaking South Africans, an intense desire to be left alone to cultivate their budding gardens; and in Australia the same feeling was, if possible, stronger, by reason of her greater exposure to the red rays of the rising sun of Japan— though the discomfort of a similar situation moved New Zealand to take the opposite line of fostering her relations with the United Kingdom and standing for an effective implementation of the principle of collective security through the agency of the League of Nations. As for the English-speaking Canadians, notwithstanding their pride in their membership in the British Commonwealth, and in the distinctive position which this gave them in the Western Hemisphere, they were inclined, like their North American neighbours in the United States,[1] to feel themselves entitled, as of right, to the enormous privilege of freedom from involvement in European entanglements. For the Australians and New Zealanders, an equivalent degree of security against the menace of aggression from Asia, so far from being an established right, was a rather remote aspiration, and they therefore had to console themselves, as best they might, with the unconvincing hope that Japan's appetite for aggression would be sated and not whetted by her attack on China[2]—while the opposite hope was cherished by some Indian and Burmese nationalists, whose sympathies were uneasily divided between their fellow Asiatic victims of imperialism in China and their other fellow Asiatics in Japan, whose aggression against China might be condoned if it should prove to have been a prelude to an attack on the European rulers of subject Asiatic peoples.[3] In anticipation, these hotheaded and short-sighted Indian and Burmese patriots did not foresee that 'liberation', when conferred by Japan, might turn out to be a synonym

---

[1] See above, pp. 1–7 and 18–20.   [2] See below, pp. 119–23.
[3] For Pandit Nehru's views see below, pp. 69–70.

for subjugation, and that the measure meted out to China as her punishment might be doled out to them as their reward.

More idealistic, and by the same token more potent, considerations also, of course, came into play. In Eire and South Africa, in particular, there was a strong current of the feeling (also influential in the United Kingdom) that the Versailles Peace Treaty had been an iniquitous imposition (in Hitler's own phrase, a *Diktat*) of the victors on the vanquished, and that therefore any attempt by the ex-vanquished to shake off these shackles ought to be viewed with sympathy. This feeling, especially in South Africa, made it essential to prove, beyond any possibility of argument or doubt, that Nazi Germany was an aggressive Power, if the Commonwealth was to be induced to take united action against her. At the time of Germany's military reoccupation of the Rhineland in March 1936[1] it had been possible, perhaps, for the United Kingdom, had she chosen, to have acted without the Dominions' co-operation; but, when once Germany's rearmament—especially her air armament, to which Great Britain was highly vulnerable—was well under way, the United Kingdom could no longer readily contemplate challenging Germany without the Dominions' support; and this made the Dominions' attitude towards the tearing-up of the peace settlement of 1919–20 by the Nazis an important consideration in the policy of the United Kingdom. This attitude is understood to have come out in the discussions at the Imperial Conference of 1937. The Government of the United Kingdom also had to take account of the insistence in Canada that the Commonwealth should not again go to war except in a cause transcending Commonwealth interests (in the narrow meaning in which the term interests was traditionally used). Mackenzie King's statement, on 25 January 1937,[2] in the House of Commons at Ottawa, that Canada 'will not necessarily become involved in any war into which other parts of the British Empire may enter simply because we are part of the British Empire' made it essential to prove to the satisfaction of Canadian—and particularly French Canadian—opinion that any war entered upon was being fought 'against the forces of evil'—in Mackenzie King's own phrase.

(*c*) The Division of Opinion on Foreign Policy in the United Kingdom

These diverse attitudes and policies that were prevalent in 1939 in the overseas Dominions, India, and Burma had one identical effect. They operated as deterrents to any inclination, in the United Kingdom, towards incurring the risk of war by resolutely opposing aggression in the cause of collective security. Political cliques in the United Kingdom which were in any case inclined, for reasons of their own, to appease aggressors instead of

[1] *Survey* for 1936, part IV (i).   [2] *The Times*, 27 January 1937.

opposing them, found in the parallel current of feeling in the Dominions a welcome occasion for being 'drafted' (in President Roosevelt's expressive phrase) to refer urgent but awkward questions of foreign policy to partner Jorkins on the imposing plea of keeping the Commonwealth together.

There was perhaps one point—and this a cardinal one—on which an overwhelming majority of the people of the United Kingdom were in 1939 most genuinely of one mind not only with one another but with an equally great majority of the people of the Dominions, the United States, and the North-Western continental European countries from France, Switzerland, and the Low Countries to Scandinavia. The peoples of all these countries had reached, by this time, a stage of moral and social development at which war was no longer taken as a matter of course but had come to be felt as a barbarity incompatible with civilized life. This weaning of the Western peoples from the 6,000-year-old tradition of militarism in an age still hag-ridden by the institution of war was a circumstance that had entered into the calculations of the makers of the Second and Third German Reichs from the generation of Bismarck onwards. If they themselves could succeed, during this critical time of transition, in keeping the Ost-Elbisch Prussians militarized and in remilitarizing the rest of the German people in their likeness, might not the premature humanization of Germany's Western neighbours bring world-dominion within Germany's grasp?

Such German calculations confronted the Western peoples on the eve of the Second World War, as on the eve of the First, with the harrowing moral and political question of what limits they should set (if it was right to set limits at all) to the price that they would be prepared to pay for being left at peace—on the assumption, which was unproven, that peace could always be purchased at some price or other. For the sake of exemption from the barbarous evil of war, should they be prepared to sacrifice interests, and even territories, of their own, but draw the line at throwing their neighbours to the wolves? Such a standard of conduct would be Wilsonianly high but unprecedentedly Quixotic. Or should they—even those of them that had signed and ratified the Covenant of the League of Nations—abide by the established Machiavellian precept of modern Western international politics that, whatever might be the moral law for individual souls, a sovereign state, at any rate, was not its brother's keeper?

How comfortable to revert, like Canning, to the good old rule of 'every nation for itself and God for us all'. Yet was not this respectable-sounding phrase perhaps just the parliamentary language for 'The devil take the hindmost'? And, if the fiend were thus cynically invited to find his prey in the last hapless straggler, might he not retort by the practical joke of also nabbing the last but one? In current concrete terms, supposing that the United Kingdom were tamely to stand by and watch her continental European neighbours—and these neighbours' possessions and dependencies overseas—go the way of China and Ethiopia, might she not find, too late, that the aggressor Powers—now established in these new points of vantage—had thereby acquired a stranglehold on the British Commonwealth itself? Did realism continue to be realism, or did it elusively turn into a suicidal form of pedantry, when one decided to sacrifice his own vital interests rather than defend these at the cost of being unprofessionally altruistic? What would have been the Florentine maestro's ruling on this very nice point of psychology and ethics?

On the eve of 15 March 1939 the people of the United Kingdom were deeply and bitterly divided over questions of foreign policy.[1] This schism in the body politic had been steadily widening ever since it had been first cleft by the entering wedge of the Japanese action in Manchuria on 18 September 1931, and the quarrel was not merely a political but a moral one. There had been nothing comparable to it in the domestic life of the United Kingdom since the quarrel between 'pro-Boers' and 'imperialists' over the South African War of 1899–1902. In that case, as in this, one faction had self-righteously imputed to the other a moral baseness as well as a political ineptitude, and the party on whom this searing aspersion had been cast had sullenly resented it without being able to feel quite clear, in its own conscience, that the odious charge was altogether undeserved. There was, however, a piquant difference in the content of the accusation which throws light on the state of human affairs in 1939 as contrasted with 1899. Whereas the imperialists of 1899 had been held up to shame for having made war in a bad cause, and had retorted by pillorying their pro-Boer censors as unpatriotic pacifists, the appeasers of 1939, who were the imperialists' authentic heirs, were being held up to shame for being unwilling to go to war in a good cause, and they were retorting by pillorying the advocates of collective security as fire-eating war-mongers.

In the schism of 1939 there were, on both sides, unresolved contradictions and strange bedfellows. In what had been the Wilsonian camp there was still a multitude—perhaps even a majority—who, though they had been faced with the issue since 1931, did not even yet know their own minds well enough to be able to tell whether they were first and foremost champions of the League of Nations or first and foremost pacifists. It was only a minority that had so far shown the clarity and strength of mind to pluck out and cast from them either their pacifism in order to pursue their crusade for collective security or their allegiance to collective security in order to keep their pacifism inviolate. Conversely, in what had been the Conservative camp there was a corresponding sifting out of a strong-

---

[1] An account of the change in British policy brought about by the events of 15 March and an analysis of British opinion at that time will appear in a later volume of the *Survey* for 1939–46.

minded and clear-sighted minority that had made up its mind to sacrifice
either patriotism to appeasement or appeasement to patriotism from a
muddle-headed majority which was still refusing to believe that these two
good horses 'Patriot' and 'Appeaser' could no longer be driven with
propriety in double harness. The greatest clarity of vision was shown,
perhaps, by the resolute Wilsonian optants for collective security and the
resolute Conservative optants for appeasement, but the palm for moral
courage must be given to a Conservative like Anthony Eden,[1] who
resigned the Secretaryship of State for Foreign Affairs and risked a personal
breach with his party in his single-minded devotion to collective security,
and to a Wilsonian-like Lord Allen of Hurtwood who publicly rallied to
the support of Chamberlain in his equally single-minded devotion to
pacifism. For the fuddled and wavering majorities, from both camps,
there was little to be said. The short verdict on them was: 'Unstable as
water, thou shalt not excel.'[2]

This chapter would be incomplete without some attempt to describe the
respective points of view of the Conservative nucleus of the appeasers and
the Wilsonian nucleus of the champions of collective security. For the
present writer the second of these two tasks should be easy, since he has
merely to state the view he held himself, but the other task is proportionately difficult for him—and this the more so because the Conservative
appeasers differed from both their pacifist bedfellows and their inter-
ventionist opponents in being strangely inarticulate. The present writer
is therefore conscious that, in ignorance as well as out of possible prejudice,
he may be in some danger of unintentionally doing less than justice to the
case of Chamberlain and his companions.

The experience, feelings, and motives that made John Bull become a
temporary convert to appeasement were certainly complex. One element
in the situation was a change in the position and outlook of the ex-governing class of the United Kingdom during the inter-war years. From the time
of the dissolution of the monasteries to the outbreak of war in 1914 this
class had been in unbroken enjoyment of increasing wealth and power; it
had prided itself on its public spirit and had lived up to its high standards
of public service in the First World War by sacrificing more than its share
of blood as well as its full share of treasure. As its reward, it now found
itself discredited under such opprobrious names as 'the capitalists' and
'the militarists', ridiculed (which was harder still to bear) in the comical
figure cut by 'Colonel Blimp', and gleefully forewarned by its newly arisen
political opponents in the camp of Labour that it was going to be voted
out of power and then taxed out of existence. Like the rest of the British
people, this ex-governing class was eager to go to great lengths for the sake
of avoiding another great war which, like its predecessor, would be a

---

[1] *Survey* for 1938, i. 129–37. [2] Genesis xlix. 4.

catastrophe, not just for the governing class in the United Kingdom, but for the whole country and the whole world. But one of the finest passages in the creditable history of this class was the fortitude and cheerfulness with which, after its obstinate inter-war struggle to recapture its pre-1914 way of life, it resigned itself to social extinction when it became convinced at long last that appeasement was no longer compatible with public spirit.

If the instinct of self-preservation were the sole guiding instinct, then the British propertied classes would have allowed Hitler to possess all the world provided he left them with their own incomes and privileges. Quite deliberately, knowing full well the consequences of their actions, they [were] prepared to sacrifice all their possessions rather than to allow this evil to triumph. [Was] this selfishness? Seldom has a whole class committed suicide in so great a cause.[1]

The explanation of Chamberlain's policy of appeasement—and of the support which this policy received from the Prime Minister's colleagues in the Cabinet and followers in Parliament and in the electorate—is perhaps to be found in a combination of a widely shared and laudable moral judgement with a complete mistake about a crucial matter of fact. In his manifest—and manifestly sincere—horror of war as an appalling moral, as well as material, evil in itself, Chamberlain was representative of an overwhelming majority of people, not only in the United Kingdom and the overseas Dominions of the British Commonwealth, but throughout the world outside the boundaries of Germany, Italy, and Japan; and, even in the three great aggressor countries, it may be surmised that if a free vote could have been taken, not on whether war was morally indefensible or not, but on whether the voters wanted their governments to put them into war or to let them off this tribulation, a large majority would have probably voted for remaining at peace. Chamberlain was on much more contentious ground in his estimate of Hitler's policy.[2] He was unwilling to believe that the ruler of a state only a few hours' flying-time distant from the British Isles could have so utterly different an outlook on life from Chamberlain's own as to be determined to have a war for its own sake. Moreover, he took at their face value Hitler's repeated mendacious declarations that his territorial aims were limited to securing the applica-tion, where it would work in Germany's favour, of the principle of national self-determination which had been applied, in the peace settlement of 1919–20, in favour of the victorious nations without also being applied impartially where it would have benefited the vanquished nations in their turn. Assuming, as he did, that Hitler's ambitions were limited to obtain-ing for Germany something that, in German eyes at any rate, might appear to be a long overdue measure of justice, Chamberlain was, again,

---

[1] Harold Nicolson: *Why Britain is at War* (Harmondsworth, Penguin Books, 1939), pp. 135–6.
[2] This is discussed more fully in the Introduction to volume ii of the *Survey* for 1938, pp. 3–9.

unwilling to believe that disputes arising within this limited field could not be settled on the common-sense, give-and-take lines on which two business men in Birmingham would iron out some hitch in the dealings between their respective firms, or on which Sir Horace Wilson, at the Ministry of Labour in Whitehall, would promote conciliation in some dispute between private employers and employees.

In staking the fortunes of his Government, his country, and the world on this reading of Hitler's attitude and intentions, Chamberlain is not, of course, to be blamed for making an error of judgement which, by the date twelve years later when this chapter was being written, had been decisively proved to be egregious by the damning evidence of captured German official documents. Down to the night of 14–15 March 1939, the truth about Hitler's policy was still every man's guess. Chamberlain's fault here (and it was assuredly a grave one) was that, on so open a question, on which alternative answers—including the sinister one that subsequently proved to be the truth—were being actively canvassed throughout the critical pre-war years, he deliberately kept his eyes closed to unpalatably pessimistic views conflicting with his own, though these views were held, and were very convincingly expounded, by British statesmen with greater experience and understanding of foreign affairs than the Prime Minister himself possessed, and by official advisers who constitutionally had the first claim on the Prime Minister's attention on questions of foreign policy.

Moreover, he not only ignored or overrode such weighty dissenting opinions, but took immense and indefensible risks on the strength of his personal belief in the superiority of his own judgement. The classical instance was one in which the other principal parties concerned were none other than Roosevelt and Eden. In his resignation speech in the House of Commons at Westminster on 21 February 1939, Eden referred to a fundamental difference between himself and Chamberlain over a 'most important decision of foreign policy' not concerned with Italy. The nature of this decision was not divulged; but in the following May a report that Chamberlain and Eden had disagreed over relations with America was published in a New York paper in an article by an American journalist in London, Joseph Driscoll.[1] In Parliament on 20 June Chamberlain refused to give any information about his disagreement with Eden, and it was not until much later that the facts became generally known. They were as follows.

On 12 January 1938, when Eden was in France, a message from President Roosevelt was received in London asking for the views of the British Government on a proposal that representatives of certain governments should be invited to Washington to discuss the underlying causes of the

---

[1] See *Survey* for 1938, ii. 113–14, for the disclosures in this article concerning British policy towards Czechoslovakia, and for the proceedings in the House of Commons which elicited the fact that Driscoll had based his article on a talk with Chamberlain.

deterioration in the international situation. Roosevelt intimated that if, but only if, this proposal met with 'the cordial approval and whole-hearted support' of the British Government, he would proceed to the next step that he had in mind, which was to approach the Governments of France, Germany, and Italy likewise. Before Eden's return to London, Chamberlain had dispatched a reply to Roosevelt in which he had suggested that action on the proposal should be postponed because it might cut across the efforts which the British Government were making to come to an agreement with Germany and Italy. Chamberlain had mentioned, in particular, that he was prepared to grant *de jure* recognition of the Italian occupation of Ethiopia as part of a general settlement. In a letter of 17 January, Roosevelt agreed to postpone action in view of the British Government's intention of entering into direct negotiations, but took occasion to express grave concern over the suggested recognition of the conquest of Ethiopia.

Meanwhile Eden had returned to London on 15 January and had been greatly perturbed to hear of the terms of Chamberlain's note. He used his influence at Cabinet meetings to procure the dispatch of further messages to Washington on 21 January in which the President's initiative was warmly welcomed (though some doubt was expressed about the suggested procedure) and a more detailed explanation was given of the British attitude on the Ethiopian question. The more cordial note struck in these messages, however, could not alter the fact that the 'whole-hearted support' for which Roosevelt had asked was clearly not to be expected from the British Government.

This incident,[1] which was not, and clearly could not have been, made public at the time as the cause of Eden's resignation, convinced Eden that there was a 'fundamental difference' between him and Chamberlain which made it impossible for him to remain a member of Chamberlain's Government. In rebuffing a momentous overture from the President of the United States without first consulting his own Foreign Secretary, the British Prime Minister of the day had in fact staked the fortunes of the country for whose interests he bore the supreme responsibility—and, it

[1] The account here given is based on Sumner Welles: *The Time for Decision* (New York, Harper, 1944), pp. 64–9, and Winston S. Churchill: *The Second World War*, vol. i (London, Cassell, 1948, pp. 196–9; Boston, Houghton Mifflin). Welles relates that Roosevelt had originally contemplated addressing to all other governments, on Armistice Day, 1937, a message containing the suggestion that the United States should invite several other governments to join in drawing up tentative proposals for a universal agreement which would set out the essential principles that should govern international conduct and would deal with methods of limiting and reducing armaments, promoting economic security and stability, and humanizing war. This project, Welles states, was strongly opposed by some of Roosevelt's closest advisers, who recommended him first to obtain the assurance that neither the British nor the French Government would regard the proposal 'as running counter to negotiations which they already had in hand or to policies upon which they had previously determined'. Roosevelt was acting on this advice when he sounded the British Government about his plan in January 1938.

would be no exaggeration to add, the fortunes of the rest of mankind as well—on his confidence in the correctness of his personal shot in the dark at divining Hitler's true character and intentions. Nothing short of an absolute certainty that Hitler was a man of sterling goodwill and good faith would have justified a British statesman in Chamberlain's position at that date in rebuffing the American President's 'formidable and measureless step'[1] with 'a douche of cold water'[2] which effectively halted Roosevelt's move to draw after him an American people who were as blind to current international realities as Chamberlain himself into a policy of throwing the decisive weight of the United States' titanic latent strength into the international scales on the side of peace. A favourable rejoinder on Chamberlain's part would have involved, 'however tentatively, the mighty power of the United States'[3] in European affairs; and the eventual publication of the minute recording the decisions which Hitler had already taken on the eve of Armistice Day, 1937, two months before Roosevelt's offer reached Chamberlain's hands, justify Churchill's comment that 'we must regard its rejection—for such it was—as the loss of the last frail chance to save the world from tyranny otherwise than by war'.[4]

If Chamberlain's interpretation of Hitler's aims had been undisputedly correct—instead of being, as it was, always under fire of telling criticism and eventually shot to pieces by the revelation of the true facts—in that hypothetical case, no doubt, a powerful defence of his policy could be propounded. To begin with, Hitler's alleged aim of securing the political incorporation into the Reich of all contiguous German-speaking and German-feeling populations might look plausible on grounds of equity, always supposing that he was aiming at this, and this alone, for its own sake, and not as a stepping-stone to outrageous ulterior objectives. And, though the successive steps already taken by Hitler to bring Austria and the Sudetenland into the Third Reich were plain violations of treaties and (on the most indulgent verdict) recklessly irresponsible riskings of a breach of the world's peace, they might still perhaps be condoned on the ground that Germany had found, by long and bitter experience, that she could not obtain what seemed to her plain justice by any law-abiding, safe, or civilized procedure.[5] Similarly, it might seem unreasonable to attempt to continue to insist on Germany's remaining disarmed after it had become clear that the World Disarmament Conference was doomed to failure.[6]

Moreover, there were strong arguments against attempting to vindicate the letter of the law in these cases by imposing sanctions in execution of the Covenant of the League of Nations. In the British Commonwealth itself there was a school of thought—represented by such eminent minds as

[1] Churchill: *Second World War*, i. 196.　　[2] Welles: *Time for Decision*, p. 66.
[3] Churchill, op. cit. p. 198.　　　　　　　[4] Ibid. p. 199.
[5] See *Survey* for 1938, ii. 5.　　　　　　[6] See *Survey* for 1935, vol. i, part I (iii).

General Smuts[1] and Lord Lothian—who, in this contentious issue, held
that the mechanism of collective security had become practically un-
workable. For example, it had become clear that the effect of modern war
was immeasurably to increase the disparity between great and lesser
Powers, and that the mechanism of collective security could not be
operated by small states alone, however numerically formidable in the
aggregate; that such states were, moreover, inevitably nervous of taking
any initiative in operations against powerful aggressors, and, in fact, that,
if resort to aggressive war was to be checked, the burden must really fall
on an increasingly limited number of Great Powers. Of the Great Powers
of the world, Germany, Italy, Japan, and the United States had to be left
out of the calculation, and the Soviet Union was an unknown quantity
which was regarded with suspicion by conservative opinion in the United
Kingdom. As Conservatives saw it, therefore, everything would depend
on Great Britain and France, which meant that the two must march in
step or that, if either partner held back, the other must resign herself to
following suit, in view of the impossibility, for either of them, of taking
on single-handed a task which, in the prevailing constellation of international forces, might well prove beyond the compass even of their united
efforts. Even an ardent and loyal supporter of the League of Nations
might feel that the League had been killed by the failure of its members, in
1935–6, to carry through to success their attempt to vindicate the Covenant against Italy; and Chamberlain himself had taken this as a touchstone,
to judge by the reversal in his personal attitude between 9 December 1935,
when he joined his colleagues in a Conservative Cabinet in counselling
Sir Samuel Hoare to resign office, and 10 June 1936, when he scoffed at
the idea of continuing to impose sanctions on Italy as being 'the mid-
summer of madness'.[2]

This test case of the Ethiopian affair might, indeed, reasonably be held
to have demonstrated that the system for the regulation of international
affairs that had been set up after the First World War was now out of
working order. There was a real 'international anarchy'; and in these
desperate circumstances there was a strong case for Chamberlain's policy
of deciding not to hamper himself by standing pedantically on the punctilio
of acting only through the League, which the three aggressor Powers had
now all repudiated, but, instead, to seize any opportunity of persuading
Hitler and Mussolini to sit round a table with him and of making it clear
to them that, if they would play the game of peaceful change by conference methods, without naked resort to force, he was prepared to go up to,
and perhaps even somewhat beyond, the bounds of justice in the sincerity

[1] See 'The British Empire and World Peace', an address given by General Smuts at Chatham
House on 28 January 1930 (*International Affairs*, March 1930, ix. 141–53).
[2] See *Survey* for 1935, ii. 302, 463.

of his efforts to meet their demands. Yet, while the maintenance, outside the framework of the League, of round-table negotiation between the aggressors and the Western European Powers was obviously of value as far as it went, it did not touch the heart of the matter; for the perils of an international anarchy could not be conjured out of existence by the verbal act of giving a non-Genevan label to a meeting of European statesmen, since in this event Britain and France would still find themselves pitted against the same formidable gang of antagonists and would still have to play a weak hand as best they could without hope of any American backing.

The reason why the League had failed was that the enforcement of the Covenant had been backed by insufficient armed power and insufficient resolution to use such power as was available. A system of collective security had been proved, by hard facts, not to be workable on the principle of a bank, in whose operations there can normally be a safe margin of excess of liabilities over assets because the creditors may normally be counted on not all to present their claims simultaneously. The League had been found not to work because its liabilities were not fully covered; and, if it was to the credit of Chamberlain's sagacity that he had divined this weakness in the League, he had the less excuse for shutting his eyes to the truth that the same principle must govern, *a fortiori*, an uncamouflaged game of power politics.[1] The players of the old diplomacy of the pre-Genevan age had never allowed themselves, or one another, to forget that (to invert Clausewitz's dictum) 'diplomacy' was 'the conduct of war by other means', and, when they came into conference, they had always been aware that the deciding factor, in the last resort, was not justice or reason and not even the mutual desire of peaceful business men to do a deal, but armaments—of which the most potent (at any rate before the invention of the atom bomb) were allies of Great Power calibre.

The cogent criticism of Chamberlain's policy was not that he sacrificed other people's ideals to *Realpolitik*, but that he sacrificed *Realpolitik* to ideals of his own. While, down to 15 March 1939, the dissentients from Chamberlain's policy might be unable to substantiate their belief that Hitler was aiming at nothing less than world dominion, it was equally impossible for Chamberlain, on his side, to verify his own contrary conviction that Hitler had limited aims which could be met by peaceful negotiation without flagrant injustice to third parties (that Hitler might have sinister designs against Great Britain herself was a contingency that perhaps hardly came within the Prime Minister's horizon until after 15 March 1939, as seems to be indicated by certain passages in his speech of 17 March 1939). In such circumstances a pre-Genevan statesman, even in a respectable country, would have felt it his duty to take up the chal-

---

[1] For the absence, on Chamberlain's side, of the motive of maintaining the Balance of Power, which was attributed to him by the Nazis, see *Survey* for 1938, ii. 13–14 and 21.

lenge of competition in military power which the three aggressor Powers of the inter-war period had long since thrown down to their pacific-minded peers. But Chamberlain had flinched from facing the appalling truth that, in the international arena of the 1930s, competition could not be conducted in an anodyne fashion. And, hiding his head in the sand, he had been slow to rearm on his side and had allowed Hitler, unopposed, to carry one position after another—now Austria, now the Sudetenland[1]—which might be nothing more than legitimate German *terre irredente*, but might equally well be decisive strategic points on a military march towards the conquest of Europe and the world.

After an event which left Chamberlain undiscredited as an idealist but with not a leg to stand on as a *Realpolitiker*, his champions still sought (perhaps ill-advisedly) to defend him in this latter capacity by representing that his policy had gained for Great Britain the time required for just sufficient rearmament to avoid defeat in the Second World War when it came. It seems unlikely that time was gained in fact, for, after the trickle of British rearmament had started to flow at last, the great flood of German rearmament did not considerately stop flowing in order to allow the gradual growth of the British rivulet to diminish the disparity in their respective volumes.[2] In any case, if this was a major motive of Chamberlain's policy, he was gravely to blame for not warning his country of her danger, not making rearmament a question of confidence in the domestic politics of the United Kingdom, not seeing to it that it should be started in time to check Hitler at an early and vulnerable stage of his game, and, above all, not being willing—as he was unwilling right down to the ending of the 'phoney war' by the overthrow of France in June 1940—to 'go all out' in the armaments race. Hitler's open display of tell-tale anger at the modest beginnings of British rearmament after Munich suggests that an earlier British retort in kind to German rearmament might have provoked Hitler into throwing off the mask at some date, previous to March 1939, when his unopposed occupation of successive strategic points had not yet brought him to the commanding position that he was to acquire by the occupation of Czechoslovakia. If it be answered that Hitler might have retorted by attacking Great Britain there and then, the counter-answer is that, while there were many stages at which the odds were still on the Western European Powers' side, there cannot have been any stage at which Great Britain would have found herself at a greater disadvantage in fighting Nazi Germany than she was in 1940.

[1] This series of German moves had, of course, been opened by the military reoccupation of the Rhineland on 7 March 1936, and the Anglo-French acquiescence in this first step had increased the moral difficulty of taking a firm stand against those that had followed; but, at the time of the Rhineland coup, Chamberlain, though a prominent member of the Government of the day in Great Britain, had not been Prime Minister.

[2] This will be dealt with in Part V of volume iii of the *Survey* for 1938.

So far, however, from fearing that Great Britain might be overwhelmed by the weight of German armaments, it looks as though Chamberlain persistently underestimated Germany's military strength throughout his term of office, since, without ever rearming with might and main himself, he contemplated the possibility of war with Germany after the Godesberg meeting of 22–23 September 1938,[1] threw himself intrepidly across the path of Germany's further advance beyond Prague when he gave a British guarantee to Poland on 30 March 1939,[2] and publicly expressed the opinion, on 5 April 1940, in the last days of the 'phoney war', that Germany had 'missed the bus'.

No doubt the wordy warfare of domestic party politics—conducted, as it was during the unhappy appeasement period, with an acrimony unusual in Great Britain—was a contributory factor in keeping an unseaworthy policy inexpediently afloat. Chamberlain and his fellow Conservatives, on their side, were violently put off by the irritating and, as they felt, contemptible antics of their opponents. How preposterous to be abused for their unwillingness to go to war, and to be accused of basely sacrificing British as well as collective interests, by people who till yesterday had been abusing them as 'imperialists' and agitating for further reductions in the United Kingdom's armaments. What logic was there in calling for the employment of the British navy for the imposition of sanctions against Japan after having protested against the completion of the Singapore Base?[3] Were the supporters of the League of Nations really so inept as to imagine that one could get something for nothing? In the scrap of paper and drop of printer's ink that constituted the text of the Covenant, did these devotees of a latter-day secular faith really see a magic charm, serviceable as a substitute for sufficient armaments and sufficient will to use them? In pure logic, it would seem, the Conservatives had here the best of the argument, but they were poorly armed against a counter-argument *ad hominem*. Considering that Conservative administrations had been in power for all but three of the twenty-one years which had elapsed since Lloyd George's 'khaki election' of 14 December 1918, the power and responsibility of maintaining British armaments at what they judged to be the proper level had really lain all this time in their own hands, while the obstruction that they had met with from their opponents had amounted to little more than impotent words.[4]

---

[1] See *Survey* for 1938, ii. 416–19.

[2] This will be dealt with in a later volume of the *Survey* for 1939–46.

[3] See *Survey* for 1929, pp. 59–60.

[4] Baldwin pronounced judgement on his own stewardship in the following passage of a speech delivered in the House of Commons at Westminster on 12 November 1936: 'I want to speak to the House with the utmost frankness. . . . Supposing I had gone to the country and said that Germany was rearming and that we must rearm, does anybody think that this pacific democracy would have rallied to that cry at that moment? I cannot think of anything that would have made the loss of the election from my point of view more certain' (H. C. Deb. 5th ser., vol. 317, coll.

The irritation and contempt with which these opponents inspired the Conservative appeasers were, of course, returned with interest. Could these self-assured claimants to 'a doctor's mandate' really be so narrow-hearted and so lacking in vision as not to feel and see that the cause of collective security was in this generation the supreme common cause of the human race, to which all lesser causes must be subordinated by all men of goodwill? And, even if they were to take the pedestrian line that they were mere trustees for British interests, could they really be so stupid as not to perceive that, in the world as it was, in which even the strongest Power could no longer provide for its own defence unaided, the only practicable method of safeguarding British interests was to throw all their energies into a common endeavour to make a substantial success of collective security? Was it not contemptible to have fought and won the general election of November 1935 in the guise of crusaders for the popular League of Nations, and then to have thrown over the League in the Ethiopian crisis of 1935–6? Was not this a shameless exhibition of vote-catching by bamboozling the electorate, with a cold-bloodedly dishonest intention to break the vote-winning pledge when once the vote had been raked in?[1] And what moral credit could the Conservative appeasers properly claim for their last-minute conversion to a holy horror of war? Had they really turned into *bona fide* pacifists, or did they secretly reckon—like birds of the same feather in France—that the Fascist Powers were the sworn-in special constables of the well-to-do class in all countries? Had they been gulled into believing that they must choose between their class and their country? And, in this erroneous belief, had they made the immoral decision to put their class-interests first?

In these mutual recriminations the two factions in the United Kingdom were, no doubt, doing one another considerably less than justice. It was, in fact, a deplorable repetition of the characteristically British performance of frantically washing not very dirty linen in public and decrepitly trailing an actually unbroken wing. In 1939, as at the time of the 'Curragh Incident' of 1914, the inopportune and unintended but inevitable result was to lure the obstinately perverse and insatiably silly Germans into believing—and making war in the belief—that the British cock would not fight. Were not the Conservatives in favour of armaments on the understanding that these were never to be used, and the interventionists in favour of using them on the understanding that they were never to be provided? What conceivable chance of survival had a house that was so fantastically divided against itself? The Germans, of course, had no valid

---

1143–4). See, however, R. Bassett: 'Telling the Truth to the People: the Myth of the Baldwin "Confession" ', *Cambridge Journal*, November 1948, pp. 84–95, together with letter from Max Beloff and reply by R. Bassett (ibid. January 1949, pp. 237–42).

[1] For this episode see *Survey* for 1935, ii. 54–6, 65–7.

excuse for making the same mistake twice over in one lifetime, but the most plausible of their inadequate pleas was that the British were past-masters of the pestilential art of decoying through make-believe.

(iii) The Soviet Union
By Edward Crankshaw

(*a*) The Attitude of the Soviet Government and of the British and French Governments towards each other

The essential difference between Soviet Russia and the Western Powers on the eve of Hitler's occupation of Bohemia and Moravia was that the Soviet leaders were certain that it was going to happen. Further, they were certain that this still undeclared act would prove to be simply one move in a long progress of aggression. There was nothing remarkable about this since, as far as the Soviet Government were concerned, if an aggressor had not arisen it would have been necessary to invent one. That is to say, the Soviet Government had been expecting war and preparing for war ever since their inauguration in the midst of war. All that was needed, as the world economic crisis deepened and expanded, was to put a name to the aggressor-in-chief. This had long been done. The aggressor-in-chief was Germany. But what was still not clear in the Kremlin at Moscow was whether Germany would be seconded, directly or indirectly, by Great Britain and France, or whether these two countries could still be used to help stave off the evil day when Germany should attack the Soviet Union herself.

Almost certainly, the main preoccupation of the Soviet Government while Hitler was mobilizing his effectives for the occupation of Czecho-slovakia was to decide whether or not the British and the French Governments were more interested in the curbing of Nazi Germany or in the destruction of Bolshevik Russia; for subsequent events went to show that even then the collective mind of the Soviet leaders was not finally made up on this point. Stalin himself, whose mind was (for a Marxist) extra-ordinarily open to different possibilities, may well have thought that there was still a hope of roping in Britain and France at least for the purpose of slowing Hitler down; and, although it appears that Stalin's position was some distance removed from the one-man dictatorship of Hitler and Mussolini, his was always the most powerful voice in the dictatorial collec-tive which, characteristically, was Soviet Russia's special contribution to the practice of government.[1]

In March 1939, doubt of the ultimate intentions of Great Britain and

[1] See below, pp. 50–51.

France was by no means limited to the Russians; it was shared by the Germans. In fact, the Prime Ministers of Great Britain and France had, by their recent actions (above all by the Munich Agreement, arrived at without reference to the Soviet Union, who was one of the main interested parties) given even impartial observers plenty of scope for speculation about their real motives. It could reasonably be argued that Chamberlain and Daladier were less interested in defeating Hitler's immediate purposes than in reaching some kind of a working agreement with Hitler at the expense of Austria and Czechoslovakia—not merely for the sake of buying time, but also in order to keep Soviet Russia out of the councils of Europe. It did not take a very lively imagination to carry this postulate a step farther and conclude that the British and the French might very well be promising at least their neutrality in a projected German onslaught on Russia, in return for which Hitler would leave Western Europe alone.[1] The Russians were not impartial observers: even if the Western Powers had given no signs of respecting Nazi Germany more than Bolshevik Russia, the Soviet leaders—self-taught by their own application of Marx's dialectic and biased beyond redemption by their inheritance, via Lenin, of the Marxist morality—would have betted heavily on such a preference. The Western Powers, however, gave plenty of such signs; indeed, their behaviour, and particularly the behaviour of Great Britain, since 1917 had heavily confirmed the Soviet Government in their dogmatic suspicion that the overthrow of Communism, and therefore of Communist Russia, had long been, and always would be, one of their main preoccupations. The Germans took note of the Kremlin's suspicion and exploited it to the best of their ability.

Indeed, on the face of it, why should a British Cabinet, especially Chamberlain's Cabinet, not have preferred Hitler to Stalin? It seems desirable to ask this question, and in no polemical spirit, in order to get the days of March 1939 into a true perspective in space and time. Communism was the declared enemy of Chamberlainism. And without now inquiring into what Soviet Russia, as a place for Russians to live in, was actually like in 1939, we may usefully remind ourselves of what it looked like from the outside. With the Soviet Union in stupendous action against the common enemy in the battles that took place three years later, that earlier vision was first dimmed in Western eyes, then forgotten—so completely forgotten that even when victory was won and when certain aspects of the Bolshevik régime came to light which were directly opposed to all Western democratic notions of good and decent government, and when Soviet foreign policy, as it was reforged, was seen to be uniquely egocentric

---

[1] This Russian thesis is developed in *Histoire de la diplomatie*, ed. Vladimir Potemkin, trans. from Russian by Xenia Pamphilova and Michel Eristov (Paris, Librairie de Médicis, 1946–7), iii. 675, 685.

in its motives and bleakly unscrupulous in its methods, these manifestations were contemplated with the wondering gaze of discovery.

In fact, it was only rediscovery. In 1939 the peoples and the governments of Western Europe knew certain things about the Bolshevik régime which had to be rediscovered in 1949. They knew, for example, that this régime was based partly upon slave-labour of one kind and another; they knew that there was serious disaffection in the vast territories of the U.S.S.R., and that this disaffection had been punished only recently with a terror which had destroyed unknown numbers of the ablest soldiers and officials; they knew also that the Soviet Government had, as a Communist Government, declared war on bourgeois society everywhere; and although they may have doubted whether the Stalin régime was in fact still Communist in faith, they knew that it was still guided by the Marxist interpretation of history, and they had to take account of its actions, which included the maintenance and encouragement of the Comintern. Here then were facts, in the moral, military, and diplomatic spheres, which in Chamberlain's eyes made the Soviet Union as a prospective ally undesirable, unreliable, and possibly treacherous. Hitler, of course, knew these facts too: he took careful note of the fact of slave-labour for domestic application; the other facts conditioned his approach to the problem of liquidating Europe.

The attitude of the Chamberlain Cabinet was, of course, not as clear-cut and lucid as is suggested above. These facts were known, but they were caught up and inflamed by a deep unreasoning hatred of the Bolsheviks seen simply as violent revolutionaries. And the Chamberlain Cabinet never asked itself to what extent the evil aspects of contemporary Russia might be ascribable to the past conduct of the Western Powers and to what extent a more conciliatory policy might have shaken the dogmatic suspicion of the Kremlin. These are questions to which we shall probably never know the answers. But it is perhaps the greatest sin of omission of the British Conservative leaders between the two wars that they never attempted to find the answers, by practical experiment, at a time when no risks were involved. As it was, not only did they fail to try the experiment of *rapprochement*; many of their actions were a positive affront to the new régime in Russia. If the intervention and the subsequent snubbings and boycotts did not cause Soviet hostility to Britain, they at least confirmed in Russian eyes the reasonableness of that hostility. Furthermore, there can be no denying that the immense strain under which the Soviet Government laboured in their task of rehabilitating and industrializing a largely ruined country was incalculably increased by the lack of normal economic relations with Britain and the West. Out of this strain came the horrors—the rushed collectivization of the peasants, the bitter struggle with the 'deviationists', the great purges, and, bound up with all of these, the development of forced labour. Out of this strain, too, came the final confirmation, if it was needed, of the conviction that Communist Russia and the rest of the world were ultimately antagonistic.

As already remarked, it is quite impossible to decide how much milder the Stalin rule might have been if Soviet Russia, the excesses of the revolutionary years forgotten, had been unreservedly treated as an equal nation by the Great Powers of the West. It is impossible to say whether sustained demonstrations of amity would have convinced Russia's leaders, against their own teaching, that they need fear no further intervention from the West. It is impossible to say whether, had the British and French, acting on quite a short-term policy, taken Litvinov's plans for collective security seriously, the fate of the world might have been changed and Russia convinced of the practicability of normal international relations. It is impossible because these things were never tried. Russia, for better or for worse, was never given a chance to cast off her dogmatic chains. Instead they were twisted ever more closely round her, and almost everything that the Western Powers did, culminating in the Munich Agreement, confirmed the Russians in their gloomiest prognostications of the future.

Thus, in 1938, the Soviet leaders were fairly certain that Chamberlain would make some sort of a pact with Hitler; and when in the autumn of that year he did so this dramatic confirmation of their foresight strengthened them in their reading of the situation as a whole. This reading was, as we have said, evidently not adopted finally and unanimously by the Soviet Government until after 15 March. Until Hitler went into Czechoslovakia —or rather, until the attitude of the British Government towards this reckless act had been made clear by events which fall beyond the scope of this chapter—there seems to have been some hope remaining in the Kremlin that British self-interest, or perhaps the British Left Wing, would assert itself and lead to a belated bid for collective security on the lines already urged by the Russians themselves. At any rate, on the eve of the German occupation of Bohemia and Moravia, Litvinov was still in charge of the Narkomindel,[1] and he did not depart until six weeks later when, on 3 May, Molotov took over from him. This date, for want of real evidence, must be regarded as the turning-point in Anglo-Soviet relations, as far as the Soviet Union was concerned. Litvinov stood for collective security, and, it appears, he was given an unusually free hand in his quest for it. It can only be assumed that so long as he remained in office certain elements in the Kremlin had not given up hope of checking Hitler. This was the position on the eve of 15 March.

[1] i.e. The People's Commissariat of Foreign Affairs.

(b) The Machinery of Government in the U.S.S.R.

Under the new Constitution of the U.S.S.R. which had been adopted at the Eighth Congress of Soviets on 5 December 1936,[1] the highest organ of state authority was the Supreme Soviet of the U.S.S.R., consisting of two Chambers: the Soviet of the Union and the Soviet of Nationalities. The Supreme Soviet, which was supposed to meet twice a year, exercised the exclusive legislative power; decrees passed between its sessions were ratified by it as law. The Presidium of the Supreme Soviet wielded considerable authority. It convened sessions of the Supreme Soviet, interpreted the laws in force, issued its own ordinances, and had the power to rescind decisions and orders of the Council of People's Commissars (later known as the Council of Ministers) of the Union and of the Union Republics if they were not in accordance with the law. It appointed the High Command of the armed forces, and had power to declare war when the Supreme Soviet was not in session, and proclaim total or partial mobilization. It ratified and denounced treaties and appointed the diplomatic representatives of the Soviet Union abroad. The highest executive and administrative organ was, however, the Council of People's Commissars, which was responsible to the Supreme Soviet and, when the latter was not in session, to the Presidium.

Behind the constitutional (and semi-democratic) façade of the Soviet state stood the real autocratic power of the Politburo: the Political Bureau, or Political Standing Committee, of the Central Executive Committee of the All-Russian Communist Party. Under the Party's statute, the 'supreme body' was its Congress, which was supposed to meet not less than once every three years (in fact, the seventeenth Congress met in 1934, the eighteenth in 1939). In the intervals the entire work of the Party was guided by the Central Committee, which also directed the work of the central Soviet and public authorities. The Central Committee 'organized' the Political Bureau, the Organization Bureau (Orgburo),[2] and the Secretariat of the Party.[3] Thus, technically, the three most powerful bodies in the Soviet state were subsidiary organs of the Central Committee.

The Politburo decided the policy of the Party, that is to say, of the U.S.S.R.; for this policy was handed on to the Council of People's Com-

---

[1] In introducing the draft Constitution Stalin had uttered the following phrases: 'What is democracy? Democracy in capitalist countries where antagonistic classes exist is in the first analysis democracy for the strong, democracy for the propertied minority. Democracy in the U.S.S.R., on the contrary, is democracy for all. But from this it follows that the foundations of democracy are violated not by the draft of the new Constitution of the U.S.S.R. but by the bourgeois constitutions. That is why I think that the Constitution of the U.S.S.R. is the only thoroughly consistent democratic constitution in the world' (*Moscow News*, 2 December 1936).

[2] The Orgburo and the Control Commission both dealt in different ways with the internal affairs of the Party.

[3] The members of the Secretariat were Andreyev, Zhdanov, Malenkov, and Stalin.

missars for implementation. The Politburo had a membership which varied, but which was usually about a dozen.[1] Most members of the Politburo held key ministerial posts and at the same time were individually responsible for groups of inferior Ministries.[2] Thus, in this capacity, they themselves carried out the policy determined in their secret conclaves. Several well-known members of the Politburo disappeared during the Great Purge, but the core of this all-powerful body was in 1939 the same as it had been in 1934. Its rule was a tyranny by a committee of tyrants, among whom Stalin was the most influential but was not supreme.

It is desirable to have this picture of the way in which government was carried on in the U.S.S.R. because the very fact that Stalin was not a hair-trigger dictator, able to act on his own intuitions, was reflected in the public policy. If the secret history of the twenty years following the Revolution in Soviet Russia is ever written, its readers will almost certainly be struck by one thing: the amount of talk behind every apparently sudden decision. We have to imagine the august members of the highest collective in the land droning on through the night, striving patiently, with the aid of their secular bible, to arrive at the proper interpretation of the desires and motives and purposes of the representatives of countries which they had never seen and of social systems passing their comprehension.

(c) The Struggle within the Politburo

When the Bolsheviks won power in November 1917 they had two main objects: the salvation of Russia and the salvation of the world. At first the salvation of Russia was only incidental to the salvation of the world. But the emphasis changed very rapidly indeed. In the first place, the success of the October Revolution was very much more rapid, complete, and lasting than Lenin himself had expected; in the second place, the new régime was heavily attacked from outside by the Western Powers in alliance with the Russian 'Whites'; in the third place, Communists outside Russia failed abjectly. All this, at a very early stage, put the new Soviet state on the defensive, and on the defensive it had to remain. To this end a whole new strategy had to be devised within the Marxist framework.

[1] The members of the Politburo in March 1939 were J. V. Stalin (General Secretary of the Communist Party), L. M. Kaganovich (Commissar for Transport), V. M. Molotov (Chairman of Council of People's Commissars), K. E. Voroshilov (Defence), M. I. Kalinin (Chairman of the Presidium of the Supreme Soviet of the U.S.S.R.), A. A. Andreyev (Chairman of the Control Commission), A. A. Zhdanov (Chairman of the Supreme Soviet of the R.S.F.S.R.), A. I. Mikoyan (Foreign Trade) and N. S. Krushchev. L. P. Beriya (Home Affairs) and N. M. Shvernik (Chairman of the Presidium of the R.S.F.S.R.) were substitute members.

[2] Members of the Council of People's Commissars who were not members either of the Politburo or of the Central Committee were little more than Permanent Under Secretaries; while those who, like Litvinov, were members of the Central Committee but not of the Politburo were important but not powerful officials.

Broadly speaking the Marxist line until then had been permanent offensive by people with nothing to lose. Suddenly, the most successful and devoted band of Marxists in the world found themselves with a great deal to lose; the outcasts for the first time had a stake in the world, like any kulak, a base to defend, like any emperor. And this base was being violently assaulted from all sides. Even when the Western Powers had ceased trying to throw out the new régime by frontal attack they continued in their efforts to make life insupportable for it. Yet the Bolsheviks needed their help if Russia was to be rehabilitated and industrialized in a reasonable time. It was probably the long-drawn-out struggle to reconcile the aggressive irresponsibility of the outlaw with the discretion and sobriety of the respected member of society which, more than anything else, produced the tension that was always so noteworthy a feature of Soviet foreign and domestic policy and that lay beneath many of the Soviet obscurities which could not readily be explained in terms of the Russian mentality, Russian conditions of life, and Marxist morality.

Among the firstfruits of this struggle were the bringing to a head, within a few months of Lenin's death in January 1924, of Trotsky's quarrel with Stalin (due sooner or later in any case on personal grounds) and, more important, Stalin's split with Zinoviev and Kamenev.[1] Until the end of 1930, when Stalin, after discarding Rykov and Bukharin,[2] appointed Molotov Prime Minister as the constitutional mouthpiece of a united Central Committee, the press and the party records threw some light on the fight to reconcile the two extremes: the fomentation of world revolution at the expense of the recovery and development of the U.S.S.R., and the strengthening of the U.S.S.R. at the expense of world revolution. From 1931 onwards, however, this struggle was no longer openly pursued. It went underground, and in more senses than one. In the first and more obvious sense, all those who disagreed with Stalin's policy and manner (and these included the majority of the Old Bolsheviks) were driven to plotting and intriguing among themselves: they could no longer speak out. In the second and far more interesting sense, the struggle between the two viewpoints within the Government itself—inside the Politburo, in effect— was hidden from the world behind a mask of unanimity: the only indications of what was going on in the minds of the Soviet leaders were the perpetual zigzags of their policy.

[1] In the autumn of 1924 Trotsky published his *Lessons of October* in which he revealed the dissensions in the Party. A few months later he was obliged to resign the post of Commissar for War, but was appointed to less important administrative positions. In December 1925 Kamenev and Zinoviev attacked Stalin at the Party Congress, and were defeated by a large majority. Trotsky, Kamenev, and Zinoviev were all expelled from their offices and Trotsky and Kamenev from membership of the Russian Communist Party, in the course of the year 1927 (*Survey* for 1927, pp. 253–4).

[2] Bukharin was expelled from the Politburo in November 1928, Rykov in December 1930. Molotov succeeded Rykov as Chairman of the Council of People's Commissars.

It is customary to assume that Trotsky stood for world revolution, Stalin for Socialism in one country. But this is an over-simplification of the most misleading kind. All the Bolsheviks stood for world revolution, and they all understood the necessity of turning the Soviet Union into a going concern. The real conflict—of which the Stalin–Trotsky quarrel was only a minor aspect—was one of emphasis: it was unescapable and constantly recurrent. It had to be fought out every day afresh in the breasts of every member of the Central Party Committee. It was a hydra. The splits, the quarrels, the intrigues, already fatal for so many, arose not over the question of ends but over the question of means. They did not end when Stalin and Zinoviev parted company. Nor did they end in 1931 when the effective government went into perpetual secret session. They continued. They had to continue, because the question at issue was a dilemma. Socialism in one country and world revolution, the defence and consolidation of the base and infiltration into the enemy camp—these have never been mutually exclusive. There is no absolute opposition: if there were, it would have been easy for the Bolsheviks to decide which course to follow. Their difficulties in fact arose because they were compelled to follow both courses simultaneously, and the quarrels over emphasis arose in trying to strike a balance which changed from day to day. The superior position of Stalin was above all due to the combination in his character of extreme flexibility and extreme resolution, two qualities rarely found in one man, and the two qualities demanded above all others by the Russian situation. Resolution was not enough; so Trotsky and Zinoviev went. Flexibility was not enough; so Rykov and Bukharin went. Stalin remained, having gathered round him a team of men who came nearer to Marx's ideal of what a statesman should be than any of the Old Bolsheviks, with the solitary exception of Lenin. But the struggle, at first openly reflected in public opposition, continued behind closed doors; and this struggle, the conflicting elements finding a voice in now one, now another, of the dozen men who constituted the Government of the U.S.S.R., and complicated by such domestic matters as the appeasement or coercion of the peasants, remained the propulsive charge behind Soviet policy until 3 May 1939. That is to say, it was still operative on the eve of the invasion of Czechoslovakia.

(d) The Problems facing Stalin in 1924

If we now ask ourselves two questions: what did the Politburo hope for, and why did it hope for this, until the moment when it abandoned the search for collective security, we have, in order to arrive at the answers, to glance at the problems involved in the two poles of Soviet policy and consider how they affected the position of the Soviet Union in the face of the world and of Germany in particular.

By the time when the Russian masses under Lenin's leadership had weathered the Intervention and the Civil War, the position of the Bolsheviks—in their first days of power a minority party suspected by the people and loathed by practically all the revolutionaries who had helped bring about the March Revolution—was comparatively secure and heavily buttressed by the Cheka and the new Red Army. None the less, the prospect ahead was as desolate as it could be, and the main features of the wretched land to whose succour the new Government of the Bolsheviks was dedicated were the exhaustion of the people and the ruin of their economy. Thus if Lenin's Government, or any other central government, was to survive, the people had to be rested and some sort of working economy restored. Lenin, the man of the new age, immediately and melodramatically found, bulking large between him and his self-appointed life-work, the perennial problem which had conditioned Russian history since the liberation of the new Russian state from the Tatars in the fifteenth century: how to impose a central government on a land which was too vast and too primitive to be run efficiently from any one centre, populated by a people too self-willed and too anarchic to be held together by anything but a central government—in a word, how to make a nation in conditions inimical to the building of a nation. Moreover, Lenin's task was harder than that of Ivan the Terrible or that of Peter the Great, since he had to turn his unnatural nation into an active, not a passive, instrument. This was called for by the very nature of his faith.

Faced with this situation (which we may hope, for his own peace of soul, even he did not recognize in all its implications), he decided for the time being to leave the peasants in peace to work their newly acquired land and to win the co-operation, first, of the business men inside Russia and, second, of the governments of the outside world for the sake of the material assistance they might bring in the shape of trade, industrial enterprise, and loans. Thus the New Economic Policy (NEP)[1] was born, breaking the hearts of many honest Russian Socialists and causing premature rejoicing to their enemies throughout the world. Domestically the key to the whole situation lay in the attitude of the peasants, still 80 per cent. of the whole population, illiterate, recently emerged from serfdom, exhausted by famine and war, and interested in revolution (the revolution which depended ultimately upon them) only in so far as it meant the ending of war and the appropriation of the land to themselves. They supported Lenin because he promised to make their dreams come true, and he kept his promise; but in ending the war he signed away at Brest-Litovsk a great part of Russia's granary, and in letting the peasants take the land he knew very well that before long he would have to annex it to the state. The defeat of Germany had improved the Russian position

[1] See also below, pp. 416–19.

in the Ukraine; but the peace treaties created a series of independent states —Latvia, Estonia, Lithuania, and Finland—where the Tsarist eagle had flown, and thus robbed the Russians of the Baltic coastline towards which for so many centuries they had so patiently and painfully aspired. Of even greater importance than this was the forfeiture to the Poles of large Russian-speaking parts of White Russia and the Ukraine. The recovery of these western lands, which, in the eyes of the Russians, formed an integral part of the U.S.S.R., was not an item of their foreign policy, but, as it were, part of the defensive base programme. The possession by Poland of these lands meant the continuation in an exacerbated form of mutual hostility between the Poles and the Russians and was directly responsible for the equivocal Polish attitude towards Hitler's Germany, which they would otherwise have been free to face with cool heads and a single purpose. Thus the Treaty of Riga signed by Poland and Russia on 18 March 1921[1] might have been concluded for the then undreamed-of Hitler's special benefit. Its wretched consequences represented the highest trump in his hand, the possession of which added hugely to his freedom of manœuvre up to 15 March 1939, and thereafter led to fatal confusion among the anti-Nazi Powers in their belated and ridiculous attempts to patch up a working coalition. When he finally played that card, on 23 August 1939, it all but gained him the mastery of the world.

But in the early 1920s, far from recovering lost territory, the Soviet Government were plainly going to be hard put to it to retain what they had. There were separatist movements in the Caucasus and in those parts of the Ukraine that remained to the U.S.S.R., and it was precisely the oil of Baku and the soil and minerals of the Soviet Ukraine on which the recovery of the whole Union in the first resort depended. The peasants still held to their land.

Here, it might be supposed, was enough for any government, however securely based, to cope with. But, as the last straw, the Bolsheviks were saddled with the historical duty of spreading the revolution throughout the world. This was the particular care of Zinoviev, who, like all good departmental heads, put the affairs of his department—that is to say, the Comintern—above all other considerations.[2] His highest hopes were centred on Germany, still labouring under the first impact of defeat and appearing to harbour a great many of the elements regarded by Karl Marx as requisite for a successful proletarian revolution.

This, very broadly, was the situation which Lenin would have had to resolve if his death in 1924 had not spared him the task. Stalin, for reasons best known to himself, grappled with the problem, thereby winning not the gratitude which he deserved from all the Old Bolsheviks, but their hostility. With his phrase about Socialism in one country, he went to the

---

[1] See *Survey* for 1920–3, pp. 243–4.   [2] See *Survey* for 1924, pp. 172–5.

root of the matter, proclaiming his realization that for an indefinite time to come what Russia needed was another Ivan Grozny, another Peter. There was still a long way to go before there could be any convincing pretence of Socialism even in the U.S.S.R. The New Economic Policy was still in being and was not to be repealed until 1928, just before the promulgation of the First Five-Year Plan. Meanwhile the urgent task, both from an ideological and from a practical point of view, was to create a proletariat.

That indispensable adjunct to Marxist revolution did not yet exist in Russia, and therefore could not dictate. Further, without it Russia could not become industrialized and thus wage the inevitable war with a modern industrialized state. In order to create this dual-purpose proletariat, millions of illiterate peasantry had to be taken from the land and taught to read and to handle machines. In order to feed them the remaining peasantry had to produce more food per head. In order to do this, modern farming methods had to take the place of immemorial strip-cultivation. This meant mechanization and collectivization. And this in turn meant, in effect, a declaration of war on the peasants—on, that is to say, those oppressed Russian masses for whom so many revolutionaries had suffered and died. How many of the Bolshevik leaders foresaw this necessity it is impossible to say. It can only be said with certainty that Lenin foresaw it in broad outline; Stalin, head on to the problem, in greater detail. Stalin's main preoccupation now was to surround himself with younger men who could see this and other problems through his own eyes and were prepared to tackle them in his way. Thus, after the dismissal of Rykov and Bukharin, both men of a humanitarian turn of mind, the effective government in 1931 went into opposition against the people, leaving Molotov, the newly appointed Chairman of the Council of People's Commissars, as their popular mouthpiece and also as a kind of potential hostage or scapegoat. The next eight years saw a fierce and relentless struggle to turn the peasants into artisans and to create a large well-equipped army based on a brand-new heavy industry. Almost everything was sacrificed to that.

(e) THE FIVE-YEAR PLANS[1]

During the period of the New Economic Policy the ghost of the profit motive had been allowed once again to walk about the streets, but it did not long survive the death of Lenin. The First Five-Year Plan (*Piatiletka*) was inaugurated in 1928. Its task was 'the restoration of the national economy which had been destroyed by wars and the Revolution, and its reconstruction along lines of increased industrialization'.[2]

---

[1] See also below, Part II, especially pp. 416 seqq.
[2] A. Yugow: *Russia's Economic Front for War and Peace* (New York and London, Harper &

Collectivization of agriculture began in 1929 and, by the spring of 1930, 50 per cent. of farm land in European Russia had been merged into the Kolkhoz and Sovkhoz systems.

The Second Five-Year Plan was prepared in 1932, and it set the quota for the period 1933–7. This period saw the completion of the collectivization of agriculture, and a very rapid development of industrialization, with special attention to the armament industries. 'The Second Five-Year Plan proposed to double the level of national consumption.'[1]

The Third Five-Year Plan, which began in 1938, was designed to adjust to the service of the community the forces of the new economy—the new collectivized agriculture and the new industrial organization with improved transport facilities (roads, railroads, canals) and new plants scattered all over the country and especially in areas remote from the dangers of the frontier. To quote Molotov's words in his report of 1939 submitting the Third Five-Year Plan, it had 'the gigantic program of raising the level of national economy, of culture, of the general welfare'.[2]

The slogan of the Third Five-Year Plan, as of the other Plans, was to 'overtake and surpass' (i.e. the accomplishments of capitalist countries, especially of the U.S.A.). The Russians had a long way to go:

Comparative per capita *production*[3]

Products	Units	U.S.S.R.	U.S.A.	Germany	Great Britain
Electric power	kilowatt	215	1,160	735	608
Pig-iron	kilo	86	292	234	183
Steel	kilo	105	397	201	279
Coal	kilo	757	3,429	3,313	5,165
Cement	kilo	32	156	173	154
Cotton cloth	sq. meter	16	58	..	60
Footwear	pair	1	2.6	1·1	2·2

But the concrete effects of the Five-Year Plans were on a far greater scale than most Western economists were prepared to admit at the time.

It will be seen that the target had not quite been reached by 1937, but that great progress had been made. Russian economic output may not have been efficient, but at least it was effective; and it was four years later to stand up to the test of war, and was to equip and supply (with important American and British help) the largest armies ever launched upon the field of battle.

Brothers, 1942), p. 10. See also U.S.S.R., State Planning Commission of the U.S.S.R.: *The Five-Year Plan for Building up the National Economy of the U.S.S.R.*, 3 vols. (Moscow, 1929).

[1] Yugow, op. cit. p. 12. See also U.S.S.R., State Planning Commission of the U.S.S.R.: *The Second Five-year Plan* (translated from the Russian by I. B. Lasker and John Swift), Moscow, 1936.   [2] Yugow, op. cit. p. 12.

[3] Ibid. p. 36. Figures for U.S.S.R. are for 1937, for other countries mostly for 1929.

Production under the Five-Year Plans[1]

		1932		
		Plan	Actual	Per cent. achieved
All Industries	Billion roubles	43·2	43·3	100·2
Coal	Million tons	75·0	64·0	85·3
Mineral oil and gas	Million tons	21·7	22·3	102·9
Electric current	Billion kilowatts	22·0	13·4	60·9
Pig-iron	Million tons	10·0	6·2	62·0
Cotton cloth	Million meters	4,700	2,720	57·9
		1937		
All Industries	Billion roubles	102·7	95·5	92·9
Coal	Million tons	152·5	127·1	83·3
Mineral oil and gas	Million tons	47·5	30·5	79·0
Electric current	Billion kilowatts	38·0	36·4	95·8
Pig-iron	Million tons	18·0	14·5	80·5
Cotton cloth	Million meters	6,250	3,450	55·2

This great national effort was not purely economic; it was at the same time a vast rearmament programme for the war which the Soviet Government believed to be inevitable, especially after Hitler's coming to power in 1933. It was inspired by genuine patriotism; it was directed not unintelligently by the central authority of the Soviet Government, armed with the formidable weapons of the NKVD;[2] it was assisted in its early stages by an important body of foreign specialists (mainly Americans and Germans);[3] it was carried through by a huge, miscellaneous, inexpert labour force, partly paid, partly under compulsion, poorly fed and miserably housed. According to one of them, John Scott, an American, who found employment for some years in Magnitogorsk, 'Russia's City of Steel':

This was the Magnitogorsk of 1933. A quarter of a million souls—Communists, kulaks, foreigners, Tartars, convicted saboteurs and a mass of blue-eyed Russian peasants—making the biggest steel combinat in Europe in the middle of the barren Ural Steppe. Money was spent like water, men froze, hungered and suffered, but the construction work went on with a disregard for individuals and a mass heroism seldom paralleled in history.[4]

[1] Yugow, op. cit. p. 24.
[2] The NKVD (Narodny Kommissariat Vnutrennykh Del—the People's Commissariat for Home Affairs) was later known as the MVD (Ministerstvo Vnutrennykh Del—the Ministry for Home Affairs). The security and political police was a branch of this department. Formerly it was a special department—the GPU or OGPU (Gosudarstvennoe Politicheskoe Upravlenie—the State Political Administration). Still earlier, in the time of the Civil War, this special department was known as the Cheka (from Chrezvychainaya Komissiya—the Extraordinary Commission). In the days of the Tsar a somewhat similar body existed under the name of the Okhrana (the Guard).
[3] Most foreign experts had left in 1936 and 1937.
[4] John Scott: *Behind the Urals* (London, Secker & Warburg, 1942), p. 76.

To quote Scott further:

Directors and managers of industrial units were usually party members. The authority of the party among the workers was high. . . . The party was the source of initiative and energy which drove the work forward. The party sometimes blundered, and often made trouble with its unnecessary intriguing and heresy-hunting, but by and large Magnitogorsk would not have been built as quickly or as well without it.[1]

(f) Interaction of the Soviet Union's Internal Problems and International Relations

In the course of the ten years following the inauguration of the First Five-Year Plan, the war with the people took a turn which Lenin certainly and Stalin probably had not foreseen. It began with the deportation of the kulaks, coinciding with the urgent need for unskilled labour on capital enterprise in under-populated areas—or areas, even, where free men would never stay. The deportees had to be employed: the Five-Year Plan cried out for crude labour. The GPU discovered the solution. Thus, from the miserable but far from wholesale beginnings of the early Bolshevik penal camps, sprang up and flourished the colossal system of forced labour which, before very long, was to form one of the main props of the Soviet economy. The more deportees, the more widespread were their labours; the more widespread their labours, the greater was the need for more deportees—a need which first the GPU, then the NKVD, knew how to satisfy. In addition to this system the ordinary free worker (so restless is the Russian in search of better conditions) had to be restricted in his movements by sanction piled on sanction. By the time, therefore, when the great new proletariat had been created, and was in some position to dictate, its regent and *Erzieher*, the Politburo, could not, even had it so desired, abdicate in its favour. Under the flaunting, blood-red banner, 'Socialism in one Country', the great defensive base had indeed been created, but the ideals which it had been created to defend were buried under concrete and steel.

This mattered less to the new generation of Bolsheviks than might have been expected. They were closer in mind to the spirit of Karl Marx and of Lenin than most of the older Bolsheviks who had prepared and carried through the October Revolution. They had launched themselves on a course from which there could be no turning back, and the only hope for Russia, for Marxism, and for themselves was to drive on with total ruthlessness and all possible speed. Those whose humanitarian principles conflicted with the chosen course had to go. The problem which presented itself to the new autocracy was how to keep up the pace without goading

[1] Ibid. p. 69.

the people into widespread passive resistance and—at all costs avoiding any sign of hesitation (which would have invited collapse into anarchy)— subordinate all means and all ends to the supreme end of replacing the vanished subsistence economy with an industrial economy based on mechanized agriculture. In personal terms the problem was even more simple: how to keep a grip on a machine which needed wrists of iron to hold it on the road at all. There would be time to look round and think when the speed could be slackened. Meanwhile the Soviet leaders knew, or thought they knew, where they were going. They were riding on the wave of history, and history was no respecter of persons. From the teaching of Marx and Lenin they had derived a dangerous contempt for ordinary humanity and this had been augmented by their experience of absolute power. One result of this was to cause them to underrate the strength of the people and to overrate the guile and singleness of purpose of the leaders in the Western democracies. At the same time it helped them to understand the Nazis, and the Bolsheviks' appreciation of the Nazi menace was due as much to an objective understanding of Nazi motives as to the fact that they also understood the problems of absolute power and totalitarianism.

The immediate policy, obscured by traditional Russian secrecy, distorted by traditional Russian clumsiness, and dazzle-painted by traditional Russian code-signs, was simplicity itself. It was, in the words of Max Beloff,

to seek friendly contacts with Powers who could assist in the economic upbuilding of the Soviet Union; to prevent the creation of a great anti-Soviet bloc of the imperialist-capitalist Powers, and to extend the security system entered into with the Soviet Union's neighbours as an added obstacle to a new war of intervention.[1]

This policy went hand in hand with the cruel drive to industrialize the country, a drive which was called for not only in order to raise the standard of living inside Russia, but also in order to create the strong defensive base for Communism from which, in due course, the Soviet leaders would preside over the disintegration of Western capitalist and of Social Democratic society. It was generally believed, however, that this disintegration would be brought about not by direct action on the part of the Soviet Union, but as the result of future slumps and wars and local revolutions precipitated by the death agonies of the capitalist system. Since it was plainly in the interests of the Soviet Union to weaken the forces employed in such wars, the Comintern was kept in being as a multiple fifth column. The main conflict in Soviet foreign policy arose quite simply, but re-

[1] Max Beloff: *The Foreign Policy of Soviet Russia, 1929–1941*, 2 vols. (London, Oxford University Press for Royal Institute of International Affairs, 1947 & 1949) i. 12. (The two volumes will be referred to hereafter as Beloff, i, ii.)

peatedly, from the necessity of creating and maintaining friendly contacts with the Powers and at the same time working to undermine the sovereign authority of their respective governments and the harmony of their anti-Communist inclinations.

It was not until Hitler's authority was seen to be absolute and permanent, facilitated by the Comintern's own mishandling of the German Communists and confirmed by the determination of the State Department at Washington to create a free world market, that the Politburo committed itself to a clear-cut line with a single over-ruling objective, and, recognizing in Nazism the fulfilment of another phase of the Leninist–Marxist prophecy, resorted to the League of Nations as an instrument for breaking Hitler's power.[1] Not that it had any faith in the League of Nations as such: it had watched with mingled complacency and exasperation its futility in face of the menace which, until then, had affected the Soviet Union most nearly: the menace of Japan. But at least the League provided a rallying-point where the Politburo, cloaked with the highest respectability, could appeal to the self-interest of Britain and France. By collective security, whatever Litvinov may have believed, the more realistic members of the Politburo could, while remaining true to themselves, mean only one thing: the postponement of any war in which the Soviet Union would be involved, however slightly, until she was strong enough to profit by it (to say nothing of surviving it), and the assurance that when war finally came, as come it must, it would embroil and disrupt the whole of Europe without causing vital damage to the Soviet Union.

In 1933, when the agitation for collective security reached its first peak with Litvinov's submission of a draft plan to the Disarmament Conference at Geneva,[2] the Soviet Union had barely embarked on her Second Five-Year Plan. In the Far East she continued to appease Japan while demonstrating her growing local strength at every opportunity. To the West she was still wide open, and all her efforts were bent on persuading others to join with her in containing Hitler. In 1935 the Comintern declared for a united front against Fascism, while pacts of mutual assistance were signed with France and Czechoslovakia[3] (but not, of course, with Poland). There were signs that the Soviet Union was at last becoming a force to be reckoned with. Then, in 1936, the whole of Russia was convulsed by the monstrous purges through which the Politburo sought to achieve the final consolidation of its position and to ensure absolute unanimity of thought and action in high places throughout the land.[4] The purges continued until 1938, largely undoing Litvinov's earlier efforts to convince the West

---

[1] For the admission of the U.S.S.R. to membership of the League of Nations in September 1934 see *Survey* for 1934, pp. 391–404.

[2] See *Survey* for 1933, pp. 180–1, 234, 246, 278–9.

[3] See *Survey* for 1935, i. 79–82.

[4] See *Survey* for 1936, pp. 376–8; *Survey* for 1937, i. 11–22.

that the U.S.S.R. was a civilized community; so that when, in March 1938, he sought to bring about a conference of the Powers, excluding Germany, Japan, and Italy, he sought in vain.[1] Munich followed six months later. Hitler had reached the point from which he was to advance on 15 March of the following year.

(g) THE STATE OF THE RED ARMY

We have seen how the immediate well-being of the Russian people had for years been sacrificed in order to build up a heavy industry and a large and well-equipped army. When finally completed, this immense and laborious project would be embodied in a war-machine of truly formidable proportions. But it had not yet been completed; as the event proved, it was not finally complete even in 1941. In contradistinction to the German army, the Red Army depended much more on mass than on cadres. It was not a series of precision machines, each coming into full and unembarrassed operation one by one as it was finished, finally linking up into one highly articulated super-machine as strong and no stronger than the sum of its parts. It was, in keeping with the whole organization of the U.S.S.R., based rather on the conception of a highly centralized and organic whole. It also suffered from the Russian failure to co-ordinate production—that is to say, divisions almost fully equipped would be immobilized for lack of one small item of equipment running through the whole army.

More important even than this was the state of the corps of officers. The U.S.S.R., chronically short of leaders of all kinds, was hard put to it to find suitable officers in almost all ranks, and, precisely at the moment when Hitler began to show his hand, the whole Union was shuddering and almost visibly crumbling under the great GPU purges which more than decimated the ranks of the leaders, senior and junior. By that time many people inside Russia and outside were ready to assume that in the new Red Army the Russians had an organization to be proud of—and suddenly this new Red Army was torn wide open and its young, gifted, and enterprising commanders destroyed in great numbers. Here no attempt need be made to assess the troubles which lay behind those purges. It is enough for our purpose to recognize that this appalling frenzy of self-mutilation was not undertaken lightly and that the Politburo had reason to doubt the total obedience to its will of the most highly tempered organizations designed to carry out that will. In any case, at the time of the Munich Conference the Red Army was, for the purposes of a major war, in dry-dock for refitting. More than this, the commanders best able to counter the German commanders, the younger men with new ideas, had gone.

[1] See *Survey* for 1938, ii. 68, note 1.

Tuchachevsky himself had gone. Their places had been taken by dug-outs —the Voroshilovs and the Budyennys and a host of ancient formation commanders whose ideas of warfare dated back to the Intervention. Indeed, it was not until 1942 that the old comrades were purged and new generations of commanders, trained in modern war, were given their heads.

By March 1939 the parts of the military machine, or most of them, had been laboriously turned out; but the final assembly was not yet complete. There were gaps to be filled. In spite of the impressive displays of para-chutists, the Russians had next to no strategic air force and only a most inadequate tactical one. As usual, they had put all their money and energy into guns. Their artillery was the most formidable in the world. But Hitler had no intention of fighting an artillery war. The Russians had also gone in for tanks, of types that were solid and robust, but slow. It was plain that they could not use their tanks in the Guderian manner if only for lack of highly trained motorized infantry to back them up. Motor transport hardly existed—in fact, it hardly existed until American Lend-Lease came into operation many years later. All this meant that the Red Army would be slow. It was probable that the High Command in Moscow had a good intellectual appreciation of the speed with which the German army proposed to fight its wars. But it is also true to say that it would take at least a year of hard experience for the formation commanders in the field to understand practically as distinct from theoretically—to feel in their bones, as it were—just how fast the German armoured divisions would be moving—above all, how fast the follow-up infantry would be moving with their heavy anti-tank guns disguised as anti-aircraft units.

(h) Hitler's Interpretation of Soviet Policy

Hitler had a clearer idea than most foreign observers of the condition of the Soviet military machine. Quite apart from what he could deduce about the internal state of the Soviet Union from her outward manifesta-tions, he had plenty of hard facts to go on. Unlike the British and the French, or even the Czechs, the Germans had for long had every opportu-nity to examine the Soviet war-potential from the inside: the military staffs of the revisionist Powers had got together at a very early stage. The Germans had, more than any other nation, helped to develop the Soviet potential—and particularly had helped in the training and equipment of the Red Army. Sooner or later, they knew, the Red Army would be something to tremble at, but that time had not yet come. It may safely be assumed that in March of 1939 Hitler was aware of those Russian weak-nesses which did not become apparent to the world until they were revealed first by the Finnish war during the following winter and then by the German invasion in 1941.

In view of all this it must have been fairly easy for Hitler to find the answers to the questions he had to ask himself as he contemplated the absorption of Czechoslovakia: what did the Russian attempts, so purposefully snubbed, to persuade France and Britain to proclaim a joint guarantee of that country really amount to? Was the Soviet Union ready, cold-shouldered by France and Britain, to fight alone? If not, when would she be ready, and in what circumstances?

The Soviet Union, Hitler must have calculated, would have nothing to do with a war which would not lead to the recovery of the western Ukraine and western White Russia from Poland. But Poland was a part of the French security system, as Czechoslovakia was also supposed to be, and, quite apart from this, Poland was a potential enemy of Germany. If the Soviet Union were in alliance with France, to say nothing of Great Britain, what could she hope to get from Poland? It was an entrancing situation, fat with the seeds of every kind of trouble. Russia, fighting Germany on account of Czechoslovakia in alliance with the Western Powers, would be a revisionist Power fighting another revisionist Power in a struggle to preserve a general *status quo* to which she objected with all her might. And would Poland, in any case, fight with Russia as a so-called ally in support of the Czechs, some of whose lands she coveted? Would she even allow the Russians free passage through her territory? These were questions which the Russians must ask themselves before committing themselves to fight.

Further, was it conceivable in March 1939, even if Russia did desire to share in a united stand against Hitler, that France and Russia, to say nothing of Great Britain, would in fact come together in time to act in concert—remembering that Hitler would be very carefully one jump ahead from now on, so that his potential adversaries would always be meeting to discuss the best way of preventing what had already happened? No power on earth, that is to say, except Hitler's own second thoughts or an immediate ultimatum from the Western Powers, could now stop him from occupying Prague: that chance had been thrown away at Munich. Moreover, even if the Russians did feel stimulated to belated action by the sight of the Nazis in Prague, the very fact that they were in Prague would now act as a strong deterrent. Without spilling over into Poland, the Red Army, forcing the Carpathians, would have no freedom of manœuvre, and by the time they could act Hitler would have as much of Czechoslovakia as mattered in his grip; but any attempt to deploy through Poland would drive the Poles into a frenzy of opposition. The consequences of the Treaty of Riga retained their endless possibilities. And there, with France and Britain at the ringside twisting themselves into agonies of incertitude, would be as delightful a scene of chaos as could well be imagined—the sort of chaos that Hitler throve on.

(i) India and Ceylon

By H. V. Hodson

(a) INDIA

At the beginning of 1939 the mind of India was turned in upon herself. The causes of this characteristic introversion lay deep. A sub-continent of over 1½ million square miles, with a population approaching 400 millions, and girt about with strong frontiers of high mountains and wide seas, exerted a natural gravitational pull upon all its people's thinking. Hinduism, the religion of the great majority of Indians, belonged to no other country, and embodied a strictly endogamous social system, unproselytizing and impenetrable. The ancient injunction against crossing 'the black water', and the difficulties of adhering when abroad to religious taboos and prescriptions as to food and conduct, had tended to keep many of the better-class Hindus from foreign travel. But the introversion of Indian political thought applied almost equally to Muslims, among whom there was always a strain of pan-Islamism, and whose religious fellow communities stretched from North-West Africa to South-East Asia. Leaders of the Indian Muslims frequently asserted their brotherly interest in other Islamic lands and peoples, and in 1939 it was the Arabs in Palestine who especially evoked their sympathetic protests; but since the collapse of the 'Kilafat' movement for the restoration of the Caliphate[1] after the war of 1914–18 these international Islamic motives were of secondary importance in determining the cast of Indian Muslim thought. Indeed many observers suspected that they were adduced rather as sticks to beat the British Raj than because they were deeply and spontaneously felt.

India's political introversion and self-centredness were, in truth, due more to political than to religious causes. No general tradition of democracy lay beyond the history of British rule;[2] under the Moguls, as under their Hindu predecessors and the Hindu successor-states which developed with the weakening of the Mogul power, government had been a professional business of the ruling classes; and under British rule the people, mostly illiterate as they were, felt no responsibility for government, nor, therefore, for the destiny of their country in its international career. They were certainly not encouraged in a sense of international responsibility by official policy, which had treated diplomacy and defence as a special duty or privilege of the British rulers, even while internal matters were falling

---

[1] See *Survey* for 1925, i. 62–3.   [2] See above, pp. 29–32.

more and more under Indian control, and while India as a full member of the League of Nations was ostensibly taking her place in world affairs as a responsible national Power. This passive attitude towards government, so valuable to the maintenance of alien rule with the barest minimum of force, became painfully conspicuous during the Second World War, when India was in imminent danger of invasion, and a common reaction among Indians of all classes was to feel that it was the Government's business to defend them rather than theirs to help the Government by defending themselves.

What was beginning to interest people both high and low, however, and to interest many of them to the point of fanaticism, was the question to whom the power of government should be transferred when it passed from British hands. It was the blinding supremacy of this issue in Indian political eyes that chiefly accounted for India's self-centred attitude even while the world around her was beginning to collapse. Both British and Indians sensed that the last stage in the transfer of power was close at hand. After long deliberation the Parliament at Westminster had passed the Government of India Act of 1935, under which full responsible parliamentary government was to be established in the Indian provinces, subject only to specific reserve powers entrusted to the Governors, and this was to be capped by an all-Indian federal Parliament and Government, also enjoying full responsibility and freedom within its own sphere, restricted as the latter would be, however, not only by the Governor-General's reserve powers but also by retention of defence and external affairs in British hands.

Early in 1937 elections had been held throughout British India to the provincial legislatures on a franchise much wider than under the previous Constitutional Act of 1919, extending, indeed, below literacy-level. The Indian National Congress had won 711 out of 1,585 seats in the provincial lower houses, and secured independent majorities in five of the eleven provinces; in two more it could count on majorities with the aid of smaller groups of like political complexion; and in an eighth, Assam, it had as the largest party the first claim to form a government, though it held less than one-third of the seats. Only in Bengal, the Punjab, and Sind would it certainly have to yield that claim to others. These were, significantly, all provinces in which the Muslims formed a majority of the population. Outside the North-West Frontier Province, where the political position was dominated by the personality of a pro-Congress Pathan leader, Khan Abdul Ghaffar Khan, the Congress had won only a very few of the seats reserved for Muslims. The Muslim League was the largest single Muslim party, but the 1937 elections had revealed it as still a minority group of a minority community, and in no province was it able to form an independent government.

The Congress had contested the elections to the provincial legislatures, 'not to co-operate in any way with the Act, but to combat it and seek the end of it'.[1] Its successes, therefore, posed the question whether its members should accept office under the Act. The appeal of power overcame the arguments for abstention, and though Ministerial office was at first refused, save on conditions which the Governors could not possibly accept, after months of controversy Congress members formed governments in seven of the eleven provinces. The emphasis of Congress preaching had been on the need for unity among all communities and interests in India for the sake of achieving the paramount objective of independence; and this doctrine it now applied in the light of its own electoral triumph. It denied the claim of the Muslim League or anyone else to speak for the Muslims; it refused to admit to partnership in provincial governments the League or other parties which denied the Congress claim to speak on major issues with the voice of all India; and it launched, with the keen sponsorship of Pandit Jawaharlal Nehru, then President of the Congress, a campaign to convert the Muslims by the million to the Congress allegiance.

The reaction of the Muslims was so sharp as to become the dominant element in Indian political history for the next two years and more, and to create, by the time war broke out in 1939, a totally new pattern of Indian politics. In place of undisputed Congress supremacy in the political field there was a struggle for the balance of power. The demand for independence as the price of support in the war, which if made by a united India would have been very hard to resist, failed in potency and effect because of the intestine struggle for the power which independence would bring.

The prime reaction to the Congress policy was a closing of the Muslim ranks. The Muslim Premiers of the Punjab, Bengal, and Assam advised their Muslim supporters to join the Muslim League, which for the first time organized itself as a nation-wide party appealing to the masses. Mohammed Ali Jinnah became the outstanding leader not merely of the League but of Muslim self-assertion generally. In 1938 he allowed negotiations for an accommodation between the Congress and the League to break down on his claim that the League should be recognized as the only organization representing the Indian Muslims. Reports of alleged offences against Muslims by Congress Governments or their subordinates, including individual Congress members or officials, were published by the Muslim League and inflamed opinion further. The majority of the Muslims having any concern with politics grew more and more convinced that the Congress was essentially a Hindu body and that for the Muslims the fight to prevent Hindu Raj must rank at least on an equality with the fight to end the British Raj.

[1] Electoral manifesto of the Indian National Congress.

It was in the course of 1939 that Muslim League policy, following the logic of that dual struggle, took a new direction. In March of that year the Working Committee of the League appointed a sub-committee under Jinnah's chairmanship to examine schemes for assuring the Muslim position in an independent India. Those with their ears to the ground were talking more and more about a concept which to the general public was still almost unknown—Pakistan. Ideas of an independent Muslim State in North-West India had been current among Muslim intellectuals since 1930, and the name Pakistan or Pakstan had been given to it in 1933.[1] As the notion took root its scope grew, until other Muslim-majority or Muslim-ruled areas of India were included. But the Muslim League had not committed itself, and the more responsible Muslim leaders, up to 1939, were still thinking in terms of a Muslim unit in a loose Indian federal structure rather than of a sovereign Muslim nation state. In September 1939, however, the Working Committee of the League declared that Muslim India was irrevocably opposed to any 'federal objective' which

must necessarily result in a majority-community rule under the guise of democracy and a parliamentary system of government. Such a constitution is totally unsuited to the genius of the peoples of this country which is composed of various nationalities and does not constitute a national State.[2]

This paved the way for the fateful decision of the League in full session at Lahore in March 1940, when it was resolved that no constitutional plan was workable unless it embodied the principle that areas where the Muslims were in a majority should be grouped to constitute 'independent states'.

For different reasons, then, both the Congress and the Muslim League, together representing the great majority of the voters of British India, were by 1939 unequivocally opposed to furthering the Federal part of the 1935 Constitutional Act. To the Congress, it represented 'imperialism'; to the Muslim League, a Hindu majority, and probably a Congress majority, at the centre of a united India. Whether the Federation could have been made to work—with vast benefit to Indian political unity and stability when war came—if it had been brought into force in 1936 or 1937 is a matter for speculation; in fact, it was legally debarred by the refusal of many of the major states to join it, for reasons of their own interest. Consequently India continued to be governed from the centre under the 'Montagu-Chelmsford' Constitution of 1919, with minor modifications made by the 1935 Act. This confided the whole executive power to the Governor-General's Executive Council, without any reservation of sub-

[1] The name was derived from the initial letters of the regions that the new state was to comprise: Punjab, Afghanistan (i.e. the North-West Frontier Province), Kashmir, Sind. It was afterwards linked with an Urdu word, 'pak', meaning 'pure'.

[2] *Indian Annual Register*, 1939, ii. 351, quoted in R. Coupland: *Indian Politics, 1936–42, Report on the Constitutional Problem in India, Part II* (London, Oxford University Press, 1943), p. 206.

jects—though the Viceroy could veto resolutions of the majority of his Council in certain circumstances. This constitutional fact was of considerable importance after 1941, when the majority of the Council became Indian; in 1939 the majority was both official and British.

The Congress and the League were not the only political parties, nor the Hindus and the Muslims the only religious communities. Other political groups included a Liberal party with strong intellectual leadership but little popular backing, and other remnants of an earlier régime of narrower franchise; a Hindu communal party, the Hindu Mahasabha, with considerable strength in patches of British India; more than one organization of the 'untouchables' or Scheduled Castes, though none with any real political weight; and Socialist groups both within and outside the Congress. No powerful Communist party had raised its head, but Communist or near-Communist individuals were influential in the Congress Socialist wing and in certain other Left-wing groups.

Nor, of course, were the politically active Indians representative of all their fellow countrymen. The classes from whom the Indian army was recruited remained true to their traditions. Business men did not allow nationalist aspirations to handicap them in adapting their businesses to the new prospects. And the mass of the people tilled their fields or worked at their trades, ignorant of what was going on in India's capital or the chanceries of the world.

Against this background the parties decided their attitudes to the problem of approaching war. For years the Congress theme had been that India should not become an instrument of 'imperialist war', as any potential conflict among the Western Powers was dubbed. In March 1939, at the annual session of the Congress, Pandit Jawaharlal Nehru, its President and chief authority on international affairs, successfully moved a resolution declaring that 'it is urgently necessary for India to direct her own foreign policy as an independent nation, thereby keeping aloof from both Imperialism and Fascism'. Pandit Nehru's writings at that time[1] suggested some latent hesitation in equating Britain and France to the Fascist Powers. But this did not shake his conclusion, and that of the Congress generally, that India should not help Britain in the coming war. This conclusion was related to the calculation—based upon an implicit reliance upon British sea-power, which had for a century preserved India from world war—that India herself would not be the scene of hostilities. Pandit Nehru wrote in January 1938:

Who might be the aggressor against India? It is hardly likely that any European country will embark on so rash an adventure, for each country in Europe fears its European neighbour. Soviet Russia is definitely out of the picture so

[1] See Jawaharlal Nehru: *The Unity of India, Collected Writings 1937–1940* (London, Lindsay Drummond, 1948) and *The Discovery of India* (New York, John Day Co., 1946), p. 424.

far as aggression goes. . . . A Japanese invasion of India could become a practical proposition only if China has been completely crushed, and if the United States, the Soviet Union and England have all been effectively humbled. This is a large undertaking.[1]

In retrospect, after the war was well advanced, and Japan had invaded North-Eastern India, Pandit Nehru (in the summer of 1944) wrote of the pre-war situation:

The world situation seemed to be drifting towards a major conflict, with England and France as heads of a European group of nations, and Soviet Russia associated with some Eastern nations. The United States of America held aloof from both these groups. . . . Indian opinion inevitably sided with Soviet Russia and the Eastern nations. This did not mean any widespread approval of communism, though a growing number were attracted to socialist thought. The triumphs of the Chinese revolution were hailed with enthusiasm as portents of the approaching freedom of India and of the elimination of European aggression in Asia. We developed an interest in nationalist movements in the Dutch East Indies and Indo-China, as well as in the Western Asiatic countries and Egypt. The conversion of Singapore into a great naval base and the development of Trincomalee harbor in Ceylon appeared as parts of the general preparation for the coming war, in which Britain would try to consolidate and strengthen her imperialist position and crush Soviet Russia and the rising nationalist movements of the East.[2]

This, though a personal reflection, may be judged fairly representative of educated opinion in the Congress, the largest and most comprehensive Indian party. Many Congress members were even more negative in their attitude towards the impending world conflict, having adopted the doctrine of 'non-violence' propounded by Gandhi, who at this period exercised considerable influence from an unofficial position in the background of Indian politics. It must, however, be remembered that the great majority of Indians, being illiterate and very poor, cared for none of these things, knowing indeed nothing of the world beyond their own experience: and that, even to the educated minority, international affairs ranked a weak second to India's internal problems.

Characteristic of the attitude of the Congress was its intense hostility towards a bill introduced in the Imperial Parliament in April 1939 amending the 1935 Constitution to enable the Central Government to superimpose its executive and legislative authority on the provinces in an emergency. This measure was deemed (rightly, as it proved) essential for the defence of India in a major war, but to the All-India Congress Committee it was intolerable because it made 'provincial governments the helpless agents of imperialism'. The Congress also protested against the dispatch of contingents of Indian troops in the spring and summer of 1939

---

[1] Nehru: *Unity of India*, pp. 24–25.   [2] Nehru: *Discovery of India*, p. 423.

to Aden, Singapore, and Egypt 'against the declared will of the Indian people'; although every serious student of such affairs knew that India's defence could be sustained only at the periphery of the Indian Ocean area, and not on her own shores. It was this dispatch of troops overseas which led the All-India Congress Committee to call upon Congress members of the Central Legislative Assembly to refrain from attending the next session, and to warn provincial Congress Governments 'to assist in no way the war preparations of the British Government'.

The official attitude of the Muslim League was more restrained. As late as 28 August 1939, its Working Committee declared that it was 'premature to determine the attitude of the Muslims in the event of a world war breaking out'. This cautious approach appeared to be animated by several motives. Because the main source of the League's policy and power was anti-Hindu and anti-Congress feeling rather than anti-imperialism—although in Indian politics, as they were, it could not afford to be in principle less anti-imperialist than the Congress—its leaders were keeping their powder dry for the real battle for which they were preparing. The League did not suffer in singlemindedness, as did the Congress, from having half-accepted the Gandhian doctrine of non-violence. Its President, Mohammed Ali Jinnah, foreshadowing his later highly successful tactical leadership, recognized that a split between the League 'high command' and the Ministries in the Punjab and Bengal—both of which were likely to support the Government in the event of war—would be fatal to its solidarity and strength, and that from the tactical point of view the profitable course was to take advantage of the probable errors and divisions of the Congress. From beginning to end, therefore, the Muslim League's official attitude towards the war was equivocal. Here was still another example of the fact that political India saw the impending world catastrophe in the light reflected from her own interior problems.

(b) CEYLON

Ceylon's communal problem, as she approached self-government, was quite different from India's, and happily much milder. The Sinhalese formed roughly two-thirds of the population of approximately 7 millions, but they included an important minority of Christians amid the Buddhist majority. About one-third of the million-and-a-half Tamils (Hindus, also with a Christian minority) were descendants of ancient invaders, the other two-thirds being recent, and for the greater part temporary, immigrants from South India. Other important minority communities included Malayalis from the Malabar Coast, 'Moors' (descendants of Arab traders), and 'Burghers' (descendants of the Dutch).

Communal electorates, embodied in earlier Constitutions, had been abolished in favour of geographical representation, with a universal adult franchise, under a new Constitution of 1931, commonly named after the chairman of the Commission upon whose report it was based, the Earl of Donoughmore. Although the Government was headed by a Council of seven Ceylonese Ministers under the chairmanship of the Governor, executive responsibility was divided between certain officials and seven 'executive committees' of the State Council, each electing its chairman who thereby became a Minister.

The Donoughmore Constitution was the object of attack from two main quarters—from, broadly, the majority who demanded complete self-government and the abolition of the committee system, and from minorities who demanded communal representation. In November 1938 the Governor, Sir Andrew Caldecott, at the invitation of the Secretary of State for the Colonies, submitted a report on the constitutional position. He thought that the demand for a communal register and communal constituencies should be resisted, and that a Cabinet system of government should replace the committee plan. This was the stage that the constitutional controversy had reached when war began. The agitation was moderate, and, except for small groups, did not go beyond demanding, as the next stage, 'Dominion Status' for Ceylon, possibly even with some qualifications.

One special cause of difficulty arose from the presence of so many Indian estate labourers. The Ceylonese proper wished to exclude them from the vote, unless Ceylon had become their permanent family domicile. They themselves, backed by the Government of India, pressed for 'equality of rights over the whole field of rights'. The friction over this issue between the Governments of Ceylon and of India was becoming serious by 1939.

(ii) Burma

By F. S. V. Donnison

From 1886 onwards, the whole of Burma came under the rule of British India, to be governed on the Indian model; it was absorbed into an Indian rather than a British empire. British officers were few on the ground; they brought with them Indian troops and Indian subordinates, and it was only too frequently with these that the Burmese had to deal; and the gates were opened to the later immigration of Indians so that in the years before the war with Japan the Indian population numbered a million out of a total population in Burma of 17 millions.

The breakdown of Burmese isolation produced far-reaching economic changes. In the last decades of the nineteenth century the cultivation of rice expanded rapidly, until Burma became the largest rice-exporting country in the world. This expansion was largely financed by Indian capital, and before the war with Japan much of the rice-land of Burma had passed into the hands of Indian landlords by foreclosure of mortgages. Much Indian labour also came to be used in the cultivation of the crop. The rice export trade was almost entirely in the hands of the British. Teak exports increased and oil and other mineral resources were developed, but, though much of the labour in these industries was Burmese, capital and management were almost entirely foreign.

With the royal family deposed and the hereditary local or tribal chiefs supplanted by a professional and largely Burmese civil service, the old social framework of Burma was destroyed. A new aristocracy of Burmese government officers grew up, educated on Western lines at the schools and university set up by the British, owing a considerable loyalty to the British and to British ideas, and often bound to British officers by strong ties of personal friendship. Those members of the educated class who failed to enter this new aristocracy drifted mostly to the Bar and thence into the new political life that was growing up with the development of democratic government on Western lines. Such men only too frequently began their careers with a sense of exclusion; and then found that to air their grievance and lay the blame for it upon the British was an easier way than most of gaining public support.

The monastic order continued outwardly little changed; but the monks were inwardly discontented and undisciplined owing to the diminution of their influence, the transfer of their educational functions to professional teachers, and the refusal of the British (under cover of refraining from interference with religion) to exercise the disciplinary control which had formerly been a prerogative of the Burmese kings. An increasing number of the order became interested in politics, their influence being usually thrown on the side of the discontented nationalist politician and against the Administration.

The growth of Indian influence in the national economy was accompanied by Indian infiltration into most of the essential services, and for many years before the Japanese war Burma depended almost entirely upon Indians for her dock labour, conservancy services, railways, river transport, posts and telegraphs, medical and public health services (except nurses), for most of the retail trade of the country, and for a considerable proportion of the police force.

The development of the economic wealth of Burma under the British considerably raised the standard of living of her people; but this benefit was easily forgotten in contemplation of the high rewards earned by foreign management and capital, and of the dependence of the country upon Indian labour. A somewhat resentful nationalism grew up, both stimulating and stimulated by the gradual transfer of political power to which the British were committed by their policy in India. It involved the growth of anti-foreign, particularly anti-Indian, feeling, so that little or no loyalty was felt to the British connexion.

By the 1930s there had grown up a popular demand for the separation of Burma from India on the ground of the deep differences in social and religious conditions and the conflict of economic interests between the two countries. In spite of a last-moment revulsion of popular feeling, prompted by fear that separation might mean that Burma would lag behind India in her progress towards independence, Burma was in fact separated from India on 1 April 1937, the British Government giving an assurance that this would in no way jeopardize her political future.

The new Constitution followed as closely as might be the lines of that conferred upon India at the same time. The Governor was appointed by the British Government, but was required, except in regard to two categories of his functions, to act upon the advice of his Ministers, who were required to command the support of a majority in a Legislature elected on a very wide franchise. In the case of one category of excepted functions, which included the important subjects of defence, currency, and external affairs, the Ministry was not entitled to advise the Governor at all. In the case of the other, which covered mainly the responsibility laid upon the Governor to safeguard certain minorities and some of the government services, the Ministry was entitled to place its advice before the Governor, but he had the power to discard this if in his opinion it conflicted with his special responsibilities. In practice the Governor was loath to disregard the Ministers' advice for fear of precipitating a constitutional crisis. The hill areas, known as the Excluded Areas, were likewise outside the Ministers' functions. Ultimate political power in the new Burma was dangerously divided and it is unlikely that the Constitution could have long survived the resultant stresses, even had there been no war.

A number of parties, new and old, contested the first elections after separation. They did not differ appreciably in policy; they were, in fact, remarkably united in their demands for an early increase in the degree of autonomy conferred upon Burma. Their real interest lay in a study of the possible permutations and combinations of parties with a view to gaining the maximum share of the spoils of office. The small European group was ready to support any government that preserved order, followed a sound financial policy, and abstained from discrimination against minorities.

In view of future developments, the Thakin or 'Master' party merits further notice. The Thakin movement had begun about 1930. The party had Communist leanings, was strongly anti-British, and aimed at independence through revolution. Its leading members were mainly young and fanatically nationalist university students. In the first general election the party was surprisingly unsuccessful, and after a brief flirtation

with one of the older parties it returned to its more familiar role of subterranean anti-Government and industrial agitation. By 1940, however,
its activities could no longer be ignored: the party was proscribed and its
leaders arrested. Aung San, then general secretary, and certain other
leaders avoided arrest and escaped to Japan, a country which, with its
vigorous development and propaganda of 'Asia for the Asiatics' and its
repeatedly successful defiance of the Western Powers, could not but appeal
to young Burmese nationalists. Thirty other members of the party were
smuggled out to Japan soon afterwards. When the Japanese invaded
Burma in 1941–2 these young men returned with them to raise irregular
forces of Burmese against the British. It would be wrong, however, to
describe them as pro-Japanese; they were pro-Burmese, and assisted Japan
for what they could get to further their own cause.

After the first elections under the new Constitution, which were held in
1936 shortly before the separation from India came into effect, a government was formed by Dr. Ba Maw, leader of the 'Poor Man's Party', who
built up an uneasy coalition. This, with the help of the European group,
commanded a majority throughout 1937 and 1938. In 1939 the Government fell owing to the withdrawal of this group's support because of
dissatisfaction at the handling of the Burmese-Muslim riots of 1938 and of
the industrial unrest subsequently fostered by the Thakin party. 'Freedom' and 'Burmanization' were the watchwords of this, as of the two
succeeding Governments, but Dr. Ba Maw had hardly begun to feel his
strength and was always held in restraint by his dependence upon the
European group. A fresh coalition under U Pu fell after a brief period of
office, partly for its too-ready support of the British in the war and partly
as a result of intrigue. Yet another coalition was then formed by the ebul-
lient and colourful personality, U Saw, leader of the 'Patriotic Party'.
The mainspring of his policy was the demand for complete independence
as the price of co-operation in the war. U Saw soon began to feel his
strength under the new Constitution; he was building up a private army
and was well on the way to establishing a dictatorship when he went to
England to press in person his demand for a promise of immediate
Dominion status. Failing in this, he set out for Japan to see what he could
gain there. But war broke out while he was on his way and as he retraced
his steps to Burma he was arrested and detained by the British Government for his contacts with the new enemy. U Saw's place as Premier was
taken by U Paw Tun. With the Japanese war obviously imminent, the
Burmese Ministry had given up trying to draw profit from Britain's
difficulties and made an honest if belated attempt to rally Burmese public
opinion to the cause of the Allies.

While still a province of India, Burma had depended on the Indian
army for defence. But the Indian army always looked to the north-west

and Burma remained a military backwater. After separation from India a beginning was made with the creation of a separate Burmese army; but a backwater flows slowly, and the rate of progress was conditioned by the resources of the country, and by the distance and lack of interest of the British War Office, to which the administration of the new army had been transferred after separation. Up to the last, war with Japan was not expected; and it was considered that in the unlikely event of war Japan could scarcely invade Burma until she had disposed of the redoubtable Singapore, which, so it was supposed, would prove beyond her strength or at least beyond her strength to achieve quickly. If Japan should then try to invade Burma, the hills and jungle were held to be a natural defence for the protection of which the small forces in Burma would be adequate. Little or no preparation was therefore made for war, none for war on the scale of the operations that later developed in Burma. But even if the authorities had been more acutely aware of what was coming, it may well be doubted whether more resources could have been spared for Burma in view of the many demands upon British strength in the Middle East and elsewhere at that time. The unpreparedness of Burma was merely one count in the general unpreparedness of Britain for war.

(iii) South-East Asia

By Victor Purcell

(a) SIAM[1]

In 1782 the first monarch of the house that was still reigning in 1951 ascended to the throne of Siam, and his accession was followed by 150 years of generally benevolent despotism and of almost continual peace. Under King Chulalongkorn (1868–1910) there were progressive steps to adjust Siam to a new way of life. The old feudal system was abandoned and a civil service was organized, slavery was abolished, the judicial system was revised, and farming-out of taxes ceased. Many Siamese, including the royal princes, received their education abroad. The reforms were continued, though at a decelerated tempo, under King Chulalongkorn's successors, but the monarchy continued to be an absolutism with the abuses usual to such a régime, including the exercise of power by favourites. Under King Vajirawudh (Rama VI, 1910–25) favouritism was carried to extravagant lengths which aroused discontent among the foreign-educated junior officials, and this discontent was increased by the drastic pruning of the civil service by King Prajadhipok (1925–35) during the economic

---

[1] The name of the state was changed from Siam to Thailand (Maung Thai = Land of the Free) on 4 July 1939, changed back to Siam in 1945 and back again to Thailand in May 1949.

depression. In alliance with a number of army officers who had grievances against the autocratic princes, a group of these officials organized a successful *coup d'état* on 24 June 1932.

Because of the tendency of the times and of the foreign political theory that had influenced the returned students, the régime that was then inaugurated took on a democratic colour. But the revolution was not the outcome of a movement among the people; it was directed by a group calling itself the People's Party under the leadership of the able and determined Luang Pradist Manudharm,[1] a young lawyer trained in Paris. There was no bloodshed and very little disorder. King Prajadhipok accepted a provisional Constitution which was replaced in December 1932 by a permanent one. Legislative power, budgetary control, and the power to interpret the Constitution were vested in an Assembly to be elected by popular suffrage every four years from candidates of twenty-three years of age or over, satisfying certain educational and other requirements. The elective element of the Assembly was, however, limited for the time being to 50 per cent. of its membership. The King was retained as a constitutional sovereign and was defined as sacred and inviolable and the Defender of the Buddhist Faith. He could dissolve the Assembly without even the Cabinet's approval, and he had the right of veto which, however, could be over-ridden by a second vote of the Assembly. The residue of the executive power was vested in a State Council which combined the functions of a Cabinet and a Privy Council. At the first meeting of the People's Assembly held on 28 June 1932 Phya Manopakorn (Phya Mano) was appointed Chairman of the Executive Committee.[2]

Political differences appeared almost at once, and were emphasized by the unrest arising from the economic depression. An attempt to form a Nationalist Party among army officers and high officials was followed by a split in the State Council between Phya Mano, at the head of a group of moderates, and Luang Pradist, leading the progressive elements. Phya Mano denounced Luang Pradist's scheme of national economy, including land nationalization and social insurance, as communistic. The forces of conservatism rallied to Phya Mano, who followed up his attack by securing a Royal Decree proroguing the Assembly until new elections could be held. A law was then passed making Communism a crime punishable by ten years' imprisonment and a fine, and Luang Pradist was sent into virtual exile, with a pension, 'to continue his studies in France'.

With the popular sentiment prevailing, a coup, if it were to be successful, would have to be associated with the idea of progress. In the hope of averting the danger of such a coup, Phya Mano announced a programme

[1] His name is sometimes written Luang Pradit. His original name was Nai Pridi Panomyong.
[2] See Kenneth P. Landon: *Siam in Transition* (London, Oxford University Press, 1939), p. 9 and *passim* for a detailed account of the Revolution of 1932.

involving a survey of resources under the direction of an Economic Council, government control of, or participation in, public utilities, and the assignment of vacant land to the unemployed. Thus Phya Mano attempted to steal Luang Pradist's thunder. One positive achievement of his was the creation of more effective electoral machinery. His Government, however, became increasingly unpopular. It adopted a dictatorial attitude towards the Assembly and interfered with the freedom of the press. At the same time the army was brought more and more into the picture and officials of the pre-revolutionary régime were given civil service posts.

The general fear that Siam might be relapsing into a mild dictatorship prepared the way for a second *coup d'état*, while Phya Mano's inept tactics alienated the military officers in the dissolved Assembly who had helped to create the new régime and upon whom he ultimately depended for power. In the summer of 1933, Phya Bahol, with a few sailors and armoured cars, occupied the palace, which was then the seat of government, without striking a blow. It was inevitable that this coup should lead eventually to the recall to Siam of the popular Luang Pradist, and this in spite of the misgivings of the conservatives. When he reached Siam in September after six months' absence he was enthusiastically welcomed by a delegation of law students and labourers. Although he was not immediately given office in the Government, it was felt that a change of economic policy was imminent.[1]

A fortnight after Luang Pradist's return, Prince Bovaredej, a cousin of the King and an ex-Minister of War, exploiting the conservatives' fear of increased taxation and of a revival of the scheme for nationalizing land, headed a royalist revolt. This revolt was crushed by Government troops after a four-days' battle. Suspected support of this ill-starred revolt by King Prajadhipok led to his going abroad and prepared the way for his eventual abdication in March 1935.[2] The suppression of the revolt also spelt the end of the aristocracy as a governing power and opened the way for the establishment of a middle class.

In a situation of sporadic revolts and conspiracies, it was hard for a democratic system of government to gain strength. Moreover, the Assembly was still half-nominated and suffered from the indifference of the electorate at the polls and from the refusal of the Government to allow party organization among members of the Assembly. The power of the Assembly, nevertheless, was slowly growing, largely as a consequence of the weakening of the State Council owing to a struggle among the leaders

---

[1] A commission set up on his return to examine the charges of Communism against him reported (February 1934) that he was *not* a Communist.

[2] The actual occasion for the abdication was the abolition of the necessity of appending the King's signature to death warrants, which abrogated his prerogative of mercy. He was succeeded by his nephew, Ananda Mahidol, who was then a boy at school in Switzerland. King Ananda Mahidol was found shot in the royal palace at Bangkok on 9 June 1946.

for control. Under the tactful leadership of Phya Bahol the differences between the liberal elements headed by Luang Pradist and the military group under Luang Pibul[1] were smoothed over. Luang Pradist, while never making any concession in principle, came to terms with Luang Pibul as far as it was possible for a liberal to come to terms with a militarist. For a while as Foreign Minister and then, after Phya Bahol's retirement, as Minister of Finance in Luang Pibul's Government, he greatly enhanced his prestige.[2]

Side by side with progress towards democratic government went the growth of nationalism. In the spring of 1939 this culminated in an orgy of anti-foreign legislation. The press, too, was vociferously anti-foreign. This xenophobic spirit had already manifested itself in the discussions on the Labour Bill, the budget, and the Shipping Bill in mid-1938, when demands were made in the Assembly for the exclusion of foreigners from the benefit of the new regulations. These demands were countered by the spokesmen of the Government, who pointed out that foreign skill and capital were temporarily essential to the country's development. But the anti-foreign movement had also a domestic aspect created by fear of the large and ever-increasing community of Chinese in Siam.

Resentment against the Chinese could be traced to a date as recent as 1911. Before that there had never been any large-scale friction between the races. But in that year the Chinese called a strike as a demonstration against the new tax laws whereby they were called upon to pay the same capitation tax as the Siamese.[3] All shops were closed and business was completely at a standstill. For the first time the Siamese realized the Chinese grip on the economic machinery of their country and they were filled with alarm. Amongst other activities the Chinese monopolized the rice-mills and the rice export trade. They also performed many essential tasks as clerks, shop-keepers, and servants. Most of the money that they made they transmitted to China. Before 1914 they had married Siamese women, but after that they usually brought in their own women from China (needless to say, a significant development). Then, with the growth of Chinese nationalism, the Chinese Government began an educational drive intended to tie overseas Chinese indissolubly to China herself through the medium of education in the Chinese National Language (*Kuo Yü*). To counter this attempt to render the Chinese an unassimilable body in their midst, the Siamese Government insisted on primary education in the Thai language for all children in Siam. By 1939 a compromise had been reached whereby Chinese schools taught both Chinese and Thai. But

[1] Luang Pibul Songgram's name is variously spelt as Pibul, Pibun or Bipul, Songgram or Songkram, &c. His personal name was Nai Blaek Srianong.

[2] In 1941 he was not to weaken in his opposition to the Japanese demands which had then been made, and he eventually resigned from the Cabinet rather than compromise.

[3] Namely, 7 *baht* instead of 1·50. A *baht* (formerly a *tical*) was worth about 1*s.* 9*d.* sterling.

attempts to displace the Chinese as the middlemen of the country seemed to be doomed to failure by the Thai indifference to business and lack of special aptitude for it.

The Chinese in Siam at the beginning of 1939 numbered about 525,000 Chinese from China and 2 million of mixed Sino-Siamese blood, and immigration legislation had so far failed to place any effective check on their increase.[1] The persistent refusal of the Siamese Government to accept Chinese diplomatic and consular representation in Siam can be traced to the fear of centralized organization of this powerful racial minority.

In the extreme south of Siam there was a concentration of about 500,000 Malays forming an unassimilable lump. The Malay provinces of the south had revolted more than once in the eighteenth century and they might do so again.

The culminating point of Siam's long diplomatic association with Great Britain was reached in the Bangkok Treaty of 1909[2] whereby British subjects were placed under the jurisdiction of Siamese 'International Courts'. By this treaty, also, Siam transferred her suzerainty over the four Malay states of Kelantan, Trengganu, Kedah, and Perlis to Great Britain. Almost simultaneously a railway loan was negotiated between Siam and the Malay States for the development of railway communication between Siam and her southern neighbour. Since the population of these four states was Malay, there was in 1939 no discernible irredentist feeling in Siam regarding them. The progressive abolition of British extraterritorial rights in Siam which began in 1909 was completed by the conclusion of the Anglo-Siamese Treaty of Commerce and Navigation of 1937, which was the first fully equal treaty between Siam and any of the Great Powers.[3] Britain, until the Second World War, held first place in Siam's foreign trade with 37 per cent. of the total as against Japan's 11·6 per cent. Britain's capital interests in the country were far greater than those of any other country. Siamese finances, too, were tied up with the London money market—the entire public debt had been floated in London and the redemption fund was deposited in London banks or invested in sterling bonds. Finally, Siam had adhered fairly consistently to the sterling bloc.

With France, Siamese relations had varied in cordiality, but a treaty of friendship, commerce, and navigation signed on 14 February 1925 had marked the beginning of a long period of, at least, diplomatic friendliness. The *coup d'état* of 1932 did not immediately alter the atmosphere, but by 1937 goodwill was threatened by fear in Indochina of Japanese penetration of Siam and of Siam's new rearmament programme. *L'Impartial*, a

---

[1] For statistics of immigration for the eight years ending in 1925–6, see *Survey* for 1926, p. 467.
[2] See *Survey* for 1929, p. 410.
[3] See ibid. pp. 405–17 for an account of the liquidation of foreign extraterritorial privileges in Siam.

Saigon newspaper, asked: 'Is the new Constitutional Government of Siam dreaming the dreams of her ancient kings, hoping to reconstruct her large kingdom of past ages by annexing the Laos country and part of Cambodia?'[1] An Indochinese rearmament programme in turn alarmed the Siamese, though it fell far short of the Siamese programme in implementation. The Siamese having denounced the 1925 treaty, a new treaty was negotiated in December 1937 which administered a final blow to extraterritoriality and to restrictions on Siam's tariff autonomy. In the spring of 1939 there was a mutual extending of the olive branch, though this scarcely concealed the suspicions that each country entertained for the other. However, Siamese irredentism was only mildly glowing and there was no hint of demands for the return of lost territory.[2]

Siamese-Japanese relations extended back to the sixteenth century, though the diplomatic paths of the two countries had not crossed. But after the victory of Japan over Russia in 1904–5, Siam naturally became aware of the changing balance of Far Eastern politics, and in the years to come her statesmen were further to note Japan's rising power and her declared ambitions which must sooner or later bring her into conflict with the West. At the same time they remarked the growing weakness of Britain and France. In the past there had existed only two political constellations for Siamese watchers to observe; in the future there would be three. Moreover, the new constellation shone at least as brightly in the Far Eastern skies as did the original two. But when in 1933 Siam, intending perhaps to assert her neutrality, abstained from taking part in the vote of censure on the Japanese for their invasion of Manchuria,[3] she was embarrassed by the effusive thanks of the Japanese. Some observers, in the light of subsequent events, detected in the succeeding years a 'drift towards Japan', and the existence of an influential Japanese group in the Siamese administration was alleged. No proof of this, however, was forthcoming and the truth seems to be that while Siam was afraid of Japan she had no bias in her favour.[4]

When we survey the state of Siam in the first months of 1939 we see the country in the grip of an aggressive nationalism. Luang Pibul Songgram had replaced Phya Bahol as Premier, heading a government in which

---

[1] *L'Impartial*, 8 February 1937.

[2] In September 1940 Luang Pibul Songgram (or Bipul Songkram) was to open negotiations for the return of former Thailand territory from Indochina, including the provinces of Luang Prabang and Bassac in Laos and part of Cambodia, including Angkor, a total of about 28,000 square miles. (Franco-Siamese relations are more fully dealt with in the section on French Indochina—see below, pp. 86–87.)   [3] See *Survey* for 1933, p. 509.

[4] A rumour that the Japanese were, with Siamese consent, about to cut a canal through the Isthmus of Kra was circulated from time to time in the pre-war years. The facts appear to be that the construction of the canal was never seriously contemplated. The objections to it were the cost (greater than for the Panama Canal), the small advantage, strategic or commercial, and the probability that the beginning of work on it would precipitate war.

military men predominated, and Luang Pradist had become Minister of Finance. There were signs that the latter would at last be allowed to carry out his economic scheme. There was news, too, of an abortive conspiracy to restore King Prajadhipok. But there was no evidence to indicate that within three years Siam would have thrown in her lot with Japan.

In her increased armament orders Siam was influenced by the fact that her finances permitted her to buy only in the cheapest markets,[1] and though she bought destroyers from Japan and Italy, American aeroplanes were also on her list of purchases, and Britain was by no means left out of the orders. The impression given by Siam's external policy in the spring of 1939 was that she was anxious to avoid involvement in any conflict between the Powers. The fall of France and Pearl Harbour were still a long way beyond the horizon. In the meantime Siam was fully occupied with her internal affairs—in developing her economic resources,[2] in adapting herself to social and constitutional innovations, and in learning to walk as a modern state.

(b) French Indochina[3]

In the southern lobe of the great Indochinese peninsula the French advance during the latter half of the nineteenth century had created an artificial political unit, French Indochina. The French founded the colony of Cochin-China in 1858, and then in succession drew within the orbit of their protection Cambodia (1863), Tongking and Annam (1873–85), Laos (1884–93), and Kwang Chow Wan (1899). The union of these territories under the Governor-General of Indochina did not become effective until 1899. French Indochina, with an area of 286,000 square miles, had in 1938 a population of 23,030,000.[4]

In the latter part of the nineteenth century the tendency of France was towards protection in trade. Industrialists, now that French heavy industry was beginning to expand, feared overproduction and they wanted new markets. The notion that colonial production should be limited to supplying the mother country with raw materials or with non-competitive products was embodied in the law of 1892. Indochina by the same law was declared an 'assimilated' possession. It was provided that the products

---

[1] Siam's pre-war budgetary expenditure was of the order of £10 million a year, about the same as that of the London County Council for the same period.

[2] Rice was Siam's staple food and her most valuable export. Her most important mining was of tin (18,500 tons quota for 1938). The value of her rubber export was about 24 million *baht* in 1937. The country was financially sound.

[3] This word is sometimes hyphenated, Indo-China. The French word Indochine is not usually hyphenated.

[4] Composed of 16,679,000 Annamites, 2,925,000 Cambodians, 1,375,000 Thai (Laos 589,000; other Thai, 786,000), 1,017,000 Indonesians (Moï), 214,000 mountain dwellers of the north (Man and Meo), 40,000 Chams, 60,000 Malays, 326,000 Chinese (to which should be added 73,000 Sino-Annamites and 40,000 Sino-Cambodians), 43,000 Europeans, and 6,000 Indians.

of the mother country should enter the colony[1] duty-free while those of other countries were to be subject to the same duties as in France. As a general rule Indochinese produce could be imported duty-free into France. But the desire to protect French industry which spurred the French legislators was even more clearly expressed in the interpretation of the law. At first many Chinese and Japanese commodities used by the Indochinese natives were taxed only to a moderate degree, but later the duties were raised.

After the First World War many commercial companies were organized for the development of Indochina, and private capital flowed freely into the colony.[2] In 1928 a new customs law was enacted which gave Indochina a regular method of adapting her tariffs to meet colonial needs. The demands of local groups of traders, industrialists, &c., were to be considered as tacitly approved unless the home Government came to a decision to the contrary within a very short time.

As it turned out, however, the Act of 1928 led to the enforcement of even harsher protectionist measures. The demands of the European interests in Indochina surpassed those expressed at home. New tariffs were established for foreign commodities even higher than those in France. The result was the increased isolation of the country and the exclusion of many Chinese and Japanese articles which had hitherto been able to enter.

Unfortunately for reform, the new customs law came into effect at the moment that the great world depression began. The depression engendered extremely autarkic economic systems in the world on a national or imperial basis. This tendency was an encouragement to a protectionist policy, and there was a danger that French imperial economy would be transformed into a closed economy. In particular, it was thought by many critics that it was a mistake to try to separate Indochina from her geographic setting. The character of her agricultural and industrial products and the needs and customs of the natives made easy access to the markets of the East essential. These ideas gained ground and Indochina's special position was recognized by degrees in subsequent laws and trade treaties with foreign countries.[3]

The French have always nourished a deep reverence for their own culture and institutions and have only with great difficulty been brought to believe that the extension of these to other people, however alien and remote, could bring anything but benefit to the recipients of the favour. Equality they conceded, and they did not tend to segregate themselves

[1] Cochin-China was the only part of Indochina technically a colony; the other provinces were protectorates.
[2] In 1938 the total value of foreign investments in Indochina was U.S.$384 million, 95 per cent. of which was held by Frenchmen.
[3] In 1936-8 slightly over half of Indochina's imports came from France and her empire, which took roughly the same percentage of her exports.

racially as did the British in their colonies, but it must be the equality of fellow Frenchmen who were well and truly assimilated to the Gallic model. In the late nineteenth century the political and cultural assimilation of a colony to France was very much favoured by French opinion, but misgivings on this score manifested themselves even before 1900 and voices were lifted to give a warning against the futility and injustice of attempting to destroy the culture of the local races which, whatever its defects, was admirably suited to their needs. Opinion began to change, but only very gradually, and with the change of opinion came a modification of policy.

Equally slow was the growth of a belief that the local population should share in the government of the country. By 1909, however, the French Chamber of Deputies stated in an order of the day that 'it is suitable to prepare gradually and wisely an advisory participation by the natives in public affairs'. Native and French representatives already sat side by side in the Colonial Council of Cochin-China. This was also the case in the Great Council of Economic and Financial Interests, organized in 1928. In other Indochinese countries wholly native assemblies were set up.[1]

Meanwhile the Annamite mind had been reacting to French colonialism according to its own instincts and logical processes. (It should be remembered that Annam had for two millenia been under Chinese influence; while Cambodia and Laos had inherited an Indian tradition.) Resistance to the political and cultural advance of the French had existed from the very beginning of the latter's penetration. The financial burdens caused by putting Indochina 'on a paying basis' and the incitements to Asiatic consciousness caused by the Japanese victory over Russia in 1904–5 and, later, by the Chinese Revolution, gave an impulse to nationalist feeling, and conspiracies and acts of violence became an almost daily occurrence.

In the decade following the First World War discontents in Annam piled up. The burden of the complaints was that the assistance given by Indochina to France and to French interests was not reciprocated, and that the Annamites were not given an opportunity to acquire the training and experience necessary for them to direct their own destinies.

Organized nationalism in Indochina at the time of the outbreak of the war in Europe in 1939 was confined to the Annamite countries. It regarded the Cambodians and Laos as naturally subject peoples. But there

---

[1] The Indochinese Union was brought into being by a decree of 11 November 1887. It consisted of five states: the colony of Cochin-China, the protectorates of Annam, Cambodia (including the territory around Battambang ceded by Siam in 1907), Tongking and Laos, and Kwang Chow Wan, leased from China. The whole country was under a Governor-General, assisted by a Secretary-General, and each of the states had as its head an official bearing the title of Resident-Superior, except in the case of Cochin-China, which, being a direct French colony while the others were only protectorates, had a Governor at its head. Cochin-China was represented in France by one deputy. (*Statesman's Year Book*, 1939, p. 922, and Charles Robequain: *The Economic Development of Indo-China* (New York, Oxford University Press, 1944), p. 9.)

were several factions in the movement and little co-operation among them. They were united in their dislike of French rule, but could not agree on a programme. There was a breach between the older and younger generations of nationalists, each group heartily disliking the other. Moreover, the almost routine misappropriation of party funds and other malpractices that distinguished nationalist politics did not enhance the credit of the movement.

There were some nationalist parties which aimed at reforms along democratic lines and not at a violent breach with France. Such were the Tongkingese Party of Pham Quynh and the Constitutionalist Party of Bui Quang Chieu. The revolutionary elements in 1926 had formed another party, the Viet Nam Cach Manh Bang, comprising two increasingly divergent elements, the nationalists and the Communists. Cantonese influence began to predominate. By 1929 the party had lost strength and influence and finally died when the Communists broke away from it during that year.

A more vital and enduring organization was the National Annamite Party (Viet Nam Quoc Dan Dang), which was Tongkingese. It was small in membership (only about 1,500) and was modelled upon the Chinese Kuomintang founded by Sun Yat-sen. It appealed to youth and it was from the outset a terrorist group. It issued propaganda addressed to students, employees, and the army, and it endeavoured to secure feminist support. Its attempts to link forces with similar groups in Siam came to nothing, but it had succeeded in 1930 in establishing relations with the Kwangtung and Yunnan branches of the Kuomintang. In January 1929 it attempted unsuccessfully to assassinate Pasquier, the Governor-General, and a month later succeeded in murdering Bazin, head of the Labour Recruiting Bureau. Police investigations following the murder revealed that of this hitherto unknown party 50 per cent. of the members were in government service.

Finding the police hot on their trail, the Quoc Dan Dang decided prematurely to launch their programme of intensive action, and a series of acts of violence resulted. A mutiny took place at Yen-Bay; at Hanoi bombs were thrown at the Commissariat; the sub-prefect of Vinhbao was assassinated. But action by the French authorities, including an aeroplane attack on the party leaders (which also killed 200 innocent villagers), was successful, and in 1933 the party was reported dead as an organized group.

The programme of the Annamite Communist Party, founded in 1925 by Nguyen Ai Quoc,[1] was first to assure Annam's independence under a democratic bourgeois régime and then, as a second step, to integrate it

---

[1] Nguyen Ai Quoc was to appear again in 1942 as Ho Chi Minh, the nationalist leader. He had assumed this name in about 1932.

with the Soviet Union. Nguyen Ai Quoc was Moscow-trained and he worked with Borodin[1] in Canton. In 1927, when the Kuomintang was purged of its Communists, Nguyen Ai Quoc had to fly with Borodin to Russia. Here Nguyen Ai Quoc was entrusted with the task of establishing Communism in Indochina. His task was facilitated by the permission that the Cantonese authorities gave to his followers to organize in Canton providing that they confined their efforts to attacking French imperialism. Nguyen Ai Quoc's great problem was to reconcile the differences between the Marxist-Leninists and the 'conservative' Communists who broke away in 1929 to form their own party. Moscow's influence had been decidedly one of restraint (at this stage at least); it disapproved of terrorism and favoured co-operation with the nationalist movements.[2]

Both in the colony and in France, the severity with which the authorities suppressed the nationalist and Communist movements came in for strong criticism. The more tolerant attitude towards these movements, which had been adopted when the Front Populaire came into power in France in 1936, proved to be but a brief interlude. Activity was soon forced underground again. The two prisons in Indochina in which thousands languished were condemned by the critics, both in France and elsewhere, for their appalling lack of hygiene and care.

Laos had been the last large area to become part of French Indochina. This had led to clashes with Siam, who tended to claim suzerainty over all countries where Thai dialects were spoken. French diplomacy had in 1868 recognized Siamese sovereignty over the Cambodian provinces of Angkor and Battambang, and this encouraged the Siamese to encroach more and more along the Menam valley. The British were disposed to back the Siamese claims. The French protectorate over Laos was not established until the conclusion of the Franco-Siamese treaty of 3 October 1893, under which Siam renounced all claims to territory on the left bank of the Mekong. Friction had developed almost immediately over the execution of the treaty. Negotiations were reopened and in 1902 a new treaty was signed. All that France obtained was a slight rectification of frontier in return for a limitation of her extraterritorial rights in Siam. Another treaty followed in 1904 by which Siam renounced all the sovereignty that she still retained over the Laos in Bassac and that part of the kingdom of Luang Prabang located on the right bank of the Mekong, and by a treaty of 1907 Siam ceded to France the Cambodian regions of Battambang, Siemreap, and Sisophon. The results of this treaty were, on the one hand, territorial advantages for France and, on the other, diplomatic gains for Siam, who was willing to make sacrifices in order to get rid of foreign sovereignty on her soil. The Siamese-French treaty of February 1925 marked the end of France's judicial rights in Siam,[3] and also estab-

---

[1] Soviet political adviser.   [2] *Survey* for 1927, pp. 354-5.   [3] See above, p. 80.

lished a new régime on the Indochinese-Siamese frontier on a footing of substantial equality and provided, *inter alia*, for the demilitarization of zones adjoining the frontier.[1] From 1907 onwards Franco-Siamese relations seem steadily to have improved in spite of the activities of Annamite nationalists in Siam.

More important than Japan's military victory over Russia and the alarm felt in consequence for the safety of Indochina was the indirect influence it had over Annamite youth. Japan became the leader of the Yellow Peoples, replacing China as the cultural head of the Asiatic hegemony. (It was reported that the Annamites planted the Japanese lotus in their paddy fields to celebrate the Japanese victory of Tsushima.) However, it gradually became clear to Annamite nationalism that Japan no more accepted the Chinese, the Indians, or the Annamites as their co-equals than the Annamites accepted the equality of the Laos or the Cambodians. Russia and China thereupon displaced Japan as the object of Annamite hero-worship.

Indochinese-Japanese relations on the diplomatic level had long been excellent. In the field of commerce Japan had always bought more from Indochina than she sold there, but the depression had revealed the amazing development of Japan's industry and export trade. The fall of the yen and the cutting down of Indochina's rice and coal exports to Japan brought home to the Indochinese industrialists the desirability of having a trade treaty with Japan, which the French had hitherto avoided. A temporary treaty was signed in Paris in May 1932.

The French saw in Japan a fellow enemy to the subversive elements that were causing them trouble in Indochina. At the same time they saw that economically Japan was a threat to their interests. There were in Indochina in 1938 only about 400 Japanese all told, and the comparative absence of another country's nationals in one's midst is always an aid to good feeling with that country. But in 1939 the French-owned Haiphong–Kunming railway, which was in fact a very important gateway to Southern China, became a subject of contention in consequence of the Sino-Japanese war. Moreover, a series of Sino-Indochinese commercial and immigration agreements, partly agreed upon in 1930[2] but not finally put into effect until 1935, was a source of friction between Japan and Indochina, for by the terms of the agreements munitions might be shipped across Tongking at the wish of the Chinese Government, free of transit duty. The blockade of the Chinese ports in 1937 had caused the Haiphong–Kunming and Hanoi–Langson railways to carry an ever-increasing

---

[1] Detailed provisions relating to the frontier régime were laid down in a supplementary convention of 25 August 1926, which also provided for the establishment of a Franco-Siamese Permanent High Commission of the Mekong. This Commission held its first session in January 1928. For these Franco-Siamese agreements see *Survey* for 1929, pp. 417–21.

[2] See *Survey* for 1930, p. 349.

portion of China's military supplies. In the course of 1938 Japan and France had agreed that the frontier should be open only to goods contracted for before July 1937. The prohibition was modified in some cases, but in 1938, after further Japanese protests, the Indochinese authorities stopped all transit to China over the Yunnan Railway. Then, following up this success, the Japanese in February 1939 announced their occupation of Hainan Island, thus blocking the Indochinese port of Haiphong. In reply the French reopened the Yunnan Railway to Chinese war materials on 20 March.

On 1 April 1939, the Japanese occupied the Spratly Islands, about half way between Saigon and North Borneo, in spite of the fact that France had given notice of the occupation of the islands and had suggested arbitration. Thereafter, very belatedly, the French began to strengthen the Indochinese defences. Hitherto they had been deterred from this course by the Conservative party in France, which feared the Chinese more than the Japanese because of the strong Communist element in China.

(c) Malaya

In the year 1939 Malaya meant only three things to the world at large —rubber, tin, and the Singapore Base. Actually it was much more than this. It was a prosperous modern country won from the jungle by British and Chinese enterprise; it was the meeting-place of three great races, the Chinese, the Indian, and the Malaysian; it was a unique experiment in governing a plural society. Altogether Malaya had a first-class importance in Asiatic politics and world strategy.

The two industries mainly responsible for Malaya's rise to prosperity were tin and rubber. The first was an age-old trade which had expanded its output enormously at the turn of the nineteenth and twentieth centuries, and the second had been created by British enterprise from seeds brought from Brazil in the 1870s and expanded to meet the demands of a new invention, the motor-car.

To find labour for these industries it was necessary to import it from abroad, since the Malay was content with his own smallholding of paddy or coconuts and was usually disinclined to work in tin mines or on rubber estates. Chinese and Southern Indians came to Malaya in increasing numbers until in 1938 there were as many Chinese as there were Malays (over 2 millions of each) and about 700,000 Indians.[1]

Wages were low (50–70 Malayan cents, or 1s. 2d. to 1s. 5d., was a common daily wage in the rubber industry early in 1939) but sufficient to attract immigrant labour. This great growth of immigration was bound to cause complications at some time or other. The Indians were mostly Tamils

[1] By 1941 the Chinese had outnumbered the Malays by 100,000. For Chinese immigration into Malaya before 1926, see *Survey* for 1926, pp. 458–64.

working on the rubber estates and were not regarded as a threat to the livelihood of the natives, but the Chinese, with their superior energy and initiative, were in a different category. Many thousands of them worked in the tin mines and a smaller number on rubber estates, but thousands also displayed an uncanny skill at establishing themselves as traders and middlemen. The Malays were to an increasing extent displaced economically by Chinese pressure, and they would also have lost a great deal of their land to the industrious immigrant had they not been protected by the law of Malay Land Reservations. The ambitions of the Chinese, however, were confined mainly to making money and returning as soon as possible to China and they were willing to leave the cares of administration to the British. It was said of the Chinese that they did not care who held the cow so long as they milked it.

In spite of the apprehensions of the Malays and the resentment felt by Malayan-born Chinese at being regarded as interlopers in the country of their birth, the relationship between the two races—and indeed between all races—was harmonious under British rule.[1] The Malay-Chinese clashes, involving the death of scores of persons, including women and children, which were to be a disturbing feature of the months immediately after the Japanese surrender in 1945, and which were a direct outcome of the Japanese policy of setting the Malays against the Chinese, were entirely unknown in the pre-war decades.

The Malays in 1939 had no political parties and little political consciousness; the politics of the Indians were imported, not domestic, and referred only to nationalism in India. With the rise of nationalism in China the Kuomintang had become very active in South-East Asia and had encouraged both the immigrants and the Malayan-born Chinese to identify themselves with their ancestral country and not with the country they lived in. The Chinese law of citizenship was the *jus sanguinis* and not the *jus soli*. The tendency of this was to create an *imperium in imperio*, and in consequence the Governments of the Malay States[2] were not willing to permit the organization of the Kuomintang in Malaya. After repeated representations by the Chinese Government, a compromise was found in 1931[3] whereby it was made legal in Malaya to be a member of the Kuomintang in China, but the organization of branches in Malaya was still prohibited. In spite of this the Kuomintang continued to be active and was the main force behind the Chinese Distress Relief Fund which, after the outbreak of the Sino-Japanese War in 1937, remitted huge sums to China. The Kuomintang also encouraged the boycott of Japanese goods. Youthful

[1] For the disturbances among the Chinese in Singapore in 1927, which precipitated the introduction of legislation restricting Chinese immigration, see *Survey* for 1926, pp. 462–4.

[2] i.e. of the Straits Settlements, the Federated Malay States, and of each state outside the Federation.

[3] The Lampson-Wang Agreement.

Chinese agitators calling themselves the Anti-Enemy-Backing-up Society (AEBUS) attempted to enforce this boycott by direct action—for example, by tarring the goods of traders suspected of dealing in Japanese goods. But the affiliations of 'AEBUS' were with the Communists, whose hatred of the Japanese was their one bond with the Kuomintang.

After the purge of the Communists from the Kuomintang in 1927[1] the two parties had become bitterly hostile to one another, but before 1930 the Malayan Communist Party had not been of much importance. From 1930 onwards, however, it exerted its influence more and more, especially through its control of the so-called General Labour Union, a self-appointed body which operated very largely through intimidation. The General Labour Union was behind a number of large-scale strikes. The Malayan Communist Party was almost exclusively Chinese. There were a number of Malay and Indian Communists but these did no more than carry out the orders of the Chinese leaders.

Owing to the diversity of the elements of the population and the migratory nature of the Chinese and Indians, the growth of democratic institutions in Malaya had been slow. The heterogeneous nature of the political units was a handicap in welding Malaya into a unit. In 1896 four of the Malay States (Perak, Selangor, Negri Sembilan, and Pahang) had been federated under British suzerainty. In 1909 the suzerainty over the four northern states—Kelantan, Trengganu, Kedah, and Perlis—had been transferred from Siam to Britain by the Treaty of Bangkok.[2] It had been hoped that the four northern states and Johore would join the Federation, but the tendency of the latter to become an amalgamation, with consequent loss of sovereignty to its units, had deterred the others from joining. The British therefore decided upon a scheme of decentralization whereby most of the control was handed back to the states. The machinery of the Federation was, however, retained for matters of common interest to the four states.[3]

---

[1] See *Survey* for 1927, pp. 331–57.

[2] See also above, p. 80.

[3] For a country only the size of England (without Wales) Malaya had a very complex constitutional history.

Penang (Prince of Wales Island) was ceded by Kedah to the East India Company in 1786; a strip on the mainland, named Province Wellesley, was added in 1800. Singapore island was ceded by Johore to the Company in 1819. Malacca was obtained from the Dutch by exchange in 1824. Labuan was founded in 1846. These, together forming the Straits Settlements, were in 1867 transferred from the control of the Indian Government to that of the British Colonial Office.

Perak came under British protection in 1874 when the Sultan agreed to ask for and to act on the advice of a British Resident on all questions other than those touching on Malay religion and custom. Similar treaties followed with Selangor (1874); Sungai Ujong (1874)—this state and others adjoining it were later combined to form Negri Sembilan; Pahang (1888), and Johore (1914). These states (with the exception of Johore) in July 1895 accepted federation, and the Federated Malay States came into being on 1 January 1896.

The Governor of the Straits Settlements was *ex officio* High Commissioner of both the Federated

By 1939 it was already clear that the centralized advisory authority was proving ineffective, and the states were tending to build up barriers between one another.

The Straits Settlements, comprising Singapore (which included for administrative purposes Christmas Island and the Cocos-Keeling Islands in the Indian Ocean), Penang (including Province Wellesley), Malacca, and Labuan, had a Legislative Council with thirteen official and thirteen unofficial members presided over by the Governor, who had a casting vote. Eleven of the unofficial members were appointed by the Governor—five Europeans, three Chinese, one British Indian, one Malay, and one Eurasian—while two European members were elected, one by the Chamber of Commerce in Singapore and the other by the Chamber of Commerce in Penang. The Federal Council of the Federated Malay States (created in 1909) was, after the adoption of the Decentralization Policy, composed of sixteen official members (including the High Commissioner), and twelve nominated unofficial members. Of the unofficial members four were Malays, five Europeans, two Chinese, and one Indian. Several of the State Councils of the Federated and Unfederated States also had European and Chinese and, usually, Indian representation (two Chinese and one Indian representative in the case of Perak, Selangor, and Negri Sembilan).

The legislature aimed at being representative, but was by no means of a democratic nature. How to introduce a franchise into a country with such diverse elements and with such a fluid population was a great problem. Education in the administrative language, English, was provided at cheap rates in government or grant-in-aid schools; Malay education of primary grade was free in the Malay States; primary Tamil education was provided free on the larger rubber estates. The Chinese provided their own education through the medium of *Kuo Yü* or 'National Language'[1] in Chinese schools which received government grants-in-aid. Vocational training was emphasized in the 1930s and higher education was provided at Raffles College and at the King Edward VII College of Medicine in Singapore.

Malaya's astonishing prosperity received a set-back in the trade depression of 1930–2, and the disadvantage of having all the eggs in one basket (or, more correctly, two baskets) became apparent. Besides tin and rubber the only products of importance in Malaya were copra and pine-

and Unfederated Malay States (the latter being Kelantan, Trengganu, Kedah, Perlis, Johore, and Brunei in Borneo).

Under the treaty of 1895 a Resident-General was appointed as the agent and representative of the British Government to act under the High Commissioner; in 1910 the Resident-General was replaced by a Chief Secretary. Since the Chief Secretary had become the virtual ruler of the Federation, under the decentralization scheme the post was abolished and a Federal Secretary, junior in precedence to the four Residents of the Federation, appointed.

[1] See above, p. 79.

apples. Restriction of rubber output had been tried earlier although not with entire success,[1] but learning from errors of the past the British interests now got into touch with the Dutch and French and after prolonged negotiations the International Rubber Regulation Agreement was brought into force in June 1934. The scheme successfully restricted exports from producing countries, and with the help of a general trade recovery raised the price to a figure that earned a fair profit on well-managed estates.[2] Similarly, the tin industry was safeguarded by the International Tin Committee which was able by the creation of buffer stocks and other methods to maintain a stable price of between £200 and £230 a ton.[3]

The trade of the Straits Settlements had been built up on the principle of complete freedom of trade in both imports and exports. By the 1930s, however, the sudden growth of Japanese competition with Britain and other countries, especially in textiles, brought about a situation in which the Straits Settlements were concerned, in the interests of British trade, to modify this policy. It was clear that in the absence of restriction of Japanese imports Japan would, within a limited space of time, have obtained a practical monopoly of the bazaar trade of Malaya. The same conditions were developing in the Netherlands Indies. The ability of the Japanese to out-distance their competitors was due to the depreciation of the yen in relation to the Malayan and Dutch currencies, to low wages in the factories, as well as to efficient management and up-to-date equipment. The Japanese would accept no reasonable compromise and the Colonial Powers were faced with the alternative of protecting their trade or of being practically driven out of the markets whose prosperity they had so largely created. There had been moderate Imperial Preference in Malaya since 1932, but it was too small to have any appreciable effect on Japanese competition.

Yet the interests of Lancashire not being immediately the same as those of the Singapore merchants, the Textiles (Quotas) Ordinance met strong unofficial opposition in the legislature and had to be passed with the use of the vote of the official members in 1934. Under this ordinance imports of Japanese textiles into Malaya might equal the average level of the years 1927 to 1931, but might not exceed it. The effect of this was that, whereas Japan's percentage share of total textile imports into Malaya in 1933 had been 68·1 as compared with 17·7 for the United Kingdom, it had by 1938 dropped to 18·6 per cent. as compared with 40·52 per cent. for the United Kingdom.

To a community with a very low purchasing power Japanese goods were undoubtedly a boon and the restriction of their importation might reasonably have been regarded as a grievance. However, the Chinese

---

[1] See *Survey* for 1930, pp. 473-7.   [2] See *Survey* for 1935, i. 351-61.
[3] See *Survey* for 1930, pp. 481-4; *Survey* for 1935, i. 362-71.

were engaged in an anti-Japanese boycott, while the Malays and Indians were silent on the subject.

The total value of the manufactured goods imported into Malaya in 1935 was 247 million Malayan dollars.[1] Of this total 29·7 per cent. came from the United Kingdom, 13·6 per cent. from other Empire countries, and only 3·6 per cent. from Japan.

During the pre-war period one-third of Japan's total iron imports came from Malaya. The Japanese operated iron mines in Trengganu and Johore. In 1937 Malaya exported 1,166,300 tons of iron-ore and in 1938 1,580,900 tons, almost entirely to Japan. In the state of Trengganu the duty on iron-ore from the mines amounted to two-thirds of the total expenditure on public works and social services. The Japanese also worked bauxite and a low quality manganese.

The Japanese community in Malaya in 1938 was small (not more than 7,000) and not at all obtrusive. Its members were for the most part middlemen—merchants, shopkeepers, keepers of small hotels, photographers, barbers, masseurs and masseuses—but there were also some fishermen. They were well-behaved and law-abiding, though those who studied them closely often noticed a suspiciousness in their attitude and not uncommonly a scarcely concealed arrogance. The police were well aware that a great many of them were engaged in espionage.

The defence of Malaya was looked upon primarily as the responsibility of the United Kingdom Government and Malaya's part was mainly to make financial contributions towards the cost. The decision to build a naval base at Singapore had been approved by the Imperial Conference in 1921. Construction was begun in 1923, but was checked during Ramsay MacDonald's first Government; it was, however, resumed in 1925. A further check occurred in 1929 under the second Labour Government, but the base was virtually completed in 1938 at a cost of approximately £20 million.[2] The official opening took place on 14 February 1939. Malaya contributed over £12 million to Imperial Defence between the two wars.[3] The Sultan of Johore had made a gift of £500,000 towards the cost of the base in 1935.[4]

But although the monetary contributions to defence were considerable, Malaya's man-power in 1939 was not organized for war. There was a small garrison of regular soldiers in Singapore and an Indian battalion was stationed at Taiping in Perak. The latter was eventually to be replaced by the Malay Regiment which had been raised in 1932 and was still in

[1] The value of the Malayan dollar was fixed at 2s. 4d. sterling.

[2] Hector Bywater in Daily Telegraph of 23 December 1938. See also Survey for 1929, p. 59.

[3] H.M.S. Malaya, still in commission in 1939, was a gift to the Imperial Government by the Federated Malay States in the First World War.

[4] There was no general realization of the fact that the effectiveness of the base must depend on Britain's ability to maintain an adequate fleet in Eastern waters.

training. A small force of engineers had been added to the 700 or so men of the Malay Regiment in 1938. The Johore Military Forces amounted to about 400 men. Apart from the garrison, reliance was placed mainly on the Volunteer Forces, which included naval and air arms but which amounted in total strength to only a few thousand men. The Volunteers were mostly British or Malays, but there were Chinese companies in the Straits Settlements. In February 1939 a Defence Secretary was appointed for Malaya, together with a Director in charge of Air Raid Precautions (A.R.P.).[1] In the event of war it was contemplated that Malaya's function would be to provide raw materials for the war effort and to act as a 'Dollar Arsenal' with which to buy war materials in countries outside the sterling bloc. It was not visualized that Malaya would be directly involved in the war that now seemed inevitable. The fall of France was a catastrophe that had not appeared, even vaguely, in the crystal of the future. While it was realized that, for Japan, Singapore would be a glittering strategic prize, it was believed that she would, in the event of war, have to seek it by frontal attack from the sea: a back-door attack from the land seemed in 1939 to be utterly out of the question.

(d) The Netherlands Indies (Indonesia)[2]

In the spring of 1939 the Japanese were aiming at the creation of a Chinese-Japanese-Manchukuo economic bloc. To be really effective the proposed economic bloc would have to include a large tropical area. This fact was well known to the Japanese, and it was also not missed by the Dutch, who happened to be in possession of the tropical area obviously indicated—an enormous empire of 733,000 square miles stretching east and west over a greater distance than the entire width of the United States, and with a population of about 66 million.[3]

The Netherlands Indies, which had been under Dutch control for three centuries, was extremely rich. It supplied about 31 per cent. of the world's copra, 17 per cent. of its tin, 33 per cent. of its rubber, over 20 per cent. of its sisal, and 29 per cent. of its palm oil, in addition to large supplies of tea, cane sugar, and coffee, together with 85 per cent. of the world's pepper, and practically all of its requirements in quinine. The foreign capital (mostly Dutch) invested in the country was estimated at between U.S. $1,000 million and 1,500 million.

[1] In June 1939 an Anglo-French Defence Conference took place in Singapore.
[2] Netherlands India was the official name for the territory. It was usually known in English as the Dutch East Indies, the Netherlands Indies, or N.E.I. Indonesia was the name in favour with the nationalists, and it was also used in many official connexions by the Dutch. For a general description of Netherlands India in its international setting in the decade following the end of the First World War, see *Survey* for 1926, pp. 438–56.
[3] The population of Java alone had grown from 4½ million in 1815 to nearly 29 million in 1900, and to 42 million in 1930.

A policy of rapid democratization had been pursued in the Netherlands Indies throughout the 1920s and 1930s. The Volksraad, which met for the first time in 1918, had been established in 1916 as a move towards giving the Indonesians their due place in public affairs.[1] It was to be composed of a minimum of thirty-nine members, half of whom (ten Indonesians and nine others) were to be elected by indirect suffrage. The Volksraad had at first only advisory powers, but it was subsequently endowed with co-legislative powers.[2] From 1929 it had the power of initiating legislation (though this was rarely exercised) as well as the power of amendment and the right of petition. Nationalism, which was developing rapidly, found one of its expressions in the proceedings of this body.

It had traditionally been the deliberate policy of the Dutch to maintain the native social order, but, as Furnivall pointed out in 1939, the centre of gravity had been displaced—the system hung down from above instead of standing firmly on its base. Pressure from outside had led to communal ownership of land, distorting native tenures and ideas of long-holding, and dissolving the normal bonds of social life. Cheap imports had destroyed the native economic system and straitened the sphere of native arts, and during the 300 years of passive acquiescence in European superiority there had been an inevitable degradation of the native culture.

Then, when occasion allowed, there was a reaction in the form of Nationalism, a fever of the body politic trying to throw off the ills impairing its vitality; and the Nationalist leaders, dazzled by Western superiority and trying to copy the West in things in which the secret of its strength was thought to lie, are contributing still further to break down the native social order.[3]

Compared with India and the Philippines the Indonesian nationalist movement began late. Reasons for this included the facts that native society had been left comparatively undisturbed until the appearance of private enterprise in the 1870s, that the islands outside Java and the Moluccas had not been effectively occupied until after 1900, and that the Dutch had been slow in introducing Western education for any considerable number of Indonesians. But the economic development of Indonesia from the beginning of the century had attracted to the archipelago a large

[1] See *Survey* for 1926, p. 446.

[2] By the terms of the revised Netherlands Constitution of 1922 and of a special *Indische Staatsregeling* of 1925, the Governor-General was to exercise administrative power except in so far as specific functions might have been reserved to the Crown by the Constitution or by the law, but the legislative power formerly exercised by the Governor-General in Council was transferred to the Governor-General and Volksraad in respect of all internal affairs of Netherlands India. The Parliament at The Hague, however, still reserved the power of direct legislation in regard to Netherlands India, as well as the right to ratify the budget and annul ordinances passed at Batavia even when these solely concerned internal affairs (see *Survey* for 1926, pp. 446–7).

[3] J. S. Furnivall: *Netherlands India: a Study of Plural Economy* (Cambridge University Press, 1939), p. 459.

number of Dutch Europeans, both officials and non-officials, of humbler status than was normal in British colonial territories, and these had brought their politics with them. The European example was extremely influential in inspiring the nationalist movement, but it was at the same time a source of weakness since it tended to divide the nationalist leaders from the mass of the Indonesian people.[1] It was not until 1910 that the nationalist movement first manifested itself as such, and it was then associated with a plan for the economic independence of the natives, especially from Chinese middlemen. *Boedi Oetomo* (Beautiful Striving), an association started by Indonesians in 1908, had for its main object the furtherance of popular education, though it gradually took on a more political character. It was, however, before very long eclipsed in popularity by a second society, the *Sarekat Islam*, which had its origins in the depressed conditions of the batik industry in central Java in 1910, and which imported a religious element into the movement. This society was at the outset moderate in its programme, striving for a self-governing Indonesia within the Dutch Empire, but it assumed a more radical spirit as time went on. Radical elements among the Europeans and Dutch Eurasians (which in 1914 formed the Indian Social Democratic Union) influenced the nationalist movement greatly during its development. A constantly increasing influence upon the nationalist movement was also exercised by the 'study clubs' organized by Indonesian students returning from Europe.

Directly the Volksraad opened it became the scene of turbulent oratory and unrestrained criticism of the Government. At one time a Radical bloc was formed which comprised not only the *Sarekat Islam*, *Boedi Oetomo*, and *Insulinde* (a Eurasian party) but also the Indian Social Democratic Party. Between 1920 and 1927 the influence of Communism began to be felt more and more upon the nationalist movement, and in November 1926 and January 1927 there were Communist insurrections which, however, were easily suppressed.[2] As Amry Vandenbosch wrote: 'Since communism is the antithesis of nationalism, what took place can probably best be explained as either communism using nationalism, or nationalism using communism for its own purposes.'[3] The suppression of the Communist outbreaks put an end to the tendency of the nationalist movement to seek and hope for foreign aid.

In the years preceding the outbreak of the war in Europe the nationalist movement assumed a great complexity. Nationalist parties with varying aims and methods proliferated, and in 1928 a federation of them was organized. This did not function smoothly owing to certain fundamental

[1] E. S. De Klerck: *History of the Netherlands East Indies* (Rotterdam, Brusse, 1938), ii. 500–1.
[2] See *Survey* for 1926, pp. 445–56.
[3] Amry Vandenbosch: *The Dutch East Indies*, 3rd edition (Berkeley, University of California Press, 1944), p. 320.

differences in aim among the members. Indian nationalism had a considerable influence on the movement, and a programme of *swadeshi*, or the domestic manufacture of goods that had hitherto been imported, was adopted to strengthen the economic front. In 1936 the nationalists succeeded in steering through the Volksraad a resolution requesting the Dutch Government to call an imperial conference in order to draft a plan for according self-government to Indonesia within the Dutch imperial framework.

Reaction to the nationalist movement among the Dutch took a number of forms. The Vaderlandsche Club, formed in 1929 to champion the interests of the European population and to keep the empire inviolate, attracted members in large numbers. But when Mussert, the leader of the National Socialists in Holland, came to the Netherlands Indies in 1935 he found little support and the movement in this part of the world expired in 1937. At the same time a liberal section of the Dutch population organized itself in sympathy with the more moderate nationalist aims. Another group came into being with both European and Indonesian members to advocate a federal structure as the best means of bringing the various parts of the empire into relationship. Conservative groups among the Indonesians themselves meanwhile advocated the strengthening of the powers of the sultans, and one movement was in favour of the autonomy of the Moluccas within the Netherlands political connexion.

Three nationalist leaders who were destined to achieve great prominence after the war of 1942–5 were in the spring of 1939 in internment. Soekarno (born in 1901) was arrested in 1933 and interned in Flores, and in 1937 was transferred to Bencoolen in Sumatra. Sjahrir (born in 1909) and Mohammad Hatta were interned on the island of Banda Neira between the Celebes and New Guinea.

A feature of great interest in the decade 1929 to 1939 had been the increasingly Indonesian orientation of the Eurasians. They numbered nearly 200,000 and the clerkships in private business and the lower positions in the government service were regarded as their patrimony. Denied right to land ownership and suffering from social disabilities, these Indo-Europeans were tending more and more towards sympathy with the nationalists.[1] This was also the case with others of mixed blood, notably the Indochinese and the Indo-Arabs.

Meanwhile the trade union movement, which had originated during the First World War, had grown rapidly in strength and had, quite naturally, fallen under the influence of nationalism. For years there was a struggle for control of the movement between the Communists and the Muslim

[1] There were in 1930 in the Netherlands Indies 242,000 Europeans and persons assimilated to Europeans in legal status (including Eurasians, 7,000 Japanese, and nearly 9,000 natives). See Vandenbosch, op. cit. p. 7.

nationalists, but the suppression by the Government of the disorders at the end of the 1920s put a virtual end to Communism as an overt force.

Next to the nationalist movement, the main domestic preoccupation of the Netherlands Indies Government was with the Chinese problem, and this problem had also its international implications. Dispersed through the Indies were a million and a quarter Chinese.[1] As elsewhere, they were the middlemen of the country as well as being labourers in tin mines and on plantations. With the rise of the nationalist movement in China and the establishment of the power of the Kuomintang, the Chinese Government took an increasingly active interest in their nationals abroad, and they made no distinction between the *Sinkhehs* (or *Sinkehs*), or immigrants from China, and the *Peranakans*, or Indochinese, all of whom were Chinese citizens by the Chinese *jus sanguinis*. This situation was embarrassing enough in itself, but the renewal of the war between China and Japan in 1937 brought fresh difficulties. The Chinese Government immediately called for financial aid from the Chinese abroad. The Netherlands Indies Government permitted the sale and purchase of Chinese bonds but did not permit public action or propaganda. The Chinese also engaged in an extensive boycott of Japanese goods.

As regards relations with Japan, the Japanese commercial penetration of the Netherlands Indies became a reality during the trade depression, assisted by the depreciation of the yen and the continued adherence by the Dutch to the gold florin. In 1933 the Japanese share of the imports into the Netherlands Indies reached 32 per cent., while Japan purchased only 5 per cent. of the Netherlands Indies produce. The Government then took action, and by the imposition of quotas they recovered a great deal of the market for the Netherlands and other Western countries. But this, of course, was not without cost to those natives who could afford only the cheap Japanese goods.

There was also much apprehension among the Dutch over the increasing number of Japanese ships trading in Netherlands Indies inter-island waters. Friction was caused between the Netherlands and Japan by the break-up of a shipping conference arranged at Kobe in 1935 to debate the question, owing to Japanese insistence that the Japanese language should be the official language of the conference. In the following year, however, an agreement was reached for the division of the shipping business between the two countries.[2]

The outstanding incident of Netherlands-Japanese relations during the last few years before 1939 took place in the Japanese House of Representatives in March 1937, when Heigoro Sakurai of the Minseito Party stated that Dutch New Guinea was in an undeveloped state and inquired whether the Government did not think it advisable to open negotiations with the

---

[1] See *Survey* for 1926, pp. 464–5.   [2] See Vandenbosch, op. cit. pp. 399–401.

Netherlands Government in order to secure a perpetual lease of this territory as a means towards the solution of Japan's population problems. The
Premier, General Hayashi, replied that the matter would be carefully
considered, but added that Japan had no territorial ambitions in the
Netherlands Indies.[1] In 1937 Tanichiro Yoshida of the Japanese Foreign
Office visited the Indies, apparently in an attempt to dispel Dutch fears
that there was a secret clause in the Japanese-German Anti-Comintern
Pact of 1936 providing for the division of the Netherlands Indies into
spheres of influence.[2]

So far the Japanese 'Southward Policy' had been little but talk, but the
occupation by Japan of the Spratly Islands on 1 April 1939 gave a sudden
reality to it. This action brought Japan nearer to the Indies and reduced
the value of Hongkong and of the French naval bases in Indochina. The
Dutch were also concerned because the date of Philippine independence
had recently been fixed by the United States for 1946.[3]

In spite of the ominous signs, the Netherlands Government were still
not prepared in 1939 to enter into alliances for the protection of the Dutch
territories. The Netherlands had strongly supported sanctions against
Italy in 1935,[4] but when these failed she fell back on her old policy of strict
isolation and neutrality. Though the security of the Netherlands Indies
was to be one of the chief subjects of discussion at the Franco-British
Defence Conference to be held at Singapore in the summer of 1939, the
Dutch Premier thought it desirable to give an assurance to the public and
the world that the Netherlands would not be represented at the Conference, as that would be against the Dutch policy of absolute neutrality and
isolation.

Taking all in all, the Netherlands Indies in the early months of 1939 had
reason enough for apprehension regarding the future. The territory was
completely isolated and, in terms of modern armaments, undefended.[5] Nor
in case of war could the Government rely with any certainty upon the
united will of the Indonesians, under Dutch leadership, to defend their
country against an invader.

(e) THE PHILIPPINES

The Tydings–McDuffie Act, which was passed by the United States
Congress on 24 March 1934,[6] provided that the Philippines should become

---

[1] Ibid. p. 404.   [2] See *Survey* for 1936, p. 387, note.
[3] See below, p. 100.   [4] See *Survey* for 1935, ii. 81, 188, 276, 472–3.
[5] The expenditure of the Netherlands Indies Department of War had been reduced from
about 76 million florins in 1929 to 50 million in 1933. Since then the Indies appropriation for
defence had steadily mounted and was to be 126 million for the army and navy in 1940 (Vandenbosch, op. cit. pp. 349–50).
[6] See *Survey* for 1933, p. 571; and, for the text of the Act, *Documents* (R.I.I.A.) for 1934,
pp. 429–42.

independent on the fourth day of July immediately following the expiration of a period of ten years from the date of the inauguration of the Government under a new Constitution. Accordingly, more than 200 Filipino delegates from all parts of the Islands assembled at Manila in July 1934 and drew up a Constitution which received the approval of the President of the United States on 24 March 1935 and of the Philippine people, voting in a plebiscite, on 14 May 1935. A Commonwealth of the Philippines was created with Senator Quezon as first President, and the former American Governor-General became a High Commissioner on 15 November 1935.[1]

The Tydings–McDuffie Act provided for a graduated tax on exports from the Philippines to the United States, beginning with 5 per cent. of the standard United States duty when the Commonwealth had been in existence for five years and increasing by 5 per cent. each subsequent year until it reached 25 per cent. of the standard rate.[2] At the same time the United States immigration laws were applied to Filipinos, and the annual quota was limited to fifty until the attainment of independence, after which the Asiatic exclusion clause was to apply to Filipinos in the same way as to other inhabitants of the barred zone.[3]

There was a great deal of controversy immediately after the passing of the Act of 1934 as to whether the date for independence should be advanced or deferred, but finally on 28 November 1938 President Roosevelt approved a report of the Preparatory Committee on Philippine Affairs (composed half of Filipinos and half of Americans) whereby 4 July 1946 was fixed as the date on which the Islands were to become independent and a provision was made for a system of economic preferences for the Philippines to continue until 1961. It may be noted that American producers of sugar, tobacco, fats, &c., stood to profit by the termination of free trade between the United States and the Philippines, and American Labour Unions had feared the competition of Filipino immigrants. The country was therefore being given its independence as the result of a curious combination of characteristic American idealism and the self-interest of the American business man.

In view of the tariff provisions of the Act of 1934, it must be explained that since 1909 the economy of the Philippine Islands had been effectively tied to that of the United States by the establishment of free trade between the two countries. This had originally been done in spite of the protests of the Philippine people, through their representatives in the Assembly, that free trade would in the future be highly prejudicial to the economic interests of the Philippine people and might hinder their attainment of independence. The result of the policy was, as had been foreseen, to trans-

---

[1] See *Survey* for 1935, i. 335–6.   [2] See *Survey* for 1933, p. 567.
[3] Ibid. p. 568. For the Asiatic exclusion clause of the U.S. immigration laws, see *Survey* for 1924, p. 477.

form the Philippines into an economic as well as a political dependency
of the United States.

During the forty years of American rule the population of the Philippines had more than doubled, and in the spring of 1939 it was 16 million
in an area of 116,000 square miles (nearly as great as that of Great Britain
and Ireland). The territory was thought to be capable of supporting
three times as many people as it then contained. Tremendous advances
had been made in education, health, and public works. The total trade
had grown from $34 million for 1899 to nearly $250 million for 1938.
American trade, however, had increased in that period from 16 to 75 per
cent. of the total. The pattern of trade followed that of the colonial
development familiar in various areas throughout South-East Asia. To the
United States went agricultural raw materials and products, and from the
United States came the industrial products vital to an undeveloped economy. The Filipinos were completely dependent on free access to the
United States market.

The scale of United States investment in the Philippines before the war
was not to be compared with the investments of the British and Dutch in
their Asiatic colonies, since it amounted in 1935 to only $258 million, or
approximately 60 per cent. of the total foreign investment in the Islands.[1]
The smallness of the total investment indicated the low level of industrialization. The economy of the Philippines was primarily agricultural, but
of the 18·6 million hectares of arable land only 4·26 million were under
cultivation in 1937. Sugar was said to be over-produced, but both manila
hemp and copra could probably be sold in the world market at a profit,
and possibly also sisal and tobacco. The annual *per capita* income of the
Filipinos in 1939 was estimated by Manuel Roxas, then Secretary of
Finance, at $40. The average wage of Filipino workers in industry was
45 cents a day and for agricultural workers the cash income was about
25 cents a day. With the economy tied to high-cost United States commodities, real income was still very low even though it had been gradually
rising.

In the country districts there was widespread restlessness with sporadic
eruptions, the symptoms of a chronically unhealthy agrarian system. A
large number of agricultural workers were employed on *haciendas* owned
by individuals or by the Church to which they were bound by debt or
necessity. The landlord or his agent reaped practically all the profits.
The Government's attempts to alleviate the situation were hindered by
the great cost of buying up the estates, and by the fact that the new way of

---

[1] According to the Bureau of Insular Affairs. The U.S. Tariff Commission, however, placed
it at $200 million, while the Department of Commerce valued it at only $151 million. The first
two estimates included the holdings of Americans domiciled in the Islands. See Helmut G.
Callis: *Foreign Capital in Southeast Asia* (New York, International Secretariat, Institute of Pacific
Relations, 1942), pp. 10–11.

life offered to the Filipino was often not congenial to him. A sounder scheme of amelioration was the transference of labour from densely crowded areas to virgin lands of Mindanao which had already been begun on a small scale.

To improve the lot of the industrial worker a social justice programme, associated with the name of President Quezon, had been inaugurated and a number of laws passed,[1] while the Government had in 1938 leased the huge Buena Vista estate and converted it into a laboratory for co-operative experiments.

The Chinese (117,000 in 1939 as against 44,000 in 1918) controlled the retail trade of the Philippines and by their prominence in warehousing and marketing, including the monopoly of rice distribution, and their network of credits, could exert pressure on the millions of Filipinos who had relied upon them since early Spanish times for many necessities of life. In spite of the application to them of the United States exclusion laws, their numbers were always increasing through illegal entry. The sympathy felt in the Philippines for the Chinese in their war against the Japanese was to a great extent neutralized by the resentment felt at the role played by their nationals in the Philippines.[2]

In Davao there was in 1939 an almost solid Japanese community of 18,000 (out of a total of 29,000 Japanese in the Philippines) occupying 60,000 hectares of land and engaged in the hemp-growing and copra industries.[3] The encroachment of the Japanese upon the fish industry in the Islands was so spectacular that it had led to a popular demand that it be curbed by law before this essential food supply was monopolized by them. Friction between Japanese fishermen and the authorities was common, and it culminated in a serious incident in 1934 when the crew of the *Haiun Maru*, a Japanese power fishing boat, threw a patrol of the Philippine Constabulary which boarded it into the sea. Japan refused to extradite the offenders, and would give no real redress.

During the period 1934–8 Japanese imports into the Philippines had averaged $13 million in value (about 2 per cent. of the total) as against an average Philippine export to Japan of $7,350,000. This was not large, but when the Philippine-United States 'free trade' came to an end the situation might be different. Japanese methods of indoctrinating Filipinos with their ideas had not differed greatly from those employed elsewhere. Delegations of Filipinos—newspapermen, teachers, legislators, business

---

[1] These laws included one which created a Court of Industrial Relations, and others providing for a National Security Administration, an Eight-hour Labour Law, and a Collective Bargaining Law.

[2] Chinese investments in the Philippines in 1932 were estimated by the Chinese Consul-General at P201 million [P = Philippine peso = 50 cents (U.S.)].

[3] See J. R. Hayden: *The Philippines: a Study in National Development* (New York, Macmillan, 1942), p. 717.

men—were entertained in Japan, and similar Japanese delegations returned the visits. Prominent Filipino lawyers and business men were associated with Japanese enterprises in the Philippines. There had developed in the Islands a small but active group whose members were aggressively campaigning to hasten the day when a Japanese orientation should replace the existing relations with the United States. Numerous young Filipinos were learning Japanese, and at least one of them had attended the Imperial Military Academy. These activities increased the uneasiness felt in circles that were aware of Japan's designs in Asia.

As far back as 1908 President Theodore Roosevelt had referred to the Philippines in the strategic sense as 'our heel of Achilles'. The growing threat of Japan in pre-war years gave rise to conflicting statements among important Philippine groups regarding both the desirability and necessity of curbing Japan. One school of thought held that the Philippines, if independent, might escape becoming involved in the coming crisis. This division of opinion resulted in a hopeless deadlock which prevented the Islands from making adequate military preparations. The Tydings–McDuffie Act contained a clause requesting the President of the United States 'at the earliest practicable date, to enter into negotiations with foreign powers with a view to the conclusion of a treaty for the perpetual neutralization of the Philippine Islands, if and when Philippine independence shall have been achieved'. In view of the strategic importance of the Islands to the United States, it was not surprising that the 'practicable date' had not arrived by the spring of 1939.

However, the Philippine Government were not altogether inactive. A National Defence Act had been passed by the First National Assembly on 31 December 1935. President Quezon, in supporting the act, explained that it was imperative that the plans should reach fruition 'by the time the beneficent protection of the United States shall have been withdrawn'. Only ten years, he said, were available in which to initiate and complete the development of the defence structure.

The Defence Act provided for an army of two elements: a regular force of approximately 10,000 men, including the Philippine Constabulary with a strength of 7,000 and a reserve that would be augmented each year by approximately 40,000 men who had received five and a half months of intensive training. By the end of 1937 two semi-annual classes of trainees, numbering 36,601, had been trained and transferred to the reserve. During 1938, 33,247 additional reserves were trained.

As an adjunct to the Philippine army, the defence plan called for an 'Off-shore Patrol' of small fast torpedo boats. A relatively small fleet of vessels, General MacArthur had declared, manned by crews thoroughly familiar with every foot of coastline, would compel a hostile force to approach cautiously and in small detachments. There was also to be an

Army Air Corps operating in conjunction with the Off-shore Patrol. The original defence plan called for a hundred trained aviators by 1946.

It was true of defence as of all other matters that, in the spring of 1939, the Philippine Government had their eyes firmly fixed on the date 4 July 1946. That the hour of trial was to come long before that date, and that the whole world issue would have been decided nearly a year earlier, was perhaps a truth that only a sibyl could have foreseen.

(iv) China

By Arnold Toynbee

(a) THE JAPANESE ATTACK ON CHINA AND THE CHANCES OF ITS SUCCESS
OR FAILURE

At the moment when the last chapter in the series of events in Europe leading up to the Second World War was opened by Hitler's occupation of Prague, China found herself in as difficult and dangerous a plight as any that she had previously experienced in her long history. She was not only already at war but had been at war since 1931, while, since 1911, she had also been going through a domestic upheaval which was not merely political and economic but was a social and a cultural revolution as well. The year 1939 found her standing at bay, dislodged from her traditional footholds and divided against herself.

The Japanese attack on China, which had been launched on 18–19 September 1931, had at first been confined in its range to the four north-eastern provinces in Manchuria and to Shanghai;[1] but on the night of 7–8 July 1937 the undeclared war between China and Japan had entered on a new phase[2] in which the aggressors had extended their field of opera-tions to the heart of China inside the Great Wall and had widened their objective from the limited aim of seizing Manchuria to the titanic enter-prise of overthrowing the National Government of China, as well as the Communist régime in the north-west, and thus bringing the whole Chinese world under Japanese domination.

By the spring of 1939 the Japanese had succeeded in occupying the principal centres of population and lines of communication in Eastern China as far south as the Wuhan group of cities (Hankow, Wuchang, and Hanyang) at the midpoint of Intra-mural China where the Han River joins the Yangtze. The Wuhan cities had fallen on 25–26 October 1938;[3] on 21 October, a separate Japanese expeditionary force, dispatched by sea,

---

[1] See *Survey* for 1931, pp. 420–72; *Survey* for 1932, pp. 432–515; *Survey* for 1933, pp. 478–84.
[2] See *Survey* for 1937, i. 180–240.
[3] *Survey* for 1938, i. 513.

had occupied Canton;[1] while, at the opposite extremity of the now vast theatre of military operations, the Japanese, as early as 1937, had thrown out a tentacle north-westward into Shansi, and on beyond into western Inner Mongolia.[2]

From their own point of view, the Japanese might have little ground for congratulating themselves on their achievements up to date. Their occupation, even as far as it extended, was a very loose-meshed network which left great pockets of territory behind the front out of Japanese control. The area under effective Japanese occupation was only a small fraction of the total area of China, and the Chinese National Government, which had retreated already from Nanking to Hankow in December 1937, had eluded the invader once again in the autumn of 1938 by a second withdrawal, still farther up the Yangtze, to Chungking.[3] This new temporary capital of China lay to the west of the Yangtze gorges, in the great mountain-girt basin of Szechwan: a single province of China which, with its 50 million inhabitants, would have qualified by itself for entering the lists as a Great Power in an arena on the European scale. If the Japanese should decide to seek out the Chinese National Government in this western fortress, or to penetrate the broad belt of mountainous country between the Yangtze Valley and the south coast of China, they would pass beyond the termini even of the scanty means of modern communication that China possessed at this date, and would have to advance over trails impracticable for wheels.

Yet the Chinese, on their side, were faced with a bleak and forbidding prospect. At grips unaided, as they were, with an enemy whose industrial and technical equipment for making war in the modern Western style was incomparably superior to China's, they had now lost to this enemy the few railways, factories, and modernly equipped ports that they had possessed at the beginning of the conflict. It was true that they still had a margin of space to sell in exchange for time. The whole country had not yet fallen under the invader's control, as had happened when China had been conquered by the Mongols in the thirteenth century and by the Manchus in the seventeenth. The Japanese invasion, however, was, on a long view, a more formidable threat for China than these total conquests in the past.

The Manchus, like so many earlier waves of intruding barbarians, had been half Sinified already before ever they broke through the Great Wall, and, long before their undramatic deposition in A.D. 1911, their assimilation had been virtually complete. As for the Mongols, who had been unique among China's barbarian invaders in resisting assimilation, they had been thrown out of China, neck and crop, within eighty-seven years of the consummation of their conquest, though they had providently reinforced their own scanty numbers by drafts of Muslim and Christian

[1] Ibid. pp. 515–16.   [2] See *Survey* for 1937, i. 194–204.
[3] See *Survey* for 1938, i. 505, 513, 517.

troops and administrators from their western dominions. The Japanese were better placed than any of their forerunners for achieving the never-yet-accomplished feat of conquering China without succumbing to one or other of the two alternative nemeses of being either slowly assimilated or quickly ejected. In national consciousness and cohesion the Japanese were at least the equals of the Mongols, and in their relative numbers, as compared with the Chinese, they were so much less at a disadvantage than either the Mongols or the Manchus had been, that this point of difference might even prove decisive. Between the populations of China and Japan (not including Korea) in 1939, the disparity in sheer numbers was probably in the order of one to not more than four or five in China's favour, and the numerical advantage which China thus still had on her side was equalled, if not outweighed, by the technological advantage enjoyed by Japan thanks to her long start over China in the arduous process of mastering the Western technique of industrial production and mechanized warfare.

Thus, if the Japanese were to succeed in gaining command even of the bare key points in the still unconquered west and south of China, they might hope to condition the Chinese to a state of lasting subjection to themselves by preventing them from making any further advance in the mastery of Western technology except on lines convenient to Japan and on conditions dictated by her. Within the past thirty years the Japanese had succeeded by such methods in reducing the Koreans to being Japan's hewers of wood and drawers of water; and, though Korea was a relatively small and weak country, the Japanese might aspire to repeat their Korean achievement on a Chinese scale.

In this perilous situation China found herself without allies, for the Japanese threat to her life had come upon her at a time when she was between two worlds and was getting the worst of both of them.

By 1939 a century had elapsed since British arms had abruptly brought to an end a passage of Chinese history in which China had been a world in herself with no neighbours to cope with except amenable tributaries and innocuous barbarians. Since the Sino-British War of 1839–42, China had been dragged out of her age-long political isolation and had been forced into the international arena of a Western society that had spread its tentacles all round the globe. Instead of being the smoothly turning hub of the universe, China found herself now in the ruck of a herd of national states which were in Ishmaelitish relations with one another; and in this unfamiliar rough-and-tumble struggle for existence she had been suffering the usual fate of the weak and inexperienced.

In earlier chapters of Western history a state in China's position would have been protected in some degree against the dangers of her defenceless-ness by the more or less automatic working of a balance of power between states of a higher political and military calibre. During the nineteenth century the Turkish Empire had been saved by this play of stronger forces from a partition which she was powerless to resist by any action of her own; and at the turn of the nineteenth and twentieth centuries, when it looked for a time as though a partition of China might be the next event on the agenda of international affairs, the balance of power had in fact saved China too from political annihilation. Russia, Germany, and France had clubbed together to forbid Japan to cull the fruits of her victory in the Sino-Japanese War of 1894, and in 1898 Great Britain had checked Russia's encroachments at China's expense by leasing from China a naval base at Weihaiwei facing the base which Russia had then just acquired at Port Arthur. Thus China had surmounted one crisis at the cost of having to permit her protectors as well as her assailants among the Great Powers of the day to take one bite each out of her enormous territories; and the peace settlement, mediated by the United States after the Russo-Japanese War of 1904–5, had restored Chinese authority in Manchuria outside the Russian and Japanese railway zones. But in the new chapter of international history which had opened in 1914 the balance of power had no longer been giving China even that minimum of protection which she had received from it during the preceding twenty years.

The preoccupation of the United States, as well as the European Powers, with a First World War in which Europe had been the principal arena had given Japan a fresh opportunity for aggression at China's expense; and the hay which Japan had made while the sun shone had not all been extracted from her clutches at the Washington Conference of 1921–2 by the deft diplomatic fingers of Balfour and Hughes.[1] Thereafter, the inter-war attempt to provide a constitutional substitute for the balance of power in the shape of a League of Nations had proved of no avail to secure protection and redress for China when Japan had assailed her again in 1931;[2] and, by the time when, in 1937, Japan had extended the field of her aggression from Manchuria to China as a whole, she had far stronger grounds than she had had seven years before for expecting to enjoy a free hand. One ground for Japanese confidence on this point was the political victory which Japan had won over other states members of the League of Nations in 1930–3. A second ground was Hitler's advent to power in Germany on 30 January 1933, which had rediverted the attention of Great Britain, France, and the Soviet Union from the Far East to Europe. A third ground was the retrospective resentment of public feeling in the United States over the participation of America in the First World War. This American sentiment, which was rife in the 1930s,[3] was a godsend

---

[1] See *Survey* for 1920–3, pp. 456–71.
[2] See *Survey* for 1931, pp. 472–505; *Survey* for 1932, pp. 515–86; *Survey* for 1933, pp. 484–518.
[3] See *Survey* for 1938, i. 575–82.

for Japan because, so long as the mood might last, it promised to inhibit a Great Power which was China's friend and which was not immobilized at the time by any European entanglements from taking effective action against Japan in China's favour.

In this international situation it remained to be seen whether China could save herself by a purchase of time which appeared to offer no prospect of bringing her any allies. If China and Japan were left to fight out their conflict by themselves, which of the two was the more likely to be able to hold out the longer? In this issue the decisive factor might be the success or failure of China in maintaining a united front. On the last occasion on which China had succumbed to an invader, the conqueror's success had been due perhaps as much to dissensions among the Chinese themselves as to their adversaries' prowess. In the seventeenth century of the Christian Era, the Manchus had been given their first opening by a Chinese insurrection against the reigning dynasty of the Ming, and their second and decisive opportunity by the decision of a Chinese military commander in charge of a crucial strategic point to open the door for a Manchu invasion of Intra-mural China rather than give his allegiance to a Chinese usurper at Peking. Again, in 1917–18, at a moment when the Western Powers had been preoccupied by the First World War, at least one precariously perched and reactionary-minded Chinese politico-military clique had proved willing to accept financial help from Japan at the price of selling China's national interests to her. This disunity in face of a formidable external enemy which had proved fatal for China in 1644, and unfortunate for her in 1918, was jeopardizing her prospects once again in 1939. In the circumstances of the day, the issue presented itself in the form of two questions: Would the Kuomintang–Communist 'United Front' against Japan hold together? And would the Kuomintang be able to keep the defections of quislings in its own ranks within limits that would allow it still to vindicate its title to be a representative and legitimate national government?

(b) THE RENEWAL OF TENSION BETWEEN THE KUOMINTANG AND THE COMMUNISTS AND THE DEFECTION OF WANG CHING-WEI FROM THE KUOMINTANG

The Kuomintang–Communist United Front had been negotiated in the course of the year 1937,[1] and, while it is possible that its initiation may have been one of Japan's reasons for widening the scope of her operations in the summer of that year, it is certain that, conversely, this renewal of Japanese aggression on a larger scale helped to consummate the agreement between the two Chinese factions. The United Front was a notable achievement of Chinese statesmanship. It temporarily suspended a civil

[1] See *Survey* for 1937, i. 154–60.

war which had been lacerating China since 1927, and it produced important positive results in the sphere of military co-operation between régimes
that had previously been at war with one another as well as with Japan.
But it was never more than a precarious alliance held together mainly
by Japanese military pressure, for the two parties to it were uneasy
yoke-fellows, and it may be doubted whether, in their inmost counsels,
the Kuomintang ever abandoned their aim of asserting their authority
unconditionally over the whole of China, or the Communists theirs of
preserving a virtual independence and continuing to gain adherents at
the Kuomintang's expense in Chinese territory outside their control. In the
spring of 1939, however, the danger of a break-down of this Kuomintang–
Communist alliance was less serious for China than the recently accomplished fact of the treasonable defection of the eminent Kuomintang
politician Wang Ching-wei, who had held several of the highest offices in
both the party organization and the National Government.

Wang Ching-wei's treason was prompted partly by a personal rivalry
with President Chiang Kai-shek and partly by a difference of opinion on
major issues of policy in which Wang had not stood alone but had been
the leader of a group within the party. Despairing, it seems, of China's
military and political prospects, he and his supporters had come to feel
that an immediate surrender to Japan on Japanese terms would be less
disastrous for China than the prolongation of a struggle which, in their
view, could have no different issue in the end. They may also have been
less concerned about the national conflict between China and Japan than
about the social conflict between the Chinese Communists and the vested
interests which had so quickly gained control over the Kuomintang after its
founder Sun Yat-sen's death, and may have had it in mind that Japan,
too, was a declared enemy of Communism both at home and abroad.
Wang Ching-wei himself had at least had the courage of his convictions.
The publication of conditions for peace with China by the Japanese
Government on 22 December 1938[1] had been taken by him as an occasion
for making his way from Chungking via Indochina to the Chinese territories under Japanese occupation and entering into collaboration with the
Japanese authorities there. In this flagrant act of treason, Wang did not
carry his previous followers with him, but for Japanese purposes he was a
host in himself. He was a big enough figure in China and in the world at
large to serve as head of a puppet régime purporting to be the legitimate
Government of China as against the refugee Government at Chungking.
In March 1939 Wang Ching-wei was already negotiating with the Japanese
for the amalgamation, under his presidency, of the two less plausible local
puppet governments which the Japanese had already set up at Peking and
Nanking.[2]

[1] *Survey* for 1938, i. 497.   [2] Ibid. p. 518; *Survey* for 1937, i. 251, 255.

(c) The Kuomintang and the Communists in Theory and in Practice

These two political rifts in the Chinese ranks—one between the Kuomintang and the Communists and the other within the Kuomintang itself—were symptoms of a cultural crisis which was an even more momentous and critical issue than the life-and-death struggle with Japan. The fundamental cause of China's tribulations was the collapse of her own traditional way of life under the impact of the aggressive civilization of the West, and the Kuomintang and Communist programmes were rival nostrums for filling the vacuum which this collapse had produced.

The theoretical ideal of the Kuomintang—as originally laid down by the founder of the party, Sun Yat-sen (1866–1925), and repeated in the book entitled *China's Destiny* which was published under President Chiang Kai-shek's name in 1943—was a culturally mixed way of life in which the Chinese people were to go on living in accordance with the Confucian moral philosophy while mastering and adopting the modern Western applications of physical science to economic activities. Sun Yat-sen, like other leaders of modernizing movements in non-Western countries, had perceived that, in a non-industrial country that was setting itself to catch up with the leading industrial countries by a forced march, the state must be called upon to play a much more active part in the nation's economic life, at any rate during this phase, than it had been apt to play in countries where industrialism had grown up spontaneously as a natural development from the local economic and social conditions of the past. Sun Yat-sen therefore advocated state development and control of key industries and state supervision of private enterprise in the rest of the economic field. In taking this line, he was not inspired by Socialism or Communism, any more than Mustafā Kemāl Atatürk was in taking a corresponding line in similar circumstances in Turkey.

Sun Yat-sen did, however, come under Russian Communist influence in the last chapter of his career, and, at the prompting of the Russian Communist emissary Borodin,[1] he delivered at Canton, in 1924, a series of lectures which were afterwards published as a book under the title *San Min Chu I* ('The Three Principles of the People').[2] The two distinctive features of this work were a note of hostility towards the Western Powers to whom China was at that date still bound by 'the unequal treaties',[3] and an attempt to find a harmony between Communism and Sun Yat-sen's own programme of social reform. Though the *San Min Chu I* was hastily compiled, and bears the marks of this in the shape of unresolved obscurities and inconsistencies, it acquired and retained, among the ideological scriptures

---

[1] See *Survey* for 1926, pp. 283–4.   [2] See *Survey* for 1925, ii. 315–16.
[3] See *Survey* for 1928, pp. 413–19.

of the Kuomintang, a position like that of the *Institutes* in the Justinianean
Corpus Juris Romani. It became a party text-book, creed, and shibboleth
rolled into one. The Chinese Communists, for their part, seized on the
San Min Chu I for the sake of its indelible Communist tinge, and, after the
breach between them and the Kuomintang in 1927,[1] they claimed to be
the sole orthodox exponents and practitioners of this key work of Sun
Yat-sen's, while they denounced the Kuomintang as traitors to the principles therein set forth.

According to Chinese Communist theory, as expounded by a member
of the Chinese Communist Politburo, Wang Ching-hsiang, in October
1939, *the San Min Chu I* provided a minimum immediate programme for a
provisional period of national emancipation and democracy; but, in the
fullness of time, this was to be followed by a maximum programme extending to the overthrow of capitalism, the establishment of Socialism, and
a radical emancipation through the elimination of class divisions. The
Chinese Communists loudly proclaimed that they were completely
Communist in their ideals and their ultimate aims, and that the Chinese
revolution was part of the world revolution, even though it was not yet
full-blown; and they showed that they meant what they said by the energy
with which they propagated the Communist doctrine in their army and
among the civilian population under their rule. At the same time, in a
country whose indigenous cultural heritage had been so potent and so
long-lived that it was still a moral force to be reckoned with, even now that
it lay in ruins, the Chinese Communists could not afford to allow the
Kuomintang an undisputed monopoly of the claim to be preserving the
best elements in the Chinese heritage while adopting the best modern
innovations of alien origin. In a critique of Chiang Kai-shek's exposition
of Kuomintang doctrine in *China's Destiny*, a Chinese Communist spokesman, Chen Pai-ta, found it necessary to reply to the anti-Communist
taunt that the Chinese Communists were inspired by foreign doctrines
and were 'proud towards their own countrymen, but submissive towards
foreigners'. After nailing his party's colours to the mast of Communist
orthodoxy, Chen Pai-ta took the line that 'scientific Marxism-Leninism
demands that the Communists of every nation should work out their
political programmes and decide their policies according to their own
national conditions, and rely on their own people for salvation'; and he
went so far as to assert that the Chinese Communists were the heirs of
indigenous Chinese revolutionary traditions derived from the T'aip'ing
through Sun Yat-sen. 'The reactionaries want to abolish the progressive
traditions and preserve the backward ones, while we do exactly the reverse.'

[1] See *Survey* for 1927, pp. 334 seqq. For the Chinese Communist Party's Manifesto of 22
September 1937, pledging allegiance to Sun Yat-sen's Three Principles, see *Survey* for 1937, i.
159–60.

When we turn our attention from theory to practice we obtain a different picture of the two opposing ideological camps and of the points on which they were at issue. From this angle of vision, the Chinese Communists look still more Chinese than they claimed to be, while the Kuomintang show little trace of their Confucian professions.

In practice, at this date, the Chinese Communists were concentrating their efforts on the two immediate aims of giving the peasants possession of the land that they were cultivating,[1] and of releasing them from the grip of the local village money-lenders. These two lines of action, in which the Chinese Communists appear to have been effective as well as sincere, account both for the large measure of support that they evidently obtained from the population in the rural districts over which they had established their rule, and for the fear and hatred with which they were admittedly regarded by the Kuomintang. For the Kuomintang Party, since the death of its founder Sun Yat-sen in 1925 and the political reunification of the greater part of China under the Kuomintang banner between that year and 1928,[2] had paid for the sensational rapidity of its worldly success by becoming the captive of vested interests: rural landlords, urban merchants, and the still rare but already influential Chinese real estate dealers, bankers, and industrialists who had learned the tricks of a Western trade in the semi-Westernized treaty ports.[3] These calculating eleventh-hour converts thus deftly smothered, without managing quite to extinguish, the spark of Sun Yat-sen's own ardent liberal idealism. It was kept alive by a faithful minority whom the now preponderant conservatives found it politic to frustrate by the tactics of paying lip-service to aspirations which had never ceased to be the Kuomintang's official ideals. The stronghold of the liberal remnant in the Kuomintang was the prophet's own household —now centred round the Soong family, into which both the prophet himself and his khalifah Chiang Kai-shek had married.[4] While Sun Yat-sen's son, Sun Fo, and his widow had by this time been driven in the direction of Moscow by the cumulative effect of repeated disillusionments with the conduct of their hero's official successors, Madame Sun Yat-sen's sister, Madame Chiang Kai-shek, had forborne to break with the main body of the Kuomintang Party and had brought all her influence to bear upon steering the party course as far as possible on a liberal tack. Yet the liberalism of the Soong family was perhaps even less like Gladstone's than

---

[1] In Russia, too, of course, the peasants had been given possession of the land in the first stage of the Communist revolution there.

[2] See *Survey* for 1928, pp. 279–90. Like Moses and Muhammad, Sun Yat-sen just did not live to see his followers make conquests which dwarfed the prophet's own modest military and political achievements.

[3] Compare the capture of the Christian Church by the well-to-do class of Graeco-Roman society after the official conversion of the Roman Empire.

[4] *Survey* for 1927, p. 385; *Survey* for 1930, p. 339.

the Communism of the Chinese Communist Party was like that of Lenin and Stalin; and this transmogrification of a modern Western ideology was certainly no effective moral substitute for a traditional Chinese Confucian discipline which was honoured by the Kuomintang in the breach rather than in the observance—as was demonstrated by the proneness of this newfangled and unfledged party to personal rivalries and animosities which had been kept within bounds by the established institutions of the *ancien régime*.

(d) THE CHINESE TRADITION

That régime—which in 1939 was as dead as Pharaoh's or Caesar's, though it had been a going concern at as recent a date as the opening of the century—had been admirably adjusted in its heyday to the needs of a civilized society which had not yet encountered the West and had therefore not yet been constrained to put itself through the Industrial Revolution. Its master institution had been a professional civil service recruited competitively by examination from candidates of a class that could afford the necessary degree of education. Though that degree had been pitched high, the field of candidatures had been wide and the amount of ability that found its way into the service had accordingly been considerable. The members of the service had been held together by an *esprit de corps*, by a traditional code of professional behaviour, and by the common possession of a 'know-how' based on the accumulated experience of many centuries. Their *arcanum imperii* had been to eschew over-administration. Local government had been left to look after itself, as in the Roman Empire in the earlier days of the Principate, and the representatives of the central government in the provinces had been given a wide discretion by Peking so long as they remitted the revenues due from them and did not show themselves incompetent in coping with emergencies—which seldom arose from any but the three familiar scourges of flood, famine, and civil disorder.

This finely tempered administrative instrument for handling the relatively simple problems of a static community had been discredited by its inevitable incapacity to produce customary results under the new and unstable conditions created by China's sudden incorporation into the body social of the Western world; and the Revolution of 1911 had swept away an institution whose history could be traced back to the second century B.C. As a result, both the Kuomintang and the Communist régime in the distracted China of 1939 were having to battle with unprecedentedly stormy seas unsupported by the life-belt that had buoyed up their predecessors in calmer waters. For any Chinese government in this revolutionary age, the task of administration was bound to be unenviably difficult. The historic emergencies did not cease to arise because the traditional apparatus for dealing with them had been thrown overboard, and they were now aggravated by war and by the thousand complications introduced into the economic, social, and spiritual life of the Chinese people by intercourse with the West. One portent was the inoculation of the hitherto long-suffering Chinese masses with an exotic discontent which its Western parents had christened 'divine'. Expectations in China were rising at a time when life was becoming harder; and this widening gulf between dreams and realities would have been difficult for even the nimblest régime to straddle. The Kuomintang and Communist régimes were, however, crude and clumsy compared with the *ancien régime* which they had replaced. In spite of their mutual animosity, they were closely akin to one another in structure and origin. Both of them were copies of the self-co-opting single-party oligarchy which was the typical régime, at the time, in other countries that were going through the awkward process of Westernization, as well as in the politically more backward of the Western countries themselves. While in China, as in Russia, Turkey, Italy, and Germany, this system of government by clique might conceivably be the only practical possibility in the circumstances, it was certainly altogether inadequate for meeting the needs of a great people struggling for life.

In this melancholy and anxious situation, the past history of China, at any rate, could still offer encouragement to any Chinese who had not wholly discarded the study of Chinese letters for the pursuit of Western technology. A Chinese literatus could reflect that, in the nineteen hundred and fortieth year of an era much younger than his own, the Chinese people was more numerous and the territory of China more extensive than at any previous date in the long course of Chinese history; and that, since the dawn of that history, which was coeval with the birth of Israel and Hellas, China—unlike those two gifted but foundered forerunners of the modern West—had managed not only to survive but to grow in the course of ages to dimensions that made her, in 1939, the largest as well as the oldest of all living human communities. In spite of all present tribulations, a Chinese student of his people's past might well feel confident that whatever might happen to the West and its works 'the Middle Kingdom' would remain on the map.

(v) Japan

By Arnold Toynbee

(a) THE IMPACT OF THE WEST ON JAPAN

In 1939 Japan was one of the seven Great Powers of a society which she had entered only eighty-five years before. At that date she still shared with Russia the distinction, achieved by no other living non-Western community, of having remained master, so far, of the difficult and hazardous situation in which all non-Western communities had been placed by the impetuous onset of the Western civilization. After having dealt with this Western problem by insulating herself from the rest of the world for some two and a half centuries, Japan had reversed this policy when the undesired, yet irresistible, *acte de présence* of Commodore Perry's squadron in 1853–4 had demonstrated that isolationism was not enough, and that, at the level of technological proficiency which the Western peoples had now attained, Japan would find herself once more at their mercy if she did not learn the latest tricks of their trade—and learn these rapidly and efficiently.

A strong impression of material achievement, as measured by Western standards, was made on the minds of Western observers who visited Japan towards the end of this remarkable chapter of her history—especially if their avenue of approach, like the writer's in 1929, ran through India and China. But this first impression was immediately overtaken by a second, which was equally forcible: the Japanese had achieved their material *tour de force* at a psychological cost which was formidable and perhaps prohibitive. Japanese adults of both sexes and all classes seemed bowed down by a crushing load of care. In terms of inward well-being, their lot might be less happy than the life of a half-starved, ill-clad, poorly housed Chinese coolie or Indian ryot.

(b) The Rising Pressure of Population

The ultimate source of these grinding personal anxieties was a revolution in Japanese life which, though distinct from the cultural revolution at the beginning of the Meiji Era, had been simultaneous with it and had been caused by it at least in part. In 1873 the population of the Japanese Isles had been 31 million;[1] by 1939 it had risen to nearly 73 million;[2] and during the years 1935–40 it was still increasing at a net rate of 5·6 per cent. over the five-year period—a formidable percentage, even though not quite so formidable as the peak figure of 7·9 per cent. for the five years 1925–30.[3]

A population pressure of this degree was a new nightmare in Japan's grim history. In early days the Japanese people had found outlets for an increasing population by expanding northwards at the expense of the previous Ainu inhabitants of the Archipelago. During the 400 years preceding the establishment of the Tokugawa régime at the turn of the sixteenth and seventeenth centuries, they had kept their numbers down by means of constant and ever more destructive civil wars; under the Tokugawa Peace, they had kept them under control by other social practices

[1] A. M. Carr-Saunders: *World Population* (Oxford, Clarendon Press for Royal Institute of International Affairs, 1936), p. 261.
[2] League of Nations: *Statistical Year Book 1939/40* (Geneva, 1940), p. 16.
[3] *Encyclopedia Britannica* (Chicago, Encyclopedia Britannica Inc., 1945), vol. 12, p. 900.

and habits; and this artificially maintained stationariness of the population had been the basis of everything else in the Tokugawa system; it had been the indispensable condition for even the partial and progressively diminishing success of the Tokugawa régime's attempt to keep Japan's life frozen for a quarter of a millennium. The intention behind the Meiji Restoration was to replace a thoroughly controlled régime of isolation by a no less thoroughly controlled process of Westernization, and the statesmen of the new era achieved a remarkable measure of success in pursuing this aim; but they failed to maintain control over the movement of population. The previous check on the number of births was removed by the liquidation of former habits through the solvent of cultural change, while a new check was imposed on the number of deaths by the successful introduction into Japan of modern Western hygiene. The movement of population got out of hand, and by 1939 the economic and political problems produced by this social misfortune had become so importunate that they were threatening to deprive Japanese statesmanship of the freedom of manœuvre which it had so far managed to retain.

An increase of population on this scale would have been a serious difficulty for any country in any circumstances; and, in the circumstances of Japan in the Meiji Era, there were several features that were particularly unpropitious. Japan was meagrely endowed with natural resources for any type of economy. Less than one-fifth of her area was cultivable; the steep wooded mountains were not suitable for pastureland; and she was not much less poor than Italy in minerals.[1] These inexorable facts of physical geography set rigid and narrow limits to her production of foodstuffs and of raw materials, either for light or for heavy industry, out of her domestic resources. The rapid increase in her population under the new dispensation therefore confronted her with a necessity of either draining off the excess by finding additional land for it to colonize and cultivate, or avoiding the need for emigration by creating sustenance at home for additional mouths through an increase of productivity to be obtained by purchasing foreign foodstuffs and raw materials with Japanese manufactures. But the former of these two theoretically alternative solutions was by this time virtually ruled out.

(c) The Breakdown of Attempts to solve the Population Problem by Peaceful Means

The regions that would have suited Japanese settlers to a nicety as areas for colonization were California and New South Wales, but here the

[1] In the islands that were Japan's home territory and ancestral patrimony, there was copper, some coal of poor quality, some iron-ore, and a little oil. In 1939, the richest and most easily worked of the coal-mines and iron-mines at Japan's command were those in her puppet state of Manchukuo—especially in Southern Manchuria.

Japanese had put themselves out of court by having persisted for more than 200 years in a policy of isolation which, in the end, had proved untenable. At the opening of the seventeenth century of the Christian Era the Japanese had been a seafaring people who were learning to hold their own with the Western nations in the arts of ship-building and navigation. They were making long-distance trans-oceanic voyages, and they had as good a chance as the English or English-descended peoples of discovering and colonizing the west coast of North America and the east coast of Australia. By 1854 that opportunity had passed, and by 1939 the alternative resort of developing manufacturing industries for export had proved itself precarious.

When Japan had entered the circle of Western economic life in the last quarter of the nineteenth century, the Westernized world of the day had still been in the era of relatively free international trade with an expanding market, and Japan had found a modest but profitable niche in the manufacture of consumers' goods for economically backward Asiatic and African peoples who could not afford to buy the superior products of Western European and North American industry. By 1939, however, the change in the world's economic climate which had been started by the introduction of high protective tariffs in the United States after the Civil War and in Germany after the foundation of the Second Reich had reached a degree at which its effects for Japan were severe. The markets which she had captured during the First World War had been lost as swiftly as they had been won; and 'the economic blizzard' which had descended on the world with 'the break on Wall Street' in October 1929[1] had blasted Japan's international trade and had transferred the control of Japan's political destinies from elements whose politico-economic philosophy had been that of 'the Manchester School' to elements whose programme was to use the sword for cutting the Gordian knot.[2]

Japan was particularly hard hit by the great fall in the price of raw silk in the United States, since the rising American consumption of Japanese silk, paid for at good prices, during the preceding decade had been a windfall for Japanese farmers which had made it still just possible for them to carry on their arduous struggle to earn a bare living for their families.[3] The Japanese farming population was the main source of recruitment, not only for the rank and file of the Japanese army, but for the junior officers. These (who were drawn from the class which in Russia, at the time of their liquidation there, had been known as kulaks) were in close touch with the men under their command, who felt that their officers understood and shared the peasants' point of view, and who were therefore ready to follow their lead. Thus the economic crisis of 1929 and the following

---

[1] See *Survey* for 1931, pp. 197 seqq.   [2] Ibid. pp. 401–3.
[3] Ibid. p. 400, note.

years in the United States struck an almost direct (though, of course, quite undesigned) blow at the Japanese army, and strengthened an existing conviction in their minds that Japan's economic difficulties at home could not be solved otherwise than by foreign conquests.

The crisis over raw silk was followed by the backwash, on Japan, of the Ottawa Conference of 1932 between the states members of the British Commonwealth.[1] Though the Ottawa Agreements did not injure Japanese trade directly to any great extent, they inaugurated a revolution in the fiscal policy of the United Kingdom which also involved that country's non-self-governing colonies and dependencies. The effect was to transform the last surviving great free import market of the world into a closed area in which the British family of peoples proceeded to place themselves in a privileged economic position, by comparison with outsiders, through a carefully devised system of trade agreements and tariffs. The British Commonwealth and Empire hereby converted itself voluntarily into what the Japanese were to call euphemistically a 'co-prosperity sphere' when they subsequently sought to impose a similarly closed economic system on other East Asian countries by force of Japanese arms for Japan's one-sided advantage. On this account, the Ottawa Agreements had a powerful psychological effect on Japan as well as on other 'have-not' Powers.

(d) The Revival of Militarism

If no empty lands of suitable climate were left for Japan to colonize, and if the alternative expedient of building up industries on the basis of international trade were at the mercy of disturbing forces outside Japanese control, no course remained open for Japan (so the reinstated Japanese militarists argued) except to conquer for herself a domain, providing the necessary raw materials and markets in the necessary quantities, which Japan could exploit economically, regardless of what might happen in the world outside the limits of her co-prosperity sphere.

This idea presented itself at this juncture with all the more force because it was already familiar to Japanese minds. The determination to plunge into warfare and conquest was no new policy. All through the eighteenth century the supporters of movements for a restoration of the Imperial Power had consistently coupled with this programme for a political revolution at home the idea of aggression and expansion, and this was the policy recommended by such teachers as Yoshida Shoin, who educated the samurai leaders of the clans that restored the Imperial Power in 1868. Yoshida himself prescribed the directions in which Japan was to expand; and, after the Imperial Restoration, nothing but caution and unpreparedness held Japan back. Many leading personalities in Japan wanted to

---

[1] See *Survey* for 1932, pp. 27–34.

start on the invasion of Asia at once; and so violent was their desire that it led to a civil war in Japan (the Satsuma Rebellion of 1877) in order to decide whether war should be undertaken or not. For the new 'kulak' military class, as for the old samurai military class, in Japan, this latent policy of foreign conquest was not merely a panacea for economic troubles. On the economic plane, Japan, hard hit though she was by the world-wide depression of 1929 and the following years, was no harder hit than Great Britain and other countries that eventually weathered the storm and did so without ever having dreamed of resorting to military aggression *à la Japonaise*. Both the population problem and the food problem of Great Britain at this time were more serious than those of Japan, who had suc-ceeded in keeping up her agriculture and doubling her food production, and who, in the 1930s, was feeding 75 per cent. of her population on home-grown foodstuffs. Japan had also been paying her way in her foreign trade till 1936, when she had made the mistake of taking on more than she could cope with in simultaneously starting an expansion of heavy industry for armaments production at home and a five-year plan in Manchuria.[1] In the minds of the military class, the decisive consideration was not econo-mic or demographic but social and political. The fiasco of Japan's military adventures on the Asiatic mainland in, and immediately after, the First World War—a failure which had been registered in the diplomatic victory of the English-speaking Powers over Japan at the Washington Conference of 1921–2[2]—had dealt a serious blow at home to the Japanese military class's prestige. Throughout the 1920s, so long as Baron Shidehara's policy of playing 'the good neighbour' to the rest of the world was in the ascen-dant, the soldiers felt their power and influence progressively ebbing away. What would have become of them if the Shidehara régime had con-tinued to commend itself to the Japanese people by continuing to bring in economic dividends without calling for military sacrifices? The Japanese military class no doubt suffered the same discomfort as the rest of mankind from the economic blizzard of 1929; yet they could not but welcome the unexpected opportunity, which this tempest hurled into their laps, of retrieving their own, by then deeply compromised, social and political position.

(e) The Position and Prospects of the Japanese in March 1939

By the spring of 1939 seven and a half years had passed since Japan had at length embarked on her militarists' desperately aggressive policy; and, on a superficial view, her new leaders might seem to have justified their policy by results. In breach of the Covenant of the League of Nations and

---

[1] For Japanese economic policy during the years 1931–8, see *Survey* for 1938, i. 96–101 and 531–44.   [2] *Survey* for 1920–3, pp. 456–71.

in defiance of the public opinion of the Western world, Japan had taken from China by force of arms the whole of Manchuria with its rich deposits of coal and iron-ore and its vast cultivable areas populated by hard-working Chinese farmers in need of consumers' goods. Moreover, since the summer of 1937, the Japanese had gone on to occupy the main lines of communication and urban and industrial centres in the north-eastern quarter of Intra-mural China.[1] And, in order to wage this Sino-Japanese war—which was expanding as lustily as Japan's population—Japan had built up, at home, an imposing battery of the heavy industry that she had hitherto lacked. On the surface, Japan's position in the world in the spring of 1939 was more brilliant than it had been at any date since Hideyoshi's invasion of Korea in 1592; below the surface there was more than sufficient ground for the *malaise* that had already been furrowing Japanese faces ten years earlier, before the storm had burst or the die had been cast.

By 1939 it had become clear, for those who had eyes to see, that Japan's continental military adventure was not going according to plan. The wealth of Manchuria was authentic, and Japan now held it in her hand, but most of this wealth was potential, not tangible. Manchuria in the 1930s was in much the same economic condition as the Mississippi Basin a century earlier. Its vast latent resources could be made to yield an abundant harvest by preliminary capital expenditure on a proportionate scale. In the nineteenth century the American pioneers had been able to raise the necessary loans in a then prosperous Europe—and this with a facility that had enabled them to win the west at lightning speed. But no foreign investor was willing to finance the Japanese conquerors of Manchuria; Japan must make the indispensable capital outlay from her own resources, and the slenderness of these resources condemned the return to be slow in coming in. By 1939, the triple strain of building up a heavy industry at home, financing the capital equipment of Manchukuo, and waging an inconclusive war of aggression against China on a widening front was beginning to tell upon Japan severely. This was not a productive way of employing her surplus labour force, and was not even a left-handed way of solving her population problem; for the undesired reduction in her population that she was bringing on herself through fatal casualties on the China front was a blood-drop in the bucket by comparison with her annual excess of births over deaths from all causes.

Nor could a Japanese observer possessing 'inside knowledge' console himself with the expectation that, if Japan could hold out till she had finished developing Manchukuo and finished conquering China, she would then have reached her goal of economic self-sufficiency within an area under her own control. If the weapon required for cutting a Gordian knot

[1] See *Survey* for 1937, i. 180–225; *Survey* for 1938, i. 504–31.

had still been the antique sword, the Japanese could have been in good heart, for as swordsmiths they had had no peers except the Damascenes. In a Westernized world, however, the knot-cutting weapons were machine tools, and here Japan was at a loss. Creditable though her progress had been in the acquisition of Western technical skill during the past eighty-five years, she was still as poor in skilled metallurgists in the Western style as she was in the raw materials of their trade; and this bottle-neck, which was throttling the whole development of her new heavy industry, was of needle's-eye stringency in the machine-tool manufacturing trade, on which all other metallurgical processes were dependent.[1] In 1939 Japan was still having to purchase abroad—and this principally from the United States[2]—nearly all the high-grade machine tools and precision instruments required for divers branches of the engineering trade which she was expanding at a forced pace; and it would take her longer to make herself independent in this sphere by training technicians of the requisite skill in the requisite numbers than to attain autarky in raw materials by raising her extraction of Manchurian iron-ores to a level that would enable her to dispense with imports of foreign 'scrap'.

Thus, in 1939, Japan was still being eluded by the economic self-sufficiency that she was pursuing with such eagerness along so perilous a political path. The foreign Powers that had played havoc with her light industries by abruptly closing their markets to her after 1929 had it also in their power to frustrate her present enterprise of conquering for herself a self-contained economic domain; they could cut off supplies of key tools and indispensable raw materials for her infant heavy industry; and the aggressive foreign policy on which Japan had now deliberately embarked had given some Powers a new motive for putting a spoke in her rather shaky wheel. During the economic crisis at the beginning of the decade, the measures taken by foreign governments that had hit Japan so hard had been inconsiderate in effect without being hostile in intent, and, towards the close of the decade, the same inconsiderateness was still threatening to operate to Japan's detriment. In the early 1930s, foreign Powers had closed their markets to Japan in defence of their own national economies; in 1939 they were beginning to cut off supplies to Japan because their economic interest in earning the profits from their sales to her was now coming to be overshadowed by their military interest in building up their own heavy industries for their own use in preparation for a com-

---

[1] See below, pp. 446–52.

[2] Japan did also obtain some equipment of this indispensable kind from her own accomplice in aggression, Germany; and, from a Japanese point of view, this was a less undesirable source, so long as she had to draw upon some foreign source or other. She might have obtained what she needed in this line in larger quantities from Germany at a later date in exchange for Manchurian soya-beans; but the development of this trade was prevented by the outbreak of the Second World War and the consequent imposition on Germany of a British blockade.

ing war in Europe. At the same time, the democratic industrial Powers had now been inspired, by Japan's new career of aggression, with another motive for exerting economic pressure on Japan; and, though this other motive might also be classified, in part, as one of enlightened self-interest on a long view, it was in part more altruistic and to that extent more formidable. In the United States and Great Britain, in particular, there was a strong feeling that aggressors ought to be restrained, and their victims protected, as a matter of principle, even when the aggression was not directly threatening the English-speaking Powers' own interests in the narrow sense in which national interests had customarily been interpreted. And at the same time it was coming to be felt in these countries that, on a wider and more clear-sighted interpretation, the interests of the democratic peoples demanded the very policy which their principles prescribed, since their greatest interest was to continue to be free to follow their own way of life, and the democratic way of life might cease to be possible in a world in which aggression could be committed with impunity.

The disapproval and anxiety evoked in British and American minds by Japanese aggression had not yet issued in any positive political action, and the Japanese could find specious grounds for persuading themselves that they had little to fear from this quarter. Great Britain, after all, was wholly preoccupied by now with the threat of a new war in Europe, and the United States seemed disinclined to make the world safe for democracy at the cost of sacrificing her cherished isolation. Yet, for Japanese who were fey, the first letters of the writing on the wall were already visible. Though no third party was yet overtly helping the Chinese to resist their Japanese assailants, the Japanese army had already been brought to a standstill by the sheer size and difficulty of the Chinese terrain. This military stalemate at this stage was discouraging for the Japanese; for the conquest and domination of China were indispensable preliminaries to the establishment of an autarkic East Asian co-prosperity sphere under Japan's control. If Japan thus found herself 'bogged down' far short of her objective in China, in the exceptionally favourable conditions created for her by the isolationism of the United States and the European preoccupations of Great Britain and the Soviet Union, how was she to estimate her prospects? The military situation in China, as it stood in March 1939, was enough in itself to give Japanese minds good cause for deep despondency,[1] even before the sentence-writing angel's hand had added the word 'Nomonhan'[2] or followed it up with the announcements of a Russo-German deal in August 1939 and of the denunciation in July 1939 by the

---

[1] See above, pp. 104–6.
[2] The district on the frontier between Outer Mongolia and Manchukuo which was the scene of a clash between Russian and Japanese troops in May 1939, ending in severe defeat for the latter at the end of August 1939.

United States Government of the existing Japanese-American commercial treaty.

The irony of the situation in which the Japanese found themselves at this date was heightened by the preposterousness of their political creed. To a cold-blooded alien observer, estimating Japan's capacity for aggression statistically in terms of her material power, even her immediate programme of bringing the whole of Eastern Asia under her control by main force would have seemed a sufficiently tall order. Yet a devoutly patriotic Japanese would have been guilty of 'dangerous thought' if he had permitted himself to think of this order of the day as anything more than an instalment of Japan's predestined performance. An orthodox-minded Japanese was at this date in duty bound to believe that Japan's ultimate destiny was nothing less than the conquest of the entire world. Was Japan not the land of the gods? And had she not a very present god perpetually in her midst in the person of the reigning emperor? This self-imposed political superstition hung like a mill-stone round the Japanese people's neck. No man living, either in Japan or outside it, could have dreamed in the spring of 1939 that, within little more than six years, the myth of Japan's divinely appointed destiny, which had survived the epiphany of Commodore Perry, was to be blasted by an American atomic bomb.

c. GERMANY AND HER FIELD OF AGGRESSION

(i) The Middle East

By George E. Kirk

(a) The Historic Role of the Middle East in Geopolitics

In 1939 the Middle East[1] had a population less than twice that of the British Isles, though its area was over thirty-three times as great. The greater part of the region was sparsely populated semi-desert and the bulk of the population concentrated in limited areas. Yet the significance of the region as a whole was out of all proportion to its low population density and to the undeveloped economy which that represented.

It had been the seat of the earliest civilizations of which we have any knowledge, and had retained a place in the forefront of the culture of the times until, in the 'Middle Ages' of Western chronology, its own level had begun to decline in conditions of military and political instability. Western Europe, now beginning to forge ahead, had still needed to use the Middle East as an intermediary through which to obtain the luxury products which Farther Asia furnished in greater volume and variety than the Middle East. The importance of this entrepôt role of the Middle East, which had been increased as a result of the Crusades, was, however, greatly diminished after the discovery of the less encumbered Cape Route to the Indies, c. A.D. 1500; and the Middle East had thus become an economic backwater whose ancient native culture seemed to have reached the final stages of senility.

Yet the restless Western Europeans could not leave it entirely alone. From their embryonic commercial empires in the Indian Ocean they burrowed into the Persian Gulf and the Red Sea for trade; they had never relinquished their Mediterranean connexions with the Levant coast; and already by 1770 the British East India Company was sending its fast despatches by courier from Aleppo to Baghdād and was experimenting with a short cut by land across the narrow Isthmus of Suez which shortened by half the five-months' voyage to India by the Cape.[2] A generation later, Napoleon had invaded Egypt and had intrigued with Persia as prelimina-

---

[1] This term is used in the post-1939 British sense to comprise the Arabic-speaking lands of the Eastern Mediterranean, 'Irāq, and Arabia, together with Turkey and Persia, which are geographically and historically associated with them. The Arabic-speaking peoples are for convenience called 'Arabs' without reference to their diverse racial origins and cultural differences.

[2] Henry Dodwell: *The Founder of Modern Egypt* (Cambridge University Press, 1931), pp. 3 seqq.

ries to overthrowing the new British empire in India; and, after the final
defeat of Napoleon, Britain had sought to ensure the defence of her Indian
possessions against any jealous European Power by keeping in being the
decaying Ottoman Empire in the Middle East as a cushion interposed
between India and Europe. This policy had been generally successful
throughout the nineteenth century, though Britain had been compelled to
intervene at weak points where the outer cover of this Ottoman 'cushion'
was so tenuous, or had grown so threadbare, as to invite penetration by
other European Powers; she had reinforced these weak points—Egypt,
Southern Arabia, the Persian Gulf—with strong patches of her own
'protection' or direct control.[1] By 1900, however, the Ottoman Empire
had come under the influence of Britain's latest rival, Germany. In the
First World War Britain had accordingly broken up the Ottoman Empire
and had taken for herself mandates over Palestine and Transjordan, and
'Irāq. These Arab territories were the arms of the 'Fertile Crescent' that
spanned the thousand-miles' short cut from the Mediterranean to the
Persian Gulf and also covered the northern land-approach to the Suez
Canal, already covered to west and south by the British occupation of
Egypt and of Aden. The Levant coastlands had, for the last three cen-
turies, had a closer connexion (mainly cultural in character) with France
than with any other Western Power.[2] It was therefore natural that
France should claim the reversion of Syria and Lebanon, to which
Britain could agree the more readily as France was no longer strong
enough to challenge Britain's supremacy in the Middle East as a whole.

(b) The Nationalist Challenge to the Imperial Powers

After 1918 the first challenge to this consolidation of British and French
imperial interests had come from the Dominant Minority[3] within the
Middle East itself. The peasant-cultivators who constituted the bulk of the
population and formed the basis of the economy of Egypt and the Fertile
Crescent[4] were as little affected directly by the European influences of the

[1] Cf. generally H. S. Deighton: 'The Arab Middle East and the Modern World', *International Affairs*, October 1946, xxii. 511–20. Persia and Afghanistan were similar, but less considerable, cushions interposed between India and the expanding Russian Empire; and Britain fought two wars in the nineteenth century in the attempt to reinforce the crumbling independence of Afghanistan and prevent the infiltration of Russian influence.

[2] A. H. Hourani: *Syria and Lebanon* (London, Oxford University Press for Royal Institute of International Affairs, 1946), pp. 146–57.

[3] Cf. A. J. Toynbee: *Study of History* vol. iv (London, Oxford University Press for Royal Institute of International Affairs, 1939), pp. 5–6. (Hereafter this work will be referred to as Toynbee: *Study*.)

[4] The percentage of wage-earners employed in agriculture in the various Middle Eastern countries has been calculated for the year 1934–5 (Alfred Bonné: *The Economic Development*

nineteenth century as they had been by the succession of foreign conquerors that had dominated their lands for some 2,000 years past; but the
cities of the Ottoman Empire and Persia were the homes of an upper class
of property-owners which had in the past been sensitive to the successive
extraneous cultural influences that had played upon the Middle East. The
torpor into which this class had sunk since the Western Middle Ages was
the result of a withdrawal into itself of the Islamic civilization,[1] and of the
consequent relative insulation of the Middle East from the quickening currents of Western European activity. This torpor did not, however, betoken
any radical degeneration in the innate mental capacity of this ruling
class; and its response to the greatly increased impact of Western influence
in the nineteenth century consisted in embarking belatedly on a process of
external Westernization and modernization, and in simultaneously absorb-
ing through Western education such liberal concepts as that of the Nation,
founded on a supposed homogeneity of cultural, linguistic, or ethnic
traits, and carrying with it the claim to political independence.[2]

of the Middle East, revised edition (London, Kegan Paul, Trench, Trubner, 1945), p. 51) as
follows:

						per cent.
Turkey	.	.	.	.	.	. 82
'Irāq .	.	.	.	.	.	. 81
Transjordan .	.	.	.	.	.	. 80
Syria .	.	.	.	.	.	. 77
Egypt .	.	.	.	.	.	. 71
Cyprus	.	.	.	.	.	. 59
Palestine:						
Arabs	.	.	.	.	.	. 57
Jews	.	.	.	.	.	. 19

'Land tenure is based on a complicated and ancient system. . . . The social structure resembles
the feudal system but, with few exceptions, those who have absolute or hereditary titles to any
considerable area of land are, to all intents, absentee landlords. . . . The landlord is a receiver of
rent in cash or kind; he may even sell the right of collecting the rent to the highest bidder with
obvious consequences to his unfortunate tenants; consciously, or unconsciously, he is in effect an
exploiter of the land and his tenants. It is hardly necessary to point out that the blame for this
disastrous state of affairs rests not with the individual landlord but with an age-old social system. . . .
'But not all the land is in the possession of large landlords; there are a number of peasant
proprietors. In Egypt the 1933 figures showed that, although 39 per cent. of the agricultural
land was held in estates of over fifty acres by 0·6 per cent. of the total number of landowners, no
less than two-thirds of the landowners held, on an average, only two-fifths of an acre each. Such
minute holdings could hardly be economically sound. . . . The consequence is that throughout
the Middle East this class is in the grip of the money-lender. Although they own their land they
have not the means to improve it and are no better off than the small tenants of the large landlord
who hold only an annual lease' (B. A. Keen: *The Agricultural Development of the Middle East* (London,
H.M.S.O., 1946), pp. 13–14).
Cf. generally Alfred Bonné: *State and Economics in the Middle East* (London, Kegan Paul,
Trench, Trubner, 1948), and Doreen Warriner: *Land and Poverty in the Middle East* (London,
Royal Institute of International Affairs, 1948).
[1] Cf. H. A. R. Gibb: *Mohammedanism* (London, Oxford University Press, 1949), pp. 144–6.
[2] This 'Arab Awakening' in its early stages was the work of a (largely Christian) literate middle
class; and it was mainly after the Young Turk Revolution of 1908 that the younger generation

This nationalist movement had naturally conflicted with the Ottoman Empire, military in its origin but deriving justification, like earlier Muslim military dynasties, from the theory of a common brotherhood in Islam of which it was the divinely-appointed protector. The nationalists had indeed played their part—a subordinate part—in the final overthrow of the Ottoman Empire; but their outlook conflicted far more fundamentally with the British and French mandatory régimes that succeeded to its Asiatic provinces. These régimes were both alien and infidel; and the new influences they introduced would be likely to interfere, as the unprogressive Ottoman administration had not, with the privileged social and economic status of the property-owning Dominant Minority. In the pursuit of their own ends these European governments appeared to the local Dominant Minority to favour (to their own disadvantage) native Christians in the Levant States, European or native Christians or Jews in Egypt, and homeless Assyrians in 'Irāq, and they even promoted an immigration of European Jews into Palestine. The fact that these countries benefited considerably from European administration in such practical matters as communications, economic development, and public health did not mollify the Dominant Minority, disappointed of their political independence: for (they thought) their own economic and social privilege would be best assured by maintaining the *status quo*, or at most modifying it only at their own pace and in their own interests; whereas its rapid transformation by influences over which they had little control threatened to awaken the urban worker, and ultimately the exploited peasantry, to the organized presentation of economic claims which must encroach upon the privileges of their traditional masters.

(c) ATTEMPTS AT COMPROMISE

The efforts of the nationalist alliance of the upper and middle classes (the latter of which was growing in size and importance with the spread of education) to throw off British and French control dominated the political history of Egypt and the Fertile Crescent from 1919 to 1939. In the Turkish Republic and Persia, where direct European rule had never been established, there was a parallel movement to throw off 'unequal treaties' and the powerful European economic interests that had been established there since about 1850. Britain had soon experienced in Egypt and 'Irāq how effectively the politically minded ruling-class minority could organize and raise the unpolitical masses in revolt against foreign rule, and she had accordingly given up her respective protectorate and man-

of the (well-to-do Muslim) Dominant Minority grasped the political aspect of the movement as an instrument for increasing their own power. The names of members of the political societies formed between 1908 and 1914 are instructive in this connexion: cf. George Antonius: *The Arab Awakening* (London, Hamish Hamilton, 1938), p. 95 and footnotes to pp. 108–11.

date over these countries and placed her relations with them on a treaty basis (1922, 1924, 1930, 1936).[1] Such treaties were still unequal, it is true, but at least they had conceded sovereignty and self-government as tangible gains for nationalism; and they were regarded by the nationalists as temporarily acceptable halfway-houses, but only as such, towards the goal of complete independence.[2] France, with many misgivings,[3] was following the same course in her relations with the Levant States, though the threatening world situation in 1938–9 had given her grounds for postponing the ratification of a first treaty with Syria (1936).[4] Of the countries which had emerged from the partition of the Ottoman Empire in Asia only Palestine, because of her special problem of the clash of Zionist and Arab nationalisms, remained under direct European rule.[5]

In making these political concessions the two European Great Powers had sought with some success to retain their essential interests in the region. The Middle East remained important to them both as a line of commercial and strategic communications with the Farther East, and the command by British forces of such vital points as the Suez Canal and the Straits of Bāb ul-Mandab, and for air communications Lydda and the Persian Gulf, had been assured.[6] Doubt had been cast on Britain's ability to keep open these communications through the Mediterranean in time of war, with pointed reference to the difficulties she had encountered there in the First World War, and the 'Cape School' of strategists had advocated

[1] For the stages of this process in regard to Egypt, see *Survey* for 1925, i. 189–238; *Survey* for 1928, pp. 235–83; *Survey* for 1930, pp. 188–222; *Survey* for 1936, pp. 662–701. For 'Irāq see *Survey* for 1925, i. 466–71; *Survey* for 1928, pp. 339–42; *Survey* for 1930, pp. 317–29; *Survey* for 1934, pp. 109–213.

[2] 'The treaty of 1936 was concluded in the midst of an international crisis, at a moment when the spectre of war was already appearing.... If Egypt accepted the treaty with all that it implied in the way of restrictions on her independence, it was because she knew that they were of a transitory character . . .' (Egyptian note to Britain, 20 December 1945; text in *The Times*, 31 January 1946).

[3] An Italian observer has objectively written: 'Faced by such a state of mind French policy has always found itself handicapped to a certain degree by the wish to maintain material and moral positions which are already outmoded. While Great Britain in the other Arab countries . . . though having in mind the firmest maintenance of her own interests, has always known how to adapt her policy to the factors gradually developing in each country, and wisely to dispense (*dosare*) her interventions and her non-interventions, France, on the other hand, in Syria and Lebanon has followed a policy which, though inspired by a broad and concrete view of the general problems, has erred through excessive one-sidedness, has often neglected the details, and has often been subject to unforeseen changes, due to the influences of personalities or political elements within metropolitan France' (Cleante, pseud.: 'Siria e Libano nella politica franco-inglese', *Nuova Antologia*, August 1945, pp. 313–14).

[4] For Franco-Syrian and Franco-Lebanese relations, see *Survey* for 1925, i. 346–66 and 386–457; *Survey* for 1928, pp. 328–32; *Survey* for 1930, pp. 304–14; *Survey* for 1934, pp. 284–301; *Survey* for 1936, pp. 748–67.

[5] On this paragraph generally cf. the writer's *A Short History of the Middle East* (London, Methuen, 1948), chapter vi: 'The Struggle for Independence, 1918–39', pp. 129–93.

[6] The corresponding French strong-points were the ports of Beirut and Jibuti, and the airfield of Rayāq in Lebanon.

placing reliance in that longer but less vulnerable route. Their argument had, however, been countered by the assertion that

the question of the abandonment of the Mediterranean as Great Britain's main route to the East cannot be settled merely on the basis of its use as a waterway. To hand it over unconditionally to foreign control would have the most demoralizing effect on Great Britain's position in the Near East. . . . It would inevitably invite the invasion of Egypt . . . and the occupation of Palestine, whilst it would undermine her prestige in the eyes of the whole Moslem world.[1]

It was, however, an admitted fact that the consolidation of the Italian African Empire in 1936 had introduced a new factor into the British imperial strategy of the Middle East, though the exact implications of this new factor had not yet become evident. On the one hand, Italian forces based on the Mediterranean and East Africa could make the passage of the Eastern Mediterranean and the Red Sea extremely hazardous for Powers opposed to Italy; but, on the other hand, those Powers, having forces based on the Middle East, could readily sever the communications between Italy and her empire,[2] which was moreover desperately lacking in all the resources essential for waging war.

One of these essential resources, oil, was present in abundance in the Middle East itself. The exploitation of the Middle East oilfields had not started until the opening of the twentieth century and had not yet begun to rival that of the oilfields of the Americas. In 1937 Britain received only 22 per cent. of her supplies from the Middle East oilfields;[3] but their importance lay not in immediate production, which was being carefully husbanded, but in the immense untouched reserves, which were being progressively proved,[4] in comparison with the steadily diminishing reserves of the Americas and Russia. The United States herself, by far the world's largest producer of oil, had already begun (in 1933) to buy a footing in the Arabian fields, with results which were not to become important until the close of the Second World War. Apart from any question of willingness, the Middle Eastern countries were themselves quite incapable technically of prospecting for, extracting, and refining these oil resources, and the discovery of them thus provided a new and potent

[1] *Political and Strategic Interests of the United Kingdom.* By a study group of the Royal Institute of International Affairs (London, Oxford University Press for Royal Institute of International Affairs, 1939), p. 128.

[2] For these points, see *Survey* for 1935, ii. 249–51. See also above, pp. 26–7.

[3] Elizabeth Monroe: *The Mediterranean in Politics* (London, Oxford University Press, 1938), p. 12, note 1. France received over 40 per cent. of her oil supples from 'Irāq (ibid. p. 75).

[4] ' "Proved reserves" are based on scientific estimates of the amounts of oil remaining in the ground which have been discovered by actual drilling and are recoverable by existing economical methods. The estimates are subject to constant alteration on the basis of information from new wells, the introduction of new methods, and from price changes' (Raymond F. Mikesell and Hollis B. Chenery: *Arabian Oil* (Chapel Hill, University of North Carolina Press, 1949), p. 15, note 2).

reason why foreign Powers could not willingly relinquish their interests in this region.[1]

The established political personalities in these countries were not seriously disturbed by the discovery of these oilfields, and often welcomed them; for they were themselves sufficiently Westernized not to object to the impact of further Westernization (provided that it did not lead to such inconveniences as a general rise in the level of wages or a spread of trade-unionism), and the fact that the cost of capital development could be met from the substantial royalties paid by the oil companies made it possible to finance from the ordinary budget the costly externals of sovereignty (civil list, bureaucracy, diplomatic representation abroad, armed forces, public buildings) and still have something for such less spectacular items as public health and elementary education. The members of the new ruling class had obtained through the nationalist movement personal authority and the fruits of office; and in their satisfied state they were rapidly becoming conservative in outlook. There was a growing middle class of civil servants and professional men who were conscious of the shortcomings of their national life and anxious to remedy them by earnest and practical effort; but they were without effective organization, to an even greater degree than their kind in other parts of the world, and much of their effort had ended in frustration.[2]

(d) THE INTRANSIGENTS, AND THEIR EXPLOITATION BY THE AXIS

The divergence between political 'moderates', who were prepared to make tactical compromises with the British or French still exercising varying degrees of tutelage over their countries, and the 'extremists', who would accept nothing less than complete and immediate independence,[3]

---

[1] Writing on this topic, Freya Stark, after remarking that with the development of long-range aircraft 'the African routes became as easy as the trans-Arabian, and the endemic tumults of Arabia would not have been worth negotiating in the interests of air-transport alone', continues with her customary vividness: 'Oil came into the picture like one of those geological intrusions by which a whole landscape is changed. By its discovery the countries of Arabia have once again become what they were for two thousand years of their history, the middlemen for one of the world's most valuable products, with the addition that the product is actually located, for the most part, within their territory' ('Arab Background', *Quarterly Review*, January 1949, p. 59).

[2] Cf. A. C. Edwards on the dilemma of liberal intellectuals in Persia: 'Persia Revisited', *International Affairs*, January 1947, xxiii. 55, 57.

[3] This division into political 'extremists' and 'moderates' was far from being identical with the division into cultural 'Zealots' and 'Herodians' illustrated by Toynbee ('Islam, the West, and the Future', *Civilization on Trial* (London, Oxford University Press, 1948), pp. 187–212); cf. *Survey* for 1925, i. 6–7. For example, Ibn Sa'ūd, leader of the 'zealot' Wahhābī movement, had become a 'moderate' in international politics since he achieved sovereignty for himself in Arabia: likewise the Sanūsī chief, Saiyid Muhammad Idrīs, became internationally 'moderate' after the Second World War because he hoped to achieve sovereignty thereby. On the other hand, in each of the countries of the Fertile Crescent and Egypt there were numerous cultural 'Herodians' who became political 'extremists' because they saw no other means of securing power, whether for personal aggrandizement or in pursuit of some political principle with which they had uncompromisingly identified themselves.

extended downwards from the 'patrons' of the Dominant Minority into a 'client' stratum of lower middle class intellectuals. Since the First World War secondary and higher education had been rapidly expanded, partly as a practical necessity arising out of the attraction of the Middle East within the orbit of Western civilization with all its complexities, but secondarily also as a matter of national prestige and emulation. Insufficient care was taken, however, to relate the young men's studies to the economic and social possibilities open to them; and the result, especially in Egypt, was to cumber the labour-market with a large surplus of young *efendis*, ill equipped for making good in any profession or in commerce, and yet unfitted by their education for returning to the more modest occupations of their fathers.[1] In Palestine, where British undertakings to Zionism had denied political power to the Arab Dominant Minority, the national Leader (the Muftī of Jerusalem, Hājj Muhammad Amīn al-Husainī)[2] held almost unchallenged sway over this class. Elsewhere, however, the Dominant Minority had already won varying measures of political power, at the price of temporary acquiescence in 'unequal treaties' with the British or French; and while their favoured dependants gratefully continued their parasitic association with them, others, who found themselves excluded from these benefits or whose firmness of political principles forbade them to compromise with 'imperialism', had seceded into organizations which were subversive and semi-underground (partly because they were denied adequate constitutional expression, and partly out of innate love of intrigue and conspiracy), and formed themselves round some Leader, whom his supporters regarded as inspired and his critics as fanatical.[3]

The German and Italian Governments, for their part, had not been slow to exploit the bonds of sympathy with the extremist movements of

[1] While, on the one hand, 'it is probably not inaccurate to state that the population density of Egypt is eight times greater than that in the United Kingdom, in relation to total resources', on the other, 'the proportion of university graduates to the total population is eleven times as great in Egypt as in the United Kingdom' (K. A. H. Murray: 'Some Regional Economic Problems of the Middle East', *International Affairs*, January 1947, xxiii. 13; A. S. Eban: 'Some Social and Cultural Problems of the Middle East', ibid. July 1947, xxiii. 370–1).

[2] See *Survey* for 1934, pp. 100–9; *Survey* for 1936, p. 720, note; *Survey* for 1937, i. 568–71; *Survey* for 1938, i. 415–16, 445, 458, note.

[3] e.g. the Egyptian Muslim Brotherhood (Ikhwān al-Muslimūn), led by the school teacher Hasan al-Bannā; the Young Egypt Party (Misr al-Fatāh), led by the lawyer Ahmed Husain; the Syrian National (or Popular) Party (Hizb as-Sūrī al-Qawmī), led by Antūn Sa'āda, sometime teacher at the American University, Beirut; the Syrian League of National Action ('Usbat al-'Amal al-Qawmī), under a succession of leaders; the Arab Club (Nādī al-'Arabī) at Damascus, probably led by the lawyer-politician Nabīh al-'Azama: its president was the Berlin-trained dentist Sa'īd Fattāh al-Imām. The 'Irāqī Futuwwa (youth movement) was the legal offspring of governmental extremism; the Phalanges Libanaises, led by the chemist Butrus Jumaiyil (Pierre Gemayel), on the other hand, were inspired by the Jesuits to promote Lebanese separatism from Syria and dependence on France. For the Syrian and Lebanese organizations, cf. *Oriente Moderno*, March 1941, pp. 101–23; and for the Futuwwa, ibid. June 1940, pp. 297–302.

the Middle East which derived both from their common opposition to Britain and France and from their common attachment to the Leader-principle. Some of the Arab extremist Leaders had received part of their education in Germany; the patronage of Baldur von Schirach during his Middle East tour in 1937 could place a halo round the head of a local Leader; and Axis subsidies, so it was said, provided handsome club-rooms for impecunious societies and so afforded a material motive for unattached youth to join them.[1]

This encouragement of the extremist youth movements was only one aspect, and probably a minor one, of the Italian and German political offensive which had been waged against Britain and France in the Middle East since 1935. Extensive and costly propaganda was made through sub-sidized news-agencies, broadcasts,[2] films, and educational institutions. The German effort, following Schacht's tour in 1936, to develop reci-procal trade, buying primary products often at prices well above world prices and offering in return German armaments and manufactures, had met with considerable success.[3] By 1937 the two Great Power blocs were engaged in a political and economic struggle for the control of the Middle East from which not even those Muslim rulers could remain aloof who were most anxious to keep their domains unaffected by disturbing Euro-pean influences. The King of Saʻūdī Arabia and the Imām of the Yaman were both represented at the London Round Table Conference on Pales-tine early in 1939;[4] and while King ʻAbd ul-ʻAzīz, as far back as 1933, had made a contract with American oil interests to develop the oilfields on his east coast, the far more exclusive Imām Yahyā had made treaties with such diverse Powers as Britain, Italy, the U.S.S.R., and Japan.

(e) ATTEMPTS AT REGIONAL ALLIANCE

This increased Great Power activity had caused the countries of the Middle East to take the first step towards forming a common front among themselves, lest they should otherwise become one by one the helpless victims of rival policies which they could not influence. The break-up of the Ottoman Empire had left many unresolved disputes among the

---

[1] Bernard Vernier: *La politique islamique de l'Allemagne* (Paris, Centre d'Études de Politique Étrangère, 1939), pp. 92–95.

[2] Cf. Seth Arsenian: 'Wartime Propaganda in the Middle East', *Middle East Journal*, October 1948, ii. 419–21; Nevill Barbour: 'Broadcasting to the Arab World', ibid. Winter 1951, v. 58–59, 63. Ciano recorded how the anti-British broadcasts in Arabic from Radio Bari originated in his chance finding of a job, as a reviewer of current affairs, for the brother of a Lebanese bishop (Galeazzo Ciano: *1937–1938 Diario* [hereafter referred to as Ciano: *Diario (1937–8)*] (Bologna, Capelli, 1948), 24 January 1938).

[3] See *Survey* for 1936, pp. 526–33; *Survey* for 1937, i. 495–65; *Survey* for 1938, i. 43–69. In 1938–9 Turkey's and Persia's trade with Germany amounted to 45 and 31 per cent. respectively of their total foreign trade, and German trade with Egypt was second only to that of Britain.

[4] See *Survey* for 1938, i. 446.

successor states, which might have led to numerous little wars had it not been for the mediating influence of Britain. The Turkish Republic had disputed its frontier with 'Irāq, and had more recently forced through a rectification of its frontier with Syria.[1] Persia had been in dispute over her frontiers with both Turkey and 'Irāq.[2] Sa'ūdī Arabia had actually been at war with her neighbour the Yaman, and Ibn Sa'ūd had a twenty-year-old dynastic rivalry and boundary dispute with the Amīr 'Abdullāh of Transjordan, now the head of the Hāshimī family that had formerly ruled Mecca under the Ottomans and had since provided rulers for Transjordan and 'Irāq.[3] The relations of Egypt with the countries of Arab Asia had not been close, in spite of their common language and religion. Egyptian politicians had been preoccupied with their own efforts to throw off foreign control, and King Fu'ād had looked to Europe rather than to Arab Asia for cultural associations. It was the growing threat to the Muslim position in Palestine arising from the advancing wave of Jewish immigration under the nationalist banner of Zionism that had brought the Arab rulers together, first in an attempt to mediate between the Palestine Arabs and the British in 1936, and then more formally in the Round Table Conference of 1939.[4] While these combinations were the result of a danger existing within the Middle East, the Sa'dābād Pact made in 1937 by Turkey, 'Irāq, Persia, and Afghanistan was an attempt to avert, by mutual guarantees, the imperilling of their existence by some external Power in this period when Great Power rivalries were increasing and the League of Nations had failed to provide collective security.[5] The special position of Turkey as a bridge between Eastern Europe and the Middle East was emphasized by the fact that she was simultaneously a member of the Balkan Entente of 1934[6] and connected with the U.S.S.R. by treaties of friendship and neutrality going back to 1921.[7]

(f) The Obstacle of Internal Instability

The stability of the Middle Eastern countries vis-à-vis the perils that were threatening the world in 1939 was not enhanced by their internal political structure. While Turkey had enjoyed continuity of government

---

[1] See Survey for 1925, i. 471–531; Survey for 1936, pp. 767–83; Survey for 1938, i. 479–92.
[2] See Survey for 1936, pp. 793–803.   [3] Ibid. pp. 783–93.
[4] For the Round Table Conference, see Survey for 1938, i. 440–58. There had also been unofficial pan-Arab congresses at Jerusalem in 1931 (see Survey for 1934, pp. 99–109) and Blūdān (Syria) in 1937 (see Survey for 1937, i. 552–3, also Hourani: Syria and Lebanon, pp. 114–15). To the Arabic-speaking peoples the frontiers drawn in the Middle East after 1918 could not appear as anything but artificial, quite apart from their political objectionableness. Under the Ottoman Empire they had known no such barriers. Members of the dominant families of Syria, Palestine, and 'Irāq had studied together at Istanbul or in Europe, and many of them were intermarried.
[5] See Survey for 1936, pp. 793–803; also Francesco Cataluccio: 'Il patto di Sa'dābād', Rassegna Italiana, April 1940, p. 247.
[6] See Survey for 1934, pp. 523–30.   [7] See Survey for 1920–3, pp. 370–3.

and had made considerable progress under the dictatorship of Mustafā Kemāl Atatürk (who had died on 10 November 1938), the achievements of his Persian counterpart Rizā Shāh Pahlavī were vitiated by his succumbing increasingly to the lust for personal enrichment.[1] In Saʿūdī Arabia and the Yaman the Monarch and his nominated provincial governors ruled the people personally without the interposition of any bureaucratic administration, and his Ministers were in very fact but the servants of their master. In Transjordan also the Amīr ʿAbdullāh exercised very considerable authority, subject only to the advice of the British Resident. Between these extremes of Westernizing dictatorship in the non-Arab north and the survival of patriarchal traditions in the Arabian Peninsula, Egypt and the countries of the Fertile Crescent exhibited a simulacrum of parliamentary government. The Governments of the Levant States were severely limited by the power of the French High Commissioner, and their conduct might therefore not be regarded as typical. In sovereign Egypt and ʿIrāq, on the other hand, British influence had become indirect; and though Britain's representatives could in fact—as war-time history was to show—when backed by armed force make and unmake governments, such extraordinary and (within the terms of normal diplomatic relations) illegitimate authority had not been exercised since Britain had recognized the sovereignty of ʿIrāq and Egypt by the Treaties of 1930 and 1936 respectively. Kings Fuʾād and Faisal had utilized to the full the powers conferred on them by their respective Constitutions to guide their infant Parliaments, and, if their conduct had (by Western standards) not always been strictly constitutional, their influence had been on the whole salutary; for the weakness of the parliamentary régimes had been apparent in their lifetimes and became more glaringly evident after their deaths had left their two adolescent sons Fārūq and Ghāzī on their respective thrones. Egyptian parliamentary life was dominated by the Wafd Party which, after the British Protectorate had been worn down in 1922 by action on the widest political front, had emerged as the principal party, despite repeated secessions from its ranks. It was in fact the only party with an effective country-wide political machine, and it consequently claimed to represent, and certainly in normal circumstances commanded the votes of, the Egyptian 'common man'. In contrast, the other parties were fragmentary groupings round some upper-class notable, representing

---

[1] Arthur C. Millspaugh: *Americans in Persia* (Washington, Brookings Institution, 1946), chapter iii; but cf. A. C. E., after a nine-months' visit to Persia in 1948–9 wrote : 'It is interesting to find that the renown of . . . the late Shah . . . is now not only admitted, but emphasized, even by the intelligentsia who support the present constitutional régime. For the magnitude of Riza Shah's achievements are there for all men to see; while the hatreds engendered by his tyranny are being forgotten. He is regarded in Persia today as the greatest sovereign since that almost legendary Prince, Shah Abbas I. The Majlis recently conferred upon him the honorific title of "The Great" ' (*The World Today*, September 1949, v. 393–4).

privileged interests with no roots in the people. Unfortunately the second leader of the Wafd, Muṣṭafā an-Naḥḥās, had entered upon a conflict with the prerogative of the Crown that laid him open to the charge of seeking a personal dictatorship; and a term of Wafdist government in 1936-7 had merely carried the feud over to the new reign of King Fārūq, had provoked an important secession from within the Wafdist ranks, and had brought political gang-warfare on to the streets, while the primary duty of good administration was neglected.[1] In 'Irāq the parliamentary situation was even less satisfactory, and far more unstable than in Egypt. Parties had never been more than embryonic, and had been abolished 'as a gesture of national unity' when 'Irāq became independent in 1932. Government was thus dominated by the personal rivalries and constant regroupings of a few score members of the landowning and mercantile oligarchy. Every government, by means of manipulated elections, packed Parliament with its own supporters, and so blocked the only constitutional device by which it could be overthrown, viz. a vote of no-confidence. After King Faisal's death in 1933 recourse to unconstitutional methods of forcing a Cabinet to resign had become common, and the powerful tribes and the army had been successively invoked as the *deus ex machina*. After the military *coup d'état* of October 1936, rival groups of army officers had played a prominent part in engineering changes of government,[2] and a heady militarist nationalism was having a disturbing effect on the education of the younger generation.

(g) Economic Problems

In the decadence of the seventeenth and eighteenth centuries the economy of the Middle East had sunk almost to the level of subsistence farming and handicrafts, except in certain favoured areas of the Levant where there was an interchange of goods with Europe.[3] The strengthening of contacts with Europe in the nineteenth century brought about a great expansion of trade, and in particular the Nile Valley, the most densely populated area of the Middle East, adopted a monoculture of cotton which was profitable in normal times but left Egypt's 16 millions (in 1937) without an assured food supply if the international exchange of goods were interrupted. In other parts of the Middle East also periodical crop failures or breakdowns in distribution, partly due to the backward

[1] Royal Institute of International Affairs: *Great Britain and Egypt 1914-1936*, Information Dept. Papers, no. 19 (London, Royal Institute of International Affairs, 1936); Philip Graves: 'The Story of the Egyptian Crisis', *Nineteenth Century*, March 1938, p. 297.

[2] Cf. Majid Khadduri: *Independent Iraq, a Study in Iraqi Politics since 1932* (London, Oxford University Press for Royal Institute of International Affairs, 1951), pp. 71-137.

[3] Cf. H. A. R. Gibb and Harold Bowen: *Islamic Society and the West*, vol. i, 'Islamic Society in the Eighteenth Century', part i (London, Oxford University Press for Royal Institute of International Affairs, 1950), pp. 258-71, 295-6, 307-8.

methods employed generally (except in the Jewish sector of Palestine with its European combination of industry and intensive agriculture), were liable to cause scarcities of essential foodstuffs which the cupidity of cultivators and merchants would artificially aggravate. In normal times these conditions roughly regulated themselves at the cost of much hardship to the poor; but in the First World War Syria, under Ottoman military government, had suffered a serious famine, and a Power using the Middle East as a base in any future war might expect similar embarrassments.

(h) The Special Problem of Palestine

The growth in Palestine of an energetic Jewish community, composed mainly of recent immigrants from Eastern and Central Europe and amounting in 1939 to 29 per cent. of the total population,[1] had presented a formidable economic challenge to the Palestine Arabs and a difficult political problem to the British mandatory. Political Zionism had been the product of at least three converging forces: the age-old religious hope of a return to the Promised Land; the desire to escape from persecution in Eastern Europe, which had been aggravated since 1880 by the growing nationalism of the majority-peoples of that region; and the spread of the same nationalist tendency to some Jewish thinkers,[2] awakening their desire to create a self-governing Jewish nation. During the First World War British (and American) statesmen had somewhat lightly made promises of a Jewish national home in Palestine,[3] the consequences of which had borne heavily on a generation of harassed British administrators.[4] The Balfour Declaration—'a solemn engagement . . . on . . . the Romantic plane of history, where . . . obstacles become dwarfed from an exalted bird's eye view'[5]— had emerged from an inextricable tangle of Zionist, British, and United States romanticism and statecraft. The original

---

[1] Their numbers had increased from 84,000 in 1922 to 411,000 at the end of 1938. 58·9 per cent. of the Jewish immigrants into Palestine from 1919 to 1938 inclusive were of Polish, Russian, Rumanian, or Lithuanian citizenship (Great Britain, Colonial Office: *Report on the Administration of Palestine and Transjordan*, 1938 (London, H.M.S.O., 1939), p. 231; Palestine Government, Department of Migration: *Annual Report*, 1938 (Jerusalem, Government Printing Office, 1939), p. 70).

[2] Such as Leon Pinsker, author of *Auto-Emancipation* (1882) and especially Theodor Herzl, who wrote *Der Judenstaat* under the impact of the *affaire Dreyfus* in 1896. It would be interesting to know what proportion of latter-day Zionists would regard as adequate the assertion 'that Judaism has always been a peculiar amalgam of nationalism, ceremonialism, messianism, and God-intoxication . . .' (a reviewer in *Zionist Review*, 19 January 1951, p. 20).

[3] In a document in which 'one nation solemnly promised to a second nation the country of a third', as Arthur Koestler puts it (*Promise and Fulfilment* (London, Macmillan, 1949), p. 4).

[4] 'Without that absurd National Home business Palestine would have been a country easy to rule and pleasant to live in. For the Jews Zionism was a messianic inspiration. For the British Administration it was simply a damned nuisance' (ibid. p. 10).

[5] Cf. ibid. p. 20.

Zionist draft,[1] which had contained no reference whatever to the Arabic-speaking Muslims and Christians who then constituted 90 per cent. of the population of Palestine, had been modified by the British Government to provide some protection for elementary Arab rights. Romanticism had rapidly tarnished 'in a sort of hangover after the debauch of imagination',[2] as the impatient Zionists, claiming a superior right to Palestine[3] and overweeningly complacent in their European 'culture',[4] were met on four occasions between 1920 and 1933 by violence at the hands of the Arabs who, having refused to accept the Balfour Declaration as the basis of the Mandate, were precluded from having any constitutional influence on the immigration policy of the Mandatory Power. Successive British commissions of inquiry had admitted that the Arabs had some reasonable grievances, and a doctrine had been evolved of a 'double undertaking' to Jews and Arabs to which the British Government had to 'give effect in equal measure';[5] but the efforts to strike a balance had been frustrated by the intransigence of both the Arab and the Zionist political leaders. The beginning of the Nazi persecution was followed by a great wave of Jewish immigration into Palestine,[6] which in 1936 was countered by an Arab rebellion, enjoying sympathy and some support from the neighbouring Arab countries.[7] A new British attempt at compromise, the Royal Commission's partition plan of 1937, both failed to satisfy Zionist ambitions and aroused the Arabs to renewed rebellion on a more serious scale.[8] In the opening months of 1939, therefore, the British Government, under the shadow of the Munich Agreement, were making a final attempt to bring the two communities to compromise; and, when they refused, Britain was compelled by the menacing international situation to treat the question in terms of *raison d'État* and to buy a respite for herself by an appeasing

[1] Text in Chaim Weizmann: *Trial and Error* (New York, Harper & Brothers, 1949), p. 203.

[2] Koestler, loc. cit.

[3] Cf. Weizmann, op. cit. p. 280, for Curzon's rejection of the Zionist proposal that a paragraph of the Preamble to the Mandate should begin with the words 'Recognizing the historic rights of the Jews to Palestine . . .'.

[4] 'The Jews . . . may tend to look down on the inferior intellectual attainments of the Arabs, but they do not hate them. Let the Arabs publish some learned journals, open a few art galleries and form a symphony orchestra, and the Jews will positively love them' (*Zionist Review* Jerusalem correspondent, 10 October 1947, p. 5); cf. Sir Ronald Storrs: *Orientations* (London, Nicholson & Watson, 1943), pp. 360–9.

[5] The Prime Minister, Ramsay MacDonald, 3 April 1930 (H. C. Deb. 5th ser., vol. 237, col. 1466). The Zionists rejected this notion of equal weight being given to the Arabs of Palestine 'as against the entire Jewish people' as an 'insidious exclusion, by implication, of the relationship between Palestine and world Jewry' (Weizmann, op. cit. p. 325).

[6] Between 31 December 1932 and 31 December 1935 the estimated Jewish population had increased by 84·8 per cent., 76·2 per cent. being due to migration and only 8·6 per cent. to natural increase (Palestine Government, Department of Statistics: *Vital Statistics Tables, 1922–45* (Jerusalem, Government Printing Office, 1947), pp. 1* and 84*).

[7] The Zionists' protests at the 'interference' of the neighbouring Arab States were characteristically inconsistent with their contention that Palestine was the concern of 'the entire Jewish people' (Weizmann, loc. cit.).   [8] See *Survey* for 1938, i. 414–79.

concession to the Arab world;[1] for the Zionists, however infuriated, could obviously be relied on not to make common cause with their Nazi persecutors, whereas the hostility of the Arab world (however ineffectual in purely military terms) presented immediately a formidable threat to the vital British position in the Middle East. Zionists and their non-Jewish supporters, not content with condemning the 1939 White Paper as a 'Palestine Munich', did not subsequently scruple to deny that it had any excuse in terms of expediency;[2] but, under the spell of their narrowly focused vision, they studiously refrained from allowing themselves to consider to what extent, in default of the White Paper policy, Arab political agitation, strikes, sabotage, &c., might have interfered with the British Middle East war-effort in 1940–2 and consequently with the Persian supply-route to the U.S.S.R.—and what the ultimate consequences might then have been, for the National Home, for world-Jewry, and for all mankind.[3]

(ii) Spain and Portugal
By Martin Wight

(a) NATIONALIST SPAIN

The German destruction of Czechoslovakia in March 1939 coincided with the end of the Civil War in Spain. Barcelona had fallen to the Nationalists on 26 January, the Germans entered Prague on 15 March, the Nationalists took Madrid on 28 March.[4] 'After three centuries of

---

[1] Oliver Stanley, President of the Board of Trade in 1939 and afterwards Colonial Secretary, was somewhat equivocal about the hopes that had been entertained that 'tempers might fall, accommodations might begin' between Jew and Arab as a result of the White Paper; contrast his statement on 31 July 1946 (H. C. Deb. 5th ser., vol. 426, col. 981) with that on 25 February 1947 (ibid. vol. 433, col. 1924).

[2] Political Declaration of the 1945 World Zionist Conference, paragraph 4 (*Zionist Review*, 17 August 1945, p. 6); cf. Weizmann, op. cit. pp. 403, 410.

The two Labour M.P.s Richard Crossman and Michael Foot found it necessary to their thesis *A Palestine Munich?* (London, Gollancz, 1946, p. 26) to represent Rashīd 'Alī's pro-Axis *putsch* in 'Irāq in 1941, which might have found much greater support in other Arab countries had it not been for the appeasing effect of the White Paper on moderate Arab nationalism, as 'of no strategic significance'; but Crossman's judgements on Palestine were anything but consistent. Contrast: 'In 1939 we had to impose the White Paper because the Arab world might have joined the Axis in the years of the war. . . . It may be it was a perfectly good strategic necessity, though an unpleasant one' with: 'This was a British policy of which, I had hoped, every decent Englishman is by now heartily ashamed' (25 February 1947, H. C. Deb. 5th ser., vol. 433, col. 1984; *New Statesman & Nation*, 10 March 1951, p. 274).

[3] Cf. in a different context General Catroux: *Dans la bataille de Méditerranée* (Paris, Julliard, 1949), p. 116: 'Si les Alliées voulaient ne pas perdre la bataille de la Méditerranée — et sans doute, par suite, la guerre. . . '. Churchill in May 1941 rejected the suggestion that the defence of Singapore was more important than that of Egypt (*Second World War*, iii. 375, 379).

[4] See *Survey* for 1938, i. 277, 306. Franco's ceremonial entrance into Madrid took place on 19 May.

inactivity', wrote Ciano, 'Spain thus again becomes a living and dynamic factor'.[1] It was a wishfully rhetorical exaggeration of the truth that, after a century and a half as a small and weak Power, Spain now had a government with expansionist ambitions and the desire to play a part in international politics.[2]

The Spanish Civil War ended the era of 'the generation of '98'—the period of profound intellectual and moral debate concerning the renovation of Spain and her place in European society, which followed her defeat in the Spanish-American War and her loss of the last remnants of the old Spanish Empire. The Spanish writer, Angel Ganivet, had said in 1897 that, though the loss of Gibraltar was a standing offence, Spain should acquiesce in it; for England as a purely maritime Power was less dangerous to the liberties of other countries than continental Powers, and being now satisfied and defensive had the same interests in international order as a weak state like Spain.[3] But the Nationalist movement, like the Fascist Revolution in Italy and the Nazi Revolution in Germany, brought a renewal of foreign claims and ambitions. Since 1815 Britain and France had had a common interest in the weakness of Spain; the new Spanish Government intended to repudiate this servitude. On the eve of his victory Franco said that Spain held the keys of the Mediterranean and that henceforward Mediterranean affairs would not be settled without her.[4] But the rejection of foreign interference and international isolation was inseparable from the desire for expansion. From the earliest days of the rebellion Franco had claimed that he was come to restore the lost imperial mission of Spain. The third point of the Falangist programme declared: 'We have a will to empire. We affirm that the full history of Spain implies

---

[1] Galeazzo Ciano: *Diario 1939 (–1943)*, 2 vols., 4th edition (Milan, Rizzoli, 1947), 22 February 1939. An English version in one volume with title *Ciano's Diary 1939–1943*, edited by Malcolm Muggeridge, was published in 1947 (London, Heinemann). (This work will be referred to hereafter as Ciano: *Diario (1939–43)*.)

[2] Though the great Spanish Monarchy was partitioned as a result of the general war of 1702–13, Spain sustained the role of a Great Power under a Bourbon dynasty throughout the eighteenth century. Her loss of Great Power status may be dated from her defeat by the French Republic in the War of the First Coalition (1793-5) and the Treaty of San Ildefonso of 1796 which reduced her to a French satellite; and she subsequently failed to obtain recognition as a Great Power at the Congress of Vienna (see C. K. Webster: *The Congress of Vienna, 1814–1815* (London, Bell, 1934), pp. 61, 75).

[3] Ángel Ganivet: *Idearium Español* (Buenos Aires, Espasa-Calpe Argentina, 1943) trans. as *Spain: an Interpretation* (London, Eyre & Spottiswoode, 1946), pp. 87–90: 'Amongst all the nations of Europe, Spain is, after Italy, the one most interested in England's naval supremacy being maintained for a long time to come.... It seems absurd, no doubt, that our own interests are linked up with those of the one nation with whom we have genuine grounds for ill-feelings, but in the recognition and acceptance of such anomalies lies at times the highest political wisdom.' Cf. E. Allison Peers: *Spain in Eclipse, 1937–1943* (London, Methuen, 1943), pp. 165–6.

[4] Declaraciones a Manuel Aznar, 31 December 1938 (*Palabras del Caudillo* (Barcelona, Fe, editado por la Delegación Nacional de Falange Española Traditionalista y de las JONS, 1939), p. 312). Cf. Camilo Barcia Trelles: *Puntos cardinales de la política internacional española* (Barcelona, Fe, 1939), pp. 474–6.

an empire. We demand for Spain a pre-eminent place in Europe.'[1] With the victory of the Nationalist Government, Spain's will to empire, her imperial and Catholic mission, became the constant theme of propaganda.[2] There was a war party among the Falangists and the army, and the new Government intended a policy of territorial aggrandizement as circumstances might allow. When Suñer visited Italy in June 1939 he told Ciano that Spain meant to recover Gibraltar, for so long as the British flag flew there she would not be a completely free and sovereign nation, and also to square accounts with France, by expansion in Morocco.[3]

The ambitions of Nationalist Spain were not confined to the Mediterranean. The imperial and Catholic mission pointed to the former empire that Spain had found and ruled for two centuries in the New World and the Pacific. Ibero-American cultural unity had attracted intellectuals and scholars and been the subject of institutes and conferences ever since the Spanish American countries had joined with Spain to celebrate the fourth centenary of the discovery of America, and Pan-Hispanism was one of the ideals canvassed by the generation of '98. The word 'Hispanity' was coined before the Civil War, on the model of 'Christianity', to comprise and characterize the whole of the Hispanic peoples.[4] Its first meaning was conservative and cultural: the ideal of Spain and her daughters being moved by the same Catholic, nationalist, and authoritarian spirit and unanimously repudiating the doctrines of the French Revolution and Yankee materialism. But irredentism does not remain confined to the literary plane. *Hispanidad*, like *Deutschtum* and *romanità*, was a concept

---

[1] Official translation of the 26 Points of Falange, reproduced in Arthur F. Loveday: *World War in Spain* (London, Murray, 1939), appendix iii, p. 184. There is another version in Allan Chase: *Falange: the Axis Secret Army in the Americas* (New York, Putnam, 1943), p. 14.

[2] See Peers: *Spain in Eclipse*, pp. 98–100.

[3] Ciano: *Diario (1939–43)*, 5 June 1939. In a memorandum to Hitler of June 1940, Franco defined his territorial demands as Gibraltar, French Morocco, the Oran zone of Algeria, and the enlargement of Rio de Oro and Spanish Guinea. (See memorandum by the German Ambassador in Madrid, 8 August 1940, in *The Spanish Government and the Axis: Documents*, Department of State Publication 2483 (Washington, U.S.G.P.O., 1946), p. 3. [This collection will be referred to hereafter as *Spanish Government*.]) In the same month Franco began his occupation of Tangier.

The last serious attempt by a Spanish Government to recover Gibraltar had been the great siege of 1779–83 during the American War of Independence. From the British point of view in 1939, if command of the sea was unable to prevent the loss of Gibraltar, it could at any time occupy the Canary Islands in exchange, from which control of the Atlantic routes and the western entrance to the Mediterranean could be maintained. (See Churchill: *Second World War*, ii. 460, 552, 563).

[4] By Ramiro de Maeztu, a political philosopher who was the precursor of Falangism, in his *Defensa de la Hispanidad* (Madrid, Fax, 1934). The terms Ibero-American, Hispano-American, and Pan-Hispanic were for the most part interchangeable, giving the advantages of imprecision. 'Hispano-American' illustrated the ambiguity on both sides of the hyphen. On the one side, did Hispanity include Portugal and Brazil? According to Maeztu it did (ibid. pp. 19–20), and it was often thus used in Falangist propaganda. 'Ibero-American' avoided this ambiguity. On the other side, Hispanic America was normally used for convenience to cover the Philippines as well (cf. Trelles, op. cit. pp. 165–6, 184–5).

whose political value lay in its elasticity of content and purpose. If Spain could replace France as the intellectual leader, and perhaps even the United States as the political leader, of the Latin American countries, she would not only be redeeming them spiritually but also strengthening her own international position; and Falangist writers hoped that Spanish aggrandizement in Africa might be backed by a political, economic, and cultural alinement with the great Hispanic bloc of America.[1] 'With regard to the Hispano-American countries', said the third point of the Falangist programme, 'we will aim at unification of culture, of economic interests and of power. Spain claims a pre-eminent place in all common tasks, because of her position as the spiritual cradle of the Spanish world.'[2] But at the moment of Franco's victory, Hispanity still had no existence outside the sphere of Nationalist propaganda, except for the obscure and impalpable influence of the *Falange Exterior* as an auxiliary to the Nazi fifth column in Latin America.[3]

But the foreign ambitions of the Nationalist Government, when its authority was at last established throughout the territory of Spain, were limited by physical exhaustion and political instability. The country was economically devastated. Suñer told Ciano in June 1939 that Spain was at the end of her resources, that in certain regions there was famine, and that she needed two or preferably three years of recovery before she could enter a war at the side of the Axis.[4] Franco told Ciano in the following month that at least five years' peace were necessary, and that many observers considered this an optimistic estimate.[5] Spain was as much divided, beneath the hardening crust of the totalitarian state, as she had been when the Civil War began. The proletariat and large parts of the peasantry remained potentially hostile to the new régime. Catalonia and the Three Basque Provinces were punished by the abolition of their autonomy. The Government instituted reprisals against the defeated Republicans which became a secular heresy-hunt against Reds. The Nationalist movement itself was deeply divided. The Falangists, themselves a collection of radicals and *arrivistes*, soon came near to ousting the

[1] See Ramiro Ledesma Ramos: *Discurso a las juventudes de España* (Madrid, La Conquista del Estado, 1935), p. 72.

[2] Loveday: *World War in Spain*, appendix iii, p. 184.

[3] The only published account of the Falange overseas is Chase: *Falange*, of which the reliability is questionable.

[4] Ciano: *Diario (1939–43)*, 5 June 1939.

[5] See conversation between Ciano and Franco at San Sebastian, 19 July 1939 (Galeazzo Ciano: *L'Europa verso la catastrofe* (Milan, Mondadori, 1948), p. 440; *Ciano's Diplomatic Papers*, ed. Malcolm Muggeridge, trans. Stuart Hood (London, Odhams Press, 1948), p. 291. [This work and the English translation will be referred to hereafter as 'Ciano: *Europa*' and 'Eng. version'.]). Ciano used the argument of the Spanish need for recuperation in his vain attempt, at Obersalzberg on 12 August 1939, to dissuade Hitler from immediate war (see memorandum of conversation between Hitler and Ciano: *I.M.T. Nuremberg*, xxix. 49 (1871–PS); trans. in *Documents* (R.I.I.A.) for 1939–46, i. 178; cf. *N.C.A.* iv. 515, viii. 523).

conservative Traditionalists from power in the Government and the Party. The monarchists were dissatisfied. The army despised the Falange. Business men opposed the doctrinaire economic policy of the Falangist Radicals. The Church was suspicious of the Government's association with Nazism. The Government was split by personal and inter-departmental feuds, and quickly became bogged in graft and inefficiency. Like the classic dictators of history and unlike his contemporary patrons and exemplars, Franco had arrived at civil power by way of military command, and if he showed a talent in the new and unfamiliar field it was perhaps that of balancing upon the rivalries of politicians and generals, of adjusting their antagonisms and playing them off against one another. But for positive reasons also domestic reconstruction took precedence of foreign adventures. The Government prided itself on plans for national unity and social reform: Franco 'wishes—to use Mussolini's formula—to go out to the people'.[1] And at the same time Spaniards individually were absorbed in scraping a living, in black-marketing, in obstructing or adapting themselves to Falangist innovations, in seeking revenge, or escaping it. The single common wish was that there should be no renewal of fighting.[2]

(b) Portugal and Spain

Franco's victory placed the two countries of the Iberian Peninsula in the middle of a diplomatic chain joining Germany and Italy on the one side with Great Britain on the other. The Nationalist cause established an unusual community of sentiment between Spain and Portugal; Franco was in close dependence upon the Axis; Portuguese policy was traditionally based upon a British alliance.

Spain and Portugal possessed a tradition of mutual hostility like that of England and Scotland before the Union of 1707. The lesser Power was always conscious of a threat to its independence, the greater Power intermittently resumed the tendency to complete the political unification of a natural geographical whole.[3] The only Hispano-Portuguese Union in history was effected by Philip II of Spain in 1580, and undone in the War of Secession of 1640–68. After this the ancient Anglo-Portuguese alliance, which had been first contracted in the fourteenth century, took on a new importance. For England, Portugal was a maritime buffer state and a

[1] Conversation between Ciano and Franco, San Sebastian, 19 July 1939 (Ciano: *Europa*, p. 443; Eng. version, p. 293).

[2] For varying pictures of Spain between the end of the Civil War and the outbreak of the World War see Salvador de Madariaga: *Spain*, 2nd edition (London, Cape, 1942), pp. 421–9; Peers: *Spain in Eclipse*, pp. 123–37; Herbert Feis: *The Spanish Story* (New York, Knopf, 1948), chapter i.

[3] See *Survey* for 1937, ii. 202. There was the difference that Portugal had an independent history in the world not less glorious than that of Spain, while Scotland only obtained her full influence on Western Civilization as a result of the Union with England.

bridgehead against Spain of the same kind as the Low Countries were against France. For Portugal, the English alliance was the guarantee of her independence.[1] The Napoleonic Wars provided the classic example of the alliance in action; they also produced a Portuguese *irredenta*, for in the Hispano-Portuguese War of 1801 the Spaniards took the frontier town of Olivença, and in spite of a clause in the Treaty of Vienna of 1815 never restored it to Portugal.[2] In the nineteenth century the ideal of Iberian unity was revived in new shapes, and canvassed in Portugal as well as in Spain; the Right thought of it in terms of dynastic union, the Left in terms of republican federation; and the English alliance was still the ultimate sanction of Portuguese independence.[3]

Confidence between the two Peninsular states was only assured when there was a similarity of régimes, and partly for that very reason their political swings did not often synchronize. The triumph of the Nationalists in the Spanish Civil War created a harmony of this kind for the first time since the fall of the Portuguese monarchy in 1910. That event had made Portugal a demagogic republic while Spain remained a conservative monarchy. In 1926 Portugal moved to the right with the military revolution which inaugurated the authoritarian 'New State', but five years later the Spanish monarchy collapsed and was succeeded by a republic with Left-wing and Iberianist tendencies.[4] From the beginning of the Spanish Civil War the Portuguese Government supported the Anti-Communist and Catholic cause of the Nationalists.[5] This marked the ascendancy of ideological over traditional political considerations, for although a Spanish Republican victory perhaps carried the danger of a union of Iberian Soviet republics, Falangist propaganda also played with a unification of the Peninsula.[6] Salazar may have hoped for the position of

[1] See Edgar Prestage: 'The Anglo-Portuguese Alliance', in *Transactions of the Royal Historical Society* (1934), xvii. 69 seqq. 'Portugal must be either an autonomous limb of the Iberian body or a disguised and hardly more autonomous limb of the British Empire' (Madariaga: *Spain*, p. 195); it is to be noted that this is a Spaniard's way of putting it.

[2] Vienna Congress Treaty, 1815, article 105 (Sir Edward Hertslet: *The Map of Europe by Treaty 1814–1891* (vols. i–iii, London, Butterworth, 1875, and vol. iv, London, H.M.S.O., 1891), i. 268). See also H. V. Livermore: *A History of Portugal* (Cambridge University Press, 1947), pp. 390–1, 402.

[3] Cf. Granville's conversation with the Spanish Minister on 19 February 1873 (*British Documents on the Origins of the War 1898–1914*, ed. G. P. Gooch and Harold Temperley (London, H.M.S.O., 1926–38), vol. i, no. 69 (enclosure no. 1). (This work will be referred to hereafter as Gooch and Temperley.)

[4] The following dates may be noted: *Portugal*: 1910, fall of the monarchy; 1926, military revolution establishing General Carmona's dictatorship; 1928, Salazar appointed Finance Minister; 1932, Salazar became Premier; 1933, new Constitution. *Spain*: 1923, Primo de Rivera became dictator; 1929, fall of Primo; 1931, flight of Alfonso XIII and establishment of the republic; 1933, general election and swing to the Right: 1936, outbreak of the Civil War (see *Survey* for 1937, ii. 10–23).

[5] Ibid. 208; *Survey* for 1938, i. 360, note 2.

[6] Cf. Ramos: *Discurso a las juventudes de España*, p. 72.

precedence and patronage with Franco that Mussolini once possessed in relation to Hitler,[1] but as soon as the Nationalists had won the war the reversal of roles became probable. In the moment of victory, on 18 March 1939, Franco concluded with Portugal a treaty of friendship and non-aggression.[2] Outwardly it confirmed the solidarity of the two régimes; the Portuguese Government may have hoped that it could be regarded also as a measure of reassurance. The abolition of Catalonian and Basque autonomy by the Nationalists in the following month was not an encouraging example of their Iberian policies for a country that was on the eve of celebrating the tercentenary of its national rising against the Spanish yoke.

(c) SPAIN AND THE AXIS POWERS

The success of Franco's rebellion had been very largely due to Italian and German intervention on his side, and with his victory the main international question concerning Spain became the extent of her future dependence on the Axis.[3] In Spain itself there were different attitudes towards the two Axis Powers. Ciano noted, at his interview with Franco in July 1939, that although the Spaniards approved of the Rome–Berlin system they were anxious to 'underline a distinct difference in their feelings towards Italy and towards Germany'.[4] There were two main reasons for this. Germany was suspect as being the more powerful and incalculable ally and the greater threat to Spanish independence.[5] And Catholic sentiment, which was probably the strongest of all the several impulses within the Nationalist movement, was implicitly hostile to National Socialism. The Spanish hierarchy had vehemently supported the rebel cause, but once victory had restored it to its privileges the more prudent policy of the Vatican was likely to prevail.[6] Even a Falangist fanatic like Suñer had Catholic prejudices against the Nazis,[7] though he afterwards became their champion in Spanish politics.

The Spanish policies of the Axis Powers themselves were correspondingly different in their scope and intensity. (It is possible indeed that they had originally expected a *coup d'état* and some street-fighting, not a three years' civil war, but having once become committed could not draw back.) Italy had adopted Franco's cause as a vital interest of her own; for Germany it was subordinate to wider ends. Italy had sent infantry and played

[1] See *Survey* for 1934, p. 328.

[2] *Survey* for 1938, i. 360–1; Peers: *Spain in Eclipse*, pp. 144–5.

[3] For the strategic anxieties of the French in view of a possible association of Spain with the Axis, see *Survey* for 1937, ii. 148–50, 188–9.

[4] Ciano: *Europa*, p. 440; Eng. version, p. 291.

[5] 'Franco and his advisers know that the country is not in a position to go to war. At the same time they are afraid of Germany and very friendly with Italy': letter from Sir Samuel Hoare to Lord Halifax, 11 June 1940 (Lord Templewood: *Ambassador on Special Mission* (London, Collins, 1946), p. 34).

[6] See *Survey* for 1937, ii. 218–21.   [7] Ciano: *Diario (1939–43)*, 9 June 1939.

the larger part at sea; Germany had sent air forces and specialist troops. Italian expenditure on the Civil War was probably greater than German,[1] and Italian intervention was throughout the more ostentatious.

For Germany the Civil War had appeared at first mainly as a new chapter in Italo-Franco-British rivalry. In his conference with his commanders on 5 November 1937 Hitler said that German interests lay, not in seeing a total victory won by Franco, but in prolonging the war and encouraging its extension into a conflict between Italy, France, and Britain, during which Germany could settle the Czech and Austrian questions.[2] German help to Franco seems to have been prompted by a desire less for his victory than for technical war experience, and for the purposes of political warfare against the democracies by encouraging the frame of mind that accepted Hitler as Europe's defender against Bolshevism. But there were important economic advantages to be had in Spain: the commercial treaty of 16 July 1937 between Germany and the Nationalists had a secret protocol providing for German collaboration in the economic reconstruction of Spain, especially in the development of minerals and raw materials,[3] and the Germans soon began getting what they wanted. The strategic advantages of a Fascist Spain became worth serious consideration a little later. In August 1938 the Luftwaffe Intelligence was planning to use the German Condor Legion in Spain to bomb Bordeaux and Marseilles if France went to war in defence of Czechoslovakia.[4] On 27 March 1939 the victorious Franco formally adhered to the Anti-Comintern Pact,[5] and on 31 March concluded a treaty of friendship with Germany. This committed each Power to the most benevolent neutrality if the other were engaged in war, expressed their desire to increase their economic relations, and was supplemented by secret pacts providing for naval co-operation and

---

[1] At the time of Mussolini's visit to Munich in September 1937 the Germans claimed to have spent quite as much on the Spanish War as the Italians (Compte rendu du troisième entretien de Mussolini avec Bülow-Schwante [September 1937] in *Documents secrets du Ministère des Affaires Étrangères d'Allemagne*, translated from the Russian by Madeleine and Michel Eristov [referred to hereafter as *Documents secrets* (Eristov)] (Paris, Éditions Paul Dupont, 1947), vol. iii (*Espagne*), no. 3, pp. 22–23). A month later, in his conversation with Ribbentrop at Rome on 6 November 1937, Mussolini said that Italian expenditure in Spain had been $4\frac{1}{2}$ milliard lire, and German expenditure, according to Göring, about $3\frac{1}{2}$ milliards (Ciano: *Europa*, p. 221; Eng. version, p. 144). For general estimates of the final Spanish war debts to Italy and Germany see Thomas J. Hamilton: *Appeasement's Child* (New York, Knopf, 1943), p. 140; Charles Foltz: *The Masquerade in Spain* (Boston, Houghton Mifflin, 1948), p. 140.

[2] Hossbach Memorandum, 10 November 1937 (*I.M.T. Nuremberg*, xxv. 411–12 (386–PS); *D.Ger.F.P.*, series D, i. 36–37; *Documents* (R.I.I.A.) for 1939–46, i. 23); cf. *N.C.A.* iii. 303.

[3] *Survey* for 1937, ii. 193–4; Feis: *Spanish Story*, p. 22, note.

[4] Report on 'extended Operation Green' by Intelligence Division of Luftwaffe General Staff, 25 August 1938 (*I.M.T. Nuremberg*, xxv. 390 (375–PS); *N.C.A.* iii. 287). In May 1939 Ribbentrop thought the Spaniards would be useful to pin down some French divisions in the Pyrenees (see conversation between Ciano and Ribbentrop, Milan, 6–7 May 1939, in Ciano: *Europa*, pp. 430–1; Eng. version, p. 285; *Documents* (R.I.I.A.) for 1939–46, i. 166).

[5] *Survey* for 1938, i. 360.

for a measure of German control over the Spanish police, press, and propaganda.[1] But Hitler had found the Spaniards tiresome and unreliable to deal with[2] until it became urgent to capture Gibraltar and shut the Mediterranean in the second half of 1940; he regarded Spain as a strategic sideshow and Germany's Spanish policy remained empirical and without high expectations.[3]

Italy had signed a secret treaty with the Nationalists as early as 28 November 1936, which assured the Nationalists of Italian support in preserving the integrity of Spain and her colonies and in re-establishing order in Spain, provided for co-operation between the two Powers in the Western Mediterranean, and pledged each to neutrality if the other went to war or became the victim of sanctions.[4] Mussolini had two main interests in Franco's victory. Nationalist Spain would be an ally against France; he originally intended to retain a naval and air base in the Balearics as long as possible in order to cut French sea-communications with North Africa.[5] But he planned to use Spain also for his 'march to the Ocean'; Italy and Spain would partition North Africa, Italy taking Tunisia and Algeria, Spain taking Morocco and Gibraltar, and giving Italy permanent transit facilities across Morocco to the Atlantic.[6] He was hoping to conclude an alliance with Franco as soon as the war was won.[7] The Fascist Government urged the Germans to conclude a pact

---

[1] Feis: *Spanish Story*, pp. 19, 22. This treaty was not ratified until 29 November 1939. The reason for its not being published in *Spanish Government* is not apparent.

[2] 'As concerned Spain, Germany, on the basis of the experiences gained during the Civil War, was clear about the fact that one could not make progress with the Spanish without quite concrete and detailed agreements. . . . In any case he [Hitler] was not convinced that Spain had "the same intensity of will for giving as for taking." . . . Economically Germany had given out many hundreds of millions for Spain. He (the Führer) had taken the stand that the payment of this debt should be left alone during the war, however that it would have to be taken up again after the victory of Franco. Whenever the Germans demand the payment of the 400 million debt incurred during the Spanish Civil War, this is often interpreted by the Spanish as a tactless confusing of economic and idealistic considerations, and as a German, one feels toward the Spanish almost like a Jew, who wants to make business out of the holiest possessions of mankind' (see notes of the interview between Hitler and Ciano on 28 September 1940 in *Spanish Government*, pp. 17, 18–19).

[3] Cf. the reference to Spain in Hitler's speech to his commanders of 22 August 1939 (*I.M.T. Nuremberg*, xxvi. 339 (798-PS); trans. in *Documents* (R.I.I.A.) for 1939–46, i. 444; cf. *N.C.A.* iii. 582).

[4] For text of treaty see *Documents secrets* (Eristov), vol. iii (*Espagne*), no. 1; *Documents* (R.I.I.A.) for 1939–46, i. 5–7.

[5] Conversation between Mussolini and Ribbentrop, Rome, 6 November 1937 (Ciano: *Europa*, p. 222; Eng. version, pp. 144–5). In the event, however, Italian as well as German troops were all withdrawn from Spanish territory in May and June 1939, though the Italians left behind most of their heavy material (*Survey* for 1938, i. 356–60).

[6] Ciano: *Diario (1939–43)*, 14 June 1939: cf. Leonardo Simoni, pseud.: *Berlino, Ambasciata d'Italia 1939–1943* (Rome, Migliaresi, 1946), pp. 140, 142. See below, pp. 191–3.

[7] Ciano: *Diario (1939–43)*, 8 January 1939. When Suñer visited Italy in June it was agreed that 'the alliance is a fact in our minds; it would be premature, for the moment, to put it in a protocol' (ibid. 5 June 1939).

with Spain, but Ciano was anxious that if this were to be published the existence of the Italo-Spanish pact of 1936 should be announced first: 'otherwise people will say that Italy makes war in Spain and Germany profits from it'.[1] There was latent jealousy between the two Axis Powers, but Mussolini was perhaps less afraid of German ascendancy in Spain than in the Balkans, and the conclusion of the Spanish War was a condition for his own annexation of Albania.[2] The Italians wanted Spain to be a member of the Axis, but connected more intimately with Rome than with Berlin; Italy's position in the Axis would be enhanced if she became the indispensable mediator, the pivot on which the Axis swung.[3] Mussolini prided himself on messages from Franco that resembled the reports of a subordinate,[4] and early in 1939 it seemed to the still sanguine eyes of Ciano that the Spanish victory bore only Mussolini's name, and that on the Ebro, at Barcelona, and at Malaga the foundations of a new Roman Mediterranean Empire had been laid.[5]

(d) THE PORTUGUESE AND SPANISH EMPIRES

In the First World War Spain was weak and divided on the question of intervening against her ancient enemy and despoiler, and remained neutral. Portugal, however, was drawn into the struggle of the Great Powers by her British alliance. In 1930 Spain was even weaker than in 1914 through the ruin of the Civil War, but she desired to enter the impending Great Power conflict in the hope of territorial aggrandizement. Portugal, however, was to remain neutral. This change in the reaction of the two Peninsular states to a general war marked their swing away from the Britannocentric system of world order that was now collapsing into the orbit of the new revolutionary Powers.

The swing reflected not only the interests of Spain and Portugal as European states but still more the position of their overseas empires. These two had first in Western Christendom discovered the transoceanic world and divided it between them. While Portugal had ruled the South Atlantic and the Indian Ocean, Spain had ruled the North Atlantic, the

[1] Ibid. 27 January and 8 February 1939. Ciano considered it important for Italian prestige that his own visit to Spain in the summer of 1939 should take place before Göring's (ibid. 21 April 1939).   [2] Ibid. 3 March 1939.

[3] During Suñer's visit to Italy in June 1939 Ciano intervened to smooth Suñer's relations with the German Ambassador in Rome (ibid. 10 June and 14 June 1939).

[4] Ibid. 8 January 1939. Mussolini's desire for influence in Spanish affairs was seen in his repeated advice to Franco against restoring the monarchy (ibid. 5 March, 11 March, 5 June 1939; Ciano: *Europa*, p. 442; Eng. version, p. 292).

[5] Ciano: *Diario (1939–43)*, 26 January and 22 February 1939. After his meeting with Franco at San Sebastian on 19 July 1939 Ciano recorded with enthusiasm that Franco was completely dominated by Mussolini, expected instruction and directives from him, and wanted him to visit Madrid, 'whereby Spain would be definitely united to the destiny of the Roman Empire' (Ciano: *Europa*, p. 446; Eng. version, p. 295). However, what the Italians wanted was a treaty, and Franco did not concede it.

Caribbean, and the Pacific.[1] But their empires had had contrary natures
and suffered contrary fates. The Portuguese Empire was oceanic in
character. It was the organization of Portuguese naval predominance in
the Indian Ocean, where it came into contact (except along the east coast
of Africa) with stable and populous civilizations that it could hope neither
to conquer nor to subvert, the Islamic and the Hindu. It remained therefore a system of bridgeheads, fortresses, and trading-stations, like Hormuz
and Goa, Malacca and Macao. The Spanish Empire by contrast was
primarily continental in character. It was established in Central America
and the Andes upon the ruins of the two feeblest non-Western civilizations
which the West had encountered in the course of its expansion, the Aztec
and the Inca. In due course the vice-royalties and *audiencias*, where
Spanish colonists ruled an indigenous population, could transform themselves into independent states, for which the Portuguese Empire offered no
counterpart except in the single case of Brazil. Both the Spanish and
Portuguese Empires suffered severely from the depredations of their
successors in the struggle for European hegemony. Both took part in the
partition of Africa in the nineteenth century. But it was because of this
contrast between them that by the beginning of the twentieth century a
Spanish empire had ceased to exist except for a few insignificant territories
acquired during the past century and a half along the west coast of Africa,[2]

---

[1] It will be noted that the dividing line from pole to pole 370 leagues west of the Cape Verde
Islands, agreed between the Portuguese and Spanish sovereigns by the Treaty of Tordesillas in
1494, corresponded unintentionally to the geopolitical conceptions of the twentieth century (see
above, pp. 12–14). It recognized the unity of the South Atlantic basin, a unity that received its
classic illustration six years later when in 1500 the Portuguese Cabral accidentally discovered
Brazil on his way to the Cape of Good Hope. The Treaty of Tordesillas modified Pope Alexander
VI's bull of 4 May 1493. This had drawn a dividing line down the Atlantic 100 leagues west of
the Azores, which was more in accordance with the distorted map of the world in Mercator's projection. (J. Dumont: *Corps universal diplomatique du Droit des gens* (Amsterdam, 1726), vol. iii, part ii,
pp. 302–3; Ludwig Pastor: *The History of the Popes*, English translation edited by F. I. Antrobus,
vol. vi (London, Kegan Paul, 1898), pp. 160–1).

[2] In 1939 the Spanish Empire consisted of the *Canary Islands*, which were administratively part
of Spain, and the following territories from north to south along the western coasts of Africa:
(1) the Spanish northern *Zone of Morocco*; (2) the Spanish south-western Zone of Morocco, or
Ifni; (3) the colony, protectorate, and occupied territory of *Rio de Oro* and *Adrar* (sometimes collectively known as the Spanish Sahara); (4) *Spanish Guinea*, both continental and insular, with
its capital at Fernando Po. These Spanish African possessions all dated from the later nineteenth
century, with the exception of the islands of Fernando Po and Annobon, which had been ceded to
Spain by Portugal in 1778, and the varying string of *presidios* along the Moroccan coast from
Melilla in the east, occupied in 1597, to Ceuta in the west, originally Portuguese but retained by
Spain after Portugal resumed her independence in 1668. (See *Spanish and Italian Possessions*:
Independent States, Peace Handbooks issued by the Historical Section of the Foreign Office, vol. xx
(London, H.M.S.O., 1920), nos. 122–5.) The original Spanish Empire had been finally liqui-
dated when the United States compelled Spain to renounce her sovereignty over Cuba, Puerto
Rico, Guam, and the Philippines by the Treaty of Paris of 1898. This meagre 'second Spanish
Empire' ranked in 1939 eighth in area and ninth in population among the colonial empires of the
world (see Royal Institute of International Affairs: *The Colonial Problem* (London, Oxford
University Press for R.I.I.A., 1937), p. 9, table i).

while the skeleton of the Portuguese thalassocracy sung by Camoens still stretched, recognizable though picked clean of flesh, from the Azores to the Malay Archipelago and the China Seas.[1] In 1939 Portugal had an empire to save, Spain had an empire to regain.

Even after Spain had ceased to be a Great Power, Britain considered it necessary for her control of the Atlantic that Portuguese independence should be maintained under British protection.[2] But outside Europe British and Portuguese interests clashed in the nineteenth century as they had in the sixteenth. The Portuguese desire to link Angola with Mozambique, across what is now Rhodesia, conflicted with the British desire for a Cape to Cairo territorial belt and occasioned the British ultimatum to Portugal of 1890.[3] Not only the expansion, even the integrity of the Portuguese overseas possessions had to be weighed against British interests in the balance of colonial power throughout the world. In 1898 Britain concluded a secret convention with Germany dividing the Portuguese colonies into two spheres of influence as a prelude to the possibility of partition.[4] The consistency of British policy was not vindicated, nor were Portuguese fears allayed, by Britain's reaffirmation of the Ancient Treaties, including the guarantee of Portugal's colonial possessions, in 1899.[5] The Revolution of 1910, which overthrew the Portuguese monarchy, weakened Portugal's international position, and revived German pressure; and between 1912 and 1914 Britain and Germany were engaged in renewed negotiations for the prospective partition of the Portuguese Empire.[6] The outbreak of the

[1] In 1939 the Portuguese Empire consisted of the *Azores* and *Madeira*, which were administratively part of Portugal, and the following territorial possessions along the oceanic route opened up by Vasco da Gama and his predecessors and successors: (1) In the South Atlantic: (a) the *Cape Verde Islands*, (b) *Portuguese Guinea*, (c) the islands of *S. Tomé* and *Principe* in the Gulf of Guinea, (d) *Angola* or Portuguese West Africa; (2) in the Indian Ocean: (a) *Mozambique* or Portuguese East Africa, (b) *Portuguese India*, consisting of the scattered territories of Goa, Damao, and Diu; (3) in the farther Indies: (a) *Macao* in China, at the mouth of the Canton River, the forerunner of Hongkong, (b) *Portuguese Timor*, the eastern part of the island of Timor in the Malay Archipelago. All these possessions dated from the sixteenth century, though Angola and Mozambique had been considerably extended during the partition of Africa in the later nineteenth century; and the Portuguese Empire had suffered no losses more recent than, in the Indian Ocean, the conquest of Thana, Bassein, and Chaul on the Indian mainland by the Mahrattas between 1737 and 1740, and, in the South Atlantic, the establishment of Brazilian independence in 1822. (See *Portuguese Possessions*, Peace Handbooks issued by the Historical Section of the Foreign Office, vol. xix (London, H.M.S.O., 1920), and *Persian Gulf: French and Portuguese Possessions*, vol. xiii of the same series, nos. 79–81. The Portuguese Empire ranked in 1939 fifth in area and seventh in population among the colonial empires of the world (see Royal Institute of International Affairs: *The Colonial Problem*, loc. cit.).
[2] See Edgar Prestage: 'The Anglo-Portuguese Alliance', in *Transactions of the Royal Historical Society* (1934), xvii. 95–97.
[3] See R. I. Lovell: *The Struggle for South Africa, 1875–1899: a Study in Economic Imperialism* (New York, Macmillan, 1934), pp. 216–18.   [4] Gooch and Temperley, vol. i, nos. 90–92.
[5] Ibid. vol. i, no. 118, with editorial note (pp. 93–95). See also vol. viii, chapter lxii, and Harold Temperley and Lillian M. Penson (edd.): *Foundations of British Policy from Pitt (1792) to Salisbury (1902)* (Cambridge University Press, 1938), pp. 512–16.
[6] Gooch and Temperley, vol. x, part ii, chapter xcv. Sir Arthur Nicolson described these

First World War freed Portugal from these dangers, and she was drawn into the conflict on the side of her traditional protector.

Her reward was three-quarters of one per cent. of the German war indemnity, and the return of the Kionga triangle in northern Mozambique which Germany had seized in 1894.[1] But the real advantage she gained from the victory of the Allied Powers was the expulsion of Germany from Africa. German East Africa, which had marched with Mozambique on the north, was transformed into a British mandated territory; German South-West Africa, which had marched with Angola on the south, was transformed into a South African mandated territory. The Portuguese Empire was thus relieved from the most dangerous pressure upon it for two and a half centuries, and the British alliance correspondingly declined in urgency. At the same time it became clear that if the alliance did not express a common interest there would be little sentiment to sustain it. The period of Portuguese national renaissance under Salazar naturally produced a reaction against dependence on a foreign Power, which happened to coincide with a decline in the international position of that Power. Salazar's policy towards the Spanish Civil War and the Non-Intervention Agreement, approximating to that of Germany and Italy, was in some degree a declaration of independence from Britain.[2]

Nevertheless Portugal had no common interest with the Axis. If as a Catholic and authoritarian Power she supported Franco, equally as a Catholic and a weak colonial Power she must fear the rise of Nazi Germany.[3] Germany indeed no longer had a foothold in Africa, but it was possible that some colonial settlement with Britain might reinstate her there—some arrangement involving Portugal's interests arrived at without her full participation, that would resemble the Anglo-German negotiations before 1914.[4] This anxiety had receded by the time of the German seizure of Prague, but it was only replaced, when the Spanish Civil War ended, by the ambiguous and disturbing aspects of Franco's dependence on the Axis. The Portuguese Government might suspect, if they could not know for certain, that the Spanish Nationalists considered it 'fundamental to Spanish policy and to the Axis to take Portugal out of the sphere of British influence'.[5] Therefore, while signing the treaty of friendship with the

negotiations as 'the most cynical business that I have come across in my whole experience of diplomacy' (Harold Nicolson: *Sir Arthur Nicolson, Bart., First Lord Carnock* (London, Constable, 1930), p. 393). Cf. *Survey* for 1929, pp. 277–8; *Survey* for 1937, ii. 203–4.

[1] See *A History of the Peace Conference of Paris*, ed. H. W. V. Temperley [referred to hereafter as *H.P.C.*] (London, Oxford University Press for British Institute of International Affairs, 1920), ii. 243–4.   [2] See *Survey* for 1937, ii. 208, 241–2, 244–5.

[3] Portugal had not failed to see the implications also of the Italian conquest of Ethiopia: see *Survey* for 1935, ii. 80, 86, 190.

[4] For the British proposal to Germany of a new colonial régime in the conventional zone of the Congo Basin Treaties, see below, pp. 164–5.

[5] Suñer's words recorded by Ciano: *Diario (1939–43)*, 5 June 1939. 'Difficult as this may be, he intends to exert his efforts in this direction, and asks for our collaboration.'

victorious Franco, Portugal was concerned to emphasize discreetly her former ties.[1] In March 1939 she was entering upon the difficult policy of balance between the new understanding with Spain and the ancient alliance with England that she was to maintain throughout the coming war, the only Small Power that remained in treaty relations with the two contending coalitions.

(iii) Switzerland, the Low Countries, and Scandinavia
By Martin Wight

Switzerland, the three states of the Low Countries,[2] and the four states of Scandinavia[3] were in 1939 the West European neutrals *par excellence*. With the exceptions of Belgium and Luxembourg, whose neutrality had been violated by Germany, they had escaped involvement in the First World War. They were distinguished from Spain, who had also been a neutral, by their uniform success as parliamentary democracies,[4] and by the pacific and internationalist character of their foreign policies, in which the elements of prestige and competition for power had perhaps a smaller part than in any other states in the world. It was neither innocence nor inexperience in international politics that separated them from the contemporary Great Powers and the repining ex-Great Powers like Spain. Four of these small states, Switzerland, the Netherlands, Denmark (to which Norway and Iceland were then united), and Sweden, had approximated to Great Powers in the early centuries of modern history.[5] Belgium and Luxembourg, whether as parts of the Spanish Empire, or of the Austrian Empire, or as independent states, had been the northern cockpit of every general war. If these eight countries appeared to stand out from

---

[1] *Survey* for 1938, i. 360, note 2.

[2] The Netherlands, Belgium, and the grand duchy of Luxembourg.

[3] Geographically the word means Denmark, Sweden, and Norway; it is here used to include also Iceland, which was united with Denmark by a political bond, but not to include Finland, which is treated among the Eastern European states: see below, pp. 206 seqq.

[4] It was noticeable to the political scientist that they were all constitutional monarchies except Switzerland, which was a federal republic. Denmark and Iceland shared the same monarch.

[5] In so far as the term 'Great Power' can be made relevant to the rudimentary international system of the fifteenth and sixteenth centuries, the Swiss Confederacy had been an expansionist Great Power from their defeat of Burgundy in the war of 1474–7 down to their defeat by the French at the battle of Marignano in 1515. The United Provinces had been a Great Power from the time of their successful war of independence against Spain, which ended in 1609, down to their exhaustion and eclipse by their overmighty ally England in the War of the Spanish Succession of 1702–13, though they had suffered a permanent diminution in power within this period as a consequence of the French invasion of 1672. Denmark had been a Great Power from her defeat of Lübeck in 1535, which destroyed the Hanseatic thalassocracy and gave Denmark command of the Baltic, down to her own defeat by the Catholic League at the battle of Lutter in 1626 and her consequent withdrawal from the Thirty Years War at the Peace of Lübeck in 1629. Sweden had been a Great Power from her intervention in the Thirty Years War in 1630 down to her defeat by Russia in the Great Northern War of 1699–1721.

the international struggle for power in attempting to base their foreign policies on rational and co-operative principles, it was to no small extent because they had had an historical experience of the frustration of the strong and the despoliation of the weak.

In two respects they had a common character and a common interest in the world of 1939. They were all buffer states precariously wedged between the flanks of Great Powers,[1] and incapable of self-defence; and half of them had extensive territorial possessions outside Europe, which each individually would be incapable of protecting. Their traditional policy for maintaining their independence was one of neutrality; but after the First World War they had adopted another, based on the hope that the existing balance of power, on which their independence rested, might be permanently stabilized and grow into a system of collective security. The conflict between the two policies had been the theme of their foreign history as the League of Nations rose and fell.

(a) GUARANTEED NEUTRALITY: SWITZERLAND, BELGIUM, LUXEMBOURG

Switzerland and the Low Countries were distant descendants of that Middle Kingdom of Lotharingia which had arisen in the ninth century A.D. to separate the Kingdoms of the Western and the Eastern Franks, and had remained in one form or another a permanent feature of European political geography between France and Germany.[2] For a brief period

---

[1] The four Lilliputian states of Western Europe, Andorra, Monaco, San Marino, and Liechtenstein, which were so small that their sovereignty was dubious and they were not commonly considered subjects of international relations, were also vestigial buffer states and owed their survival mainly to this character. The republic of Andorra was a buffer state between France and Spain, and had now become their joint protectorate (L. Oppenheim: *International Law*, 6th edition, ed. H. Lauterpacht (London, Longmans, Green, 1947), i. 176, 232). The principality of Monaco had originated as a buffer state between France, Savoy, and Genoa; since the cession of Savoy and Nice to France by Italy in 1860 it had been an enclave in French territory, and probably had the status of an independent state in close alliance with France (ibid. i. 175, note 4, 232). The republic of San Marino had originated as a buffer state between the duchy of Urbino and the lordship of Rimini; it had then become embalmed as an enclave, first within the States of the Church, and later within the kingdom of Italy, and was now an Italian protectorate (see W. Miller: 'Democracy at San Marino', *History*, April 1922, pp. 1–16; Oppenheim, op. cit. i. 176, 232). The principality of Liechtenstein had originated as a buffer state between Austria and Switzerland; it was probably a fully sovereign state, but had been refused admission to the League of Nations in 1921 apparently because of its small size, and had entered a customs union with Switzerland in 1923 whereby it entrusted Switzerland with its representation abroad (Oppenheim, op. cit. i. 232, note 2, 169, note 4). The fifth Western European state of a similar archaic minuteness was the Vatican City, which, however, had a different origin and character (see *Survey* for 1929, pp. 453–4).

[2] See Toynbee: *Study*, i. 37–9, iii. 349, note 2. 'The guaranteed neutrality of Belgium and the guaranteed neutrality of Switzerland are alike survivals or revivals—it is hard to say which they should be called—of the instinctive feeling which, in the ninth century, called the Lotharingian Kingdom into being' (E. A. Freeman: *The Historical Geography of Europe*, 3rd edition, ed. J. B. Bury (London, Longmans, Green, 1912), p. 304; cf. pp. 290–2). The demilitarization of the Rhineland under the Treaty of Versailles was the most recent expression, in 1939, of this persisting feature of the European political balance.

in the fifteenth century this middle belt, which was then represented by the Swiss Confederation and the Burgundian dominions, had been more powerful politically and militarily than the territories it divided. The Burgundian state had collapsed first, largely as a result of conflict with the Swiss, and the Swiss Power itself only survived another forty years.[1] After that it sank into the position of a buffer state between France, Austria, and the Spanish Power in Italy; and developed a policy of neutrality which was proclaimed as a principle at the beginning of the General War of 1672–1713, when in 1674 the Confederation declared that it would regard itself as a neutral state and intervene on neither side.[2] Since then the only substantial violations of Swiss neutrality had been during the General War of 1792–1815, at the hands both of France and of the Allies. In 1815 the neutrality of Switzerland and the inviolability of her territory were guaranteed by the Powers at Vienna, and for the first time the neutrality of a small state became part of the public law of Europe.[3] Swiss neutrality survived the international revolutions of the nineteenth century and the First World War; it was reaffirmed in the Treaty of Versailles;[4] and though the seat of the League of Nations was fixed at the Swiss city of Geneva,[5] and Switzerland became a member of the League, her peculiar status was recognized by a Council resolution in 1920 which exempted her from the necessity of taking part in military operations under the Covenant.[6]

Switzerland and Belgium were both buffer states, but Switzerland had been a barrier while Belgium had been a corridor. Switzerland was the mountain fortress of Europe, seldom violated by foreign arms; Belgium was the principal battlefield of every war. Switzerland, from the beginning of modern times, was an independent state; Belgium was an outlying province of a distant empire, first the Spanish and then the Austrian.[7]

---

[1] Burgundy became a European Power through its dynastic union with Flanders in 1384. The Burgundian Power was at its height from the conclusion of the Anglo-Burgundian alliance in 1419, which enabled it to hold the balance between France and England in the last phase of the Hundred Years War, down to its defeats by the Swiss at Grandson and Morat in 1476, and by the Duke of Lorraine in alliance with the Swiss at Nancy in 1477. The Swiss Power was at its height from these victories over Burgundy down to its own defeat by the French at Marignano in 1515.

[2] See Edgar Bonjour: *Geschichte der schweizerischen Neutralität* (Basel, Helbing & Lichtenhahn, 1946), translated and abridged by M. Hottinger as *Swiss Neutrality: its History and Meaning* (London, Allen & Unwin, 1946).

[3] Webster: *Congress of Vienna*, p. 134; Act of 20 November 1815 (Hertslet: *Map of Europe by Treaty*, i. 371–2).   [4] Article 435 (see *Survey* for 1925, ii. 217).

[5] Covenant of the League, article 7.

[6] A. J. Toynbee: *The World after the Peace Conference* (London, Oxford University Press for British Institute of International Affairs, 1925), pp. 37–38; cf. *Survey* for 1935, ii. 87.

[7] The growth of Switzerland as an independent state was identical with its growth as a political unit. Swiss statehood may be dated from 1389, when the Habsburgs were compelled to sign a treaty with the Confederation on an equal footing, and renounced feudal suzerainty over each of its members; though Swiss independence from the Empire was not effected until 1499 *de facto*, or 1648 *de jure*. The existence of Belgium as a political unit dates from 1579, when the union of Arras alined those provinces of the Netherlands that remained loyal to Spain against those that

The neutrality of Switzerland was a traditional principle of Swiss policy which, after several centuries, received recognition from the Great Powers. The neutrality of Belgium was imposed by the Great Powers on a reluctant small state at the moment of its creation in 1831. It was finally guaranteed by three Treaties of London of 1839.[1] But this status, which had originally been resented as a violation of sovereignty, and had later not altogether come to be accepted as an advantage, was destroyed by the German invasion of 1914, and was abrogated implicitly by the Treaty of Versailles.[2] Belgium was the only one of the small Western Powers, apart from Denmark, to obtain territory at Germany's expense, in the acquisition of Eupen-Malmédy.[3] Like the other Small Powers, she now sought an alternative form of security by joining the League of Nations;[4] but unlike them she was an Occupying Power in the Rhineland, and consequently needed to concert her policy with France in a military agreement of limited scope that was signed in 1920.[5] An equivalent of Belgium's old status was not found until the Treaty of Locarno in 1925 gave her the guarantees of Britain, France, Italy, and Germany for her frontiers under the Versailles Settlement.[6]

Luxembourg was the third of these small states to have gained an inter-national guarantee. Like Belgium and Holland it had been part of the Burgundian inheritance,[7] and descended with the Belgian provinces from the Spanish to the Austrian Habsburgs. In 1815 it was created a grand duchy, to be within the German Confederation but joined to the Nether-lands in a personal union. The Luxemburgers disliked Dutch rule as much as the Belgians, and revolted with them in 1830, desiring to be incorporated in the new Belgian state. The Great Powers, however, partitioned Luxembourg between Belgium and the Grand Duke, that is, the King of the Netherlands. In 1842 Luxembourg joined the Prussian *Zollverein*. When Prussia defeated Austria and dissolved the Germanic Confederation in 1866, the control of the grand duchy became a subject of contention between Prussia and France, and was the *occasion manquée* of the Franco-Prussian War. The Treaty of London of 1867, however, established Luxembourg as a perpetually neutral state under a collective

continued the struggle for independence as the Union of Utrecht, but 250 years elapsed before Belgium became a state in 1831.

[1] Hertslet: *Map of Europe by Treaty*, vol. ii, nos. 153 and 183–5, article vii of the treaty or the annex in each case. See *Survey* for 1920–3, p. 65.

[2] Ibid. pp. 65–67; *H.P.C.* ii. 189–90; *Survey* for 1925, ii. 170.

[3] *H.P.C.* ii. 190–1.

[4] Toynbee: *World after the Peace Conference*, p. 37.

[5] *Survey* for 1920–3, p. 71; *Survey* for 1936, p. 353.

[6] Article 1 of the Treaty of Locarno (see *Survey* for 1925, ii. 440–2); cf. ibid. pp. 56–57.

[7] The annexation of Luxembourg in 1441 marked the zenith of Burgundian power. Previously Luxembourg had been a not insignificant principality, which had given Bohemia a dynasty producing four Emperors between 1308 and 1437 and nearly anticipating the Habsburgs as the dynasty of the Empire. It had been raised from a county to a duchy in 1354.

guarantee of the Great Powers;[1] but the customs union with Germany remained. During the prosperity and industrial development of this régime, the city which had hitherto been a fortress of the Germanic Confederation acquired still greater importance as a centre of modern communications.[2] The grand duchy was accordingly invaded by Germany two days before the invasion of Belgium in 1914 and remained in German occupation throughout the First World War.[3]

But unlike Belgium, Luxembourg was incapable of being a belligerent, and was refused a place at the Peace Conference. Both France and Belgium hoped to annex it; the Luxemburgers wished for continued independence and neutrality. The Treaty of Versailles abrogated the customs union with Germany, and in 1922 Luxembourg entered a customs union with Belgium. But a political settlement was lacking. As with Belgium, so with Luxembourg, the Versailles Treaty compelled Germany to recognize the termination of the régime of neutrality and to adhere to whatever arrangements the Allied and Associated Powers might make to replace it;[4] but no such arrangements were made, and Luxembourg therefore claimed that the treaty of 1867 was still in force. In 1920 she entered the League of Nations, but her plea that her status as a neutral might exempt her from military obligations under the Covenant was rejected.[5] In 1926 Luxembourg asked to become a party to the Locarno settlement, but Britain decided that to guarantee the grand duchy was not a vital British interest. Luxembourg therefore fell back upon the claim to neutrality under the continued existence of the treaty of 1867, a neutrality which Britain regarded as terminated when Luxembourg joined the League. Like Switzerland, Luxembourg acted upon this policy when sanctions were applied against Italy in 1935.[6]

The events of 1935–6, when the League failed to prevent the Italian conquest of Ethiopia and Germany destroyed the Locarno system by

[1] Hertslet: *Map of Europe by Treaty*, iii. 1801–5. See C. R. M. F. Cruttwell: *A History of Peaceful Change in the Modern World* [referred to hereafter as Cruttwell: *Peaceful Change*] (London, Oxford University Press for Royal Institute of International Affairs, 1937), pp. 188–90. In 1890 the throne passed from the Ottonian branch of the Nassaus, who ruled the Netherlands, to the Walramian branch, represented by the Duke of Nassau Weilburg, in accordance with the Nassau Succession Agreement of 1783 and Article 71 of the Vienna Congress Treaty (see Hertslet, op. cit. i. 253 and iii. 2013–15).

[2] 'By the end of the nineteenth century five railways and nine main roads radiated from the capital towards the chief strategic points on the French, German, and Belgian frontiers. In French hands it secures the defence of the Moselle line and facilitates an advance down that river. In 1914 its possession by Germany was essential for the Schlieffen plan: it was the essential link between the offensive and defensive wings of her armies, and by opening the way to the gap of Stenay imperilled the whole of the Meuse from the north' (Cruttwell: *Peaceful Change*, pp. 184–5). Cf. *H.P.C.* ii. 188.   [3] See *H.P.C.* ii. 184–9.

[4] Article 40; *Survey* for 1920–3, pp. 68–71. For Luxembourg's peculiar position, sovereign on the political plane but non-sovereign on the economic plane, cf. *Survey* for 1934, p. 404, note.

[5] Oppenheim: *International Law*, i. 224, note 3.

[6] *Survey* for 1935, ii. 231–2.

remilitarizing the Rhineland, removed the foundations on which Switzerland, Belgium, and Luxembourg had based their post-war policies and
drove them back upon their traditional neutrality. Belgium was particularly threatened by the resurgence of Germany. Geography had already
once made her a victim of German aggression; she had profited territorially from the dismemberment of Germany in 1919; and the division
between the Walloons and the Flemings, which gave her something of the
character of a bi-national state, might seem to offer special advantages to
German propaganda and penetration. It was perhaps a misfortune from
the German point of view that while Flemish nationalism, with its Teutonic
sentiments and pro-German sympathies, was the best lever to hand for
disrupting the Belgian state, the most conspicuous and successful Fascist
leader to arise in Belgium, Degrelle, was a Frenchman by birth, and his
Rexist Party was almost entirely supported by lower middle class Walloons.[1] Nevertheless, the Belgians felt the danger of their position acutely,
and in 1936 there was a revolution in Belgian policy, designed to reverse
the developments of 1914 and to recover a guaranteed status.[2] It was so
far successful that in 1937 Britain and France both declared that they
considered Belgium relieved of her obligations under Locarno, but their
own guarantees to Belgium as still binding upon themselves; and Germany
countered with a guarantee of Belgian inviolability in different and more
equivocal language.[3] It was on this uneasy three-legged stool that Belgium
was balanced in 1939. The country as a whole clung to neutrality as the
least imperfect protection against invasion that could be found. The
Government knew that invasion was only to be feared from Germany and
attached proportionate value to the British and French guarantee. But
the desire not to endanger neutrality by offending Germany, which was
emphasized particularly by King Leopold and his entourage, precluded
Belgium from engaging in the staff talks with France and Britain which
were essential for her military defence. Luxembourg, for her part, had in
1936 sought a defensive agreement with Belgium,[4] and in 1937 once more
approached Britain and France for guarantees, which were refused.

Switzerland was in a happier position. Her neutral status had remained without interruption part of the public law of Europe; it had
been recognized by the League of Nations; and when the League collapsed
it was necessary only to redefine it. In May 1938 the sessions of the League
Council and Assembly that dealt with the *de jure* recognition of Italian
sovereignty over Ethiopia recognized also the Swiss intention not to
participate henceforth in any sanctions,[5] which virtually released Switzer-

---

[1] For the zenith of the Rexist movement in 1936 see *Survey* for 1936, pp. 36–37.
[2] See ibid., pp. 351–60. The military agreement of 1920 with France had already become
obsolete when the Allied occupation of the Rhineland ended in 1929.
[3] See *Survey* for 1937, i. 346–68.   [4] See *Survey* for 1936, p. 354, note 2.
[5] *Survey* for 1938, i. 152; Bonjour: *Swiss Neutrality*, p. 118.

land from the obligations of the Covenant and acknowledged her return to her pre-existing status of perpetual neutrality. She seemed to have been peculiarly endangered by the Anschluss, which left her encircled on three sides (as Belgium and Luxembourg were not) by the Axis Powers. But it was in her geographical strength as a mountain island that her real security lay; this alone had guarded her neutrality in the First World War, and might do so again in the new dangers of 1939.[1] Belgium and Luxembourg, in contrast, were facing a new European war in which they could scarcely hope to escape invasion, the one with renewed guarantees from the Great Powers, the other with nothing but her unsupported claim to the neutrality of 1867; but guarantees of neutrality were to prove again as worthless as they had in 1914, and the difference in status between Belgium and Luxembourg was not to prevent them from being overwhelmed in common.[2]

(b) Neutrality without Guarantees: the Netherlands and Scandinavia

The Scandinavian countries, like the Low Countries, had a long tradition of political unity. From 1397 to 1520 the three kingdoms of Denmark, Sweden, and Norway (of which Iceland was then a dependency) had been joined in the Union of Kalmar.[3] Denmark and Norway had remained united down to 1814, when as part of the Vienna settlement Norway had been transferred to Sweden, leaving Iceland, however, united to Denmark. It was not until 1905 that Norway seceded and became an independent state, and not until 1918 that Iceland obtained the equivalent of British Dominion status, becoming an independent kingdom joined to Denmark by a personal union.[4] The Scandinavian countries, like the Netherlands, had a traditional policy of neutrality which had never been written into the public law of Europe,[5] but consisted in the refusal to enter into alliances

---

[1] Hitler's plans in 1939 do not seem to have provided for the invasion of Switzerland, though when he said that she would tenaciously defend her neutrality he was saying what he said also about the Low Countries. See minutes of conference between Hitler and Ciano, 12 August 1939 (*I.M.T. Nuremberg*, xxix. 42 (1871–PS); *N.C.A.* iv. 509); also Hitler's speech to his commanders-in-chief, 22 August 1939 (*I.M.T. Nuremberg*, xxvi. 342 (798–PS); *N.C.A.* iii. 585). Cf. Directive no. 1 for the Conduct of the War, 31 August 1939 (*I.M.T. Nuremberg*, xxxiv. 457 (126–C); *N.C.A.* vi. 935). For these three texts see also *Documents* (R.I.I.A.) for 1939–46, i. 172, 443, and 499.

[2] For a contemporary estimate of German interests in this connexion see *Survey* for 1937, i. 350.

[3] On the historical significance of the Union of Kalmar, see Toynbee: *Study*, ii. 175–6. Iceland had been an independent republic from A.D. 930 to 1263, when the Scandinavian colonists swore allegiance to the King of Norway.

[4] See Cruttwell: *Peaceful Change*, pp. 91–95; *Survey* for 1920–3, pp. 232–3.

[5] At the time of obtaining her independence in 1918, Iceland made a declaration of perpetual neutrality, and in consequence never joined the League of Nations; but the declaration was unilateral and had no validity in international law (Oppenheim: *International Law*, i. 218, note 1; Cruttwell: *Peaceful Change*, p. 184). In 1855, during the Crimean War, Britain and France had

with Great Powers. They had not taken part in any war between Great Powers since 1815, and in particular they had maintained their neutrality during the First World War.[1] Yet they were not without profit from that upheaval. It destroyed the two Great Powers from whom they had most to fear. For fifty years the Low Countries and Denmark had lived under the shadow of Germany; for 200 years Sweden had lived under the shadow of Russia; and in 1919 Germany and Russia were equally exhausted and diminished. The Scandinavian states even benefited territorially from a victory in which they had not participated. At the peace settlement the Great Powers awarded Spitsbergen to Norway,[2] and, as a result of a plebiscite in 1920, restored Northern Slesvig to Denmark.[3] By contrast Sweden failed to regain, from a newly independent Finland, the Åland Islands which she had ceded to Russia along with Finland in 1809.[4] But Sweden was in a different position from Norway, an Atlantic Power, and Denmark, who had a front on two seas: Sweden alone was a wholly Baltic Power, and faced wholly east; they had only a German problem, she had a Russian problem too. Thus her disappointment over the Åland Islands was far outweighed by the advantage of having the sister state of Finland interposed between herself and her hereditary enemy, and the Baltic no longer dominated by any Great Power, but ringed by the small and peaceful succession states of the Russian Empire.[5]

The Netherlands and the Scandinavian countries, except Iceland, became original members of the League of Nations, and were the most earnest supporters of the twin policies of collective security and disarmament.[6] In Denmark, alone of all the states in the world, a principal issue of domestic politics in the 1920s was the reduction of her exiguous armed

guaranteed the integrity of Sweden and Norway; and in 1907 Britain, Germany, France, and Russia had guaranteed the integrity of the newly independent Norway (Gooch & Temperley, vol. viii, chapter lxiii). These guarantees, however, had not imposed neutrality, and Norway had in 1922 denounced the treaty of 1907 (*Survey* for 1920–3, pp. 231–2).

[1] Only one of them had been involved in any kind of European war since 1815: Denmark, in the war of 1864 against Prussia and Austria resulting in the loss of Schleswig-Holstein. The Netherlands, however, like Britain during the nineteenth century, had compensated for her abstention from European adventures by a number of colonial wars of which the most important was the conquest of northern Sumatra in the protracted Achinese War of 1873 to 1904.

[2] The settlement of the Spitsbergen question was not dealt with in the *History of the Peace Conference*. For the statement of the Norwegian case to the Peace Conference, see David Hunter Miller: *My Diary at the Conference of Paris* (privately printed, 1924–6), xvii. 479–83; cf. James T. Shotwell: *At the Paris Peace Conference* (New York, Macmillan, 1937), p. 181, note. The recognition of Norwegian sovereignty was effected by a treaty of 1920 (see *Survey* for 1920–3, p. 230; *Survey* for 1924, pp. 258, 462; *Survey* for 1925, ii. 226). The Soviet Union recognized Norwegian sovereignty over Spitsbergen in 1924, and voluntarily adhered to the treaty of 1920 in 1935. See *The Norseman*, March–April 1947, pp. 83–90.

[3] See *H.P.C.*, vol. ii, chapter iv, part i.   [4] See *Survey* for 1920–3, pp. 234–8.

[5] Ibid. pp. 229–30. Finland entered the Scandinavian group diplomatically in 1924 (*Survey* for 1924, p. 461). See further below, p. 246.

[6] See Toynbee: *World after the Peace Conference*, p. 37; *Survey* for 1920–3, p. 231; *Survey* for 1935, ii. 79–81.

forces into a police force;[1] while Iceland, alone of all the states in the world, had neither army, navy, nor fortifications. In their habit of mutual discussion and co-operation the Scandinavian countries came to resemble the British Commonwealth of Nations; and there was a certain parallel between the Ottawa Conference of the British empire in 1932 and the Oslo Conference of the Scandinavian Powers in 1930, to which Holland, Belgium, and Luxembourg also were parties. By the Oslo Convention these six states agreed not to increase their mutual tariffs without prior consultation.[2] But the convention had little economic importance, since the mutual trade of the group was only one-fifth of the aggregate of their foreign trade; and as the international tension increased after the Nazi Revolution in Germany, the existence of 'the Oslo Powers' reflected no more than a consciousness of the desirability of co-operation between them in the face of common dangers which, in fact, made effective co-operation impossible.[3]

When the League of Nations collapsed, the Netherlands and the Scandinavian countries had no traditional guaranteed neutrality to try to return to. They adopted a common policy concerning the raising of sanctions against Italy, reluctant to abandon the hope of collective security until the last;[4] they endeavoured to renovate the Oslo Convention;[5] but apart from that they had no alternative to the *sauve-qui-peut* of rearmament.[6] Holland, however, redefined her obligations under the Covenant, announcing in 1937 that she would not allow the passage of troops across her territory under Article 16 of the Covenant, since this would inevitably involve her in hostilities,[7] and hoping thus to approximate to the position which Switzerland had enjoyed, with the consent of the League, since 1920. She also took the lead in persuading the Oslo Powers to recognize the Italian conquest of Ethiopia.[8] When Hitler offered in 1937 to guarantee the integrity and neutrality of Holland as well as Belgium, the Dutch replied that the inviolability of their territory was an axiom which could not be made the subject of international agreement.[9] Against the Swiss and Belgian policy of neutrality with guarantees, they asserted the alternative policy of neutrality without guarantees.

Dutch policy sought neutrality more positively than did Scandinavian policy, because if a new conflict between Germany and the Western Powers had now to be taken for granted, the Netherlands and the Scandinavian countries varied in the degree of their vulnerability. The Nether-

---

[1] See *Survey* for 1924, pp. 73–77; *Survey* for 1929, p. 32, note.
[2] See *Survey* for 1931, p. 154, note 2; *Survey* for 1932, p. 38. Finland joined them in 1932.
[3] See *Survey* for 1937, i. 99.   [4] See *Survey* for 1935, ii. 472–4.
[5] See *Survey* for 1937, i. 96–99.
[6] See *Survey* for 1936, p. 121, with further references there given.
[7] See *Survey* for 1937, i. 349, note.   [8] See *Survey* for 1938, i. 145–6.
[9] See *Survey* for 1937, i. 353.

lands was the most immediately exposed, and there was every reason to expect that in another general war she would resume her role of 1572 and 1672 and 1793 rather than that of 1914. In the First World War, German strategy had required the invasion of Belgium in order to turn the French left wing, and it had been difficult to distinguish between Belgium and the Low Countries as a whole because of the 'Maastricht appendix', a promontory of Dutch territory which ran south almost to Liége, halving the distance along which Belgium and Germany might otherwise have had a common frontier. Dutch neutrality had rested throughout, not on the strength of the Dutch army, but on the German calculation that it was better to keep Holland as 'the last air-hole through which we can breathe'.[1] In 1939, however, the strategic importance of the Low Countries had changed. Since 1919 Belgium had greatly strengthened the defences along her eastern or German frontier, which formed a continuation of the Maginot Line along the Franco-German frontier. As in 1914, therefore, Germany had been compelled to invade Belgium in order to turn the French left, so in a new conflict with France it might be expected that she would be compelled to invade the Netherlands in order to turn the Belgian left. But there was another possibility which the Netherlands had to consider. If it were German policy to wage a war of conquest only in the east, accompanied by a containing war against the Western Powers, the position of 1914 might be reversed, and German strategy might leave Belgium inviolate, but attack and occupy Holland, in order to establish air and naval bases against England along the Dutch coast. In fact, however, German war plans did not distinguish between the two countries, and assumed that they would jointly become a theatre of war. The Blomberg directive of 24 June 1937 used the assumption that their neutrality would be violated by France and Britain.[2] By August 1938 the Luftwaffe was urging that the Low Countries 'would, *in German hands*, represent an extraordinary advantage in the prosecution of the air war against Great Britain as well as against France'.[3] At the military conference of 23 May 1939 Hitler declared that the Dutch and Belgian air bases must be occupied by force: 'declarations of neutrality must be ignored'.[4]

[1] The words are Moltke's, in a memorandum of December 1912; see C. R. M. F. Cruttwell: *A History of the Great War, 1914–1918* (Oxford, Clarendon Press, 1934), p. 8.

[2] See *I.M.T. Nuremberg*, xxxiv. 744 (175–C); trans. in *Documents* (R.I.I.A.) for 1939–46, i. 13; cf. *N.C.A.* vi. 1011; cf. the Luftwaffe plan study of 2 June 1938 (*I.M.T. Nuremberg*, xxxviii. 415 (150–R); *N.C.A.* viii. 270).

[3] Report on 'extended Operation Green' by Intelligence Division of Luftwaffe General Staff, 25 August 1938 (*I.M.T. Nuremberg*, xxv. 391 (375–PS); *N.C.A.* iii. 287–8).

[4] Minutes of conference of 23 May 1939 (*I.M.T. Nuremberg*, xxxvii. 550 (079–L); trans. in *Documents* (R.I.I.A.) for 1939–46, i. 274; cf. *N.C.A.* vii. 850. Hitler implicitly contradicted this for tactical purposes in his conference with Ciano of 12 August 1939 (*I.M.T. Nuremberg*, xxix. 41–42 (1871–PS); trans. in *Documents* (R.I.I.A.) for 1939–46, i. 172–3; cf. *N.C.A.* iv. 508–9; and Peter de Mendelssohn: *The Nuremberg Documents* (London, Allen & Unwin, 1946), p. 115).

Denmark had been one of the first countries to be threatened by German revisionism after 1933, with regard to Northern Slesvig,[1] and her interests were affected by the German denunciation of the Versailles régime for the Kiel Canal.[2] In the Netherlands, Mussert's National Socialist movement had gained slight parliamentary successes between 1935 and 1937;[3] and the Norwegian eponym of all the quislings, who never obtained a single seat in the Storthing for his party, entered into close relationships with Rosenberg in 1939.[4] Denmark and Norway were scarcely less exposed than the Netherlands as a strategic position between the Great Powers. Together they flanked the North Sea over against Britain, resuming their historic political association with one another on the plane of modern naval and air strategy; Norway, moreover, from the viewpoint of an encircled continental Germany, was a coastline running northwards far beyond the Shetlands straits, and offering in Trondhjem and Narvik accessible and ice-free harbours on the open Atlantic.[5] Although it seems that German policy up to the outbreak of the Second World War preferred to plan for Scandinavian neutrality, it was clear that, once war began, the occupation of the desirable Danish and Norwegian bases might present itself either to Germany or Britain as a surer method than assuming their neutrality or denying them to the enemy.[6] Sweden, by contrast, had some hope of profiting from the geographical exposure of her neighbours; for if war between Germany and France were to be waged across the Low Countries, and if war between Germany and Britain were to be waged along the coasts of the North Sea, over the bodies of Denmark and Norway, then war between Germany and Russia might also follow its historic path along the southern shores of the Baltic, over the bodies of Poland and the three continental Baltic states, and

[1] See *Survey* for 1933, pp. 171–3; *Survey* for 1936, p. 43 and note.

[2] See *Survey* for 1937, i. 376.

[3] See Bartholomew Landheer, ed.: *The Netherlands* (Berkeley, University of California Press, 1943), pp. 129–30. Mussert's movement, like Degrelle's, attained the zenith of its influence in 1936.

[4] See Rosenberg's report on the political preparation of the Norway action, 15 June 1940 (*I.M.T. Nuremberg*, xxv. 26–27 (004–PS); *N.C.A.* iii. 20).

[5] See memorandum by Doenitz on base in Norway, 9 October 1939 (*I.M.T. Nuremberg*, xxxiv. 159–61 (005–C); *N.C.A.* vi. 815–16) and lecture by Jodl at Munich, 7 November 1943 (*I.M.T. Nuremberg*, xxxvii. 636 (172–L); *N.C.A.* vii. 924–5). Hitler's occupation of Denmark and Norway in 1940 has a resemblance to Napoleon's forcing the Danish-Norwegian Kingdom to join the Continental System by the Treaty of Fontainebleau in 1807; but Napoleon's prime motive was economic, Hitler's was strategic.

[6] See minutes of conference between Hitler and Ciano, 12 August 1939 (*I.M.T. Nuremberg*, xxix. 42 (1871–PS); trans. in *Documents* (R.I.I.A.) for 1936–46, i. 173; cf. *N.C.A.* iv. 509) and Rosenberg's report on the political preparation of the Norway action, 15 June 1940 (*I.M.T. Nuremberg*, xxv. 28–29 (004–PS); *N.C.A.* iii. 22. Hitler told Quisling on 16 and 18 December 1939 that he preferred Scandinavian neutrality). Cf. extract from Naval War Diary, questionnaire on Norway bases, 3 October 1939 (*I.M.T. Nuremberg*, xxxiv. 422–5 (122–C); *N.C.A.* vi. 928) and sources given in preceding footnote.

Sweden might become an immobilized buffer state, the still centre of the spinning northern world.[1] As for Iceland, since she became independent in 1918 she had been happy, above all nations, in having practically no international relations, and only the keenest insight could have foretold that in 1939 she was on the verge of a strategic revolution that would make nonsense of her neutrality and place her in the most exposed position of all the Scandinavian countries, a pawn between continents, the prize not only of the giants of the past, Britain and Germany, but also of the giants of the future, the Soviet Union and the United States of America.[2]

(c) THE OVERSEAS EMPIRES

The dependence of these small countries on the Western society of which they were part was equally apparent in the vulnerability of their colonial possessions. Those of them which possessed oceanic sea-boards, Denmark, Norway, Sweden, Holland, and Belgium, had all taken part in that general expansion of Western Civilization which Ranke likened to the respiration of a single body.[3] Iceland as a political unit was itself the product of Scandinavian expansion in the Dark Ages before Western Civilization had become a coherent entity.[4] Switzerland and Luxembourg alone, because they were land-locked, had been precluded from sharing in this movement. By 1939 Sweden had abandoned her overseas possessions.[5] But Denmark still retained sovereignty over the vast North American island of Greenland.[6] The Netherlands still possessed a

[1] See *Survey* for 1936, p. 533. The importance of Sweden to Germany was not as a strategic position but as a source of iron and nickel ore, and the safeguarding of this was to be one of the reasons for the occupation of Denmark and Norway; see directive for 'Fall Weserübung', 1 March 1940 (*I.M.T. Nuremberg*, xxxiv. 729–32 (174–C); *N.C.A.* vi. 1003–5) and lecture by Jodl at Munich, 7 November 1943 (*I.M.T. Nuremberg*, xxxvii. 366 (172–L); *N.C.A.* vii. 924.

[2] For this revolution in Iceland's position see two articles in *Bulletin for International News* (Royal Institute of International Affairs): 'American Troops in Iceland', 26 July 1941, xvii. 948–51, and 'Iceland: a Political & Geographical Note', 22 August 1942, xix. 742–6. Cf. the hypothetical position of Iceland if Western Civilization's place in history had been taken by a Scandinavian civilization, as 'the inevitable stepping-stone, in mid-ocean, between the European and American half' (Toynbee: *Study*, ii. 441).

[3] Leopold von Ranke: *History of the Latin and Teutonic Nations, 1494–1514*, revised translation by G. R. Dennis (London, Bell, 1909), p. 19.

[4] See Toynbee: *Study*, ii. 291–2, 354–60.

[5] In the seventeenth century Sweden took part in the Western colonization of North America: New Sweden flourished on the banks of the Delaware River from 1638 to 1655, when it was conquered by New Netherlands. In the eighteenth century Sweden had trading stations on the West Coast of Africa. In 1939 the most recent non-European possession of Sweden had been the West Indian island of St. Bartholomew, which was ceded to Sweden by France in 1784, and remained in Swedish hands until it was repurchased by France in 1877.

[6] In 1939 the Danish overseas possessions consisted of the *Faroes*, which were constitutionally an integral part of the kingdom with representation in the Rigsdag, and *Greenland*, a colonial possession. The Scandinavian colonists of Greenland formed a republic until 1261, when they swore allegiance to the King of Norway; at the dissolution of the Danish-Norwegian union in 1814 Greenland, like Iceland and the Faroes, was not mentioned and was consequently retained

world empire stretching from Curaçao in the west to New Guinea in the east, which she had won from the Portuguese in the seventeenth century, which had not been cripplingly diminished by British depredations in the eighteenth and nineteenth centuries, and which in the two generations before the First World War she had extended and consolidated.[1] Belgium possessed a great African empire as a result of her share in the partition of Africa in the late nineteenth century.[2] And Norway, the youngest of them as an independent state, had immediately shown the same Western tendency towards expansion by acquiring various unappropriated islands in the Arctic and Antarctic, and only a few weeks before Hitler's entry into Prague and the ensuing transformation of Bohemia and Moravia into a German protectorate, had annexed a vast sector of the Antarctic Continent many times larger than the Greater Reich itself.[3]

The Western Small Powers and the Western Great Powers were even more closely interdependent in the political geography of their overseas possessions than in that of their metropolitan territories on the continent of Europe.[4] The colonial empires of the Small Powers were uniformly indefensible by their mother countries. The Dutch possessions in the East Indies, like those of Portugal,[5] were impossible to protect against Britain, and Dutch policy was based on that premiss. The Belgian Congo was encircled on three sides by British and French territories and took for

by Denmark (for the Norwegian claims arising out of this see *Survey* for 1920–3, p. 232, and *Survey* for 1924, pp. 461–2). Apart from Greenland the most recent extra-European possessions of Denmark had been the three West Indian islands of St. Croix, St. Thomas, and St. John, which had been purchased by the United States in 1917. The Danish colonial possessions ranked in 1939 ninth in area but tenth in population among the colonial empires of the world (see Royal Institute of International Affairs: *The Colonial Problem*, p. 9, table i).

[1] In 1939 the Netherlands Empire consisted of (1) *Netherlands India*, comprising the islands of Java, Sumatra, Celebes, the Moluccas, the great part of Borneo, half New Guinea, the Timor archipelago, and a number of smaller islands; (2) *Netherlands West Indies*, comprising Surinam or Netherlands Guiana on the South American mainland, and the island of Curaçao with its dependent islands. The Netherlands Empire ranked in 1939 sixth in area but second in population among the colonial empires of the world (see *The Colonial Problem*, loc. cit.).

[2] In 1939 the Belgian Empire consisted of (1) the *Belgian Congo*, which had been annexed by Belgium from the King of the Belgians in 1908; (2) *Ruanda-Urundi*, formerly part of German East Africa, but acquired by Belgium as a mandated territory in 1920 and administratively united with the Congo. The Belgian Empire ranked in 1939 third in area but sixth in population among the colonial empires of the world (see *The Colonial Problem*, loc. cit.).

[3] In 1939 the Norwegian overseas possessions consisted of: (1) in the Arctic: (a) *Svalbard*, the archipelago comprising Spitsbergen, Bear Island, and adjacent islands, acquired by Norway in 1920 (see above, p. 158), (b) *Jan Mayen Island*, annexed in 1929; (2) in the Antarctic: (a) *Bouvet Island*, occupied in 1928 and annexed in 1930 after a diplomatic dispute with Britain, (b) *Peter I Island*, annexed in 1931, (c) the sector of the Antarctic Continent lying between 20° W. and 45° E., known as *Queen Maud Land*, which was annexed on 14 January 1939 (see 'Norwegian Claims in the Antarctic', *The Norseman*, January–February 1947, pp. 1–4). The Norwegian overseas possessions (with the exception of Queen Maud Land) ranked in 1939 lowest among the colonial empires of the world, being eleventh both in area and in population (see *The Colonial Problem*, loc. cit.).   [4] See above, pp. 24–25.   [5] See above, pp. 148, 149 and note 1.

granted good relations with them.[1] Norwegian claims in the Antarctic had been developed in agreement with Britain. And the Netherlands West Indies, like Danish Greenland, were held at the good pleasure of the United States.

These empires were not only as vulnerable as their mother countries; they were in several cases more valuable. The importance to a conqueror of the mother countries lay in their strategic position rather than in their wealth or industry, but the Netherlands Indies and the Belgian Congo, standing high among the world's producers of strategic raw materials and foodstuffs, were worthy objects of cupidity in themselves. The small colonial Powers were inevitably in a more difficult and dangerous position than the great ones. The disproportion between their weight in the world and their possessions marked them down for attack.[2] On 15 March 1939 Germany was still occupied with the destruction of the Versailles Settlement in Europe, but her colonial claims had been a discreet accompaniment to her European policy,[3] and just as in Europe her aim was nothing so conservative as the recovery of the frontiers of 1914,[4] so it was clear that when the moment came to look overseas she would not be satisfied with a simple recovery of her former colonies. Italian ambitions outside Europe had been temporarily satisfied by the conquest of Ethiopia, and Japan was temporarily absorbed in the conquest of China, but these were steps that took the conquerors nearer to the defenceless European empires in Africa and East Asia. The Small Powers knew that their empires were held on sufferance from the Western Great Powers; and remembering the Anglo-German agreements about the Portuguese Empire before the First World War,[5] they might well wonder whether the policy that had abandoned Manchuria to Japan, Ethiopia to Italy, and Austria and Czechoslovakia to Germany, might not possibly lead towards the attempt to satisfy German colonial claims at the expense of the smaller colonial empires.

It was rumoured that an Anglo-German colonial settlement involving the Small Powers had been discussed when Halifax visited Hitler in November 1937, and Spaak then declared that Belgium would defend the Belgian Congo by all the means at her disposal.[6] The rumour was not

---

[1] Unlike the Belgian Congo, the two great Portuguese colonies in Africa had extensive ocean frontiers. Angola was contiguous along half its continental frontiers with South African and British territory; along the other half it marched with the Belgian Congo itself. Mozambique was wholly bounded on its landward side by South African and British territory.

[2] Cf. Adolf Hitler: *Mein Kampf*, 2 vols. in 1, 305th–306th edition (Munich, NSDAP, 1938), pp. 152–3; *Mein Kampf* (trans. James Murphy), 2 vols. in 1 (London, Hurst & Blackett, 1939), p. 127. (Hereafter the original and translation will be referred to as *Mein Kampf* and 'tr. Murphy'.)

[3] Cf. *Survey* for 1937, i. 33, 326, 340.

[4] 'Die Grenzen des Jahres 1914 bedeuten für die Zukunft der deutschen Nation gar nichts' (*Mein Kampf*, p. 738; tr. Murphy, p. 530; cf. pp. 736 and 529 respectively). See below, p. 335.

[5] See above, pp. 149–50.

[6] *Survey* for 1937, i. 368, note 1. Cf. Erich Kordt: *Wahn und Wirklichkeit*, 2nd edition (Stuttgart,

without foundation. Although Halifax talked of the colonial issue on that occasion only in general terms,[1] three months later Henderson presented Hitler with a written suggestion about it from the British Government, which was to be kept secret from Britain's allies the French and still more from the Belgians, the Portuguese, and the Italians.[2] The suggestion was for a new colonial régime in an area of Africa roughly corresponding to the conventional zone of the Congo Basin Treaties. Each Power would remain solely concerned for the administration of its own territories there, though subscribing to certain principles for the promotion of civilization; but there would at the same time be a redistribution of colonies, and Germany would once more have African territory under her sovereignty.[3] It was not clear whether the British Government had in mind simply the return to Germany of Tanganyika, under mandatory forms, or whether the territorial interests of other Powers would be affected. Hitler's reply was that he wanted the restoration of Germany's former colonies, not a complicated international system; he did not want to involve other countries, and anyway would Belgium and Portugal agree? 'Sir Nevile Henderson declared that he believed that Portugal and Belgium, and presumably France and Italy too, would in the end co-operate in the settlement.'[4] The British proposal does not seem to have been pursued after the German conquest of Austria, which occurred a week later. The Western neutrals had to trust that Britain, being traditionally more sensitive to disturbances of the balance of power in Africa and the Indian Ocean than in Central Europe, would thenceforward recognize in her policy that the great empires overseas were reciprocally dependent upon the security of the smaller.[5]

Union Deutsche, 1948), pp. 90–91, who places Henderson's proposals on the colonial question in the autumn of 1937.

[1] *D.Ger.F.P.*, series D, i. 55 seqq.

[2] Ibid. pp. 240–9; Ministry of Foreign Affairs of the U.S.S.R.: *Documents and Materials relating to the Eve of the Second World War from the Archives of the German Ministry of Foreign Affairs* (Moscow, Foreign Languages Publishing House, 1948), vol. i, no. 3. (This collection will hereafter be referred to as *Documents . . . from the Archives of the German Ministry of Foreign Affairs*, publ. by the U.S.S.R.)

[3] *D.Ger.F.P.*, series D, i. 242–3, 246. The conventional basin of the Congo, an enlargement upon the geographical basin, was defined by the Berlin General Act of 26 February 1885, article 1 (2) and (3), as extending on the Atlantic side between 2° 30′ South Latitude and the mouth of the river Logé in Angola, and on the Indian Ocean side between 5° North Latitude and the mouth of the Zambesi (*British and Foreign State Papers* (London, H.M.S.O.), lxxvi. 9; cf. S. E. Crowe: *The Berlin West African Conference, 1884–1885* (London, Longmans, Green, 1942), pp. 108 seqq.). Henderson mentioned the latter boundaries specifically in his talk with Hitler. The conventional basin of the Congo covered the Belgian Congo, the British territories of Uganda, Kenya, Nyasaland, and Northern Rhodesia, the British mandated territory (formerly German) of Tanganyika, half Indian Somaliland, and half the Portuguese colony of Mozambique, as well as fringes of French Equatorial Africa, Ethiopia, and Portuguese Angola.

[4] *D.Ger.F.P.*, series D, i. 247.

[5] Cf. A. J. Toynbee: 'The Issues in British Foreign Policy', *International Affairs*, May–June 1938, xvii. 321–2.

(iv) France
By D. R. Gillie

(a) LOSSES AND DESTRUCTION IN THE FIRST WORLD WAR

The outlook of the French people in March 1939 was more influenced than that of any other in Europe by the losses and destruction of the First World War.[1] The number of births had started falling at an earlier date in France than in any other European country—that is to say, from 1880—and although the fall was much more gradual than was later to be the case with other nations, this meant that the French soldiers who fought between 1914 and 1918 were drawn from smaller families than in Britain or Germany. Thus the proportion of the French people between the ages of fifteen and thirty-five in 1911, that is to say, the section of the nation which was to bear the heaviest losses on the battlefield, was 22·5 per cent., while that of the peoples of the United Kingdom was 25·3 per cent. and that of Germany 26·6 per cent. It has been calculated that 1,325,000 French lives were lost in the First World War and that this represented 18·2 per cent. of Frenchmen of military age, while the German loss of 1,855,000 represented 15·5 per cent. and the United Kingdom's loss of 744,000, 8·8 per cent.[2]

The effect of the war on French population was, however, even greater than these figures suggest, for, owing to the catastrophic decline of the birth-rate during the four years of the war in which civilian life was disrupted to a much greater extent than was the case in the territories of France's neighbours, the excess of deaths, civil as well as military, over births in the decade 1911 to 1921 was 2,582,000. This fall of the birth-rate in the years 1915–19 was reflected twenty years later in a scarcity of young mothers, so that while the decade 1921–30 (during part of which the French birth-rate was higher than that of the United Kingdom) provided a surplus of 714,000 births over deaths, the decade 1931–40 gave a surplus of 125,000 deaths over births. During the very years when France was required by the aggressiveness of Nazi Germany to adopt a bold policy, with its concomitant risk of heavy loss of life in battle, the number of French births was sinking from 722,000 in 1932 to 612,000 in 1938, to be followed by a slight rise (613,000) in 1939, as a result of first timid legisla-

---

[1] For population statistics the following works have been used: Michel Huber and others: *La population de la France* (Paris, Hachette, 1937); Charles Rist and Gaëtan Pirou: *De la France d'avant guerre à la France d'aujourd'hui* (Paris, Librairie du Recueil Sirey, 1939); Alfred Sauvy: *Richesse et population* (Paris, Payot, 1943) and *Bein-être et population* (Paris, Éditions Sociales Françaises, 1945); Robert Debré and Alfred Sauvy: *Des Français pour la France* (Paris, Gallimard, 1946)

[2] Quoted from W. Winkler by Arthur L. Bowley in *Some Economic Consequences of the Great War* (London, Thornton Butterworth, 1930), p. 41. A slightly higher figure for French casualties during the First World War was given in the official records of the United States War Department: see below, p. 404, note 4.

tive steps to encourage parenthood and put down abortion. During the
years 1936–40 the intake of young men into the armed forces in each
yearly contingent (the intake, that is to say, of men born during the First
World War) sank from an average of 240,000 to a paltry 120,000, so that
in 1935 the term of military service had to be raised from one year to two,
not in order to strengthen the French army but in order to maintain its
effectives.[1]

Just as the impression created by the human losses of the First World
War was to be intensified on the eve of the Second, so was that of the
material losses, though in a less striking degree. For years the spectacle of
reconstruction was encouraging rather than the reverse. But when the
completion of the restoration of Rheims Cathedral[2] was solemnly celebrated in 1938, between the Anschluss and the Munich crisis, the occasion
could not but make men ask themselves whether the work of reconstruction
would not prove to have been carried out in vain.

(b) The French Attitude to the Population Problem

One of the most important effects of the destruction of French lives
during the First World War was the heavy loss of precisely those young
men who distinguished themselves by character and initiative, and who
were therefore in the van of battle. Certainly the history of the 1930s
suggests that in political life the younger generation was not replacing the
older with a sufficient number of men of equal calibre. Had the moral
climate of France been one favourable to the development of bold political
and economic leadership, this might well have been less noticeable.
Leaders are made as well as born. But it was precisely the moral climate
that was affected, partly by a reaction against the immense effort of four
and a half years and partly by the shifting of the balance in the population
structure in favour of the elderly. Before 1914, generation had been succeeding generation in France with only the slightest numerical advantage
to the young; this advantage disappeared in the years following the First
World War.

This phenomenon did not prevent a brilliant display in literature and
the arts, but it did prevent the germination of new political and economic
ideas;[3] it undermined self-reliance in a changing world, and predisposed
against the acceptance of those risks which were implied in the very
policy by which France hoped to guarantee her security, namely, by
alliance with the weaker states to the east and south-east of Germany.

[1] See *Survey* for 1935, i. 135–9.
[2] In the very heart of the city there were blocks still not rebuilt, while only the nave of the
second church of Rheims, St. Rémy, had been reroofed.
[3] Only in the 1930s did social and political problems begin to replace aesthetics and problems
of individual morality in the work of young writers.

The attitude of the French to their own population problem was an instance of this static state of mind. The sense that young Frenchmen were becoming additionally precious because rare, that the body of the French nation no longer filled the same space in the world as before, that national victory had been bought at too high a price (and therefore that France's allies were her debtors), that another victory bought at the same price would be an irremediable disaster, underlay both the thoughts and the instinctive reactions of Frenchmen throughout the twenty years between the two wars. Yet it was most rarely that the problem was faced, or that campaigns in favour of an intelligent population policy were treated, except on the eve of the Second World War, as anything but a comic fad.

The one way of stating the population problem which had some measure of popular appeal was that of General Mangin, who declared that France was a nation not of forty millions but of a hundred and that the North African and black troops that had fought so well in the war were the heralds of the greater France that was to be. Unfortunately, this argument created complacency and, as will be seen later, did not even lead to the development of French colonial policy which it implied.

Until 1939 there was no serious attempt at a policy for the encouragement of parenthood nor a sufficient attack on the problem of the high death-rate, not only of infants but of men in the prime of life.

Nor was there a coherent policy of immigration. That the population of France was in 1939 slightly in excess of that of France and Alsace-Lorraine in 1911 was due to massive immigration. The decade 1921–30 alone saw 1,811,000 foreigners settle in France and the number of foreigners recorded in the census of 1931 was 2,715,000 as compared with 1,160,000 in 1911. Largely owing to naturalization, the figure had fallen to 2,198,000 in 1936. This big influx, it will be noted, did little more than replace the losses of the years 1914–18.

While in boom periods immigration was encouraged, the attitude prevailed that immigration was the privilege of the immigrant. During the slump in 1934 efforts were actually made, in the supposed interest of fuller employment for Frenchmen, to send back to their countries of origin miners who had been established for many years in France and who had already founded families there. The protests then raised, largely in the first instance on grounds of humanity, began at last to awaken public opinion to the problem. On the other hand, the lack of any policy aiming at the assimilation of the immigrants or at preventing them from forming compact masses—in the case of the Italians near their own frontiers—provoked xenophobia. This contained a justifiable element, for, so long as no French policy counteracted the tendency, there was a real danger of large areas of Southern France being colonized by her neighbour. Italian consuls exercised control comparable to that of French authorities over

Italian immigrants; Italian-born women were induced to return to their country of origin for the birth of their children so that France should have no claim over those whose schooling was to be paid for out of French taxes. The reflection that, when the French farmer was called up to go to the front, the Italian or the Spanish labourer would remain on the farm provided an additional motive for French pacifism.

(c) THE ECONOMIC POSITION

Since there was a failure to appreciate France's need of her immigrants, there was necessarily also a failure to perceive the possibilities that they opened up to her. France and her territories overseas provided scope for economic expansion, with the help of immigrant labour, on a much greater scale than was achieved between the two wars.

France, having taken the place of the United States as the recipient of the unemployed energies of the rest of Europe, might have been expected to follow the American example of expansion had it not been for the lack of enthusiasm due to her age structure.

It is true that considerable changes took place in France's economic structure. Although agricultural production did not decline, about 1,300,000 agricultural workers (both farmers and labourers) went into other professions, and for the first time in her history the population classified by French statisticians as urban (communes of more than 2,000 inhabitants) exceeded that classified as rural (not necessarily agricultural). In 1936 the proportion was 52·4 per cent. to 47·6 per cent. But manufacturing industry was far from being the principal beneficiary. Commerce and transport, the liberal professions, and public services expanded to a greater extent than industry. It is, however, true that, in industry, metallurgy and mechanical construction expanded at the expense of textiles and the clothing industry. The production of steel doubled, from 4,870,000 to 9,700,000 tons between 1913 and 1929, the high peak of the boom. At the same time France's trade with her overseas territories increased from 10·16 per cent. of her total imports in the years 1911–13 to 26·6 per cent. in the years 1934–6, and from 13 per cent. of exports to 31·9 per cent.

But here again the stability of the country, the much prized balance between town and country, set a brake on the development of new power. Except in Indochina[1] there was no development of industry in the colonies. In Metropolitan France the lack of an expanding market constantly produced objections to the development of her overseas territories, which should have been the greatest subject of pride and satisfaction. Even the success of French West African banana groves aroused fears for the

[1] See above, pp. 82–83.

marketing of home-grown fruit. Obstacles were set in years of big production to the importation of the wine and corn of Algeria, which was
theoretically part of France. Few colonial products escaped duty. Even
the industry of Indochina aroused disquiet. Effective obstacles were put
in the way of developing industry in North Africa, with catastrophic
results during the Second World War. When the decision had to be taken
whether or not to transfer the Government and as much as possible of the
army to North Africa in 1940 the argument weighed heavily that not only
would it be impossible to replace a rifle, a machine gun, a bullet, or a shell
in the Maghrib: there was not even an industry that could provide shirts,
boots, or buttons.

A France with a growing population would have been faced with none
of these difficulties. An expanding economy would have found ever more
reasons for expanding the economy of her overseas territories. As it was,
the much vaunted balance of her population at home prevented not only
the generation of, but the appetite for, power. An eighteenth-century
douceur de vivre, the more warmly appreciated because of the incomparable
effort and terrible sufferings in the common cause of the years 1914–18,
had its logical sequence in an eighteenth-century mercantilism which
thwarted the finest energies of France's colonizers. Mercantilism is a form
of planning, and planning was not even provided with the necessary eyes
in France, for of all civilized countries she had the most inadequate
statistics—a fact of the greatest political as well as economic moment.[1]

France herself remained predominantly a country of small towns from
which the energy was ebbing, while the power of the vote remained. The
small shop and the artisan received artificial protection from the state,
while the great provincial banks which had supported local energy and
initiative were swallowed up by the banks of Paris in the early stages of the
financial and economic crisis which began to be felt in 1930. Marc
Bloch, reviewing the causes of defeat in the late summer of 1940, wrote:
'Let us admit that what has been conquered in us is the little town of which
we were so fond, its waste of time, its short-sighted political squabbles, its
preference for what it knows already, and its distrust of all surprises.'[2]

It was this section of the French people which prevented France in the
1930s from making use of her great financial strength to follow the
example of the United States and Belgium in voluntary devaluation, and
so almost painlessly ending her crisis and avoiding the bitter social con-

[1] In Charles Rist and Gaëtan Pirou's *De la France d'avant guerre à la France d'aujourd'hui* the
author of the chapter on industry, Marc Aucuy, complains that the detailed results of the census
of 1931 are not yet available. The figures given on p. 168 for the numbers of foreigners in France
are the most authoritative, but others exist with divergences of over half a million.

[2] Marc Bloch: *L'étrange défaite* (Paris, Éditions de Franc-Tireur, 1946), p. 167. This little
book on the French defeat and its causes by the great medieval historian who was shot by the
Germans on 26 June 1944 is the best introduction to the whole subject.

flicts which took place in 1936–7 at the very moment when she needed to gather her strength for the coming conflict. Paul Reynaud, not absurdly, called the 1936 elections the result of the franc at 65½ milligrammes of gold. Pierre-Étienne Flandin, who referred on one occasion to the 'sordid materialism' of Marxist doctrine and at the same time could speak as if he identified the gold-parity of the franc with the moral integrity of every young Frenchman, could write as late as 1944 and publish in 1947 the following sentence:

The remedy (devaluation) which was probably best for a country like the United Kingdom, whose prosperity was largely based on exchange and its accessory profits (financing, insurance, shipping), became poison for a country like France which is naturally autarkic, and in which the stability of the consumers' revenue was the guarantee of the normal remuneration of producers.[1]

(d) Right and Left in Politics

This clinging to stability in an unstable world was the counterpart in economic policy of the monotonous insistence on security in foreign policy and was to prove as self-defeating. It had a most serious effect on the moral temper of the conservative classes in France on the eve of the Second World War. The conservatives in France had their full share of government in the 1920s and 1930s: first in the form of the Bloc National from 1920 to 1924; second from 1926 to 1932, after the forces of the Left had been divided in the financial crisis of 1925–6, and again, after similar divisions of the Left, from 1934 to 1936 and from 1938 to 1940. The only period which corresponded to the Baldwinian years of complacent, but at least contented and socially peaceful, prosperity over large areas of Britain was that from 1926 to 1929. The subsequent years were marked by the failure of the conservative forces of France to find solutions for her economic and financial problems, and this failure necessarily generated social discontent and social conflict. The fruit of this failure only became fully apparent with the successive and unsuccessful devaluations under the governments of the Front Populaire, whose own errors to some extent masked those of their predecessors. Balm for the shattered hopes of 1929 and for the undermined self-confidence of the middle-class conservatives was found by putting all the blame on the bourgeois intellectual who led the Socialists, Léon Blum, against whom the hatred of many Frenchmen reached an extraordinary degree of venom. This, however, could not restore the lost self-confidence while it did add greatly to the difficulty of forming a united national front.

The economic and financial restoration under a brilliant leader drawn

---

[1] Pierre-Étienne Flandin: *Politique française 1919–1940* (Paris, Les Éditions Nouvelles, 1947), footnote on pp. 61–62.

from the French middle classes, Paul Reynaud, who was at the Ministry of Finance from November 1938 till March 1940, could not undo the moral mischief that had been done. Reynaud had been for many years the Cassandra of French politics, perpetually pointing out the errors of his colleagues in financial, economic, military, and foreign policy. He had barely escaped defeat in the elections of 1936, and his obvious satisfaction in rubbing in the mistakes of others did not make him loved. Intellectually his position as a voice in the wilderness was similar to that of Winston Churchill, except that his interests were even wider, but he had not the long ministerial past of the Englishman, the same qualifications as a leader, or the same experience in action. He had not the gift of winning forgiveness from those whom he had proved wrong. His triumph, therefore, did nothing to restore the morale or satisfy the bitterness of those whose interests he had served. Nor could an economic and financial recovery in the ever-darkening shadows of approaching war restore that sense of healthy national energy which had been recovered for a moment under Poincaré, but had been dissipated by nine years of difficulty during which four or five different but always abortive policies had been tried.

On the Left disillusion was also the dominant note in March 1939. Three times Radicals and Socialists had won victories together at the polls, on the third occasion with the Communists included in the alliance —in 1924, 1932, and 1936. Three times the alliance had broken down in the face of economic and financial problems—in 1926, 1934, and 1938. The alliances were based in every case on purely political and mainly negative objectives, so that the recurrent failures were not difficult to foresee. The divergences arose over problems which should have been the primary concern of both parties, but in the handling of which neither shone. They were hampered by a hardened doctrinal passion in the service of which there was real devotion. The disillusionment of 1938 was all the more bitter because the hopes of 1936 had been greater than those of the earlier years. The tandem bicycles ridden out of town on Friday evenings by young couples with their children in trailers had become the symbols of a new hope of a world of peace and of forty-hour weeks, a hope in complete disagreement with the implications of the loudest slogan of the same period—'Cannons for Spain'. By March 1939 the long week-ends had gone and there was no Republican Spain to which to send cannons. The Left had realized as few of its hopes in twenty years as the Right.

As a result of this double failure of Right and Left in French politics (which reached its bitter climax at a time when, in England, life had for years looked cheerful except in the areas of permanent unemployment) movements had arisen on the extreme wings which sought hope not only outside the nation's institutions, but also in the example of and in association with other nations.

On the extreme Right[1] the Action Française was drifting from Monarch-
ism into Fascism, from self-reliant nationalism into xenophobia under
foreign patronage. It was not a movement capable of very great development, because of its reliance on fading traditions. Its leader, Charles
Maurras, cultivated a violence of invective which did not stop short of
incitement to murder and in 1935 nearly cost Léon Blum his life.[2]

The Croix de Feu of Colonel de la Rocque secured a far bigger following
than the Action Française, partly because it provided the middle class with
a means of escaping from an individualism which had grown frightening
in twentieth-century conditions, through organizations some of which did
at least a certain amount of useful social service. If the Croix de Feu had
had leaders with political vision and competence it might have been a
grave danger to the Republic; but either from a structural defect, or from
the lack of comprehension of modern problems in the social groups from
which it was drawn, or through the chance mingling of respectable scruple
and incapacity amongst its leaders, it did not, as it turned out, threaten
anybody. The Croix de Feu was the instrument rather than the ring-
leader in the riots of 6 February 1934,[3] which were probably planned and
certainly prepared by the Action Française; its political idol turned out to
be President Doumergue.

But the Croix de Feu was none the less to have a great influence on
French history. Though de la Rocque's Fascism proved no more effective
than the grand old Duke of York's military tactics, his organization provided the bogy which brought together Socialists and Communists in
street demonstrations after the riots of 6 February 1934 and in a pact of
united action in August of that year, and in the following year it provided
the motive which induced the left wing of the Socialist Radicals, led by
Daladier, the Premier who fell as a result of the riots, to bring their whole
party into the Front Populaire. Ultimately, though many members of the
Croix de Feu were to prove themselves courageous patriots during the war,
the many hundreds of thousands who followed the lead of this essentially
anti-parliamentary though anodyne movement were to provide strong support for Marshal Pétain's anti-parliamentary government. The principal
effect of de la Rocque's efforts in the period under review was to prepare
the ground for a great Communist success in 1936.

The most resolute characters who had joined the Croix de Feu in the
hope of carrying out a *coup d'état* left it in the course of the years 1935 and
1936 to join the new French People's Party founded by the expelled Communist leader Jacques Doriot. Simultaneously the extreme elements of the
Action Française were being drawn into the small terroristic organization,

---

[1] On the political leagues belonging to the extreme Right, see *Survey* for 1935, ii. 36–38.
[2] Ibid. p. 37, note.
[3] See *Survey* for 1934, p. 387; *Survey* for 1935, ii. 36.

the Comité Secret d'Action Revolutionnaire (C.S.A.R.), known popularly as the Cagoulards, led by Deloncle and patronized by Marshal Franchet d'Espérey. Doriot's movement was a more frankly fascist and more popular rival to the Action Française. The C.S.A.R. was a purely conspiratorial organization that placed bombs where it was thought they would be attributed to Communists, and probably provided the murderers who killed the two Rosselli brothers in France in June 1937 at the behest of Rome.[1] That the inspiration behind these movements was not necessarily unpatriotic was shown by the fact that men drawn from their ranks were members of the Resistance movement after 1940. Franchet d'Espérey's attitude from the moment of military defeat in 1940 onwards was to be the exact opposite of that of the more republican Pétain. In an atmosphere of depression and discouragement these extremists at least reacted, but they were to prove schools principally for active collaboration. The Cagoulards had the infamous responsibility for bringing back into French politics not merely instigation to violence but carefully plotted crime.

On the extreme left the Communists had for almost twenty years been building up a movement more firmly knit, more doctrinally schooled, and with a broader basis than any movement on the extreme Right. It is true that for a time the Croix de Feu, reorganized as the Parti Social Français, had a larger membership than the Communists, but this was paid for by a total inability to act. The Communist Party had its moments of decline and defeat, but it never lost its power of recovery and renewal. It ejected its heretics without ever losing seriously in substance. It was to prove its capacity for survival under persecution and showed even before 1939 an astonishing power of manœuvre and of applying casuistry to mass tactics.

The French Communist Party had been launched on an international basis, the clamant heir of the most violent French anti-militarism and anti-colonialism, despising the Marseillaise, and employing such slogans as 'Poincaré-la-guerre'. It fought the 1936 elections, however, with posters reproducing the bas-relief of 'la Marseillaise' from the Arc de Triomphe, and calling for a 'free, strong and happy France' which to the masses certainly suggested a thoroughly national attitude. Once its interpretation of Marx became sufficiently supple to shed the foreign jargon and make possible its own style of hard-hitting French with Jacobin reminiscences, it found the national garb not difficult to wear, and it was in harmony with deep instincts in the French working class. The change was probably mainly the work of Maurice Thorez and Jacques Duclos, who in

[1] The responsibility for this murder had not been decided twelve years later. In 1944 Anfuso, then Italian Ambassador to Berlin, Colonel Emanuele, and Major Navale were tried for the crime. Anfuso was sentenced to death *in absentia*, the other two to life imprisonment. In a re-trial, held in Perugia in October 1949, Anfuso was found not guilty, and against Emanuele and Navale the verdict was 'charges not proven' (*Observer*, 16 October 1949).

a historic press conference in 1935 did their best to persuade the French
and foreign press that the Communist Party was neither in favour of unconstitutional action nor in any sense under non-French control.

That Communist Party leaders were as much devoted to the welfare of
France as any other Frenchmen is indeed a reasonable view, but it is at
least as certain that they identified the national cause with the success of
the Soviet Government's policy. Stalin, by consenting to the publication
of an official Russo-French statement in support of the Franco-Soviet
Pact of 2 May 1935[1] in which he specifically stated his approval of French
efforts for rearmament, had implicitly acknowledged (at the request of
a French Foreign Minister) that he had influence in France. But at the
moment when the Nazi menace was alarming both the Government of the
Soviet Union and French opinion, and when the constant demonstrations
of the Croix de Feu were alarming the entire French Left, the Communists
had an ideal opportunity to convince the other parties of the Left that they
constituted a new world which could restore the balance of the old both in
home and foreign politics. For the Communists this meant that they could
at last achieve those electoral alliances without which, under the French
single-member electoral, and multi-party political, system, any political
group was condemned to under-representation.

It was not as evident as it seemed, later, that it should have been that the
Communist motives for national solidarity might at the shortest possible
notice become motives for an opposite attitude, with their newly won
certificates of national virtue still operative in the eyes of their followers.

Meanwhile the Communists reaped manifold advantages. As members
of the victorious electoral alliance they increased the number of their seats,
but they declined to enter the Government and, in fact, played a part more
like that of an opposition than a government party. Not having to resolve
practical problems, they could create for themselves the reputation of
being the only members of the Front Populaire alliance who remained
loyal to the promises made to the electorate. They could, in particular,
strengthen their position inside the trade unions in preparation for later
conquests. They could, in fact, take advantage both of the deep social
fissures dividing the French proletariat from other classes and of the
national spirit of the masses to make a bid for monopolizing the French
revolutionary tradition with its national associations.

The Communist Party's unique relationship to trade unionism was of
great advantage to them in this. The older French syndicalist tradition
insisted that trade unions must be entirely independent of political parties

---

[1] In a communiqué issued on 15 May 1935 after talks in Moscow between Stalin, Molotov,
Litvinov, and Laval, for the purpose of determining in greater detail the implications of the Pact
of 2 May. The exact words were: 'M. Stalin understands and fully approves the policy of national
defence adopted by France to maintain her armed forces at the level required for security'
(*The Times*, 16 May, *Temps*, 17 May 1935).

and made trade union and political offices incompatible. This was the doctrine of the Confédération Générale du Travail (C.G.T.), from which the Communist trade unionists had split to form the Confédération Générale du Travail Unitaire (C.G.T.U.), at the same time that the Communist Party was created. When the C.G.T. and C.G.T.U. merged in March 1936, it was the doctrine of the C.G.T. that theoretically prevailed, but it was not really possible to suppose that the habits and personal links of Communist trade unionism would disappear, even if the intention had existed among the Communists that they should. The cuckoo in the nest became apparent when Ambroise Croizat became a deputy while remaining, in spite of protests, secretary-general of the metallurgical trade union.

The Communist trade union influence increased with the influx of unschooled workers into the unions and with the enthusiasm for strikes, and declined as the new members fell off and the belief in strikes disappeared, but the presence of the Communists inside the C.G.T. henceforth made it possible constantly to question the authority of the old C.G.T. elements. The Communists above all maintained a source of steady recruitment from the working class into the higher ranks of the party. This source had almost dried up in the case of the Socialist Party, who respected the old C.G.T. principle and had no organic link with the unions. Its leaders, when not bourgeois, were usually the sons of workers who had risen through scholarships.

In proportion as the Communist claim to be not only the true, but the actual, representatives of the proletariat became increasingly plausible, especially in the Paris area, it strengthened the estrangement, dating from 1848, between the working class and the other classes of the community, not only by preaching the doctrine of class war to the workers behind the screen of nationalism, but also by its effect on the middle and upper classes. A new excuse was found for those strong elements in the bourgeoisie to whom the trade union movement had always been an irreconcilable enemy to be fought and to whom their own class was the nation. The success of the Communists in the big towns at the municipal elections of May 1935 immediately influenced middle-class opinion with regard to the Franco-Soviet Pact signed on 2 May and undermined the campaign originally launched by Barthou (murdered on 9 October 1934)[1] in favour of a foreign policy which would take no more account of the internal régime of the Soviet Union than it would that of Italy.[2] As Communist strength grew, it became at least arguable that foreign policy and internal policy could no longer be treated separately. The ablest formulation of

---

[1] See *Survey* for 1934, p. 550.

[2] For Barthou's project for an Eastern European Pact of Mutual Assistance, see *Survey* for 1934, pp. 347–51; *Survey* for 1935, vol. i, part I (iv).

the case for Munich came from Thierry Maulnier in an article much commented on at the time although it appeared only in *Combat*,[1] a review with a small circulation. The article is the more worthy of attention because its author ultimately recognized the necessity of offering a barrier to Hitler and, under the Occupation, rejected the policies recommended by his earlier mentor Charles Maurras. He wrote in November 1938 that the outcome of any war could not but be a defeat for France since the alternative was between a German and a Soviet victory. He had certainly in mind that if the first alternative would mean an avowed foreign domination of France, the second would mean an indirect foreign domination through a French minority controlling industry with the trade unions as its instrument, as well as the state by means of a party.

The strength of the Communists in the years 1936–9 had another most important consequence. While every other party in the state was divided between pacifists and those who advocated resistance to the Nazis, the Communists alone were united—not, however, behind either pacifism or what the pacifists called 'bellicisme', but behind a policy which accepted all risks in defence and support of the Soviet Union. For the time being, and indeed from as far back as 1934, this policy involved a common front with all who opposed Hitler, though without the implication that was self-evident to men like Léon Blum that opposition to Germany made necessary above all association with England. Apart from one deputy of the Right, de Kérillis, the Communists alone voted against the Government on the Munich issue on 5 October 1938.[2] The Socialists, to maintain their unity, abstained from voting. It thus came about that the *bellicistes* took it for granted that the working class could be mobilized for war with the help of the Communist Party. Few took into consideration that the Communists at the crucial moment might reverse this attitude and become, as was to happen, a peace party within a few weeks of the declaration of war, spreading confusion in the minds of those who had been accustomed for the last four years to consider that the causes of social emancipation and of resistance to Hitler were one.

Thus, in March 1939, the traditional parties of the French Republic, paying belatedly for the immense national sacrifice that had apparently come to an end twenty years before, were, on both Right and Left, suffering from a sense of frustration due to repeated failures, which in turn were due to inability to renew ideas. On either wing groups, having the recommendation of novelty and on the whole youth, were responding to the attraction of foreign poles, which seemed to be, but were not in all cir-

[1] No connexion with the newspaper which was appearing in 1948 under the same title.
[2] Georges Bonnet, however (*De Washington au Quai d'Orsay* [referred to hereafter as Bonnet: *De Washington*] (Geneva, Bourquin, Éditions du Cheval Ailé, 1946), p. 298), notes that of the 75 votes cast against the Government in the Chamber on this occasion, 73 were Communist and 2 'isolés'.

cumstances, irrevocably opposed. The sharp party divisions of the self-confident France of 1914 had not been burdened with foreign associations.

(e) THE FRENCH EMPIRE[1]

One other aspect of French affairs, which was to have the greatest importance in the course of the war, must be mentioned before passing to military and foreign policy in the strict sense of the word. The enhanced

---

[1] In 1939 the French Empire consisted of the following colonies, protectorates, and dependencies:

Africa

1. *North Africa* (a) Algeria, occupied in and after 1830; administered, since 1881, as three departments of the metropolitan territory of France with territories under military government in the southern hinterland; (b) Tunisia, since 1881 under a French protectorate, with a native government; (c) French Zone of Morocco (i.e. the greater part of the Sultanate of Morocco), the occupation of which began in 1907; administered as a protectorate since 1912 under the terms of a treaty of that year with the Sultan.

2. *French West Africa* consisting of a federation of seven colonies under a Governor-General, and the mandated territory of Togo. The Federation included the colonies of Senegal (acquired between 1736 and 1889), which had autonomous institutions and representation in the Parliament in Paris; French Guinea (acquired in 1843); the Ivory Coast (1843); Dahomey (1893); Mauretania (1893); French Sudan (1893); Niger and its dependencies (1912); and the District of Dakar and its dependencies (separated from Senegal by decree in 1924). Dakar was the administrative centre and the principal port for the whole territory and a French naval and air base; the harbour was to become the scene of a famous incident during the war. The territory of the colony of Upper Volta, which was reconstituted after the war, had been distributed in 1933 between Niger, French Sudan, and the Ivory Coast.

The mandated territory of Togo, comprising two-thirds of the former German colony assigned by the Treaty of Versailles to France, was closely linked to the Federation—the Governor-General of the Federation being *ex officio* High Commissioner of Togo—but retained its separate entity both financial and administrative.

3. *French Equatorial Africa.* The French Congo, acquired since 1841, was divided in 1910 into the three colonies of Gabon, Middle Congo, and Ubangi-Shari. In 1920 the Chad Territory, formerly a dependency of Ubangi-Shari, was made a separate colony. By a decree of 1934 the Federation of French Equatorial Africa became a single colony and the four former colonies became territories. The mandated territory of the French Cameroons (the greater part of the former German colony) was constituted an autonomous territory by decrees of 1921 and 1925.

Practically the whole of the Sahara came within the French sphere in virtue of an Anglo-French Declaration of 21 March 1899 recognizing the right of France to all territory west of the Nile Basin.

4. *French Somaliland.* This small colony on the East African coast, acquired in 1864, contained the port of Jibuti, which was founded in 1888 (the year in which the territory was delimited by agreement with Great Britain) and which became the terminus of the railway to the Ethiopian capital, Addis Ababa.

5. *Islands off the East Coast of Africa*: (a) Madagascar, declared a protectorate in 1890 and a colony in 1896; (b) the archipelago of the Comoro Islands attached, with the status of a colony, to the general government of Madagascar since 1914; (c) Réunion, a French possession since 1643, with an autonomous government and representation in the Parliament in Paris.

Asia

1. *French India*, consisting of the five provinces of Pondicherry (founded by France in 1674 and continuously in her possession since 1814), Karikal, Chandernagore, Mahé, and Yanaon. The government was autonomous, with representation in the Parliament in Paris.

2. *French Indochina* (see above, pp. 82–84). The colony of Cochin-China and the protectorates of

importance attached by French opinion to the French overseas Empire and the increase of imperial trade have already been mentioned, as well as the contradiction between colonial economic development, on the one hand, and the demographic stability of a metropolitan France still almost able to provide her own food supply, on the other. Throughout the years between the wars the French conception of the relationship between France and the Empire, and of the course that political emancipation should take, remained fundamentally different from that of Britain. The relationship was symbolized in French minds by the representation (on, it is true, haphazard and unrealistic lines) of the colonies and of Algeria in the French Chamber and Senate.[1] It was little noted that the populations with the most highly evolved cultures of their own, the North African Muslims and the Annamese, had not found a place in the French Parliament. The colonies were considered as external provinces of France, which would ultimately be integrated in a wider nationhood, just as

Annam, Cambodia, Tongking, and Laos were occupied between 1862 and 1884. The territory of Kwang Chow Wan had been held under lease from China since 1900.

America (all colonies with autonomous governments):

1. *St. Pierre and Miquelon*, small rocky islands off the south coast of Newfoundland, acquired in 1635.
2. *Guadeloupe*, one of the Leeward Islands, acquired in 1634, with five dependencies consisting of smaller islands.
3. *Martinique*, in the Windward Islands, acquired in 1635.
4. *French Guiana*, on the north-east coast of South America, acquired in 1626. The territory of Inini was separated from Guiana by decree in 1930.

Australasia and the Pacific (all colonies with autonomous governments):

1. *New Caledonia*, with several dependencies consisting of smaller groups of islands; acquired between 1854 and 1888.
2. *New Hebrides*, administered under Anglo-French Condominium since 1906.
3. *Islands in the East Pacific*, acquired between 1841 and 1881. The principal groups were the Society Islands (including Tahiti, the administration centre), the Marquesas, the Tuamotu Archipelago, the Gambier or Mangareva group, the Austral Islands, and Rapa. The total area of the French Establishments in Oceania was estimated at 1,544 square miles.

The Mandated States of Syria and Lebanon

The 'A' Mandate over Syria and Lebanon, assigned to France by the Treaty of Versailles, had not yet been juridically extinguished in 1939, since France had not ratified the treaties of 1936 providing for the replacement of the mandatory régimes by autonomous governments (see *Survey* for 1936, pp. 748–58, 766–7), and these territories were still under French military occupation.

The French Empire ranked in 1939 first in area and third in population among the colonial empires of the world (Royal Institute of International Affairs: *The Colonial Problem*, p. 9, table i).

[1] Algeria was represented by three deputies each for the departments of Oran and Constantine and four deputies for the department of Algiers and by three senators. Of the colonies, each of the islands of Réunion, Guadeloupe, and Martinique sent two deputies and one senator to Paris; French India sent one deputy and one senator; while Senegal, Cochin-China, and French Guiana sent one deputy each. The remaining colonies with some autonomous institutions (French Somaliland, Madagascar, St. Pierre and Miquelon, New Caledonia, and the French Establishments in Oceania) were represented in the Parliament in Paris. All the colonies of French Equatorial Africa, except Senegal, which were ruled by Governors-General with autonomous institutions, and the territories of the French Empire which were protectorates or were held under mandate, were likewise not represented in Paris.

German-speaking Alsace, Italian-speaking Corsica, and Celtic Brittany had been at the time of the Revolution. When and how this would happen were questions that were rarely asked. The overseas territories were governed under a highly centralized system, and there was no encouragement of autonomous political life. The party labels of the colonial deputies were those of the homeland. There was no root in the French political past from which the idea of dominions could naturally spring. The habit of looking to Paris was inculcated on the principle of 'France one and indivisible'. Though there was educational progress there was singularly little political or constitutional change. There was thus no preparation for a situation in which the overseas territories would be called upon to make independent judgements of the situation in opposition to those of the central national Government. One new development, however, was to prove of quite unexpected importance. West Indian Frenchmen of negro descent were being recruited for the French colonial service and appointed to posts in West and Equatorial Africa. One of them, M. Eboué, had reached the rank of Governor in the Chad Province. The status of these men was clearly incompatible with any alinement of French policy with that of Nazi Germany, and of this they were aware.

(f) National Defence

Although the age of retirement for French generals had been fixed at sixty-eight, a man who reached that age in 1924 was the most influential person in French military policy throughout the period between the two wars. This was Marshal Pétain. Technically this was possible because there was no retiring age for Marshals of France, but he owed his great position to popular support, in spite of the severe judgement passed on his limitations by Joffre, Foch, and Poincaré. While to students of the First World War it was clear that victory was ultimately due to the spirit of the offensive, and that, without a general who thought primarily in offensive terms and without troops prepared to advance to the assault, the opportunity of the summer of 1918 would have been lost, perhaps fatally, the memory of the French people was of the cost in human lives of the offensives launched at intervals throughout the war. It was not easy for the ordinary soldier who returned to his home with memories of thousands of dead comrades in the mud or strung on barbed wire entanglements to realize that Verdun had been saved by the battle of the Somme. Still less was it easy for the families of the dead. A general's error in sending men over the top is always more obvious than the alternative error of keeping them in the trenches.

In the early months of the First World War, when France's casualties were heaviest and inflicted the greatest shock, the errors in the application of the doctrine of the offensive were most clear. Pétain was not only the French general least associated with the doctrine of the offensive, he was also the man who had put an end to the mutinies of 1917 with firm humanity and had redressed the soldier's grievances.[1] For once Paul Valéry was speaking on behalf of the masses of France, when, welcoming Pétain to his seat in the French Academy, he declared that his was the superlative genius able to perceive the truth to which most of his colleagues were blind—that fire-power kills. The popular French judgement was that a Foch might bring victory but might also destroy the nation in the process. Pétain's extraordinary health and longevity not only prolonged his influence at an age when only the most exceptional gifts could have made his mind highly receptive to new ideas, but also left him the sole representative of victory, apart from Franchet d'Espérey, who had won his battles on a distant front and whose political attitude made him much less acceptable to Republicans than his rival.

The doctrine of the defensive received additional support from the comprehensible desire of Frenchmen to see reversed the tendency that had extended military service up to three years for every male member of the French nation on the eve of the First World War. This was all the more natural because in 1929, when military service was about to be reduced to one year,[2] the nation, at the height of a boom, was working up to the limit of its man-power. Military opinion opposed the reduction (which in practice was to be, for most recruits, to ten months) because it in fact made impossible the continuance of the occupation of the Rhineland. It was also, combined with growing economic depression, to reduce the pressure that favoured immigration. Thus the combined desires to save men in battle and to shorten the time spent by every citizen in uniform, backed by the conservative and defensive instincts of an old soldier in his seventies, turned the Maginot Line, originally conceived in relation to offensive strategy, into an excuse for having neither the means nor the ideas for winning a war. Behind these fortifications France was popularly believed to be safe; why therefore intervene in Germany, why have allies at the other end of Europe, why serve for a whole year in the army? Already in 1932 Jean Prévost was warning the readers of his *Histoire de France depuis la guerre*[3] that 'confidence in the cuirasse' might again bring disaster on France as it had done at Crécy and at Agincourt.

The reduced number of conscripts with the colours gave added importance to the professional elements in the army. This might have been expected to promote those military doctrines, which found a brilliant

---

[1] Pétain was also one of the few infantry officers in the French High Command.
[2] The law providing for the reduction of the period of military training had been promulgated on 31 March 1928 and was to take effect from 1 November 1930 (*Survey* for 1929, p. 31, note).
[3] Paris, Rieder, 1932, p. 338.

exponent in Colonel Charles de Gaulle,[1] favouring the creation of a highly mechanized and armoured striking force. But a number of factors militated against these ideas. In the parties of the Left, Jaurès's idea of a militia on the Swiss model still held the field. The de Gaulle doctrine seemed to offer a new opportunity for the creation of a politically powerful military caste. Anti-militarism remained an extremely strong emotion in the working class. Serving soldiers had no vote. One of the most popular songs at the Front Populaire rallies, until the victory of 1936 brought the responsibilities of office, was that in honour of the soldiers of the 17th Regiment who mutinied when used to maintain order in 1907 during the troubles in the wine-growing south.

The memory of the conflict between the Republic and the army during the Dreyfus case was not only lively on the Left. It had also made the average professional officer extremely anxious to avoid conflict with the Government or with public opinion on any subject. The merits of defiance of orders in certain circumstances which, as typified in Nelson, had been praised by de Gaulle in 1932 in his book *Le fil de l'épée*,[2] were not widely appreciated in military circles, and there was no repetition of the resignation of generals which before 1914 had effectively called attention to defects in military preparedness. The effect on de Gaulle's own career of his intellectual activity was not an encouraging example. Marc Bloch has described[3] as one of the intellectual weaknesses of the period between the two wars the favour bestowed by university teachers on the *bon élève* who was by definition also the docile student who did not contradict his professor. This, as he points out, was no less true of the army than of the university.

The reorganization of the army on new lines was also hampered by the economic crises which successive governments tried to solve by deflation and retrenchment throughout the early years of the Hitler Government in Germany. Military doctrines which required a transformation of armament could not easily be accepted by governments which were engaged in trying to balance the budget by reducing expenditure. Thus the statement of the French Government on 17 April 1934, putting an end to the disarmament negotiations and declaring that France would henceforth assure her security by her own resources,[4] was followed by a reduction of armament credits from 600 to 400 million francs. Pétain, as Minister for War in 1934 (at the age of seventy-eight), proved totally unable or unwilling to use his immense authority on behalf of the army's needs. The credits were increased to 800 million francs for 1935 under General

---

[1] Charles de Gaulle: *Vers l'armée de métier* (Paris, Berger-Levrault, 1934).
[2] Paris, Berger-Levrault, 1932.
[3] In *L'étrange défaite*, pp. 131–44.
[4] See *Survey* for 1935, i. 27–28.

Maurin, Pétain's successor as Minister for War, and finally a supplementary credit of 1,885 million francs was accorded for 1935 and 1936.

It was not, however, till the Blum Government came into office with its doctrine of curing the depression by spending that on 7 September 1936 a credit of 14 milliard francs was accorded[1] and later increased to 31 milliard. But apart from a necessarily slow departure, the utilization of these credits was hampered in the initial stages by labour conflicts and the rigid application of the forty-hour week (which involved the increase of railway staffs by 70,000 men). It was not till Paul Reynaud took control of financial and economic affairs in November 1938 that the release of energy already described gave an impetus to rearmament. But even with these credits the army was in such financial straits that there was cheese-paring of other essential expenditure, so that men called up in September 1938 during the Munich crisis found a shortage of boots and in many cases had to join their units in town shoes, an experience which had an unfortunate effect on morale in the following year.

Finally the nature of the military problems to be solved required co-ordinated thinking on the use of all three arms, in other words a general staff of national defence. Although the title of Minister of Defence had been created as far back as 1932 and was used as often as that of Minister for War by occupants of the office, and although General Gamelin had been given the title of Chief of the General Staff of National Defence at the beginning of 1938, no organization for national defence ever really came into existence. This was particularly unfortunate for the air force, which had been in decline throughout the 1920s and, when finally given equality with the other two arms and an independent Ministry in 1929, had never acquired a doctrine or a tradition of its own except that of valour. In the five years preceding March 1939 three entirely different programmes succeeded one another under different Ministers, and in 1939 the Government and the General Staffs were aware, as they had been in each succeeding crisis, that France was disastrously weak in the air. On the other hand, the navy was perhaps the best that France had ever possessed, though its use was only possible if its bases could be adequately protected or if the centre of resistance could be transported overseas, which was not the case.

In March 1939 French opinion was prepared at the best for a defensive war. It was tormented by fear of crippling casualties. It was divided between growing doubts as to the efficacy of its armed forces and comfort drawn from the assertions of Pétain and Weygand that its army was incomparable.[2] It placed illusory hopes in the Maginot Line, which it

---

[1] Paul Reynaud: *La France a sauvé l'Europe* (Paris, Flammarion, 1947), i. 339; *Survey* for 1936, p. 148.

[2] It has sometimes been taken for granted that at that time Churchill (because of later utter-

supposed extended from Switzerland to the sea, though in fact it had not been completed beyond the point where the Belgian frontier joined the French. At the very moment when the inevitability of conflict darkened the sky, Pétain was recommending to the public in a long preface General Chauvineau's book *Une invasion est-elle encore possible?*[1] which claimed to prove that reinforced concrete fortifications could be built faster than they could be destroyed by bombardment.

The army's doctrine was based on the *Instruction sur l'emploi tactique des grandes unités* of 12 August 1936, a code compiled by a committee presided over by General Georges. This replaced the *Instruction* of 1921, which had been compiled by Pétain. The 1936 code asserted:

> Without underestimating the importance of the progress made [since 1921] in the domain of means of combat and transport, the committee responsible for the present Instruction is nevertheless of the opinion that this progress of a technical character has not seriously modified the essential rules laid down by its predecessors in the sphere of tactics. It has in consequence recognized that the body of doctrine objectively established on the morrow of victory by eminent commanders who had just occupied the highest posts should remain the charter of the tactical use of our large formations.[2]

This text probably betrays as much frustrated anxiety as complacency. The French army commanders knew that they must wait at least until the summer of 1940 for tanks, probably later for aeroplanes, and later still for formations trained in the use of these arms. They knew that the defences of France were incomplete and that the army had not yet the equipment necessary for the rapid advance into the Low Countries planned for the eventuality of a German breach of Dutch and Belgian neutrality.

(g) Foreign Relations

Jean Giraudoux, looking back in 1939 across the twenty years of peace, wrote:[3]

> All our treaties whether of victory or even of defeat had been signed in confidence and in hope. The treaties of 1815, which dismantled our natural frontiers, were received by the majority in the country with a sigh of relief. The Treaty of Frankfurt in 1871 provoked only one reaction in France, the desire for revenge. The treaty of our greatest victory, on the other hand, that of Versailles, had been beaten into shape under the device 'Security'. It was not a question

---

ances—see e.g. *Second World War*, i. 265, where he says: 'The German armies were not capable of defeating the French in 1938 or 1939') shared these views on the strength of the French army, but it should be noted that a statement made by him in March 1936 (ibid. p. 163) that 'the French army is the strongest in Europe' was qualified by the words immediately preceding it: 'Today, for this year, probably for part of 1937, the French army . . .' &c.

[1] Paris, Berger-Levrault, 1939.
[2] Reynaud: *La France a sauvé l'Europe*, i. 339.
[3] In 'Pleins Pouvoirs', *Nouvelle Revue Française*, 1939, p. 36.

of obtaining this security for some years, for the period required to overhaul a country worn out by the war, but of eternal security. We wanted centuries of security, to be able to go in security to the end of the world and to the Last Judgement.

It was with this exigency of fatigue that France began her twenty years of struggle for repose until her energies had recovered.

France's problem in international affairs was to secure against German revenge the backing of at least Great Britain if not America on her western flank, the support of a continental ally or allies on her eastern flank, and at least the neutrality of the countries which Germany would wish to bring into action against her on her southern flank and athwart her communications with her overseas territories. At the beginning of the twenty years of peace the divergences of outlook on this problem among Frenchmen, though considerable, were not such as to make their general harmonization appear impossible. The Right thought in terms of old-fashioned alliances, the Left in those of collective security. France's position on the Continent was such after her victory that it seemed as if the two systems could be merged, and during Barthou's brief tenure of power in 1934 they seemed to be on the point of combining in the shape of a grand alliance which would have the at least passive support of the majority of the Powers at Geneva.[1]

By that time, however, another divergence in French views was becoming apparent, that between, on the one hand, the pacifists of both the Right and Left who dreamed of a Scandinavian France, rich, brilliant, without foreign entanglements and permanently neutral and, on the other, those who realized that France was potentially too rich and actually too weak and poor to achieve any such happy condition; that the neutrals whom France envied owed their happiness to the fact that France and Britain had not abdicated; that none of the traditional political ideals of France could be realized, nor her material interests protected, without the acceptance of her traditional responsibilities. In addition to this split in the outlook of the main body of the nation, a third view was held, as has been already pointed out,[2] by the Communists for whom the Ark of the Covenant was in Moscow and not in Paris.

This change of polarization in views on foreign policy was due first of all to the phenomena of fatigue, frustration, and division in internal affairs and the growing sense of military weakness that have already been described. But the growth of pacifism was also due to frustration and ambiguity in the sphere of foreign policy. After her disappointment over the abortive triple alliance of France, Great Britain, and the United States,[3] France made the discovery that in Britain's post-war mood it was

---

[1] See *Survey* for 1934, pp. 339–43, 387–8; *Survey* for 1935, i. 58–90.
[2] See above, pp. 174–8.   [3] See *Survey* for 1924, pp. 2–16.

impossible to combine the organization of European peace, either on the lines of the Geneva Protocol (the ideal of the Left) or on those of continental alliances (the ideal of the Right), with any form of alliance with Great Britain.[1] The result was the Locarno compromise,[2] whose advantages, it became increasingly apparent in the 1930s, lay with Germany.

Locarno marked an important stage in the relaxation of France's close ties with the new or greatly enlarged states lying between Germany and the Soviet Union. This had, however, other and most important causes. The French yearning for security was not the attitude of leadership which compelled respect. France's stable and self-contained economy was not able to provide the dynamic impulsion that the peasant states of the Danube and the Vistula required from a Great Power either in ideas, capital, or the attraction of a market. Here the problem that arose was not unlike that of France's economic relations with her colonies. Finally France's cultural prestige among her allies was not of the character that many Frenchmen supposed, and provoked, when its inefficacy was discovered, some bitterness and disappointment. Not only was the class that spoke or read French in the countries concerned in process of social and economic dissolution, but French literary and artistic culture during the period between the two wars was from the point of view of the majority of the inhabitants of any country the most esoteric in the world. The German commercial traveller in Poland, Rumania, or Yugoslavia had not to compete with Frenchmen of his own class and he provided a more comprehensible and relevant example of a higher state of economic and cultural evolution than the French lecturers and diplomats.[3]

The first concrete fact that awakened French opinion to the weakening of France's Eastern alliances was the German–Polish Pact of January 1934.[4] It had, however, been preceded by France's own abandonment of earlier positions through her participation in the four-Power pact proposed by Mussolini in 1933.[5] That lost ground could be recovered was shown by the reception given to Barthou during his tour of the capitals of the Little Entente.[6] Barthou's murder, however, created a position which was to produce the most catastrophic effects not only on France's allies but on French opinion. He was succeeded by Laval, who in theory was pursuing his predecessor's policy but in fact was doing his utmost to make this policy unnecessary by finding an alternative through understanding

---

[1] *Survey* for 1924, pp. 16–64; *Survey* for 1925, ii. 2–10.   [2] See ibid. pp. 20–66.

[3] How deep were French illusions on this subject appeared when French political deportees met Poles and Czechs in German concentration camps and were surprised both at the cultural level of a Polish workman, although there were hundreds of thousands of them in France, and of the almost total ignorance of French among the Slavs.

[4] *Survey* for 1934, pp. 386–7; *Survey* for 1935, i. 60–61.

[5] See *Survey* for 1934, pp. 207–21.

[6] Ibid. pp. 347–9; *Survey* for 1935, i. 60–66.

with Germany.[1] Here began that rapid devaluation of the meaning of plain words and plain sentiments which ended with Georges Bonnet explaining to his electors that France had not abandoned Czechoslovakia. Neither Frenchmen nor France's allies were to know what France stood for. This demoralizing ambiguity was to mark all French governments except those of Blum until the actual outbreak of war. But in French eyes the ambiguities of French action were fully paralleled by those of a Great Britain capable of signing the Anglo-German naval agreement on 18 June 1935,[2] thereby condoning Germany's overt breach of all the military clauses of the Treaty of Versailles three months before[3] and dissipating the attempts of French diplomacy to make a reality of the Stresa agreement.[4]

At this point the contradiction between the Franco-British alliance and France's attempt to secure alliances in the rear of Germany was paralleled by a similar contradiction between the first objective and the necessity of preventing Germany securing alliances in France's rear. First of all, the French Right acquired the conviction that Britain's demand for sanctions against Italy[5] had imposed on France an enemy in the Alps and the Mediterranean. Two years later the Left was to feel that Britain, by her insistence on non-intervention in Spain, had imposed on France both moral disgrace and an enemy in the Pyrenees.[6]

Between the Italian attack on Ethiopia and the Spanish Civil War had occurred the failure of France to intervene, and of Britain to support France in intervention, when Germany remilitarized the Rhineland.[7] Since this event had been provoked by France's ratification of the Franco-Soviet Pact,[8] British failure to react was one more example of Britain's refusal to support France in her search for continental allies. But here the reaction on France of her own *gran rifiuto* was to have the gravest consequences. She had missed her last chance of action on her own initiative, not least because there was an election due in a few weeks. The unreality of democracy as practised in the West could not have been more blatantly revealed. After ratifying an alliance with the greatest Power east of Germany, France had lost the power to intervene effectively on behalf of any Eastern ally. She was, in fact, left alone with an ally unable, if a war broke out, to contribute, on her own admission, as many troops as in the terrible first three months of the war of 1914–18 when France had suffered her heaviest casualties.

That France was again to stem the first rush of the German armed forces was a thought that worked like a poison in French minds in the years of peace that remained. Britain had seemed unaware in the Italian

---

[1] See *Survey* for 1935, i. 72–85.
[2] See ibid. pp. 178–93.
[3] Ibid. pp. 140–2.
[4] Ibid. pp. 156–69.
[5] See ibid. ii. 212–39, 271–9.
[6] See *Survey* for 1937, ii. 141–5.
[7] See *Survey* for 1936, part III (i).
[8] Ibid. pp. 252–6.

crisis that, if sanctions led to war, it was France who would mobilize every man in his prime while Britain prepared her armies at her leisure. That Britain would fight to the last Frenchman needed no German formulation to occur to French minds. It covered with fatal facility France's own failures, and gave a moral consecration to the habit of inaction when Austria was annexed[1] and the claims of Sudeten Germans were pleaded on the analogy of Savoy and Nice. In the dark days of September 1938, when Londoners were digging trenches in the park, Parisians were being called to the colours without even enough military boots to go round. Flandin, who had advocated action in 1936 when the German regiments marched into the Rhineland[2], was now declaring, on street posters, that war was a criminal folly.[3] Twenty years of diplomacy, twenty years of politics, twenty years of military service by age-group succeeding to age-group had failed to secure the just fruits of the sacrifice of 1,320,000 French lives on the battlefield. That an astounded and shocked Daladier, on his way back from Munich, should drive down the Rue Lafayette between cheering crowds was not really surprising.[4] It was more surprising that after France had received almost without emotion the news that German troops had occupied Prague, the majority of Frenchmen should have slowly and soberly faced the issue before them.

(v) Italy[5]

By Katharine Duff

(a) Italy's Unreadiness for War in 1939

'Between 1935 and 1940 we shall find ourselves at a point which I should call a crucial point in European History—we shall be in a position to make our voices heard, and to see, at last, our rights recognized.' The crisis thus foretold by Mussolini in his speech before the Chamber of Deputies on 26 May 1927[6] had come to pass, but the voice which claimed most attention in Europe at the moment did not come from Italy. In

---

[1] See *Survey* for 1938, vol. i, part II (ii).

[2] See *Survey* for 1936, pp. 283, 287–8, 294–5, 297, 299.

[3] See *Survey* for 1938, ii. 436.   [4] Ibid., p. 451.

[5] The most important documents available at the time of writing for the history of Italian foreign relations from 1936 to 1943 were the diaries and diplomatic papers of Count Galeazzo Ciano, Mussolini's son-in-law and Italy's Foreign Minister. Their unique character, however, makes it essential to regard them with a critical eye. Ciano was a small man and his relations with Mussolini were not such as to make his evidence entirely trustworthy. For the greater part of the years 1938–43 Ciano was a devoted disciple; at the end of his life he suffered from a feeling of desertion and of injustice at the hands of the man whom he had served to the best of his abilities. There is no ground for doubting the authenticity of the documents, and many statements in them are confirmed from other sources, but equally there is no certainty that Ciano did not revise part of the diaries in order to show himself in a favourable light compared with Mussolini.

[6] *Survey* for 1927, pp. 120–1.

1927 Mussolini may well have hoped that during the next ten years Germany would revive, and France decline, enough to enable him to drive a hard bargain with the 'satisfied' countries, and to ensure Italy at least equal weight with France in the balance of the four European Powers; but at that time he thought Hitler too humble or questionable an imitator even to deserve the gift of a signed photograph;[1] and it was with mixed feelings that he had since watched the rise of his fellow dictator.

Nor had Mussolini succeeded in equipping Italy with adequate armaments, industrial capacity, raw materials, foodstuffs, financial reserves, or political and social cohesion for her to plunge boldly into the world-wide game of power politics for which the Nazis were setting the pace. Neither imperial expansion nor even the defence of Fascist ideology was a cause to arouse a mood of heroic enterprise and endurance throughout Italy; and many Italians who had taken pride in the establishment of the Empire, and in the victory over sanctions, were now feeling the strain of the drive for autarky[2] and of two and a half years' undeclared war in Spain, and were uneasily conscious of a drift towards war in alliance with the Germans, whose unpopularity in Italy was far older than the Nazi revolution.

On the other hand, it is difficult to over-estimate the effect on the Italian people of the imposition of economic sanctions. By the use of skilful propaganda Mussolini had succeeded in convincing a large number of Italians that the economic possibilities for Italy in Ethiopia were immense; and the political cynicism that was rife in Italy not only during the Fascist régime but since the age of the Renaissance made Italians blind to the truth that their aggression against Ethiopia was a crime that excited genuine indignation abroad, and that the ideal of collective security, embodied in the League of Nations, was precious to many non-Italians, both for its own sake and because the League was felt to be the sole bulwark against a second world war. Italians unconsciously gave themselves away by readily jumping to the conclusion that sanctions were nothing but a move in the game of power politics, and this naïvely cynical assumption united Italy behind Mussolini to an extent which was never recognized outside Italy, any more than it was recognized inside Italy how ugly Italian aggression looked in foreign eyes. Great, though assuredly unwarranted, bitterness was felt against Great Britain on this score, a bitterness which lasted long after the conclusion of the Anglo-Italian Agreements of 1937 and 1938 and which still found expression after 1943 even among Italians who were in general friendly to Great Britain. At the same time the failure to impose sanctions on a conclusive scale probably encouraged Mussolini's belief in the weakness and divided counsels of the Western Powers. On the ordinary Italian the psychological

---

[1] See Mario Donosti, pseud.: *Mussolini e l'Europa* (Rome, Edizioni Leonardo, 1945), p. 80.
[2] See *Survey* for 1938, i. 91–96.

effect was far more important than the economic, and this abiding resentment helped to make possible the acceptance of the Axis policy which was
so alien to Italian sympathies and which Mussolini himself only adopted
after long hesitation.

Moreover, Fascism still had its enthusiasts, and many Italians had
acquired a vested interest in it. The Government could rely on the
acquiescence of the general public and prevent any effective opposition
from taking shape, while criticism of foreign policy from within the higher
ranks of the Fascist Party was apt to peter out into mere grumbling. King
Victor Emmanuel shared his subjects' distaste for Germany; but the
shadow of power remaining to him, after he had let the monarchy be
harnessed to Fascism, gave him no influence with Mussolini, who resented
the existence of even a potential rival to his supremacy. The most vigorous
challenge to the Axis policy came from the Catholic Church, and in
January 1939 the Fascist Government expected a major crisis over the
Vatican's objections to their anti-Semitic legislation.

Even if the opponents of an Italo-German alliance were not strong
enough to restrain Fascist Italy from entering war as an aggressor, her
chances of success in such a war were poor, in view of the country's
economic situation, and of widespread unwillingness to engage in war.
Mussolini's powers were deteriorating, and his autocratic methods, his
preoccupation with petty administrative routine, and the poor quality of
his lieutenants did not make for far-sighted and efficient government or
for the training of statesmanlike successors to the ruling generation. The
Fascist 'hierarchy' was in fact notorious for corruption, stupidity, and
irresponsibility, though ability and courage had by no means died out in
Italy, as the Resistance movement was to show a few years later.

The economic situation at this time is discussed elsewhere in this
volume.[1] As for the imposing and loudly advertised array of armed
strength evolved in sixteen years of Fascism, though it was by no means all
bluff, its shortcomings were already causing anxiety at Rome. In the
Ethiopian and Spanish wars the Italian forces had gained battle experience, under less exacting conditions than might be expected in future, at
the cost of war weariness and a heavy drain on material and financial
reserves. Besides, since 1936, Mussolini had undertaken far-reaching
schemes for the reorganization and rearmament of all three services, and
the next peak of preparedness would not be reached for two or three years.
And, while Italians were being encouraged to think in terms of the offensive spirit, a war of movement, and General Douhet's theory of intensive
air warfare,[2] they were also reminded that a war of attrition would be
contrary to the 'iron laws' of Fascist economy.[3]

[1] See below, pp. 398 seqq.   [2] Cf. Reynaud: *La France a sauvé l'Europe*, i. 439.
[3] See 'Le forze armate dell' Italia fascista', in *Rassegna Italiana*, June–September 1939, pp.

Mussolini himself appears to have been of the opinion that, in a war with France alone, the defences of either side would prevent decisive fighting on the Alpine frontier or in North Africa, while, even against Jibuti, French reinforcements were making an attack more difficult though not impossible. In the air, and at sea, he expected that Italian forces would prove equal or superior to those of the French, but that such a war would be a long one unless it were to spread to the rest of Europe, or of the world.[1] He did not, in fact, consider this an ideal moment for a Franco-Italian, still less a general, war, and, though he was prepared to take the risk of war in his dealings with France, he appears to have treated it as possible rather than probable. He did not want war till the end of 1942, by which time he hoped that Italy would have renewed all her artillery; that she would have eight new and modernized battleships in commission, twice the existing number of submarines, and a native army half a million strong in a pacified and self-sufficient Ethiopia; that the autarkic programme for the home country would be half-way to completion; that the exhibition of 1942 would have replenished foreign exchange reserves; and that as many as possible of the Italians living in France would have been repatriated.

This breathing-space could also be used to extort strategically important colonial concessions from France, and to encourage any tendency to disintegration in rival countries, such as agitation among minorities and colonial peoples, anti-Semitism, pacifism, or even that 'Bolshevism' against which Mussolini had so long been crusading in Spain.[2] Unlike Hitler, he does not seem at this time to have thought in terms of a peak of Axis strength during which the attack must be made or not at all.

(b) Mussolini's Territorial Ambitions

By the beginning of 1939, more than half the 'crucial' years foretold in 1927 had gone by, bringing Italy first the 1935 Agreement with France[3]— which, explicitly at least, gave her very little of value, required concessions from her over Tunisia, and had never been ratified—and then an Ethiopian empire that had still to be pacified, let alone made profitable. Mussolini's ambitions soared far higher than this. Italy, as he displayed her in the Augustan Exhibition of 1937, was a dynamic and resurgent

1–380, especially the two articles entitled 'La dottrina — lo spirito' by Generals Pariani and Valle, Under-Secretaries respectively for War and Air.

[1] For purposes of comparison it may be added that Gamelin had planned to attack the Italians on both the Alpine and North African fronts, but feared that French unpreparedness might only allow him to do so in North Africa (M. G. Gamelin: *Servir* (Paris, Plon, 1946), i. 134).

[2] See Mussolini to Hitler, 'Cavallero Memorandum' of 30 May 1939 (*I.M.T. Nuremberg*, xxxi. 156–9 (2818–PS); extracts trans. in *Documents* (R.I.I.A.) for 1939–46, i. 170; cf. *N.C.A.* v. 453–5). See also Ciano: *Diario (1939–43)*, 8 January 1939.

[3] See *Survey* for 1935, i. 91–118.

'Have-Not' Power, setting out to regain her Roman inheritance by establishing a Mediterranean and African empire. As things were, the Mediterranean, far from being her empire, was her prison; Corsica, Malta, Tunis, and Cyprus formed that prison's bars, while Gibraltar and Suez guarded its gates, and Greece, Turkey, and Egypt were ready to complete the chain encircling her. Determined, first to break her prison bars, and then to 'march to the ocean'—without free access to which she must be considered only half independent[1]—Italy might push towards the Indian Ocean by linking Libya with Ethiopia through the Sudan, or towards the Atlantic through French North Africa.

In either case the opposition of France and Great Britain must be faced. No claims against Great Britain had been officially formulated, nor do they figure in Ciano's *Diary* of this time, or in his letter of 2 January 1939 to Ribbentrop,[2] but it was understood that they might include the cession of Malta, the demilitarization and internationalization of Gibraltar or its return to Spain, and a condominium in the Sudan.[3] Parity of empires was a theme which appeared, for instance, in Ciano's Chamber of Deputies speech of 30 November 1938, and in the Fascist Chamber's reply to the King's speech on 18 April 1939.[4] At the moment Mussolini appears chiefly to have been interested in how far the British were able and willing to resist Axis expansion, whatever direction it might take, and especially in the waxing or waning of British solidarity with France.

On the mainland of Europe, Albania was the only immediate territorial objective. Italian plans for the Middle East and Levant[5] were also, for the time being, in the background. Mussolini had declared himself Protector of Islam in 1937,[6] but the anti-British propaganda of Radio Bari had been soft-pedalled since the conclusion of the Anglo-Italian Agreement of April 1938.[7] Minor incidents of 1938 and 1939 show the Fascist Government preparing to raise an anti-British fifth column among the Italian community in Egypt,[8] welcoming an inquiry from King Fārūq as to whether the Axis would support him if an Egyptian declaration of neutrality led to direct or indirect intervention by Great Britain,[9] and allaying 'Irāqī suspicions that Italian colonization in Libya might break the continuity of Islamic communities in the Mediterranean.[10]

---

[1] See Giuseppe Bottai: *Vent' anni e un giorno (24 luglio, 1943)* (Milan, Garzanti, 1949), pp. 123, 127.

[2] See Ciano: *Europa*, pp. 392–4; Eng. version, pp. 258–9; cf. *Documents* (R.I.I.A.) for 1939–46, i. 150.

[3] See Maxwell H. H. Macartney: *One Man Alone* (London, Chatto & Windus, 1944), p. 10.

[4] *Giornale d'Italia*, 1 December 1938, 19 April 1939.

[5] See Monroe: *Mediterranean in Politics*, chapter iv.

[6] *Survey* for 1936, p. 17, note.

[7] *Survey* for 1938, i. 137–43; text in *Documents* (R.I.I.A.) for 1938, i. 141 seqq.

[8] See Ciano: *Diario (1937–8)*, 3 January 1938.

[9] See ibid. 23 February 1939.   [10] See ibid. 4 January 1939.

It was against France that Fascist demands and hostility were now being concentrated.[1] Here again, no official definition of these demands had been made in public. In private, however, Mussolini had outlined them to Ciano on 8 November 1938 and 8 January 1939, and to the Grand Council, first on 30 November 1938 and then, with special emphasis, on 4 February 1939 in the political testament which he entitled 'The March to the Ocean'. His aims may be summed up as follows: 'Corsica: autonomy, independence, annexation; Tunis: statute for the Italians, autonomy for the Bey, Italian protectorate;[2] Jibuti: free port and railway, administration of the colony in condominium, cession; Suez Canal: a large share in the administration.'[3] Mussolini deliberately omitted Savoy as being outside the circle of the Alps, and neither historically nor geographically Italian, and Nice, because this would only mean a minor rectification of frontier, and the cession of a town now thoroughly French.[4] Corsica, on the other hand, in spite of French penetration, must not be renounced, for reasons of strategy as well as of geography, history, race, and language. In Jibuti, territorial claims stood the best chance of settlement partly because Great Britain would have no occasion to fear changes in the Mediterranean *status quo*. The questions of the Tunis Statute, the Jibuti port and railway, and the Suez Canal could all, in the opinion of the Fascist Government, be settled by negotiation, but anything further would need very different methods of settlement, and must wait upon events.[5]

[1] Reynaud's memoirs (*La France a sauvé l'Europe*, i. 178–9) contain a revealing glimpse of French and Italian attitudes regarding the dispute. When visiting Rome in October 1936, Reynaud had warned Ciano that it was unwise to encourage the enemies of France all over Europe, as the French army was the bulwark of Italian independence. What would become of that independence if France were to disappear? Ciano, probably nettled by this assumption of superiority, replied that France would, of course, always be there, leaving Reynaud to guess that he would not object to see her power somewhat diminished. (On Italian susceptibility to real or fancied slights from the French, see Gaetano Salvemini: *Mussolini diplomate* (Paris, Grasset, 1932), pp. 77–78.) Another Italian motive is indicated by the reply of an Italian general when one of the diplomats at Rome had tackled him with arguments similar to Reynaud's: 'Oui ... mais la proie est si belle!' (Reynaud, loc. cit.).

[2] Mussolini had also thought of a condominium for Tunisia (see Ciano: *Diario (1937–8)*, 8 November 1938).

[3] Ibid. *(1939–43)*, 8 January 1939.

[4] Ibid. *(1937–8)*, 8 and 30 November 1938 and ibid. *(1939–43)*, 8 January 1939. In November, Mussolini claimed Nice as well.

[5] See ibid. *(1937–8)*, 8 November 1938. The annexation of the Canton Ticino also figured among Mussolini's more distant plans (ibid. 30 November 1938). More extensive ambitions still are indicated by his proposal (recorded by Ciano on 14 June 1939) for an Italo-Spanish agreement providing that, in an eventual division of spoils, Italy should receive Algeria and Tunisia, and permanent transit facilities over a Morocco entirely under Spanish control. And, in a note addressed to Hitler on 7 July 1940, Italy aspired to take the place of Great Britain and France in the Levant, 'Irāq, Egypt, the Sudan, Aden, and Equatorial as well as North Africa; also to control oil supplies in the Middle East, and to annex Corfù and Northern Epirus (see Simoni: *Berlino, Ambasciata d'Italia*, p. 142); cf. Ciano's conversation with Ribbentrop on 19 June 1940 (Ciano: *Europa*, pp. 563–4; Eng. version, pp. 373–4).

(c) MUSSOLINI'S EUROPEAN POLICY, AND RELATIONS WITH THE WESTERN POWERS

Mussolini's dreams of an overseas empire were combined with a strong desire to vindicate Italy's precarious claim to the status of European Great Power, in relation to Germany as well as to Great Britain and France, and with an equally strong conviction that Italy could never afford to be 'odd man out' in Europe. Moreover, all his clamour for treaty revision, in the hope of extending the Italian Empire and breaking French hegemony, in no way diminished his determination (shared by his fellow countrymen whether Fascist or not) to defend the Versailles *status quo* at Trieste and on the Brenner. Hopes still survived at this time in France and Great Britain that alarm at the growing strength of the Third Reich might yet restrain him from throwing in his lot irrevocably with the Nazis. Nevertheless, in spite of his well-deserved reputation for opportunism and 'realism', the consequences of his own policy and the events of recent years left him very little freedom of action.

For more than ten years after he came into power, Mussolini's bark had been on the whole worse than his bite.[1] If, on the one hand, he displayed the ranting aggressiveness of the self-made leader of a comparatively newly established Power,[2] on the other he pursued something much more like the pre-Fascist policy of making the most of limited diplomatic and military assets by elaborate manœuvring.[3] He had preached militarism and the revision of the Versailles Settlement, carried on his feud with France, established his political influence over Hungary and the Balkans,[4] bombarded Corfù,[5] and forcibly Italianized the South Tyrol,[6] but he had also sought to establish friendly relations with Great Britain, and associated Italy with peaceful institutions such as the Locarno Treaties and even the League of Nations. This apparent moderation, however, was not, of course, inspired by moral scruples which many Italians, who did not otherwise see eye to eye with Mussolini, would have agreed with him in discounting cynically as 'Anglo-Saxon attitudes' that were ridiculous in so far as they were not hypocritical. Nor did Mussolini's own attitude mean that he would let slip any favourable opportunity for fishing in troubled international waters and picking up any unconsidered trifles that he might be able to acquire with a reasonable chance of not being involved in a first-class war.

[1] See *Survey* for 1927, pp. 115–24; *Survey* for 1930, pp. 16–22.
[2] See the study of Mussolini in Sir Arthur Salter's *Personality in Politics* (London, Faber, 1947), pp. 226–38.
[3] See the description of Italian technique in Harold Nicolson's *Diplomacy* (London, Thornton Butterworth, 1939), pp. 151–3.
[4] See *Survey* for 1926, pp. 146, 156 seqq.; *Survey* for 1927, pp. 155–60, 166, 172, 298; *Survey* for 1928, pp. 147–61.
[5] See *Survey* for 1920–3, pp. 348–56.   [6] See *Survey* for 1927, pp. 185–201.

The Nazi Revolution of 1933 did not mark a turning-point in Italian policy. Fascist pressure for treaty revision had left the door open for a *rapprochement* with Germany which became increasingly noticeable after the Nazis' partial election triumph in 1930;[1] but the Italians at first underestimated the powers and ambitions of both Reich and Führer,[2] and Nazi designs on Austria put a serious strain on relations. Mussolini, who had already in 1931 sided with France to oppose an Austro-German Customs Union,[3] formed an 'Italo-Austro-Hungarian Triangle' by means of the Rome Protocols of 17 March 1934.[4] He sent troops to the Brenner frontier after the murder of Dollfuss on 25 July 1934;[5] and joined with Great Britain and France in several attempts to support the independence of Austria and restrain German rearmament, such as the declarations on Austrian independence of 17 February and 27 September 1934,[6] and the Stresa Conference of 11–14 April 1935.[7] These moves, however, did not mean the abandonment of his 'revisionism' or his desire for a European Directory of Four, both of which motives were visible in the original Italian proposal for the Four-Power Pact of 7 June 1933.[8]

It was at this point that Italy came into conflict with the Western Powers.[9] Italian spokesmen were afterwards to assert that the promise of a free hand in Ethiopia had formed an unwritten complement to the Franco-Italian Agreements of 7 January 1935, and even that the Fascist Government had assumed till too late that, as the price of support against Hitler, Great Britain as well as France would condone Italy's action; a misunderstanding alleged to have arisen because the British Prime Minister and Foreign Secretary had given Italy no explicit warning at the Stresa Conference.[10] It is also probable that the Anglo-German naval agreement of 18 June 1935[11] led Mussolini to draw conclusions about the lack of unity between Great Britain and France, and about British consciousness of the growing strength of Germany, which influenced him in favour of risking his war of aggression against Ethiopia and thereafter moving into the German camp.

---

[1] See *Survey* for 1930, pp. 16, 21, 95, 123, 125, 128–30; *Survey* for 1932, p. 260.

[2] See *Survey* for 1933, pp. 198–202; *Survey* for 1934, pp. 328–31.

[3] See *Survey* for 1931, part III A.

[4] See *Survey* for 1934, pp. 487–507; text in *Documents* (R.I.I.A.) for 1933, pp. 396–8.

[5] See *Survey for* 1934, pp. 474 seqq.   [6] See ibid. pp. 442–8, 454–5, 484–7.

[7] See *Survey* for 1935, i. 156–61.

[8] See *Survey* for 1933, pp. 206–20; text in *Documents* (R.I.I.A.) for 1933, pp. 240–9.

[9] Mussolini is reported to have told Hitler at Munich that if the League had imposed oil sanctions he would have been forced to withdraw from Ethiopia in a week (Paul Schmidt: *Statist auf diplomatischer Bühne 1923–45* (Bonn, Athenäum-Verlag, 1949), pp. 342–3, 416).

[10] See *Survey* for 1935, i. 106, 108–9, 109–10, note; Bottai: *Vent' anni*, pp. 124–5; Ciano: *Diario (1937–8)*, 24 December 1938; Gayda in the *Sunday Dispatch*, 26 March 1939; Salter: *Personality in Politics*, pp. 236–7; Massimo Magistrati: 'La Germania e l'impresa italiana di Etiopia', *Rivista di Studi Politici Internazionali*, October–December 1950, pp. 563–606.

[11] See *Survey* for 1935, i. 178–93.

Between 1936 and 1939, against a background of growing tension throughout Europe, attempts were made to patch up relations between Italy and the Western Powers. Mussolini had entered into the Anglo-Italian Agreements of 2 January 1937 and 16 April 1938, but the negotiations begun with France in April 1938 were broken off almost at once, as he would accept no agreement covering Spain or associating France in any way with the Anglo-Italian *modus vivendi*.[1] Irritated by reports that war material was reaching Republican Spain through France, he declared, in his Genoa speech of 14 May 1938, that France and Italy stood 'on opposite sides of the barricades'.[2] Both France and Great Britain had recognized Italian sovereignty over Ethiopia, and the Anglo-Italian Agreement had been brought into force on 16 November 1938; but hopes that this would be the prelude to a general European settlement had not been fulfilled.[3] Mussolini in fact told Ciano at the time that the exchange of ratifications left Fascist policy unchanged. In Europe, it would remain based on the Axis; in the Mediterranean, collaboration with the British would continue as long as possible, but France would remain right outside this, and it was from France that Italy would now make demands[4]—a policy which was revealed to all the world only a fortnight later by Ciano's speech in the Fascist Chamber and by the accompanying vociferations from his audience.[5]

(d) The Rome–Berlin Axis: Italian Hopes and Fears

Meanwhile the Nazis had courted Italy with very different results.[6] Friendly gestures culminated in Ciano's visit to Germany in October 1936, when a secret protocol was signed, co-ordinating policy with regard to a number of current problems,[7] and in Mussolini's reference to the Axis in his Milan speech of 1 November.[8] In the early stages of the *rapprochement*, both Ciano and Attolico, the Italian Ambassador in Berlin, were more effective in promoting the Axis policy than they afterwards were in restraining it, when its dangers became apparent.[9] Italy joined the Anti-Comintern Pact on 6 November 1937,[10] having previously entered into

---

[1] See Ciano: *Diario (1937–8)*, 11 and 30 May 1938; Ciano: *Europa*, pp. 326–7, 337; Eng. version, pp. 211–12, 217–18.

[2] *Survey* for 1938, i. 155.   [3] See ibid. pp. 158–63.

[4] See Ciano: *Diario (1937–8)*, 16 November 1938.

[5] *Survey* for 1938, i. 164–5.

[6] See *Survey* for 1936, pp. 575–83; *Survey* for 1937, i. 28–55, 324–46; see also Elizabeth Wiskemann: *The Rome–Berlin Axis* (London, Oxford University Press, 1949).

[7] The existence of this protocol is revealed in Ciano's conversation with the German Foreign Minister, Neurath, on 21 October 1936 (Ciano: *Europa*, pp. 87–92; Eng. version, pp. 52–55).

[8] See *Survey* for 1936, p. 582.

[9] According to Sir Nevile Henderson (*Water under the Bridges* (London, Hodder & Stoughton, 1945), p. 183) Attolico used to say that Italy would be better off as a good second to Germany than as a bad third in an ineffectual Anglo-Franco-Italian *entente*.

[10] See *Survey* for 1937, i. 43–44, 46 seqq., 301 seqq., 336.

negotiations with Japan for a pact of neutrality and consultation;[1] and she announced her withdrawal from the League of Nations in the following December.[2] Mussolini went to Germany in September 1937; Hitler paid him a return visit in May 1938, and proposed a military assistance pact, which the Duce was not yet ready to accept. Secret economic protocols were concluded on 14 May and 18 December 1937,[3] and the Italian military intelligence service began to supply information to Germany.[4] But, though the two Powers concerted their policy on a number of issues, especially the war in Spain, with regard to many others they acted independently or even competed and intrigued against each other. Each Government had its moments of alarm at the rashness of the other. Indeed, those who watched Germany and Italy from other countries were apt, by turns, to exaggerate either the automatic unity of the partnership or its instability.

Axis solidarity was proclaimed loudly and incessantly in public, while, in conversations between Nazi and Fascist leaders, both sides used the argument that, unless Germany and Italy remained united, the Western Powers would destroy first one and then the other.[5] On the other hand, the slightest hint that Germany might draw closer to Great Britain or France was enough to revive the Fascist Government's fears of isolation;[6] and they were at pains to dissuade Nazi leaders from such a course, one of their more dramatic gambits being Mussolini's present to Hitler in October 1936 of copies of British official documents secretly obtained in London.[7] They also advised against accepting a settlement based on colonies and access to raw materials.[8] The Concert of European Great Powers may still have had its attractions for Mussolini, but the available documents do not show that he made any real effort towards bringing it about.

Long before he had come to power, Hitler had 'conceived a profound admiration for the great man beyond the Alps',[9] and expressed his conviction that so ruthless an enemy of Marxism, freemasonry, and the international press, could not but share his own feelings about 'World Jewry',

---

[1] Dealt with in a later volume of the *Survey* for 1939–46.   [2] *Survey* for 1937, i. 35–36.

[3] For text of second protocol see *D.Ger.F.P.*, series D, i. 142–6.

[4] Evidence of this was produced at the trial, in 1945, of General Roatta, who had been at the head of the Italian military intelligence at the time (see Italian press of 5 January 1945).

[5] e.g. Hitler's conversation with Ciano on 24 October 1936 (Ciano: *Europa*, p. 93; Eng. version, p. 56; cf. *Documents* (R.I.I.A.) for 1939–46, i. 1).

[6] See Ciano: *Europa*, pp. 186–9; Eng. version, pp. 122–4, apropos of a proposal of June 1937 that Neurath should visit London; also a report to Berlin from Hassell, the German Ambassador in Rome, on 31 December 1937, describing Italian reactions to the news that Neurath had called on the French Foreign Minister as the latter passed through Berlin on his way to Eastern Europe (*D.Ger.F.P.*, series D, i. 161–2, and Ciano: *Diario (1937–8)*, 5 December 1937).

[7] See Ciano: *Europa*, pp. 78, note 1, and 94; Eng. version, pp. 46, note 1, and 56.

[8] See Mussolini's conversations with Hans Frank on 23 September 1936, and with Göring on 23 January 1937 (ibid. pp. 75, 79, 129, and 44, 47, 82 respectively).

[9] *Mein Kampf*, p. 774; tr. Murphy, p. 544.

the driving force behind these three evils.[1] Convinced that the most skilful choice of partners for each phase of German expansion was from those states whose interests compelled them to travel the same road for the time being, quite irrespective of whether they were reputed to be heredi- tary 'friends' or 'enemies' of Germany, or of what the next international alinement might be, Hitler had decided on Italy as Germany's only possible ally, other than Great Britain, and had even thought of a German– British–Italian alliance.[2] During the Disarmament Conference crisis in the late autumn of 1933[3] he was already expecting Italy to mediate between him and the Western Powers, because her role in Europe would be ended 'if Germany were condemned to complete impotence',[4] but his decision to side with Italy, not Great Britain, in the Italo-Ethiopian con- flict is reported to have cost him some regrets, and he was not unconscious of the Italians' military and economic shortcomings, or of their lack of enthusiasm for the Axis. He still admired Mussolini,[5] but felt that, if any- thing happened to him, Italian loyalty could not be counted on.[6] A more usual feeling in Germany was to suspect Italian loyalty to an alliance with or without Mussolini, and to pass round the anecdote of the cabaret entertainer who announced the popular waltz 'You Can't Stay True' as the Italian national anthem.

Mussolini, for his part, was morbidly anxious to give the Germans no cause to accuse him of repeating the Italian 'betrayal' of 1915. He was determined to prove that Fascist Italy was 'no longer the Italy of the *combinazioni*, Italy the whore of the democracies'.[7] On the other hand, he had never returned Hitler's admiration. After the Venice meeting in 1934 he had called him an imbecile, and told Badoglio that it was no good working with a man who had talked and talked unceasingly about Austria and letting war loose upon Europe.[8] Hitler cut a shabby figure amid the uniformed pageantry of Fascism on that occasion, but, in September 1937, it was his turn to show off the military and industrial wonders of his régime.[9]

---

[1] *Mein Kampf*, pp. 721 and 519 respectively.

[2] Ibid. pp. 698, 720, 755 and 505, 518, 541 respectively.

[3] See *Survey* for 1933, pp. 291–317.   [4] *N.C.A.* v. 576 (2907–PS).

[5] After Munich Hitler told Attolico that he had only brought himself to endure the hours of negotiation by keeping his eyes fixed on the Duce (Donosti: *Mussolini*, p. 132).

[6] This was one of the reasons for war with Poland that Hitler gave to his Wehrmacht leaders on 22 August 1939 (see *I.M.T. Nuremberg*, xxvi. 338 (798–PS); trans. in *Documents* (R.I.I.A.) for 1939–46, i. 443; cf. *N.C.A.* iii. 581).

[7] Ciano: *Diario (1937–8)*, 16 November 1937; cf. ibid. 7 November 1937, 17 July 1938.

[8] Reynaud: *La France a sauvé l'Europe*, i. 179.

[9] Not long afterwards, Mussolini is reported to have told his Grand Council (when proposing that Italy should withdraw from the League of Nations) that this was the century of the Germans, and that it was evidently better to be with them than against them (see Camillo M. Cianfarra: *The Vatican and the War* (New York, E. P. Dutton, 1945), pp. 109–10). The story lacks confirmation from Ciano, but, even if apocryphal, is extremely characteristic. According to Bottai (*Vent' anni,*

Fascist policy regarding Austria during the last months before the Anschluss certainly suggests that Mussolini had taken to heart his recent experience of Nazi might.[1] As late as 3 May 1937, in a conversation with Neurath, he expressed the hope that, while Austria, being a German state, could, of course, not pursue an anti-German policy, the Agreement of 11 July 1936[2] would none the less allow her to maintain her independence, 'in the shadow of mighty Germany';[3] but he admitted to Ribbentrop on 6 November that he was prepared to let events take their natural course.[4] He did not, however, expect the Nazis to act so soon; and believed that they had promised, in September, both that he would be warned in advance of German intervention,[5] and that the façade of Austrian independence would be maintained.[6]

As for Hitler's next victim, Czechoslovakia, it was made clear to the Germans in May 1938 that her future was a matter of complete indifference to the Italian Government.[7] They would neither hinder nor actively support German designs.[8] Hitler had not expected any objection from them, but it was true that, for the moment at least, the Anglo-Italian Agreement blocked one of the opportunities for an attack on Czechoslovakia discussed by Hitler in November 1937—namely, that Italy should engage both Great Britain and France in war over Spain.[9] However,

pp. 112–13), Ciano went to Berlin hoping to maintain Italy's cherished freedom of manœuvring and came back disappointed, but comforting himself with hopes that Italy would be able to check the revival of Germany and Germanism until she could lead the Latin world in the struggle against them.

[1] See *D.Ger.F.P.*, series D, i. 225–7, 517–18, 533, 537 (no. 315), 542, 570–2 (nos. 348–50), 582–3, 585, 591 (no. 373), 612.   [2] See *Survey* for 1936, pp. 450–6.

[3] Ciano: *Europa*, p. 176; Eng. version, p. 116; cf. *D.Ger.F.P.*, series D, i. 419. For the September stage of Mussolini's progress towards non-interference see ibid. pp. 458–9, 463–4, and Ciano: *Diario (1937–8)*, 24 February 1938.

[4] Ciano: *Europa*, p. 224; Eng. version, p. 146; cf. *Documents* (R.I.I.A.) for 1939–46, i. 25–26. Shortly afterwards Ghigi, the newly appointed Italian Minister to Austria, was told that his role would be that of 'a doctor who must give the dying man oxygen without letting his heir see what is happening. In case of doubt, we are more interested in the heir than in the dying man' (Ciano: *Diario (1937–8)*, 24 November 1937).

[5] Ribbentrop repeated this assurance on 6 November 1937.

[6] See Ciano: *Diario (1937–8)*, 18 February 1938; Massimo Magistrati: 'L'Anschluss austro-tedesco da Berlino', *Rivista di Studi Politici Internazionali*, January–March 1948, pp. 77–106.

[7] See Ciano's statement of 26 May 1938 to the German Ambassador in Rome, Mackensen (*D.Ger.F.P.*, series D, ii. 345–6).

[8] See a minute by Weizsäcker, State Secretary in the German Foreign Ministry, of 12 May 1938 on the results of Hitler's visit to Rome (ibid. i. 1110).

[9] See the 'Hossbach Memorandum' of 10 November 1937 on the conference in the Reichskanzlei of 5 November 1937 (*I.M.T. Nuremberg*, xxv. 402–13 (386–PS); trans. in *D. Ger.F.P.*, series D, i. 29–39; *Documents* (R.I.I.A.) for 1939–46, i. 16–25; cf. *N.C.A.* iii. 295–305). A note by Hitler's adjutant, Schmundt, on some 'observations of the Führer' made in April 1938 suggests that Hitler, before going to Italy, thought of seeking an understanding with Mussolini, in return for supporting Italy's African claims; but documents prepared at the time by the German Foreign Ministry (*D.Ger.F.P.*, series D, i. 1097, 1104, 1110) emphasize the point that Italy was entering a phase of consolidation, and thus stood in no urgent need of Axis support. In the event, the South Tyrol, not Africa, was made the token of German goodwill.

Hitler's own 'Operation Green' directive of 30 May 1938 still counted on Italy's 'unequivocal attitude on our side' as a restraining influence on France.[1] A Luftwaffe directive of 25 August 1938 reckoned Italy among the benevolent neutrals, if war were to break out,[2] but Mussolini, during the September crisis, went so far beyond neutrality in his public and private declarations of solidarity with Germany[3] (while doing very little to enable Italy to honour his promises, had this suddenly been required of her) that he had good reason to be thankful when the Munich Conference offered him the opportunity to escape from this predicament, and even to appear in the gratifying role of mediator between Germany and the West.[4]

Since then Italy had linked herself still more closely with the Axis. Discrimination against Jews, first adopted as a policy in July 1938, was extended. In October Mussolini had not yet been ready to commit himself by accepting German proposals for a military alliance, including Japan, but by the New Year of 1939 he had decided that Italy should enter a tripartite pact to be signed if possible at the end of January. And whereas, before the Nazi Revolution, the well-established power of the Western democracies had held his aggressiveness in check, any signs in 1938–9 that those countries were recovering strength and initiative merely stimulated his desire for an alliance with Germany, not for self-defence (which he himself had admitted was unnecessary), but 'to change the map of the world'.[5]

By this time, the extent of Mussolini's demands itself formed an awkward barrier to a settlement with the Western Powers. Moreover, how might Italy expect to fare as an ally of the Western Powers, in the war which Mussolini now considered inevitable? And would it not be suicide on the part of Fascism to turn the balance of power against Nazism, even supposing this to be possible?

On recent form, Germany was the most promising horse to back and a German victory would have the advantage that the price of Italian help could be paid from newly conquered territory, without Germany having to sacrifice anything she held already. Italy had a contribution to make both in man-power and through her control of the Central Mediterranean and her power to threaten French communications with North Africa; and the recent proposals for an alliance had come from the Nazi side.

---

[1] *I.M.T. Nuremberg*, xxv. 436 (388–PS, item 11); trans. in *D.Ger.F.P.*, series D, ii. 359; *Documents* (R.I.I.A.) for 1939–46, i. 31; cf. *N.C.A.* iii. 317.

[2] *I.M.T. Nuremberg*, xxv. 382 (375–PS); *N.C.A.* iii. 281.

[3] See *Documents on British Foreign Policy 1919–1939*, ed. E. L. Woodward and Rohan Butler. Third series (London, H.M.S.O., 1949), ii. 600 (no. 1186). [This collection will be referred to hereafter as *D.Brit.F.P.*] See also *D.Ger.F.P.*, series D, ii. 670, 804–5, 881–2, 977, 993, and Ciano: *Diario (1937–8)*, 25 September 1938.

[4] See *Survey* for 1938, ii. 427 seqq., also Ciano: *Diario (1937–8)*, 29–30 September 1938.

[5] See Ciano: *Europa*, pp. 373–8, 392–4; Eng. version, pp. 242–6, 258–9; *Documents* (R.I.I.A.) for 1939–46, i. 146–50, 150–2.

Mussolini felt that the existence of the Axis, even without an alliance, had been of value—for instance, in helping to modify British policy towards Italy—and that, both before and during the approaching war, it would provide indispensable protection for Italy's rear. Moreover, he had learnt from Ribbentrop, in October 1938, first that, in return for the two proofs of friendship she had given to Germany, it would be Italy's turn to benefit during the next phase of Axis policy, a phase during which 'all our energies' could be 'directed against the Western Democracies'; and secondly, that Hitler held convenient views about the timing of Axis policy, in that, though he considered that the Axis was ready to fight at once, he did not expect war for the three or four years which he needed to perfect German rearmament.[1]

The Fascist Government were not, however, blind to the fact that Germany was becoming an uncomfortably dynamic and dominant partner. Hitler's unfeigned and lasting gratitude for Mussolini's acceptance of the Anschluss[2] became one of Italy's few assets in dealing with Germany, but the Italian people suffered intense alarm and bewilderment at this shift in the balance of Axis power,[3] and Mussolini had no better consolation for them than to say that 'when an event was fated to happen it is better that it should happen with one's consent than in spite of it'.[4] In October 1938, he had reassured the National Council of the Fascist Party on the subject of Italo-German relations by arguing that Germany had common frontiers with eleven other countries besides Italy, that it was in her interest to be friendly with Italy, and above all, that Pan-Germanism was strictly racial. Hitler had, for instance, told the British at Munich that he would not take a single Czech, no, not for his weight in gold.[5] Much emphasis was laid on the independence of German and Italian spheres of influence. Nazi leaders had repeatedly assured the Fascist Government that the Mediterranean was destined to be an Italian sea and the Alps to be Italy's inviolable northern frontier, even though this involved sacrificing the German minority in the South Tyrol; and Mussolini had himself told Ribbentrop that the focusing of interest on the Mediterranean and overseas colonies had made Sicily the geographical centre of the Empire.[6]

Nevertheless, even if the Italians could rely on Nazi Germany keeping her word, or at least being more tempted to expand to the east and west than to the south, these pledges left a wide debatable land between the Julian Alps, the Carpathians, and the Black Sea, in which Italy as well as

---

[1] Ciano: *Europa*, pp. 373–8; Eng. version, pp. 242–6; *Documents* (R.I.I.A.) for 1939–46, i. 146.
[2] Schmidt: *Statist auf diplomatischer Bühne*, p. 382.
[3] Monroe: *Mediterranean in Politics*, p. 239.
[4] Benito Mussolini: *Scritti e discorsi*, vol. xi (Milan, Hoepli, 1938), p. 226.
[5] See Filippo Giolli: *Come fummo condotti alla catastrofe* (Rome, Editrice Faro, 1945), p. 76.
[6] In their conversation of 6 November 1937; see Ciano: *Europa*, p. 224; *Documents* (R.I.I.A.) for 1939–46, i. 25–26.

Germany had long been interested, and where Germany was now establishing economic and political pre-eminence. German competition had already hindered Italy in recovering her trade with South-Eastern Europe after the removal of sanctions,[1] and a Greater Germany with Danubian and Balkan states in her exclusive orbit could penetrate through the Balkans to Italy's Mediterranean, and, more alarmingly still, through Croatia and Slovenia to the Adriatic. This was a question apt to cause both the Fascist Government and Italian public opinion the most acute anxiety. Hungary merely formed part of the outer zone of Italy's defences, but the very thought of 'a Swastika in the Adriatic' was intolerable.[2]

(e) ITALIAN ATTEMPTS AT A REINSURANCE POLICY

It was perhaps significant that in September 1938 Mussolini had made a tour of Venezia Giulia, including Trieste, and had repeatedly emphasized Italy's good relations with Yugoslavia and the loyalty of the Slovenes in Italy. As in earlier days, he sought for satellites in Danubia and the Balkans, and though these could no longer be marshalled openly against Germany, he hoped to form a group which, while associated with the Axis, would depend more closely on Rome than on Berlin. As Ciano put it on his return from Yugoslavia in January 1939: 45 million Italians, 16 million Yugoslavs, 11 million Hungarians, and 32 million Poles could surely achieve something, between them all.[3] Italian good offices might, it was also hinted, facilitate harmonious relations between Germany and the lesser satellites.

The Italian *rapprochement* with Yugoslavia, towards which Italy had made the first advance with French encouragement as early as the end of 1934, had been consolidated by the pact of 25 March 1937;[4] and close relations were maintained with Hungary after the disappearance of Austria. The Fascist Government intended to complete a 'Rome-Budapest-Belgrade Triangle' by reconciling Yugoslavia and Hungary, and they had hopes, though more remote, of achieving a triangular manœuvre with Hungary and Rumania. The tendency to discourage Hungarian territorial claims against Yugoslavia and Rumania and to support the idea of a common frontier between Hungary and Poland in Sub-Carpathian Ruthenia again brought Italian policy into conflict with Germany.[5] It was hoped that understandings with Hungary, Yugoslavia,

---

[1] See *Survey* for 1937, i. 459–65; *Survey* for 1938, i. 43–69.
[2] See Ciano: *Diario (1939–43)*, 17 March 1939. It was also suspected in Rome that Germany might exploit Hungarian ambitions in the direction of the Adriatic (Ciano: *Diario (1937–8)*, 3 October 1938), or draw the Slavs into an alliance against Italy (ibid. 21 April 1938).
[3] Giolli, op. cit. p. 115.
[4] See *Survey* for 1934, pp. 537–77; *Survey* for 1937, i. 465 seqq.
[5] See also *Survey* for 1938, ii, chapter vii, section v and ibid. iii, part I, section v.

Rumania, and possibly Poland would provide Italy with foodstuffs and raw materials.[1] During 1938, however, trade was hindered by currency difficulties and by changes in economic structure due to Italian autarky and the industrialization of South-Eastern Europe, as well as by German competition.

At the same time Italy had been fostering Yugoslav suspicions of Greece and Turkey, and encouraging Yugoslavia, and probably also Bulgaria, to gravitate towards the Bosporus and Aegean.[2] Support of Yugoslav claims to Salonika was to compensate for Italian pre-eminence in the Adriatic and annexation of Albania. But, though Yugoslavia at this stage was cast for the part of ally, the Croat terrorist leader, Pavelić, was still in Italy, apparently under some form of restraint, and the spring of 1939 was to show how easily the Fascist Government could reverse their policy and begin conspiring with the Croats, as soon as they lost confidence in the Yugoslav Government's attitude towards the Axis.[3]

In the Western Mediterranean Mussolini planned to establish an Italo-Spanish understanding within the framework of the Axis. He meant to back the Nationalists till the Republicans were utterly defeated, and therefore to block any proposal for mediation or a compromise peace. He had no intention of leaving troops in Spain when once the Civil War was over, but he already counted on General Franco as a reliable 'subordinate', and proposed to conclude an alliance, which, in the event of war with France, would secure to Italy the use of naval bases in the Balearics, and of the three airfields which the Italians had themselves constructed there.[4] The secret pact of 28 November 1936[5] already forbade alliances or understandings with hostile third parties and the use of the territory and territorial waters of one party for operations by third parties against the other. Were one of the parties to be involved in a conflict or in collective sanctions, the other would maintain benevolent neutrality and afford trade and transport facilities. The pact also provided for co-ordination of policy, especially in the Western Mediterranean, for mutual assistance, and for co-operation in economic matters. For the time being, Germany and Italy had a common interest in attracting Spain to the Axis for immediate use against France and England, but (besides Italian attempts at reinsurance inside the Axis) points of conflict might arise later, especially in Morocco.

---

[1] See Ciano: *Diario (1939–43)*, 8 January 1939.

[2] Ibid. *(1937–8)*, 24 November 1938; see also the Italo-Yugoslav conversations of 26 March and 6–7 December 1937, 17 June 1938, and January 1939 (Ciano: *Europa*, pp. 158, 233, 330–1, 411; Eng. version, pp. 102–3, 152, 214, 271).

[3] See Ciano: *Diario (1939–43)*, 9 March, 2 April 1939.

[4] Ibid. 8 January, 5 March 1939; Ciano: *Europa*, p. 222; Eng. version, pp. 144–5.

[5] For text see *Documents secrets* (Eristov), vol. iii (*Espagne*), no. 1; trans. in *Documents* (R.I.I.A.) for 1939–46, i. 5–7.

(f) The Personality of Mussolini

Mussolini's eventual adoption of the Axis policy, despite all its dangers and humiliations for Italy, was perfectly in keeping with the curious combination of calculation and impulsiveness in his completely amoral character. He was, it is true, the last man to be carried away by fanatical devotion to Nazism or any other ideology. For him, men and ideas meant little or nothing except in so far as they served or thwarted his own purposes.[1] He was the first to admit the frequent contrasts between his professions as a revolutionary Socialist and his policy as a Fascist dictator.[2] But though there was so much in him of the political soldier of fortune, predatory and unscrupulous, but conscious that his resources were limited, and quick to change his policy as his interests seemed to him to require, this side of his personality was nevertheless often submerged by uncontrollable fancies and ambitions, vitriolic hatreds, and a most childish vanity.[3] It was this Mussolini who told one of his biographers: 'What have I done so far? . . . Order must be given to this nation. Then I shall have accomplished something. Then I shall be somebody. . . . I dream of leaving my mark on Time, like a lion with his claws!'[4] His early struggles left him with a deep grudge against Church, king, and middle class, and with a lifelong tendency to claustrophobia, acquired or aggravated in prison. He never forgave the French for the treatment which Italy received in the peace settlement of 1919–20, or the Greeks for the incompleteness of his triumph in the Corfù incident.[5] His craving for speed and movement was exemplified by the Fascist maxim 'He who stands still is lost', and by his own handling of motor-cars and aircraft. Many of the characteristics which justly made Mussolini's personality alien to non-Italian conceptions of a great national leader were familiar to Italians, who recognized—and, less excusably, accepted—in him a typical inhabitant of the Romagna.[6]

[1] Giuseppe Prezzolini: *Fascism* (London, Methuen, 1926), pp. 61–62. See also D. A. Binchy: *Church and State in Fascist Italy* (London, Oxford University Press for Royal Institute of International Affairs, 1941), pp. 100 seqq.; and the memorandum of 11 February 1925 by Mussolini's former collaborator and subsequent enemy Cesare Rossi, quoted in Gaetano Salvemini: *The Fascist Dictatorship* (London, Cape, 1928), p. 412.

[2] For Mussolini's Socialist period see Gaudens Megaro: *Mussolini in the Making* (London, Allen & Unwin, 1938).

[3] To quote Robert Louis Stevenson's description of the Master of Ballantrae: 'To think that this great force for evil should be swayed by the same sentiment that sets a lassie mincing to her glass.'

[4] Margherita Sarfatti: *Mussolini, l'homme et le chef* (Paris, Albin Michel, 1927), p. 365; Megaro, op. cit. p. 327.   [5] See *Survey* for 1920–3, pp. 348–56.

[6] Mussolini's tendency to rhetoric and his liking for violent action had distinguished the Romagnoli for centuries; and no Italian found any difficulty in understanding the post-war strength of the Communist movement in Emilia. It was considered perfectly natural for the Romagnoli to favour the political party which was most inclined to violence. For twenty years they had been Fascists, in 1951 they were Communists. In addition to a liking for violent action

He boasted freely of his delight in violence for its own sake;[1] if his followers were more violent than he, he was apt to comply with them rather than resist them. He was not always bold in argument with a single person, when he was not sure of having the upper hand, but he took pleasure in bullying the representatives of small nations. His self-confidence expanded in front of a large audience, though insufficient applause was apt to send him away in the sulks, and a show of enthusiasm to give him (expert in mass propaganda though he was) a false idea of public opinion.

What remained constant throughout his career and in all his varying moods was his contempt for his fellow men—not least among them for his fellow Italians, his relish for political and diplomatic methods that were Machiavellian in the more derogatory sense of that word, and his insatiable appetite for power. For wealth, unlike most of the Fascist hierarchy, he cared very little; he had a genuine affection for his family, and the achievements of his régime in public works and public health should not be passed over. But his ruling passion was not to promote the social welfare of the Italian people, but to win glory—in the most benighted traditional meaning of the term—for a deified Italy that was identified in his mind with a deified Benito Mussolini, Duce of the new Roman Empire; statesman, soldier, and athlete; lord of 8 million bayonets and a sky-darkening air force; reclaimer of the Pontine Marshes, and defender of the lira. The Italians were for Mussolini simply the means to Italy's and her Duce's greater advancement, a means which (at least in his later years) he found more and more exasperatingly inadequate.

But the resplendent figure which Mussolini wished to present to the world was, considered from another point of view, only a little journalist from Romagna who had made himself dictator of the weakest of the Great Powers in a period of world crisis, and would fall as rapidly as he had risen, the instant that luck, vitality, or political cunning were to fail him. Already he had begun to fear that one or other of his party comrades might supplant him. Sixteen years of power had increased his megalomania and instability, and impaired his judgement and initiative. Believing himself a great administrator, he pored over routine, and fussed over the baton of a drum-major when the whole machine of government and rearmament needed overhauling.

One reason for his turning to the Axis was that he clung to his dreams of empire as obstinately as the baboon that was trapped by its own grip of the bait. He hoped to support his popularity by offering the Italians

---

Mussolini possessed great oratorical powers, and until his last years he used them in combination with a magnificent voice to great effect. His speeches, when read, contain little meat and consist largely of boastful rhetoric, but their effect was impressive.

[1] See e.g. Mussolini: *Scritti e discorsi*, vi. 66.

national prestige and their share of the loot, and in that way to steal the thunder of the party extremists. A reconciliation with the Western Powers would have been a most distasteful hunk of humble pie, with little advantage for Italy as compared with the danger of estranging Germany, the Power that most alarmed and fascinated the Duce. On the contrary, by the diplomatic sleight-of-hand on which he particularly prided himself, he hoped to make Italy safer inside the Axis than outside. One of his motives for urging Italian intervention in the First World War in 1915 had been that a neutral Italy would have to face the hostility of whichever side won; and he had also thought of war as a means of national regeneration.[1] In 1939 there was good reason to suspect whither 'realism' and his feud with the Western Powers, fear and ambition, the creed of 'dynamism', and his growing inclination to the line of least resistance, would lead him.

(vi) Eastern Europe
By Martin Wight

Eastern Europe in March 1939 was a belt of small countries lying between Germany and Italy on the one side and Russia on the other: a buffer zone along Germany's eastern flank, as Switzerland and the Low Countries and Scandinavia were a buffer zone along her west and north.[2] From the Barents Sea in the north to the Aegean Sea in the south there straggled a line of states, which varied in size, but were all small and weak compared with the Great Powers on the west and the east.[3] At the beginning of March 1939 they numbered fourteen.[4] A year earlier there had been fifteen, but Austria had disappeared under pressure from the West, and under the same pressure, on 15 March 1939, Czechoslovakia dissolved, leaving in its place the doubtfully sovereign successor state of Slovakia. This illustrated the ambiguity of a buffer zone, which may be created as a

---

[1] Emil Ludwig: *Mussolinis Gespräche mit Emil Ludwig* (Berlin, Paul Zsolnay, 1932), pp. 87–88.

[2] See above, pp. 151–2.

[3] Italy had a population of 44 millions; Germany had 69 millions before the Anschluss, 76 millions after it, 80 millions after the annexation of the Sudetenland; the U.S.S.R. had 166 millions. The largest of the states of Eastern Europe was Poland, with about 33 millions; next came Rumania with 18 millions, Czechoslovakia before her partition in 1938–9 with 15 millions, and Yugoslavia with nearly the same. But the numerical balance of nationalities was much more adverse to the peoples of Eastern Europe in their relation to the Great Powers than the numerical balance of the populations of their states. Most of the Eastern European states were not nationally homogeneous, and conversely there were still German minorities outside Germany. There were only about 22 million Poles, 13 million Rumanians, 11 million Yugoslavs (Serbs, Croats, and Slovenes combined), 10 million Czechoslovaks, and 10 million Hungarians. This enumeration omits the largest nationality of Eastern Europe, the 36 million Ukrainians, of whom the great majority were incorporated in the U.S.S.R.

[4] From north to south: Finland, Estonia, Latvia, Lithuania, the Free City of Danzig, Poland, Czechoslovakia, Hungary, Rumania, Yugoslavia, Bulgaria, Albania, Turkey (of which only a fraction lay in Europe), Greece.

MAP OF EASTERN EUROPE

————————	Frontiers March 1939
– – – – –	Frontiers 1919
xxxxxxxx	Curzon Line (showing A & B)
··············	Frontiers of the Munich Settlement 1938
/////////////	Frontiers of Hungary-Croatia and the Dual Monarchy pre 1914

EASTERN EUROPE IN MARCH 1939

barrier or containing wall, but is liable to be transformed, by a political subsidence, from a watershed of power into an extent of low-lying flats, open to inundation by the floods from either side.

This belt of small states had come into existence through the rolling back of previous imperial floods. It was a new aspect of Eastern Europe. In 1914 there had been no such belt; more than half these states had not existed; to the north of the Carpathians the great empires of Germany, Austria-Hungary, and Russia marched together, and it was only in the lower Danube valley and the Balkans that there was a knot of half a dozen small countries forming a buffer zone between Russia and Austria-Hungary on the north and the shrinking Ottoman Empire on the south.[1] A hundred years earlier, at the Peace Settlement of 1815, these too had not existed, and the whole of Eastern Europe from the Gulf of Finland to the island of Crete had been partitioned between Prussia, Russia, Austria, and Turkey.[2] Of these four military empires, only the Austrian and the Ottoman had their historic capitals and centres of gravity within Eastern Europe. For Prussia and Russia, Eastern Europe was a frontier region offering advantages for expansion.[3] The historical retrospect must be carried back half a century before 1815 to catch sight of a purely Eastern European state to the north of the Carpathians, the old kingdom of Poland, still unsubmerged by the advancing tide of the Great Powers. And behind the Prusso-Russian partition of Poland (1772–95) lay the long and brilliant history in which Poland herself had once been a Great Power, had crushed the *Ordensstaat* of the Teutonic Knights, had stretched in union with Lithuania from the Baltic to the Black Sea, had invaded Russia and held Moscow, and had at last surrendered the mastery of the Baltic to a Sweden that was also a Great Power.[4]

[1] The small states of Eastern Europe in 1914 were: Rumania, Serbia, Montenegro, Bulgaria, Albania, Turkey, Greece.

[2] There were three exceptions: the republic of Cracow, a vestige of Poland, neutralized from 1815 till 1846 in the interstice between Russia, Austria, and Prussia; the principality of Montenegro (see below, p. 210, note 2); and the Ionian Islands, conquered from the French by the British in 1809, and a British protectorate from 1815 to 1864. But the history of Eastern Europe had not been as favourable as that of Western Europe to the survival of Lilliputian states on the scale of Cracow, Montenegro, and the Free City of Danzig. Cf. above, p. 152, note 1.

[3] Its attraction was illustrated by two almost simultaneous developments in Prussian and Russian history. In 1701 the Elector Frederick of Brandenburg, when he at last attained royalty, took his kingly title from his duchy of Prussia, because it lay beyond the confines of the Empire, and staged his coronation in the ducal capital of Königsberg. In 1703 the Tsar Peter the Great of Russia founded the city of St. Petersburg on the Gulf of Finland as a new capital to replace Moscow; and the capital was not restored to Moscow until 1918.

[4] Poland was a Great Power from her dynastic union with Lithuania under Wladislaw II Jagellon in 1386, and her consequent defeat of the Teutonic Order at the battle of Tannenberg in 1410, down to her defeat by Gustavus Adolphus of Sweden in the Swedo-Polish War of 1617–29, which ended with the Truce of Altmark, and was the Baltic prelude to Swedish intervention in the Thirty Years War. Sweden was a Great Power from this defeat of Poland, and her consequent intervention in the Thirty Years War, down to her own defeat by Russia in the Great Northern War of 1699–1721. Cf. above, p. 151, note 5.

All this belt of states, then, had come into existence since 1815, and half of them as late as 1918. The First World War, with its prologue in the Balkan Wars of 1912–13, had caused a political rearrangement of Europe on a scale more extensive than any before. Four empires, the Ottoman, the Romanov, the Habsburg, the Hohenzollern, had collapsed. Seven new sovereign states appeared in Eastern Europe. Finland,[1] Estonia,[2] and Latvia[3] had never before been independent states. Albania had nominally become an independent state in 1912 through the First Balkan War, but in 1918 her independence was still to be established and her frontiers still to be defined.[4] Lithuania,[5] Poland,[6] and Czechoslovakia[7]

---

[1] The pagan barbarian Finns were conquered by the Swedes in 1154. Finland remained part of the kingdom of Sweden until 1809, when it was ceded to Russia under the Treaty of Frederiks-hamn. It was an autonomous grand duchy connected with Russia until 1917 when it declared itself an independent republic; formal recognition of its independence was granted by Soviet Russia in January 1918 (*H.P.C.* vi. 287).

[2] The pagan barbarians of Estonia were conquered by the Danes from 1219 onwards. The province was sold by Denmark to the Teutonic Order in 1346. It was annexed by Sweden from the Teutonic Order in 1561, and ceded by Sweden to Russia under the Treaty of Nystadt in 1721. It declared itself an independent republic in 1917; its independence was recognized by Soviet Russia in the Treaty of Dorpat of 1920 (ibid. vi. 295; *Survey* for 1920–3, p. 240).

[3] Latvia approximately covered the former provinces of Livonia and Courland, which were conquered from their pagan barbarian inhabitants by the Teutonic Order from 1158 onwards, and were ceded to Poland in 1561. Livonia was ceded by Poland to Sweden under the Treaty of Altmark in 1629, and by Sweden to Russia under the Treaty of Nystadt in 1721, an indicator of the transference of Baltic ascendancy between these three Powers. Courland was a duchy under Polish suzerainty from 1561 to 1795, when Russia annexed it in the Third Partition of Poland. Latvia declared itself an independent republic in 1918; its independence was recognized by Soviet Russia in the Treaty of Riga of 1920 (ibid.).

[4] From the seventh to the fourteenth centuries Albania was variously under the rule of the Bulgarian, Byzantine, and Serbian Empires, and of Latin princes. There was a period of dis-united native rule from 1359 to 1392, when Albania was conquered by the Turks. Albania declared its independence of Turkey in 1912 during the First Balkan War; see below, pp. 250–1.

[5] Lithuania was the last heathen Power in Europe before the twentieth century. It was converted to Christianity in 1386 when its grand duke became king of Poland, and remained united with Poland until it was annexed by Russia in the partitions of Poland. It negotiated its independence with Germany, as occupying Power, in 1917–18; its independence was recognized by Soviet Russia in the Treaty of Moscow, 1920 (*H.P.C.* vi. 302–5; *Survey* for 1920–3, p. 251).

[6] Poland was one of the members of Western Christendom from the tenth century, first as a duchy and from 1300 as a kingdom. It was successively partitioned between Russia, Prussia, and Austria in 1772, 1793, and 1795. With the exceptions of the Napoleonic grand duchy of Warsaw (1807–14), the nominally autonomous 'Congress' kingdom of Poland under the Tsar (1815–31), and the republic of Cracow (1815–46), there was no Polish state from 1795 till the declaration of an independent Polish republic in 1918. The independence of Poland was recognized by Soviet Russia in the Treaty of Riga of 1921 (*H.P.C.* vi. 322).

[7] Bohemia, with its dependencies of Moravia, Silesia, and Lusatia, was a member of Western Christendom from the ninth century, acknowledged the suzerainty of the Empire from 950, finally became a kingdom in 1198, and developed into one of the seven original electorates of the Empire. In 1526, by the election of a Habsburg as Bohemian king, it was finally united dynastic-ally with Austria. After the Bohemian revolt of 1618 had been crushed at the battle of the White Mountain in 1620, Bohemia was deprived of its independence as an elective monarchy in 1621 and merged for 300 years into the hereditary Habsburg dominions. Slovakia had been included in the Bohemian-Moravian state in the ninth century, but at the end of that century was con-quered by the Magyars and remained for 900 years incorporated in Hungary. Czechoslovak

were reattaining independent statehood after a long disappearance. Rumania,[1] Yugoslavia,[2] and Greece[3] were expanding towards the fulfilment of a national self-determination that was only a century old. Austria and Hungary were by the same process being forcibly reduced from imperial into national states, and Hungary was simultaneously recovering an independent national existence;[4] Bulgaria was being shorn of

union and independence were established simultaneously in 1918 (ibid. iv. 105–6, 112–14, 261–5, 270).

[1] The Rumanian principalities of Wallachia and Moldavia grew up on the frontier of Eastern Christendom in the thirteenth century. Wallachia was made tributary to the Turks in 1391, Moldavia in 1513; and they remained the only parts of Eastern Christendom (Russia apart) which were not formally annexed to the Ottoman Empire. By the Treaty of Paris in 1856 they were placed under the guarantee of the Great Powers, and Turkish suzerainty became only nominal. In 1859 they united *de facto*, in 1862 *de jure*, to form the principality of Rumania. Its independence was recognized by the Treaty of Berlin in 1878, and in 1881 it became a kingdom.

[2] The duchy of Croatia grew up on the Adriatic frontier of Western Christendom in the ninth century, became a kingdom in 924, and was united dynastically with Hungary in 1102, remaining so for 800 years. Serbian principalities grew up on the corresponding frontier of Eastern Christendom from the ninth century; a kingdom of Serbia uniting them was established in 1217; it became the dominant Power of Eastern Christendom under Stephen Dushan (1331–55) who assumed the imperial title in 1346. In 1389 Serbia was conquered by the Turks at the battle of Kosovo; it remained tributary till 1459 when it was reduced to a pashalik. The prince-bishopric of Montenegro alone maintained a desperate and uncertain independence from the Turks, in tenuous continuity with the Old Serb kingdom of Zeta. The Serbian War of Independence in 1804–13 brought the grant of a limited autonomy by the Treaty of Bucharest in 1812. This autonomy was gradually enlarged until the independence of Serbia was recognized by the Treaty of Berlin in 1878; in 1882 it became a kingdom, and Montenegro followed suit in 1910. In 1918 Serbia and Croatia united to form the Serb-Croat-Slovene kingdom, and were joined by Montenegro (*H.P.C.* iv. 112–14, 196–204).

[3] Greek national consciousness was based on the tradition of the Byzantine Empire, the original and presiding Power of Eastern Christendom, which was destroyed by the Western Crusaders in 1204, and after an imperfect restoration was finally conquered by the Turks in 1453 (see William Miller in *Byzantium*, ed. Norman H. Baynes and H. St. L. B. Moss (Oxford, Clarendon Press, 1948), pp. 326–9). The Greek War of Independence of 1821–9 led to the establishment of an independent Greek kingdom by the Treaty of London of 1832—the earliest of the Ottoman Empire's successor states.

[4] Hungary became a member of Western Christendom at the end of the tenth century, and a kingdom in 1001. In the twelfth century it was engaged in struggle with the Byzantine Power in the south, and in the fifteenth century with its successor the Turkish Power. In 1526 Hungary was conquered by the Turks at the battle of Mohács. It was consequently partitioned into three: three-quarters of Hungary was occupied and annexed by the Turks; Transylvania became a semi-independent principality under Turkish suzerainty; the nominal Hungarian crown, together with the north-western fringe of Hungary, for which tribute was paid to the Turks, passed in 1526–7 to the Habsburgs. In the war of 1683–99 which ended with the Treaty of Karlowitz, Austria reconquered Hungary and imposed suzerainty on Transylvania. In 1687 Hungary was changed from an elective into a hereditary monarchy; by the Pragmatic Sanction of 1723 it was declared an integral part of the Habsburg dominions; in 1849 it was administratively amalgamated with the Austrian Empire. By the *Ausgleich* of 1867 the Austrian Empire was transformed into the Dual Monarchy of Austria-Hungary: Hungary became a sovereign state equal with the Austrian half of the monarchy, united thereto by the dynasty and by the common services for foreign policy, finance, and war, but otherwise independent; home rule was granted by Hungary to Croatia, but Transylvania was reduced to an integral part of Hungary. The abdication of the last Habsburg in November 1918 made Hungary for the first time since 1526 a fully independent state (*H.P.C.* iv. 118–19, 487–8).

territory as the price of defeat.[1] The final destruction of the Ottoman
Empire in Europe had been accomplished in the two Balkan Wars of
1912–13; it was now confirmed, at the same time as the remainder of the
Ottoman Empire dissolved in Western Asia, by the creation of a national
Turkey.[2] The most ephemeral among these national revenants or new
arrivals was the Ukraine, which appeared as an independent state from
the ruins of the Russian Empire, existed for less than a year under the
shadow of Germany's eastern conquests, and was then swallowed up again
in the Russian Power as a member of the Soviet Union—tracing a path
which was to be followed or approached within a generation by most of
the other successor states of Eastern Europe.[3]

(a) National Conflicts

The territorial revolutions of Europe before 1918 normally diminished
the numbers of states and increased their size by annexations or mergers,

[1] Bulgaria was a member of Eastern Christendom from the ninth century, and at two periods,
from 893 to 972, and again from 1186 to 1258, it became the dominant Power of Eastern Christendom. It was conquered by the Turks in 1393. As a result of the revolutionary movement which
culminated in the outbreak of 1875 and the Russo-Turkish War of 1877–8, the Treaty of Berlin
of 1878 established Bulgaria and Eastern Rumelia as two autonomous provinces tributary to the
Turks. In 1885 the two provinces established a united principality of Bulgaria. In 1908 Bulgaria
proclaimed its complete independence as a kingdom.

[2] The European frontier, i.e. Eastern Thrace up to the Maritsa, which was attained by Turkey
in the Treaty of Lausanne of 1923 (*H.P.C.* vi. 108–9), was virtually the same as that she won for
herself from Bulgaria in the Third Balkan War and confirmed by the Treaty of Constantinople
of 29 September 1913 (*British and Foreign State Papers*, cvii. 706–21).

[3] Ukrainian national consciousness in its extreme form is based on the memory of the principality of Kiev, which was converted to Orthodoxy at the end of the tenth century and became the
original Power of Russian Christendom. In 1240 it was conquered by the Mongols. The principality of Galicia or Red Russia remained the only autonomous representative of the future
Ukraine, until it was annexed by Poland in 1349. Lithuania extended its frontiers to the mouth
of the Dnieper in 1363; in 1386 it united with Poland, and thus the greater part of the Ukraine
was incorporated in the Polish kingdom. In the sixteenth century Cossack communities grew
up on the Dnieper, becoming the nucleus of the new Ukrainian nation. They developed into
a semi-independent Power, and transferred their allegiance from Catholic Poland to the
Orthodox Moscow Tsar by the Pereyaslavl Agreement of 1653. By the Treaty of Andrusovo
of 1667 Poland and Russia partitioned the Ukraine along the Dnieper line. After Pugachev's
rebellion of 1773–4, the Russian Government deprived the Cossacks of their liberties in 1775, and
in 1781 Little Russia, i.e. left-bank Ukraine or the Ukraine east of the Dnieper, was absorbed
administratively into the Russian Empire. In 1793 Russia acquired right-bank Ukraine by the
Second Partition of Poland. In November 1917 the Ukraine declared its independence; this was
recognized by the Central Powers on 1 February 1918, and on 8 February by the first Treaty of
Brest-Litovsk the Ukraine became their economic protectorate. In the anarchy following the
German evacuation in 1919 a Ukrainian Soviet Republic was consolidated, which became in
1923 the second largest and most important constituent of the Soviet Union.

'It is hardly possible then to discuss the question of a distinctive "Ukrainian" nationality and
its origins, before a peculiar combination of historical factors operating between 1590 and 1700
produced a community on the borderland of the Polish realm which became united by common
economic and political circumstances, the vast majority of whose members confessed the Orthodox Greek faith, and which made use of a form of Russian speech—itself continuously subject to
modification and adaptation in accord with the circumstances of day-to-day social and economic life' (W. E. D. Allen: *The Ukraine: a History* (Cambridge University Press, 1940), p. 65).

and the most notable triumphs of the national principle, the union of Italy by Piedmont and of Germany by Prussia, also had this effect. There was no precedent for the creation of half a dozen new small states, suddenly, simultaneously, and *ex nihilo*. The Peace of Westphalia in 1648 created two new sovereign states by recognizing the Swiss Confederation's independence from the Empire and the United Provinces' independence from Spain, but this was the formal recognition of long-established facts. The Treaty of Berlin in 1878 also created two new sovereign states, Serbia and Rumania, laying as well the foundations of a third in Bulgaria, and this was the most important stage in the fragmentation of Eastern Europe before its climax in 1918; but Serbia and Rumania were already thriving autonomous principalities before their independence was recognized, unlike any of the new states of 1918 with the doubtful exception of Finland. The nearest analogy to the multiplication of states in 1918 was the attainment of legal independence by the states of Germany when the Holy Roman Empire was abolished in 1806.[1] But this gave juridical sanction to an independence which they had already possessed in fact since the Westphalian settlement of 1648; moreover, it was part of a process that was already driving them into a new and stricter dependence upon France, through the creation and extension of the Confederation of the Rhine. Cut adrift from a conservative Great Power, the small states were immediately swept under the harsher protection of a revolutionary Great Power. In Eastern Europe in the twentieth century the same process was at work, but was spread over thirty years. For here the ground had been more completely cleared than in Western Europe at the beginning of the nineteenth century. The successor states of Eastern Europe owed their existence to a unique circumstance, the destruction or disablement of all the adjacent Great Powers, and they remained independent only until Germany and Russia resumed their ineluctable predominance.

If this was the condition for the establishment of the successor states, the cause lay in the extreme doctrine of nationality, that a common language meant a single nation, and that every nation had the right to form a single independent state. The rearrangement of Eastern Europe in 1918 was the most extensive triumph of national self-determination, and was to provide the classic example of its limitations. When the Western European creed of linguistic nationalism was carried into Eastern Europe, it came to a region whose national groupings had not undergone the historical develop-

---

[1] Sixteen German states were original members of the Confederation of the Rhine; twenty-six originally outside it; see Albert Sorel: *L'Europe et la Révolution Française*, vii. 52–53. By the Act of the Confederation of the Rhine on 17 July 1806 the sixteen signatories seceded from the Empire; Napoleon then declared that he no longer recognized its existence, and on 6 August Francis II abdicated the imperial dignity. The Confederation of the Rhine was eventually joined by every German state except Austria, Prussia, Hesse-Cassel, and Brunswick (James Bryce: *The Holy Roman Empire*, new edition, revised (London, Macmillan, 1904), p. 409, note l).

ment and discipline which in the west had produced the nationalist creed itself. Stable nationality had been the product of slow growth and favourable conditions. Every nation had a fringe, however small, of partially assimilated elements which in other circumstances might adhere to other nations; and conversely, it had proved possible in Western Europe, in the histories of Switzerland and Belgium, for a purely political nationality to be created out of linguistically heterogeneous elements. But in other historical conditions, linguistic nationalism offered the possibility of breaking up nations into their component elements, and either keeping them separate or putting them together again in different combinations.

The history of Eastern Europe had been unfavourable to the development of stable nationality for the very reason that the history of Western Europe had been favourable. Western Europe, in the farthest extremities of the European peninsula, was sheltered and insulated by Eastern Europe, whose history was punctuated by the flow of invasions from the east and their reflux from the west. For Eastern Europe lies across the neck of the European peninsula between the Baltic and the Black Sea; the Baltic coasts are a section of the great plain that stretches from the Rhine delta, scarcely interrupted by the Urals, to Siberia; and the Danubian basin, though partially sheltered by the Carpathians, is the terminus of the steppes that stretch through Central Asia and the Zungarian Gate to Mongolia. Along these avenues came the successive migrations that subverted and replenished the civilizations of the Mediterranean and Europe. Within the lifetime of Christendom Western Europe had been sheltered from the onslaughts of the Mongols and the Turks, because Eastern Europe had taken the brunt of them;[1] and the Tatar invasion governed the historical development of Russia as the Turkish invasion governed the historical development of the Balkans and the Danubian basin. Within the same span Eastern Europe had undergone continuous pressure from the stronger societies of the west, invasions that were slower but more deeply penetrating than the nomadic irruptions from Asia. Polish eastward expansion had conditioned the history of Lithuanians, White Russians, and Ukrainians; German eastward expansion had conditioned the history of the Poles themselves, the Baltic peoples, Czechs, Slovaks, Magyars, Yugoslavs, and Rumanians; Scandinavian eastward expansion had conditioned the history of the Finns, the Baltic peoples, and of the earliest Russian state.

Eastern Europe was divided into two regions by the Carpathians: to the north the Baltic basin, to the south the Danubian basin with its Balkan appendage. Each had its subdivisions, but there was the general difference between them that south of the Carpathians there were natural

---

[1] 'It is hardly an exaggeration to say that the civilization of Western Europe is a by-product of the Byzantine Empire's will to survive' (Norman Baynes, in *Byzantium*, ed. Baynes and Moss, p. xxxi).

frontiers that might have provided the moulds for national communities, in the Baltic region there was none. The Powers that had grown up on this unvaried plain—the *Ordensstaat* of the Teutonic Knights, Lithuania, Poland, the Swedish Empire, Prussia—had fluctuated wildly in extent, having no frontiers save where their colonists could be planted or where their armies stood. The oscillation of the Polish-Soviet War of 1920, which first took Pilsudski's armies into Kiev, then brought the Red Army antistrophically to the gates of Warsaw, and finally carried the returning Polish forces to rest along the Riga Line which became the Polish eastern frontier, was only the most recent illustration in 1939 of this principle,[1] providing the most conspicuous contradiction of the nationalistic principle that was the basis of the new settlement.

South of the Carpathians there were natural frontiers and geographical units. Bohemia was compact within its quadrangle of mountains, though Moravia lay open to the south-east through Lower Austria. Great Hungary with its back against the curve of the Carpathians and facing south across the Save was a geographical unit comparable to France with its back to the Atlantic and its face towards the Rhine.[2] Transylvania was made by nature for a lovelier Switzerland, and had in the seventeenth century played such a role; the Rumanian principalities lay like another Low Countries at the mouths of the Danube; the Mediterranean peninsula of Greece was a second Italy. But none of these corresponded with a national bloc. Bohemia and Moravia contained a population two-thirds Czech, a third German; of Great Hungary only half the population had been Magyar; Transylvania contained half Rumanians, a third Magyars, and the rest Germans; the Rumanian principalities failed to include one-third of the Rumanian nation.[3]

Not only were there minorities. There were also sub-nationalities, potential nations whose inclusion in larger national states in 1919 or whose erection into separate states were equally the source of political difficulties. Such were the Austrians in relation to the Germans. Such were the Slovaks in relation to the Czechs.[4] Such, according to many Poles, were the Lithu-

[1] *H.P.C.* vi. 274-8, 318-22. The great historical example of this Polish-Russian dialectic was the Hundred Years War that ruined the old Polish kingdom. It carried Ivan the Terrible to the shores of the Baltic in the Livonian War of 1558-83; it then brought Poland back in an attempt to conquer Russia during the Muscovite Time of Troubles (1603-13) which culminated in the Polish occupation of Moscow in 1610-12; it finally took Russia advancing westwards again in her first annexation of Polish territory under the Treaty of Andrusovo in 1667, which was the precursor of the Polish partitions.

[2] 'If Hungary had been ruled by national Kings in the seventeenth, eighteenth, and nineteenth centuries, she might well have solved her national problem as completely as France did' (C. A. Macartney: *Hungary and her Successors* . . . *1919–1937* (London, Oxford University Press for Royal Institute of International Affairs, 1937), p. 35; cf. p. 487).

[3] In 1914 the population of Rumania was 7 millions, and there were nearly 3½ million Rumanians in Hungary.

[4] *H.P.C.* iv. 245-8, 270; Macartney: *Hungary and her Successors*, pp. 94–110.

anians in relation to the Poles.[1] The South Slavs, who were distributed in
a belt south of the Danube from the Black Sea coast to the Julian Alps,
were a spectrum of intermerging sub-nationalities: Bulgarians, Macedonians, Montenegrins, Serbs, Croats, Slovenes. The two states that became
established after 1919, Bulgaria and a Serbia enlarged to include the
remainder of the South Slavs, showed the chief lines of linguistic division.
But Macedonia, where the South Slavs intermingled with the non-Slav
Greeks and Albanians, remained a spiritual *terra nullius*, a land of contention between Yugoslavia and Greece, who divided the greater part of it
between them, Bulgaria, who had historic claims to it, and Albania,
because a third of the Albanian nation lived there:[2] a province which
other Powers had a continual interest in inflating into an independent
state. The possibility of regrouping the South Slavs was the main origin
of the continual projects for a Balkan federation. Yet in Macedonia, more
clearly than anywhere in the Balkans, nationalist categories were irrelevant
to the life of the people. 'Macedonian peasants describe themselves as
Turks, Greeks, Bulgarians or Serbs according to political circumstances,
and no one knows what the truth is, not even the peasants themselves.'[3]

The largest example of a sub-nationality was afforded by the Ukrainians
or Ruthenes in relation to the Great Russians. North of the Carpathians
the Ukraine was a greater and more dangerous political counterpart to
Macedonia. It was a submerged nation, politically visible in the second
largest constituent republic of the U.S.S.R., but running far out westwards
beneath the frontiers of the Versailles states, comprising two-thirds of
Poland east of the Curzon Line and a sixth of Poland's total population,
lapping over the Carpathian watershed towards the Danube in the
northern fringe of Slovakia itself and in Carpatho-Ruthenia, which was
the caudal appendage of Czechoslovakia, and interpenetrating with the
Rumanian provinces of Bukovina and Bessarabia.[4] Yet there were almost

---

[1] *H.P.C.* vi. 278–9; *The Cambridge History of Poland*, ed. W. F. Reddaway, J. H. Penson,
O. Halecki, R. Dyboski, vol. ii (Cambridge University Press, 1941), pp. 522–4; Walter Kolarz:
Myths and Realities in Eastern Europe (London, Drummond, 1946), pp. 108–10. Lithuanian was
a totally different language from Polish, but the Polish case for federating or incorporating
Lithuania with Poland was based on the tradition of the Polish-Lithuanian Union preceding the
partitions of Poland.

[2] The population of Albania was just under one million. The Albanian minority in Yugoslav
Macedonia just across the frontier was nearly half a million.

[3] Hugh Seton-Watson: *Eastern Europe between the Wars, 1918–1941* (Cambridge University
Press, 1945), p. 311. Cf. H. N. Brailsford: *Macedonia* (London, Methuen, 1906), pp. 99–103, and
Elisabeth Barker: *Macedonia: its Place in Balkan Power Politics* (London, Royal Institute of Inter-
national Affairs, 1950), pp. 9–12.

[4] At the beginning of 1939 the distribution of Ukrainians in Europe was approximately as
follows: in the U.S.S.R. (primarily in the Ukrainian S.S.R.), 31 millions; in Poland, 5 millions;
in Rumania, half a million; in Czechoslovakia, half a million; in Hungary (as a result of the first
partition of Czechoslovakia), 38,000. See *Bulletin of International News*, 14 January 1939, p. 5,
with correction on p. 13, and C. A. Macartney: *National States and National Minorities* (London,
Oxford University Press for Royal Institute of International Affairs, 1934), appendix iii.

as many gradations of Ukrainian national consciousness as of South Slav. Eastern Galicia was the centre of the most Westernized and anti-Russian Ukrainian national movement, which had formerly been encouraged by Austria-Hungary to embarrass Russia. The Ukrainian peasants of Volhynia and Rumania were pro-Russian. 'Even so, there remained in the Polish–Russian borderlands numbers of peasants without clearly defined national character, who described themselves as "people from here" (*tutejszi*).'[1] Those of Carpatho-Ruthenia were non-national and partly Magyarized, as unconcerned whether the Ruthenes were to be identified with Ukrainians as the East Galician nationalists were indignant if Ukrainians were identified with Great Russians.[2] The Ruthenians, along with the White Russians,[3] were the only Eastern European nationalities at the disposal of the Paris Peace Conference which were regarded as so backward politically that they could not be erected into states but must be placed under tutelage. Therefore Carpatho-Ruthenia was given to Czechoslovakia,[4] and the Great Powers recognized Poland's seizure of East Galicia and her acquisitions at the expense of Soviet Russia.[5] Poland dishonoured her obligation to grant autonomy to East Galicia; Czechoslovakia with some reason postponed the fulfilment of hers towards Carpatho-Ruthenia.

The eastward expansion of Western Christendom from the eighth to the fourteenth centuries had created in Eastern Europe a social stratification along lines of linguistic nationality. There was a widespread German bourgeoisie, and in parts a Polish or Magyar aristocracy, which were alien in speech and culture from the peasantry. There were in consequence many great cities different in nationality from the countrysides in which they stood. Danzig was a German port for a Polish hinterland, Memel a German port for a Lithuanian and White Russian hinterland. Vilna was disputed between Lithuania and Poland because Lithuanians predominated in the surrounding province and Poles in the city itself; but the argument really lay between two non-Western and therefore in Western eyes inferior peoples, for Lithuanians and Poles together were outnumbered in the city by Jews, and in the region round by White Russians.[6] Lwów,

---

[1] H. Seton-Watson: *Eastern Europe*, pp. 321–2.

[2] 'Ruthenus' was a medieval Latinization of the Russian name. It was officially adopted for the Ukrainians of Austria and Hungary by the Austrian Constitution of 1849 (Allen: *Ukraine*, p. 248). On the development of the Ruthene question see Macartney: *Hungary and her Successors*, pp. 206–11.

[3] The White Russians of Eastern Europe, like the Ukrainians, were potentially a *terra irredenta* of a constituent republic of the Soviet Union. At the beginning of 1939 there were approximately 5½ million White Russians in the White Russian S.S.R; 1½ million in Poland; 36,000 in Latvia; 4,000 in Lithuania.   [4] *H.P.C.* iv. 272–3.

[5] Ibid. vi. 283, note.

[6] See *Survey* for 1920–3, p. 255, note 2, and *The Baltic States*, prepared by the Information Department of the Royal Institute of International Affairs (London, Oxford University Press for Royal Institute of International Affairs, 1938), p. 89, note 3. The Lithuanian claim to Vilna

once Lemberg, the capital of East Galicia, gave Poland her best claim to that province, since it was a Polish island in a Ukrainian sea. In the industrial region of Upper Silesia, on the other hand, the towns were largely German, the countryside largely Polish. Trieste was an Italian port with a Slovenian hinterland, Fiume an Italian port with a Croatian hinterland—the Danzig and Memel of the Adriatic.[1] The same principle was illustrated by the great Danubian metropolis of Vienna itself, which had never produced a native Austrian bourgeoisie, and in the last half century of the Habsburg Monarchy had instead acquired one predominantly composed of Jews.[2] These towns were incapable of being fitted into a framework of national states without social mutilation: like the Hellenistic cities, their only happy political setting was that of an oecumenical empire. Since they could be claimed on national grounds with equal plausibility or lack of it by two contestants, they were among the most acute causes of international conflict. And Vienna, which pre-eminently among East European cities had had its international character guaranteed for many centuries as a great imperial capital, was the source of a form of social conflict more corroding and insidious than international war, the anti-Semitism that Hitler had learned from Schönerer and Lueger and taken to Berlin to become the central feature in the policy of the German Government.

The same mingling of peoples that could combine provinces of one nationality with capitals of another produced also national leaders of different origin from the nations they championed. The social anomaly of great men who are in origin peripheral to the society they dominate, as Napoleon was a Corsican and Stalin a Georgian, had many examples in Eastern Europe. Kemāl Atatürk was of Albanian and Macedonian descent,[3] Pilsudski of Lithuanian. The Hungarian Prime Minister Gömbös 'was of German origin, and caused some amusement by his unsuccessful attempts to prove a Hungarian noble pedigree'.[4] His successor Imrédy, who made anti-Semitism a legislative programme in Hungary, was compelled to resign in February 1939 when confronted with the

rested principally on historical grounds, however, since Vilna had been the capital of Lithuania down to the Union of Lublin in 1569.

[1] Smyrna at the end of the First World War just failed by the numerical test to repeat this pattern as the Greek port for a Turkish hinterland, though in everything except numbers the Greeks there predominated over the Turks (see A. J. Toynbee: *The Western Question in Greece and Turkey* (London, Constable, 1922), pp. 133–4). This was before the Turks had driven out the Greeks in the Anatolian War of 1919–22.

[2] See Franz Borkenau: *Austria and After* (London, Faber, 1938), pp. 93–102.

[3] On the resemblance between Atatürk and Venizelos, who was born an Ottoman subject in Crete, see the *Survey* for 1930, p. 167. A critic has commented at this point: 'The test of Ottoman Turkish nationality was linguistic and cultural, not strictly racial. Atatürk was not felt to be "peripheral" any more than we felt Lloyd George, Bonar Law and Ramsay MacDonald to be peripheral.'

[4] H. Seton-Watson: *Eastern Europe*, p. 193.

evidence that he derived from a Jewish great-grandfather.[1]   The Slovak leader Tuka, for many years the most influential figure of the Slovak People's Party after its founder Hlinka, was a renegade Hungarian who had learned Slovak when approaching middle age.[2]   The romantic Codreanu, founder of the Iron Guard and extoller of Rumanian nationalism, was of Ukrainian and German descent with the real name of Zilinsky.[3] His Hungarian counterpart Szálasi, leader of the Hungarian Nazis and champion of Magyar racial purity, was of mixed Armenian, Slovak, and German origin.[4]   The elevation of the Vienna destitute and 'Bohemian corporal'[5] to the supreme power in the German Reich was only the most distinguished Eastern European example, and the least extreme or ridiculous, of a national leader having begun as a frontiersman or an alien.[6]

There ran through Eastern Europe, however, an older and deeper division than the divisions of nationality. For the neck of land between the Baltic, the Adriatic, and the Black Sea was the region of the historic frontier between Western Christendom and the two Eastern Christendoms of Byzantium and Russia; and there still lay across it, beneath the political frontiers, the line between Catholics and Protestants on the one side and the Orthodox Churches on the other.[7]   This cultural and religious frontier

[1] See Elizabeth Wiskemann: *Undeclared War* (London, Constable, 1939), p. 22.

[2] See H. Seton-Watson: *Eastern Europe*, p. 410; R. W. Seton-Watson: *A History of the Czechs and Slovaks* (London, Hutchinson, 1943), p. 334. Tuka was a marginal example of the type, for he probably never genuinely exchanged his Magyar for a Slovak national loyalty. For contrasted views of his trial for treason in 1929, see R. W. Seton-Watson, op. cit. p. 335, and Macartney: *Hungary and her Successors*, pp. 132, 140.

[3] See Wiskemann: *Undeclared War*, p. 55; *Survey* for 1937, i. 424.

[4] Wiskemann: *Undeclared War*, p. 16.

[5] This was Hindenburg's phrase for Hitler before the Nazi Revolution (J. W. Wheeler-Bennett: *Hindenburg: the Wooden Titan* (London, Macmillan, 1936), p. 407).

[6] Cf. Macartney: *National States and National Minorities*, p. 10. 'The immensely complicated problem of nationality in this area is well illustrated by a story which is supposed to have occurred at Geneva in 1924. The League was discussing a minorities question, and someone suggested that, as between Greece and Albania, language was the true criterion; that is to say, the language which a man spoke in his own home. It then transpired that the rulers of these two countries each belonged, by this criterion, to his opponents' country; Bishop Fan Noli, then Prime Minister of Albania, was said to speak Greek at home (though he is the greatest living Albanian scholar), while the President of the Greek Republic, Admiral Kondouriotis, a member of one of the Albanian families long settled in Hydra, habitually spoke Albanian in his own home circle' (Vandeleur Robinson: *Albania's Road to Freedom* (London, Allen & Unwin, 1941), p. 35).

[7] The frontier had indefinable salients eastwards in the Uniat or Greek Catholic Churches, which had reunited with the Holy See while retaining the Byzantine rite. These were among the conquests of the Counter-Reformation. The two most important were the Ruthenian Catholic Church, which was created at the Synod of Brest in 1596 as an instrument of Polish ecclesiastical imperialism in the Orthodox provinces of Poland, and the Rumanian, which was created by the Synod of Alba Julia in 1698 to serve a similar purpose for the Habsburgs in Transylvania (for the latter see R. W. Seton-Watson: *A History of the Roumanians* (Cambridge University Press, 1934), pp. 124–5). They soon became limited to the subject nations, distinguishing them from their Polonized Catholic or Magyarized Calvinist governing classes. They were thus, like the Orthodox Churches themselves, authentic expressions of the Ukrainian and Rumanian nations, and had an important role in the nationalist movements, but were correspondingly weakened

passed approximately down the eastern or Russian frontiers of the four Baltic States; bisected Poland along the Curzon Line,[1] which was the only part of this frontier to have been delimited by an international authority; separated Carpatho-Ruthenia from Slovakia; followed the frontier between Hungary and Rumania; and then cut through northern Yugoslavia in the arc that divided the Catholic Croats from the Orthodox Serbs, following up the line of the Save to the west and swinging south down the Dalmatian coast to beyond Dubrovnik.[2]

This frontier was a line of potential nationality as well as of religion, since in Eastern Europe the two were not fully differentiated. It was along this line that Poland and Yugoslavia were to fracture in the course of the Second World War. To have overpassed it in self-aggrandizement was Poland's chief internal cause of weakness in 1939, as was shown by her fear of a Ukrainian nationalism radiating from Carpatho-Ruthenia.[3] It was the principal cause of weakness also of Yugoslavia, for it provided one of the two main lines of differentiation on the South Slav spectrum. The frontier between Croatia, Slovenia, and Dalmatia, on the one side, as parts of the Catholic West, and Serbia and Bosnia on the other, seemed still in 1939 no less real and enduring than the linguistic frontier between Yugoslavia and Bulgaria, and a united state of Serbs and Bulgars was scarcely less of an intrinsic possibility than the united state of Serbs and Croats.[4]

once independence was achieved. In March 1939 the Uniat Church in Ruthenia and Polish Galicia numbered about 4 millions, and in Rumania about 1½ millions. The other Uniat Churches in Eastern Europe were numerically insignificant. See Donald Attwater: *The Catholic Eastern Churches*, revised edition (Milwaukee, Wisconsin, Bruce, 1937), pp. 279–82, statistical summary.

[1] The Curzon Line was the minimum eastern frontier, on ethnographical principles, within which the Supreme Council on 8 December 1919 authorized Poland to establish a permanent administration. See *H.P.C.* vi. 275, 322; *Survey* for 1920–3, p. 251; S. Konovalov: *Russo-Polish Relations* (Princeton, N.J., University Press, 1945), p. 34 and appendixes 3 and 4; L. B. Namier: *Facing East* (London, Hamish Hamilton, 1947), pp. 109–13. Almost half the area of Poland (64,000 square miles out of 150,000) and one-third of the population (10½ millions out of 33 millions) lay between the Curzon Line and the frontier finally won by the Treaty of Riga in 1921.

[2] The line was faintly continued on the farther side of the Adriatic across Italy from the Gargano peninsula to Gaeta. This was the frontier between Byzantine Italy on the south and the kingdom of Italy on the north from the ninth to the eleventh centuries (Toynbee: *Study*, iv. 343–4, 610–11); and it was reflected, from the twelfth to the nineteenth centuries, in the more northerly frontier between the kingdom of the Two Sicilies or of Naples and the Papal States. This ancient cultural boundary was not erased by the Risorgimento, and the Duce of Fascism succeeded in obliterating it as little as King Alexander the Unifier succeeded in obliterating the analogous boundary in Yugoslavia.

[3] This cultural frontier roughly traced the western edge of the submerged Ukrainian nation. The word 'Ukraine' means frontier or border. It had originally referred to the southern marches of the Russian world (which were under Polish-Lithuanian rule) over against the Tatars of the Crimea (Allen: *Ukraine*, pp. 64–65). But by the twentieth century the Ukraine had been transformed into the Russian world's western march over against Western European civilization.

[4] Toynbee: *World after the Peace Conference*, p. 70, note 1.

(b) SOCIAL CONFLICTS

The national antagonisms of Eastern Europe were largely also social antagonisms, and the vertical conflict between states was often bound up with a horizontal conflict between classes. The principal social characteristic of Eastern Europe was the absence or weakness of an indigenous middle class. It was the consequence of the retarding of commercial development over ten centuries by invasion, warfare, and the deadening rule of the Turkish Empire—another aspect of how the growth of Western Europe had been purchased by the stunting of Eastern Europe. But in many cases this catastrophic history had done more than prevent the growth of a middle class, it had altogether destroyed the aristocracy and governing class; and in so far as a governing class in the widest sense is normally the bearer of a nation's traditions and historical consciousness, this had made it possible to divide the peoples of Austria-Hungary into the 'historic' and the 'unhistoric' nations.[1]

In this respect the Eastern European nations fell into four classes. (1) The flowering states of Balkan Christendom had been cut short by the Turkish conquest in the fourteenth century, which destroyed their aristocratic and nascent middle classes. The resurgence of these nations against the Turkish Empire in the nineteenth century reciprocally destroyed the Turkish official and aristocratic class, leaving entirely peasant states with a governing class of the first generation. To this there were two exceptions. The Greeks never fully became an unhistoric nation, for they had soon made themselves indispensable to their conquerors and established a privileged position as the administrative and commercial class of the Ottoman Empire in Europe. Independent Greece, because of its geographical position and tradition, was a maritime and commercial nation, accessible to sea-power; and thus, though the heir of that Greek Empire which was the core of Eastern Christendom, it became the most Western in sentiment of the Turkish successor states.[2] In Rumania, again,

---

[1] The distinction was coined in Vienna, apparently by Karl Renner, at the beginning of the twentieth century. It was equally applicable to the Ottoman and Russian Empires. The historical nations *par excellence* of Eastern Europe were the Germans, the Italians, the Turks, and the Russians. The Magyars and the Poles in Austria-Hungary, and the Greeks in the Ottoman Empire, were also among the historical nations, because their national traditions had never been lost and they had retained or acquired a privileged position. All the rest were the unhistorical nations: in Austria-Hungary, the Czechs and Croats (despite occasional recognition of their historical rights), the Slovaks, Ruthenes, Rumanians, Slovenes, and Serbs; in the Ottoman Empire in Europe, the Bulgars, Serbs, Rumanians, and Albanians; in the Russian Empire in Europe, the Ukrainians, White Russians, Lithuanians, Letts, Estonians, and Finns.

[2] Cf. Monroe: *Mediterranean in Politics*, pp. 22–23. It is to be remembered that although modern Greek nationalism appealed to the tradition of the Byzantine Empire, the heart of Byzantine Orthodox Christendom had been not Greece but Asia Minor; Greece had been an outlying fringe over against the Western world, included in the patriarchate of Rome down to 732, and afterwards encroached upon and occupied by French and Venetians.

there had developed a landowning class of partially Greek origin which was allied with Jews and the foreign interests that exploited the oilfields. (2) In Central Eastern Europe, which comprised both the north-eastern bulwark of Eastern Christendom and the eastern tier of Western Christendom, the decisive event had been not the Turkish conquest but the Mongolian invasion two centuries before. It had depopulated the Rumanian principalities and Hungary and Poland; and the rulers of Poland and Hungary had called in German colonists to repair the damage. At the same time the ruling classes of the Ruthenes, Slovaks, and Rumanians, in so far as they existed, were either Polonized or Magyarized. (3) The Czech Lands, Bohemia and Moravia, were *sui generis*. Unlike Poland and Hungary, they were part of the medieval Reich, and the Mongolian invasion did not reach them. They were very completely colonized and developed by German artisans and traders; and they maintained a highly developed national independence until they elected a Habsburg king in 1526. Their attempt to reject the Habsburg succession at the beginning of the Thirty Years War brought defeat, conquest, and national submergence. A process of Germanization and Catholicization effaced the native Bohemian aristocracy as surely as the Turkish conquest destroyed the native aristocracies of the Balkans, and the Czechs joined the unhistoric nations. (4) The Baltic was the colonial domain of medieval Western Christendom, where pagan barbarians had been subjugated, in Finland by the Swedes, and in Livonia and Prussia by the Teutonic Order. In these countries there was a native peasantry under an alien governing class. The Lithuanians alone of these barbarians maintained their independence by uniting with Poland, at the price of becoming rapidly Polonized, and the pattern recurred.

But the accumulated heritage of national strife and injury that had divided Eastern Europe for centuries into the historic and the unhistoric nations gave them all alike a sharper and deeper historic consciousness than the nations of Western Europe. The Germans preserved the memory of their defeat by the Poles and Lithuanians at Tannenberg in 1410, to avenge it at last in Hindenburg's and Ludendorff's victory over the Russian army on the same field in August 1914.[1] The Magyars sought to redeem the disaster at Mohács, the 'Flodden of the East' where the Turks slaughtered the Hungarian king and chivalry, by making it part of the

---

[1] Tannenberg 'is a German island in a Slav sea. Yet this island contains one of the sacred places of a people to whom the sword is a symbol of moral virtue. Moreover, the place commemorates the triumphant revenge taken by the German nation for the terrible defeat inflicted upon Teutonic chivalry five centuries before. It might be thought that all recollection of defeat would have been lost in the course of five hundred years. The victory of Tannenberg in 1914 revealed that it had merely been lying dormant. Patriotic songs and military marches prevented the emotional and historic appeal of the Eastern Marches from becoming moribund' (Ian F. D. Morrow: *The Peace Settlement in the German-Polish Borderlands* (London, Oxford University Press for Royal Institute of International Affairs, 1936), p. 217).

legend of their defence of Christendom.[1] The peasantries of the unhistoric peoples, even during the period of their national submergence, kept alive the traditions of their past. The Serbs had a cycle of ballads that told the story of their conquest by the Turks at Kosovo; and though the Czech literary tradition became virtually extinct in the century after the battle of the White Mountain, the Bohemian serfs who rose in revolt against their German masters in 1775 sang Hussite songs.[2] Like the Irish, the only Western nation with a comparable experience, these peoples regained their freedom because they lived among their ancient wrongs and glories. History was the stuff of their politics, and all their politics turned back to history.

It was as if one should drive along the South Downs, turning off the main road and following by-roads in to the downlands at Sullington and Washington and Steyning, and should find buildings where persons involved in the tragedy of Richard II had but newly cast aside their garments in mourning, where the sound of their weeping was hardly stilled.[3]

There was a far greater affinity than in Western Europe between the extreme assertions of fanatical nationalists and the purposes of governments, and the foreign policies of the Eastern European states were directed by historical claims and memories to an extent that would have been paralleled in the west only if the basic object of British policy had been the recovery of Guienne and Normandy. The truncated Hungary of Trianon would not abandon a fraction of the historic rights of the Crown of St. Stephen; the inflated Rumania of Trianon was sustained by the Dacian myth; the Polish Republic was haunted by the kingdom of the Jagellons, Bulgaria by the empire of the Asens and the earlier empire of Tsars Symeon and Samuel, the Serbs of Yugoslavia (but not the Croats or Slovenes) by the empire of Stephen Dushan; and the Albanians found compensation for their present weakness in their claim to be 'the original and autochthonous race of the Balkans', for whom the Slavs were but immigrants of yesterday, and to possess, not only Skanderbeg, but also Pyrrhus of Epirus and Alexander the Great.[4] The only Eastern European nations that escaped the self-imposed burden of a mighty past were Latvia, Estonia, and Finland, and even among the Finns there were those who

---

[1] Cf. Zoltán Gerevich in *La Hongrie et la civilisation*, edited by Georges Lukács (Paris, La Renaissance du Livre, 1929), p. 66. For the arrogance and impolicy of the Hungarian ruling class which led to the defeat of Mohács, and the reaction thereto of the subject Croats, see R. W. Seton-Watson: *The Southern Slav Question and the Habsburg Monarchy* (London, Constable, 1911), p. 19 and note 5. Like Tannenberg, Mohács was afterwards avenged on the same spot, by the great Imperialist victory over the Turks in 1687.

[2] R. J. Kerner: *Bohemia in the Eighteenth Century* (New York, Macmillan, 1932), p. 279.

[3] Rebecca West: *Black Lamb and Grey Falcon: a Record of a Journey through Yugoslavia in 1937* (London, Macmillan, 1941), i. 523; cf. i. 157.

[4] Brailsford: *Macedonia*, pp. 271-2. Cf. Robinson: *Albania's Road to Freedom*, pp. 11-12.

dreamed of a Greater Finland that would include the whole of East Karelia and the Kola peninsula.[1]

The middle class of Eastern Europe was supplied since the Middle Ages by the Germans, but latterly also by the Jews. In March 1939 the Jews were still a predominantly Eastern European people, and had been so since about 1800; the end of this chapter of the *Galuth* was now at hand. They had been first settled in Poland by Casimir the Great in the fourteenth century; and in the nineteenth, driven from behind by the persecution of the Russian Government and attracted from in front by an incipiently liberal society and the opportunities of commercial advancement, had migrated into Hungary and Rumania, taking over the middle-class functions which the Magyars in particular were unwilling to perform for themselves.[2] The Jews as a minority afforded the extreme of contrast with the Germans: they had no fatherland, no Great Power protected their interests, they were predestined victims of class and nationalist spite, and to pillage them became an international interest, which Germany skilfully exploited.

This absence of established indigenous middle classes determined the social history of the Eastern European states, and the absence of bourgeois civilization conditioned in its turn their political history. Except in Czechoslovakia and Finland there were neither the social foundations nor the moral traditions of constitutional government; in Hungary alone there was a tradition of parliamentary institutions, but it was oligarchic and illiberal. At the end of the First World War the appearance of the successor states in the comity of nations was applauded by the West. They had the indefeasible certificate of national self-determination, they added the claim to be democratic republics and constitutional monarchies, and it was easy to see them collectively through a haze of Masaryk and Venizelos, as if Eastern Europe were a nursery of liberal statesmen. By March 1939, in all of them except Finland and perhaps Czechoslovakia, parliamentary government had been replaced by some degree of dictatorship.[3] It was then perhaps too little understood that it had been the destiny

---

[1] For a study of this archaistic nationalism see Kolarz: *Myths and Realities in Eastern Europe.* Cf. H. Seton-Watson: *Eastern Europe*, chapter viii.

[2] The chief Jewish minorities of the world at the end of 1938 were as follows: in the United States, 4,700,000; in Poland, 3,345,000; in the Soviet Union, 3,180,000; in Rumania, 800,000; in Hungary, 480,000; in Germany with Austria, 475,000; in Palestine, 440,000; in the United Kingdom, 370,000; in Czechoslovakia, 315,000. See Arthur Ruppin: *The Jewish Fate and Future*, trans. E. W. Dickes (London, Macmillan, 1940), chapter ii, especially p. 35.

[3] *Finland*: unbroken parliamentary government from 1918 onwards, with restriction of civil liberties in 1930-2 to meet the Fascist Lapua movement. *Estonia*: dictatorship 1934-40, under President Paets and General Laidoner. *Latvia*: dictatorship 1934-40, under the Prime Minister Ulmanis, who became President 1936. *Lithuania*: dictatorship 1926-40: under the Prime Minister Voldemaras 1926-9, under President Smetona 1929-40. *Poland*: parliamentary government 1919-26, Witos as leader of Peasant Party. Dictatorship 1926-39: under Pilsudski 1926-35, the rule of the Colonels 1935-9 (triumvirate of President Móscicki, the Commander-

of the successor states to come to birth in an upheaval that destroyed constitutional government throughout the greater part of the world, and Eastern Europe only failed to attain to what half Western Europe failed to preserve. The rule of the Macedonian Terrorist Organization in Bulgaria,[1] the atrocities of the Polish pacification of Eastern Galicia in 1930,[2] the Rumanian plundering and misgovernment of Bessarabia,[3] were not only in the tradition of Turkish and Ukrainian history; they also prefigured the kind of government which was soon, after this interlude of independence, to be imposed on Eastern Europe once more from without, and they reflected at the same time the internal conflicts that made this possible. From Poland to the Balkans there was a gulf between the peasant masses and the ruling class, with resentment and often real misery below, police oppression, brutality, and corruption from above. Eastern Europe was in a pre-revolutionary condition, and its social conflicts became in some degree polarized in terms of the antagonism between the two adjacent revolutionary Great Powers. The ruling classes, who were to prove susceptible to the counter-revolutionary propaganda of Germany, already feared, exaggerated, and inadvertently contributed to the masses' susceptibility to the revolutionary propaganda of Russia.

A peasant who complained of an act of injustice was denounced as a 'Communist', sent before a military court, beaten from time to time, and sentenced

in-Chief Smigly-Rydz, the Foreign Minister Beck). *Czechoslovakia*: parliamentary government, the Agrarian Party being the dominant factor in successive coalitions, from 1919 till after the first partition in 1938; authoritarian democracy 1938–9. *Austria*: parliamentary government 1919–33 (Seipel as Christian Socialist Chancellor 1922–4, 1926–9). Dictatorship 1933–8: under Dollfuss 1933–4, under Schuschnigg 1934–8. *Hungary*: Communist régime under Bela Kun 1919, White Terror and restoration 1919–20. Horthy as Regent 1919–45. Nominal parliamentary government and veiled dictatorship 1919–45: Prime Ministers Bethlen 1921–31, Gömbös 1932–6, Darányi 1936–8, Imrédy 1938–9, Teleki 1939–41. *Rumania*: parliamentary government 1919–37, Liberals under Bratianu in power 1922–8, National Peasants under Maniu 1929–31 and 1932–3. From 1930 King Carol II (1930–40) acquired personal ascendancy. Anti-Semitic ministry of Goga 1937; royal dictatorship 1937–40. *Yugoslavia*: parliamentary government 1921–8, Serbian Radical Party under Pasić, Croat Peasant Party under Radić; Radić assassinated 1928. Royal dictatorship under King Alexander 1929–34, continued under Prince Regent Paul 1934–41 (Stoyadinović Prime Minister 1935–9). *Bulgaria*: parliamentary government 1919–23, with Stamboliski as leader of Peasant Party and Prime Minister; Stamboliski murdered 1923. Succession of governments controlled by terrorist Macedonian Revolutionary Organization 1923–4. Military dictatorship 1934–5, under Velchev and Georgiev. Royal dictatorship 1935–43 under King Boris II (1918–43). *Albania*: council of regency 1920–4; rebellion by Ahmed Bey Zogu 1925, who ruled as president of the republic 1925–8, and as King Zog 1928–39. *Greece*: Venizelos Prime Minister 1917–20. King Constantine, restored, 1920–2; King George II, under army rule, 1922–3. Republic 1924–35, Venizelos Prime Minister 1928–32. King George II (1935–47) restored by military coup 1935; constitutional monarchy 1935–6, dictatorship under General Metaxas 1936–41. *Turkey*: exclusive rule of Republican People's Party from 1923 onwards, under President Kemāl Atatürk 1923–38, under President Inönü after 1938.

[1] See below, p. 248 and note 3.

[2] See especially the *Manchester Guardian*, 14, 22, 24, and 25 October, 17 November, and 29 December 1930; H. Seton-Watson: *Eastern Europe*, p. 335. The intention of a full treatment of the Ukrainian question, which was declared in the *Survey* for 1932, p. 368, note 1, was not fulfilled.   [3] H. Seton-Watson: *Eastern Europe*, pp. 148–9, 336–8.

either to prison or to forced labour under military discipline. . . . A peasant who did not like to have his daughters raped or his property stolen by a gendarme must be a 'Bolshevik'.[1]

Almost every state in Eastern Europe was liable, under pressure or shock, to fracture along horizontal lines.

Eastern Europe was an agrarian region, and its nations were self-consciously peasant nations. Czechoslovakia was the only one in which more than half the population was not engaged in agriculture.[2] They were mostly overpopulated, and agricultural under-employment was for them what industrial unemployment was in the west. This was a subsidiary motive for the spread of industrialization since 1919. But the main cause of industrialization was the application of nationalist principles to economic life. The establishment of the successor states meant economic as well as political fragmentation. Of two great economic units one, the Russian Empire, was deprived of its most industrially advanced provinces along its European frontier; the other, Austria-Hungary, which had united the middle Danube valley in a single customs area, was broken up into five separate economic units divided by tariff barriers.[3] Feeble efforts at Danubian economic co-operation in the later 1920s were a failure; and the world depression accelerated the drive towards autarky, through the artificial development of agriculture by Czechoslovakia and Austria, and of industry by the agrarian states. The consequence was a general reduction of Danubian trade and of Eastern European trade as a whole. For the states of Eastern Europe were not economically complementary, and they were left with a large surplus of agricultural produce for which they had to find external markets. The pressure of this economic necessity, growing heavier through the 1920s, delivered them into the hands of the Great Power that was ready to take their exports, and had enabled Germany, by March 1939, to effect an economic conquest of South-Eastern Europe that fore-shadowed political conquest.

---

[1] Ibid. pp. 149–50; cf. pp. 153, 241, 262–3, 317, 337, and Wiskemann: *Undeclared War*, pp. 98, 107–8.

[2] These were the approximate percentages of the occupied population who were engaged in agriculture in 1939: Finland, 60; Estonia, 60; Latvia, 66; Lithuania, 77; Poland, 63; Czechoslovakia, 34; Hungary, 55; Rumania, 73; Yugoslavia, 75; Bulgaria, 80; Greece, 61; Turkey (the whole country), 82. In Albania, the most primitive, almost the entire population was engaged in pastoral farming and stock-raising.

[3] The economic unity of the Habsburg Empire was an ambiguous matter: it was largely a function of economic backwardness and the low standard of living of the Empire's inhabitants. 'Much more was heard of the natural economic unity of the Monarchy after 1918 than before it' (C. A. Macartney: *Problems of the Danube Basin* (Cambridge University Press, 1942), p. 78. The evils of economic nationalism led to controversies involving a retrospective justification of the Habsburg Empire. Thus Frederick Hertz (in *The Economic Problem of the Danubian States* (London, Gollancz, 1947)) claims that there was a decline in the national income of the successor states, in contradiction to Colin Clark in *The Conditions of Economic Progress* (London, Macmillan, 1940), pp. 127–36.

(c) THE VERSAILLES SETTLEMENT

The new states which thus appeared in Eastern Europe in 1918, precociously nationalist, socially divided, and economically unbalanced, were also precarious internationally. The strength of the Versailles Settlement was in its conformity to national self-determination. Its weakness lay in its disconformity to the foreseeable balance of power.

The Versailles Settlement was only a recognition of the new system of Eastern Europe.[1] That system dated from 1918, not 1919; the national revolutions had preceded the Paris Peace Conference; and the main decisions of the conference, more than those of any previous conference at the end of a general war, were determined by forces outside the control of the conference itself. The new system had been created from below by a single overmastering political impulse, that of nationalism; and so far as could be seen in March 1939 the change was permanent. The revision of the Versailles Settlement was then in full swing, but it did not appeal back from the national principle to the pre-national principle of dynasticism. It claimed rather to be the fulfilment of nationalism, succeeding by the manipulation and perversion of the national principle as that was understood in 1919.

Democratic nationalism, like all great political forces, supplied also the dominant conception of political justice of its time; and its fruition in the collapse of the eastern empires had the character, for those involved in it, of a tremendous act of emancipation.[2] Like its great predecessors 1789 and 1848, the year 1918 brought the sense of revolutionary fulfilment, the beginning of a new age, the bliss of springtime or of dawn.[3] This intoxica-

[1] The term 'Versailles Settlement' was strictly a misnomer in relation to Eastern Europe, since the Versailles Treaty of 28 June 1919 was limited to Germany, affecting Eastern Europe only by the definition of Germany's eastern frontier. The treaties by which the Allies gave juridical form to the new system of Eastern Europe were the Treaty of St. Germain-en-Laye of 10 September 1919 with Austria, the Treaty of Neuilly-sur-Seine of 27 November 1919 with Bulgaria, the Treaty of Trianon of 4 June 1920 with Hungary, and the Treaty of Lausanne of 24 July 1923 with Turkey (replacing the Treaty of Sèvres of 10 August 1920).

The Versailles Treaty is printed in *H.P.C.* iii. 100 seqq. The Austrian and Hungarian treaties are printed ibid. v. 170 seqq.; the Bulgarian treaty, ibid. v. 305 seqq. The two Turkish treaties are not printed in *H.P.C.*, and will be found respectively in Treaty Series No. 11 (1920), *Treaty of Peace with Turkey: signed at Sèvres, August 10, 1920*, Cmd. 964, and Treaty Series No. 16 (1923), *Treaty of Peace with Turkey, and other instruments: signed at Lausanne on July 24, 1923*, Cmd. 1929.

[2] The most brilliant brief description of this process within Austria is by L. B. Namier: 'The Downfall of the Habsburg Monarchy', *H.P.C.* vol. iv, chapter i, part iii; see especially pp. 90, 113.

[3] 'For the old Turkey had gone and its successor had no interest in Empire, and Russia was a Union of Soviet Republics, and the Hapsburgs were fallen; and the treaties of Versailles and Trianon and St. Germain had set the small peoples free. Freedom was for these peoples an ecstasy.... Finland, Estonia, Latvia, Czecho-Slovakia and Yugoslavia, they were all like young men stretching themselves at the open window in the early morning after long sleep' (West: *Black Lamb and Grey Falcon*, ii. 494). Cf. T. E. Lawrence: 'It felt like morning, and the freshness of the world-to-be intoxicated us' (suppressed introductory chapter to *Seven Pillars of Wisdom*, quoted in *The Letters of T. E. Lawrence*, ed. David Garnett (London, Cape, 1938), p. 262, and in a

tion was itself perhaps the most important political circumstance of the Peace Conference, especially in its dealings with Eastern Europe, and the reaction from it was one of the most important aspects, cause as much as effect, of the rise of Nazi Germany. The same dialectic that had led from the Festival of the Federation to the Terror and the Empire, and from Lamartine and Bakunin and Mazzini to Louis Napoleon and Bach and Cavour, led also from the liberated Eastern Europe whose most splendid figure was Masaryk to the Eastern Europe of March 1939, dominated by the Eastern European expatriate who had become Führer of the German Reich.

It was a subsequent achievement of Hungarian and German revisionist propaganda to represent the Versailles Settlement as a bleak reversal by which the under-dogs of the old régime became the top-dogs of the new.[1] But many more of the states, and millions more of the population of Eastern Europe, obtained by it national freedom and national fulfilment than were brought under alien rule. There was no parity between the revisionist and the satisfied states. There were nine 'victorious' nations: Finland and the three Baltic States, which had risen independent out of the ruins of the Russian Empire; Poland; Czechoslovakia, Rumania, and Yugoslavia, the principal successor states of the Habsburg Empire; and Greece.[2] The defeated nations were five: Germany, Austria, Hungary, Bulgaria, and Russia.[3] Germany and Russia were in a different class from

later version in T. E. Lawrence: *Oriental Assembly*, ed. A. W. Lawrence (London, Williams & Norgate, 1939), p. 142).

In Siberia the spring came rather earlier, round about 1904: 'The youth of the revolutionary generation coincided with the youth of the labor movement. It was the epoch of people between the ages of eighteen and thirty. Revolutionists above that age were few in number and seemed old men. The movement was as yet utterly devoid of careerism, lived on its faith in the future and on its spirit of self-sacrifice. There were as yet no routine, no set formulae, no theatrical gestures, no ready-made oratorical tricks. The struggle was by nature full of pathos, shy and awkward. The very words "committee", "party" were as yet new, with an aura of vernal freshness, and rang in young ears as a disquieting and alluring melody' (Leon Trotsky: *Stalin*, translated from the Russian by Charles Malamuth (London, Hollis & Carter, 1947), pp. 53–54). In Germany it came of course with the Nazi Revolution: see Hitler's speech at Munich of 19 March 1934 (*The Speeches of Adolf Hitler, April 1922–August 1939*, trans. and ed. N. H. Baynes [referred to hereafter as Hitler: *Speeches* (Baynes)] (London, Oxford University Press for Royal Institute of International Affairs, 1942), i. 212).

[1] 'In the national field, a complicated system of hierarchies had, as we have seen, evolved in many districts. The 1919 settlement roughly reversed the earlier positions, with the single exception that the Ruthenes remained national under-dogs after 1919, as they had been before it' (Macartney: *Problems of the Danube Basin*, p. 120; cf. pp. 151–2, 108–9; and Toynbee: *World after the Peace Conference*, pp. 60–61).

[2] Albania fell into neither class, having been neither a belligerent in the war, nor anything but an object of policy; and her frontiers as finally delimited did not greatly differ from those of 1913. She certainly had a grievance about the Albanian minority in Yugoslav Macedonia, but was precluded by her weakness from pursuing a revisionist policy.

[3] Turkey was also on the losing side in the First World War, as registered in the Treaty of Sèvres, 1920; but arose victorious from the Graeco-Turkish War of 1919–23, as registered in the Treaty of Lausanne, 1923.

the states of Eastern Europe: they were Great Powers, and their revisionism took a revolutionary and imperialist form unconnected with the rectification of the alleged injustices of the Peace Settlement. Austria was not
a revisionist state in the pure sense. She was a state lacking the will to
existence, since her original wish had been for an Anschluss with Germany,[1]
which had been forbidden by the Allies;[2] and lacking also the means to
existence, since she had to be kept alive in her early years through the
artificial respiration of League loans.[3] From then on Austria scarcely had
an active foreign policy, and furthermore she obtained an accession of
territory, at the expense of Hungary, in the Burgenland, which put her
paradoxically in the class of territorial gainers.[4] The two chief revisionist
states of Eastern Europe were Hungary and Bulgaria, but their revisionism
differed. Bulgaria's defeat in 1918, unlike Hungary's, was the second in
seven years, and her discontent was consequently less embittered and
more resigned.[5] Moreover, Bulgaria had extraordinary ties with Yugoslavia. The tradition of Stamboliski and of Velchev was one of collaboration with Yugoslavia tending towards a South Slav Union, and for this
reason Bulgaria nearly became a signatory of the Balkan Pact of 1934.[6]
There was never any question of Hungarian accession to the Little Entente.
Hungary had no Stamboliski and no Velchev. For the cleavage between
victorious and revisionist Powers was less important than the older cleavage
between the historic and the unhistoric nations. The deepest grievance of
the Germans and the Hungarians was not that the settlement had done
them an injustice, but that it had deprived them of their age-old right of
ruling over other peoples.[7] And the force of this older distinction was
illustrated again by the one Power of Eastern Europe that combined the
advantages of being both a historic and a victorious nation, Poland.

The criticism of the Versailles Settlement that it created as many new
minority problems as those it solved[8] was fallacious. The problems it
created were not numerically comparable with those it solved: they were

---

[1] *H.P.C.* iv. 119; Borkenau: *Austria and After*, p. 206.

[2] *H.P.C.* iv. 391–2, i. 347, ii. 13–14.   [3] *Survey* for 1920–3, p. 316.

[4] *H.P.C.* iv. 382–3; *Survey* for 1920–3, pp. 304–7.

[5] Ibid. pp. 333–4. The first defeat had been inflicted by Greece, Serbia, Rumania, and
Turkey in the Second Balkan War of 1913. Like other contrasts between them, the difference
in the quality of their revisionism may not have been unconnected with the fact 'that Bulgaria
has the most equalitarian social structure in Eastern Europe, and Hungary the least' (H. Seton-
Watson: *Eastern Europe*, p. 130).

[6] *Survey* for 1934, pp. 524–5.

[7] On the ambiguity of justice, see *H.P.C.* iv. 439–42. 'It is surprising how often one finds the
same nationalist German declaring that to cut off East Prussia from the Reich was impossible
but that it was absurd to question the practicability of *Deutsch-Böhmen*' (Elizabeth Wiskemann:
Czechs and Germans: A Study of the Struggle in the Historic Provinces of Bohemia and Moravia (London,
Oxford University Press for Royal Institute of International Affairs, 1938), p. 86).

[8] 'There are no fewer suppressed minorities to-day in the various successor states of the Austrian
Empire than existed before its disruption' (Borkenau: *Austria and After*, p. 83). Cf. the reply of
the Allied and Associated Powers to Hungary of 6 May 1920, in *H.P.C.* iv. 422.

of a different order. The revolutions of 1918 liberated the national majorities; and it was this great and broadly irreversible achievement that
brought into existence the problem of the minorities. The national
doctrine in the form in which it actually triumphed in Eastern Europe
from 1918 onwards was too extreme to carry within itself the principle of
its own correction. 'The most certain test', said Acton in a famous sentence,[1] 'by which we judge whether a country is really free is the amount
of security enjoyed by minorities.' On this test the new system of Eastern
Europe, taken as a whole, failed to establish freedom: it established only
the rights of national majorities. And the history of this failure, of this
acquiescence in a partial freedom, illustrated another profound saying of
Acton's:

> The greatest adversary of the rights of nationality is the modern theory of
> nationality. By making the State and the nation commensurate with each other
> in theory, it reduces practically to a subject condition all other nationalities that
> may be within the boundary. . . . The combination of different nations in one
> State is as necessary a condition of civilised life as the combination of men in
> society.[2]

The oppression of minorities in Eastern Europe under the Versailles
Settlement was part of a process that speedily transformed nationalism
into its own opposite. For the assertion of the rights of national majorities
at the expense of those of minorities led to the assertion of the rights of the
largest national majority at the expense of those of all the other nationalities together, and the subordination of the peoples of Eastern Europe to
the will of 80 million Germans. It was along the sharpest bend in this
spiral path that Hitler walked in the six months between his declaration
before Munich that he did not want to rule a single Czech[3] and his
annexation of Bohemia and Moravia as belonging to the living-space of
the German people.[4]

[1] In 'The History of Freedom in Antiquity', *The History of Freedom and Other Essays* (London,
Macmillan, 1907), p. 4.   [2] 'Nationality', ibid. pp. 297, 290.

[3] 'And I have further assured him that at the moment when Czechoslovakia solves her
problems, that means when the Czechs have come to terms with their other minorities, and that
peaceably and not through oppression, then I have no further interest in the Czech state. And
that is guaranteed to him! We want no Czechs!': speech in the Berliner Sportspalast, 26 September 1938 (Hitler: *Speeches* (Baynes), ii. 1526; *Documents* (R.I.I.A.) for 1938, ii. 259).

[4] See preamble to the decree regulating the status of the Protectorate of Bohemia and Moravia,
16 March 1939 (*Reichsgesetzblatt*, 1939, part i, p. 485; *N.C.A.* viii. 404 (051–TC); *Documents*
(R.I.I.A.) for 1939–46, i. 62).

The contradiction between 'national' and 'territorial' aggrandizement was the theme of
Hitler's conversation with Csáky on 16 January 1939. Hitler upbraided Hungary for her folly
in having asserted her demands during the first partition of Czechoslovakia in the form of
national claims and not of territorial acquisition. Hungary's assertion of the national principle
had embarrassed German diplomacy: had she co-operated with Germany on the territorial
principle Hitler would have been able to laugh at Chamberlain (report of conversation
between Hitler and Csáky, 16 January 1939, in *Documents secrets* (Eristov), vol. ii (*Hongrie*) no.
25.) Similarly, when he saw Tiso on 13 March 1939, Hitler said that 'in the decisions which he

But although the national principle was the basis of the Versailles Settlement, its details showed many modifications in the interests of strategy and economics. For the settlement was not only the redrawing of frontiers in accordance with a principle, but also a decision imposed by victors on vanquished as the result of a general war. Consequently it was exclusively in the interests of the victors that the modifications of the national principle were made.[1] The geographical and historic unit of Great Hungary was partitioned on the overriding principle of nationality.[2] The geographical and historic unit of Bohemia and Moravia was preserved in defiance of nationality, on the ground that a purely Czech state would be neither economically nor strategically viable.[3] In September 1938 the Munich Agreement unravelled the Versailles Settlement and created a purely Czech state; its dissolution and disappearance six months later perhaps vindicated the wisdom of the Peace Conference.[4]

The victorious states extended their frontiers to include in general all their adjacent *terre irredente*. This optimum expansion could be attained only by swallowing alien minorities.[5] The defeated states were correspondingly deprived of groups of their nationals, or in the case of Germany were not allowed to be joined by groups which on the principle of self-determination desired to do so.[6] This enforced separation applied

took at Munich [he] . . . was not playing power politics, but was working for the good of the German people' (German Foreign Ministry minute of interview between Hitler and Tiso, 13 March 1939 (*I.M.T. Nuremberg,* xxxi. 152 (2802–PS); translation in *Documents* (R.I.I.A.) for 1939–46, i. 48; cf. *N.C.A.* v. 445).

[1] 'When once, during the next creative bout in 1919, a Polish diplomat expounded to me the very extensive (and mutually contradictory) territorial claims of his country, and I inquired on what principle they were based, he replied with rare frankness: "On the historical principle, corrected by the linguistic wherever it works in our favour" ' (L. B. Namier: *1848: The Revolution of the Intellectuals*, Raleigh Lecture on History, 1944, from the Proceedings of the British Academy, vol. xxx (London, Geoffrey Cumberlege, Oxford University Press), p. 66). Cf. *Survey* for 1920–3, p. 228, note 3.

[2] *H.P.C.* iv. 418–19.   [3] Ibid. pp. 276–7.

[4] The inter-war history of Bohemia and Moravia as a geographical unit was reversed by that of Anatolia. In the Anatolian War of 1919–23 the Turks triumphantly vindicated the national unity of Anatolia against the will of the Allies by the expulsion of the Greek minority and the erasure of the Smyrna enclave contemplated by the Sèvres Treaty (*H.P.C.* vi. 53–54, 110). After the Second World War Czechoslovakia followed this violent example in an attempt finally to solve her minority problem.

[5] Minorities formed the following approximate percentages of the total population of the Eastern European states in 1938: Finland, 11; Estonia, 12; Latvia, 23; Lithuania (excluding Memel), 16; Poland, 31; Czechoslovakia, before the first partition (viz. other than Czechs and Slovaks), 33; Hungary, 10; Rumania, 25; Yugoslavia (viz. other than Serbs, Croats, and Slovenes), 12; Bulgaria, 10; Albania, perhaps 5; Greece, 12; Turkey in Europe (excluding Istanbul, which had a considerable Greek minority), none.

[6] Nearly one-third of the Hungarian nation were outside Hungary's Trianon frontiers: 1½ million in Rumania, three-quarters of a million in Czechoslovakia, half a million in Yugoslavia; in Trianon Hungary there remained 7 millions. The situation was less marked in Neuilly Bulgaria, which contained 5¼ million Bulgars; outside its frontiers there were half a million, or a whole million if Bulgaro-Macedonians be included; 360,000 in Rumania; 70,000 pure Bulgarians and half a million Bulgaro-Macedonians in Yugoslavia; 82,000 Macedonians in Greece. Of

a fortiori to groups that were non-contiguous. East Prussia was separated from Germany, but remained under her sovereignty; the German Bohemian enclaves were separated from Austria and passed under Czechoslovak sovereignty; the Magyar enclave in Transylvania was separated from Hungary and passed under Rumanian sovereignty. But it applied also to contiguous groups. Austria and the Bohemian Germans were not allowed to join Germany; Danzig and Memel were detached from East Prussia; districts with Magyar majorities in Slovakia and the Voivodina were severed from Hungary. The country most sorely thus pared and sheared was Hungary, the country most unnaturally swollen was Poland.

The separation of East Prussia from Germany was established primarily on national grounds, since the intervening provinces of Poznania and Pomorze had Polish majorities, and secondarily on the economic ground of giving Poland access to the sea. The popular term 'Corridor' emphasized the artificiality of this arrangement, by its cutting off a German province from the body of Germany. The tradition and habit of continental Great Powers made it impossible that Germany, or the rest of the world, should learn to regard the German colony of East Prussia as an island, whose separation was no greater a hardship than that imposed by nature between Italy and Sicily, or on the further shore of the Baltic between Sweden and Gottland.[1] The urge to territorial unity had been the strongest force in Prussian history; it would inevitably continue; and it could be foreseen that, when the balance of power shifted, the Polish Corridor would prove the most ineffective balk between the massing waters on either side.[2] When Hitler took possession of Memel on 23 March 1939 he refused to cross the Polish Corridor, but came instead by sea, sailing from Swinemünde in the *Deutschland* at the head of the German war fleet, and going ashore in a torpedo boat. 'It is said that on the trip he was violently sea-sick, and that this hardened his determination to obtain from the Poles an overland connexion with East Prussia'.[3]

Albanians, a third lived outside the frontiers of Albania, half a million in Yugoslavia, and 19,000 in Greece. Of Turks, there were 18 millions in Turkey; over half a million in Bulgaria, 190,000 in Greece. For the German minorities in Eastern Europe, see below, p. 332, note 2.

[1] Cf. L. B. Namier: *Diplomatic Prelude 1938–1939* (London, Macmillan, 1948), p. 17, note 1. On the colonial character of East Prussia see *H.P.C.* ii. 289–90, and Morrow: *The Peace Settlement in the German–Polish Borderlands*, pp. 223–5.

[2] See *H.P.C.* ii. 210, vi. 255–6. The Nazi Government made early provision for the development of East Prussia as a war base (see Brauchitsch's memorandum of 29 September 1934: *N.C.A.* vi. 280–1 (3585–PS)), and if the annexation of Danzig had preceded the attack on Poland it would have had to be carried out from East Prussia (see *I.M.T. Nuremberg*, xxxiv. 481–3 (137–C); translated in *Documents* (R.I.I.A.) for 1939–46, i. 97; cf. *N.C.A.* vi. 949–50).

[3] Namier: *Diplomatic Prelude*, p. 88; *Daily Telegraph*, 24 March 1939. Hitler 'once told Raeder: "On land I am a hero, but at sea I am a coward" ' (Anthony Martienssen: *Hitler and his Admirals* (London, Secker & Warburg, 1948), p. 2). 'The seizure of West Prussia is the most pardonable theft Berlin ever committed. . . . Even Napoleon, when he beat Prussia to earth, did not venture to reverse this inevitable outcome of the geographical situation. . . . Now that the lapse of a century has cemented more firmly than ever the union between West Prussia and the

East Prussia itself possessed two contiguous *irredente*. Danzig lay at its western end at the mouth of the Vistula, an ancient German commercial town that was Poland's historic gateway to the sea.[1] Memel lay at the north-eastern corner of East Prussia at the mouth of the Niemen, a minor Prussian seaport that could provide the only outlet to the sea for the new state of Lithuania.[2] Both of these, by a compromise between their German national character and the economic claims upon them of Poland and Lithuania respectively, were given a degree of autonomy. Danzig became a true buffer state, being made a free city under the protection of the League of Nations; and its preservation became a vital interest of Polish policy. Memel was given a degree of local autonomy under Lithuanian sovereignty; this status was not less a vital interest for Lithuania, and was less likely to be maintained only inasmuch as Lithuania was smaller and weaker than Poland.

Czechoslovakia was the only victorious state that was land-locked, having no direct access to the sea at all, though, after Germany had resumed command of the Baltic, Poland and the Baltic States were forced strategically into a similar position.[3] Just as Poland was defensible only on the assumption that Germany and Russia would not combine against her, so Czechoslovakia was defensible only on the assumption that she would not have to sustain unaided the joint attack of Germany, Poland, and Hungary; and the time came when these assumptions were not granted. Poland ensured the enmity of Germany by her acquisitions under the Versailles Treaty, of Russia by her conquests in 1920.[4] Czechoslovakia

German lands on either side of it, we should be ill-advised if we departed from Napoleon's precedent. . . . If every other question in Europe had been justly solved, West Prussia would suffice in itself to plunge all Europe into another war' (A. J. Toynbee: *Nationality and the War* (London, Dent, 1915), p. 75).

[1] Danzig grew from a fishing-village into an important port between the tenth and twelfth centuries. It was captured by the Teutonic Order in 1308, and became a member of the Hanseatic League in 1361; in 1466 it was ceded by the Order to Poland under the Treaty of Thorn. It remained a free city under Polish suzerainty from 1466 until acquired by Prussia at the Second Partition of Poland in 1793; the First Partition in 1772 cut it off from Poland by Prussia's acquisition of a 'Prussian corridor', viz. West Prussia, connecting Brandenburg with East Prussia, and it was preserved in this precarious detachment until 1793 by Russian jealousy of Prussia. In 1807 it was detached from Prussia by Napoleon under the Treaty of Tilsit, and re-erected into a free city under French protection; in 1814 it was recovered by Prussia. In 1919 it was erected again into a free city under the protection of the League of Nations (see *H.P.C.* ii. 291–3, 366–7, 383, 391–2; vi. 257–61; Morrow: *The Peace Settlement in the German-Polish Borderlands*, chapter ii).

[2] Memel was founded by the Teutonic Order in 1252, and remained part successively of their *Ordenstaat* and of the succeeding duchy and kingdom of Prussia down to 1919. It was then ceded by Germany to the Allied and Associated Powers, but was seized by Lithuania in 1923, to whom sovereignty was conveyed in 1924 on condition that Memel should have local autonomy (*H.P.C.* ii. 290–1, 366–7, 383, 391; vi. 247–8; *Survey* for 1920–3, pp. 256–61; Morrow, op. cit. chapter xiii).

[3] J. F. C. Fuller: *The Second World War, 1939–45* (London, Eyre & Spottiswoode, 1948), p. 48.

[4] 'Germany, indeed, would always have causes for dispute with Poland. It was, however, possible and desirable to reduce these causes to the minimum demanded by justice. In such

ensured the enmity of Germany by incorporating the Bohemian Germans who had wished when the Habsburg Monarchy dissolved to remain part of a 'German-Austria' which had voted for union with the Reich;[1] of Poland, because in 1919–20 she seized Teschen from Poland;[2] of Hungary, because the drawing of her southern frontier had been heavily weighted against Hungary. Poland was chiefly vulnerable from Germany, with Pomorze lying between two parts of the Reich, defensible only by means of a general war. Czechoslovakia too was chiefly vulnerable in relation to Germany. While Czechoslovakia was strong, her position could be compared to a spring-board for Bolshevik aggression or a base for French bombers according to the current anxieties of German propaganda;[3] but when she became weak, her Bohemian head was fastened between the German jaws of Austria and Silesia.

It therefore became an important part of both Polish and Czechoslovak policy to break this encirclement by establishing territorial contiguity with friendly states. Czechoslovakia had desired a corridor separating Austria and Hungary and establishing a common frontier with Yugoslavia, but the Peace Conference rejected such a subordination of national to strategic principles.[4] Czechoslovakia had originally desired also a common frontier with Russia.[5] This was prevented when the Polish conquest of East Galicia and the Treaty of Riga created instead a common Polish-Rumanian boundary.[6] Czechoslovakia nevertheless acquired Carpathian Ruthenia, and, though its original purpose was denied her, it became the centre of her strategic system. Through Ukrainian territory on either side of the Carpathians, Poland and Czechoslovakia stretched long fingers down to touch Rumania.

It is Slovakia and Ruthenia [said Beneš in 1933] which have rendered possible the whole conception of our foreign policy in collaboration with Poland,

circumstances the Poles would be wise to avoid all possible cause of quarrel with Russia, even if it meant in some cases recognizing Russian claims whose justice they disputed. Above all, it was dangerous to take advantage of Russia's temporary weakness and annex border peoples without securing a free expression of their wishes. Such action, as it separated Russia and Germany in space, would bring them together in spirit and might easily result in a new and this time perhaps a final Partition of Poland from which no human power could save her' (H. J. Paton in *H.P.C.* vi. 240. This prophecy was published in 1924).

    [1] See Wiskemann: *Czechs and Germans*, p. 83; A. J. P. Taylor: *The Habsburg Monarchy 1809–1918*, 2nd edition (London, Hamish Hamilton, 1948), p. 250.   [2] *H.P.C.* iv. 356–63.
    [3] Cf. Hitler's Reichstag speech of 28 April 1939: 'a bridge to Europe for Bolshevik aggression', 'a bastion extending into the German Reich' (Hitler: *Speeches* (Baynes), ii. 1612–13; *Documents* (R.I.I.A.) for 1939–46, i. 222–3; cf. Hitler: *Speeches* (Baynes), pp. 1488, 1519, 1597, and *Survey* for 1935, i. 296).
    [4] See *H.P.C.* iv. 273–4; T. G. Masaryk: 'Independent Bohemia', confidential memorandum of April 1915, in R. W. Seton-Watson's *Masaryk in England* (Cambridge University Press, 1943), p. 129; Macartney: *Hungary and her Successors*, pp. 51–53.
    [5] See *H.P.C.* iv. 273; R. W. Seton-Watson: *Masaryk in England*, pp. 45, 23. Cf. *Survey* for 1937, i. 406.
    [6] *H.P.C.* i. 335–9; iv. 104–5, 135; vi. 266–74, 283, note; *Survey* for 1920–3, pp. 271–2.

Roumania, and Yugoslavia, and it is that collaboration which makes us, in the eyes of France and of all Western Europe, a force in the whole policy of Central Europe. We shall therefore never allow our territorial link with Roumania to be cut.[1]

Ruthenia was the strategic turn-table of Eastern Europe. It offered contiguity alternately between Czechoslovakia and Rumania, which was its function from 1919 to 1938, as the land-bridge of the Little Entente; or between Communist Hungary and Soviet Russia, which was the reason for Bela Kun's attempt to conquer it in 1919;[2] or between conservative Hungary and conservative Poland, a contiguity which was brought about in March 1939. And if its Ukrainian national character ever led to its union with the Soviet Ukraine, it would give the Soviet Power territorial access by a broad avenue between Poland and Rumania to Czechoslovakia and Hungary, a bridgehead over the Carpathians towards the great Danubian plain.

(d) International Politics of Eastern Europe

The new system in Eastern Europe, which was confirmed and defined by the Versailles Settlement, illustrated, almost in a laboratory form, the politics of a *Kleinstaaterei*, the workings of a congeries of small states whose destiny is ultimately determined not by themselves but by Great Powers outside.

When once the general war had shattered the eastern empires, the new states came into existence through the will and exertion of their own nationals. But, immediately, they became objects of Great Power policy, and were cast for a role in wider schemes than they themselves controlled. They were first conceived of as a barrier to German expansion eastward, which would prevent the German conquest and penetration of Russia that had been consummated in the Peace of Brest-Litovsk in March 1917, and would balance the Germans of Austria and Prussia.

The condition of stability in the territorial rearrangement of East Europe [wrote H. J. Mackinder about Christmas 1918] is that the division should be into three and not into two State-systems. It is a vital necessity that there should be a tier of independent States between Germany and Russia.[3]

This consideration had been put forward by the representatives of the new states themselves when they had sought Allied support and recognition during the war.[4] But as the focus of Western apprehension shifted from

---

[1] Speech at Nové Zámky, 7 December 1933 (Macartney: *Hungary and her Successors*, p. 249).

[2] *H.P.C.* i. 356; iv. 139, 160, 489; vi. 246.

[3] Sir Halford J. Mackinder: *Democratic Ideals and Reality* (Harmondsworth, Penguin Books, 1944), p. 118.

[4] Cf. Masaryk's war-time memoranda, in R. W. Seton-Watson's *Masaryk in England*, especially pp. 130, 193–6.

prostrate Germany to revolutionary Russia, the tier of Eastern European states acquired a new function as a *cordon sanitaire* protecting Central and Western Europe against the Bolshevik danger from the east. This purpose was believed to be fulfilled by Poland in the Polish-Russian war of 1920 (although Poland had herself provoked it), when the French sent Weygand to save her from defeat at the battle of Warsaw.[1] France was the chief architect of the dual conception of the new Eastern Europe. It was the last phase of her tradition of making alliances in the rear of the Habsburg or German enemy. Once her aim had been to encircle that single enemy, and her alliances had been with other Great Powers, the Valois and Louis XIV with Turkey, Richelieu with Sweden, the Third Republic with Nicholas II. Now she was reduced for allies to unstable satellites of whom Poland was the chief, and simultaneously their function was doubled: no longer to encircle one Great Power, but to separate two Great Powers, the traditional masters of those satellites and each alone potentially more powerful than France herself. This system in Eastern Europe could last only so long as Germany and Russia were in collapse. With their recovery, the political value of the successor states would depreciate at the moment when the French need for them matured, France would be compelled to seek more substantial allies, and the balance of Europe would be restored to the hands of the Great Powers.

Eastern European politics were haunted by the longing for collective independence in international affairs, and by the fancy of political self-sufficiency. The conception of the Little Entente was 'of an organization of Central Europe in which our liberated countries have been their own masters, without the predominating influence or domination of any Great Power'.[2] This was the purpose also of the Balkan and Baltic Ententes. The illusion was always pursued, and never attained, that there might be built up in Eastern Europe an autonomous third force, a neutral bloc that would itself have the defensive weight of a Great Power. Polish policy aimed in successive phases at creating such a grouping, whether it were a Baltic constellation or one stretching south to the Danube, based on the Polish alliance with Rumania. It was indeed the fallacy of France's policy in Eastern Europe that she sought from her allies the performance of functions that in the long run were within the capacity of a Great Power alone. But there is no political avoirdupois by which an aggregation of small states can be made to equal a Great Power. The Eastern European blocs never stood the strains for which they were devised. The centrifugal pull of the Great Powers was too strong, and one or other of the small states

---

[1] *H.P.C.* vi. 318. Cf. Winston S. Churchill: *The Aftermath* (London, Butterworth, 1929), chapter xiii.

[2] Beneš, speech at Nové Zámky, 7 December 1933 (Macartney: *Hungary and her Successors*, p. 249).

would always give preference to its Great Power relationships over its relations with its putative allies. Only once in history had the states of Eastern Europe displayed a collective independence, when the Balkan League in 1912 defied the Concert of the Powers in order to partition the Ottoman Empire in Europe. But that adventure had been moved by a dynamic and aggressive purpose. The history of the Versailles system in Eastern Europe showed in microcosm, what the League of Nations showed in the world at large, that sovereign states are incapable of disciplined co-operation for a long period in defence of a static international order.

This failure to attain effective independence was with the Eastern European states from the beginning. They had come into existence under a kind of tutelage, not only political but juridical as well. For all of them were compelled to accept international obligations, supervised by the League of Nations, for the treatment of their minorities. This system of international servitude was confined to the states of Eastern Europe. It was intensely resented, partly as an infringement of the new-won sover-eignty, and particularly because the Great Powers were exempted from it. The minorities system was regarded as preventing the assimilation and encouraging the disloyalty of minorities, weakening the unity of the state and institutionalizing intervention. The minority treaties were consistently violated by governments, and the protection of minorities by the Council of the League faded simultaneously with every other expression of the League's authority. Intervention on behalf of minorities then became a German monopoly, more arbitrary and oppressive than anything Eastern Europe had suffered under the League of Nations.[1]

The attraction and influence of the Great Powers was the chief cause of Eastern European disunity. Within Eastern Europe itself the organization of states on the national principle gave some promise of a period of stability, because the majority of states were satisfied, and were capable of holding down the dissatisfied. The revisionist issue therefore became of less importance than the differences between the victor states. Thus the successful imperialism of Poland was a more consistently disturbing factor than the frustrated imperialism of Hungary throughout the twenty years which culminated, in March 1939, in their achieving territorial contiguity along the crest of the Carpathians. But these differences were only in-creased to a decisive magnitude through their exploitation by the Great Powers. The Little Entente and the Balkan Entente did not fall to pieces from within, but were prised asunder by external influences. It was

[1] On the whole subject see *H.P.C.* vols. v, chapter ii, and iv. 434–5; *Survey* for 1920–3, pp. 213–25; Macartney: *National States and National Minorities*; Jacob Robinson and others: *Were the Minorities Treaties a Failure?* (New York, Institute of Jewish Affairs, 1943). The only other state (counting Turkey as an Eastern European state) which was subjected to similar international obligations for the treatment of its minorities was 'Irāq, when the British mandate ended and she entered the League of Nations in 1932 (*Survey* for 1934, pp. 208–11).

remarkable that the two revisionist states, Hungary and Bulgaria, acted as allies of Great Powers, not as allies of one another. Hungarian revisionism was geared into German revisionism, so that the Magyars resumed their role under the Dual Monarchy of 'the obedient advanced guard of Berlin',[1] but Bulgarian revisionism was not similarly geared into Hungarian: in so far as Bulgaria was not a client, first of Italy and later of Germany, her policies and alliances were confined to her immediate neighbours.

The system of Eastern Europe illustrated all the particulars of a balance of power. Finland, Estonia, and Latvia formed a simple buffer belt. Their backs were to Russia, their faces to the sea, which gave them Britain as a neighbour as well as Germany;[2] though Finland was also an advanced zone of the Scandinavian neutral bloc, into which she dovetailed strategically through her retention of the Swedish Åland Islands, and which she insulated from Russia through her acquisition of the Petsamo Corridor to the Arctic Ocean.[3] But below Latvia the buffer belt became politically complex, with a double tier of states, widening out to become three deep where Austria and Hungary and Rumania lay between the source of the Danube in Germany and its mouths in the Euxine. The belt ended in another inland sea, where Greece and Turkey like the Baltic States had Britain as a neighbour. But they had these advantages over the Baltic republics, that they were peninsular not continental states; they were divided from Germany and Russia by the whole depth of the Balkans and the Danube valley, and Turkey's common frontier with Russia was marked by the Black Sea and the natural barrier of the Armenian mountains; and in the Mediterranean, but not in the Baltic, Britain was dominant Power.

Thus the international politics of Eastern Europe were shaped by the search for or the dread of territorial contiguity,[4] the fear of encirclement,

[1] Masaryk: 'Independent Bohemia', confidential memorandum of April 1915, in R. W. Seton-Watson's *Masaryk in England*, p. 130.

[2] In the two decades ending in March 1939 Britain and Germany accounted for half the exports and three-quarters of the imports of Estonia and Latvia (see Royal Institute of International Affairs: *The Baltic States*, pp. 125–7, 164–7).

[3] On the Åland Islands dispute see *Survey* for 1920–3, pp. 234–8. Finland obtained the Petsamo Corridor from Russia by the Treaty of Dorpat of 1920, although it had not formed part of the previous grand duchy of Finland (see Royal Institute of International Affairs: *The Baltic States*, pp. 226–7, 240). The Corridor was to be retained by Finland under the Treaty of Moscow of 12 March 1940 (*Finland Reveals her Secret Documents on Soviet Policy, March 1940–June 1941* (Blue-White Book of Finland) ed. H. J. Procopé (New York, W. Funk, 1941), p. 35), but was retroceded to Russia by the Treaty of Paris of 10 February 1947 (*The World Today*, December 1946, ii. 584; April 1947, iii. 198, map). Russia thereby regained a common frontier with Norway.

[4] Stalin emphasized the importance of common frontiers in the interview he gave to Roy Howard on 1 March 1936. 'History shows that when some State is intent on making war against any other State, even though not adjacent, it begins to seek frontiers across which it could reach the frontiers of the State which it desires to attack. Usually the aggressive State finds such frontiers. It finds them either with the aid of force, as in 1914 when Germany invaded Belgium

the desire for alliances with Powers in the rear of a potentially hostile neighbour.[1] These, however, were features common to every balance of power. The peculiarity of Eastern European politics was provided by the minorities. They were of three kinds.[2] First, there were border minorities contiguous with the state to which they would have preferred to belong, and these provided the greatest danger of disintegrating the state within which they were included. The extreme example was Czechoslovakia, with German minorities strung continuously along her Bohemian and Moravian frontiers. Secondly, there were scattered enclaves at a distance from the state to which they owed spiritual allegiance, a potential fifth column in every international crisis; and it was Germany who had the advantage both in the number of such German minorities and in the power of exploiting them. Thirdly, there were regions of mixed population, usually in frontier regions, whose loyalty was doubtful. The classic example was Macedonia, but there were many others, such as the Voivodina between Yugoslavia and Hungary, Transylvania between Hungary and Rumania, the Dobruja between Rumania and Bulgaria, Bessarabia between Rumania and Russia. The existence of these minorities gave a tenseness and ferocity to international relations in Eastern Europe which had no counterpart in Western Europe, unless it were in the relations between the Irish Free State and Northern Ireland.

They determined, moreover, the characteristic wars of Eastern Europe. These tended to be horizontal as well as vertical, war within states as well as war between states. Guerrilla warfare rising into civil war could be carried on for long periods without a declaration of war between governments, because the irregular and terroristic bands who waged it could be disowned by the state in whose interest it was conducted. War of this kind had become endemic in Eastern Europe with the growth of the national movements under the Ottoman Empire; and by a curious verbal transplantation the characteristic form of political activity in Western parliamentary states, the *committee*, had provided the name for the bands of irregular soldiers who represented the characteristic political activity of Eastern Europe, the *Comitadji*. With the dissolution of the eastern empires after the First World War this form of warfare spread, being the natural form of strife in states with an inflamed nationalism and minority problems; it was the most concrete expression of what was meant in

in order to deal a blow to France, or it "borrows" such a frontier, as Germany did with regard to Latvia, for instance, in 1918, in attempting to break through to Leningrad across Latvia. I do not know what specific frontiers Germany could adapt for her purposes [*sc.* of aggression against Soviet Russia], but I think those willing to lend a frontier to her can be found' (*Manchester Guardian*, 5 March 1936).

[1] See L. B. Namier: *Conflicts* (London, Macmillan, 1942), p. 14, on 'the "sandwich system" of international politics'.

[2] See H. Seton-Watson: *Eastern Europe*, pp. 269–72.

Western Europe by 'the Balkanisation of Central Europe'.[1] During most of 1919 and 1920 the whole of Eastern Europe was in the throes of this irregular warfare, and it appeared again within the frontiers of dissolving Czechoslovakia between Munich and March 1939. At that date, when they were at the meridian of their success in utilizing it over this fair field for aggression that lay beyond their eastern frontiers, the Germans did not see that it was to become, in the form of partisan warfare during the Second World War, a principal means of breaking up their Eastern European empire and transferring its fragments to the allegiance of the rival Eastern European Great Power.[2]

A balance of power has its proper laws of libration. Insight into their nature can provide foresight, of the kind which was often claimed and displayed between the First and Second World Wars as a property of the Marxist analysis of social conflicts. In a memorandum written as early as February 1925 the Historical Adviser to the British Foreign Office described the successive derangements of the Eastern European balance of power which, if unprevented, would lead to another Anglo-German war.

It is the real interest of this country [wrote J. W. Headlam-Morley] to prevent a new alliance between Germany and Russia, an alliance which would no doubt be cemented by an attack on Poland. We cannot now be indifferent if Germany breaks through upon the east and there begins to acquire a new accession of territory and strength which would inevitably in the future be brought to bear upon the Rhine. . . . Has anyone attempted to realize what would happen if there were to be a new partition of Poland, or if the Czecho-slovak State were to be so curtailed and dismembered that in fact it disappeared from the map of Europe? The whole of Europe would at once be in chaos. There would no longer be any principle, meaning or sense in the territorial arrangements of the continent. Imagine, for instance, that under some improbable condition, Austria rejoined Germany; that Germany, using the discontented minority in Bohemia, demanded a new frontier far over the moun-

---

[1] 'It now looks as if the Near East were infecting conflicts of nationality in Western Europe with the ferocity of fanaticism which it has imported into its own. Before the War, the ancient conflicts of interest between Ulstermen and Catholics in Ireland or Germans and Poles in Silesia were waged with some restraint, and bloodshed was uncommon. In 1921 both these and other zones of national conflict in the West were a prey to revolutionary bands, semi-official bashy-bozuks, regular combatants whose activities were disavowed while approved by their govern-ments, and all the other indecencies familiar in the Armenian vilayets or Macedonia. This moral Balkanisation is also unmistakable, and it is more dangerous than the political and economic manifestations of the tendency' (Toynbee: *The Western Question in Greece and Turkey*, pp. 26–27).

[2] Liddell Hart finds in T. E. Lawrence the first great modern commander to recognize this mode of warfare and to embody it in his strategy in the Arabian campaign of the First World War. 'For orthodox concentration, Lawrence substituted dispersion. For battle, he substituted a creeping paralysis—produced by intangibility and ubiquity. But he did more than paralyse the Turks. He foreshadowed what I believe will be the trend of the future—a super-guerrilla kind of warfare' (B. H. Liddell Hart, in *T. E. Lawrence by his Friends*, edited by A. W. Lawrence (London, Cape, 1937), p. 184). Cf. the same author's *T. E. Lawrence—in Arabia and After* (London, Cape, 1934), p. 438; and Julian Amery: *Sons of the Eagle* (London, Macmillan, 1948), pp. 165–9.

tains, including Carlsbad and Pilsen, and that at the same time, in alliance with Germany, the Hungarians recovered the southern slope of the Carpathians. This would be catastrophic, and, even if we neglected to interfere in time to prevent it, we should afterwards be driven to interfere, probably too late.[1]

It is the purpose of the rest of this chapter to trace the working-out of the inherent weakness of the Versailles system in Eastern Europe, thus early recognized, and counteracted by no supporting and containing influences from outside. For the detailed narrative of the German conquest of Czechoslovakia, of the Sudeten problem, the Munich Conference, the Vienna Award, and the final seizure of Prague, the reader is referred to the second and third volumes of the *Survey of International Affairs* for 1938. All that is attempted here is to show how the general European crisis of March 1939, which is the theme of the present volume, arose, by degrees which in retrospect acquired the delusive texture of inevitability, out of the unstable constellation of power in Eastern Europe; how that constellation of power was governed by its own laws, by the principles of irredentism and of political alliance, by the problem of national minorities and the importance of common frontiers; how the attempts of the Eastern European states to combine, from the Little Entente to the Polish-Rumanian project for a neutral bloc, were doomed to failure; and how, with the abdication of responsibility by the remoter Great Powers in Western Europe, the destinies of Eastern Europe were decided by the contiguous Great Powers, and above all by Germany and Russia.

(e) THE DELIMITATION OF EASTERN EUROPE AGAINST SOVIET RUSSIA

The struggles for national self-determination were the principal internal theme of Eastern European politics in the immediate aftermath of the First World War. But they were overshadowed in importance by an external theme: the delimiting of an eastern frontier for Eastern Europe over against Russia. Bolshevik Russia was at that time considered a greater danger to Europe than defeated Germany; and moreover, in its aspect as the Russian Empire in dissolution, Bolshevik Russia offered handsome opportunities for territorial acquisition by the contiguous states, and for the expansion of the influence of the Western Great Powers.

The most powerful of the successor states, and the chief instrument of the anti-Bolshevik policy of the Allies (particularly of France) was Poland. In 1918–19 Poland conquered East Galicia and overthrew the Ukrainian authorities there. The Supreme Council then authorized her to occupy the territory on condition of giving it autonomy; and then again granted her a twenty-five years' mandate for it; and when the Poles repudiated

---

[1] Sir James Headlam-Morley: *Studies in Diplomatic History* (London, Methuen, 1930), pp. 183–4, quoted by permission of Messrs. Methuen.

both of these proposals for placing them under an international obligation, the Supreme Council in 1923 at last assigned East Galicia to Poland in full sovereignty.[1] In 1920 Poland transgressed the defensive role allotted her by the Allied Great Powers and invaded the Soviet Ukraine. The ensuing war, in which the Poles first captured Kiev and the Russians nearly captured Warsaw in return, ended with the Treaty of Riga in 1921, whereby Poland secured extensive tracts of the Ukraine and White Russia, far beyond the Curzon Line, the provisional eastern frontier laid down for her in 1919 by the Allies in Paris.[2]

Rumania had already obtained territorial advantage from the dissolution of the Russian Empire. When the Central Powers imposed the Treaty of Bucharest on her in May 1918, they gave her a free hand to absorb Bessarabia, 'an absolutely unique example of a country crushingly defeated in war, yet aggrandized at the expense of one of her own allies'.[3] Rumania's national claims to Bessarabia were good, though they were quickly nullified as far as the will of the population was concerned by her brutal misgovernment. The annexation was recognized by the Supreme Council;[4] it remained an obstacle to normal relations between Rumania and the Soviet Union until the latter entered the League in 1934.[5] One reason for the Polish conquest of East Galicia in 1919 was to establish a common frontier with Rumania,[6] and in 1921 Poland and Rumania formed a defensive alliance against Russia,[7] an alliance that remained the only constant factor in Eastern European diplomacy down to the outbreak of the Second World War. Together the two Powers, one of them a Baltic state and the other a Danubian and Black Sea state, held the neck of Europe against the Bolshevik menace from the east.

South of Rumania, the delimitation of Eastern Europe rested not so much with the Eastern European states themselves as with the Western Great Powers, whose sea-power here gave them something in the nature of a common frontier with Russia. The Danubian delta and the Black Sea Straits represented the line at which they had held the southward advance of Russia in the nineteenth century. The Danubian and Straits questions were connected geographically as well as historically, because the Danube,

---

[1] *H.P.C.* i. 335–8; iv. 84–85, 95, 103–5, 135; vi. 245–6, 272–4, 283, note; *Survey* for 1920–3, p. 282. According to Macartney (*National States and National Minorities*, p. 199) this was 'the only instance in which an attempt was made to apply the mandatory principle in Europe'. But Italy was offered the mandate for Albania (see below, p. 250).

[2] *H.P.C.* vi. 275, 318–22; *Survey* for 1920–3, p. 254.

[3] R. W. Seton-Watson: *A History of the Roumanians*, p. 520; cf. *H.P.C.* iii. 50; iv. 220.

[4] *H.P.C.* iv. 139–40, 228–9; *Survey* for 1920–3, pp. 273–8.

[5] *Survey* for 1924, pp. 263–5; *Survey* for 1927, pp. 297–300; *Survey* for 1934, p. 378. The Soviet Union was not recognized by Rumania until her admission to the League, when the Bessarabian question was tacitly shelved (ibid. p. 392).

[6] *H.P.C.* i. 337; vi. 269.

[7] *Survey* for 1920–3, pp. 271–2. The treaty was renewed in 1926 (*Survey* for 1926, p. 154).

which was the greatest waterway of Eastern Europe, had its ultimate mouth not at Sulina but at the Dardanelles.[1] The Danube was potentially contested between the two Danubian Great Powers, Germany (formerly Austria-Hungary) and Russia; and the Small Power most concerned was Rumania, who after recovering Bessarabia in the north from Russia and the Dobruja in the south from Bulgaria[2] held sovereignty over the whole of the Danubian delta. The Black Sea Straits were potentially contested between Russia, the dominant Power in the Black Sea, and Britain, the dominant Power in the Mediterranean; and the Small Power most concerned was Turkey, who had throughout modern history possessed sovereignty over both shores of the Straits.

The simultaneous collapse of Austria-Hungary, Russia, and the Ottoman Empire in 1918 enhanced the influence of the Western Powers in the Danube and the Straits, or, to use the language of the Western Powers, made possible an unprecedented degree of internationalization for these regions. The Danube had first been internationalized by the Paris Congress of 1856, which set up a European Commission of the Great Powers and Turkey (together with Rumania after 1878) to administer the mouths of the Danube, and a Riparian Commission to supervise the whole course of the river above its mouths. The Riparian Commission was disliked by Austria-Hungary and soon discontinued; the European Commission proved one of the most successful experiments in international collaboration, a European institution that grew with the independence of the Rumanian state, in the interstice between the Russian, Austrian, and Ottoman Empires.[3] By the Versailles Treaty in 1919 the European Commission, whose powers extended over the maritime Danube as far up as Braila, was confirmed; it was to consist of Britain, France, Italy, and Rumania. A new International Commission was foreshadowed for the fluvial Danube, from Braila up to Ulm, to consist of Britain, France, Italy, and the riparian states, two representatives, however, being assigned to the 'German riparian states', for France at that time was hoping that Germany would break up.[4] These provisions were embodied and established

---

[1] Cf. Grigore Gafencu: *Préliminaires de la guerre à l'Est de l'accord de Moscou, 21 août 1939, aux hostilités en Russie, 22 juin 1941* (Fribourg, Egloff, 1944), p. 84 [transl. by Fletcher Allen with title *Prelude to the Russian Campaign* (London, Muller, 1945)]. Russia had twice had a Danubian frontier, through the possession of Southern Bessarabia: between the Russo-Turkish Treaty of Bucharest in 1812 and the Treaty of Paris in 1856, and between the Treaty of Berlin in 1878 and the Treaty of Brest-Litovsk in 1918.

[2] *H.P.C.* iv. 12, 414, 433, 449–50.

[3] See *International Affairs*, Peace Handbooks issued by the Historical Section of the Foreign Office, vol. xxiii (London, H.M.S.O., 1920), no. 149 (*International Rivers*, by Georges Kaeckenbeeck), pp. 30–36.

[4] Treaty of Versailles, articles 346–7; *H.P.C.* ii. 107–8; iv. 274, 435. Similar international commissions were established for the Elbe (representing Germany, Czechoslovakia, Britain, France, Italy, and Belgium), and the Oder (representing Poland, Germany, Czechoslovakia, Britain, France, Denmark, and Sweden).

in the Definitive Statute of the Danube in 1922.[1] The non-riparian Great
Powers thus obtained a predominating influence in the Danube régime,
which met with increasing opposition from Rumania;[2] and within a few
years Russia and Germany were demanding to be admitted to the European Commission.

The régime for the Black Sea Straits, which had been based on international agreement since the London Convention of 1840, was another
index of the balance of power. Russia's interest in the Straits was more
vital than that of the other Powers, and since she was always inferior in
naval strength to Britain and France it was her normal policy to prevent
entry into the Black Sea for foreign fleets rather than to secure exit from it
for her own. Moreover, the Straits régime involved the security of Turkey
in a much greater degree than the Danube régime affected that of any
Danubian Small Power. When in 1918 Russia and Turkey both collapsed,
control of the Straits and of the Black Sea passed to Britain and France,
who used it to intervene directly against the Soviet Government by supporting Denikin and Wrangel in Southern Russia, and indirectly against
Turkey by encouraging the expansionist aims of Greece. The twelfth of
Wilson's Fourteen Points had declared that 'the Dardanelles should be
permanently opened to the ships and commerce of all nations under international guarantees'; but when the United States refused a mandate for
the Straits,[3] they were jointly occupied instead by Britain, France, and
Italy, which meant the preponderance of Britain as the strongest naval
Power and the growing jealousy of the other two.[4] By the Treaty of
Sèvres which the Allies imposed on Turkey in 1920, Eastern Thrace (including Gallipoli and most of the northern shore of the Sea of Marmara)
was added to Greece, so that the only part of the former European Turkey
remaining under Turkish sovereignty was Constantinople and its hinterland. Full freedom of passage through the Straits was established for the
first time; a Commission of the Straits, comparable to the European Commission of the Danube, was created to administer them; and both sides
of the Straits, whether under Greek or Turkish sovereignty, were created
a demilitarized zone in which Britain, France, and Italy alone could maintain troops.[5]

The Treaty of Sèvres was never ratified and was at once made obsolete
by the Kemālist revival in Turkey. The Western ascendancy in the
Straits produced by reaction an alliance between Nationalist Turkey and
Soviet Russia, signed at Moscow in 1921, which proclaimed the freedom
of the Straits to be guaranteed under a statute drawn up by a conference

---

[1] *Survey* for 1920–3, pp. 328–32.   [2] *Survey* for 1925, ii. 165–6.
[3] *H.P.C.* vi. 26–28. This solution of the Straits problem had apparently first been proposed in
Toynbee's *Nationality and the War*, pp. vii, 375–8.
[4] *H.P.C.* vi. 64.   [5] Ibid. pp. 60–63.

of the littoral states of the Straits and the Black Sea: that is to say, excluding the Western Powers and giving Turkey and Russia a preponderant
voice.[1] When in 1922 the Turks drove the Greek invaders out of Anatolia
and themselves advanced into the Straits demilitarized zone as far as
Chanak, Britain was abandoned by France and Italy and the foundations
of the Sèvres settlement were swept away. The Mudania armistice of
1922 embodied a compromise, whereby the Allies conceded that Eastern
Thrace should be restored to Turkey and Turkey accepted the British
conception of the freedom of the Straits.[2] At the subsequent Lausanne
Conference the conflict of interests between the Western Powers and Russia
became uppermost, with Turkey in a position of detachment. The Western
Powers wanted the Straits to be open to a limited number of warships,
which would give themselves access to the Black Sea at the price of giving
Russia similar access to the Mediterranean; Russia wanted the Straits to
be closed to all warships. Turkey was prepared to come to terms with the
Western Powers; Eastern Thrace was restored to her, and the Lausanne
Treaty of 1923 included a Straits Convention with the following provisions: (1) Freedom of passage was established for merchant vessels in peace
and war. (2) Freedom of passage was allowed to all warships in time of
peace, except that no Power might send a fleet into the Black Sea larger
than the largest fleet of a littoral Power (which meant that, though no
single fleet larger than the Soviet fleet might pass the Straits, a combination of hostile fleets was still possible). (3) The shores of the Dardanelles
and the Bosporus only were demilitarized (and not, as under the Sèvres
Treaty, of the Sea of Marmara as well). (4) An international Straits
Commission was established to see that the provisions concerning the
passage of warships were carried out. (5) Turkish security was protected
by permission to close the Straits to enemy ships in a war in which she was
herself belligerent, and by a joint guarantee of the freedom of the Straits
and the security of the demilitarized zones by Britain, France, Italy, and
Japan. This treaty struck a balance between the predominance of the
Western Powers and Turkish national interests; Soviet Russia signed it
under protest and did not ratify it.[3]

The diplomatic links between Russia and Turkey were renewed as a
result of the conflict of interests between Britain and Turkey over the
question of Mosul, on the Turco-'Irāqi frontier; and in 1925 a Russo-
Turkish treaty of friendship and neutrality was signed at Paris.[4] Thenceforward Turkey alone of the Eastern European states, through the strength
of her strategic position and the sagacity and sobriety of her policy, and by

---

[1] *Survey* for 1920–3, pp. 370–2.
[2] *H.P.C.* vi. 38–39, 104–6.
[3] Ibid. pp. 108–10; *Survey* for 1920–3, pp. 374–6; *Survey* for 1936, pp. 595–8.
[4] *Survey* for 1925, i. 525; ii. 66. This treaty was renewed in 1929 and 1931 (*Survey* for 1931,
pp. 340–1), and again in 1935, and was denounced by the Soviet Government in 1945.

not leaning heavily to one side or the other, succeeded in combining an independent course and tolerable relations with all the neighbouring Great Powers, of whom the two most important for her were Russia and Britain.[1]

(f) THE ASCENDANCY OF FRANCE

The Allied Great Powers confirmed and established the small states of Eastern Europe as a barrier to Bolshevik Russia and a counterpoise to defeated Germany. The centre of this system was Poland. Being twice the size in population of any other Eastern European nation, and relying on her historic traditions as the dominant Power of Eastern Europe in the fifteenth and sixteenth centuries, she now aspired to the rank of Great Power.[2]

Poland aimed to be supreme in the Baltic region. The Baltic had become for a brief interval what it had not been before in modern history: a sea without a Great Power on its shores. Before 1914 it had been dominated by the German navy at the expense of the second Baltic Great Power, Russia. Russia had now lost her Baltic seaboard, except for less than a hundred miles, largely icebound, where Leningrad lies at the head of the Gulf of Finland. Of Germany's Baltic predominance the main instrument had been the Kiel Canal,[3] which was opened by the Versailles Treaty to all nations at peace with Germany, though its continuance under her sovereignty was an assurance of restored dominion.[4] There being

---

[1] Turkey had a common frontier with Britain all along her western and southern coasts where she bordered a sea in which Britain was the dominant Power; with France, on the southern border of Anatolia where she marched with the French mandated territory of Syria; with Italy, through the Italian possession of the Dodecanese. She made a treaty of friendship with Italy in 1928, which, however, had little foundation or consequence (see below, pp. 253-4); and another with France in 1930 (*Survey* for 1930, p. 316), which was followed, after the cession to Turkey of the Sanjaq of Alexandretta in 1938, by a Franco-Turkish declaration of mutual assistance (*Survey* for 1938, i. 491). Turkey did not form diplomatic ties with Britain until the eve of the Second World War, which resulted in the Anglo-Franco-Turkish treaty of alliance of 19 October 1939.

[2] The Poles numbered 19 millions in 1919; the Rumanians, the next largest, were $11\frac{1}{2}$ millions; the three Yugoslav peoples together, 10 millions; the Czechoslovaks collectively, 9 millions. On Poland's 'brevet rank as a Great Power', cf. Toynbee: *World after the Peace Conference*, pp. 35-36; *Survey* for 1926, pp. 20 seqq.; *Survey* for 1933, pp. 184-5, 206, 218; *Survey* for 1934, p. 409; *Survey* for 1936, pp. 393-4.

[3] See Toynbee: *Nationality and the War*, pp. 339, 347-58.

[4] Treaty of Versailles, articles 380-6; *H.P.C.* ii. 199-201; *Survey* for 1920-3, pp. 233-4. By the Treaty of Versailles (article 195) Germany had further to demolish all fortifications along her Baltic coastline. 'The Baltic has served many successive lords, but the Germans, in the later Middle Ages the German Hansards, and in modern days the German Reich, have wielded an unrivalled supremacy. One of the two gates into the sea, the Kiel Canal, belongs to Germany alone; the other, that through Scandinavian waters, she can practically close at will. Her Baltic coastline, which for seventy years stretched from Flensburg as far as Memel, was broken only from 1919 to 1939 by the short strips amputated at Versailles. Even then her ten ports on the Baltic formed a galaxy unrivalled by any other State' (W. F. Reddaway: *Problems of the Baltic* (Cambridge University Press, 1940), p. 104).

from 1919 to 1933 no active Great Power on the Baltic, the new Poland,
which controlled the Vistula, could claim the role. In October 1920, in the
flush of victory over Russia, Poland seized Vilna from Lithuania.[1] Like
Poland's other acts of violence this created its train of bad blood. Lithuania in consequence refused to establish diplomatic relations with Poland,
their common frontier remaining in a state of blockade for eighteen years.[2]
Her tradition of hostility towards Poland set up a corresponding tradition
of diplomatic amity with Soviet Russia,[3] and it was assisted by the Riga
Treaty, which separated Lithuania from Russia by a belt of territory that
gave Poland a common frontier with Latvia.[4] In 1923 Lithuania in her
turn flouted the Allied Powers and compensated herself by seizing Memel,
whose status had remained indefinite. The Allies could only recognize the
Lithuanian *fait accompli* as they had recognized its Polish precedents, and
they assigned the sovereignty over Memel to Lithuania on condition that
it should be constituted an autonomous area.[5]

From Rumania and Poland, the chain of Russia's frontier states continued north in Latvia, Estonia, and Finland; like Poland they had reason
to fear Russia, because they had won their independence at her expense,
and even after it had been recognized by the Soviet Union their relations
with her remained bad. Poland might seem their natural protector and
ally, and Polish policy aimed at forming a Baltic Union under her hegemony; but the aim was frustrated by her bad relations with Lithuania and
the suspicions aroused by her aggressive policy. In 1924 Finland entered
the Scandinavian group, since her historic links were with Sweden,
and the loss of the Åland Islands, in the Scandinavian political atmosphere,
was not intolerable;[6] and after 1925 the Baltic States turned their attention to a triple bloc between themselves.

The Polish-Rumanian alliance was the only internal diplomatic link
between the Baltic and Danubian regions; the Carpathians formed a
political as well as a physical barrier. Poland, whose existence involved
bad relations with Germany and Russia, whose aggression had established
a frontier with Russia in which Russia could never acquiesce and had
made an enemy of Lithuania, lived in bad relations also with Czechoslovakia, with whom she had an overriding common defensive interest
against Germany. The dispute centred upon Teschen, which was partitioned between the two in 1920; and the Poles felt that the Czechs had
taken advantage of Polish weakness during the Russo-Polish War to extract

---

[1] *H.P.C.* vi. 309; *Survey* for 1920–3, pp. 250–6.
[2] *Survey* for 1934, pp. 412–13. See below, pp. 268–9.
[3] *Survey* for 1920–3, p. 249; *Survey* for 1927, pp. 225–6; *Survey* for 1934, p. 412.
[4] *Survey* for 1920–3, pp. 243–4.
[5] Ibid. pp. 256–61.
[6] Ibid. p. 241; *Survey* for 1924, p. 461. See above, p. 158. On the Åland Islands dispute see
Survey for 1920–3, pp. 234–8.

concessions which could not have been obtained in times of peace.[1] North
of the Carpathians the main centre of unrest was Poland, an 'historic
nation' temporarily victorious and encroaching upon its neighbours;
south of the Carpathians the source of unrest was Hungary, an historic
nation temporarily defeated and seeking the restoration of its historical
rights in revisionist claims upon its neighbours. In 1920–1 the three leading successor states of the Dual Monarchy, Czechoslovakia, Yugoslavia,
and Rumania, formed the Little Entente against Hungarian revisionism
and the danger of a Habsburg restoration.[2] The Little Entente remained
for seventeen years the diplomatic skeleton of the Eastern European system.
What clothed it with flesh, and at the same time provided an external link
between the Danubian and Baltic regions, was the French alliance.
A military alliance between France and Poland was signed in 1921, after
General Weygand's mission had saved Poland from military collapse in
the Russo-Polish War.[3] In 1924 a treaty of friendship and alliance was
signed between France and Czechoslovakia.[4] These two alliances, between
France on the one hand and Poland and Czechoslovakia on the other,
were embodied in the Locarno Pact of 1925 in the form of treaties of
mutual guarantee.[5] But the Locarno Pact already weakened the Versailles
system in Eastern Europe by the distinction it made between Germany's
western frontier (which was multilaterally guaranteed by Germany,
France, Belgium, Britain, and Italy) and Germany's eastern frontier,
which Britain refused to guarantee, and which thus seemed to be recognized as possessing a less sacrosanct character. The French system of
alliances was completed by a Franco-Rumanian alliance in 1926[6] and a
Franco-Yugoslav alliance in 1927.[7] This series of treaties marked the high
point of Eastern Europe as a political ridge or wall. Thenceforward it was
subject to steady Italian erosion, unwittingly preparing for German
expansion ten years later.

(g) The Ascendancy of Italy

Though the immediate history of the Turkish and Russian successor
states after the First World War was similar, and drew them together,
their circumstances soon became different. Soviet Russia was pillaged,
ostracized, suspected, and feared, for she had adopted a creed that accentuated the old antagonism between Holy Russia and Europe, and she never

---

[1] *H.P.C.* iv. 348–67; *Survey* for 1920–3, pp. 210, 299; *Survey* for 1924, pp. 457–8; *Survey* for
1935, i. 279–86. There was a slight *rapprochement* in 1925 (*Survey* for 1925, ii. 247–50).

[2] *H.P.C.* iv. 428, 436, 493–6; *Survey* for 1920–3, pp. 287–303.

[3] Ibid. pp. 272–3.   [4] *Survey* for 1924, p. 441.

[5] *Survey* for 1925, ii. 52, 55, 451–2. It was the Franco-Czechoslovak treaties of 1924 and 1925
(the latter an integral part of the Locarno Pact) that France evaded and dishonoured at Munich.

[6] *Survey* for 1926, pp. 156, 485–7.

[7] Ibid. pp. 156–7; *Survey* for 1927, pp. 154–5, 162–3, 539–41.

lost her potential status of Great Power. Nationalist Turkey liquidated the heritage of the Ottoman Empire, repulsed her invaders, and transformed herself into a well-conducted national Small Power on the Western model. Greece endeavoured to wring gains from Turkey's weakness as Poland did from Russia's, and between 1919 and 1922 followed a brief dream of eastern expansion,[1] but the Anatolian sea-board proved a Curzon Line she could not pass. She was once more confined to a Balkan policy, and her foreign policy became concerned again with relations with Yugoslavia and Bulgaria to her north.[2]

Greece, Yugoslavia, and Rumania had the same kind of common interest against Bulgarian revisionism that Yugoslavia, Rumania, and Czechoslovakia had against Hungarian. But there were certain differences. There were ties between Bulgaria and her victors which had no counterpart in the case of Hungary; and there were larger disagreements between the victors than in the case of the Little Entente, so that a Balkan Entente was not concluded until 1934. The main tie between Bulgaria and her victors was that with Yugoslavia. It was Stamboliski's policy to establish a Balkan federation based on the unity of the South Slav peoples, and though he was thrown from power before he could advance towards his aim, the ideal remained deeply rooted in the Bulgarian mind. The Balkan vortex was centred not on Bulgaria itself so much as on Macedonia, the indeterminate region where the frontiers of Yugoslavia, Greece, and Bulgaria all met, and here the conflict of interests was triangular. Bulgaria had irredentist claims to Serbian Macedonia, and became the headquarters of the Internal Macedonian Revolutionary Organization (IMRO), although she was herself the worst victim of that body.[3] Bulgaria's chief loss by the Neuilly Treaty was Western Thrace, and she had constant claims upon Greece for access to the Aegean through Dedeagatch or a similar port.[4] But Yugoslavia likewise had southward-thrusting claims against Greece, for access to the Aegean at Salonika, and these for many years were the cause of bad relations between the two.[5]

But just as the relationships of the Baltic states were ultimately determined by the positive pressure or the negative attraction of Germany and Russia, so the relationships of the Danubian and Balkan countries were not self-determining. Before 1914 Balkan politics had been overshadowed

---

[1] On Venizelos's dream of creating 'a real *Magna Graecia*' (*sic*) in Asia Minor see *H.P.C.* iv. 452–3.   [2] See *Survey* for 1920–3, pp. 333–8.

[3] IMRO was founded in 1896 to liberate Macedonia from Turkish rule and unite all Macedonians for that purpose irrespective of their nationality. After the First World War it became the main instrument of Bulgarian revisionism against Yugoslavia, until it was suppressed by Velchev in 1934. It was the European prototype of a liberation movement which degenerates into a terrorist organization. See J. Swire: *Bulgarian Conspiracy* (London, Hale, 1939); H. Seton-Watson: *Eastern Europe*, pp. 247–51, 312–16; Barker: *Macedonia*, pp. 16 seqq., 36–45.

[4] *H.P.C.* iv. 456–9; *Survey* for 1920–3, pp. 338–40.

[5] Ibid., pp. 340–3; *Survey* for 1926, pp. 165–77; *Survey* for 1928, pp. 183–7.

by Austria-Hungary and Russia. After 1918 Russia's influence was temporarily in abeyance; but with the disappearance of Austria-Hungary, whom the Italians considered as their ancient enemy, Italy immediately stepped into the Austro-Hungarian role as the dominating influence and disturbing factor in South-Eastern Europe. In the 1920s Mussolini's flamboyant and provocative part in European politics was comparable to that played at earlier times by Kaiser Wilhelm II or Napoleon III,[1] and an overture to that about to be played by a more considerable dictator north of the Alps. Italian policy in South-Eastern Europe was consistently malignant in that it pursued opportunist designs of hegemony which Italy herself lacked the strength to fulfil, a prestige policy of rivalry with France, with the aim and effect of exacerbating conflicts and promoting new hatreds.

Like Greece, Italy had aims of aggrandizement in the Aegean at Turkey's expense. These were first realized when she occupied the Dodecanese and Rhodes in the Italo-Turkish War of 1911–12. Her pledge to evacuate them only when the Turkish evacuation of Libya was complete allowed her to be in continued occupation of the islands when the First World War brought the opportunity of a more extensive partition of Turkey.[2] By the secret Treaty of London of 1915 Italy was to obtain the Adalian sector of Anatolia and the Dodecanese in full sovereignty, despite previous disclaimers of an intention of annexing Greek islands.[3] By the Venizelos–Tittoni agreement of 1919, Italy agreed to cede the Dodecanese to Greece, and to hold a plebiscite in Rhodes when Britain ceded Cyprus; this agreement was to have simultaneous effect with the Treaty of Sèvres, by which Italy obtained an enlarged sphere of Anatolia. But Italy's Anatolian dreams along with those of Greece were blown away by the Kemālist renaissance in Turkey. In 1922 she accordingly denounced the Venizelos–Tittoni agreement as invalidated by the nullity of the Treaty of Sèvres; and under the Treaty of Lausanne of 1923 she finally secured the sovereignty of the Dodecanese, a modest but satisfying balance out of her Near Eastern speculations,[4] but at the expense of creating lasting hostility in Turkey and Greece.

[1] *Survey* for 1927, p. 115.

[2] For the original connexion between the Dodecanesian and Libyan questions see *Turkey in Asia*, Peace Handbooks issued by the Historical Section of the Foreign Office, vol. xi (London, H.M.S.O., 1920), no. 64 (*Islands of the Northern and Eastern Aegean*), pp. 19–20; and *Spanish and Italian Possessions: Independent States*, vol. xx of the same series, no. 127 (*Italian Libya*), pp. 22–26, with appendixes.

[3] For the text of the secret Treaty of London of 1915, see *H.P.C.* v. 384–91. Italy's territorial claims in Asia Minor were defined by the Agreement of St. Jean de Maurienne of 1917, which, however, never obtained the necessary consent of Russia (ibid. vi. 18–22).

[4] Ibid. pp. 31, note, 37–38, 117; *Survey* for 1924, pp. 470–1. The Dodecanesian question, which was originally entangled with that of Libya, at this stage became entangled with that of Jubaland (*Survey* for 1924, pp. 465–8).

The nearer and more urgent object of Italian policy was to succeed to the inheritance of Austria-Hungary. The irredentist formula was 'Trent and Trieste', which meant in effect the Brenner frontier and control of the Adriatic. By the secret Treaty of London of 1915 Italy was conceded the Brenner frontier, and had this gain confirmed at the Peace Conference on grounds of strategic necessity, although it meant not only the redemption of the Italian Trentino but also the acquisition of the purely German South Tyrol or Alto Adige, and the drawing of a frontier that put the new Austrian Republic at Italy's military discretion.[1] It was an index of Austrian weakness that the Fascist Government's ruthless policy of denationalization against the German minority in the South Tyrol,[2] unparalleled in pre-war Austrian policy in the Trentino, did not, as it would have done between states of a more equal size, cause permanent bad relations, or prevent Austria from becoming an Italian satellite.

Control of the Adriatic involved two separate aims—control of Albania, and control of Istria with the Croatian and Dalmatian coasts. Albania was a principal strategic position of Eastern Europe, one of the historic gateways between Western Europe and the Balkans, controlling also, by the splendid harbour of Valona, the Straits of Otranto leading into the Adriatic. Albanian independence from a hostile Power was as vital an interest for Italy as the independence of the Low Countries for Britain. The declaration of Albanian independence in 1912 during the First Balkan War was accepted by the Great Powers as preferable to the partition of Albania between Serbia and Greece, because Austria-Hungary and Italy had determined on the creation of an Albanian buffer state. In 1913 Albania was accordingly recognized by the Great Powers as a sovereign principality, to be neutralized like Belgium under their guarantee.[3] With the outbreak of the First World War this status was never confirmed, and in Italian policy the buffer state quickly developed into a bridgehead. In November 1914 Italy occupied Valona, and by the secret Treaty of London of 1915 she was to acquire the port, with a protectorate over Albania. At the Peace Conference she was offered a mandate over Albania, but she returned it in 1920, chiefly because of the success of Ahmed Bey Zogu in playing on a small scale the role of a Mustafā Kemāl as leader of the forces of Albanian nationalism against foreign intervention. By an Italo-Albanian agreement of 1920 Italy withdrew her troops from Albania,

---

[1] *H.P.C.* iv. 280–7.

[2] *Survey* for 1927, pp. 185–201.

[3] Organic Statute of the Albanian State, 29 July 1913, clause 3 (Gooch and Temperley, vol. ix, part ii, no. 1186; G. F. de Martens: *Nouveau recueil général de traités*, 3rd ser., vol. ix (Leipzig, T. Weicher, 1938), p. 650). The Great Powers had accepted the principle of Albanian autonomy on 20 December 1912 (Gooch and Temperley, vol. ix, part ii, no. 403), and the settlement of Albania had been reserved for their decision by the Treaty of London of 30 May 1913, article iii (Martens, op. cit. viii. 16).

retaining only the island of Sasseno which dominated the Bay of Valona.[1] In the same year Albania was admitted to the League of Nations, without the question of her neutralization having been revived.[2]

The frontiers of Albania were fixed in 1921.[3] At the same time the Allied Great Powers declared that the violation of Albania's frontiers or independence 'might constitute a danger for the strategic safety of Italy', and that if Albania should appeal to the Council of the League because her independence was endangered the Great Powers would 'recommend that the restoration of the territorial frontiers of Albania should be entrusted to Italy'.[4] Italy thus secured a reversionary interest in Albania amounting to a contingent mandate.[5] The delimitation of Albanian frontiers upon the spot was not completed until 1926,[6] and the process involved sharp conflicts of interests between Italy on the one side and Yugoslavia and Greece on the other, giving occasion for the first assertion of Italian power and prestige by the Fascist Government. In 1923 Italy took advantage of the murder of an Italian general engaged in the delimitation of the Graeco-Albanian frontier to deliver an ultimatum to Greece, followed by the bombardment and occupation of Corfù, one of the most important strategic points in the Mediterranean, which had been neutralized since 1864.[7] This act of violence marked the international début of Italian Fascism, and left an enduring impression on Greek minds.[8] The condonation of the Polish seizure of Vilna now had its fruit in the first defiance of the new international order and of the League of Nations by a Great Power.

[1] See J. Swire: *Albania: the Rise of a Kingdom* (London, Williams & Norgate, 1929), pp. 322–4. Sasseno had been a dependency of Corfù and Paxo when these islands were neutralized on the cession of the Ionian Islands by Britain to Greece in 1864 (see below, note 7). In 1914 Italy prevailed upon Greece to cede Sasseno to Albania (*British and Foreign State Papers*, cvii. 889).

[2] See *H.P.C.* iv. 338–47; Oppenheim: *International Law*, ii. 231, note 1; Robinson: *Albania's Road to Freedom*, pp. 41–46.

[3] *Survey* for 1920–3, pp. 343–8.

[4] Declaration by the Governments of the British Empire, France, Italy, and Japan, in regard to Albania, 9 November 1921 (*League of Nations Treaty Series*, xii. 383; *Survey* for 1927, pp. 166–7).

[5] See Robinson: *Albania's Road to Freedom*, p. 46.

[6] See *Survey* for 1925, ii. 282–8.

[7] See *Survey* for 1920–3, pp. 343–8; George Glasgow: *The Janina Murders and the Occupation of Corfu* (London, Anglo-Hellenic League, 1923). Corfù, Paxo, and their dependencies had been neutralized when Britain ceded the Ionian Islands to Greece, by the Treaty of London, 1864, article ii (Hertslet: *Map of Europe by Treaty*, iii. 1592; cf. Cruttwell: *Peaceful Change*, pp. 11, 55). This neutrality was violated by the protecting Powers themselves, Britain, France, and Russia, when they occupied Corfù in 1916 (see G. F. Abbott: *Greece and the Allies 1914–1922* (London, Methuen, 1922), pp. 85–86, and J. W. Garner: *International Law and the World War* (London, Longmans, Green, 1920), ii. 241 seqq.). It appears, however, that after the First World War Corfù automatically resumed its neutral status, since the Treaty of London, 1864, remained in force, and that in this respect the Italian act of aggression in 1923 was aggravated, though it was not an aspect of the matter to which Britain and France could conveniently advert (see Quincy Wright in *The American Journal of International Law*, 1924, xviii. 104–8, who does not mention, however, the Allied violation of Corfiote neutrality in 1916).

[8] See Monroe: *Mediterranean in Politics*, pp. 179–80.

By the secret Treaty of London of 1915 Italy was to succeed Austria-Hungary in possession of Trieste, Gorizia, Istria, and half the Dalmatian coast, as well as Valona in Albania, on strategic grounds which would have put 750,000 Yugoslavs under Italian rule. The corollary of this policy was intense Italian hostility to the enlargement of Serbia into an Adriatic Yugoslav state.[1] Italian claims were whittled down by the Peace Conference, leaving as their residue the unsettled question of a buffer-state of Fiume, which by the Italo-Yugoslav Treaty of Rapallo in 1920 was at length erected into a free city.[2] It took Germany twenty-one years to extinguish the Free City of Danzig, and then at the cost of precipitating a European war; it took Italy only four to extinguish Fiume: an index of the difference in strength between a defeated Germany and a victorious Italy, a resolute Poland and a weakened Yugoslavia, as well as the difference between the constellations of European power in 1923 and 1939. One of the first achievements of the Fascist Government was to take over the inheritance of d'Annunzio by incorporating Fiume in Italy *de facto*; and in 1924 Yugoslavia was compelled to consent to the partition of the territory, Italy gaining the chief advantage.[3]

As a result of the Peace Settlement, therefore, Italy gained important positions in Eastern Europe, which enabled her to pursue an active policy of intervention and disruption that was the conditioning factor in Balkan and Danubian politics until she was eclipsed by Nazi Germany.

Now Italy can only move in an easterly direction [said Mussolini after the Fiume Agreement in 1924], the fact being that on the west there are national states which have taken definitive form and to which we can send nothing except our labour. . . . Therefore the lines for the pacific expansion of Italy lie towards the east.[4]

Italian policy pursued four related aims: the extension of a virtual protectorate over Austria in the north and Albania in the east; the isolation and disruption of Yugoslavia, which was not only contiguous but was also the strongest of the Balkan Powers, by fomenting the Croat question in the north and the Macedonian question in the south;[5] the support of the revisionist Powers, Bulgaria and Hungary; and consequently opposition to Yugoslavia's ally France as dominant Power in Eastern Europe. These aims were pursued not only by diplomatic means, but secretly, by the subsidizing of Fascist and terrorist groups in other countries, and illegally,

---

[1] On Italian opposition to the recognition of the Serb–Croat–Slovene state, see *H.P.C.* iv. 131, 206–7; v. 158–9.

[2] *H.P.C.* iv. 301–35.   [3] *Survey* for 1924, pp. 408–22.

[4] Ibid. p. 442.

[5] 'Albania and Bulgaria were separated by Jugoslav Macedonia, to parts of which each advanced claims on ethnical grounds. From Durazzo to Salonica, across Albania, Jugoslav and Greek territory, had once gone the "Via Egnatia", highway of Imperial Rome for the domination of the Balkan Peninsula' (H. Seton-Watson: *Eastern Europe*, p. 367). Italy promised Albania a common frontier with Bulgaria (Swire: *Bulgarian Conspiracy*, p. 214).

by arms-running in contravention of the Peace Treaties. In the Szent Gotthard incident of January 1928, Italy was implicated in the smuggling of machine-guns to Hungary; and in January 1933 the socialist workmen at the Austrian arms factory at Hirtenberg exposed a similar smuggling of rifles and machine-guns, probably destined not only for Hungary but also for the Heimwehr in Austria.[1] Italy patronized and financed both IMRO, the Macedonian terrorist organization, and Ustaša, its Croatian counterpart. In 1929 the Ustaša leader Pavelić had to flee from Yugoslavia, Ustaša and IMRO concluded a formal alliance, and thenceforward Pavelić lived mainly in Italy or Hungary.[2] The international revolutionary policy of Fascist Italy culminated in the murder of Alexander of Yugoslavia in 1934.

The Italian forward policy first became overt in 1926, when Mussolini rejected a French and Yugoslav proposal of a tripartite treaty between France, Italy, and Yugoslavia for the stabilization of the Balkans.[3] In November 1926 Italy and Albania signed a treaty of friendship and security, which the British Minister in Tirana regarded as incompatible with Albanian independence[4] and which initiated a crisis that lasted for a year. In April 1927, Italy and Hungary signed a treaty of friendship and arbitration.[5] Yugoslavia replied by securing, on 11 November 1927, the signature of her treaty of friendship and arbitration with France, which completed the links between France and the Little Entente.[6] On 22 November 1927 Italy and Albania signed a defensive alliance, which was the outward expression of the increasing Italian hold over the military and economic organization of Albania.[7] In 1928 Italy secured treaties of friendship with Turkey and Greece, by which she hoped to consolidate her influence in the Eastern Mediterranean.[8] For Turkey this was a reinsurance against her treaty of 1925 with the Soviet Union,[9] as well as an attempt to avert Italian expansionist claims; for Greece it served to bring pressure to bear on Yugoslavia for a settlement of the Salonika dispute.[10] But Turkey and Greece did not abate their suspicions of Italian imperial-

---

[1] *Survey* for 1928, pp. 161–7; *Survey* for 1933, p. 247, note 2; *Survey* for 1934, p. 494, note 2. There are versions of these obscure incidents in George Seldes: *Sawdust Caesar* (London, Barker, 1936), pp. 264–7, and G. E. R. Gedye: *Fallen Bastions* (London, Gollancz, 1939), pp. 74–76.

[2] *Survey* for 1934, p. 559, note 3; Swire: *Bulgarian Conspiracy*, especially pp. 49, 169–70, 223–4; Macartney: *Hungary and her Successors*, p. 374. See also Cecil F. Melville: *Balkan Racket* (London, Jarrolds, 1942), chapter i.   [3] *Survey* for 1927, p. 154.

[4] Ibid. pp. 156, 169–71. On the incident of the British Minister, see H. Seton-Watson: *Eastern Europe*, p. 371; Swire: *Albania*, p. 473; Robinson: *Albania's Road to Freedom*, pp. 76–77; cf. *Survey* for 1927, p. 173.

[5] Ibid. p. 159. The corresponding entente between Italy and Bulgaria was not enshrined in a treaty, but was crowned by the marriage of Tsar Boris to an Italian princess in 1930 (*Survey* for 1930, p. 156, note 2).

[6] *Survey* for 1927, pp. 162–3.   [7] Ibid. pp. 163, 182–3.

[8] *Survey* for 1928, pp. 158–61.   [9] Ibid. p. 158.

[10] Ibid. p. 185.

ism, their memories of Anatolian claims, of the Dodecanese and Corfù;[1] and when the Graeco-Turkish *rapprochement* which Italy had striven for as the third side of her East Mediterranean triangle was finally achieved in 1930,[2] it proved to be, not an instrument of Italian designs, but the most enduring bulwark of the *status quo* in Eastern Europe.[3]

In 1932 Turkish policy as a conservative Power was crowned by her entry into the League of Nations.[4] It was under the combined leadership of Greece and Turkey that the tendency towards Balkan unity now acquired new momentum, as a reaction against the division of the Balkan states between the French and Italian systems. An unofficial Balkan Conference was set up of the six Balkan states, Yugoslavia, Rumania, Bulgaria, Albania, Greece, and Turkey, which held annual sessions from 1930 to 1933.[5] They failed of any lasting political agreement, because of the Bulgarian revisionism that refused to sign any general Balkan treaty involving recognition of the *status quo*. The only result of the movement towards Balkan unity was the conclusion in 1934 of the Balkan Pact, by which Yugoslavia, Rumania, Greece, and Turkey mutually guaranteed their frontiers against aggression by a Balkan state, and also against a Balkan state which joined another Power in aggression against a signatory.[6] The latter clause quickly disclosed that the interdependence of the Balkan Powers did not outweigh their several dependence upon non-Balkan Great Powers: Turkey qualified the Pact by insisting that she would not be obliged to go to war with Russia on behalf of Rumania, because of the Russo-Turkish treaty of 1925, and Greece by insisting that she would not be obliged to go to war with any Great Power, meaning Italy.[7] The Pact was open to the adherence of the other two Balkan countries, but they never joined. The omission of Albania already impaired the Entente in its character of a united front against the Great Powers. Albania had shown a disposition to join, having in 1931 so far emancipated herself from Italian supervision that she refused to renew the treaty of 1926, but by 1934 Italy had resumed sufficient control to forbid her signing the Pact.[8] The omission of Bulgaria gave the Balkan Entente as

---

[1] *Survey* for 1925, i. 526, note 3; *Survey* for 1934, p. 330; *Survey* for 1925, ii. 83 and note 2; *Survey* for 1936, pp. 601–2. 'Italy's historical objectives are Asia and Africa', Mussolini's speech of 18 March 1934.

[2] *Survey* for 1930, pp. 157–68.

[3] Cf. *Survey* for 1931, pp. 326–9; *Survey* for 1934, pp. 518–19. This was the only one of the treaties between Eastern European Powers which survived the Second World War (*The Times*, 6 April 1948).

[4] *Survey* for 1934, pp. 216–20.

[5] See *Survey* for 1930, pp. 145–56; *Survey* for 1931, pp. 324–40; *Survey* for 1934, pp. 508–11.

[6] Ibid. pp. 526–7.

[7] Ibid. pp. 527–8. The contingency foreseen by the Turks was that in a war between Russia and Rumania, Bulgaria might be drawn in on the Russian side, and Turkey thereby obliged to go to war against Bulgaria and Russia.

[8] *Survey* for 1934, pp. 523; note 2, and 535–6.

purely anti-revisionist an appearance as the Little Entente, and nullified its character as an embryonic Balkan federation by leaving a dissident state in a key position, as a foothold for any Great Power.[1] The isolation of Bulgaria, however, was by no means as complete as that of Hungary. Her relations with Yugoslavia, against whom she had the largest territorial claims, were by turns fratricidal and fraternal, and in 1933 and 1934 the latter tendency was so marked that it alarmed Greece and Turkey.[2] The formation of the Balkan Entente encouraged the *coup d'état* in Bulgaria in 1934 by Velchev and Georgiev, who at long last suppressed IMRO and drew tighter the bonds with Yugoslavia.[3] But the overthrow of Velchev by Boris in 1935 meant that the policy of Bulgaro-Yugoslav *rapprochement* was brought to fruition by other hands, and with other implications.

From 1930 until 1934 Italian influence in Eastern Europe moved towards its zenith, at the same time as the rivalry between the French and Italian systems was becoming blurred and eclipsed, first by the world economic crisis, and then by the resurgence of Germany. These causes produced a tendency towards consolidation in the Danubian region as well as in the Balkans, though fainter and less successful. Czechoslovak policy had consistently sought to renew economic collaboration between the Danubian states (Czechoslovakia, Austria, Hungary, Yugoslavia, and Rumania), on a basis of acceptance of the existing frontiers, and the need was sharpened by the world crisis. In 1931 Austria proposed to improve her own economic position by concluding a customs union with Germany. France and Czechoslovakia energetically opposed the project and secured its defeat on the ground that it must lead to the forbidden political union.[4] They were joined in their opposition by Italy, the first occasion that French and Italian interests in Eastern Europe had coincided,[5] and for the next three years Italy was establishing her own control over Austria. France and Czechoslovakia replaced the proposal for an Austro-German customs union by a Danubian customs preference plan, associated with the name of Tardieu, which would consolidate French influence in Central Europe; but this was wrecked on the opposition of Italy and Germany.[6] Italy had one thing in common with Germany, opposition to the extension of French influence in Eastern Europe, as she had one thing in common with France, opposition to the extension of German influence.

In February 1933, a fortnight after Hitler's accession to power in Germany, the states of the Little Entente signed a Pact of Organization, by

---

[1] On the importance of Bulgaria's strategic position, see *H.P.C.* iv. 444–6; *Survey* for 1934, p. 512.
[2] Ibid. pp. 513–16; cf. pp. 352–3; *Survey* for 1936, p. 601.
[3] Ibid. pp. 531–2; H. Seton-Watson: *Eastern Europe*, p. 374.
[4] *Survey* for 1931, pp. 36–38, 297–323.
[5] Ibid. pp. 243, note 3, and 319–20.
[6] *Survey* for 1932, pp. 22–23; *Survey* for 1933, p. 205, note 3; *Survey* for 1934, pp. 487–9.

which they renewed their original bilateral treaties of alliance in perpetuity, and set up a Permanent Council of Foreign Ministers to unify their foreign policy.[1] This was the high point in the consolidation of the Little Entente. A month later Mussolini proposed a Four-Power Pact between Italy, France, Britain, and Germany which would formally replace the French hegemony in Eastern Europe by a directory of the Great Powers, among whom France would be in a minority, and from whom Russia was excluded. The four Powers were to promote the revision of the peace treaties and to concede equality of armaments by degrees to Germany, Austria, Hungary, and Bulgaria. The plan was a logical conclusion of Italy's policy of prestige, revisionism, and rivalry with France. It was vigorously countered by the Little Entente and Poland, and successfully emasculated by the French, so that the Four-Power Pact that was finally signed in June 1933 had been deprived of its original features and rendered safely innocuous.[2] As the project for an Austro-German customs union prefigured the Anschluss, so the Four-Power Pact prefigured Munich. But now France and her allies were still able to stave off what they feared, and Italy, lacking the strength to reorganize and control the Concert of the Powers as Germany did five years later, fell back instead on the consolidation of the small revisionist states of Eastern Europe.

The year 1934 shook the structure of Eastern Europe to its foundations. In 1933 Dollfuss had suspended parliamentary government in Austria, seeking, by one of those political moves so frequent in international affairs, to avert the effects of the Nazi Revolution in Germany by imitating it.[3] The janissaries in the Austrian dictatorship were Starhemberg's *Heimwehr*, who were financed from Italy, and were scarcely less the Italian faction in Austria than the Austrian Nazis were the German faction; and Dollfuss cultivated the patronage of Italy. In February 1934 he suppressed the Social-Democrats in a brief civil war, and finally transformed Austria into a Fascist state.[4] He had the support and encouragement of Mussolini, who had his own grievance against the Social-Democrats of Austria for their exposure of the Hirtenberg scandal.[5] A month later Austria signed with Italy and Hungary the Rome protocols, providing for consultations on matters of policy and economic co-operation.[6] This crowned Italian policy towards her Danubian satellites, and successfully prevented the formation of a common front against Germany.[7] When, in July 1934, Dollfuss was murdered in the Nazi *putsch* in Austria, Italy mobilized four divisions on the Italo-Austrian frontier and declared her intention of defending Austrian independence.[8] It was the culminating point of

---

[1] *Survey* for 1933, pp. 203–5.
[2] Ibid. pp. 208–21; cf. Beloff, i. 90–1.
[3] *Survey* for 1934, pp. 435–6.
[4] Ibid. pp. 456–67.
[5] See H. Seton-Watson: *Eastern Europe*, p. 376.
[6] *Survey* for 1934, pp. 487–507.
[7] *Survey* for 1933, p. 205, note 3.
[8] *Survey* for 1934, pp. 471–5.

Italian power in Eastern Europe between the wars. Thenceforward her power ebbed, as she dissipated her forces in Africa and Spain, until in less than four years she accepted the German annexation of Austria.

The Franco-Italian competition for the hegemony of Eastern Europe had, however, one last violent act. French policy in 1934 concentrated on establishing a *rapprochement* with Italy against Germany, and this involved a settlement of the feud between Italy and Yugoslavia. Yugoslavia had seen with alarm the increase of Italian control over Austria, which, when it was coupled with Italian control over Albania, threatened to encircle Yugoslavia on three sides, as Germany was later to encircle successively Czechoslovakia and Poland. In 1933 and again in July 1934 Yugoslavia had declared that if Italian forces entered Austria, Yugoslav forces would follow suit.[1] French attempts to establish an understanding with Italy produced a *refroidissement* between France and Yugoslavia. In October 1934 King Alexander of Yugoslavia sailed to Marseilles to meet Barthou, the French Foreign Minister, and was there assassinated.[2] The purpose of his mission died with him, whether he went to warn France that Yugoslavia must have equal rights with France and Italy in any international arrangement to safeguard Austria, or to inform France of the prospects of the Balkan Pact, or in connexion with Barthou's plans for an Eastern European pact.[3] The assassination laid bare the nature of Italian policy in the Balkans: it was the fruit of Italian and Hungarian patronage of Croat terrorists, it had been organized from Italian and Hungarian territory, and after the murder Italy refused to extradite Pavelić or to put him on trial;[4] and by a twist which showed the unity of the attack on Yugoslavia the assassin himself was a Bulgarian member of IMRO.[5] France was concerned to prevent international repercussions that would endanger a *rapprochement* between herself, Italy, and Yugoslavia; she therefore put pressure on Yugoslavia not to accuse Italy, and secured in exchange that Italy would not shield her satellite Hungary. In this way the League Council achieved a compromise.[6]

[1] Ibid. pp. 341, 475–6, 556–7 and note.
[2] Ibid. pp. 537–77.
[3] Ibid. p. 538.
[4] Ibid. pp. 560–1.
[5] See Swire: *Bulgarian Conspiracy*, pp. 33–34, 291–2. 'The Croats and Macedonians trained in Italy and Hungary who killed King Alexander of Yugoslavia represented the highest point of expertise in terrorism that man has yet attained' (West: *Black Lamb and Grey Falcon*, i. 365).
[6] 'In thus composing a political dispute which had been embittered by an inveterate national feud, envenomed by a dictated Peace Settlement, and brought to a head by a series of violent "incidents" culminating in the assassination of the head of one of the two states concerned, the League of Nations had achieved a remarkable success' (*Survey* for 1934, p. 573). 'The "solution" of the Marseilles incident, acclaimed by many well-meaning people as a "triumph of the League of Nations", was in point of fact a peculiarly discreditable piece of "secret diplomacy"' (H. Seton-Watson: *Eastern Europe*, pp. 377–8).

(h) THE ASCENDANCY OF GERMANY

Inherently weak and divided, weakened and divided further by ten years of Polish imperialism, Italian intervention, and Macedonian terrorism, Eastern Europe was ripe for German expansion. The Nazi Revolution threw its ripples outwards to disturb first the Baltic and Danubian regions, where Germany was herself a Power, and then the Balkans from which she was divided by a double or triple layer of intervening states. International revolutionary terrorism passed from Italian-sponsored hands into German, where it was more firmly and purposefully wielded. The French system of alliances in Eastern Europe, devised to meet this contingency, was at once distorted and soon destroyed by it. For the German revival produced a diplomatic revolution, which called in Soviet Russia to replace Poland as the Western Powers' counterweight to Germany;[1] relieved Poland herself of the fear of encirclement, Rumania of the pressure of Russia, and Yugoslavia of the pressure of Italy, so beginning the disintegration of the Little Entente;[2] at length drew Italy into Germany's wake, and sealed off Eastern from Western Europe.

The Powers most immediately menaced by the Nazi Revolution were Austria and Poland: Austria, because the Anschluss was the declared aim of Hitler's policy;[3] Poland, because Germany had never acquiesced in the losses of territory along her eastern frontier. But the diplomatic revolution in the Baltic was spectacular. For Poland, Nazism was an ambiguous phenomenon. It offered an opportunity of dividing Poland's enemies, since the new German régime was anti-Bolshevik and repudiated the entente with Soviet Russia that had been the basis of Weimar foreign policy. Nazism showed goodwill towards Poland, not only in Germany, but also in Danzig, where the Nazis captured political control in May 1933.[4] Moreover, Pilsudski hated Russia more than Germany, and there seemed an affinity between his illiberal régime in Poland and the reactionary and anti-Communist aspects of the Nazi régime in Germany. In March and again in November 1933 Pilsudski proposed military preventive measures against Hitler to France, which France rejected.[5] This alternative blocked, Poland accordingly signed in January 1934 a ten years' non-aggression pact with Hitler, the first crack in the French system in Eastern Europe.[6]

---

[1] See however Beloff, i. 140: 'The French generals, and such professional diplomats as Alexis Léger, regarded a Franco-Soviet agreement as desirable mainly in order to destroy any bonds which might remain between the U.S.S.R. and Germany, and to strengthen the position of Poland and Roumania. The Red Army was not thought of as a serious supplement to the armed might of France and her allies.'

[2] Cf. *Survey* for 1934, pp. 341–2.   [3] See *Mein Kampf*, p. 1.

[4] *Survey* for 1933, p. 187; *Survey* for 1935, i. 213–15.

[5] Namier: *Diplomatic Prelude*, pp. 97, note 3, and 439; Beloff, i. 92, note 1.

[6] *Survey* for 1933, pp. 183–6; *Survey* for 1934, pp. 327–8; *Survey* for 1935, i. 204 seqq.

The Polish-German *rapprochement* made its consequences felt immediately on the states contiguous with Poland. Its first effect was a revival of Polish hostility to Czechoslovakia, which gave the Polish-German Pact the appearance of covering an understanding for the joint satisfaction of Polish and German irredentist claims on Czechoslovakia.[1] Its second effect was to excite the three Baltic States into collaboration. On 17 February 1934, Latvia and Estonia, already alarmed by the threat of the Nazi Revolution to themselves as possible German *irredente*, had signed a defensive alliance modelled on the Balkan Pact and the Little Entente Pact of Organization.[2] But the more particular consequence of the Polish-German Pact was to encircle Lithuania. Lithuania had hitherto carried on a feud with Poland over Vilna and with Germany over Memel, a double policy which was possible only so long as Poland's own attention was divided between hostility towards Russia and hostility towards Germany. The Polish-German Pact was a junction of Lithuania's enemies, putting Lithuania in a position which foreshadowed that in which Poland herself was afterwards placed by the German-Soviet Pact of 23 August 1939. This stimulated Lithuania into joining the Estonian-Latvian Pact on 12 September 1934.[3] The third effect was to confirm Russia's tendency towards joining the anti-revisionist camp, which led to her admission to the League of Nations on 18 September 1934.[4] This move was preceded by the recognition of the Soviet Union *de jure* by Hungary, Czechoslovakia, Rumania, Bulgaria, and Albania, which left Yugoslavia as the only Eastern European state that had still not established full diplomatic relations with Russia.[5]

The diplomatic revolution was crowned by Soviet Russia's pacts of mutual assistance with France of 2 May 1935,[6] and with Czechoslovakia of 16 May 1935,[7] which finally alined her among the anti-revisionist Powers. With this rearrangement of forces the political subsidence of Eastern Europe was accomplished. Instead of a barrier it became a

---

[1] *Survey* for 1935, i. 288-98.   [2] *Survey* for 1934, p. 411.
[3] Ibid. pp. 414-15.

[4] Ibid. pp. 388-404. The Russian reaction to the Polish–German Pact was guarded (see *Survey* for 1935, i. 62-63, 279, and Beloff, i. 140), but a little later its aggressive purpose was assumed by European Communists in the broad and undiscriminating lines of their world-picture. Cf. R. Palme Dutt: *World Politics, 1918–1936* (London, Gollancz, 1936), pp. 268-9, 297-302.

[5] By Hungary on 6 February 1934; by Czechoslovakia and Rumania, after a meeting of the Permanent Council of the Little Entente, and with Yugoslav approval, on 9 June; by Bulgaria on 23 July; by Albania on 17 September (*Survey* for 1934, pp. 391-2; Beloff, i. 131, note 2). The recognition by Rumania did not involve any settlement of the Bessarabian question (*Survey* for 1934, pp. 378, 382). Yugoslavia continued to refuse recognition because of the personal repugnance for the Bolshevik régime of King Alexander and after him of his brother the Regent Prince Paul, with their Tsarist connexions and upbringing; and diplomatic relations between Yugoslavia and Soviet Russia were not established till 24 June 1940.

[6] *Survey* for 1935, i. 79-81.   [7] Ibid. p. 82.

valley, imperfectly traversed by the ridge of Czechoslovakia. But the
Franco-Soviet Pact, which for France was the core of that eastern pact
she had been seeking as a counterpart to Locarno, was declared by Germany to be inconsistent with Locarno, and served as the occasion for the
German remilitarization of the Rhineland on 7 March 1936.[1]

There followed the working-out of logical consequences: the elimination
of French influence in Eastern Europe and the substitution for it of German domination. The process was not imposed on the Eastern European
countries solely by the changing relations between the Great Powers.
It was accelerated by their own weaknesses and mistakes. Their economic
weaknesses made them ripe for the German trade drive that preceded the
establishment of Germany's political control. Their political mistakes prevented them from forming a united front against German diplomacy.

The world economic crisis had revealed one of the main deficiencies of
the French system in Eastern Europe: that it was a diplomatic arrangement without basis in economic interest. The depression brought the
countries of Eastern Europe to the verge of ruin by accentuating their
constant problem of disposing of their agricultural surpluses. Their trade
fell catastrophically. France was incapable of taking their agricultural
exports, being herself agriculturally self-sufficient, or of supplying their
need for industrial goods. The French system could not be widened into
a general economic and political association with Western Europe,
because Britain had adopted a policy of imperial protection with the
Ottawa Agreements and refused to undertake political or economic commitments in Eastern Europe. Soviet Russia was herself one of the world's
great primary producers, nor was her industrial productivity yet capable
of meeting Eastern European needs for imports. Her economic interests
competed with those of Eastern Europe instead of being complementary.
Yugoslavia and Rumania were developing an important market in Italy, but
they sacrificed it in support of collective economic sanctions against Italy
in 1935, and no alternative outlet was given them.[2] The predestined market,
the predestined supplier of industrial goods for Eastern Europe was Germany, and although the Western Powers regarded this as a danger, they
did nothing adequate to avert the fatality. In 1936 the German economic
conquest of Eastern Europe began under the direction of Schacht.[3] The
Eastern European countries were offered an unlimited demand for the

[1] *Survey* for 1936, pp. 252–66. Though the Franco-Soviet Pact was signed on 2 May 1935, it
was not ratified by the French Chamber till 27 February 1936, and by the French Senate until
12 March 1936. But what Germany was exploiting was not the formal process of treaty ratification but the irreparable clash of interests between the Western Powers and Italy over the Italo-
Ethiopian War. For the German argument on the incompatibility of the Franco-Soviet Pact
with Locarno, see *Survey* for 1935, i. 84–89.

[2] *Survey* for 1935, ii. 228, 235–6, 484; *Survey* for 1936, p. 468; Wiskemann: *Undeclared War*,
pp. 154–5.

[3] *Survey* for 1936, pp. 526–33.

greater part of their produce, and prices well above the level of the world
market. Their trade rose again rapidly from the trough into which it had
fallen during the world crisis, economic life quickened, employment improved, and the standard of living went up. These short-term advantages
were immense, and governed the considerations of every politician in
Eastern Europe. But the economic revival was directed towards and
dominated by Germany. The trade it stimulated was always bilateral,
with Germany in the economically more powerful position. In return for
the German market, the countries of Eastern Europe were forced to purchase, not goods that they wanted, but goods that Germany was equipped
to produce, which were to an increasing extent inessentials. In return for
the high German prices, they were repeatedly forced to raise the exchange-
rate of the Reichsmark with their currencies, and their internal price-levels
rose correspondingly, making it cumulatively difficult for them to find
alternative economic associations.[1] Eastern Europe became penetrated
with German commercial and technical missions, the *avant-garde* of political
and military control.

The remilitarization of the Rhineland debilitated the French system of
alliances, as it was meant to do, making it impossible for France to come to
the aid of her allies by invading Germany across a frontier zone which was
both unfortified and of vital economic importance to Germany.[2] France
could no longer be the policeman of Eastern Europe by such a measure as
the occupation of the Ruhr. The immediate effect of this stroke was to
unknit the Polish-German entente and draw Polish policy once more towards France. On the day that German troops marched into the Rhineland, the Polish Government renewed their assurances of fidelity to the
French treaty, declaring that in the event of war Poland would be at
France's side, and decided to take the same military measures as France.[3]
Even the timidity and failure of French policy in that crisis did not decisively alienate Poland, whose policy from now on was to maintain her
position in French eyes as the original ally in Eastern Europe, preferable
to the U.S.S.R., and to hold the balance between the groups of Great
Powers, a role appropriate to a weak Great Power and one which had been
played by Italy in the 1920s. But Poland tried also to combine the
policy of detachment with the advantages of acting as Germany's jackal,
and she continued to play with revisionist forces in Eastern Europe, and to
show hostility to Russia, to the Little Entente, and above all to Czechoslovakia.[4]

---

[1] *Survey* for 1937, i. 459–65.   [2] *Survey* for 1936, pp. 10, note 1, 262, 478, note 3.
[3] Léon Noël: *L'agression allemande contre la Pologne* (Paris, Flammarion, 1946), pp. 128–9;
Namier: *Diplomatic Prelude*, pp. 440–2; J. W. Wheeler-Bennett: *Munich: Prologue to Tragedy*
(London, Macmillan, 1948), p. 287.
[4] *Survey* for 1936, pp. 393–401. 'The new Polish policy was to maintain Poland's position as a
Great Power by oscillating between the other Powers of Europe in response to the successive

From 1936 to 1938 Germany's policy concentrated on expansion to the south-east, and in the Baltic the balance of power shifted for the time being without violence. The Anglo-German naval agreement of 18 June 1935, by which Britain condoned German violation of the naval restrictions of Versailles, had given Germany once more the command of the Baltic, and led naturally to the refortification of the Baltic coast.[1] The process culminated in the German resumption, on 14 November 1936, of full sovereignty over the Kiel Canal.[2] The policy of *détente* with Poland was extended to Lithuania, and in August 1936 a comprehensive commercial treaty was signed between Germany and Lithuania.[3] And German influence reached out, in the form of a visit by a man-of-war, to confirm Finland's diplomatic inclination towards Germany.[4]

In the Danubian region the change from Italian to German ascendancy was speedily seen. After the breakdown of the Stresa front and the formation of the Italo-German entente in 1936, Austria could no longer rely on Italian protection, and Italy, because of the financial strain of the Ethiopian War, could no longer finance the *Heimwehr*.[5] In July 1936 Germany forced a pact upon Austria which transformed her from an Italian into a German satellite, and placed two pro-Nazis in Schuschnigg's Cabinet.[6] At the same time full German pressure was turned on Czechoslovakia.[7] Though Germany did not denounce the German–Czechoslovak arbitration treaty that went with the Locarno Pact, the validity of that treaty in the changed circumstances was evidently questionable;[8] and Hitler's peace offers after the reoccupation of the Rhineland did not mention Czechoslovakia. In the Czechoslovak general election of May 1935 Henlein's Sudetendeutsche Partei won an impressive victory, polling more votes than any other single party, and the support of two-thirds of the Sudeten German population.[9] A strong lever for the disruption of the Czechoslovak State was thus to Hitler's hand, and its

changes in the balance between the non-Polish forces' (ibid. p. 394). 'His [Beck's] aim, in a dangerously tense European situation, was to preserve Poland's (seeming) freedom of action, and to continue the non-stop acrobatic performance of balancing between Germany and Russia' (Namier: *Diplomatic Prelude*, p. 92; cf. p. 42).

[1] *Survey* for 1935, i. 178–88; cf. Churchill: *Second World War*, i. 109–10.

[2] See *Survey* for 1937, i. 373–5, 379–80; cf. extract from *History of the German Navy, 1919–1939* (*I.M.T. Nuremberg*, xxxiv. 175 (017–PS); *N.C.A.* vi. 824).

[3] *Survey* for 1936, p. 538.   [4] Ibid. pp. 534–5.

[5] Ibid. p. 413; *Survey* for 1938, i. 184–5.

[6] *Survey* for 1936, pp. 450–4, 478–9; 'Primarily it was an Italo-German agreement about Austria, in which the latter was forced to concur' (Gedye: *Fallen Bastions*, p. 193).

[7] *Survey* for 1936, pp. 469–86.   [8] *Survey* for 1938, ii. 63, note 2.

[9] The three largest parties were the Sudetendeutsche Partei, 1,249,530 votes; the Czechoslovak Agrarians, 1,176,593 votes; the Czechoslovak Social Democrats, 1,034,774. The Sudetendeutsch National-Socialist Party had been dissolved on 4 October 1933; Henlein had founded the Sudetendeutsche Heimatfront on 30 September 1933, and this changed its name to Sudetendeutsche Partei before the general election of May 1935 (see *Survey* for 1936, pp. 491–3; Wiskemann: *Czechs and Germans*, chapter xiv).

character was made apparent when, on 21 June 1936, Henlein demanded in a speech at Cheb that the German minority should have rights, not individually, but corporately as a racial group: a claim which the minority treaties of 1919 had not dreamed of, making the minority an *imperium in imperio*, and which in the next two years was to disrupt and subjugate the states of Eastern Europe.[1] It was symbolic that Masaryk had resigned the Czechoslovak presidency in December 1935. Perhaps the greatest European statesman of the twentieth century, he had embodied, as nobody else could, the better features of the peace settlement. Beneš succeeded him, assuming full power at the moment when his lifework was to be tested.[2]

In Europe Czechoslovakia was isolated. From her French ally she was divided by the breadth of the Germany she feared; and the remilitarization of the Rhineland meant that even if France still had the will to help her, she could not do so except by a full-scale war against Germany. From her Russian ally she was separated by the strip of Ukrainian territory which had been brought under Polish and Rumanian sovereignty after the war, though it was less than a hundred miles across. For Poland and Rumania one of the problems of politics was whether to allow Russian troops to advance over their territory to the assistance of Czechoslovakia. Poland, who herself had an alliance with neither Czechoslovakia nor Russia, and whose relations with both indeed were unfriendly, was determined to refuse this; to her, the Czechoslovak–Russian entente represented a partial encirclement and a threat to Eastern Galicia.[3] Rumania, however, was in alliance with Czechoslovakia, and since 1934 had improved her own relations with Russia; moreover, she had signified her approval of the Soviet–Czechoslovak Pact.[4] In Rumania there was a sharp conflict of policies (similar to that going on in France) between the advocates of strengthened links with France, Czechoslovakia, and Russia, and those who feared to offend Germany—a cleavage between those who feared Germany more than Russia, and those who feared Russia more than Germany. The leader of the former group was Titulescu, a man of extraordinary clear-sightedness and frankness, for many years the director of Rumanian foreign policy, next to Beneš the chief architect of the Little Entente, and himself the chief architect of the Balkan. But like Wilson and Venizelos, he pursued his triumphs abroad to the neglect of his position at home; and his fall from power in August 1936 was a sign of the changing political wind as unmistakable as the fall of Litvinov three years later.[5] The succeeding régime continued the construction of the Bukovina–Transylvania railway which would give communication between the Soviet Union and

---

[1] *Survey* for 1936, pp. 498–9; Wiskemann: *Czechs and Germans*, pp. 249–51. Cf. the same author's *Undeclared War*, pp. 32–33, 152.

[2] Wiskemann: *Czechs and Germans*, pp. 238–42.   [3] *Survey* for 1935, i. 280.

[4] Ibid. p. 82, note 3; *Survey* for 1936, pp. 522–4.

[5] Ibid. pp. 517–19.

Czechoslovakia,[1] but it refrained from committing Rumania to diplomatic co-operation as the middle link.

During 1936 and 1937 German pressure was remorselessly tearing the Little Entente apart. Germany bore hard upon Czechoslovakia; Poland drew off Rumania; Italy drew off Yugoslavia.[2] Czechoslovakia leaned increasingly on her alliance with Russia; Yugoslavia alone of the states of Eastern Europe refused to renew diplomatic relations with Russia; Rumania was as divided on the Russian issue as France. Czechoslovakia was the main obstacle to German control of Eastern Europe, both as a strategic fortress and as a resolute democracy, and the pressure upon her was proportionate to the obduracy with which Beneš and his people refused to serve German interests.[3] Into the German–Czechoslovak vortex were drawn Hungary and Poland, in hope of territorial gain. Hungary's revisionism, with German encouragement, turned away for the time being from the south and east towards her northern frontiers, relieving the pressure on Yugoslavia and Rumania and weakening for them the value of the Little Entente.[4] It became the object of Hungarian diplomacy to trade a renunciation of Hungarian territorial claims on Yugoslavia for a Yugoslav promise of neutrality if Hungary went to war with Czechoslovakia, to associate Germany with this through a German guarantee of the Hungaro-Yugoslav frontier, and to obtain staff talks with Germany for a combined attack on Czechoslovakia.[5] Poland maintained her bad relations with Czechoslovakia.[6] Polish diplomacy at this time aimed at recultivating the French and Rumanian alliances (without offence to Germany) and indulged grandiose and chimerical hopes of forming a neutral group in Eastern Europe, with a repetition of the motive of anti-German consolidation that had inspired the Rome bloc.[7] In September 1936 Beck sought a *rapprochement* with Lithuania, but was rebuffed. Rumanian policy, under Titulescu's successor Antonescu, also aimed at strengthening Rumanian-Polish relations, a renewal of the old *cordon sanitaire* of 1921, which afforded

[1] See H. Seton-Watson: *Eastern Europe*, p. 391.

[2] *Survey* for 1936, pp. 502–7; *Survey* for 1937, i. 405–14.

[3] Ibid. pp. 343–4. There is nothing in the Nuremberg Documents to support Seton-Watson's contention that 'if Beneš had been willing to follow the examples of Beck and Stojadinović, Hitler would have been willing to leave the "Sudeten Germans" where they were' (*Eastern Europe*, p. 392). From the Hossbach Memorandum of 10 November 1937 onwards (see *I.M.T. Nuremberg*, xxv. 409–10 (386–PS); trans. in *D.Ger.F.P.*, series D, i. 35; *Documents* (R.I.I.A.) for 1939–46, i. 21–22, cf. *N.C.A.* iii. 301), it is the conquest, not the neutralization, of Czechoslovakia that is the immediate objective.

[4] *Survey* for 1936, pp. 441, 457–8, 506. When Darányi and Kánya visited him on 25 November 1937, Hitler advised that Hungary should not scatter her energies in different directions but should follow a single line—in Czechoslovakia (see *Documents Secrets* (Eristov), vol. ii (*Hongrie*), no. 3).

[5] Ibid. nos. 3 to 24. It seems that none of these ends was formally attained.

[6] *Survey* for 1935, i. 296–8; *Survey* for 1936, pp. 395, 401, note 1, 506; *Survey* for 1937, i. 344, 383, 386, 406.

[7] *Survey* for 1936, pp. 393–401; *Survey* for 1937, i. 383.

these two countries the illusion of pursuing an independent line, and served Germany's purpose by weakening the existing diplomatic structure of Eastern Europe.[1] Small Powers cannot pursue a successful policy of reinsurance *inter se* against an aggressive Great Power; that requires association with another Great Power. At the same time Yugoslavia was forming unprecedented economic ties with Germany, and unprecedented diplomatic ties as well as the old economic ties with Italy. The murder of Alexander in 1934 had been the turning-point in Italo-Yugoslav relations;[2] from then on, with the German shadow lengthening towards the Adriatic, Mussolini vigorously pursued a policy of reinsurance with Yugoslavia, which was interrupted but not ended by Yugoslavia's participation in sanctions during the Ethiopian War. In Stojadinović Mussolini had his Colonel Beck, and the two signed a pact of friendship in March 1937 which was the Adriatic counterpart of the German-Polish treaty of 1934. A treaty which, if King Alexander had negotiated it, would have crowned his work by securing from Italy a recognition of Yugoslavia's right to exist on the other shore of the Adriatic, now had the appearance of a weakening of the Little Entente for the sake of an impolitic and frivolous association with the Axis.[3]

Rumania and Yugoslavia were signatories of the Balkan Pact as well, and their policies of detachment or of vacillation towards the Axis prevented the consolidation of that *entente*. Greece already had defined her commitments under the Balkan Pact to exclude the danger of being drawn into war with a non-Balkan Power, particularly Italy.[4] Bulgaria fell earliest and most completely under the economic domination of Germany, and resumed her old role as German fulcrum in the Balkans.[5] When Yugoslavia and Bulgaria signed a simple pact of eternal friendship in January 1937, it might have been the fruition of the great tradition of Stamboliski and Alexander and Velchev, a drawing together of the Byzantine Slavs against the age-long exploitation and aggression of the West, had not both Yugoslavia and Bulgaria been ruled by unpopular dictatorships, whose policies were already following the lines dictated by their German masters.[6] The only country of the Balkan Entente whose policy was shaped in freedom from the German pressure was Turkey, the Eastern European state with the smallest territorial commitment in Eastern Europe and the only

---

[1] *Survey* for 1936, pp. 524–6; *Survey* for 1937, i. 410–12. 'In those bygone years the Polono-Rumanian *cordon sanitaire* had been desired by France as a means of preventing Russia from joining hands with Hungary and Germany; in 1936 the same Polono-Rumanian combination was desired by Germany as a means of preventing Russia from joining hands with Czechoslovakia and France' (*Survey* for 1936, p. 525).

[2] *Survey* for 1934, p. 328 and note 3.

[3] *Survey* for 1937, i. 407, 465–85; Wiskemann: *Undeclared War*, pp. 120–1. For the unpopularity of the Italo-Yugoslav pact in Serbia cf. West: *Black Lamb and Grey Falcon*, ii. 46.

[4] *Survey* for 1936, pp. 519–20.   [5] Ibid. pp. 531–2.

[6] Ibid. pp. 512–16; H. Seton-Watson: *Eastern Europe*, p. 390.

one that had the advantages as well as the dangers of a common frontier, not only with Russia, but also with the Western Powers.

The remilitarization of the Rhineland in March 1936 had reverberated to the farther end of Eastern Europe and been followed within four months by the remilitarization of the Black Sea Straits. This was a demand raised regularly by Turkey since 1933,[1] and by 1936 the Great Power guarantee of Turkish security under the Lausanne Treaty had lost all its value. The diplomacy which led to the Montreux Conference of June–July 1936 gave Turkey the moral prestige of pursuing treaty revision by peaceful methods. But a conference called originally for the purpose of allowing Turkey to remilitarize the Straits went on to modify the conditions of passage through the Straits, which Russia wished to alter in her own favour. Like the Lausanne Conference in 1923, the Montreux Conference developed into a conflict of interests between Britain and Russia, but with France now on the Russian side; Turkey once again held the balance, having gained her objective in principle (the remilitarization of the Straits now, as it had been the restoration of Eastern Thrace in 1923) before the conference began. Russia had greatly increased in power and prestige since Lausanne, and now desired egress from the Straits for the purpose of secure communication with her French ally. Britain wished to loosen the Turkish reliance on Russia, and to obtain compensation for permission to Russia to send her fleet into the Mediterranean, which would affect the Mediterranean balance of power. But Britain at Montreux was isolated, and the Montreux Convention of July 1936 established a new régime for the Straits on the following terms: (1) The principle of freedom of passage for merchant vessels through the Straits was reaffirmed. (2) Non-Black Sea Powers might send only light surface vessels into the Black Sea, with a limitation on their aggregate tonnage; but Black Sea Powers might send capital ships of any size into the Mediterranean. (3) The International Straits Commission was abolished and its functions were transferred to Turkey. (4) Turkey was allowed to close the Straits in time of war or of an imminent threat of war. (5) Turkey was given permission to remilitarize the Straits immediately.[2] The role of malcontent played by Russia at Lausanne was played at Montreux by Italy, for the limitation of her influence in the Mediterranean was the common aim of Turkish, Russian, and British policies; she therefore neither attended the conference nor signed the convention. The Montreux settlement struck a balance between the interests of Russia, once more given formal recognition as dominant Power in the Black Sea, and the national security of Turkey; and as it marked the end of the period in which Italy could speak of her 'historic objectives in Asia' and dream of an ascendancy in the Aegean, so it adumbrated the conflict for the control of the Balkans which

---

[1] *Survey* for 1936, pp. 600–3.   [2] Ibid. pp. 603–45.

five years later was to be the main factor in disrupting the German–Soviet entente.[1]

(i) THE ANSCHLUSS

Since the formation of the Rome–Berlin Axis in 1936 the Anschluss had been virtually inevitable. A small state which is a buffer between two Great Powers that are hostile may succeed in retaining its independence, since this will be the interest also of the weaker Great Power. But if the Great Powers establish an entente, the buffer state is likely to be partitioned. This was the case with the German conquest of Austria on 11–12 March 1938. The Anschluss was a veiled partition; for although its most obvious aspect was the annexation of the Austrian Republic to the Third Reich,[2] it brought also the recognition by Germany of the Brenner frontier and the abandonment to Italy of that part of the Austrian nation which had been annexed by Italy in 1919 and had been living, submerged and persecuted, in the South Tyrol.[3]

The moment the Nazis successfully set up their standard in Vienna [wrote Namier in 1935], the whole of Central and South-Eastern Europe, from the Bohemian Mountains and the Carpathians down to the Adriatic, Greece, and the Straits, would be aflame, and the political balance of Europe would be destroyed.[4]

The overturning of the balance of power by the Anschluss was like that produced by the French invasion of Italy in 1796; the conquests of the small states by the expanding Power became cumulative, one making the next more easy and more certain, until the vacuum between the Great Powers was filled up, and within eighteen months the Soviet Union signed her Campo Formio. By annexing Austria, Germany thrust herself forward down the Danube, and found a common frontier with Hungary and Yugoslavia.[5] The Czech provinces were encircled along four-fifths of the length of their frontiers.

The Austrian Anschluss . . . not only achieved a national aim of long standing, but also contributed to the strengthening of our military power by creating a definite improvement in our strategic position. Whereas, hitherto, Czechoslovak territory had thrust up into Germany in a most menacing way (a wasp-waist in the direction of France and an air base for the Allies, particularly for Russia) now Czechoslovakia in turn was also held in a pincer-grip. Her own

---

[1] Cf. Molotov's conversations with Hitler and Ribbentrop on 13 November 1940 (U.S. Department of State: *Nazi-Soviet Relations 1939–1941: Documents from the Archives of the German Foreign Office*, ed. R. J. Sontag and J. S. Beddie [referred to hereafter as *Nazi-Soviet Relations*] (Washington, U.S.G.P.O., 1948), pp. 244–6, 252–3); Gafencu: *Préliminaires de la guerre à l'Est*, pp. 136–7.

[2] *Survey* for 1938, i. 185–223.   [3] Ibid. p. 218.

[4] *Manchester Guardian*, 28 June 1935, reprinted in L. B. Namier's *In the Margin of History* (London, Macmillan, 1939), p. 33.   [5] *Survey* for 1938, i. 220–1.

strategic position had now become so unfavourable that she was bound to fall victim to an energetic attack before effective help could reach her from the West.[1]

Hitler had not always intended to conquer Austria before Czechoslovakia; five months earlier he had declared the necessity of conquering them simultaneously;[2] and on 21 April, five weeks after the fall of Vienna, when the tide of suicides had scarcely ebbed in the conquered capital,[3] and the Terror was only beginning to become routine, he began the detailed consideration of the attack on Czechoslovakia.[4] Three days later Henlein raised the standard of revolt within Czechoslovakia by a speech at Carlsbad in which, not tentatively as at Cheb in 1936, but with all the authority of the triumphant Reich behind him, he demanded administrative autonomy as well as legal personality for the German folk-group, and their right to 'profess German nationality and German political philosophy': the dismemberment of the democratic republic by the establishment of a Nazi totalitarian régime in its German area.[5] He asked also for 'a revision of Czechoslovak foreign policy, which had led the country into the ranks of the enemies of the German people'. During the night of 20–21 May, in view of reports of German troop concentrations, Beneš ordered a partial mobilization.[6] This angered Hitler and made him advance his plans; on 30 May he wrote: 'It is my unalterable decision to smash Czechoslovakia by military action in the near future.'[7]

The derangement of the balance of power altered the relationships of the small states not only with Germany but also among themselves. The jackals improved their positions and looked for pickings. Poland had contemplated a military occupation of Lithuania to offset the Anschluss; but

---

[1] Lecture by General Jodl at Munich on 'The Strategic Position in the Beginning of the 5th Year of War', 7 November 1943 (trans. from *I.M.T. Nuremberg*, xxxvii. 634–5 (172–L); cf. *N.C.A.* vii. 923). Cf. Borkenau: *Austria and After*, pp. 327–30.

[2] 'For the improvement of our politico-military position our first objective, in the event of our being embroiled in war, must be to overthrow Czechoslovakia and Austria simultaneously in order to remove the threat to our flank in any possible operation against the West' (Hossbach Memorandum of 10 November 1937).

[3] See Gedye: *Fallen Bastions*, pp. 305–7, 349–50; *Survey* for 1938, i. 226, with criticism in Namier: *Conflicts*, pp. 107–8. T. G. Masaryk's first book, published at Vienna in 1881, had been *Suicide as a Collective Social Phenomenon of Modern Civilization*.

[4] See Plan for Operation 'Green' (code name for the invasion of Czechoslovakia), summarizing a conversation between Hitler and Keitel of 21 April 1938 (*I.M.T. Nuremberg*, xxv. 415–17 (388–PS, item 2); trans. in *D.Ger.F.P.*, series D, ii. 239–40; *Documents* (R.I.I.A.) for 1939–46, i. 26–27; cf. *N.C.A.* iii. 306–8). See also *Survey* for 1938, ii. 141–2.

[5] See *The Times*, 25 April 1938; cf. *Survey* for 1938, ii. 94–97.

[6] See *Survey* for 1938, ii. 122–5.

[7] See revised directive for 'Operation Green', 30 May 1938 (*I.M.T. Nuremberg*, xxv. 434 (388–PS, item 11), trans. in *D.Ger.F.P.*, series D, ii. 358; *Documents* (R.I.I.A.) for 1939–46, i. 30; cf. *N.C.A.* iii. 316). Cf. Jodl's diary, undated entry (*I.M.T. Nuremberg*, xxviii. 373 (1780–PS); *N.C.A.* iv. 363) and Keitel's evidence (*I.M.T. Nuremberg*, x. 509). See also *Survey* for 1938, ii. 143–4.

she sent instead an ultimatum on 17 March demanding the establishment of normal diplomatic relations.[1] Russia warned Poland that in the event of an armed Polish attack on Lithuania, she reserved the right to take action.[2] Hungary and Bulgaria could not be compelled to remain subject to the restrictions of a peace settlement which Germany had triumphantly destroyed. On 31 July Bulgaria signed a non-aggression pact with the Balkan Entente at Salonika, which recognized her equality of status in the matter of armaments and full sovereignty over her frontiers, without her joining the Balkan Entente or renouncing her revisionist claims.[3] On 22 August a similar agreement was signed at Bled between Hungary and the Little Entente.[4] These agreements might have had the character of Small Power consolidation against the German menace, if Bulgaria was not already as much the vassal of Germany as she had been ten years before of Italy; and if Hungary was not half-transformed, willy-nilly, politically as well as economically, into a *gleichgestellte Hilfsmacht*.[5] The Anschluss had stimulated both the German and the Hungarian Nazis inside Hungary and increased German pressure and propaganda; in May 1938 Horthy replaced Darányi by Imrédy, in order to stem Hungarian National Socialism, but Imrédy, like Dollfuss and Carol and Stojadinović, could pursue no policy except an imitation of the threatened disease whose effect was not to immunize the subject but to prepare the way for the real thing. The only sign of vitality in the Little Entente during the summer when the Czechoslovak crisis was mounting was the number of young Yugoslavs who offered their services to the Czechoslovak legation and consulates in the event of war. They were the most enthusiastic visitors at Prague in July at the last great festival of the national gymnastic association, the Sokols, coming to the aid of Masaryk's country as once Masaryk had embroiled himself at the Agram trial, when the former Europe was sliding to its ruin, in the cause of the Serbs and Croats.[6] But, as in almost every such crisis, it was not the Small Powers but the Great who in the end settled the Czechoslovak question.

[1] See *Survey* for 1938, iii, part II, section ii.
[2] See Joseph E. Davies: *Mission to Moscow* (London, Gollancz, 1942), pp. 191–2; Potemkin: *Histoire de la diplomatie*, iii. 643–4.
[3] See *Survey* for 1938, iii, part IV, section i.
[4] *Survey* for 1938, ii. 290–1.
[5] The Bled Agreement was disagreeable to Germany, since it suggested a *rapprochement* between Hungary and the Little Entente; Kánya was at pains to assure Ribbentrop that Hungary's renunciation of the use of force under the agreement was not intended by her to become effective. See memoranda of conversations between Ribbentrop, Imrédy, and Kánya on 23 August 1938 and between Ribbentrop and Kánya on 25 August 1938 (*I.M.T. Nuremberg*, xxxi. 135–9 (2796/7–PS); trans. in *D.Ger.F.P.* series D, ii. 609–11, 623–4; cf. *N.C.A.* v. 430–3). See also *Survey* for 1938, ii. 295–8.
[6] See Wiskemann: *Undeclared War*, p. 123; H. Seton-Watson: *Eastern Europe*, p. 394; Gedye: *Fallen Bastions*, pp. 428–9.

(j) The First Partition of Czechoslovakia

The first partition of Czechoslovakia in September–November 1938 was the consequence of an unfought war which overthrew the Versailles Settlement and made Germany undisputed master of Eastern Europe.[1] This crisis subjected the policies of the Powers of Eastern Europe (no less than those of the Western Great Powers) to a telling strain, and provided an alternative pattern of forces for the true war that broke out a year later. The decisive factor was the policy of the Western Powers, their determination to render the Franco-Czechoslovak alliance inoperative,[2] the fate of Eastern Europe thus being decided once again by forces beyond Eastern Europe; but next most important were two factors within Eastern Europe, the policies of Poland and of Czechoslovakia herself. Polish policy was purely opportunist, what Beck naïvely called a policy 'of independence'. In appearance it was based on an equal fear of Germany and of Russia, and it toyed again in September 1938 with the chimera of a neutral bloc between them, inflated now into 'a Helsinki–Bucharest axis',[3] as if Poland by standing on a chair could make herself a Great Power. But with war imminent it became clear that Poland was not holding the balance between Germany and Russia: though Germany was the more immediately dangerous of the two, it was towards Germany that Poland inclined, and towards Russia that her hostility was the more active. There was another factor at work, the desire for immediate territorial advantage. If Germany fought Czechoslovakia alone, Poland would join Germany in defeating and dismembering Czechoslovakia; although Poland's military measures might not be concerted with Germany's and she might feel herself to be acting independently.[4] Even if France honoured her alliance with Czechoslovakia, Poland would give to Noël, the French Ambassador in Warsaw, no assurance of neutrality.[5] Here the French system of alliances finally jammed in its own contradictions. Poland, bound to France by an alliance directed mainly against Germany, would join Germany in attacking France's other ally Czechoslovakia, even when France in defence of Czechoslovakia went to war with Germany. The Poles explained this by

[1] For an exact prediction of this, written before October 1937, see the *Survey* for 1936, pp. 479–81.

[2] '. . . the representatives of the two Governments were guided by a desire to find a solution which would not bring about a European War, and, therefore, a solution which would not automatically compel France to take action in accordance with her obligations', Chamberlain in the House of Commons at Westminster, 28 September 1938, describing the Anglo-French discussions of 18 September (H.C. Deb. 5th ser., vol. 339, col. 16; *Documents* (R.I.I.A.) for 1938, ii. 281).　　[3] Noël: *L'agression allemande contre la Pologne*, p. 209.

[4] See *Survey* for 1938, iii, part I, section iv (c).

[5] Noël, op. cit. p. 217. The Polish Opposition believed, however, that if France stood by Czechoslovakia Poland would be compelled to follow suit; see Namier: *Diplomatic Prelude*, p. 447, note 2. The Polish White Book contains, on the Munich crisis, nothing but one extract each from Hitler's Nuremberg and Sportpalast speeches (cf. ibid. p. 33).

the arguments that Czechoslovakia was bound to break up anyway, that it was Poland's interest in this event to recover her stolen territories, that it was France's interest to see Poland thus strengthened and aggrandized as the leader of the Eastern European neutral bloc between Germany and Russia:[1] the combined arguments of necessity, covetousness, and misjudgement that are the fully matured substitute for adherence to principle. But probably more important was Poland's dislike of Czechoslovakia's Soviet ally. To fight against Germany on Czechoslovakia's side would almost certainly mean fighting on Russia's side, with the danger of having to grant passage to the Soviet army and air force, and to this Poland would in no circumstances consent.[2] In the last resort Poland was not equally balanced between Germany and Russia: she would co-operate with Germany against Russia,[3] but in no circumstances would she co-operate with Russia against Germany; the reverse of Czechoslovak relations with those Powers.

Poland's own claims upon Czechoslovakia were limited to Teschen. But she held out her hands southwards to Hungary, whose desire to dismember Czechoslovakia was second only to Germany's, and to Rumania, who had an essential part in the defence of Czechoslovakia as a link between her and Russia. With Rumania Poland had a common frontier; with Hungary this was still to create. The urge towards contiguity between Poland and Hungary was the small core of reality and achievement within the Polish project of a neutral bloc, and it had a partial aim of widening the barrier between Germany and Russia. It was to be won by Hungary's expanding once more to her old frontier on the crest of the Carpathians, which would be the fulfilment of her utmost revisionist claims against Czechoslovakia, the reincorporation not only of the Magyar *irredente* but also of Ruthenia and perhaps Slovakia as well.[4] For Poland, what mattered was the extinction of Ruthenia as a centre of potential Ukrainian nationalism; and if the province was recovered by Hungary, the Hungarians could be depended upon to eradicate that. But this implied the collapse of the Little Entente, that Yugoslavia and Rumania would not go to the aid of Czechoslovakia. Hungary had sought an assurance of neutrality from Yugoslavia in exchange for an abandonment of her claims on Yugoslavia, and she had also sought an undertaking from Mussolini to attack Yugoslavia if Yugoslavia attacked Hungary.[5] It does not seem that formal engagements were obtained in either case. Stojadinović was cautious: both to Hitler, when he

---

[1] Bonnet: *De Washington*, pp. 256–7.

[2] See *Survey* for 1938, ii. 132–4; cf. Noël: *L'agression allemande contre la Pologne*, p. 22.

[3] The limits to Poland's co-operation with Germany became much more definite after Munich (see *Survey* for 1938, iii, part II, section i (*b*) (5)).

[4] Hitler had apparently promised this to Darányi and Kánya when they visited him on 25 November 1937 (see *Documents secrets* (Eristov), vol. ii (*Hongrie*), no. 12).

[5] See *Survey* for 1938, ii. 292–4.

visited Berlin in January 1938, and afterwards to the French,[1] he had re-affirmed Yugoslavia's commitments to the Little Entente. The Anschluss probably deflected Yugoslav policy several points towards the Axis, and as the Czechoslovak crisis was being kindled and fanned through the summer, Yugoslavia was informing the Italians that she would not intervene in a Hungaro-Czechoslovak conflict provided that Hungary left the initiative in aggression either to Germany or to the appearance of Czecho-slovak provocation.[2] Italy, too, was non-committal: if Yugoslav relations with the Axis were good, a Yugoslav attack on Hungary would not occur.[3] For Italy was hoping to draw Yugoslavia into the Rome bloc,[4] and even to extend Italian patronage discreetly as far north as Warsaw. It was Mussolini who, speaking at Trieste on 18 September 1938, first publicly widened the Sudeten controversy to include the Hungarian and Polish minorities in Czechoslovakia, and these subsidiary claims had his ostentatious support in his speech-making tour throughout Northern Italy during the height of the crisis.[5]

Rumania alone of the Little Entente Powers had no common frontier with the Axis, and alone had a common frontier with Russia; this gave her policy a greater independence towards Germany. Moreover, her vital interest in the Little Entente was as much greater than Czechoslovakia's or Yugoslavia's as her Hungarian minorities were greater than theirs. Yet Rumanian policy was paralysed by the complementary terrors of Germany as an aggressor and of Russia as an ally. A Hungarian attack upon Czechoslovakia in league with Germany was different from the Hungarian revisionism against which the Little Entente had been formed seventeen years before: it might bring German forces across Hungarian soil to the frontiers of Rumania.[6] Russian assistance to Czechoslovakia would certainly bring the Soviet air force, if not the Soviet army, across Rumanian soil: Rumania would become a German-Russian battleground, and there was no confidence that when the war was over the Soviet forces would retire once more behind the Bessarabian frontier. On this great issue of the missing strategic link in the Franco-Czechoslovak-Soviet alliance, Rumania prevaricated and temporized.[7] In March 1938 Litvinov had replied to a question about it with a phrase something like: 'If the non-aggressive nations take up that problem seriously it can be solved. . . . "Where there's a will there's a way" '; which had been interpreted as

---

[1] *Survey* for 1938, ii. 293; cf. *Documents secrets* (Eristov), vol. ii (*Hongrie*), nos. 24 and 9; and *Survey* for 1937, i. 409, 484–5.

[2] See *Documents secrets* (Eristov), vol. ii (*Hongrie*), no. 21; Ciano: *Europa*, pp. 328–9, 359; Eng. version, pp. 213, 233.

[3] See *Documents secrets* (Eristov), vol. ii (*Hongrie*), no. 22.

[4] Ibid.

[5] See *Survey* for 1938, ii. 338 and *Documents* (R.I.I.A.) for 1938, ii. 239–43.

[6] See *Documents secrets* (Eristov), vol. ii (*Hongrie*), no. 18.

[7] *Survey* for 1938, ii. 132, 276–81.

meaning that if necessary Russia would violate Polish and Rumanian territory to reach Czechoslovakia.[1] But Soviet policy was still ostensibly hoping for collective action. On 2 September 1938 Litvinov proposed to the French chargé in Moscow,[2] and Maisky proposed to Churchill, for transmission to the British Foreign Office, that Rumanian reluctance should be overcome through the agency of the Council of the League acting under Article XI of the Covenant.[3] British and French aversion to the League of Nations and collective action relieved Rumania from the odium of rejecting this proposal. She could now entrench herself strategically behind the non-completion of the Bukovina–Transylvania railway, which might make it impossible for Soviet troops to reach the Bohemian front in under three weeks,[4] and legally behind the clause of the Polish-Rumanian alliance that obliged her to concert her Russian policy with Poland.[5] Thus with her left hand Poland restrained Rumania from the defence while with her right hand she beckoned Hungary to the attack.

The Czechoslovak plan of defence against Germany assumed the alliance with France in the west and the consequential alliance with Russia in the east, and, if attack came from Hungary as well, the older alliance with the Little Entente Powers too. The Czechoslovak General Staff calculated that it could hold up the Germans, and even if necessary the Hungarians, for from three to six months, giving time for the arrival of Russian support by way of Rumania and for a French assault upon the Rhineland.[6] The foundation of this plan was destroyed by France's betrayal of her obligations. In June 1938 Hitler had written: 'I shall, however, only decide to take action against Czechoslovakia if, as in the case of the occupation of the demilitarized zone and the entry into Austria, I am firmly convinced that France will not march and therefore Britain will not intervene either.'[7] The British, however, who had taken upon themselves to mediate, and the French who were allies of Czechoslovakia, intervened on the side not of Czechoslovakia but of Germany herself, issuing the ultimata to Czechoslovakia that broke her moral resistance. The first ultimatum, on 21

[1] Press conference in Moscow, 17 March 1938 (*The Times*, 18 March 1938); cf. *Survey* for 1938, ii. 67–68; Davies, *Mission to Moscow*, p. 191; Beloff, ii. 122–3. This intention was later expressly denied by Litvinov (Bonnet: *De Washington*, p. 200).

[2] *Survey* for 1938, ii. 278.

[3] Ibid. p. 279. For a general estimate of Soviet policy at this time see Beloff, ii. 163–6.

[4] *Survey* for 1938, ii. 280.

[5] Bonnet: *De Washington*, p. 201, where the clause is wrongly cited as 4 instead of 2: see the treaty printed in the *Survey* for 1920–3, pp. 504–5.

[6] See Gedye: *Fallen Bastions*, p. 368. The opinion of British military authorities was that Czechoslovakia might hold out at most for one month. One of the reasons for German-Hungarian staff talks urged by Hungary in April 1938 was that a simultaneous Hungarian attack on Czechoslovakia would forestall the arrival of Russian parachutists in Slovakia and Ruthenia: see *Documents secrets* (Eristov), vol. ii (*Hongrie*), no. 14.

[7] General strategic directive of 18 June 1938 (*I.M.T. Nuremberg*, xxv. 446 (388–PS, item 14); trans. in *D.Ger.F.P.* series D, ii. 473; *Documents* (R.I.I.A.) for 1939–46, i. 34; cf. *N.C.A.* iii. 324).

September, declared that if Czechoslovakia rejected the Anglo-French plan for the cession of the Sudetenland that resulted from Chamberlain's visit to Berchtesgaden on 15–16 September, Britain and France would disinterest themselves in her fate.[1] Beneš accepted this in the hope of gaining time to buy off Poland and Hungary, who were concentrating their forces along the Czechoslovak frontiers; 'I have made plans', he said, 'for all eventualities.'[2]   On the same day, 21 September, Poland demanded that the question of the Polish minority in Czechoslovakia should be settled immediately in the same way as the Sudeten German question, and denounced the Polish–Czechoslovak minorities treaty of 1925.[3] On 22 September Hungary made a similar demand for the Hungarian minorities[4] and there were demonstrations in Warsaw for a Polish-Hungarian frontier.

The increase of Hitler's demands at Godesberg on the same day,[5] the apparent stiffening of the Western Powers in consequence, and Czechoslovakia's mobilization on 23 September, afforded the Czechs a momentary release from the four-Power pressure, and it seemed that an anti-German coalition might at last be formed.   On 21 and again on 23 September Litvinov, who was then at the League Assembly at Geneva, reaffirmed Soviet commitments to Czechoslovakia within the framework of collective security under the Covenant, and conditional upon the fulfilment of the Franco-Czechoslovak treaty.[6]   On 23 September Russia warned Poland that she would denounce the Soviet-Polish non-aggression pact if Poland invaded Czechoslovakia.   In these circumstances Beneš's plan for buying off Poland was put into operation.   On 22 September he had addressed to Mościcki, the Polish President, a personal letter accepting Polish claims in principle and consenting to immediate negotiations; this was delivered on the 25th.[7] Beck rejected the proposal, desiring a spectacular humiliation of Czechoslovakia.[8]   Beneš afterwards said that this provided him with 'the last and decisive reason' for capitulating to Germany, in spite of Russian support.[9]

[1] *Survey* for 1938, ii. 355–63.

[2] Broadcast of 22 September 1938 (*Documents* (R.I.I.A.) for 1938, ii. 226).

[3] *Survey* for 1938, iii, part I, section iv (*c*). The Polish note to Czechoslovakia is printed in L. B. Namier's *Europe in Decay: a Study in Disintegration, 1936–1940* (London, Macmillan, 1950), pp. 286–7.   [4] *Survey* for 1938, iii, part I, section v (*b*).

[5] At Godesberg Hitler assumed the championship of the Polish and Hungarian claims: see *Survey* for 1938, ii. 376–91.

[6] *Documents* (R.I.I.A.) for 1938, ii. 224–5, 233–4. For a discussion whether the Soviet Government went beyond their treaty commitment in their offer of help to Czechoslovakia, see *Survey* for 1938, ii. 369–72.

[7] Printed in Namier: *Europe in Decay*, pp. 289–90; cf. *Survey* for 1938, iii, part I, section iv (*c*). Bonnet (*De Washington*, pp. 258–9, 364–6) says that on the night of 24–25 September Beneš agreed at French instigation to cede Teschen, on condition that Poland would change camps and resume the policy of an ally of France, affording Czechoslovakia if not military co-operation at least a benevolent neutrality.

[8] See Noël: *L'agression allemande contre la Pologne*, p. 234.

[9] See letter from Beneš to Namier of 20 April 1944 (Namier: *Europe in Decay*, p. 284).

While Polish policy remained brutal and predatory, the Little Entente Powers were trimming. Their aim was to stay neutral;[1] it was clear that they would not in any case commit themselves until the Western Powers were committed, that is to say, until the war had begun. On 23 September the Rumanian Minister in Rome told Ciano that Rumania was resisting, and would continue to resist, Soviet demands for the free passage of Soviet troops; that she approved the return to Hungary of the purely Magyar parts of Czechoslovakia, though she would deprecate Hungarian claims on Slovakia; and that in the event of war between Russia and Poland she would support Poland, giving her alliance with Poland precedence over her commitments to Prague.[2] On 24 September the Yugoslav Government banned public meetings in an attempt to suppress the mass demonstrations which were not only in favour of Czechoslovakia but also against Stojadinović. The next day Stojadinović agreed in principle to a Rumanian proposal for a joint declaration by the two Powers, to be made verbally to the Hungarian Government, that they would accept a rectification of Czechoslovak-Hungarian frontiers in Hungary's favour if it was limited to regions with a majority of Magyar inhabitants, but that they could not remain unmoved by a Hungarian annexation of Slovakia.[3] At the request of Berlin this *démarche* was never made;[4] the project of it was the last throe of the Little Entente.

The dictate of the Great Powers overrode all. On 29 September the heads of the two Axis Powers and the two Western Powers met at Munich, and agreed on a partition of Czechoslovakia that differed only illusorily from Hitler's Godesberg demands.[5] This was imposed on the Czechoslovak Government the same evening, with unusual brutality, by the second Anglo-French ultimatum.[6] The Poles, in such an extremity, deserted by all their allies, and with an enemy crouched behind every frontier, would probably still have fought. The Czechs, cautious, circumspect, self-possessed, submitted. Beneš's decision was based on a cool estimate, not only of the strength of Czechoslovakia's enemies, but also of the balance of forces within the country. For the leaders of the army and the Agrarians,

[1] Cf. the Yugoslav Minister's opinion given to Ciano in Rome on 13 September 1938 (Ciano: *Europa*, pp. 358–9; Eng. version, p. 233). See also Alexander Henderson: *Eyewitness in Czecho-Slovakia* (London, Harrap, 1939), pp. 226–8: Henderson drove from Czechoslovakia through Hungary and Yugoslavia to Italy between 24 and 30 September.

[2] Ciano: *Europa*, pp. 364–5; Eng. version, pp. 236–7.

[3] See N. P. Comnène: *Preludi del grande dramma* (Rome, Edizioni Leonardo, 1947), pp. 109–11, 119–20.

[4] Ibid. pp. 155–6, 137; cf. Hubert Ripka: *Munich: Before and After* (London, Gollancz, 1939), p. 145. See also *Survey* for 1938, iii, part IV, section ii.

[5] *Survey* for 1938, ii. 437–44; *Survey* for 1938, iii, part I, section i. For text of Agreement see *D.Brit.F.P.*, 3rd Series, ii. 627–9.

[6] See Hubert Masařík's report in Ripka: *Munich*, pp. 224–7, also *Survey* for 1938, ii. 444–7.

the dominant political party, regarded the loss of the Sudetenland as a lesser evil than the intervention of the Red Army in the guise of an ally.[1] If Czechoslovakia had taken up arms in defiance of the Munich Powers she would have depended on the sole assistance of the Soviet Union. This would have bound her to the Bolshevik Power in an ideological struggle against the West, captained by Nazi Germany, which would have fulfilled the assertions of Nazi propaganda and perhaps prevented any ultimate assistance from the Western Powers. For all the traditional slavophily of the Czechs, the Czechoslovakia of Masaryk and Beneš (like the Bohemia of the Prmzyls and the Luxemburgers) was a Western not a Byzantine state, and it was the Western Powers that had stood sponsors at her rebirth in 1918. The Western Powers had betrayed her; the isolated assistance of Russia was dangerous in the degree in which it was not doubtful, and repudiated by half the country; and thus Czechoslovakia was forced back upon the last hope of small nations, that by compliance to their neighbours they may earn a tolerated neutrality.[2] Yet speculation will always play with the contingency of her having resisted, whether it would have accelerated the outbreak of war between the Great Powers, and whether these Powers would then have assumed different alinements.[3]

The Munich settlement was the introduction to the Second World War, and prefigured many of its consequences. The three conspicuous absentees from the Munich Conference were Czechoslovakia, Poland, and Russia, and each omission had its distinct importance. The settlement was the fruition of the tendency towards the establishment of a Great Power directory in Europe, disposing arbitrarily of the territories and interests of minor Powers, which Czechoslovakia and Poland had together checked in 1933. While it marked the spurious zenith of Italy's claim to be a Great Power, with Mussolini as the mediator and peacemaker of Europe,[4] it marked also the end of Poland's pretensions to be a Great Power: the first gloss upon Beck's policy of plagiaristic bullying was his not being invited to Munich. Russia too was not invited; and though this new exclusion from

[1] 'To fight with Russian support alone was to court civil war in Czechoslovakia itself' (Wheeler-Bennett: *Munich*, p. 175; cf. pp. 81–82, 127–8). The Prime Minister and the Ministers of Defence and of the Interior were all Agrarians. There is evidence suggesting that the Prime Minister, Hodža, who was a Slovak, was pursuing a policy throughout the crisis that was at variance with Beneš's (see ibid. pp. 55, note 2, 121–2, and *D.Brit.F.P.*, 3rd series, i. 519–20, 524).

[2] Cf. Syrový's broadcast of 30 September 1938 (*Survey* for 1938, ii. 446–7; *Documents* (R.I.I.A.) for 1938, ii. 326–8).

[3] Cf. Churchill: *Second World War*, i. 237. 'I have always believed that Beneš was wrong to yield. He should have defended his fortress line. Once fighting had begun, in my opinion at that time, France would have moved to his aid in a surge of national passion, and Britain would have rallied to France almost immediately.'

[4] 'The point which Italian observers particularly like to emphasize is that . . . the fact that the leaders of two of the great democracies appealed to Signor Mussolini at the last moment to save the situation shows that they have at last realized Italy's value as the keystone of a Europe organized for peace' (Rome correspondent, *The Times*, 30 September 1938).

Eastern Europe lasted only eleven months, it strongly confirmed her hostility to the Western Powers and affected her future relations with them.[1] The Munich settlement marked the end, not only of the French system of alliances, but of the long history of French influence in Eastern Europe of which they were the most recent expression, an influence that stretched back four centuries to the founding of the entente between Francis I and the Grand Signior after Pavia, and still farther, to the Angevin dynasty in Poland and Hungary and the Peloponnese, to its designs upon Byzantium, and to the revolution in Papal policy which in the thirteenth century placed the brother of St. Louis upon the throne of Sicily.[2] It marked the beginning of the end of British influence in Eastern Europe apart from the peninsular outposts of Greece and Turkey, an influence that was not redeemed by the guarantees to Poland and Rumania in 1939, and finally disappeared in the barren agreements at Yalta in 1945. And it marked the end of Czechoslovakia as the only Western parliamentary state in the heart of Europe. Betrayed and discarded by the Western Powers, she sank into a satellite and then a protectorate of Nazi Germany, and came ten years later by another path, through the Second World War and its aftermath, to that exclusive dependence upon Russia which she had rejected in September 1938.[3]

The partition of Czechoslovakia proceeded smoothly and rapidly. The German occupation of the Sudetenland was carried out between 1 and 10 October; on 13 October the International Commission in Berlin of the four Munich Powers together with the nominal representation of Czechoslovakia, which provided a veil of decency for the transaction and deferred to every German demand,[4] decided to dispense with plebiscites in the ceded zones; on 20 November the final frontier was determined by a German-Czechoslovak protocol. The line of demarcation approximated to Hitler's Godesberg demands: it followed mainly ethnographical considerations, but also gave Germany strategic advantages, placing the rump

---

[1] See *Survey* for 1938, iii, part III, section iii (*c*).

[2] Charles of Anjou (1226–85) was invested with Sicily as a papal fief by Clement IV in 1266. He ruled the undivided kingdom until 1282; after the revolt of the island, he and his house ruled in Naples alone until 1435, they were suzerains or rulers of the principality of Achaia from 1267 to 1377, and titular emperors of Romania from 1313 to 1373. His house ruled in Hungary from 1308 to 1387, and in Poland from 1372 to 1398.

[3] 'We should not accept lessons in democracy and constitutionalism from those who are responsible for Munich, who bargained about our existence with Hitlerite Germany, and wholly undemocratically and illegally tore up the treaties of alliance and friendship with Czechoslovakia' —reply of the Czechoslovak Prime Minister, Gottwald, to the joint American, British, and French note condemning the Communist *coup d'état* in Czechoslovakia, 27 February 1948 (*Manchester Guardian*, 28 February 1948).

[4] 'The Munich settlement gave Germany all she immediately wanted. In applying the Agreement, every contentious point was decided in Germany's favour': Halifax, speech at Leeds, 20 January 1940 (Viscount Halifax: *Speeches on Foreign Policy* (London, Oxford University Press for Royal Institute of International Affairs, 1940), p. 347. For an account of the work of the International Commission see *Survey* for 1938, iii, part I, section ii.

of the Czech Lands at her discretion.[1] While Bohemia was being thus partitioned for the first time in its history, and Henlein's followers were celebrating their reunion with a Reich to which they and their ancestors had never belonged, the northern and southern frontiers of Czechoslovakia were caving inwards. Here history spun backwards to 1919–20, and territories she had gained then were wrenched from her. On 30 September, as soon as it was plain that Czechoslovakia was abandoned and prostrate, Poland presented an ultimatum demanding surrender of the Teschen district:[2] the reversal of the Czechoslovak annexation of Teschen while Poland was preoccupied in 1920. On 1 October Czechoslovakia yielded, and between 2 and 12 October Poland occupied a territory in which, by Czech estimates, the Czechs were 53·5 per cent. and the Poles only 33·5 per cent. of the population.[3] On 1 October Hungary demanded negotiations with Czechoslovakia on frontier revision. The negotiations were conducted between the Slovaks and the Hungarians at Komárno (Komárom) from 9 to 13 October, when they broke down because of the extensiveness of Hungarian demands.[4] On 12 October Hungary had already resorted to military action, and a small-scale irregular war ensued for several weeks in eastern Slovakia and Ruthenia, the Hungarian-Czechoslovak war of 1919 in reverse.[5] As in 1919, the conflict was not fought out in a straight issue between the two Small Powers; one of them had the military superiority, the other had the backing of the Great Powers, and the latter triumphed.[6] After further abortive direct negotiations, the Czechoslovak and Hungarian Governments submitted the dispute to the arbitration of Germany and Italy; and thus it was that in the Belvedere Palace in Vienna, on 2 November, Ribbentrop and Ciano traced a new Hungaro-Czechoslovak frontier, completing the partition of Czechoslovakia.[7] The injustice of 6 per cent. of the Magyar nation having been incorporated in Czechoslovakia was now rectified by incorporating 20 per cent. of the Slovak nation in Hungary.[8]

[1] It transferred to the Reich a tenth of the Czech people (719,127) together with 2,806,638 Sudeten Germans.

[2] See *Survey* for 1938, iii, part I, section iv (c). The ultimatum is printed in Namier: *Europe in Decay*, pp. 297–300.

[3] 123,000 Czechs, 77,000 Poles, 20,000 Germans, and 11,000 other foreigners, mostly of Polish nationality (*D.Brit.F.P.*, 3rd series, iii. 225).

[4] See *Survey* for 1938, iii, part I, section v (c).

[5] See A. Henderson: *Eyewitness in Czecho-Slovakia*, pp. 248–54. The irregular war did not end with the Vienna Award but went on until January 1939, and appeared along the Polish as well as the Hungarian frontiers of Czechoslovakia (Ripka: *Munich*, pp. 506–8). On the Hungarian-Czechoslovak war of 1919, see *H.P.C.* i. 354–5; iv. 160; F. J. Vondracek: *The Foreign Policy of Czechoslovakia, 1918–1935* (New York, Columbia University Press, 1937), pp. 34–40.

[6] On the military weakness of Hungary compared with Czechoslovakia at this time see the report of the conversation between Hitler and Csáky at Berlin on 16 January 1939, when Csáky admitted that Hungary without German help was militarily impotent (see *Documents secrets* (Eristov) vol. ii (*Hongrie*), no. 25). [7] See *Survey* for 1938, iii, part I, section v (f).

[8] The Vienna Award transferred to Hungary 859,885 Czechoslovak subjects, of whom 505,808

At Vienna as at Munich the absentees were important, and the most conspicuous were the two Western Munich Powers, in contradiction to the annex to the Munich Agreement which envisaged a quadripartite settlement of the Polish and Hungarian claims. The exclusion of Britain and France from Eastern Europe now received its first diplomatic expression.[1] Hungary had wanted Poland to be an arbitrator with Germany and Italy; Czechoslovakia demanded that if Poland, then also Rumania. The Small Powers therefore were once again excluded and Poland was once again one of them. The question at issue in the Vienna Award was the establishment or not of the Polish-Hungarian common frontier, which meant the disposal once again, as in 1919, of Ruthenia. It was the object of Hungary and Poland that Hungary should regain her old Carpathian boundary with minor frontier rectifications in Poland's favour, and they were supported by Italy; the policy of the Rome bloc joined hands with the policy of the Polish bloc. Poland tried to bring Rumania into the partition of Ruthenia, but Rumania was prevented by the fear of Hungarian revisionism turning next to Transylvania: the last negative expression of the common interest that had created the Little Entente.[2] Once again the consolidation of the satellites was ambivalent: to Germany, the Polish-Hungarian common frontier was represented as strengthening an anti-Soviet group that would be ancillary to German policy; but its main motive was perhaps anti-German, barring the road to the east.[3] The Vienna Conference revealed the latent conflicts within the Axis, Italy supporting Hungary, but Germany supporting Slovakia with preponderant voice. The Award mutilated Slovakia and Ruthenia more arbitrarily than the partition of Bohemia, but preserved a rump Ruthenia, like the rump Czechoslovakia of which it remained a part, for an instrument of German purposes.

(k) From Munich and Vienna to Prague

The new Czechoslovakia was from the outset a German puppet state. Its natural defences and prepared fortifications had been surrendered; strategically and economically it was not viable, and existed at German discretion; and Germany from the outset was preparing for its complete annexation.[4] The Czechoslovak Government used the popular fury against

were Magyars, 276,287 Slovaks, the remainder Jews, Germans, and Ruthenes (*D.Brit.F.P.*, 3rd series, iii. 225–6).

[1] 'Munich represents a decisive turning-point in the history of Central Europe. The Powers of the Rome–Berlin Axis on that occasion took into their hands the settlement of the outstanding questions in Central Europe, as the Western Powers themselves have recognized': Csáky to the Budapest Correspondent of the *Popolo d'Italia*, 21 December 1938 (*Documents* (R.I.I.A.) for 1938, i. 252).   [2] See *Survey* for 1938, iii, part I, section v (*d*).

[3] See Michael Winch: *Republic for a Day* (London, Hale, 1939), p. 228; Ripka: *Munich*, p. 499; Namier: *Diplomatic Prelude*, p. 37.

[4] See *Survey* for 1938, iii, part I, section iii. Hitler's secret directive of 21 October 1938 laid down 'the liquidation of the remainder of the Czech State' as the object of the German armed

the Western Powers to co-operate with the Axis. On 5 October Beneš resigned the presidency and on 22 October left the country.[1] Two internal developments in Czechoslovakia followed upon Munich, the achievements of a demagogic radicalism stimulated by Germany. The first was the federalization of the country, the second the partial establishment of a Fascist system. In the German grip Czechoslovakia disintegrated into its component nationalities, and their autonomist tendencies, hitherto latent or frustrated, came to fulfilment. On 6 October an autonomous government was set up for Slovakia;[2] on 11 October another for Ruthenia,[3] which having lost its old capital, Užhorod, to Hungary, was now compelled to set up a new capital in the wretched village of Chust. On 17 November a new Constitution was adopted for the whole country, in which the name Czechoslovakia became Czecho-Slovakia, and autonomy statutes for Slovakia and Ruthenia were formally enacted on 21 November.[4] In the Czech Lands there was a constitutional revolution: a fusion of political parties into two groups with the elimination of the rest and a concentration of power in the hands of the executive.[5] But the two new autonomous governments, lacking roots and traditions of independence, were more under German influence than that of Prague. In Slovakia, where there had always been a clerical and authoritarian tradition, a totalitarian régime was established, under the Slovak Populist Party with its Hlinka Guard modelled on the Nazi SS. Slovakia became in some degree the model Nazi satellite state, eclipsing Hungary: the leader of the German minority, Karmasin, was made Secretary of State for German Affairs and virtually supervised the Government.[6] Ruthenia was so backward as to be incapable of effective self-government; Vološin, the elderly Uniat priest who became Premier, was as little prepared for such an eminence as Hácha, the elderly judge who had succeeded Beneš as President of Czechoslovakia; a semi-Fascist régime was set up under the inspiration of the Ukrainian nationalists, with anti-Semitic measures and a storm-trooper organization named Sič, modelled on the Hlinka Guard;[7] but the importance of Ruthenia was as an advanced position for further German expansion.

'Par un curieux renversement du destin', wrote Coulondre in December 1938, 'la Tchécoslovaquie, établie comme un bastion pour contenir la poussée allemande, sert aujourdhui de bélier au Reich pour enfoncer les

forces second only to the defence of the German frontiers. 'It must be possible to smash the remainder of the Czech State at any time if it should be inclined to pursue a policy hostile to Germany' (*I.M.T. Nuremberg*, xxxiv. 480 (136–C); *Documents* (R.I.I.A.) for 1939–46, i. 38; cf. *N.C.A.* vi. 947–8).

[1] See *Survey* for 1938, iii, part I, section vi (*a*).   [2] Ibid. (*b*).
[3] Ibid. (*c*).
[4] The non-hyphened form 'Czechoslovakia' will continue to be used here throughout.
[5] See *Survey* for 1938, iii, part I, section vi (*d*).
[6] Ibid. (*b*).
[7] Ibid. (*c*).

portes de l'Orient.'[1] Through the conquest of Austria and Czechoslovakia Germany had encircled Hungary on the west and north, and
virtually annexed her economically to the Reich, a subjection for which
Hungary's meagre territorial acquisitions did not compensate. More
striking was the new position of Poland. Poland was, next to Czechoslovakia herself, the chief and most immediate loser by the Munich and
Belvedere settlements; and this went far beyond her loss of prestige
through her exclusion from a share in them. As the Anschluss had encircled Czechoslovakia on three sides, so the conversion of Slovakia and
Ruthenia into German satellites encircled Poland on three sides, putting
her in her turn at a strategic disadvantage which Beck had failed to foresee. The first note of the new theme was sounded when on 24 October
1938, a little more than three weeks after the conference at Munich,
Ribbentrop summoned Lipski, the Polish Ambassador in Berlin, and presented him with a demand for the cession of Danzig to the Reich and an
extraterritorial road and railway across the Polish corridor.[2] Being drawn
more closely than she willed into the German wake, a danger which it was
her folly not to have avoided long before her own territorial integrity was
brought into question, Poland now felt a common interest with the other
major Power that had been excluded from the Munich and Vienna settlements, and leaned to the east. On 26 November 1938, in order to contradict reports that Poland was about to join the Anti-Comintern Pact,
Poland and Russia issued a joint communiqué reaffirming their non-
aggression pact of 1932.[3]

The most evident threat to Poland was not the pressure upon her
western frontiers but the autonomous Ruthenia, which became, from
Munich to March 1939, the fulcrum whereby Germany sought to break
up the remaining structure of Eastern Europe. In Ruthenia Germany set
on foot a Ukrainian nationalist movement, and the little backward province, which had been a bridge between Czechoslovakia and Rumania,
and was to become for a brief period the bridge between Hungary and
Poland, was promoted into an irredentist centre, a Ukrainian Piedmont,
whose attractive force was intended to spread far beyond its own exiguous

---

[1] Despatch to Bonnet of 15 December 1938 (France, Ministère des Affaires Étrangères: *Le livre jaune français. Documents diplomatiques 1938–1939* . . . [referred to hereafter as *Livre jaune français*] (Paris, Imprimerie Nationale, 1939), no. 33); cf. Namier: *Diplomatic Prelude*, p. 37.

[2] See *Survey* for 1938, iii, part II, section i (*b*) (5). Yet it was not Poland, but Lithuania, who was marked down by Germany as the next victim after Czechoslovakia: the directive of 21 October 1938 defined the task of the German armed forces as being, after the protection of the Reich's frontiers and the liquidation of the remainder of the Czech State, the seizure of Memel (*I.M.T. Nuremberg*, xxxiv. 477–8 (136–C); trans. in *Documents* (R.I.I.A.) for 1939–46, i. 38; cf. *N.C.A.* vi. 947). A month later, on 24 November, Keitel signed a supplementary instruction which added the occupation of Danzig as a further task: 'The assumption is a lightning occupation of Danzig, exploiting a favourable political situation, not a war against Poland' (*I.M.T. Nuremberg*, xxxiv. 481–2 (137–C); trans. in *Documents* (R.I.I.A.) for 1939–46, i. 97; cf. *N.C.A.* vi. 949).

[3] See *Survey* for 1938, iii, part II, section i (*b*) (5).

frontiers, among the oppressed Ukrainians of Eastern Poland and the great body of the nation in the Soviet Ukraine.[1] From October 1938 onwards the German press called it Carpatho-Ukraine, and on 31 December this change of name became official.[2] Here the wheel of history tended backwards, not to the confused struggles of 1919, but to the brief apogee of German power in the preceding year, when between the signing of the Brest-Litovsk Treaty and the collapse of the German front in the west a vassalized autonomous Ukraine made an avenue for the German armies as far east as the Don.[3] For eighteen years Poland had expected and feared the irredentist influence upon her Ukrainian population from the Russian east; it now appeared from the German south. From here it endangered the industrial reservoir round Sandomierz, the Central District or Triangle of Security with its back to the Carpathians, which had been chosen and developed precisely because of its remoteness from the German and Russian frontiers alike. On 8 December 1938 the Ukrainian National Democratic Party in Poland demanded the kind of autonomy now obtained by Slovakia and Carpatho-Ukraine: a separate army, and a share in the control of foreign relations. Poland was threatened by the same combination of external encirclement and internal disruption that had destroyed Czechoslovakia, and the latter was the more alarming.[4]

The partition of Czechoslovakia not only marked the limit of German revisionism according to the national principle, beyond which it would move into imperialism. It also stirred up the small revisionist states, the minorities, the sub-nationalities of Eastern Europe. For the first time the national principle had been invoked for its new purpose of disintegrating the successor states that had formerly been built upon it; the Croats in Yugoslavia, like the Ukrainians in Poland, were excited by the spectacle of Slovak and Ruthenian autonomy.[5] And for the first time German revision-

[1] For first-hand accounts of Carpatho-Ukraine from January to March 1939 see Winch: *Republic for a Day* (reviewed in Namier: *In the Margin of History*, pp. 181–5) and A. Henderson: *Eyewitness in Czecho-Slovakia*, pp. 274–87.

[2] Ripka: *Munich*, p. 243, apparently referring to an enactment of the Czechoslovak Parliament. The change was confirmed or effected by a decree of the Ruthenian Government on 2 January 1939, though the name Carpatho-Russia still remained a valid alternative (*The Times*, 3 January 1939; *Manchester Guardian*, 19 November 1938).

[3] Ripka: *Munich*, p. 325. The Central Powers recognized the Ukraine as an independent sovereign state on 1 February 1918; on 8 February it became their economic protectorate by the first Brest-Litovsk Treaty; on 1 March the Germans occupied Kiev and reinstated the Ukrainian government overthrown by the Bolsheviks; by the middle of May the German and Austro-Hungarian occupation of the Ukraine was complete, and the German evacuation did not take place until after the Western armistice of 11 November 1918 (see Allen: *Ukraine*, pp. 286–306).

[4] Cf. Ciano: *Diario (1939–43)*, 25 February 1939. A common fear of the Greater Ukraine agitation underlay the Polish-Russian joint communiqué of 26 November 1938. Russia and Poland now found the same interest in standing shoulder to shoulder over the prostrate Ukrainian nation that Russia and Prussia had had throughout the nineteenth century in standing shoulder to shoulder over the prostrate Polish nation.

[5] On 15 January 1939 the Croat Opposition, at Zagreb, passed a resolution demanding the settlement of the Croat question in accordance with the principle of self-determination.

ism had provided subsidiarily a degree of satisfaction for a small revisionist
Power; Bulgaria's appetite was sharpened by the extension of Hungary's
frontiers. These movements offered a variety of opportunities to German
policy; but while Germany was concentrating on the final destruction of
Czechoslovakia, and beginning her pressure upon Poland, she aimed at a
general consolidation of her mastery over South-Eastern Europe rather
than the promotion of new divisions. As in 1936, when she had first
isolated Eastern Europe from the West, her exploitation of the field was
inaugurated by Schacht's tour of the Danubian and Balkan capitals as
Minister of Economics,[1] so in the last quarter of 1938 Germany's ascendancy was celebrated and cemented by Schacht's successor Funk in a
similar journey.[2] Ribbentrop, when he met Mussolini and Ciano in Rome
on 28 October 1938, numbered among 'other countries which want to
form still closer bonds with the Axis' not only Hungary but Yugoslavia
and Rumania also.[3]

Nevertheless, German diplomacy here was not unimpeded by obstacles,
and at the end of the year and the beginning of 1939 there appeared
throughout the Danube valley a faint tremor of resistance. These states
attempted, while maintaining their subservience to Germany in foreign
policy, to establish increased control and independence in domestic
affairs. A German trade mission to Bucharest in November and December
failed to obtain the long-term commercial agreement it was seeking,[4]
and on 30 November the Iron Guard leader Codreanu, who had been in
prison since April, was murdered by Carol only a week after Carol's
return from a visit to Berchtesgaden. Hitler was intensely indignant, and
Gafencu believed, with characteristic self-dramatization, that his appointment as Foreign Minister on 23 December was to handle a situation in
which there might be a German 'punitive expedition' down the Danube.[5]
Throughout the winter Rumania was the most active of all the Eastern
European Powers in the pursuit of solidarity, being not yet contiguous with
Germany and paralysed into subordination, nor so remote from danger as
Greece and Turkey, who left the initiative in other hands. But solidarity
against Germany was less easy to achieve than solidarity against Bulgaria, and the only concrete result of Gafencu's busy journeyings to foreign
capitals was the meeting of the Balkan Entente at Bucharest on 22 Febru-

[1] *Survey* for 1936, p. 529, note 1.
[2] *Survey* for 1938, i. 50–55.
[3] Ciano: *Europa*, p. 375; Eng. version, p. 244. Cf. Ciano: *Diario (1939–43)*, 8 January 1939:
'closer relations with Yugoslavia, Hungary, Rumania, and possibly Poland, for the purpose of
ensuring raw materials'.
[4] *Survey* for 1938, i. 55–56.
[5] See Grigore Gafencu: *Les derniers jours de l'Europe: un voyage diplomatique en 1939*, revised edition
[referred to hereafter as Gafencu: *Derniers jours*] (Paris, Egloff, 1947), p. 39 [trans. by Fletcher
Allen with title *The Last Days of Europe* (London, Muller, 1947)]; cf. *Survey* for 1938, iii, part IV,
section iii.

ary 1939, which reaffirmed the existing frontiers against any revisionist claims.[1]

The Yugoslav alliance was still of cardinal importance to Italy. On 8 January 1939 Mussolini definitely included the annexation of Albania in his programme of expansion, but it was to depend on Yugoslav support, and Yugoslavia for her part was to be encouraged in the conquest of Salonika.[2] From 18 to 23 January Ciano visited Yugoslavia and conferred with Stojadinović. At Germany's request Ciano asked whether Yugoslavia might join the Anti-Comintern Pact; on Italy's account he proposed the Albanian partition; and to both suggestions Stojadinović responded favourably.[3] But in the general elections of 11 December 1938 Stojadinović had been virtually defeated: the dictatorship had gone far towards transforming the Croat autonomous movement into a Yugoslav national opposition backed by the majority of Serbs as well;[4] and on 4 February 1939 Stojadinović was compelled to resign, and Axis influence in Belgrade was shaken. 'With the removal of Stoyadinovich', wrote Ciano, 'the Yugoslav card has lost for us 90 per cent. of its value.'[5] Mussolini now decided, 'if the Stoyadinovich policy still holds, to go ahead with the partition of Albania between us and Yugoslavia; if not, then occupation of Albania by us without Yugoslavia, and, if necessary, even against Yugoslavia'.[6]

The satellite whose relations with Germany were most ambiguous was Hungary. Hungary strongly resented not having obtained Ruthenia under the Belvedere Award and believed that she had been deprived by German meanness of her just demands. Her feelings were vented in the continuance of terroristic attacks along the Slovak and Ruthenian frontiers, and in criticism of Germany in political speeches and in the press. This in turn angered both Hitler and Mussolini.[7] In December the Hungarian Foreign Minister Kánya, whom Hitler regarded as an enemy of Germany, was succeeded by Csáky; and on 13 January 1939 Csáky had a stormy interview with Hitler, from which he withdrew, however, with the assurance that Hitler no longer forbade a Hungarian occupation of Ruthenia.[8]

---

[1] See Ripka: *Munich*, p. 322; Gafencu: *Derniers jours*, pp. 148–50.

[2] See Ciano: *Diario (1939–43)*, 8 and 15 January 1939.

[3] Ibid. 17 and 19 January 1939; and Ciano: *Europa*, pp. 407–12; Eng. version, pp. 268–72. See also *Survey* for 1938, iii, part IV, section iii.

[4] See H. Seton-Watson: *Eastern Europe*, pp. 236–7. 'The final result was announced as being 1,643,783 votes for the Government and 1,364,524 for the United Opposition—and it should not be forgotten that this was the Government estimate of the votes' (Wiskemann: *Undeclared War*, p. 125).

[5] Ciano: *Diario (1939–43)*, 7 February 1939. Ribbentrop, however, was complacent in the belief that Cincar-Marković, the Yugoslav Minister in Berlin, who was now promoted to be Yugoslav Foreign Minister, was pro-Axis (ibid. 6 February 1939; Germany, Auswärtiges Amt: *Dokumente zum Konflikt mit Jugoslawien and Griechenland* (Berlin, Deutscher Verlag, 1941), no. 34).

[6] Ciano: *Diario (1939–43)*, 5 February 1939.

[7] Cf. ibid. 10 January 1939.

[8] See *Survey* for 1938, iii, part I, section x (a). See also report of conversation between Hitler

Three days before his meeting with Hitler, Csáky announced that Hungary had accepted an invitation to join the Anti-Comintern Pact;[1] and on 2 February Russia broke off relations with Hungary on the ground that Hungary had now virtually lost her independence.[2] Rumania was pleased by this further alienation of two of the three Powers that had claims on her territory. On 14 February Imrédy was forced to resign by the increasing unpopularity of his subservient policy towards Germany; the discovery of a Jewish streak in the ancestry of the anti-Semitic politician suggested the capricious but ineluctable destiny against which his country itself was fighting in vain. He was succeeded as Prime Minister by Teleki, but Csáky retained his post. Hungary formally signed the Anti-Comintern Pact on 24 February, the fourth adherent and the first Small Power on the roll; on the same day Teleki dissolved the Hungarian Nazi Party in the hope of insulating his domestic from his foreign policy. It seemed at the time as if the German occupation of Prague in March might have been decided upon partly 'in order to break the insubordination being shown at the time by most of Germany's smaller neighbours to her east and south'.[3]

Rumania had long wished to secure the same unrestricted sovereignty over the mouths of the Danube that Turkey obtained in 1936 over the Black Sea Straits. As early as 1925 Rumania had sought the abolition of the European Commission of the Danube and its replacement by the International Commission, and her discontent was increased by the success of Turkish diplomacy at Montreux.[4] Moreover, Russia had been demanding representation on the European Commission since 1925, and Germany since 1927.[5] When in November 1936 Germany denounced the provisions of the Versailles Treaty concerning international waterways, and withdrew from the international river commissions, she struck a decisive blow at the international régime for the Danube.[6] The Rumanian campaign against the European Commission obtained its objectives at the Sinaia Conference of August 1939, when the Commission renounced all its powers which

and Csáky, 16 January 1939, in *Documents secrets* (Eristov), vol. ii (*Hongrie*), no. 25. On 27 February Csáky sent a servile and deprecatory message to Berlin that the Hungarian desire for Ruthenia was based only on economic reasons: see report of conversation between Weizsäcker and the Hungarian military attaché, 27 February 1939 (ibid. no. 26).

[1] This had been prepared by Ciano's visit to Budapest on 19–22 December 1938.

[2] *Manchester Guardian*, 3 February 1939. Russia discriminated between the Small and Great Powers of the Pact, and the representation of Hungarian interests in the Soviet Union was appropriately entrusted to Japan, one of the three Powers whose invitation to Hungary to join the Pact had caused the severance of Russo-Hungarian relations (ibid. 9 February 1939).

[3] Wiskemann: *Undeclared War*, p. 92; cf. pp. 62, 237.

[4] *Survey* for 1925, ii. 165–6; *Survey* for 1937, i. 372, note; Jean Duvernoy: *Le régime international du Danube* (Paris, Pédone, 1941), pp. 130–6.

[5] Sir Osbert Mance: *International River and Canal Transport* (London, Oxford University Press for Royal Institute of International Affairs, 1944), p. 67.

[6] *Survey* for 1937, i. 368–80; Mance, op. cit. p. 55.

were incompatible with Rumanian sovereignty.[1] On 1 March 1939 Germany was at last admitted to the European Commission. But the régime of 1856 was now virtually dead; Rumania had been engaged in destroying a European guarantee of her own independence; and the way was cleared for a conflict, to control the mouths of the Danube, between Germany and Russia.

(l) THE SECOND PARTITION OF CZECHOSLOVAKIA

'It was clear to me from the first', said Hitler afterwards, 'that I could not be satisfied with the Sudeten-German territory.'[2] The Munich frontiers of Bohemia and Moravia were not viable for Czechoslovakia, but neither were they likely to remain acceptable to Germany: a Czech salient still deformed her eastern frontier, and proclaimed the strategic desirability of straightening the line between the southern tip of Silesia and the north-eastern tip of the Ostmark.[3] On 16 January 1939 Hitler told Csáky that between October and March no military operation was possible in Europe.[4] This pointed, for the final conquest of Czechoslovakia, to the month in which in previous years Germany had reintroduced conscription, had remilitarized the Rhineland, and had conquered Austria. Throughout the winter of 1938–9 the fulfilment of what had been only half achieved at Munich was in preparation. The military and economic plans were complete; the German fifth column inside Czechoslovakia was highly organized; the diplomatic pressure on the Prague Government was constant.

But it was through a national *Auflösung* that the destruction of Czechoslovakia was designed.[5] By the beginning of 1939 the three component parts of the state were ceasing to function within a common framework, and were assuming separate international existences. Ruthenia as the base for a Nazi Ukrainian agitation was exacerbating the relations of Prague with Poland and Hungary. The Nazi exploitation of Slovak separatism was preparing the opportunity for German intervention; the Slovak extremists were given the role in the second act that had been played by Henlein's party in the first. In February 1939 their agitation for Slovak independence reached its height. The Prague Government had to decide whether to acquiesce in the disintegration of the Czechoslovak State, or to

---

[1] Duvernoy, op. cit. pp. 141–3.

[2] Hitler's conference with his Commanders-in-Chief, 23 November 1939 (*I.M.T. Nuremberg*, xxvi. 329 (789–PS); trans. in *Documents* (R.I.I.A.) for 1939–46, i. 529; cf. *N.C.A.* iii. 573).

[3] 'Geographically the situation was already made clear by the fact that Bohemia and Moravia were enclosed by Germany, and Germany could never tolerate in her own territory a hotbed of unrest', minutes of a conference between Hitler and Tiso, 13 March 1939 (*I.M.T. Nuremberg*, xxxi. 151 (2802–PS); trans. in *Documents* (R.I.I.A.) for 1939–46, i. 48; cf. *N.C.A.* v. 444).

[4] See *Documents secrets* (Eristov), vol. ii (*Hongrie*), no. 25, p. 79; *Documents* (R.I.I.A.) for 1939–46, i. 194.   [5] *Livre jaune français*, no. 65.

take action which might precipitate a crisis. On 6 March they intervened in Ruthenia,[1] and on 9 March in Slovakia,[2] dismissing the Ministers who were most active in the separatist movements. These acts were the last attempts of a government in Prague to assert its authority throughout the territories of the Czechoslovak Republic.

The situation was now ready for German intervention. Under strong Nazi pressure, and the threat of seeing their country handed over to Hungary, the Slovak Diet voted the independence of Slovakia on 14 March.[3] The people of Bratislava received the declaration of independence with apathy and pessimism. It was the last tribute to the republic of Masaryk and Beneš that the separation of the Slovaks from the Czechs had to be carried through by German violence and could not be invested with any appearance of spontaneity. On the same evening the Government in Chust followed suit and proclaimed the independence of Carpatho-Ukraine.[4] The previous midnight the Ruthenes had sent a telegram to Hitler asking him to accept Carpatho-Ukraine as a German protectorate, but this was never answered.[5] For less than twenty-four hours the Ruthenian province became for the first and last time in its history an independent state, the republic of Carpatho-Ukraine, cut loose from Czechoslovakia, not yet reabsorbed in Hungary, but seeming, as the last mutilated embodiment of the hopes of a free Ukrainian nation, like a faint echo of the Ruthenian principality of Galicia on the farther side of the Carpathians, which in the second half of the thirteenth century, at the flood-tide of the Mongolian invasion, had been the last representative of the old Kievan Russian world.[6]

On the evening of 14 March Hitler summoned Hácha to Berlin, and in the interview that was held in the early hours of the following morning, the most notorious and brutal as well as the best attested to which Hitler ever subjected a foreign statesman, he forced Hácha, by the threat of the immediate destruction of Prague from the air, to sign an agreement which 'placed the fate of the Czech people and of their country in the hands of the Fuehrer of the German Reich'.[7] At dawn that day, 15 March, the

[1] See *Survey* for 1938, iii, part I, section x (c).   [2] Ibid. (b).
[3] Ibid. section xi (a).   [4] Ibid.
[5] See Winch: *Republic for a Day*, pp. 280–1; *Livre jaune français*, no. 66.
[6] See Allen: *Ukraine*, pp. 38–40; Toynbee: *Study*, vi. 310, note 2. 'In twenty-four hours we lived in three different States. We woke up in the Czechoslovak Republic. By the evening Carpatho Ukraine was a free land. Next day the Hungarians came in. The Germans, who had occupied Prague early that morning, were, it was announced, "not interested" in Carpatho Ukraine, and thus the little Republic, which all Europe believed was to be the germ of a Great Ukraine, was crushed at birth' (Winch, op. cit. p. 276). See also Anne O'Hare McCormick in the *New York Times*, 17 March 1939.
[7] See *Survey* for 1938, iii, part I, section xi (d). For text of the agreement see *Dokumente der deutschen Politik*, initiated by the Deutsche Hochschule für Politik and continued by the Deutsches Auslandswissenschaftliches Institut (Berlin, Junker and Dünnhaupt, 1940), vol. 7, part 2, pp. 498–9; trans. in *Documents* (R.I.I.A.) for 1939–46, i. 56; cf. *N.C.A.* viii. 402 (049–TC).

German army invaded Czechoslovakia from all sides, advancing rapidly through heavy snow; and in a proclamation to the German people Hitler declared that 'Czecho-Slovakia has ceased to exist'.[1] He himself entered Prague in the evening, shortly before the streets had been cleared by the imposition of a curfew, and slept the night in the Hradčany. From there on 16 March he issued a decree annexing Bohemia and Moravia and creating them a Protectorate.[2] Of protectorates in Europe there had been none hitherto except at one time or another the diminutive insterstitial states of Andorra and Monaco, San Marino and the Ionian Islands, the republic of Cracow and the Free City of Danzig.[3] The reduction of so ancient and considerable a territory as Bohemia and Moravia, which even in its Habsburg servitude had remained juridically a kingdom, to a status which was primarily a legal instrument of Western expansion against the Islamic world and among primitive peoples, showed a more advanced stage in the dissolution of Western society than the Balkanization which was already infecting it from Eastern Christendom[4]—its colonialization. The Western Powers would no longer monopolize the prestige of imperial possessions, for Germany would provide herself with colonies and protectorates in Europe.[5]

When the independence of Slovakia was declared on 14 March, Hungary instantly sent an ultimatum to Prague, demanding the withdrawal of Czech troops from Ruthenia.[6] While Hácha was on his way to Berlin the Czech Government accepted the ultimatum in substance, and on the same evening Hungarian troops cautiously began the invasion of Ruthenia. For the next two days they moved slowly up the mountain valleys in a blizzard, being resisted by Ukrainian guerrillas. Vološín offered the country to Rumania, himself fleeing thither. But Rumania was in panic; she had mobilized in the expectation that the Hungarian invasion of Ruthenia would be followed by an invasion of Transylvania, and in the fear of Bulgarian movements in the south; and with the very structure of her state seeming in danger, she contented herself by occupying only a few Ruthenian frontier communes.[7] On 16 March the Hungarians captured Chust and reached the Polish border, and Teleki proclaimed the annexa-

---

[1] See *Survey* for 1938, iii, part I, section xi (*e*). For text of proclamation see *Dokumente der deutschen Politik*, vol. 7, part 2, pp. 499–500; trans. in *Documents* (R.I.I.A.) for 1939–46, i. 57; cf. *N.C.A.* viii. 402–3 (050–TC). Wheeler-Bennett (*Munich*, p. 346) dramatically makes Hitler write this proclamation in the Hradčany; but it was dated from Berlin and given out over the wireless by Goebbels at 6 a.m. on 15 March, several hours before Hitler had left his own capital.

[2] Text of decree in *Dokumente der deutschen Politik*, vol. 7, part 2, pp. 501–6; *N.C.A.* viii. 404–6 (051–TC); *Documents* (R.I.I.A.) for 1939–46, i. 62–5.

[3] Oppenheim: *International Law*, i. 175–6 and note 4. See above, pp. 152, note 1, and 208, note 2.

[4] See above, pp. 238–9.

[5] *Mein Kampf*, pp. 153, 742; tr. Murphy, pp. 127, 533.

[6] See *Survey* for 1938, iii, part I, section xi (*b*).

[7] *Livre jaune français*, no. 73, p. 97; Ripka: *Munich*, pp. 389–90; Wiskemann: *Undeclared War*, pp. 64–66.

tion of Ruthenia in Budapest. On 19 March the occupation was officially completed, though fighting continued for some days. Hungary once more stretched to the Carpathian crests, and the common frontier with Poland was achieved.

Slovakia like Ruthenia was fully independent only for a day, but it was not its fate to be annexed. On 15 March, while Hitler was on his way from Berlin to Prague, Tiso begged him by telegram to take Slovakia under his protection; on 16 March, by another telegram, Hitler formally complied.[1] From that date onwards German troops entered Slovakia and occupied all the positions of strategic importance. A treaty of protection was signed in Vienna on 18 March and in Berlin on 23 March, whereby Germany virtually took over the defence and foreign relations of Slovakia.[2] In Berlin a secret protocol was added, making Slovakia an economic as well as a political protectorate of the Reich, and establishing *de facto* a customs union between them.[3] Nevertheless, German protection for Slovakia was provisional and equivocal. It did not prevent Hungary from invading south-eastern Slovakia on 23 March, while German attention was occupied with the seizure of Memel, and taking possession of the Ung valley railway line with several towns. The Hungarians argued that this occurred some hours earlier than the signature of the German-Slovak treaty in Berlin, but the subsequent fighting went on until the end of the month.[4]

The price paid by Hitler for the acquisitions of March 1939 was the abandonment of his Ukrainian designs. He told Brauchitsch on 25 March[5] that he no longer entertained immediate plans for establishing a Ukrainian state.[6] This was the necessary condition for a German-Russian *rapprochement*, and it is not impossible that Hitler already saw its advantages in that respect.[7] The extinction of the Ukrainian Piedmont relieved Eastern

---

[1] See *Survey* for 1938, iii, part I, section xi (*f*). For text of telegrams see *Dokumente der deutschen Politik*, vol. 7, part 1, p. 9; trans. in *Documents* (R.I.I.A.) for 1939–46, i. 49, note 1. Namier (*Diplomatic Prelude*, pp. 71, 415) wrongly gives the date of Tiso's request to Hitler as 16 March.

[2] See *Survey* for 1938, iii, loc. cit. For text of treaty see *Dokumente der deutschen Politik*, vol. 7, part 1, pp. 12–13; trans. in *Documents* (R.I.I.A.) for 1939–46, i. 83–84; cf. *N.C.A.* iv. 18–19 (1439–PS). In terms of the constitutional organization of the British Empire, the difference in status between Slovakia and the Protectorate of Bohemia and Moravia was now that between a protected state and a colonial protectorate.

[3] Confidential Protocol concerning Economic and Financial Collaboration between the German Reich and the State of Slovakia (*I.M.T. Nuremberg*, xxxi. 121–3 (2793–PS); trans. in *Documents* (R.I.I.A.) for 1939–46, i. 84–86; cf. *N.C.A.* v. 427–8).

[4] *The Times*, 29 March 1939. A Slovak-Hungarian frontier agreement was signed on 4 April, giving Hungary the full extent of her claims; but the Slovak Government continued to protest against it and frontier clashes continued to occur.

[5] See *Survey* for 1938, iii, part I, section xi (*h*).

[6] 'The Fuehrer does *not* want to go into the Ukraine. Possibly one could establish a Ukrainian State. But these questions also remain open' (*I.M.T. Nuremberg*, xxxviii. 274 (100–R); *N.C.A.* viii. 84).

[7] In Stalin's speech to the Eighteenth Congress of the C.P.S.U. (B.) on 10 March 1939 there was a confident reference to the unlikelihood of 'the gnat, namely, the so-called Carpathian Ukraine', annexing 'the elephant, that is, the Soviet Ukraine' (J. Stalin: *Problems of Leninism*, trans.

European politics of what had been their most disturbing and imponderable factor since Munich. The common Polish-Hungarian frontier meant relinquishing what had been virtually a common German-Rumanian frontier, and this was conceded now by Germany with a show of deference to Hungarian and Polish wishes.[1] Nevertheless, when the dust of collapsing Czechoslovakia had settled, and the new pattern of power could be clearly seen, the small states, severally and collectively, found their positions decisively weakened. Hungary was enslaved by her territorial gains, and lay in vassalage with the Germans now along her northern as well as her western frontier. Rumania was threatened more gravely by the German-Hungarian combination than she had been by the German control of the Ruthenian corridor; Magyar imperialism had been fleshed along the north, and might next be encouraged to turn to the east.[2] In the emotional repercussions of the fall of Prague, Rumania signed a long-term commercial treaty with Germany on 23 March of the kind that she had refused in December; it made Rumania an economic vassal to Germany, but it might imply a German guarantee of her frontiers.[3] Yugoslavia too felt the premonitions of national disintegration. The reaction of the Serbs was characteristically more positive than that of any people in Eastern Europe; there was now increasing demand in Belgrade for a Serbo-Croat government of national union. But in Croatia there were

from the 11th Russian edition (Moscow, Foreign Languages Publishing House, 1945), pp. 603-4); but there is no evidence that Stalin was anticipating Hitler's gesture. On this speech see further below, pp. 530-1.

[1] In his Reichstag speech of 28 April 1939 Hitler described how the Vienna Award had been unsatisfactory to Hungary and Poland, and continued: 'It was a fact that perhaps only one single state was interested in the preservation of the *status quo*, and that was Rumania; the man best authorized to speak on behalf of that country told me personally how desirable it would be to have a direct line of communication with Germany perhaps *via* the Ukraine and Slovakia. I mention this as an illustration of the feeling of being menaced by Germany from which the Rumanian Government—according to the American clairvoyants—are supposed to be suffering. But it was now clear that it could not be Germany's task permanently to oppose a development or actually to fight for the maintenance of a state of affairs for which we could never have made ourselves responsible. The stage was thus reached at which in the name of the German Government I decided to make a declaration to the effect that we had no intention of any longer incurring the reprobation of opposing the common wishes of Poland and Hungary as regards their frontiers, simply in order to keep open a road of approach for Germany to Rumania' (Hitler: *Speeches* (Baynes), ii. 1619). This passage probably affords evidence not for what Carol said to Hitler but for what had been one of the less explicit of Hitler's several purposes in establishing an autonomous Carpatho-Ukraine.

[2] As it did the following year. The Second Vienna Award, on 30 August 1940, gave northern Transylvania to Hungary.

[3] 'Twenty-one years earlier, in May 1918, the victorious Central Powers had imposed a treaty upon Roumania which, if very much harsher in detail, was not dissimilar in principle.... Shrewder people now began to speak of the three types of German protectorate since March 15th. The first, in Bohemia and Moravia, had comprised the complete subjection of the Czechs; the second had provided the Slovaks with diplomatic representation and a territorial guarantee, which was promptly followed by a Hungarian invasion and the cession of Slovak territory to Hungary; the third was established by the commercial treaty with Roumania' (Wiskemann: *Undeclared War*, pp. 93, 95).

still two minds about the Slovak model of autonomy under the German
hand, and the Italians anxiously saw the German shadow creeping forward over Fiume and Trieste and the Adriatic.[1]

· The country most immediately menaced was Poland. The disappearance of the Ukrainian danger from Ruthenia was altogether nullified by
the appearance of German troops in Slovakia, a cruder and more massive
threat.

The bloodless solution of the Czech conflict in the autumn of 1938 and spring
of 1939 and the annexation of Slovakia rounded off the territory of Greater
Germany in such a way that it now became possible to consider the Polish
problem on the basis of more or less favourable strategic premises.[2]

The encirclement of Poland was illustrated and emphasized, in the opposite quarter, by the German seizure of Memel from Lithuania on 23 March,[3]
the colophon to the violent events of March 1939. 'Henceforth the Germans overflowed with "generosity" towards Lithuania, hoping to find in
her, because of Vilna, an ally against Poland: another Slovakia on her
northern flank.'[4]

The new position was incisively drawn in a report by the United States
military attaché in Berlin.

The military and strategic advantages which Germany has gained by the
occupation of Bohemia, Moravia, and Slovakia are enormous. Strategically
Germany has placed herself between Poland and Hungary and definitely and
forever prevented joint Polish-Hungarian action against her. Further, in case
Germany desires to move against Poland, she now commands the gateway to
Krakow, Limburg, and the Russian Ukraine. Her new position now places her
armies on three sides of Poland, poised for a quick and telling blow. With
respect to Hungary, Germany also threatens Budapest from the north and west
and her armies are in a position to march directly into the fertile plains of
Hungary, or through Hungary to Roumania. The occupation of the mountainous Ruthenia by Hungary becomes unimportant in the light of Germany's
new strategic position.[5]

[1] See ibid. pp. 128–30; Ciano: *Diario (1939–43)*, 16 and 17 March 1939. In Belgrade, democratic Serb public opinion was probably a less potent force at this juncture than the Yugoslav
army (mainly Serb in its upper ranks) which two years later was to carry out the *coup d'état* of
25 March 1941.

[2] Jodl's lecture at Munich on 'The Strategic Position in the Beginning of the 5th Year of War',
7 November 1943 (*I.M.T. Nuremberg*, xxxvii. 635 (172–L); *N.C.A.* vii. 923–4). Cf. Hitler's
speech to his military commanders, 23 November 1939: with the erection of the Protectorate 'the
basis for the conquest of Poland was laid' (*I.M.T. Nuremberg*, xxvi. 329 (789–PS); trans. in
Documents (R.I.I.A.) for 1939–46, i. 529; cf. *N.C.A.* iii. 573). See also Namier: *Diplomatic
Prelude*, pp. 85–86.

[3] See *Survey* for 1938, iii, part II, section iii (*e*).

[4] Namier: *Diplomatic Prelude*, p. 88. The relevant documents are in *Dokumente der deutschen
Politik*, vol. 7, part 2, pp. 531–61.

[5] Report of the U.S. military attaché in Berlin, 20 March 1939 (*N.C.A.* vi. 396 (3618–PS)).
The position was described in remarkably similar words by the diplomatic correspondent of the
Manchester Guardian, 16 March 1939.

Henceforward the Small Powers might join the German column or they might seek help in undischargeable guarantees from the anti-German Great Powers; but the illusion of an Eastern European neutral bloc, which had survived the first partition of Czechoslovakia, was finally dead. Thus the Polish-Hungarian common frontier was deprived of its main purpose by the very circumstances of its achievements.[1] It was the mark of Hitler's tactical genius that the laying aside of his long-term Ukrainian plans brought such immense immediate advantages; or it was an illustration of how, when a Great Power is on the spring-tide of aggrandizement, the defensive manœuvres of Small Powers are likely to turn back upon themselves and become tributaries of the common flood; 'for the nature of Power is, in this point, like to Fame, increasing as it proceeds; or like the motion of heavy bodies, which the further they go, make still the more haste'.[2]

Twice in the past Bohemia had been the protagonist in a European crisis. The Hussite Revolution in the fifteenth century was not only the revolt of nascent Czech nationalism against German ascendancy; it was also the first in the series of national revolutions conceived in terms of moral or intellectual ideals of freedom, which ran through Western history and culminated in the national movements and Wilsonian doctrines of 1918; and in the international effect of its extreme religious and social manifestations it played the same part in relation to the Conciliar Movement that Bolshevism afterwards played in relation to the League of Nations.[3] Bohemia defied German Catholicism once again in the first quarter of the seventeenth century, when by dissolving its connexion with the Habsburg Monarchy and electing a Protestant prince as king it precipitated the Thirty Years War. In the Hussite War the Bohemians maintained their independence and indeed their military superiority against Europe for seventeen years, and at last negotiated a compromise with the Council of Basel, the Compacts of 1436, by which their religious autonomy was recognized. At the beginning of the Thirty Years War they asserted their independence against the forces of the Counter-Reformation for only two years, and then in the catastrophic defeat of the White Mountain for-

---

[1] One of the last people to deceive himself about its value as a reinsurance against Germany was Mussolini. When German plans for the final partition of Czechoslovakia became known belatedly in Rome on 14 March, 'he sought a recompense in the advantages which Hungary will have by achieving a common frontier with the Poles, and he instructed me to tell Budapest to move boldly. But to me this seems very little' (Ciano: *Diario (1939–43)*, 14 March 1939).

[2] Thomas Hobbes: *Leviathan*, chapter x.

[3] The identification of Hussitism with Bolshevism was a favourite theme of Nazi propaganda. 'Once, indeed, during the Hussite wars the Czechs had gained a temporary independence. They used it like the Bolsheviks, burning and ravaging, until the Germans rose and crushed them', Hitler's interview with G. Ward Price on 17 September 1938 (Hitler: *Speeches* (Baynes), ii. 1503; cf. Hermann Rauschning: *Hitler Speaks: a Series of Political Conversations with Adolf Hitler on his Real Aims* (London, Thornton Butterworth, 1939), p. 46, and Wiskemann: *Czechs and Germans*, p. 278).

feited it for three centuries. The third time the Czechs became the centre of a European crisis, in the prologue to the Second World War in the twentieth century, they were victims rather than protagonists, and their part was acquiescence not resistance: in September 1938 they obstructed the will of the Great Powers for only a week, and in March 1939 they submitted without a blow. So decisive had become the disparity between Great Powers and Small through the growth since the fifteenth century in the power and organization of the modern state, and so hard was it now for the lesser peoples to preserve their independence. But the liquidation of small states, which Hitler advocated,[1] sharpened the rivalry between Great Powers in a way he could not control. Sixty years earlier Bismarck had said that if the Habsburg Monarchy broke up, Russia would try to get possession not only of Galicia but of all the Austrian Slavs.

As to Bohemia, the eternal battle-field of Europe, the great plateau whence come all the rivers that water us, the vast natural fortress erected by God in the centre of our continent—Bohemia in the hands of Russia would mean our enslavement, Bohemia in our hands would mean war without mercy or truce against the Empire of the Tsars. You see that the survival of Austria is necessary for our own existence.[2]

Hitler's statecraft knew none of the limited aims and the moderation of his predecessor's, for it was indeed the fulfilment of the deeper moral qualities, the violence, deceit, and arrogance of Bismarck's policy; and the triumph of 15 March 1939 carried within itself all the consequences that Bismarck had foreseen.

(vii) Germany
By Martin Wight

The Nazi annexation of Bohemia and Moravia in March 1939, together with the conquest of Austria the year before, was a renewal and fulfilment of German history. The Third Reich, which had been erected on the foundations of the Second Reich but within more contracted boundaries, now suddenly assumed the aspect of the ancient Reich, expanding to its eastern confines and claiming its inheritance. As the Napoleonic Empire

[1] For Hitler's impatience with 'all the rubbish of small nations [Kleinstaaten-Gerümpel]' see The Goebbels Diaries, trans. and ed. Louis P. Lochner (London, Hamish Hamilton, 1948), p. 279; cf. Rauschning: Hitler Speaks, pp. 46, 128, and the same author's Germany's Revolution of Destruction, trans. E. W. Dickes (London, Heinemann, 1939), pp. 208–10.

[2] Bismarck to Saint-Vallier, the French Ambassador, on 14 November 1879 (Documents diplomatiques français (1871–1914), 1st series, vol. ii (Paris, Imprimerie Nationale, 1930), no. 476, p. 583). This is apparently the source of two sayings widely attributed to Bismarck during the Czechoslovak crises of 1938–9: 'Bohemia is a fortress erected by God in the centre of Europe', and 'the master of Bohemia is the master of Europe'.

had invoked the Carolingian tradition, so Hitler's Greater Germany appealed to the Ottonian tradition.[1] The annexation of Bohemia and Moravia re-established the eastern frontiers of the Saxon and Salian Emperors, and was undertaken with explicit reference to a 'thousand-year-old historical past'.[2] The previous summer, after the Anschluss with Austria, the imperial regalia of the Holy Roman Empire had been brought back from Vienna to Nuremberg, now the seat of the annual *Parteitag*, the new community-festival of the German people.[3]

I have caused the insignia of the old German Empire to be brought to Nuremberg [said Hitler], in order that not only our own German people but also a whole world may bethink themselves that more than half a millennium before the discovery of the New World already a mighty Germanic-German Reich was in existence. . . . The German Reich has slumbered long. The German people is now awakened and has offered itself as wearer of its own millennial crown.[4]

The appeal to the Ottonian tradition was a new and more potent mode of asserting the secular German claim to overlordship in Europe, and especially among the peoples of Eastern Europe. Ribbentrop told Matsuoka[5] that 'the new German Reich would actually be built up on the basis of the ancient traditions of the Holy Roman Empire of the German Nation, which in its time was the only dominant power on the European Continent'.[6] When Hitler upbraided the Hungarian Foreign Minister Csáky in January 1939 for Hungarian complaints of the injustice of the Vienna Award of the previous November, he said that the Hungarians thought about nothing but the thousand-year-old realm of St. Stephen, but he himself would override these pretensions in the name of the ancient Germanic Empire.[7] But all these claims showed the present remoulding the past in

---

[1] For example, on 2 July 1938 Himmler made a ceremonial visit at midnight to the tomb of Henry the Fowler at Quedlinburg, and this shrine became the object of regular SS pilgrimages.

[2] See the preamble to the decree of 16 March 1939 regulating the status of the Protectorate of Bohemia and Moravia (*Dokumente der deutschen Politik*, vol. 7, part 2, p. 502; *N.C.A.* viii. 404; *Documents* (R.I.I.A.) for 1939–46, i. 62–63). Cf. Hitler's historical excursus in his Reichstag speech of 28 April 1939 (*Speeches* (Baynes), ii. 1610–11; cf. *Documents* (R.I.I.A.) for 1939–46, i. 220–1).

[3] Cf. Hitler: *Speeches* (Baynes), i. 205–6; ii. 1470. The regalia had reposed at Nuremberg from 1424 until 1796, when they were moved to Vienna to be out of reach of the French. They were formally given back into the custody of the city of Nuremberg on 6 September 1938.

[4] Nuremberg speech, 12 September 1938 (Hitler: *Speeches* (Baynes), ii. 1498–9). The claim that the Third Reich was to last a thousand years seems to have arisen not only from the intoxication of talking in millennia but also from projecting the *tausendjährige geschichtliche Vergangenheit* into the future. Four years earlier Hitler said: 'It is our wish and will that this State and this Reich shall continue to exist in the coming millennia' (Nuremberg speech, 10 September 1934: ibid. i. 627).

[5] Japanese Minister for Foreign Affairs, 1940–1.

[6] Notes on talk between Ribbentrop and Matsuoka, 5 April 1941 (*I.M.T. Nuremberg*, xxix. 82 (1882–PS); *N.C.A.* iv. 527).

[7] Compte rendu de l'entretien de Hitler avec Czaky, 16 janvier 1939 (*Documents secrets* (Eristov), vol. ii (*Hongrie*), no. 25, p. 76).

its own image. For the Reich whose suzerainty Bohemia had acknowledged since the tenth century, and which had nearly reduced Hungary to dependence in the eleventh, had been something other than a German national state, and it was not until the later fifteenth century, in response to nascent German nationalism, that the words 'of the German Nation' were formally added to the title of the Holy Roman Empire.[1] Hitler's early conquests had a more immediate impetus than medieval memories. They were the liquidation of a non-national past, in which the German people had been separated into many weak states or divided between Bismarck's Empire and Austria–Hungary. They were the final repudiation of the Habsburgs, 'the effete and degenerate dynasty'[2] that had been an obstacle to German unity, and the fulfilment of the *grossdeutsch* policy which it had been Bismarck's work to frustrate. The appeal to the old Reich was the reconciliation of Germany with her past by the myth that the *injuria temporum* had only been an historical interlude.

(a) THE NATIONAL SOCIALIST REVOLUTION

The ingredients of Hitler's success were a national resurrection after defeat, a militaristic tradition, a messianic leader. The factors had coexisted before, but in the case of Nazi Germany they had acquired a peculiar potency. The obvious and superficial aspect of the Nazi movement was that of a national revival after defeat. Its most potent myths in conquering Germany were those of the *Dolchstoss in den Rücken*, the army stabbed in the back by the civilian November traitors, the fiction that Germany had not been militarily defeated in the First World War;[3] and of the *Versailler Diktat*, the Allies imposing mutilation, servitudes, and tribute upon Germany by force and treachery.[4] Its most potent claim in recovering for Germany the position to dominate Europe was *Gleichberechtigung*, the restoration of Germany's equality of rights in the international community, the ending of the servitudes of Versailles.[5]

But the promulgation and acceptance of these myths pointed to a disturbance in Germany and Europe far more deep-seated than any impulse to restore national prestige. The proudest claim of the Nazi

---

[1] By Frederick III. On the character of the first Reich see G. Barraclough: *The Mediaeval Empire: Idea and Reality* (London, Philip, Historical Association publications, General Series G17, 1950).   [2] *Mein Kampf*, p. 573; tr. Murphy, p. 421.

[3] *Mein Kampf*, vol. i, chapter x and pp. 583–92; tr. Murphy, pp. 428–35. For the inadvertent English origin of the legend of the stab in the back see Wheeler-Bennett: *Hindenburg*, pp. 167, 229, 238.   [4] *Mein Kampf*, pp. 523–4; tr. Murphy, pp. 389–90.

[5] 'As regards their foreign policy the National Government consider their highest mission to be the securing of the right to live and the restoration of freedom to our nation. Their determination to bring to an end the chaotic state of affairs in Germany will assist in restoring to the community of nations a State of equal value and, above all, a State which must have equal rights,' proclamation by the Government to the German Nation, 1 February 1933 (Hitler: *Speeches* (Baynes), i. 114–15).

movement was that it accomplished a true revolution in Germany—a transformation, the victory of a *Weltanschauung*, compared with which the 'Revolution' of 1918 was no more than a change of government.[1] The analogue for the National Socialist *Machtergreifung* was not the July Revolution of 1830,[2] but the great French Revolution itself; and the General War of 1939–45 was to be the war of the German Nazi Revolution as the General War of 1792–1815 was the war of the French Revolution.

France [said Hitler in 1934] carried her great Revolution beyond her borders with the conception of the nation. With the conception of race, National Socialism will carry its revolution abroad and recast the world. . . . This revolution of ours is the exact counterpart of the great French Revolution. And no Jewish God will save the democracies from it.[3]

The year 1939 was the one-hundred-and-fiftieth anniversary of the French Revolution, and Fascist philosophers had already announced that the era inaugurated by the French Revolution had come to an end.[4] But the resemblance between the National Socialist and French Revolutions was exhausted by their being termini of the same epoch and their disruption of the international order. For the National Socialist Revolution was a new portent in European history. Hitherto the great revolutions of the West had effected or confirmed the transfer of power to a new class, with a corresponding extension of political and social liberties. This had been true both of revolutions within an established state, like the English in the middle of the seventeenth century and the French at the end of the eighteenth century, as well as of revolutions that were bound up with a war of national independence, like the Dutch at the end of the seventeenth century and the American in the eighteenth. But the National Socialist Revolution was neither the revolution of the middle class, like its Western predecessors, nor the revolution of the proletariat, as its Russian contemporary claimed to be. It was a revolution (and in a rudimentary way this was true also of its Italian Fascist precursor) conducted by a class that had not before attained size or prominence in European history, and which had to be described by a word abrogating the ordinary conceptions of class. It

[1] Cf. Hitler's speech at Munich of 19 March 1934) Hitler: *Speeches* (Baynes), i. pp. 211–12).
[2] Cf. *Survey* for 1933, pp. 112–14.
[3] Rauschning: *Hitler Speaks*, p. 230; cf. the same author's *Germany's Revolution of Destruction*, p. 73. On the value of Rauschning as an authority see H. R. Trevor-Roper: *The Last Days of Hitler*, 2nd edition (London, Macmillan, 1950), pp. 4–5.
[4] See Mussolini: *La dottrina del fascismo*, in *Scritti e discorsi*, viii. 83–84 (translated in Michael Oakeshott: *The Social and Political Doctrines of Contemporary Europe* (Cambridge University Press, 1939) p. 175). By 1939 the abrogation of the French Revolution had become the stock-in-trade jointly of Fascists and Nazis, but there seems to have been originally a difference of attitudes, the Italians regarding the French Revolution with the spite of the impoverished aristocrat, the Germans with the emulation of the *parvenu* (cf. above, p. 193, note 1, and below, p. 351, note 7). It was the Italians and not the Germans who imitated and dismissed the French Revolution by reckoning a new chronological era from their Fascist Revolution.

was a revolution of the *déclassés*, of those elements which had lost their place in society, their traditions, their loyalties.[1]

Germany was unique in the material it offered for a revolution of this kind. The defeated army of the First World War had dissolved into the military adventurers whose crimes of violence marked the politics of the early Republic, the men of the *Freikorps* and the Vehmic courts, the murderers of Kurt Eisner and Erzberger and Walther Rathenau. These demobilized and unemployable soldiers were the original source of the National Socialist Movement, and Hitler himself, the *Gefreiter des Weltkrieges*, was their exemplar. But the rank and file of a mass movement were supplied by the deracinated middle class, whose final destruction came in the inflation of 1923. And this accession of numerical strength was confirmed and made overwhelming when the world economic crisis of 1929–31 raised the figures of the unemployed in Germany to 5 millions and gave the National Socialist Party its first great parliamentary success.[2]

But though the National Socialist Revolution was occasioned by the defeat of Germany in the First World War, it had its roots much deeper, and while in one aspect it seemed a perversion, in another aspect it was a fulfilment of German history. It posed with a new sharpness the problem of whether there is any method of drawing up an indictment against a whole people, the question in what way a modern nation can be held responsible for its capture and debauch by a totalitarian party, and whether successful revolt against a totalitarian government armed with the civil, military, and propaganda power is technically possible. It was the first concern of Nazi propaganda to identify the German people with National Socialism, to diffuse and generalize responsibility, to involve the nation morally in the actions of its rulers. Every nation is, indeed, in an ultimate sense reflected in the government which it tolerates,[3] and the character of opposition within a totalitarian state can only be inferred from the vigour of its political life before the curtain has fallen. The Nazi Party never obtained a majority in a free election;[4] but in the last year before it attained power it had become the largest party in the Republic, and the democratic parliamentary parties were incompetent to combine against it.

[1] Cf. Konrad Heiden: *Der Fuehrer: Hitler's Rise to Power*, trans. Ralph Manheim (London, Gollancz, 1944), pp. 17, note, and 280. (See also below, p. 305, note 5.)

[2] In the general elections of September 1930, National Socialist representation in the Reichstag rose from 12 to 107 (*Survey* for 1930, p. 8).

[3] 'Toute nation a le gouvernement qu'elle mérite' (Joseph de Maistre: *Lettres et opuscules inédits*, 6th edition (Paris, Vaton, 1873), i. 264: letter of 15 August 1811).

[4] In the general elections of July 1932, the Nazis won 37·4 per cent. of the votes and 230 seats, becoming the strongest single Reichstag party. In the elections of November 1932 their strength receded: they won 33·1 per cent. of the votes and 196 seats. This was the last free election in Germany. At the next election, on 5 March 1933, Hitler had been Chancellor for over a month, the Reichstag Fire had given occasion for the arrest of all the Communist deputies, and the Terror was already in being. Even now the Nazis gained only 44·1 per cent. of the votes, with 288 seats.

Opposition within the Third Reich was heroic and sometimes saintly in individual terms, but its overriding characteristic, as of the opposition to William II and his Chancellors, to Bismarck, and to Frederick William IV, was political weakness and futility. Bismarck had obtained the surrender and abdication of the Liberals in 1866, which destroyed Prussia's last chance of developing into a parliamentary democracy. Hitler received the surrender and abdication of the Centrum, which had first sabotaged the Weimar Republic by its high-minded confessional opportunism, and in the end destroyed the last chance of parliamentary resistance to the Nazi Revolution by voting for the Enabling Law of 16 March 1933 that set up the dictatorship—the Centrum 'which had defied Bismarck and beat him, and now crawled Catholic and universal before Hitler'.[1]

Only the Social Democrats were loyal to the republic which they had failed to defend and by a final gesture, impotent but noble, voted unitedly against the bill. But even the Social Democrats went on to show the fatal weakness which had destroyed German liberties. When in May 1933 the Reichstag was recalled to approve Hitler's foreign policy, the Social Democrats did not repeat their brave act: some abstained, most voted with the National Socialists.[2]

Four months before Hitler seized Prague, the impotence of whatever forces of traditional decency may have been supposed to have survived in the Third Reich was vividly shown in the anti-Jewish pogrom of November 1938, the worst outbreak of domestic savagery in Germany since the massacres of 30 June 1934.[3]

In the Frankfurt National Assembly in 1848 Wilhelm Jordan had concluded his proclamation of the aims of German nationalism with the words 'Freedom for all, but the power of the Fatherland and its weal above all'.[4] This cry had since then been the theme of German history, and it culminated in Nazi propaganda. The Third Reich was a system of government by terror, but it was nevertheless deeply popular. It fulfilled for the Germans collectively their most profound and ambiguous wishes: a restoration of self-confidence which was the resumption of national arrogance, the completion of internal unity by the suppression of minorities, the union of all German-speaking peoples in a Greater Reich through the subjugation of the Slavs. The Nazi Revolution, like the French Revolution, continued the main course of the national life at the same time that it widened its banks and deepened its channel. It gathered up all

But the Nationalists of Papen and Hugenberg, who were in coalition with the Nazis, had 52 seats; and the coalition thus had 340 seats out of a total of 647—a bare majority in the Reichstag of just over 51 per cent. (*Survey* for 1933, pp. 142–4.)

[1] R. T. Clark: *The Fall of the German Republic* (London, Allen & Unwin, 1935), p. 487; cf. pp. 74–76, 306, 312–13, 485.

[2] A. J. P. Taylor: *The Course of German History* (London, Hamish Hamilton, 1945), pp. 212–13.

[3] Cf. Michael Power: *Religion in the Reich* (London, Longmans, Green, 1939), pp. 159–60.

[4] See Namier: *1848: The Revolution of the Intellectuals*, p. 88.

the forces of German history, the military fanaticism of the Prussian army, the unscrupulous tenacity of the Junkers and their hatred of the Poles, the demand for economic empire of the industrialists and their middle-class supporters, the 'Austrian mission' wherewith the Habsburg Monarchy had justified its ascendancy in Eastern Europe, giving all these a demonic drive and intensity through a mass support they had not previously possessed. The intensification brought many trends to the point where their fulfilment passed over into their reversal. The Third Reich consummated the unification of Germany by Prussia, and finally erased the ancient *Länder* of the Reich as the French Revolution erased the ancient provinces of the French Monarchy.[1] But at the same time it destroyed the historic Prussia. The Social-Democratic Prussia which had been the bulwark of the Weimar Republic was destroyed by Papen's *coup d'état* in July 1932, the prologue to the Nazi *Machtübernahme*; the old Prussian aristocracy was superseded by a new Nazi élite of South German and Rhineland origin, and was itself in July 1944 to provide some of the last ineffectual opponents of the Austrian Führer's régime. But in a more important way the Third Reich reversed Bismarck's work, inheriting the *kleindeutsch* Reich he had built to exclude the German Austrians, and replacing it by the *grossdeutsch* Reich that came into existence with the conquests and annexations of 1938.

Although the National Socialist Revolution was a German phenomenon, it was no less a crisis of the civilization of which Germany was part.

The evils of Nazi Germany were most disturbing and menacing not in those features which might have been peculiar to Hitler or to the Teutonic mind, but those which are liable to occur in other lands and systems, those moreover which some men were predicting, without any thought of Germany, in the nineteenth century.[2]

National Socialism was the German, and most virulent, form of Fascism, but Fascism neither began nor ended in Germany. It was a universal phenomenon, which had first seized power among a people more cultivated and more intelligent than the Germans, in a country with more ancient traditions of civilization and which had been, moreover, for twenty centuries the seat of the Catholic Church. There were similarities between the Italy that succumbed to Mussolini and the Germany that fell

---

[1] 'Many people ask why we are abolishing the German States. I can only answer: "I do not know why we are doing this. I only know that I must do it. You lose the past and gain the future"', Hitler's speech to German students at Munich, 26 January 1936 (*The Times*, 28 January 1936). The *Gleichschaltung* of the *Länder* began with the law for co-ordinating the German states of 7 April 1933 (*Survey* for 1933, p. 147), and was completed with the law on the reconstruction of the Reich of 30 January 1934. The *Länder* were replaced in effect by the *Gaue* or tribal districts, units of Nazi Party organization (see Hitler: *Speeches* (Baynes), i. 266–76; Stephen H. Roberts: *The House that Hitler Built* (London, Methuen, 1937), pp. 67–70, 91–97; and Toynbee: *Study*, vi. 109).

[2] H. Butterfield: 'Reflections on the Predicament of Our Time', *Cambridge Journal*, October 1947, p. 12; cf. *Survey* for 1933, pp. 120–1.

under Hitler. Both had attained national unification later than the other states of Western Europe—only two generations before the First World War. Neither had traditions of parliamentary government. Both were dissatisfied with the consequences of the First World War: Germany as being defeated, Italy as having barely vindicated her claim to be a Great Power, and as having acquired (though one of the victors) rewards far smaller than she had claimed. These circumstances made Italy and Germany alike more susceptible to the disease of extreme nationalism in its new totalitarian form. But the disease was endemic in Western Civilization as a whole.

When Gibbon reflected upon the barbarian invasions that overthrew the Roman Empire, he concluded that

cannon and fortifications now form an impregnable barrier against the Tartar horse; and Europe is secure from any future irruption of Barbarians; since, before they can conquer, they must cease to be barbarous. Their gradual advances in the science of war would always be accompanied, as we may learn from the example of Russia, with a proportionable improvement in the arts of peace and civil policy; and they themselves must deserve a place among the polished nations whom they subdue.[1]

In the century after Gibbon wrote, the possibility of an external barbarian invasion of Europe, resembling that which overturned the Roman Empire, was removed altogether through the extension of European civilization over the entire globe, leaving no barbarian penumbra of the old kind at all. But the pressure upon European civilization of masses imperfectly assimilated to it did not disappear. It was now provided by the vast increase in population that accompanied the Industrial Revolution. In the four generations between Gibbon and the First World War the population of Europe was more than trebled, and the population of North America multiplied fifty-fold.[2] How free institutions could survive the rise of the

[1] Edward Gibbon: *The History of the Decline and Fall of the Roman Empire*, edited by J. B. Bury, 2nd edition (London, Methuen, 1901), iv. 167. The impossibility of new barbarian invasions was a frequent theme with eighteenth-century writers. 'Le temps s'écouloit, et de nouveaux peuples se formoient dans l'inégalité des progrès des nations. Les peuples policés environñés de barbares, tantôt conquérans, tantôt conquis, se mêloient avec eux: soit que ceux-ci reçussent des premiers leurs arts et leurs loix avec la servitude, soit que vainqueurs ils cédassent à l'empire naturel de la raison et de la politesse sur la force, la barbarie diminuoit toujours' (A. R. J. Turgot: *Discours sur les progrès successifs de l'esprit humain, prononcé en Sorbonne le 11 décembre 1750*, in *Œuvres* (Paris, 1808), ii. 65–6). 'In modern war the great expence of fire-arms gives an evident advantage to the nation which can best afford that expence; and consequently, to an opulent and civilized, over a poor and barbarous nation. In ancient times the opulent and civilized found it difficult to defend themselves against the poor and barbarous nations. In modern times the poor and barbarous find it difficult to defend themselves against the opulent and civilized. The invention of fire-arms, an invention which at first sight appears to be so pernicious, is certainly favourable both to the permanency and to the extension of civilization' (Adam Smith: *The Wealth of Nations*, book v, chapter i, part i (edited by Cannan, ii. 202).

[2] In 1770 the population of Europe was about 150 millions, in 1914 about 460 millions, in 1933 about 519 millions. In 1770 the population of North America was perhaps 2 millions, in

masses was the preoccupation of the greatest nineteenth-century political thinkers who remained outside the socialist movement, of Tocqueville and Mill, Burckhardt and Acton, and they generally expressed the danger in terms of the opposing extremes of Caesarism and Communism. But in 1919 Rathenau interpreted the revolutionary mass-movements that accompanied the First World War as 'a vertical invasion of the barbarians',[1] and ten years later Ortega y Gasset developed the idea into a famous book and described 'the revolt of the masses' as the governing tendency of the age.[2] His book was a broad interpretation of Fascism, then already an established feature of European politics, and the National Socialist Revolution in Germany confirmed many of his predictions.[3]

Among the Germans there was a self-conscious barbarian tradition, a certain aloofness from European civilization, the recollection that it was German tribes who overthrew the Roman Empire in its decadence and inaugurated the new medieval era to which the name 'Gothic' was once generally given and to whose supreme mode of expression it still applies. In the sixteenth century German national consciousness became definite and impassioned through hostility to Papal Rome. Arminius was already

1914 about 100 millions, in 1933 about 137 millions. See A. M. Carr-Saunders: *World Population* (Oxford, Clarendon Press, 1936), pp. 19, 42; José Ortega y Gasset: *The Revolt of the Masses*, authorized translation from the Spanish (London, Allen & Unwin, 1932), pp. 54, 119.

[1] 'Die Völkerwanderung von unten nach oben hat begonnen' (Walther Rathenau: *Der Kaiser* (Berlin, Fischer, 1919), p. 54). '... wir die lange Epoche der—vertikalen—Völkerwanderung betreten, in der die Ebene der Welt-zivilisation sich senkt' (W. Rathenau: *Kritik der dreifachen Revolution* (Berlin, Fischer, 1919), p. 41). Cf. a letter written by Macaulay 'in the last years of his life' to an American friend (quoted in Arthur Bryant: *Macaulay* (London, Davies, 1932), pp. 144–7): 'Either some Caesar or Napoleon will seize the reins of Government, with a strong hand, or your Republic will be as fearfully plundered and laid waste by barbarians in the Twentieth Century as the Roman Empire was in the Fifth; with this difference, that the Huns and Vandals who ravaged the Roman Empire came from without, and that your Huns and Vandals will have been engendered within your own country by your own institutions.'

[2] José Ortega y Gasset's *La Rebelión de las Masas* was published in 1930, and translated as *The Revolt of the Masses*. 'The rebellion of the masses is one and the same thing with what Rathenau called "the vertical invasion of the barbarians"' (p. 57). 'The European who is beginning to predominate—so runs my hypothesis—must then be, *in relation to the complex civilisation into which he has been born*, a primitive man, a barbarian appearing on the stage through the trap-door, a "vertical invader"' (ibid. p. 95; cf. p. 89).

[3] Cf. Toynbee: *Study*, v. 335; vi. 56–57. 'There was a time when the most frequent method of completely replacing a governing class was a barbarian invasion. Barbarians invaded a country, conquered it, governed it and crushed the previous inhabitants. Thus we may say that an event in foreign politics became an event in domestic politics. On another occasion I shall have no difficulty in establishing some interesting analogies between the ancient barbarian invasions and the consolidation of Fascist movements in modern states. By this I do not mean, as many do, that Fascism is barbaric because it is based on one class rather than another. My meaning is rather that it is barbaric because it mobilizes and marshals all the relics of primitive barbarism that still survive in modern man, whether plebeian or aristocratic. It frequently succeeds also in contaminating many of its political opponents, who, struggling against Fascism by Fascist methods, become barbarians themselves—Red barbarians' (Ignazio Silone: *The School for Dictators*, trans. from the Italian by Gwenda David and Eric Mosbacher (London, Cape, 1939, p. 88; cf. pp. 135–6; New York, Harper, 1938; Toronto, Nelson; Clarke Irwin, 1939)).

being made into a national hero as Hermann;[1] and Gibbon recorded the patriotic remark of a Prussian count of his own day, 'that most of the Barbarian conquerors [of the Roman Empire] issued from the same countries which still produce the armies of Prussia'.[2] But a self-conscious barbarian tradition, which began as a harmless literary archaism, insensibly degenerated into a genuine neo-barbarism equally self-conscious. After the War of Liberation against Napoleon extreme German nationalists harked back to the traditions of the ancient Teutons, which in their belief involved anti-Semitism, the proscription of persons of Slav descent, and the replacement of the French invention of the guillotine by beheading with the axe. A hundred years before Hitler came to power, Heine, in the most astonishing political prophecy of the nineteenth century, foretold a German Revolution which would make the French Revolution seem like an innocent idyll, when Thor and the old stone gods would arise from the forgotten ruins and wipe from their eyes the dust of centuries, there would appear 'Kantians as little tolerant of piety in the world of deeds as in the world of ideas, who will mercilessly upturn with sword and axe the soil of our European life in order to extirpate the last remnants of the past', and there would be aroused again the ancient German eagerness for battle, which Christianity had not entirely quenched, and 'which combats not for the sake of destroying, not even for the sake of victory, but merely for the sake of the combat itself'.[3] And on a visit to Germany in 1924, when Hitler was a prisoner in Landsberg-am-Lech and his movement had collapsed, D. H. Lawrence saw the gangs of German students, youths and girls, with their rucksacks, 'their non-materialistic professions, their half-mystic assertions', as loose scattered tribal bands, and understood intuitively that the inflation and the occupation of the Ruhr had completed what the war had begun, that the old hope of peace and production was broken, and that the Germans had subconsciously apostasized from Europe.

The old flow, the old adherence is ruptured. And a still older flow has set in. Back, back to the savage polarity of Tartary, and away from the polarity of civilized Christian Europe. This, it seems to me, has already happened. And it is a happening of far more profound import than any actual *event*. It is the father of the next phase of events.[4]

[1] C. V. Wedgwood: *The Thirty Years War* (London, Cape, 1938), p. 46.

[2] Gibbon, op. cit. iv. 343, note 7.

[3] Heinrich Heine: *Religion and Philosophy in Germany*, trans. by John Snodgrass (London, Trübner, 1882), pp. 159–62. This was first published in 1834. Heine's perception that 'the German revolution will not prove any milder or gentler because it was preceded by the "Critique" of Kant, by the "Transcendental Idealism" of Fichte, or even by the Philosophy of Nature' (ibid. p. 158), was independently elaborated by George Santayana in *Egotism in German Philosophy*, 2nd edition (London, Dent, 1939).

[4] D. H. Lawrence: 'A Letter from Germany', in *Stories, Essays, and Poems* (London, Dent, Everyman's Library, 1939), pp. 282–6. 'A Letter from Germany' was first published in the *New Statesman* of 13 October 1934, which, however, wrongly gave the date of the letter as 1928 instead of 1924.

Hitler came back to capture and organize the *Wandervögeln*. His central conception of his historic mission lay in the claim that the Nazi movement was a new barbarian inroad, coming to end another outworn civilization and to replace it by a rejuvenated culture built on the principles of race.

'They regard me as an uneducated barbarian', he exclaimed jubilantly. 'Yes, we are barbarians! We want to be barbarians! It is an honourable title. *We* shall rejuvenate the world! This world is near its end. It is our mission to cause unrest.' He then launched into a verbose exposition of what he called an 'historical necessity'. Barbarian forces, he claimed, must break into decadent civilizations in order to snatch the torch of life from their dying fires.[1]

Hitler was the first overlord of Europe to reject the ancient title of Emperor that embodied the claim to universal dominion. Charles V was elected to the imperial dignity in succession to his ancestors; Gustavus Adolphus and Louis XIV aspired to it; Napoleon assumed it; Bismarck's king nationalized it. Hitler's chosen title of Führer of the German *Volk* represented a ruder source of authority than the Roman *imperium*: the charismatic leadership of the tribe.[2] At the height of his power he wrote to Mussolini:

Above all, Duce, it often seems to me that human development has only been interrupted for fifteen hundred years and is now about to resume its former character. That destiny should have given to the two of us so eminent a position in this struggle binds me year by year more closely to you.[3]

When Alaric and Gaiseric sacked Rome they were not animated by memory of the Greek barbarians who had sacked the Minoan capital some 2,000 years before; nor were the Greek barbarians consciously imitating their predecessors, the authentic Aryans, who had previously invaded and destroyed Sumerian Civilization. The development in National Socialism of a barbarians' historical memory and purpose that

---

[1] Rauschning: *Hitler Speaks*, p. 87; cf. Trevor-Roper: *Last Days of Hitler*, pp. 53–54. In *Mein Kampf* (p. 433; tr. Murphy, pp. 329–30) Hitler displayed a mood of historical prudery, declaring that it was outrageously unjust to describe the old pagan Germans as barbarians: they were only handicapped by the severity of the climate in their northern wilderness.

[2] Hitler also repudiated the name of dictator, which implied something different from leader (see Rauschning: *Hitler Speaks*, pp. 196–9, and Franz Neumann: *Behemoth: the Structure and Practice of National Socialism* (London, Gollancz, 1942), pp. 73–75). 'I am not the Head of the State in the sense of being either Dictator or Monarch: I am the Leader of the German People! I could have given to myself—of that folk may be convinced—quite other titles. I have kept my old title and I will keep it so long as I live, because I do not wish to be anything else and never think of becoming anything else. The old title contents me,' speech at Munich, 8 November 1938 (Hitler: *Speeches* (Baynes) ii. 1559). On 27 June 1939 it was decreed that official appointments were thenceforward to be made in the name of the Führer simply, not, as previously, in the name of the Führer and Chancellor.

[3] Unpublished letter of Hitler to Mussolini, 29 December 1941, quoted in Wiskemann: *Rome-Berlin Axis*, p. 263. The name 'the Gothic Line' for the last German line of defence in Italy in 1944 seems to have been a deliberate reference to the defence of the Gothic Kingdom of Italy against Belisarius, the great precursor in the sixth century A.D. of the Allies' Italian strategy during the Second World War.

spanned a millennium and a half was one of the most remarkable evidences of human progress.[1]

But just as National Socialism was not the only form of Fascism, so the Fascist revolutions of Europe were not the first mass-movements of the twentieth century and did not establish its first totalitarian régimes. They had their precursor and their exemplar in the Communist Revolution in Russia. The connexion between Fascism and Communism at first appeared to be dialectical: the Fascist dictators claimed to be saving their countries from the dangers of Bolshevism. But from the outset their techniques for the revolutionary seizure of power and its totalitarian consolidation were modelled upon those of the Bolsheviks; and by the beginning of 1939, when the Soviet régime was over twenty years old, the Fascist régime in Italy over fifteen years old, and the National Socialist régime was at the height of its power after a bare six, it was becoming apparent to discerning observers that their similarities were greater than their contrasts, and that they might be represented as gradations in a single phenomenon of militant national Bolshevism.[2] Hitler did not invent the phrase 'National Socialism', but he was the first European statesman to perceive that socialism and nationalism are two aspects of the same revolt of the masses, and to found his policy upon their identification.[3]

[1] The analogy often made between Hitler and Alaric or Attila was imperfect, because at the time when Hitler declared war on it Western Civilization was not yet organized into a universal state whose capital city it was his achievement to sack. The indigenous barbarians of twentieth-century Europe were comparable, in terms of relative chronology, to the Cimbri and Teutones who invaded the Roman world three-quarters of a century before the establishment of the Roman Empire. But in their character, their impact upon the minds of their contemporaries, and the social degeneracy to which they bore witness, the resemblance of the Fascist revolutions was rather to the Catilinarian conspiracy. Hitler was Catiline become triumvir; and one of his subjects wrote secretly in 1941 that 'the most significant event in the twentieth century is the rise of the Catilinian power-state' (Theodor Haecker: *Journal in the Night*, translated from the German by Alexander Dru (London, Harvill Press, 1949) p. 165). It may be noted that, just as the German Communists named their party after Spartacus, so the Nazi leaders had a sense of historical affinity with the period of the dissolution of the Roman Republic, which was expressed in an enthusiasm for the blond and blue-eyed dictator Sulla, lieutenant and supplanter of Marius, the victor in the Cimbrian War (see Rauschning: *Germany's Revolution*, p. 92, and his *Hitler Speaks*, p. 257).

[2] Cf. Michael Polanyi: 'Collectivist Planning' in *The Contempt of Freedom* (London, Watts, 1940), pp. 27 seqq.

[3] He laid this down at the very outset of his career in a speech of 12 April 1922: ' "National" and "social" are two identical conceptions. . . . At the founding of this Movement we formed the decision that we would give expression to this idea of ours of the identity of the two conceptions: despite all warnings, on the basis of what we had come to believe, on the basis of the sincerity of our will, we christened it "National Socialist". We said to ourselves that to be "national" means above everything to act with a boundless and all-embracing love for the people and, if necessary, even to die for it. And similarly to be "social" means so to build up the State and the community of the people that every individual acts in the interest of the community of the people and must be to such an extent convinced of the goodness, of the honourable straightforwardness of this community of the people as to be ready to die for it' (Hitler: *Speeches* (Baynes), i. 15). On the assimilation of Communism and nationalism cf. L. B. Namier in *H.P.C.* iv. 77–78, and *In the Margin of History*, p. 76; E. H. Carr: *Nationalism and After* (London, Macmillan, 1945), p. 19; and

The connexion between Russian Communism and German National Socialism was particularly close. Germany was the original home of the international socialist movement; the German Social Democratic Party was the original mass-party[1] and was the world's greatest Marxist party before 1914; and after its foundation in 1920 the German Communist Party was the largest Communist party outside Russia. It was to the German working class above all that the Russian Bolsheviks looked, in their first triumphs, for the seizure of state power that would turn the Russian Revolution into the world revolution. But German Communism was to have a different role, as the pace-maker of the National Socialist movement. It was from Communism that Hitler learned most of his techniques of revolutionary agitation;[2] and the Communist Party, though perpetually engaged in civil brawls with the Nazis, collaborated with them to make parliamentary government in the Weimar Republic impossible and to neutralize Germany's feeble indigenous democratic elements. 'The twin enemies of western civilization do their work nobly; they split and make impotent the only force that is perhaps capable of saving it.'[3] From 1931 onwards, when the Republic entered its death-agonies, the co-operation between Communists and Nazis became explicit, a tactical alliance comparable to the future Nazi–Soviet Pact. By adopting under Stalin's orders a *politique du pire* the Communists lent their strength to the last push that brought the Nazis into power, supporting the Nazi agitation for a plebiscite in Prussia in 1931, voting in alliance with the Nazis a motion of no-confidence in the Braun Government in the Prussian Diet in June 1932, joining a Nazi strike against the Berlin transport board in November 1932.[4] As Napoleon was the Child of the Revolution, so Hitler claimed: 'I am not only the conqueror, but also the executor of Marxism.'[5]

(b) HITLER

The creator and personification of the National Socialist Revolution was Hitler himself. To those whose temperament and circumstances did

Franz Borkenau: *Socialism: National or International* (London, Routledge, 1942), *passim*. The phrase 'National Socialism' had originated with Friedrich Naumann (1860–1919), who founded the Nationalsozialer Verein in Germany on 23 November 1896. Naumann also coined the phrase 'Mitteleuropa' (see below, p. 334 and note 1).

[1] Cf. Karl Otten: *A Combine of Aggression: Masses, Élite, and Dictatorship in Germany*, trans. by Eden Paul and F. M. Field (London, Allen & Unwin, 1942), pp. 176–7.

[2] *Mein Kampf*, pp. 45–46, 541–2; tr. Murphy, pp. 49, 401. See below, pp. 321–2.

[3] R. T. Clark: *Fall of the German Republic*, p. 206.

[4] See Franz Borkenau: *The Communist International* (London, Faber, 1938), pp. 342–7, 376; Heiden: *Der Fuehrer*, pp. 331–2, 363–6, 388, 412–13.

[5] Rauschning: *Hitler Speaks*, p. 185. 'In 1930 Hitler surprised a circle of his friends by asking them if they had read the just-published autobiography of Leon Trotzky, the great Jewish leader of the Russian Revolution, and what they thought of it. As might have been expected, the answer was: "Yes ... loathsome book ... memoirs of Satan. ..." To which Hitler replied: "Loathsome? Brilliant! I have learned a great deal from it, and so can you"' (Heiden: *Der Fuehrer*, p. 245. Quotations by permission of Messrs. Victor Gollancz and Curtis Brown).

not expose them to the magnetism of his personality, he was a being so mean in his appearance, so uncultivated in mind and expression, so debased in his moral purposes, that the first mistake made by his contemporaries was to underestimate his power and ability. In the last months of the Republic the myth of Hindenburg's loyality to the Constitution had its obverse in the myth of Hitler's mediocrity.[1] Many German politicians thought that it would be good for the Nazis to form a government: within a few months their incompetence would be exposed, their prestige broken, and they would be laughed out of politics.[2] Even after Hitler's accession to power it was easy to see him as the expression of a social phenomenon, and to concentrate on the social phenomenon rather than on the individual. His colleague Otto Strasser called him 'the cork of the German Revolution',[3] and one of the earliest biographies published abroad was called *Hitler the Pawn*.[4] But the object of this depreciation had himself already written: 'It will often be found that apparently insignificant persons will nevertheless turn out to be born leaders.'[5]

Few of the revolutionary titans of history were so completely merged in their revolutions as Hitler, and found their identity so exclusively in their role as the revolution's mouthpiece and personification. Cromwell was in many ways the representative Puritan Englishman of the seventeenth century, but apart from becoming general and Protector he played a respectable role as a local magnate, and the core of his life was an individual spiritual struggle. Napoleon was the consolidator of the French Revolution, but only because he had first been its *condottiere*, and his genius, even if it had not brought him supreme power, would in any circumstances have assured him a degree of military and political leadership. Lenin was the maker of the Russian Revolution, but only because he was already pre-eminent as a Marxist ideologue and social scientist. Mussolini, a smaller figure, had had a career as a journalist before he entered politics, and after his fall from power he wished to reconstruct for himself a private life. Hitler was an anonymity of the Vienna slums who became the conjurer and medium of a mass revolution; besides this he was nothing. It was as if the historical requirements for revolutionary leadership in twentieth-century Germany had been pared away until there remained neither

[1] Cf. the impression Hitler made on Dorothy Thompson in 1932 (Dorothy Thompson: *I Saw Hitler* (New York, Farrar and Rinehart, 1932), pp. 13–14).

[2] See the views attributed to Meissner and Papen in Heiden: *Der Fuehrer*, p. 422. Severing, the Prussian Minister of the Interior, privately expressed a similar opinion in 1932.

[3] Quoted in Rudolf Olden: *Hitler the Pawn* (London, Gollancz, 1936), p. 411. Otto Strasser himself was one of the earliest shipwrecks of the German Revolution: he quarrelled with Hitler and left the Party on 4 July 1930 (R. T. Clark: *Fall of the German Republic*, pp. 322–3; Otto Strasser: *Hitler and I*, trans. from the French by Gwenda David and Eric Mosbacher (London, Cape, 1940), p. 127). His abler brother Gregor remained to be murdered on 30 June 1934.

[4] Olden, op. cit.; see especially p. 403. Rudolf Olden was formerly Political Editor of the *Berliner Tageblatt*. [5] *Mein Kampf*, p. 650; tr. Murphy, p. 473.

moral stature, nor accepted social status, nor autonomous professional
and intellectual skills, but only an intensity of concentration upon the
revolutionary task itself. It was characteristic of the First World War,
which was the first war of the masses, that its hero in every country was
not a great commander but an Unknown Soldier.[1] Hitler repeatedly
declared himself the unknown soldier of Germany—'only a nameless
German soldier, with a very small zinc identification number on my
breast'[2]—not buried under wreaths in the national shrine but walking his
country for revenge.[3] When people called him, half contemptuously,
'the drummer of national Germany', he accepted the metaphor with pride.[4]
In this self-identification with the German masses he found his power and
intoxication. Apart from it, his figure loses its outline and becomes
smudged. Journalists strove with little success to find in him the personal
idiosyncrasies that commend leaders to their peoples. When we seek a
precise picture of his early life and ambitions, his artistic talents, his recrea-
tion, his personal and emotional relationships, his stunted marriage with
Eva Braun, we are met by blurred and uncertain impressions, as if we are
dealing with a generalized symbol of mass-man rather than a particular
individual, or with a typical figure of a remote epoch; and it is fitting that
even the circumstances of his death, after twelve years of pre-eminence,
should be tinged with the same obscurity.[5] His life was drained of meaning
by the concentration upon power; and the dominating figure of his age
became nebulous, enigmatic, and legendary less through his achievements
than because he had virtually no private attributes.[6]

Nevertheless, while there would have been a revival of German nationalism anyway, and the revival would have found its leader, and all this was

[1] Cf. Pertinax: *The Gravediggers of France* (New York, Doubleday, Doran, 1944), p. 333.

[2] Speech at the Industrie–Klub, Düsseldorf, 27 January 1932 (Hitler: *Speeches* (Baynes), i.
821).

[3] Cf. Hitler's Sportpalast speech of 26 September 1938: 'And we wish now to make our will as
strong as it was in the time of our fight, the time when I, as a simple unknown soldier, went forth
to conquer a Reich and never doubted of success and final victory' (ibid. ii. 1527). 'Parties
cannot save Germany, but only a man—the unknown soldier of the World War', Goebbels in
1930 (Heiden: *Der Fuehrer*, p. 276).

[4] Speech at the Industrie–Klub, Düsseldorf, 27 January 1932 (Hitler: *Speeches* (Baynes), i.
826).

[5] This is in spite of a wealth of research and information. On Hitler's early life see Heiden:
Der Fuehrer; on his last years see Trevor-Roper: *Last Days of Hitler*.

[6] The same was true of Hitler's contemporary and rival, Stalin. 'The ordinary man is a hotch-
potch of desires. He likes eating, drinking, smoking, keeping a canary, playing tennis, going to
the theatre, being well-dressed, having children, stamp-collecting, doing his job, and many
other things besides. That is the reason he remains a nobody; he spreads himself over so many
little things. But the born politician wants nothing but power and lives for nothing but power. It
is his bread, his meat, his work, his hobby, his lover, his canary, his theatre, his stamp-album, his
life-sentence. The fact that all his powers and energies are concentrated upon one thing makes it
easy for him to appear extraordinary in the eyes of the masses and thus become a leader, in the
same way as those who really concentrate on God become saints and those who live only for
money become millionaires' (Silone: *School for Dictators*, p. 69; cf. ibid. pp. 219–20).

indeed foreseen, Hitler brought to the German Revolution the talents of a consummate political genius, which establish his claim to be regarded as the greatest European figure not since Bismarck but since Napoleon, and as the greatest German figure not since Bismarck but since Luther.[1] His power of personality was itself a decisive historical force. It built him out of nothing a position of supreme political authority, and continued to control men after the political structure had crumbled in disaster.[2] Göring fell under his spell at their first meeting in 1921 when he heard Hitler speak only two sentences; and years later, on being asked by a foreign diplomat 'Are you really afraid of him?', he replied after thought: 'Yes I think so. . . . You don't know him!'[3] Speer was fascinated by him, and Schacht confessed or pretended that he never left Hitler's presence without feeling uplifted and refreshed.[4] Nor were foreigners immune. Lloyd George was only the most eminent of the English politicians who were seduced by a visit to Hitler,[5] and even Mussolini, who began with a Latin scepticism, and became gnawed by jealousy, and experienced much cause for anger and resentment, remained under the psychological domination of the Führer.[6] Hitler's monologues, which reduced private interviews and conferences with his Ministers and generals to the level of mass oratory, did not impair his ascendancy; they were rather a means of asserting it.[7]

Of many witnesses I will cite only one—the judgment of a Canadian: 'I could listen to Hitler talk for an hour on one side of a subject and then if he turned round and for the next hour directly contradicted everything he had previously said, I would follow him and believe him. That is what I think of Hitler's persuasive powers! If he can get me that way, how much more can he get the German audiences!'[8]

[1] If Lenin is to be considered in a European as well as in a Russian context, he appears as a Robespierre whose Bonaparte was distributed between two figures: Hitler the transient demonic destroyer, and Stalin the patient despotic consolidator. For Heine's prophecy of the third German emancipator, 'the gleam of his golden armour shining through his purple imperial mantle', who would complete what Luther began and what Lessing carried forward, see *Religion and Philosophy in Germany*, p. 96. The Germans were susceptible to this kind of vaticination; it was ironical that Heine, who did it better than anyone else, should have been undervalued in Germany even before he was banned by the Nazis.

[2] Trevor-Roper: *Last Days of Hitler*, pp. 185–6, 226–7.

[3] Heiden: *Der Fuehrer*, pp. 91–92, 591; Göring's evidence, *I.M.T. Nuremberg*, ix. 237–9.

[4] See Trevor-Roper, op. cit. pp. 45–46; Rauschning: *Hitler Speaks*, pp. 188, 265. For Schacht's retrospective picture of Hitler, see Hjalmar Schacht: *Account Settled*, trans. from the German by Edward Fitzgerald (London, Weidenfeld & Nicolson, 1949), chapter ix.

[5] See *Survey* for 1936, p. 350, note 2: Churchill: *Second World War*, i. 195; Rauschning: *Germany's Revolution*, p. 103.

[6] See Wiskemann: *Rome–Berlin Axis*, pp. 82, 287. No foreign statesman has given a better description of an interview with Hitler than Gafencu in *Les derniers jours de l'Europe*, pp. 94 seqq.

[7] See Rauschning: *Germany's Revolution*, p. 248; cf. Keitel's evidence, *I.M.T. Nuremberg*, x. 485.

[8] N. H. Baynes: 'National Socialism before 1933', *History*, March 1942, p. 264; cf. *Mein Kampf*, p. 522; tr. Murphy, p. 388.

There were those, of course, who remained untouched by Hitler's magnetism, particularly the generals in Germany and Ciano among foreign politicians; but it was the others who mattered.[1]

The first of Hitler's political gifts was oratory, the handling of mass audiences by the spoken word. This was his decisive endowment, as handling armies was Napoleon's. 'Words are battles today', wrote one of Ludendorff's staff at the crisis of the First World War. 'The right word is a battle won. The wrong one is a battle lost.'[2] It was in this spirit and from the same circumstances that Hitler had learnt the arts of propaganda.[3] Judged by the range and depth of the disturbance that he could evoke, he was the greatest mass-orator in history.

Just imagine what his feelings must be when he stands, as in peacetime he used to stand, on the platform at the Tempelhofer Field in Berlin, and before him are a million Germans. This is the largest crowd that any man has ever had before him in person. You could never assemble such a crowd in a democracy, because it takes them twelve hours to march into place and twelve hours to march away.[4]

His speeches to German audiences illustrated his principles of simplicity of statement, repetition, and appeal to the brutal emotions.[5] Endlessly discursive and reiterated, regularly accusing his enemies of the crimes that he himself intended to commit against them, there was a sense in which they were all the same speech.[6] But he had another principle, equally

[1] For a general judgement on Hitler's magnetic personality see Rauschning: *Hitler Speaks*, p. 23. Ciano made the best comment for the recusants: 'I believe that at heart Hitler is glad to be Hitler, because this permits him to talk all the time' (Ciano: *Diario (1939–43)*, 19 December 1942).

[2] Colonel von Haeften: 'Two Projects for a German Political Offensive in 1918', Berlin, 14 January 1918 ('forwarded by me [Ludendorff] with the strongest possible recommendation, to the Imperial Chancellor') (Erich Ludendorff: *Urkunden der Obersten Heeresleitung über ihre Tätigkeit 1916–18*, 2nd edition (Berlin, Mittler, 1921), p. 477; trans. by F. A. Holt as *The General Staff and its Problems* (London, Hutchinson, 1920), ii. 557).

[3] See *Mein Kampf*, vol. i, chapter vi.

[4] H. R. Knickerbocker: *Is Tomorrow Hitler's?* (Harmondsworth, Penguin Books, 1942), p. 36. One of Hitler's most vivid early memories was his first sight of a mass demonstration in Vienna: 'I stood dumbfounded for almost two hours, watching that enormous human dragon which slowly uncoiled itself there before me'; and this experience, like so many others, contributed to his later armoury of mass suggestion (*Mein Kampf*, pp. 43, 536; tr. Murphy, pp. 47, 398).

[5] See the speech in the Bürgerbräu Keller, Munich, 27 February 1925, paraphrased in Heiden: *Der Fuehrer*, pp. 205–7 (it is not in Hitler: *Speeches* (Baynes)).

[6] Cf. a description of the pattern of Cromwell's speeches in Wilbur Cortez Abbott: *The Writings & Speeches of Oliver Cromwell*, vol. iv (Cambridge, Mass., Harvard University Press, 1947), p. 463: 'Yet, in a sense, it was nearly always the same speech, with variations due to time and circumstance. It often began with an historical introduction. It denounced his opponents and defended his course and that of his party, so interpreting events that whatever course they took seemed natural, necessary, even inevitable. He attacked the actions and especially the motives of his opponents vigorously, even violently, attributing to them the very ambitions and activities which, as the event demonstrated, were those which his own party put into effect. . . . He painted a dark picture of conspiracy, rebellion and new civil war, contrasting it with the peace which his own rule conferred upon his country, and offering his hearers in effect a choice between

important, that oratory should be adapted to the particular audience.[1] The success of his speeches was not limited to Germans prejudiced in favour of what they were to hear from him, for those who were prejudiced in favour of what they were to hear from him were not limited to Germany. And even for those in foreign countries not so prejudiced, when they heard Hitler's speeches of 1938 and 1939 on the wireless, the rasping voice with its suggestion of femininity and hysteria brought the communication of his baleful power.[2]

It was by his oratory that Hitler rose to power in Germany: his speeches were then what the victories in Italy were to the young Napoleon.

In January 1932 Hitler met the chiefs of the heavy industry of Western Germany at the Industrie Klub in Düsseldorf—he addressed an ice-cold audience of hard-headed business men, and at the end of the speech he had won their enthusiastic agreement. It is perhaps his greatest achievement as an orator. It is a superbly ingenious argument. That speech is a landmark in the history of National Socialism.[3]

Another decisive oratorical victory, at a more sombre domestic crisis, was the Reichstag speech of 13 July 1934. In the preceding fortnight he had murdered over a thousand people and many Nazi Party leaders; he had now to justify this to the survivors in a Reichstag where the massacre had left a score of seats empty. For perhaps the only time in his life he was heard for twenty minutes in silence, until, 'raising his right hand, forefinger pointed on high, he stood on his toes and roared: "In this hour I was responsible for the fate of the German nation and in these 24 hours I was therefore the supreme court of the nation in my own person",' and found at last the customary applause.[4]

But once Hitler was in power his speeches acquired a wider range. They were now not addressed to the German audience only, but became a series of psychological victories over British and French opinion, from the

these two alternatives.' All this is true of Hitler's speeches. But on a more general comparison between Hitler and Cromwell, the last word has been said by Sir Ernest Barker: *Oliver Cromwell* (Cambridge University Press, 1937).

[1] 'Moi, je sais toujours en face de qui je me trouve et je parle pour qui est en face de moi. . . . La valeur d'un orateur n'a qu'une mesure, en fin de compte: son efficacité. . . . L'immense erreur des partis bourgeois est de s'être entêtés à parler au peuple le langage des intellectuels. Il fallait savoir distinguer les publics différents': Hitler as quoted by Philippe Barrès: 'Hitler et l'Autriche', *Revue des Deux Mondes*, 8ᵐᵉ période, xliv (1938), p. 546, reproduced in Hitler: *Speeches* (Baynes), ii. 1707. Cf. Raeder on the nature of Hitler's speeches (*I.M.T. Nuremberg*, xiv. 35).

[2] Among other 'examples of Hitler's effect on England' at the time of the Munich crisis, it was recorded that during the Nuremberg speech of 12 September 1938 'a seven-year old boy, woken up by the wireless, rushed downstairs terrified and cried: "Stop that horrible woman screaming" ' (*The New Statesman and Nation*, 17 September 1938, p. 407).

[3] Baynes: 'National Socialism before 1933', *History*, March 1942, p. 278. The date of the speech was 27 January 1932 (Hitler: *Speeches* (Baynes), i. 777–829).

[4] Knickerbocker: *Is Tomorrow Hitler's?*, pp. 39–40. The speech is in Hitler: *Speeches* (Baynes) i. 290–328, from the version of the *Frankfurter Zeitung*; but the sentence quoted above is the more familiar translation from *The Times*, 14 July 1934 (contrast *Speeches* (Baynes), i. 321).

Friedensrede of 17 May 1933, when he made himself spokesman of the world's need for peace,[1] down to the Reichstag speech of 7 March 1936, in which, wielding a Gladstonian theme, he justified the reoccupation of the Rhineland on the grounds of moral right.[2] At this point his speeches, shifting to Germany's vital interests abroad, gained new overtones of menace, and developed every modulation between the assurance of immediate peace and the assertion of the conditions upon which alone Germany would withhold from war. Now, he said, the struggle for *Gleichberechtigung* was accomplished; in Europe Germany had no territorial claims to put forward; and he felt more than ever before the obligations towards other states which the recovery of national honour and freedom imposed.[3] Again, he said that in the three years since the Nazi Revolution the Germans had done nothing to injure any other people, had stretched out their hand to nothing that did not belong to them, had remained within their own frontiers; and if now lies were spread abroad that tomorrow or the day after tomorrow Germany would invade Austria or Czechoslovakia, these lies originated not with the peace-loving millions but with a small international gang of agitators—the Jews.[4] A little later: if he had carried out the measures for achieving *Gleichberechtigung* without consulting the Versailles Powers each time and even without informing them, it was because this made it easier for them to accept the decisions, for they would have to accept them in any case; but now that all this had been accomplished, the so-called period of surprises was at an end.[5] And then the climax, when he declared that he stood before the last problem that had to be solved, the last territorial claim he had to make in Europe, but a claim from which he would not recede; for with regard to the problem of the Sudeten Germans his patience was now at an end.[6] It was not until the seizure of Prague on 15 March 1939 that the hypnotic spell finally broke, the suggestibility of his foreign audiences was dissipated, and he won no more victories by words alone.

In the second place, Hitler possessed a kind of genius for organization. He had nothing of Napoleon's superb intellectual equipment and execu-

---

[1] Hitler: *Speeches* (Baynes), ii. 1041–58, especially pp. 1046–7; Heiden: *Der Fuehrer*, pp. 485–90.

[2] 'It is not wise to imagine that, in so small a household as Europe, there can be a permanent commonwealth of nations in which each nation has its own jurisprudence and in which each wants to uphold its own concept of law and justice' (Hitler: *Speeches* (Baynes), ii. 1273). This sentence was quoted by Professor R. W. Seton-Watson on the title-page of *Britain in Europe, 1789–1914* (Cambridge University Press, 1938).

[3] Reichstag speech, 7 March 1936 (Hitler: *Speeches* (Baynes), ii. 1300).

[4] Speech in the Lustgarten, Berlin, 1 May 1936 (ibid. p. 1322).

[5] Reichstag speech, 30 January 1937 (ibid. p. 1336).

[6] Sportpalast speech, 26 September 1938 (ibid. pp. 1517, 1526). Cf. Chamberlain's speech in the House of Commons on 28 September 1938: 'In the first place he repeated to me with great earnestness what he had said already at Berchtesgaden, namely, that this was the last of his territorial ambitions in Europe and that he had no wish to include in the Reich people of other races than Germans' (H.C. Deb. 5th ser., vol. 339, col. 22; *Documents* (R.I.I.A.) for 1938, ii. 285).

tive gifts, the capacity for unremitting work, the command of detail, the power of moving with equal mastery from one topic to another over a vast range. Hitler was a spasmodic worker, capricious and undisciplined. He disliked reading reports and memoranda, and acquired such information as he wanted by interrogating men without allowing them to advise him.[1] 'The laborious work of calculating and checking every possible detail is not to his taste. He loses patience with it, gets tired of it. In throwing out a sketch with a few strokes of genius—that is where he finds supreme satisfaction.'[2] The only subject he studied with any thoroughness was strategy, for it was his unfulfilled ambition to be as great a military strategist as revolutionary leader.[3] The only sphere in which he had detailed knowledge (and it was remarkable) was that of fortifications and armaments, which united his fascination by gadgets with his passion for immensity. He was the sciolist and café politician on a throne. But he was something more. His talent for organization consisted in his range of planning, his tenacity of purpose, and his power of making men his instruments.

Like every successful revolutionary movement, National Socialism had a double technique, of violent upheaval and rapid advance supplemented by the slower methods of infiltration and undermining. It was his mastery of the second of these that distinguished Hitler from revolutionary adventurers who, like Napoleon III and Mussolini and the majority of Hitler's contemporary dictators, have taken advantage of a transient revolutionary situation. There was a rhythm in the history of National Socialism, an alternation between advance and consolidation. The Munich *putsch* of 1923 was premature.[4] It was followed by ten years of adherence to 'legality',[5] which meant organization and infiltration.

Hitler could not overthrow in a year the Weimar Republic, but within the National Socialist organisation itself he could fashion a miniature State which, when the day of victory came, should be ready to occupy the cadres of the *Unstaat*—the State which was not worthy of the name of State—and carry on the government of the German Empire without intermission. That is the task of the years after Landsberg. And in the life of Hitler there is perhaps nothing

[1] See Heiden: *Der Fuehrer*, p. 302; Keitel's evidence, *I.M.T. Nuremberg*, x. 484–5.

[2] See Rauschning: *Hitler Speaks*, pp. 265–6; cf. pp. 183, 254–5. Hitler once confided to a fellow prisoner of his Landsberg days: 'In the last half hour, while I have been resting, I have invented a new machine-gun and an apparatus for bridge-building, as well as composing a piece of music in my head' (Kordt: *Wahn und Wirklichkeit*, p. 53).

[3] On Hitler's military gifts see Franz Halder: *Hitler as War Lord*, trans. from the German by Paul Findlay (London, Putnam, 1950); B. H. Liddell Hart: *The Other Side of the Hill* (London, Cassell, 1948), pp. 9–10, 305–9. An extreme statement of Hitler's strategical genius is in Keitel's evidence, *I.M.T. Nuremberg*, x. 600.

[4] The immediate result was Hitler's sentence to detention in a fortress at Landsberg-am-Lech from 1 April to 20 December 1924. Hitler, no less than Peter the Great and Lenin, is a conspicuous example of Toynbee's principle of Withdrawal-and-Return (see *Study*, iii. 248 seqq.).

[5] See Hitler: *Speeches* (Baynes), i. 161–2.

more remarkable than this sustained work within the party. . . . And at the time
when the fortunes of the party were at its lowest ebb, Hitler appointed a commission of jurists to work out the form of the constitution of the National
Socialist State of the future. When Hitler was asked in after years how it was
that he could hold out his arm continuously for four hours in the Nazi salute,
he replied 'Will-power . . . Göring can't do it!' *Glaube—der Sieg einer Idee—*
Faith! the Victory of an idea. It has become vulgarised through constant
repetition in countless speeches, but the appointment of that commission *just
then* must never be forgotten if you would attempt any explanation of Hitler.
The Department for Foreign Affairs, the Department for Propaganda, the
organisation of youth, the association of National Socialist teachers, the National
Socialist organisation of women, the Motor Corps, the Flying Corps, not to speak
of the SS. and the SA.—the Party should be ready when the hour struck to
supersede the *Unstaat* and to carry over its institutions into its own State.[1]

This long period of the hard work of constructive subversion is something which has no counterpart in the careers of Cromwell or Napoleon,
and is imperfectly resembled by Lenin's life in exile between 1900 and 1917.
It bore its fruit when the great advance came in 1933, the *Machtübernahme,*
the taking-over of power. But then, on a wider field and in different
circumstances, the pattern was repeated. A new period of 'legality'
began, of legality in the international sphere. The Germans' boundless
love for their own national traditions, said Hitler, made them respect the
national claims of others and desire from the bottom of their hearts to live
with them in peace and friendship; no German Government would of its
own accord break an agreement which could not be removed without
being replaced by a better one; Germany did not wish to take any other
path than that recognized as justified by the treaties themselves.[2] The
attempted *coup-d'état* in Vienna in July 1934, when Dollfuss was murdered,
was conceived of as the extension of the *Machtübernahme* to Austria; its
failure showed that the time was not ripe and that it was really the
analogue of the Munich *putsch.*

The decision for the July uprising was right, [wrote the *Gauleiter* Rainer
afterwards] but many mistakes were made in carrying it out. The result was the
complete destruction of the [Party] organization, the loss of entire groups of

---

[1] N. H. Baynes: 'National Socialism before 1933', *History*, March 1942, pp. 275–6; cf. Hitler:
Speeches (Baynes), i. 415. Baynes has written in similar terms of the way in which Constantine
the Great built for the future: 'Within the pagan Empire itself one could begin to raise another—
a Christian—Empire: and one day the walls of the pagan Empire would fall and in their place
the Christian building would stand revealed' (*Byzantium*, ed. Baynes and Moss, p. xviii).

For what is apparently the original version of the story of Hitler giving the Nazi salute for four
hours on end, see Henderson: *Failure of a Mission*, p. 40.

[2] *Friedensrede*, 17 May 1933 (Hitler: *Speeches* ((Baynes), ii. 1047, 1056; *Documents* (R.I.I.A.)
for 1933, pp. 201, 207). 'We shall triumph by the same inexorable logic of fact in our foreign
policy as in our home policy. I shall attain my purpose without a struggle, by legal means, just
as I have come to power—simply because the inner logic of events demanded it' (Rauschning:
Hitler Speaks, p. 112).

fighters through imprisonment or flight into the 'Altreich', and, with regard to the political relationship between Germany and Austria, a formal acknowledgement of the existence of the Austrian State by the German Government. With the telegram to Papen, instructing him to reinstitute normal relationships between the two States, the Führer liquidated the first stage of the battle and began a new method of political penetration.[1]

The work of international revolutionary preparation and penetration, which went forward unceasingly behind the statements of adherence to international legality, was conducted in two spheres. One was the acceleration and completion of rearmament inside Germany. As soon as he came to power Hitler 'made a clear political request to build up for him in five years, that is, by the 1.4.38, Armed Forces which he could place in the balance as an instrument of political power'.[2] With Göring's announcement of the existence of an air force on 10 March 1935, the reintroduction of conscription on 16 March 1935,[3] the secret Reich Defence Law and the appointment of Schacht as plenipotentiary-general for war economy on 21 May 1935,[4] and the formal unilateral repudiation of the Versailles armaments restrictions in Hitler's Reichstag speech on the same day,[5] the first and secret phase of German rearmament was successfully achieved.

History will know only a few examples [wrote the German general Thomas ten years later] of cases where a country has directed even in peacetime all its economic forces so deliberately and systematically towards the requirements of war as Germany was compelled to do in the period between the two world wars.[6]

The other sphere was the organization of *Auslandsdeutschtum*, of Germans in foreign countries. During the First World War the German General Staff had enunciated a principle for Imperial Germany, which is to some extent the same for all Great Powers: 'German prestige demands that we should hold a strong protecting hand, not only over German citizens, but over *all* Germans'.[7] Under National Socialism this was accomplished. The *Auslands-Organisation* (AO) and the subsidiary *Volksbund für das Deutschtum in Ausland* (VDA) became in a smaller degree to the world what the Party itself had been to Germany between 1923 and 1933.[8] In 1937

[1] Report on the events in the NSDAP of Austria between the beginning of the last stage of battle and the seizure of power on 11 March 1938, enclosed in a letter from *Gauleiter* Rainer [of Salzburg] to Bürckel, 6 July 1939 (*I.M.T. Nuremberg*, xxvi. 349 (812-PS); cf. ibid. xvi. 380; cf. *N.C.A.* iii. 589).

[2] 'History of the War Organization and the Scheme for Mobilization' (*I.M.T. Nuremberg*, xxxiv. 473 (135-C); cf. ibid. xiv. 16–18; *N.C.A.* vi. 947).   [3] *Survey* for 1935, i. 140–2.

[4] *I.M.T. Nuremberg*, xxx. 60–2 (2261-PS); *N.C.A.* iv. 934–6.

[5] *Survey* for 1935, i. 172.

[6] 'Basic Facts for a History of German War and Armaments Economy, 1923–44' (*N.C.A.* iv. 1089).

[7] Colonel von Haeften in Ludendorff, op. cit. p. 481, trans. Holt, op. cit. ii. 562.

[8] The AO was founded in 1931; its *Gauleiter* was Bohle. The VDA was the former *Verein für das Deutschtum im Ausland*, founded in 1881 and *gleichgeschaltet* in 1933. See 'Note on Auslandsdeutschtum' in Hitler: *Speeches* (Baynes), ii. 1063–79; cf. *Survey* for 1936, pp. 41–48.

the AO became a department of the German Foreign Ministry; it was partially fused with the diplomatic and consular services, and its activities acquired the shelter of diplomatic immunity. It thus became a highly developed medium for the revolutionary penetration of foreign countries by propaganda and espionage, the establishment throughout the world of fifth columns and a network of *Stützpunkte*.[1] With its control supplemented by the Gestapo, its formations and associations embraced not only Party members but all Germans in their social and professional lives, and supervised their activities in every sphere. In some places it set up paramilitary organizations, usually in the form of an *Ordnungsdienst* or police service, nominally for maintaining order among the members of the Party but capable of being used as a striking-force. There was also an attempt to direct the emigration of Germans to areas of strategic importance, like Northern Slesvig, South Africa, and Latin America, and the movement of reinforcements under the guise of tourists, technicians, and commercial travellers was highly organized.

Foreign nations and foreign statesmen [said Göring's official organ in 1937] must recognize that in the future fruitful relationships between Germany and other world-peoples can take place only on the basis of the organized activity of foreign Germans as natural agents of German culture and commerce.[2]

Within four months of the seizure of power within Germany Hitler made his first direct appeal to Germans beyond the frontiers of the Reich.[3] The official disclaimers of irredentist and imperialist purposes had already lost credit by the time the offices of the AO in Barcelona were searched and their documents seized and published by the Spanish Government after the outbreak of the Civil War in 1936.[4] Much of the organization of *Auslandsdeutschtum*, like much German organization of any kind, was supererogatory and fruitless. This was true of the immense ramifications of the Nazi Party in Latin America, and the less successful activities of the Deutsche-amerikanische Volksbund in the United States and of the Deutsche Bund in Canada. But it produced its European results in the Nazification of Danzig four months after the seizure of power in Germany,[5] the Nazification of Austria that prepared the Anschluss, the disruption of Czechoslovakia through the Sudeten Germans, the marshalling of the German minorities throughout Eastern Europe,[6] and the penetration and

---

[1] Cf. Rauschning: *Germany's Revolution*, pp. 260–1.

[2] Richard Csaki in *The Four Years Plan*, quoted in the *New York Times*, 26 October 1937 (Hitler: *Speeches* (Baynes), ii. 1072).

[3] His broadcast message to Danzig of 27 May 1933, before the Danzig elections of 28 May (Hitler: *Speeches* (Baynes), ii. 1060–3).

[4] See *The Nazi Conspiracy in Spain*, by the editor of *The Brown Book of the Hitler Terror*, trans. from the German manuscript by Emile Burns (London, Gollancz, 1937); *Survey* for 1937, ii. 127, note 1.

[5] By the elections of 28 May 1933 (*Survey* for 1933, p. 187).

[6] See below, p. 332.

paralysis of Norway.[1] These could not be so directly Hitler's achievements as was the building of the Party and the corrosion of the Weimar Republic. They followed from the impetus he gave to the natural German tendency to laborious, blind, and expansive organization. Nevertheless the spirit and the purpose were his.

Whoever imagines Socialism as revolt and mass demagogy is not a National Socialist [he said in 1934]. Revolution is not games for the masses. Revolution is hard work. The masses see only the finished product, but they are ignorant, and should be ignorant, of the immeasurable amount of hidden labour that must be done before a new step forward can be taken.[2]

Apart from its doctrinal drive and propagandist techniques, the skeleton of the Nazi system of government was gangsterism magnified to a national scale. One of its chief incentives was organized corruption; among its most powerful means of coercion were espionage and personal black-mail.[3] These were developed with an eye to their use in international politics, but their efficacy diminished outside Germany, and Hitler's foreign successes were attributable to other aspects of his genius than the conception of a comprehensive card-index of the vices of every influential person in the world. More important in its international effects was Hitler's character-istic method of government by playing men off against one another and cultivating the rivalries of subordinates. Like Franklin Roosevelt, he multiplied contradictory assignments and conflicting agencies;[4] but for reasons which were beyond the scope of Hitler's moral and political philosophy the result in Germany was not harmonious but centrifugal, and the monolithic Nazi state dissolved under the strain of war, as Trevor-Roper has described, into 'a confusion of private empires, private armies, and private intelligence services'.[5] In 1939 the process was far from com-plete, but since Hitler came to power foreign policy had been pursued through conflicting organs and involved in personal rivalries. In 1933 the ideologist of Nazi expansion, Rosenberg, was put in charge of the Foreign Policy Office of the Nazi Party, which organized foreign penetration under the guise of spreading National Socialism abroad. The official Ministry of Foreign Affairs remained under Neurath from 1932 to 1938, and preserved diplomatic appearances.[6] But Neurath had a jealous rival in Ribbentrop, who followed an independent line as Hitler's Ambassador-at-large, and at

---

[1] Cf. Churchill: *Second World War*, i. 478–9.

[2] Rauschning: *Hitler Speaks*, p. 175.

[3] Ibid. pp. 98–99, 267–70. The most important instance of the use of blackmail in high politics was in the dismissal of Blomberg and Fritsch in February 1938.

[4] See Schacht: *Account Settled*, pp. 212–13; Namier: *Europe in Decay*, p. 232.

[5] Trevor-Roper: *Last Days of Hitler*, p. 2.

[6] 'Neurath is unimaginative. Shrewd as a peasant, but with no ideas. At the moment it's his benevolent appearance that is of most use to me. You can't imagine a man like that going in for a revolutionary policy, they will say in England' (Rauschning: *Hitler Speaks*, pp. 268–9).

length replaced Neurath as Foreign Minister.[1] Göring, moreover, as chief of the Luftwaffe and president of the Council of Ministers for the Defence of the Reich, was also a prominent diplomatic figure, entertaining distinguished visitors to Berlin, and having conversations with potentates in foreign capitals. This variety of influences encouraged the illusion among British politicians that Hitler was a visionary, ill advised or only partially informed by extremist subordinates, that Ribbentrop was a sinister influence, or Göring a moderating one.[2] But in truth there was never any foreign policy in Nazi Germany except Hitler's, which inspired and included the intrigues of his Ministers; it needed no enhancement from sinister influences outside; and when the moment came it was he alone who made the decisions.

In the third place, Hitler possessed in a supreme degree the virtuosity of politics: sheer technical competence in the struggle for power. Its central source was his extraordinary strength of will. But in addition to this, his tactical elasticity and adroitness in manœuvre, his sensing of the enemy's weak points and probable reactions, his suppleness in biding his time and confusing the enemy before striking, had the Napoleonic range.[3] And though Hitler moved by intuition, and lacked anything resembling Napoleon's intellectual clarity over a wide horizon, he made power politics the object of his study; he understood the theory of it; and he has left dicta thereon as penetrating and enduring as Machiavelli's, like the principles that the masses fall victims more readily to the big lie than the small lie,[4] and that a shrewd conqueror will enforce his exactions by stages.[5]

The main source of his prestige in 1939 was his political flair, his recognition of the moment for action, what was called in Germany his *Fingerspitzgefühl*. In the succession of foreign crises since 1933 he had been constantly right when his political and military advisers were wrong. The last decision on foreign policy about which he informed the Reich Government in advance was the leaving of the League of Nations.[6] 'It was a hard decision. The number of prophets who predicted that it would lead to the occupation of the Rhineland [*sc.* by the French] was large, the

[1] Ribbentrop was Hitler's chief adviser on foreign affairs from 1932; appointed commissioner for disarmament questions in April 1934; became Hitler's Ambassador-at-large in May 1935, and in that capacity negotiated the Anglo-German naval agreement; was made Ambassador in London on 11 August 1936, without relinquishing the previous post until 1937; and became Foreign Minister on 24 February 1938.

[2] Cf. Henderson: *Failure of a Mission*, pp. 65, 69, 83–84, 176–7, 251. Cf. *Final Report by Sir Nevile Henderson on . . . the Termination of his Mission to Berlin, September 20, 1939*, Cmd. 6115 (London, H.M.S.O., 1939), paras. 18, 75–76.

[3] Hitler's capacity for biding his time was often carried to the point where it appeared like irresolution (Rauschning: *Germany's Revolution*, pp. 172, 288; Heiden: *Der Fuehrer*, pp. 293, 592). See further below, pp. 347, 348 and note 4.

[4] *Mein Kampf*, p. 252; tr. Murphy, p. 198.

[5] Ibid. pp. 759 and 544 respectively; quoted below, pp. 338–9.

[6] Lammers's evidence (*I.M.T. Nuremberg*, xi. 39).

number of believers was very small.'[1] His own decision to reoccupy the Rhineland in 1936 was made spontaneously, a couple of days beforehand, without consulting his Cabinet[2]—'once more an act thought to be impossible at that time. The number of people who believed in me was very small'.[3] As his adventures increased their scope, the opposition of the General Staff grew stronger. Throughout the conference of 5 November 1937 there was an undercurrent of doubt and disapproval from Blomberg, the Minister for War, and Fritsch, the Commander-in-Chief of the Army. They argued that France would have a military superiority on the German frontier even if she were at war with Italy, and that the Czechoslovak fortifications were comparable in strength to the Maginot Line.[4] In February 1938 Blomberg and Fritsch were accordingly removed from office, and Hitler himself became Commander-in-Chief of all the armed forces; Neurath was replaced by Ribbentrop, and Schacht was replaced at the Reichsbank by Funk. These were the outward signs of the first collision between Hitler and the army, a governmental crisis which Hitler solved with enhanced prestige by the occupation of Austria.[5] When he signed the directive of 30 May 1938 for the destruction of Czechoslovakia, Jodl wrote that

the whole contrast becomes acute once more between the Fuehrer's intuition that we *must* do it this year and the opinion of the army that we cannot do it as yet, as most certainly the Western Powers will interfere and we are not as yet equal to them.[6]

In July 1938 the General Staff submitted to Hitler a memorandum, drawn up by Beck, the Chief of the General Staff, which argued that Germany's military inferiority was such that though she might have initial successes against Czechoslovakia she would be defeated by France, and that therefore war should not be risked over the Sudetenland.[7] The memorandum provoked Hitler's anger: he dismissed Beck and replaced him by Halder. In February the generals had been unprepared for action; in the September crisis, under Halder's leadership, it was arranged that immediately upon the outbreak of war Hitler should be overthrown.[8]

[1] Hitler, speech to his commanders, 23 November 1939 (*I.M.T. Nuremberg*, xxvi. 328 (789–PS); *Documents* (R.I.I.A.) for 1939–46, i. 529; cf. *N.C.A.* iii. 573).

[2] Neurath's evidence (*I.M.T. Nuremberg*, xvi. 626); Lammers's evidence (ibid. xi. 39).

[3] *I.M.T. Nuremberg*, xxvi. 328 (789–PS); *Documents* (R.I.I.A.) for 1939–46, i. 529; cf. *N.C.A.* iii. 573.

[4] Hossbach Memorandum (*I.M.T. Nuremberg*, xxv. 413 (386–PS); *D.Ger.F.P.*, series D, i. 38; *Documents* (R.I.I.A.) for 1939–46, i. 24; cf. *N.C.A.* iii. 304).

[5] For the Fritsch-Blomberg crisis see H. B. Gisevius: *To the Bitter End*, trans. from the German by Richard and Clara Winstone (London, Cape, 1948), chapter vi, especially pp. 254–5.

[6] Jodl's diary (*I.M.T. Nuremberg*, xxviii. 373 (1780–PS); *N.C.A.* iv. 364).

[7] Interrogation of Halder, 25 February 1946 (*N.C.A.* Supp. B, pp. 1548–50); Rundstedt's evidence (*I.M.T. Nuremberg*, xxi. 33); Liddell-Hart: *The Other Side of the Hill*, pp. 39–40.

[8] Interrogation of Halder, 25 February 1946 (*N.C.A.* Supp. B, pp. 1547–60); Gisevius, op. cit. pp. 277–327; Allen Welsh Dulles: *Germany's Underground* (New York, Macmillan, 1947), chapter 4.

But now came Mr. Chamberlain, and with one stroke the danger of war was avoided. Hitler returned from Munich as an unbloody victor glorified by Mr. Chamberlain and M. Daladier. Thus, it was a matter of course that the German people greeted and enjoyed his successes. Even in the circles of Hitler's opponents—the senior officers' corps—those successes of Hitler's made an enormous impression.[1]

From Munich onwards there was no organized opposition to Hitler inside Germany for six years.

It has been said that the final failure of Hitler's politics and strategy lay in the corruption of irresponsible power and the absence of criticism 'essential to such a random genius'.[2] This is entirely true. But the attempt to estimate his political gifts involves deeper questions. There is an ultimate level of analysis on which we have to consider the standards by which we judge political achievement. Is it *virtù*, mere brilliance of execution; or service to the interests of the state; or service of values lying behind the interests of the state?[3] For the last, Hitler indeed claimed that his was not a purely national policy, it aimed at biological objectives.[4] This was the substitution of pseudo-science for the principles of Western Civilization. As to the interests of Germany, he made her the instrument of universal unsettlement, creative unrest, permanent revolution;[5] and he himself gave an unintentional verdict on this when he wrote that 'the object of a diplomatic policy must not be to see that a nation goes down heroically but rather that it survives in a practical way'.[6] There remains *virtù*. Hitler sometimes interpreted this quality at its very lowest, as mere slickness. 'Politics is a game, in which every sort of trick is permissible', he said, 'and in which the rules are constantly being changed by the players to suit themselves.'[7] But politics on this level have no criterion except success, and in the long run Hitler was not a success. If *virtù* means something more than this, that brilliant technique shall be governed by an adequate appraisal of the circumstances in which it is to be employed, then we must take into account the ambiguity of Hitler's terrible combination of realism and fanaticism.[8] For it meant that while he saw certain things with extraordinary clarity, the periphery of his lens was always liable to be fogged by nonsense. His discernment could be hampered by his creed and his temperament alike, as when he believed that the United States was undergoing a racial disintegration which would show itself in military

---

[1] Interrogation of Halder, 25 February 1946 (*N.C.A.* Supp. B, p. 1558); cf. Keitel's evidence (*I.M.T. Nuremberg*, x. 509).

[2] Trevor-Roper: *Last Days of Hitler*, pp. 254–9.

[3] Cf. W. K. Hancock: *Politics in Pitcairn* (London, Macmillan, 1947), pp. 26–27.

[4] Rauschning: *Hitler Speaks*, p. 243. 'The paramount purpose of the State is to preserve and improve the race' (*Mein Kampf*, p. 430; tr. Murphy, p. 328).

[5] Cf. Rauschning: *Hitler Speaks*, pp. 175–6, 186–8, 248–9.

[6] *Mein Kampf*, p. 693; tr. Murphy, p. 501.   [7] Rauschning: *Hitler Speaks*, p. 273.

[8] Rauschning: *Germany's Revolution*, pp. 193–4.

inefficiency,[1] or that the only outstanding men in the world were himself and Mussolini and Stalin, and the only kind of statesmanship was theirs.[2] His seizure of Prague on 15 March 1939 assumed that 'the little worms' Chamberlain and Daladier, whom he had seen at Munich,[3] had personally no reserves of purpose deeper than the level of that fatal meeting, and that England and France had no reserves of moral strength deeper than the policy of Chamberlain and Daladier. The technical criterion itself raises the question whether the fundamental flaw in Hitler's policy was not a moral impoverishment that made him misjudge the ultimate nature of the civilization he sought to destroy.

In one respect Hitler was unique among the great political adventurers of history. It was the fortune of Cesare Borgia to fulfil a pattern of statecraft already conceived by so potent a thinker as Machiavelli.[4] But Hitler, as befitting the Borgia of an age of universal semi-literacy and popular journalism, was both Cesare and Machiavelli in one; and had expressed very early in his career, under a transparent veil of detachment, the consciousness of being the rare combination of practical politician and political thinker.[5] His most enduring monument, outlasting the physical consequences of his assault upon Western Civilization, might well be *Mein Kampf*. It was a landmark in political philosophy, at the point where the justification of authority was superseded by the assertion of power, where the rule of reason was impugned by philosophic irrationalism, and where the ordered processes of government were replaced by the manipulation of the masses for the purposes of destructive revolution. '*Mein Kampf* is a handbook for revolutionaries and contains more practical advice about revolutionary tactics than all Marxist literature put together.'[6] Contemptible as literature, but nevertheless animated by barbaric force, like a gale of bad wind down an avenue of dry trees, it was perhaps the representative political book of the twentieth century.

Apart from its political content, *Mein Kampf* deserves analysis for the way in which it illustrates Hitler's psychological insight into the circumstances of his own time. He painted in it not only the broad lines of the policy he was to pursue when ten years later he was head of the German Reich, but also the state of mind in the world which would enable him to do so. He described how the masses in general fell into the sedative and

[1] See Rauschning: *Hitler Speaks*, pp. 14, 78–79.

[2] Cf. Hitler's speech to his commanders of 22 August 1939 (*I.M.T. Nuremberg*, xxvi. 339 (798–PS); *Documents* (R.I.I.A.) for 1939–46, i. 443–4; cf. *N.C.A.* iii. 582; vii. 753).

[3] *I.M.T. Nuremberg*, xxvi. 343 (798–PS); *Documents* (R.I.I.A.) for 1939–46, i. 446; cf. *N.C.A.* iii. 585; vii. 753.

[4] H. Butterfield: *The Statecraft of Machiavelli* (London, Bell, 1940), p. 130.

[5] *Mein Kampf*, pp. 231–2; tr. Murphy, p. 183.

[6] F. A. Voigt: *Unto Caesar* (London, Constable, 1938), p. 116; cf. Baynes: 'National Socialism before 1933', *History*, March 1942, pp. 272–3. For the customary depreciation of *Mein Kampf* see Heiden: *Der Fuehrer*, pp. 226–7.

feckless attitude of 'It can't happen here';[1] how the bourgeois shut their eyes to the political future, being bound to what they had inherited from the immediate past by a passive obstinacy which never passed over into active defence;[2] how when the bourgeois were brought to the point where they could no longer deny that evil exists, they could not summon the energy to fight it, but tried from a safe distance to show that such an enterprise was theoretically impossible and doomed to failure.[3] He was writing of the struggle between the Nazi movement and the bourgeois parties of the Republic, but he was also predicting the later struggle between Germany and the bourgeois world, and the psychological foundations of the policy of appeasement.[4] When he described how under the Republic his party was deprived of official protection, because the police instead of arresting the disturbers of the peace prohibited as a precautionary measure the lawful activities of the innocent,[5] he was foreshadowing the debility to which international authority was reduced by Mussolini and himself in the Spanish Civil War. He passed judgement on the foreign policies of the Western Powers before 1939 when he wrote that national spirit is more important than armaments, and that a state will have no international weight in which the main part of the population is at least passively opposed to any resolute foreign policy.[6]

But the fascination of *Mein Kampf* lies deeper than this, in the description not of Hitler's enemies, but of National Socialism and of himself. *Mein Kampf* is probably the most sustained example in political literature of the psychological phenomenon of projection, the transfer of one's own unconscious attitudes into a scapegoat. It is in this oblique and reflective sense, rather than directly, that *Mein Kampf* is the authority on National Socialist Germany. When Hitler described the Jewish-Marxist menace,[7] the picture that emerged from the intensity of his hatred was of himself, his own tactics, and his own movement. It is generally forgotten that the two famous passages in *Mein Kampf* which described the power of propaganda referred only indirectly to Hitler. The principle of the bigger the lie the greater the credibility was the principle on which the Jews had attributed the collapse of 1918 to Ludendorff,[8] and it was 'only the Jew' who realized that by an

---

[1] 'Uns kann nichts geschehen!' (*Mein Kampf*, p. 170; tr. Murphy, p. 140). Sinclair Lewis used the current cliché for his novel, *It Can't Happen Here* (London, Cape, 1935), whose theme was the capture of the United States presidency in the 1936 elections by a dictator compounded of Hitler and Huey Long of Louisiana.

[2] *Mein Kampf*, pp. 736–7; tr. Murphy, p. 529.

[3] Ibid. pp. 450 and 340–1 respectively.

[4] Cf. the acid sentences on appeasement in Namier: *Diplomatic Prelude*, pp. 60, 148.

[5] *Mein Kampf*, p. 545; tr. Murphy, pp. 403–4.

[6] Ibid. pp. 366–7 and 279–80 respectively.

[7] For the dogma of the identity of the Jew and the Marxist or Social Democrat, see ibid. pp. 54, 350–1 and 55, 268 respectively.

[8] Ibid. pp. 252 and 198 respectively.

able and persistent propaganda heaven could be represented as hell and the most miserable of lives as if it were paradise.[1] When Hitler described the Marxists' methods of mental terrorism and physical intimidation,[2] their technique of breaking up bourgeois meetings or having them suppressed as provocation against the proletariat,[3] the Social Democratic subversion of the trade union movement,[4] and the parliamentary party programmes in which every section of society was promised everything it wanted,[5] he was describing the methods by which the Nazis conquered power, and which he congratulated himself on having copied from his adversaries. The Jewish state, he said, had never had frontiers, but was distributed throughout the world, constituted exclusively from the membership of one race; and consequently the Jews already formed a state within the state.[6] For Eastern Europeans this was a description less of the Jews than of the Germans; and later in *Mein Kampf* Hitler claimed for the Germans that they, too, should possess a territorially undelimited state—

the German frontiers are the outcome of chance and are only temporary frontiers that have been established as the result of political struggles which took place at various times. . . . State frontiers are established by human beings and may be changed by human beings.[7]

And when he wrote of the imminent Jewish conquest of the world, since Bolshevism could not continue to exist without encompassing the whole earth, but would be shaken by the survival of a single independent national state,[8] he was describing the logic of Nazi imperialism, which was driven by the same fatality to conquer Czechoslovakia and afterwards to experience the penalty of failing to conquer England.[9] 'Only in the brain of a monster', he wrote, 'and not that of a man, could the plan of this organization take shape whose workings must finally bring about the collapse of human civilization and turn this world into a desert waste.'[10] In this frenzied loss of moral balance and discrimination the hater and the hated became indistinguishable, and Hitler himself said the last word on Hitler.[11]

---

[1] *Mein Kampf*, p. 302; tr. Murphy, p. 231.   [2] Ibid. pp. 45–46 and 48–49 respectively.
[3] Ibid. pp. 547–8 and 314 respectively.   [4] Ibid. pp. 51–52 and 53 respectively.
[5] Ibid. pp. 410–11 and 314 respectively.   [6] Ibid. pp. 165 and 136 respectively.
[7] Ibid. pp. 740 and 531–2 respectively.   [8] Ibid. pp. 723 and 520–1 respectively.
[9] Cf. Churchill's speech in the House of Commons of 18 June 1940: 'Hitler knows that he will have to break us in this island or lose the war' (H.C.Deb. 5th ser., vol. 362, col. 60).
[10] *Mein Kampf*, p. 68; tr. Murphy, p. 65.
[11] Besides this unintentional self-portrait *Mein Kampf* contains several prescient condemnations of Hitler's subsequent policy. 'In the case of a people like the Germans, whose history has so often shown them capable of fighting for phantoms to the point of complete exhaustion, every war-cry is a mortal danger. By these slogans our people have often been drawn away from the real problems of their existence' (ibid. pp. 633 and 462 respectively). 'The fact of forming an alliance with Russia would be the signal for a new war. And the result of that would be the end of Germany' (ibid. pp. 749 and 538). Cf. the Reichstag speech of 30 January 1937 (Hitler: *Speeches* (Baynes), ii. 1339). In another passage he wrote that if the battles of the First World

The essence of *Mein Kampf* was hatred, and the central object of the hatred was the Jews. Nazi anti-Semitism was the climax of a long tradition in Central Europe. Hitler got it from Vienna in the days of Schönerer and Lueger.[1] But his belief in the Jewish world-plot had its probable source in the Protocols of the Elders of Zion, a forgery springing from the same soil of political illiteracy and malevolence, the same half-baked semi-intellectual beliefs in world conspiracies and subterranean dictators and secret weapons, in the power and ubiquity of Jews and Jesuits and free-masons, as *Mein Kampf* itself. *Mein Kampf* was the reality of which the Protocols were the premonition.[2] But the intensity of Hitler's reaction to his first sight of a Jew, which afforded one of the most vivid pages in *Mein Kampf*,[3] was peculiar to himself; and the mounting hatred that followed was the most evil expression of his mind. His anti-Semitism transcended sociological or historical explanations, and must be interpreted ultimately in psychological and theological terms. As Marxism in its essence was a perversion of the New Testament, a secularized debasement of the Messianic story, so National Socialism was a perversion of the Old Testament, the self-appointment of a new Chosen People, appropriating the promise without the judgement.[4] Hitler's hatred of the Jews had its roots in this spiritual usurpation.[5] The Nazi demonology was indeed exploited for political purposes; as in most tyrannies, an adversary who

War had been fought not in Flanders, Poland, and the Balticum but 'in Germany, in the Ruhr or on the Maine, on the Elbe, in front of Hanover, Leipzig, Nürnberg, etc. . . . we must admit that the destruction of Germany might have been accomplished' (*Mein Kampf*, pp. 763–4; tr. Murphy, p. 547. Cf. ibid. pp. 693 and 501 respectively, quoted above, p. 319).

[1] *Mein Kampf*, pp. 107–10; tr. Murphy, pp. 93–95; cf. Borkenau: *Austria and After*, pp. 128–54, and above, p. 217. Hitler lived in Vienna from October 1907 until May 1913. Georg von Schönerer (1842–1921) was leader of German nationalism in the Dual Monarchy from 1882 to 1899, though after that the Pan-German leadership passed to his abler lieutenant, the Sudeten-deutscher, K. H. Wolf (1862–1941). Karl Lueger (1844–1910) was leader of the Catholic anti-Semitic Christian Social Party, and mayor of Vienna from 1893 to 1910.

[2] The Protocols of the Elders of Zion were an anti-Semitic plagiarism (probably forged by the Russian political police at the beginning of the twentieth century) of Maurice Joly's *Dialogue aux enfers entre Machiavel et Montesquieu* (Brussels, Mertens, 1864), which was a brilliant polemical tract against the Second Empire. On the whole subject see John S. Curtiss: *An Appraisal of the Protocols of Zion* (New York, Columbia University Press, 1942), and Heiden: *Der Fuehrer*, pp. 12–22. For Hitler's avowal of having learned from the Protocols see Rauschning: *Hitler Speaks*, pp. 235–6. The only reference to the Protocols in *Mein Kampf* is on p. 337 (tr. Murphy, p. 258): 'What many Jews unconsciously wish to do is here clearly set forth. It is not necessary to ask out of what Jewish brain these revelations sprang; but what is of vital importance is that they disclose, with an almost terrifying precision, the mentality and methods of action characteristic of the Jewish people and these writings expound in all their various directions the final aims towards which the Jews are striving. The study of real happenings, however, is the best way of judging the authenticity of those documents.' Again Hitler was gesticulating in front of a mirror: was this a judgement on the Jews and the Protocols or upon the Germans and *Mein Kampf*?

[3] *Mein Kampf*, p. 59; tr. Murphy, pp. 58–59.

[4] The two thus illustrated the approximating opposites of Futurism and Archaism (Toynbee: *Study*, v. 383–5; vi. 97–101; cf. *Survey* for 1933, p. 121, note 2; *Survey* for 1934, p. 373).

[5] Cf. Rauschning: *Hitler Speaks*, p. 232.

could be both a scapegoat and a bogy was a requirement of Fascist propaganda; and the Jewish menace was of great importance to Hitler's national and international politics as a means of brutalizing his party, of intimidating his opponents, and of cementing in his own support the German people, the governing class throughout Eastern Europe, and all those elements abroad that were infected by the anti-Semitic corruption which marks a society in crisis. Hitler's genius combined doctrinal fanaticism with the coldest consideration of expedients.[1] Nevertheless his anti-Semitism was far from being simply tactical; it was a matter of his ultimate beliefs. The last words of his will, dictated amid the ruins of his empire in the Berlin bunker on 29 April 1945, on the day before his suicide, enjoined upon his successors that they must, 'above all else, uphold the racial laws in all their severity, and mercilessly resist the universal poisoner of all nations, international Jewry'.[2]

(c) THE DIRECTION OF HITLER'S FOREIGN POLICY

Balfour had seen as early as 1916 that though Germany might be defeated in the First World War, her predominance in Central and Eastern Europe would nevertheless be enhanced if at the same time the Dual Monarchy broke up.[3] And in 1919, though Germany was temporarily defeated, her potential strength in Europe was relatively greater than it had been in 1914. For of all the continental Powers Germany had suffered least. She had waged the war wholly beyond her own frontiers.[4] Virtually single-handed, she had by 1917 accomplished the defeat of her two greatest military rivals. The defeat of the Russian Empire was confirmed by the imposition of the Brest-Litovsk Treaty upon its Bolshevik successors in March 1918. France ceased to be the greatest Allied military Power on the western front after the mutinies of 1917, and surrendered the main part to Britain, content, as Pétain said, to 'wait for the Americans and the tanks.'[5] When the war ended Germany was incapable of further military resistance; but her circumstances did not compare with the convulsions of Russia and the exhaustion of France. The Russian Empire had disintegrated far more dramatically than the German; it had lost more of its territory; it was torn by civil war, and supreme power was precariously held by a revolutionary clique whose success would be bought at the price of total exclusion from the community of nations. France, a more civilized and socially complex state than Russia, had been the main victim of the war: her richest

---

[1] Rauschning: *Hitler Speaks*, pp. 233–4.   [2] Trevor-Roper: *Last Days of Hitler*, p. 196.
[3] The Peace Settlement in Europe', memorandum dated 4 October 1916, printed in David Lloyd George's *War Memoirs* (London, Nicholson & Watson, 1933), ii. 877–88, and in Blanche Dugdale's *Arthur James Balfour* (London, Hutchinson, 1936), vol. ii, appendix ii.
[4] Cf. *Mein Kampf*, pp. 763–4; tr. Murphy, p. 547 (quoted above, p. 322, note 11).
[5] Cruttwell: *History of the Great War*, p. 416.

territories had been laid waste and the decline in her population had been accelerated.[1] In Germany the transition from empire to republic had been effected without any social upheaval; the unity of the Reich had been strengthened; the 'revolution' of 1918 had provided a classic example of a revolution that was no revolution; the governing class, the army, and the administration remained in uninterrupted control.

The principal change in Germany's position was wrought by the disappearance of the other two military monarchies of Eastern Europe, one of which, Russia, she had herself destroyed, while the third, Austria-Hungary, had been her own partner. Since the Congress of Vienna Germany had faced west. Her watch was on the Rhine, and her disputed frontier provinces were Alsace and Lorraine. Her eastern border for a hundred years had not been in question. It marched with Russia across the partitioned state of Poland, and swung back west and south along the mountain boundaries of Bohemia. But this apparently settled frontier concealed a weakness and an anomaly; for the Prussian state and the German nation differed in extent, and they converged only temporarily in Bismarck's Reich. The German Confederation of 1815 had inherited the ancient boundaries of the Holy Roman Empire, including on the one hand the Austrian and Bohemian territories of the Habsburg Emperor, and on the other hand excluding the Polish provinces of the Prussian king. When in 1866 the German Confederation was dissolved and the North German Confederation replaced it, there came into being for the first time in history a Germany which took in Polish lands and left out Bohemia and Austria.[2] Prussia–Germany, which was finally erected into the Second Reich, contained one-fifth of the Polish nation,[3] and excluded the 10 million Germans of Austria and the Sudetenland. This was the result of the *kleindeutsch* policy, a delicate balance that it was Bismarck's life-work to achieve and maintain. It required the preservation of Junker rule in the Polish provinces of Prussia, and the preservation of the Habsburg Monarchy as an independent and multi-national state under the control of its German inhabitants and their Magyar allies.

Both these objectives were destroyed by the revolution in Eastern Europe that accompanied the First World War. The fall of the Russian Empire meant the liberation of Poland and the loss of Prussia's Polish provinces. The fall of the Habsburg Empire meant the setting adrift of the Austrian and Bohemian Germans and the possibility at last of a *grossdeutsch* policy, the inclusion of all Germans in one state. The appearance of a chain of national states in Eastern Europe, from Finland to

[1] *Survey* for 1920–3, p. 59, and see above, pp. 166–71.
[2] See Taylor: *Course of German History*, pp. 49, 131.
[3] In 1914 there were approximately 4 million Poles in Prussia, 4¼ million in Austria-Hungary, and 13 million in Russia (*H.P.C.* vi. 226, note 1).

Albania, provided Germany with an entirely new arrangement of power on her eastern frontier. France, from Louis XIV to Napoleon, had been able to expand on her eastern frontier against a buffer zone of weak principalities. There was now opened up for Germany a similar buffer zone in the east. It had been first created by the settlement of Brest-Litovsk in 1918, which detached Finland, the Baltic States, Russian Poland, Bessarabia, the Ukraine, and the Caucasus from Russia. 'We saw reproduced, in the twentieth century, and five hundred miles farther east, a new version of Napoleon's plan for a Confederation of the Rhine.'[1] For a moment this German plan was frustrated by the defeat in the west, but the new situation on Germany's eastern frontier remained; and with it the certainty in due course of Germany's expansion in that direction.

The leaders of Republican Germany could acquiesce in the loss of Alsace-Lorraine and accept as final the new western frontier with France and the Low Countries. They could not assent to the surrenders in the east—the loss of Danzig; the cession of West Prussia and Posen to a new Polish Power, severing East Prussia from the body of the Reich; the cession to Poland of Upper Silesia;[2] the exclusion from the Reich of the Germans of Austria and Bohemia. Stresemann, in a celebrated letter to the ex-Crown Prince in 1925, laid down the

three great tasks that confront German foreign policy in the more immediate future—

In the first place the solution of the Reparations question in a sense tolerable for Germany, and the assurance of peace, which is an essential promise [? premiss] for the recovery of our strength.

Secondly, the protection of Germans abroad, those 10 to 12 millions of our kindred who now live under a foreign yoke in foreign lands.

The third great task is the readjustment of our Eastern frontiers; the recovery of Danzig, the Polish corridor, and a correction of the frontier in Upper Silesia.

In the background stands the union with German Austria, although I am quite clear that this not merely brings no advantages to Germany, but seriously complicates the problem of the German Reich.[3]

The Locarno Treaties of 1925 gave expression to this general line of German policy. They stabilized Germany's western frontier by mutual guarantees of the Franco-German and Belgo-German frontiers, and also of the Demilitarized Zone. But Germany refused to pledge herself to accept similarly her eastern frontiers, which she then hoped to rectify by peaceful change.[4] The French regarded the security of their eastern allies as indi-

---

[1] Churchill: *Aftermath*, p. 97.

[2] One of Hitler's earliest political successes was to predict that Germany would lose the coal-basin of Upper Silesia despite her success in the plebiscite of 1921 (see Heiden: *Der Fuehrer*, p. 94). For the plebiscite itself see *H.P.C.* iv. 261–5.

[3] Letter to the ex-Crown Prince, 7 September 1925 (Gustav Stresemann: *His Diaries, Letters, and Papers*, ed. and trans. Eric Sutton, vol. ii (London, Macmillan, 1937), p. 503).

[4] *Survey* for 1925, ii. 28.

spensable to French security, desiring the same guarantees for the Polish-German and Czechoslovak-German frontiers as for the Franco-German.[1] Britain, however, refused to extend her commitments to Eastern Europe and supported the German case; and consequently Poland and Czechoslovakia gained from Locarno only treaties of arbitration with Germany and treaties of mutual assistance with France.[2] Therefore, though the Locarno settlement opened a new period of security and confidence in Western Europe and prepared for Germany's accession to the League of Nations, it also suggested that Germany's obligation to respect her western frontier rested not upon the Versailles Treaty but upon her subsequent voluntary assent made during the Locarno negotiations, and that since she had given no voluntary consent with regard to her eastern frontier she was under no obligation to respect it. For the time being this land-scape was concealed by the mists of treaties of arbitration, obligations under the Covenant, and provisions for peaceful change in accordance with Article XIX. But it was the logical consequence of Locarno that when France made the Franco-Soviet Pact with the only Power capable of exerting an independent pressure upon Germany's eastern frontier, Hitler made this the excuse for denouncing the Locarno Pact and remilitarizing the Rhineland. The Locarno balance of power was thus translated from the language of juridical obligations into that of fortifications and arma-ments: the Siegfried Line consolidated the Franco-German frontier, and Germany prepared in security for the armed revision of her eastern frontier.[3]

German ascendancy in Eastern Europe was based upon two traditions and two concrete assets. The first tradition was that of the supremacy of the Teutonic Knights in the Balticum, of which East Prussia and the dispossessed aristocracies of German Balts in the Baltic Republics were the vestige. The social engine of this tradition was the Junker class of Eastern Germany. These were the great agrarian capitalists of the colonial lands of the east, where their forebears the Teutonic Knights, those 'consummate economists', had conquered and expropriated the Slav peoples and re-duced them to landless labourers. The words Slav and slave still remained undifferentiated in the German mind; the Slavs were the *consuetus hostis*, the hereditary enemy of Christians, as Gerbert had once called them,[4] though the Slavs had since become Christian and the German Government had returned to paganism; and exploitation of the peoples beyond the Elbe had always appeared to Germans as a civilizing mission. Bismarck's

---

[1] Ibid. p. 30.   [2] Ibid. pp. 49–61.

[3] See *Survey* for 1936, pp. 10, note 1, 261–2, 478, note 3.

[4] *Lettres de Gerbert (983–997)*, published with an introduction and notes by Julien Havet (Paris, Picard, 1889), p. 92. Cf. a remark of the Emperor William II to Sir Edward Goschen on 16 October 1910: 'I am all for the white man against the black, whether they be Chinese, Japanese, niggers or Slavs' (Gooch and Temperley, vi. 531).

Polish expropriation law of 1886 and the redoubled persecution of the Poles under Bülow were conceived as the crusade of German culture against barbarism. The *Ostbahn* of the 1840s, the first railway east of Berlin, was claimed by the Junkers as 'the greatest German thrust into Eastern Europe since the Teutonic Knights'.[1] The German frontier tradition went back through the centuries with every variation of brutality and vigour—to the Lithuanian man-hunts which were the winter pastime of the Teutonic Knights in their decadence;[2] to the Wendish Crusade of 1147 with its slogan of baptism or extermination;[3] to the summons sent out by Adolf of Holstein for settlers in the Baltic lands where he founded Lübeck,[4] and to the earlier appeal by the spiritual and temporal princes of Saxony,[5] at the beginning of the great German movement of colonization in the twelfth century, when the fertile and illimitable continent beyond the Elbe was to the northern peoples of Christendom like the land beyond the Ohio River to the United States at the time of its achievement of independence; perhaps even to the campaigns in the later eighth century when Charlemagne harried the Saxons and forced upon them in the first place the Christianity which they in turn were to force upon the Slavs.[6] Of this Prussian and Baltic tradition the chief National Socialist exponent was Alfred Rosenberg, a German Balt from Estonia, who, having been a student in Moscow at the time of the Russian Revolution, escaped and embraced German nationality, and in 1923 effected the meeting between Hitler and Houston Stewart Chamberlain.[7]

The second tradition was that of Austria, the other German Great Power. Austria had been the standard-bearer of German culture south of the

---

[1] Taylor: *Course of German History*, p. 67.

[2] Henri Pirenne: *A History of Europe*, trans. by Bernard Miall (London, Allen & Unwin, 1939), p. 476.

[3] 'Ut eos aut christiane religioni subderet, aut Deo auxiliante omnino deleret', *Annales Magdeburgenses*, sub anno 1147 (*Monumenta Germaniae Historica*, ed. G. H. Pertz, Scriptorum tomus xvi (Hanover, Hahn, 1858), p. 188); cf. *Auctarium Gemblacense*, sub anno 1148 (*Monumenta Germaniae Historica*, ed. G. H. Pertz, Scriptorum tomus vi (Hanover, Hahn, 1844), p. 392).

[4] Helmold: *Chronica Slavorum*, lib. i, cap. 57 (*Monumenta Germaniae Historica*, ed. G. H. Pertz, Scriptorum tomus xxi (Hanover, Hahn, 1868), pp. 55); cf. G. Barraclough: *The Origins of Modern Germany* (Oxford, Blackwell, 1946), p. 262.

[5] 'The Slavs are an abominable people, but their land is very rich in flesh, honey, grain, birds, and abounding in all produce of fertility of the earth when cultivated so that none can be compared with it. So they say who know. Wherefore O Saxons, Franks, Lotharingians, men of Flanders most famous, here you can both save your souls and if it please you acquire the best of land to live in' (Rudolf Kötzschke: *Quellen zur Geschichte der Ostdeutschen Kolonisation im 12. bis 14. Jahrhundert* (Leipzig, Teubner, 1912), p. 10, as freely translated in H. A. L. Fisher: *A History of Europe* (London, Arnold, one volume edition 1936), p. 203). The writer is indebted to Professor Geoffrey Barraclough for pointing him to the original of this proclamation. It might be a National Socialist pronouncement, except that the Nazis had substituted the preservation of the German race for the salvation of individual souls. Cf. Hitler's speech of 12 September 1936, quoted below, p. 336.

[6] Toynbee: *Study*, ii. 343–5; iv. 488–90. For Hitler's defence of Charlemagne's policy see *The Goebbels Diaries*, p. 280.   [7] See Heiden: *Der Fuehrer*, chapter i and p. 198.

Carpathians[1] as Prussia had been to the north. The Austrian role was historically later and more important than the Prussian, and had become formally represented by the Habsburg tenure of the imperial throne. It answered to the Turkish conquest of South-Eastern Europe, which made Austria the bulwark of Western Christendom. But just as this role was forced upon the Habsburgs, whose policy had hitherto been greedy, hesitating, and inglorious, so they sought to exploit its advantages long after its necessity had disappeared with the recession of the Turkish menace. Even in the nineteenth century, when the Austrian Empire was steadily growing weaker and more disordered, and had become the European China,[2] with all its powers of growth exhausted, unable to offer its renascent peoples anything but the duty of loyalty to an inflexible and unlearning dynasty, the pretence of a German and Catholic civilizing mission among the nationalities of Eastern Europe was maintained as the envelope for inefficiency and oppressiveness.[3]

The two concrete assets upon which German ascendancy in Eastern Europe was built were the preponderance and distribution of her population, and her economic strength. The main European demographic change of the nineteenth century was the growth of the German population to become the largest—the Russians excepted—of Europe.[4] The assertion of this numerical superiority was one of the principal themes of Nazi propaganda. But it was the political distribution of the German population that made Germany unique among the Great Powers. Never before 1938 had Germany approximated to the coincidence of state with *Volk* that was the character of other nations. The German population of Europe was not the same thing as the inhabitants of Germany.[5] Down to 1866 the bound-

---

[1] The exception is Galicia, the Austrian share of Poland, which brought the Austrian frontier, from 1772 to 1918, well to the north of the Carpathian watershed, and compensated on the north for the loss of Silesia to Prussia in 1740.

[2] 'Coningsby . . . could not comprehend how a free government could endure without national opinions to uphold it; and . . . governments for the preservation of peace and order, and nothing else, had better be sought in China, or among the Austrians, the Chinese of Europe' (Benjamin Disraeli: *Coningsby* (London, Oxford University Press, World's Classics, 1931), p. 318).

[3] See Taylor: *Habsburg Monarchy*, pp. 175-6.

[4] At the beginning of 1939 the populations of the European Great Powers were approximately as follows: Germany, 80 millions; United Kingdom, 45 millions; Italy, 44 millions; France, 42 millions; U.S.S.R., 166 millions. For the preponderance of Germany's population over those of the states of Eastern Europe see above, p. 206, note 3.

[5] The tendency towards German national unification was accompanied by the disappearance of an international society specifically comprising all German states. Until 1866 the German states, however complete their sovereignty, were included also in the Reich and its successor the Confederation. (For the exception of the Napoleonic interregnum between the abolition of the Reich in 1806 and the establishment of the Confederation in 1815, see above, p. 212, note 1.) Since 1866 there has been no such comprehensive German society, certain fragments on the circumference of the German nebula flying off into complete independence of the German Great Powers (an independence only ephemerally impaired by those Powers' conquests and annexations during the First and Second World Wars). The German Confederation was dissolved by article iv of the Austro-Prussian Treaty of Prague, 1866 (Hertslet: *Map of Europe by Treaty*, iii.

aries of the Reich, and afterwards of the Confederation, had included the great majority of Germans, though much else besides. From 1866 to 1938 the central German Power excluded a fringe of German-speaking peoples amounting to about 15 per cent. of the potential total nation. It was not until the Anschluss in 1938 that for the first time in history the frontiers of the principal German state included more than nine-tenths of the German-speaking peoples of Europe without including also considerable non-German populations, and *Grossdeutschland* came into existence.[1]

But the distribution of the German people was further peculiar in that they were not all collected in a single compact mass. There were disconnected communities of Germans scattered throughout Eastern Europe, whose inclusion in a central German state was only possible through the incorporation also of the non-German peoples among whom they formed minorities. There was a German minority in every Eastern European state except Finland, Albania, and Greece. In Estonia and Latvia there were the 'Baltic Barons', the descendants of the Crusaders who had first conquered the Baltic shore and of the Hanseatic traders who had developed it. In Lithuania there was a minority of German Protestant settlers who had fled from oppression in Germany and taken refuge in this province of the Russian Empire at the beginning of the nineteenth century. Memel was by origin a German city, and nearly one-half of the population of the Memel territory was German.[2] Poland had considerable German minori-

1722). The members of the Confederation (numbering twenty-nine after Prussia had annexed Hanover, Hesse-Cassel, Holstein, Nassau, and Frankfurt) thereupon ceased to have any form of connexion. Liechtenstein and Luxembourg have ever since retained this independence of Germany, Liechtenstein gravitating instead towards Switzerland, and Luxembourg towards Belgium (see above, pp.152, note1, and 154–7). The partially German state of Austria, transformed in 1867 into the Dual Monarchy of Austria-Hungary, survived down to 1918. Apart from these peripheral units there remained twenty-six German states. The establishment of the North German Confederation in 1867 reduced their number to five: the North German Confederation itself, Bavaria, Württemberg, Baden, and the parts of the grand duchy of Hesse south of the River Main (see, however, Hertslet, op. cit. iii. 1828, note). These five were all united into the Second Reich in 1871. In 1918 the disintegration of the Dual Monarchy of Austria-Hungary brought into existence a purely German Austrian Republic; and in 1919 the purely German Free City of Danzig was erected out of a city of the defeated German Reich (see above, p. 232, note 1). There were thus in 1919 five different German national units: Germany, Austria, Liechtenstein, Luxembourg, and Danzig.

[1] Cf. Hitler: 'On 13 March Great Germany was created and on 10 April that creation will be confirmed', speech in the Berliner Sportpalast, 28 March 1938 (*Speeches* (Baynes), ii. 1448); 'This plebiscite signifies the creation of Great Germany: now, German people, hold this Great Germany fast in your fist and never let it be wrested from you', speech at Klagenfurt, 4 April 1938 (ibid. ii. 1453); 'It is Great Germany which in these days makes its appearance at Nuremberg for the first time', speech at the opening of the Nuremberg Parteitag, 6 September 1938 (ibid. ii. 1470).

[2] See above, p. 232, note 2. Memel resembled Danzig in being a German foundation. In other respects they differed. Danzig for the greater part of its history was connected with Poland; Memel from its foundation until 1919 was with unbroken continuity part of the Prussian state. Danzig in 1919 was erected into an independent state, with certain reservations; Memel in 1924 was made an autonomous unit under Lithuanian sovereignty. The population of the Free City of Danzig was 95 per cent. German; in the Memelland, the population of the city itself was

ties in Poznán and Pomorze, mainly the result of Prussian efforts to Germanize those provinces when they had been Posen and West Prussia;[1] there was another German minority in Polish Upper Silesia; there were German colonists in what had been formerly Russian Poland, farmers and a large population of industrial workers, especially in Lodz; and farther east in Poland there were bodies of German peasant colonists who had settled at the end of the eighteenth century in Austrian Galicia, Volhynia, and Chelm. Czechoslovakia contained a larger German minority than any country, so ancient an element of the population that it was disputed whether they were colonists or original inhabitants. The majority of them were in Bohemia, Moravia, and Silesia; they mainly formed compact masses round the outer rim of those provinces, including the chief mining and industrial regions, but there were also large German enclaves elsewhere and colonies in the main towns, particularly Prague. And there were German minorities of different origin in Slovakia and Carpatho-Ruthenia, the descendants of colonists in the old Hungary. Hungary itself contained a German element only less ancient than that in Bohemia and Moravia. The medieval kings of Hungary and Bohemia and Poland, backward countries with purely agricultural economies, had encouraged German immigration, especially after the Mongol invasion of the thirteenth century, and for many hundreds of years the Germans supplied their bourgeoisies. Until the beginning of the nineteenth century almost all Hungarian towns were predominantly German, though they became largely Magyarized. In addition there were German-speaking agricultural colonies; some were of medieval origin, but most of them dated from the colonizing schemes of the Habsburgs in the seventeenth and eighteenth centuries, when South Germans or 'Swabians' were brought in to settle the country after its reconquest from the Turks.[2] They were found mostly round Budapest, north of Lake Balaton, and in the south-west. The Swabian colonies in the Voivodina had been transferred, under the Treaty of Trianon, to the successor states of Yugoslavia and Rumania. They formed the chief German minority of Yugoslavia, but there were other islands of German colonists in Croatia and Slovenia, and even a few in Serbia. Rumania was more extensively riddled with German minorities than any country except Czechoslovakia. In Transylvania were the Saxons, a body of colonists dating from the thirteenth century, who had become one of the three privileged nations of Transylvania,[3] and retained a high cultural

likewise almost entirely German, but the Lithuanians and Memellanders outnumbered the Germans in the Territory as a whole.

[1] Though there were small German colonies of medieval origin, as in Thorn, a city founded by the Teutonic Order and afterwards a member of the Hanseatic League.

[2] Macartney: *Hungary and her Successors*, p. 384.

[3] R. W. Seton-Watson: *A History of the Roumanians*, pp. 21–22, 101–3. These 'Saxons' were originally Rhinelanders and Luxemburgers (Macartney, op. cit. p. 254).

tradition and elaborate national organization; in the Banat were Swabians; in the Bukovina, in Bessarabia, and in the Dobruja were smaller German groups dating mainly from the nineteenth century. In Bulgaria there was a negligible German minority. But more than a thousand miles to the east, on the lower reaches of the Volga, was another community of Germans, established there by Catherine the Great, erected in 1923 into the Autonomous Socialist Soviet Republic of the Volga Germans, and only dispersed and expelled to Siberia by the Soviet Government in the autumn of 1941 after Hitler's invasion of Russia.[1]

The Germans were the most widespread of the minorities of Eastern Europe, and because of their connexion with the dominant Power of the Continent they became the most dangerous. Like the nation of which they were distant outcrops, they had been for the most part traditionally loyal to the governments under which they lived, economically advanced and prosperous, attached to their national language and culture, docile and valuable colonists. But with the National Socialist Revolution they underwent the spiritual revolution that had already befallen the *Reichsdeutsch*. Within a few months of the *Machtübernahme* the Nazis declared their intention of bringing into the Party all German citizens living beyond the frontiers, and of awakening in all German minorities the consciousness of being *Volksgenossen*, racial comrades, members of the German people. A *Volksgenosse* was defined as anybody of German descent and German blood; the German nation, as distinct from the German state, was claimed to embrace a population of 100 millions; and the German minorities in Eastern Europe were transformed into an international fifth column of unique power.[2]

[1] Sidney and Beatrice Webb: *Soviet Communism: a new Civilisation*, 3rd edition (London, Longmans, Green, 1944), p. 113, note 2; B. H. Sumner: *Survey of Russian History* (London, Duckworth, 1944), p. 41.

[2] Cf. above, p. 315, and further below, pp. 346–7.

The size of the German minorities in the countries of Eastern Europe, and the percentages they formed of the total populations, were in 1938, before the first partition of Czechoslovakia, approximately as follows:

		per cent.
Estonia	16,346	1·5
Latvia	62,144	3·19
Lithuania	29,231 (1923 census)	1·44
Memelland	67,671 (1925 census)	43·4
Poland	741,000	2·3
Czechoslovakia	3,231,688	22·3
Hungary	478,630	5·5
Rumania	740,000	4·1
Yugoslavia	513,472	4·2
Bulgaria	4,171	0·1

The figures for Estonia, Latvia, Lithuania, and Memelland are taken from Royal Institute of International Affairs: *Baltic States*, tables on pp. 36, 33, 30, and 94; for Poland and Czechoslovakia, from H. Seton-Watson: *Eastern Europe*, appendix, pp. 430–1; for the remainder, see

The second concrete asset upon which Germany's predominance in Eastern Europe was based was her enormous economic strength. The century that ended with the First World War had made Germany the industrial master of Europe, and with the growth of German industrialization there grew, like its shadow, the conception of Eastern Europe and the Near East as Germany's sphere of influence. In this conception, however, economic considerations were always subordinated to considerations of power. It was characteristic that the Prussian Zollverein was originally intended to promote trade between North Germany and the outer world, but became, as List desired it to be, an instrument for the economic unification of Germany for the purposes of war.[1] Thus, too, in Hitler's time the arguments for Germany's right to dominate Eastern Europe did not rest upon economic grounds. For the Eastern European countries indeed, if they were offered no alternative by the Western Powers, Germany was essential as the market for their primary products;[2] but the Eastern European countries were not essential to Germany. Compared with Germany's total trade her trade with Eastern Europe was small. The exertion of her economic supremacy in Eastern Europe was due not to economic needs, but to political purposes.[3]

The chief embodiment of the German claim to predominance in Eastern Europe had been, for about a century, the conception of *Mitteleuropa*. This was one solution of the problem of the relations between the Austrian Empire, on the one hand, and the German Confederation and Empire on the other. Essentially it asserted the need for unifying Central Europe under German leadership. List, the prophet of the Prussian Zollverein and the German railway-system, came to believe that Germany's destiny lay not westwards across the oceans but towards the Danube basin and European Turkey, and he originated the idea of the Berlin–Baghdād Railway.[4] Bruck, the German merchant who founded the Lloyd Triestino and the commercial greatness of Trieste, and became Austrian Minister of Commerce under Schwarzenberg, wished to incorporate the entire Austrian Empire in the German Confederation, so that the Germans united under the Habsburgs might become the masters of an organized Central Europe.

Royal Institute of International Affairs: *South-Eastern Europe: a Political and Economic Survey*, 2nd (rev.) edition (London, R.I.I.A., 1939), table on p. 8. The figures are in each case the official estimates; the German estimates were sometimes 30 or 40 per cent. higher (see ibid. and Macartney: *National States*, appendix iii). The Volga German A.S.S.R. in 1933 numbered 588,000 (N. Mikhaylov: *Soviet Geography* (London, Methuen, 1935), p. 222), but a third of its population was Russian or Ukrainian.

[1] Cf. Taylor: *Course of German History*, p. 63.
[2] See above, pp. 260–1.
[3] See below, pp. 484–7.
[4] There is a useful account of List's contribution to military thought by Edward Mead Earle in 'Adam Smith, Alexander Hamilton, Friedrich List: The Economic Foundations of Military Power', in *Makers of Modern Strategy: Military Thought from Machiavelli to Hitler*, edited by Edward Mead Earle (Princeton, N.J., University Press, 1944), pp. 138–52.

Bismarck's defeat of Austria, which resulted in the transformation of the Habsburg Empire by the *Ausgleich* in 1867 and in the establishment of the Second German Reich in 1871, brought into being an empirical *Mitteleuropa* through the leverage which Germany obtained over the Dual Monarchy and its Emperor. The *Ausgleich* made a German minority uppermost in Austria, and a Magyar minority uppermost in Hungary, leaving them both dependent in the last resort on the support of Berlin. The First World War welded the Central Powers more closely together, and brought *Mitteleuropa* at last fully into being, besides producing as well its classic theoretical formulation,[1] in the last years of the Habsburg Monarchy.

The War proved Austria-Hungary's value to Germany. The Habsburg Monarchy, which to short-sighted Pan-Germans (not to Bismarck) had seemed a cumbersome survival impeding the road to a reunion of the entire German nation, proved the most valuable asset for *Mittel-Europa*, the German World-Empire. Even the extremest Pan-Germans in Austria became converted to the Habsburg Monarchy. There was now a platform common to all the Austrian Germans—Austria was to be maintained, reconstructed on a German basis, and firmly fitted into the Germanic system; her policy was to be subordinated to that of Central Europe, and the entire Habsburg inheritance was to be taken over and secured by the joint strength of the German nation. Through *Mittel-Europa* the Austrian Germans returned both to the Pan-German and to the Great-Austrian idea, now reconciled with each other. They beheld themselves once more an integral part of the German nation, and as part of it resumed an 'imperialism' too wide for them in their previous isolation.[2]

There was much speculation about Nazi foreign policy in terms of these traditions of eastern expansion. When Hitler inaugurated his foreign policy by a spectacular accord with Poland[3] it was easy to assume that, being himself an Austrian, his policy would be in the Habsburg not the Prussian tradition, and that having effected his declared aim of the Anschluss,[4] he would resume the historic *Drang nach Osten* to the south of the Carpathians. The influence of Alfred Rosenberg, it is true, was supposed to be in favour of north-western expansion, towards the Balticum of which he was himself a native;[5] but the sequence of Hitler's foreign successes down to March 1939—the treaty with Poland followed by the conquest of Austria and Czechoslovakia—might confirm the first supposition. The error was to suppose that Nazi policy would confine itself to one or other of these policies as if there was an incompatibility between them.

---

[1] Friedrich Naumann: *Mitteleuropa* (Berlin, Reimer, 1915), trans. by C. M. Meredith, with an introduction by W. J. Ashley, as *Central Europe* (London, King, 1916).

[2] L. B. Namier in *H.P.C.* iv. 71.

[3] *Survey* for 1933, pp. 184–6; *Survey* for 1934, pp. 386–7; *Survey* for 1935, i. 60, 204–10. It was not known at the time that Hitler negotiated his non-aggression pact with Poland only after an offer of a similar pact to Czechoslovakia in the autumn of 1933 had been rejected by Beneš (see Beneš's letter to Namier of 20 April 1944, in Namier: *Europe in Decay*, pp. 281–2).

[4] See *Mein Kampf*, p. 1.   [5] For the 'Rosenberg Plan' see *Survey* for 1933, p. 176 and note 2.

Hitler never considered himself an heir to the Habsburgs: he was as contemptuous of their anti-national policy as he was ignorant of the problems of statecraft with which, in his own Vienna days, they had been wrestling.[1] He was *grossdeutsch* by origin, but he had become head of a *kleindeutsch* Reich, and the greater included the less.[2] His anti-Russian policy had immediate antecedents in the Habsburg rather than the Hohenzollern tradition, but he himself expressed it in terms of a pristine Germanic destiny that was pre-Habsburg and pre-Hohenzollern. His foreign policy amalgamated the Habsburg and Prussian traditions, and at the same time transcended them as Napoleon's policy transcended the traditions of Bourbon aggrandizement. The immediate aims of National Socialism went far beyond the abolition of the Versailles Treaty and the restoration of the former frontiers of the Second Reich;[3] its ultimate ambitions exceeded the historic Prussian ascendancy in the Baltic and the historic Habsburg ascendancy in the Danube valley and the Balkans. The old conception of *Mitteleuropa* was transformed and swallowed up in the new theory of *Lebensraum*.

The change had taken place in the stress and tumult of the First World War, when the collapse of the Russian Empire revolutionized German policy. For the first time in six centuries no great state stood between the Reich and the Eurasian steppes, and for six months at the supreme crisis of the war German rule had extended from the Somme to the Don.[4] This was the empire that Hitler meant to restore.

Therefore we National Socialists have purposely drawn a line through the line of conduct followed by pre-War Germany in foreign policy. We put an end to the perpetual Germanic march towards the South and West of Europe and turn our eyes towards the lands of the East. We finally put a stop to the colonial and trade policy of pre-War times and pass over to the territorial policy of the future. But when we speak of new territory in Europe to-day we must principally think of Russia and the border States subject to her.[5] . . . To-day

---

[1] See *Mein Kampf*, pp. 13–14, 100–3, 118–19, 139–43; tr. Murphy, pp. 26–27, 88–91, 102, 118–20. Cf. Hitler: *Speeches* (Baynes), i. 46, 55.

[2] See Taylor: *Course of German History*, pp. 218–19.

[3] *Mein Kampf*, pp. 736, 738–9; tr. Murphy, pp. 529, 530–1.

[4] Cf. above, pp. 211, note 3, and 282, note 3.

[5] *Mein Kampf*, p. 752; tr. Murphy, p. 533; cf. pp. 154 and 128 respectively. (The Ukraine is not mentioned by name in *Mein Kampf*.) At about the same time as Hitler wrote these words, Churchill was formulating the same objective of German policy, in his criticism of Falkenhayn's decision in 1916 to attack in the west instead of the east. 'It would appear that the true strategic objectives of Germany in 1916 were the Black Sea and the Caspian. These lay within her grasp and required no effort beyond her strength. A continued advance against the south lands of Russia into the Ukraine and towards Odessa would have secured at comparatively little cost sufficient food for the Teutonic peoples. . . . One-half the effort, one-quarter the sacrifice, lavished vainly in the attack on Verdun would have overcome the difficulty of the defective communications in "the rich lands of the Ukraine" ', Winston S. Churchill: *The World Crisis, 1916–1918*, part i (London, Butterworth, 1927), pp. 80–81, 82. The preface to this volume is dated 1 January 1927; the second volume of *Mein Kampf* was published on 10 December 1926.

there are eighty million Germans in Europe. And our foreign policy will be recognized as rightly conducted only when, after barely a hundred years, there will be 250 million Germans living on this Continent, not packed together as the coolies in the factories of another Continent but as tillers of the soil and workers whose labour will be a mutual assurance for their existence.[1]

For a century and a half Russia and Prussia had been united by the common interest of subjugating Poland. When in 1914 war broke out between Russia and Germany for the first time since the Seven Years War, the Polish problem was once more placed in the forefront of European politics. In its shadow appeared the question of the Ukraine, which had for a generation been an Austro-Hungarian interest,[2] and now became an inescapable object of German policy. The new system of power that came into existence in Eastern Europe after the First World War confirmed this: across a belt of weaker states the German return to the Ukraine lay permanently open. The former Cossack hetman Skoropadski lived at Wannsee near Berlin, exile or pretender according to circumstances; Ukrainian projects were among the Nazi stock-in-trade;[3] Rosenberg in his prospectus of foreign policy elaborated the broad statements of *Mein Kampf*;[4] and with the *Machtübernahme* the Ukrainian plans became an avowed part of German foreign policy.[5]

If we had at our disposal [said Hitler in a celebrated indiscretion in 1936] the incalculable wealth and stores of raw material of the Ural Mountains and the unending fertile plains of the Ukraine to be exploited under National Socialist leadership, then we would produce, and our German people would swim in plenty.[6]

In Hitler's secret counsels, the need for *Lebensraum* was consistently emphasized as the theme of National Socialist foreign policy. At the conference of 5 November 1937, when Hitler laid down his fundamental ideas on foreign policy and asked that they be regarded as his last will and testament, he stated the principle at the outset that the future of Germany was 'wholly conditional upon the solving of the need for space'.[7] He then examined whether the need for expansion could be circumvented either by autarky or by increased participation in world economy. Germany within her existing frontiers could attain only a very limited self-sufficiency in raw materials, and none at all in foodstuffs. The world economy was already

---

[1] *Mein Kampf*, p. 767; tr. Murphy, p. 549.

[2] H. Wickham Steed: *The Hapsburg Monarchy*, 4th edition (London, Constable, 1919), pp. 289–93; Allen: *Ukraine*, p. 251; Wiskemann: *Undeclared War*, pp. 196–7.

[3] Rauschning: *Hitler Speaks*, pp. 73, 80, 122; Beloff, i. 94.

[4] Alfred Rosenberg: *Der Zukunftsweg einer deutschen Aussenpolitik* (Munich, Eher, 1927), pp. 97–98.

[5] Cf. Allen: *Ukraine*, pp. 330–1, 341.

[6] Speech to the Labour Front at the Nuremberg Parteitag, 12 September 1936 (*Survey* for 1936, pp. 381–2 and note; Hitler: *Speeches* (Baynes), i. 929).

[7] Hossbach Memorandum, *I.M.T. Nuremberg*, xxv. 404 (386–PS); *D.Ger.F.P.*, series D, i. 30; *Documents* (R.I.A.) for 1939–46, i. 17; cf. *N.C.A.* iii. 296.

breaking down through the industrialization of backward countries and the formation of great economic empires. Therefore

the only remedy, and one which might appear to us as visionary, lay in the acquisition of greater living space—a quest which has at all times been the origin of the formation of states and of the migration of peoples. . . . If, then, we accept the security of our food situation as the principal question, the space necessary to insure it can only be sought in Europe, not, as in the liberal-capitalist view, in the exploitation of colonies. It is not a matter of acquiring population but of gaining space for agricultural use. Moreover, areas producing raw materials can be more usefully sought in Europe in immediate proximity to the Reich, than overseas; the solution thus obtained must suffice for one or two generations. . . . The question for Germany ran: where could she achieve the greatest gain at the lowest cost.[1]

He left the question unanswered in this conference, but there was only one answer, the answer he had himself given eleven years earlier in *Mein Kampf*.[2]

The conquest and dismemberment of Russia was the central aim of Hitler's foreign policy, to which all other aims were subordinated.[3] Behind the shifts of opportunism and tactics this remained constant. 'Danzig is not the object of our activities', he said in May 1939, when the Danzig crisis was maturing. 'It is a question of expanding our living space in the east, of securing our food supplies.'[4] Again, in the conference of 23 November 1939,

Our growing population demands a larger *Lebensraum*. My aim was to create a reasonable relation between the number of people and the space in which they live. . . . To relate the number of Germans to the space available is a perpetual problem. The necessary space must be secured. No calculated cleverness is of any help, a way can only be won by the sword.[5]

[1] *I.M.T. Nuremberg*, xxv. 406 (386–PS); *D.Ger.F.P.*, series D, i. 31–32; *Documents* (R.I.I.A.) for 1939–46, i. 18–19; cf. *N.C.A.* iii. 298.

[2] 'Wenn wir aber heute in Europa von neuem Grund und Boden reden, können wir in erster Linie nur an *Russland* und die ihm untertanen Randstaaten denken' (*Mein Kampf*, p. 742; tr. Murphy, p. 533).

[3] Cf. Trevor-Roper: *Last Days of Hitler*, pp. 5–7. Cyril Falls, in *The Second World War* (London, Methuen, 1948), p. 1, adduces the argument that 'the war of 1939 . . . was essentially a war of revenge. . . . It is not too much to say that German National Socialism, the Nazi creed, stood first and foremost for revenge. The other aims, the "living room" to be obtained by the subjugation of neighbouring states, the absorption of all Teutonic or allegedly Teutonic populations, the colonization of agricultural districts like the Ukraine, the control of all major industries in Europe, were either the means of consolidating the revenge once achieved or the expression of purely predatory instincts such as had always flourished in Prussia and had more recently been diffused by Prussia over all Germany.' The argument appears to be internally inconsistent as well as unsupported by the documents and history of the Third Reich. It is, perhaps, a belated example of the inability of the foreign liberal to believe the self-declared truth about Hitler.

[4] Minutes of conference of 23 May 1939 (*I.M.T. Nuremberg*, xxxvii. 548 (079–L); *Documents* (R.I.I.A.) for 1939–46, i. 272; cf. *N.C.A.* vii. 849).

[5] *I.M.T. Nuremberg*, xxvi. 329 (789–PS); *Documents* (R.I.I.A.) for 1939–46, i. 529–30; cf. *N.C.A.* iii. 574.

(d) THE CHARACTER OF HITLER'S FOREIGN POLICY

Non-aggressive states tend to seek security in collaboration, in order to preserve the balance of power. Expanding states seek to divide and rule. Deal with your enemies one by one, isolate the adversary with whom you are at present concerned, avoid general negotiations: these are the principles of all the great masters of aggressive statecraft. In its main lines Hitler's political strategy was the same as those of Bismarck, Napoleon, and Louis XIV.

In *Mein Kampf* Hitler emphasized economy of objectives in foreign policy. He attacked the *Parlamentschwätzern* who expended their indignation on the South Tyrol question instead of upon the aim of conquering *Lebensraum*.[1] 'Because we keep on howling against five or ten States, we fail to concentrate all the forces of our national will and our physical strength for a blow at the heart of our bitterest enemy.'[2] This was impressive propaganda; once the Nazis were in power, though the principle was retained, its application was reversed. It was not the bitterest enemy who was struck at, but, in an ascending succession, the weakest and most inoffensive.[3] Frederick the Great once quoted with approval the classic saying of one of the princes of Savoy: 'Mon fils, le Milanais est comme un artichaut; il faut le manger feuille par feuille.'[4] Churchill used a phrase destined to become equally famous: 'One by one, there is the process; there is the simple, dismal plan which has served Hitler so well.'[5]

It was in the application of the principle of economy of immediate objectives that Hitler's political genius was most clearly displayed. Napoleon's enemies were for the most part dynasties; Hitler's were democracies, electorates, masses with a public opinion, who had to be confused, anaesthetized, 'played along'. His chief contribution to this political art may be called the rule of the graduated dose. He had laid it down in one of the most penetrating passages in *Mein Kampf*, whose relevance only slowly broke upon the peoples of the Western Great Powers.

A shrewd conqueror will always enforce his exactions on the conquered only by stages, as far as that is possible. Then he may expect that a people who have lost all strength of character—which is always the case with every nation that voluntarily submits to the threats of an opponent—will not find in any of these acts of oppression, if one be enforced apart from the other, sufficient grounds for taking up arms again. The more numerous the extortions thus passively accepted

---

[1] *Mein Kampf*, pp. 707–11; tr. Murphy, pp. 510–12.

[2] Ibid. pp. 718 and 517 respectively.

[3] Cf. Rauschning: *Hitler Speaks*, pp. 83, 214.

[4] Frederick the Great: *Histoire de mon temps*, chapter i, in *Œuvres de Frédéric le Grand* (Berlin, 1846 seqq.), ii. 31. Cf. Albert Sorel: *L'Europe et la Révolution Française*, i. 393.

[5] Broadcast of 24 August 1941 on the Atlantic meeting with Roosevelt (Winston S. Churchill: *The Unrelenting Struggle: War Speeches*, compiled by Charles Eade (London, Cassell, 1942), pp. 235–6.

so much the less will resistance appear justified in the eyes of other people, if the vanquished nation should end by revolting against the last act of oppression in a long series. And that is specially so if the nation has already patiently and silently accepted impositions which were much more exacting.[1]

Hitler divined and exploited not only the weaknesses of his victims but also their virtues; for instance, the perseverance of the British Government in seeking a peaceful settlement of Europe and in going to extreme lengths in putting up with provocation and with actual loss of position rather than be responsible for precipitating another war. The abortive Austrian *putsch* of 1934 was a miscalculation of forces,[2] and it was Hitler's only coup before 1938 that evoked the movement of troops in opposition to it.[3] Not the least of Hitler's achievements was the success with which, as far as a foreign opinion was concerned, he glossed over both this affair and the massacres he had carried out inside Germany a month before;[4] and for the rest, the period up to March 1939 was a series of perfectly graduated triumphs, each in turn homologated or applauded by the dominant part of public opinion in the Western Great Powers—the withdrawal from the Disarmament Conference and the League of Nations on 14 October 1933;[5] the Polish-German Pact of 26 January 1934,[6] the Saar plebiscite on 13 January 1935;[7] the announcement that a German air force was once more in existence on 10 March and the reintroduction of compulsory military service on 16 March 1935;[8] the Anglo-German naval agreement of 18 June 1935;[9] the reoccupation of the Rhineland on 7 March 1936;[10] the announcement of the Rome–Berlin Axis on 1 November 1936;[11] the recognition of Franco's Government in Spain on 18 November 1936,[12] and the signing of the Anti-Comintern Pact with Japan on 25 November 1936;[13] the Anschluss with Austria on 13 March 1938,[14] and the first partition of Czechoslovakia

[1] *Mein Kampf*, p. 759; tr. Murphy, p. 544.

[2] See *Survey* for 1934, pp. 471–87. For subsequent evidence upon the German Government's implication in this *putsch* see *Ambassador Dodd's Diary, 1933–1938*, ed. by William E. Dodd, jr., and Martha Dodd (London, Gollancz, 1941), pp. 143–4, entry for 26 July 1934; affidavit of George S. Messersmith (see below, p. 346, note 1), 28 August 1945 (*I.M.T. Nuremberg*, xxviii. 255–93 (1760–PS); *N.C.A.* iv. 305–25), and report of the American Consul-General in Vienna to the Secretary of State, 26 July 1938 (*I.M.T. Nuremberg*, xxxviii. 94–96 (273–L); *N.C.A.* vii. 1094–5).

[3] The movement of four army divisions by Mussolini to the Brenner and the Carinthian border (*Survey* for 1934, p. 475). The next example of troop movements in opposition to Hitler was the partial Czechoslovak mobilization of 20–21 May 1938 (see above, p. 268). But the failure of the Austrian *putsch* of 1934 was more encouraging than otherwise for Hitler, since it showed the reluctance of the Western Powers to embark on any action more energetic than protests.

[4] *Survey* for 1934, p. 325.   [5] *Survey* for 1933, pp. 305–6.

[6] Ibid. pp. 184–6; *Survey* for 1934, pp. 386–7; *Survey* for 1935, i. 60, 204–10.

[7] *Survey* for 1934, p. 619.   [8] *Survey* for 1935, i. 140–2.

[9] Ibid. pp. 178–88.   [10] *Survey* for 1936, pp. 263–6.

[11] Ibid. pp. 581–2.   [12] *Survey* for 1937, ii. 256–7.

[13] *Survey* for 1936, p. 384. Another minor German success in the same month was the denunciation of the provisions of the Versailles Treaty relating to German waterways on 14 November 1936 (*Survey* for 1937, i. 373–7; cf. above, pp. 262, 285, and below, p. 343, note 5).

[14] *Survey* for 1938, i. 211–12.

at Munich on 29 September 1938.[1] 'The period which lies behind us', said Hitler in May 1939, 'has been put to good use. Every step taken was directed towards our goal.'[2] At which point in this sequence should resistance have been concerted by other Powers? Each one, argued on its merits, was capable of being seen as a rectification of the injustices of Versailles or a consolidation of the forces of anti-Communism. In retrospect it was clear that the remilitarization of the Rhineland was the watershed, after which events acquired a fatal downward momentum.[3] But at the time, 'we have no more desire', said Baldwin, 'than to keep calm, to keep our heads and to continue to try to bring France and Germany together in a friendship with ourselves'.[4]

Another aspect of Hitler's statecraft was his adroitness in the art of timing. The series of diplomatic coups by which he demolished the Versailles Treaty were regularly carried out on Saturdays, when the English week-end meant that the governmental machine of his chief potential opponent would be awkwardly placed for immediate action.[5] More important than the exploiting of his enemies' social routine was the exploiting of their political and military preoccupations. In the summer of 1935 the Nazis were eagerly awaiting a war between Italy and Ethiopia, reckoning that this would cause disturbances in the European situation from which they would be able to benefit:[6] it permitted them to reoccupy

---

[1] See above, pp. 270 seqq.

[2] Speech to his commanders, 23 May 1939 (*I.M.T. Nuremberg*, xxxvii. 548 (079–L); *Documents* (R.I.I.A.) for 1939–46, i. 272; cf. *N.C.A.* vii. 848).

[3] Cf. above, pp. 260 seqq. Hitler understood this well. 'Yes', he said to Schuschnigg on 12 February 1938, 'two years ago, when we marched into the Rhineland with a handful of battalions —then I risked a great deal. If France had marched then, we would have had to withdraw. . . . But now for France it is too late!' (Kurt von Schuschnigg: *Ein Requiem in Rot-Weiss-Rot* (Zürich, Amstutz, 1946), p. 43). Cf. Schmidt: *Statist auf diplomatischer Bühne*, p. 320; and Hitler's speech to his commanders of 22 August 1939: 'Reference to previous risks. . . . The most dangerous step was the invasion of the neutral zone. Only a week before, I got a warning through France. I have always accepted a great risk in the conviction that it may succeed' (*I.M.T. Nuremberg*, xxvi. 341 (798–PS); *Documents* (R.I.I.A.) for 1939–46, i. 445; cf. *N.C.A.* iii. 584); and Vocke's evidence (*I.M.T. Nuremberg*, xiii. 57). Flandin claims to have seen this at the time: 'Cette fois, l'abandon sera décisif, car il sera générateur de toute une série d'autres abandons' (*Politique française, 1919–1940*, p. 204).

[4] 9 March 1936. H.C.Deb. 5th ser., vol. 309, col. 1841 (quoted in *Survey* for 1936, p. 276); cf. Churchill: *Second World War*, i. 153.

[5] The following is the list of Hitler's Saturday crises: the withdrawal from the League on 14 October 1933; the official notification to other Governments of the re-creation of the German air force on 9 March 1935 (*Survey* for 1935, i. 140, note 1), and the announcement of conscription on 16 March 1935; the reoccupation of the Rhineland on 7 March 1936; the resumption of full control over German waterways on 14 November 1936; and the invasion of Austria on 12 March 1938 (it began on the night of Friday the 11th; the Anschluss was legally consummated on Sunday the 13th). 30 June 1934 was also a Saturday, but this was determined by the development of the stresses within the Party (see Heiden: *Der Fuehrer*, p. 592). The Ides of March 1939 fell upon a Wednesday.

[6] Affidavit by George S. Messersmith for the Nuremberg Tribunal (*I.M.T. Nuremberg*, xxx. 309 (2385–PS); *N.C.A.* v. 36–37).

the Rhineland.[1] The Spanish Civil War provided the background for the seizure of Austria and Czechoslovakia.

The political instability of the world situation, in which the occurrence of sudden incidents cannot be prevented, demands constant preparedness for war on the part of the German armed forces in order (a) to meet attacks at any time[2] and (b) to be able to exploit militarily any favourable political opportunity that may offer itself.[3]

In the autumn of 1937 the opportunity for attack on Czechoslovakia and Austria was seen as arising from the outbreak either of civil war in France or of a Mediterranean war between France, England, and Italy. 'A 100 per cent. victory for Franco was not desirable . . . from the German point of view', said Hitler at the conference of 5 November 1937; 'rather were we interested in a continuance of the war and in the keeping up of the tension in the Mediterranean.'[4] After Munich, when he had assumed a complete European hegemony, these considerations became less important, and he supplied his own diversions.

But Hitler's timing was something more than skilful opportunism. It was governed ultimately by his long-term judgement of German strength in relation to the shifting balance of European forces. On 20 February 1933 he enunciated an important principle in a speech at a meeting of industrialists:

We must first get complete power into our hands, if we want to crush the other side completely to the ground. So long as one is still gaining in power, one should not begin the struggle against the opponent. Only when one knows that one has reached the pinnacle of power, that there is no further upward development, should one attack.[5]

This was laid down with reference to the political struggle in Germany and the forthcoming election, the first of the Nazi régime. 'In Prussia we must gain another ten seats, and in the Reich another thirty-three. That is not impossible if we throw in all our strength. Then only begins the second action against Communism.' But the same principle, of waiting to strike till the moment of maximum relative strength, *der Höhepunkt der Macht*, underlay his foreign policy. In the conference of 5 November 1937 he defined the years 1943–5 as marking the zenith of German power.

---

[1] Cf. *Survey* for 1935, ii. 339–40 and 394, note 1.

[2] The preceding paragraph had laid down the assumption 'that Germany need not take into account an attack from any side'.

[3] Blomberg directive on the combined preparations for war of the Wehrmacht, 24 June 1937 (*I.M.T. Nuremberg*, xxxiv. 735 (175–C); *Documents* (R.I.I.A.) for 1939–46, i. 8; cf. *N.C.A.* vi. 1007).

[4] Hossbach Memorandum (*I.M.T. Nuremberg*, xxv. 411 (386–PS); *D.Ger.F.P.*, series D, i. 37; *Documents* (R.I.I.A.) for 1939–46, i. 23; cf. *N.C.A.* iii. 303).

[5] *I.M.T. Nuremberg*, xxxv. 46 (203–D); cf. *N.C.A.* vi. 1083. The writer is indebted to Miss Elizabeth Wiskemann for drawing his attention to this speech; she was the first to point out its importance (see Wiskemann: *Rome–Berlin Axis*, p. 18).

'After this date only a change for the worse, from our point of view, could be expected.' By that time German war preparations would have reached their highest point in relation to the counter-measures of other Powers, and the danger of German armaments becoming out of date would increase. 'The recruiting of reserves was limited to current age groups; further drafts from older untrained age groups were no longer available.' Any year could then bring a crisis in Germany's food supplies. The difficulty of keeping up large armed forces, the danger of a decline in the standard of living and a drop in the birth-rate, 'the aging of the [Nazi] movement and of its leaders', all suggested that downward trends would then begin. 'Nobody knew today what the situation would be in the years 1943–45. One thing only was certain, that we could not wait longer. . . . If the Führer was still living, it was his unalterable resolve to solve Germany's problem of space at the latest by 1943–45.'[1] It was within this chronological limit that the moment for military action might be advanced by seizing favourable contingencies, such as civil strife in France or a war between France and Italy. On 22 August 1939 Hitler told his commanders that all the factors in the European situation were now advantageous for an attack on Poland. 'For us it is easy to make decisions. We have nothing to lose; we can only gain. Our economic situation is such, because of our limitations, that we cannot hold out more than a few years.'[2] With the overwhelming of Poland the *Höhepunkt der Macht* seemed manifest. 'Time is working for our adversary', said Hitler on 23 November 1939. 'Now there is a relationship of forces which can never be more propitious, but can only deteriorate for us. . . . Today we have a superiority such as we have never had before.'[3] Perhaps it was the defect of Hitler's policy, on its own principles, that in the delicate balance between exploiting favourable opportunities and waiting for the culmination of German power relative to his enemies, he showed an increasing preference for the former;

[1] Hossbach Memorandum (*I.M.T. Nuremberg*, xxv. 408–9 (386–PS); *D.Ger.F.P.*, series D, i. 34–5; *Documents* (R.I.I.A.) for 1939–46, i. 21; cf. *N.C.A.* iii. 300–1).

[2] *I.M.T. Nuremberg*, xxvi. 340 (798–PS); *Documents* (R.I.I.A.) for 1939–46, i. 444; cf. *N.C.A.* iii. 582. It was the question of timing that produced the conflict of policy between Germany and Italy at this moment, on the eve of the war: Mussolini's *Höhepunkt der Macht* did not coincide with Hitler's. See the conference between Hitler and Ciano of 12 August 1939 (*I.M.T. Nuremberg*, xxix. 41–53 (1871–PS); *Documents* (R.I.I.A.) for 1939–46, i. 172–81; cf. *N.C.A.* iv. 508–17, with the comment in Mendelssohn: *Nuremberg Documents*, p. 169), and Hitler's letter to Mussolini of 3 September 1939 (*I.M.T. Nuremberg*, xxviii. 547–9 (1831–PS); *Documents* (R.I.I.A.) for 1939–46, i. 507–8; cf. *N.C.A.* iv. 465–6).

[3] *I.M.T. Nuremberg*, xxvi. 332 (789–PS); *N.C.A.* iii. 576. Hitler was also driven forward by a similar calculation about his own age and indispensability. On 23 August he told Henderson that he preferred war now, when he was 50, to when he would be 55 or 60 (Great Britain, Foreign Office: *Documents concerning German-Polish relations and the Outbreak of Hostilities between Great Britain and Germany on September 3, 1939*, Cmd. 6106 [referred to hereafter as Cmd. 6106] (London, H.M.S.O., 1939), no. 58). Cf. his estimate of the importance of his own personality in his speech to his commanders on 22 August 1939 (*I.M.T. Nuremberg*, xxvi. 339 (798–PS); *Documents* (R.I.I.A.) for 1939–46, i. 443; cf. *N.C.A.* iii. 582).

his long series of successes created a habit and took the edge off his judgement, and the tendency to double the stakes was inherent in a dynamic
policy.

An aggressive Power tends to independent action; it is cautious about
association with other Powers except upon its own terms; if it enters into
engagements they will be bilateral, not multilateral. 'I principi debbono
fuggire quanto possono lo stare a discrezione d'altri.'[1] Like Napoleon,
Hitler aimed at separate transactions with every Power, and avoided
general negotiations.[2] He told Halifax that 'he was a fanatical enemy of
conferences which were doomed to failure from the start. He would in no
case allow himself to be persuaded to take part in such proceedings by
statesmen who considered that a conference was due every quarter'.[3] It
was the logical inauguration of his diplomacy to withdraw Germany from
the League of Nations;[4] he inevitably advanced towards the destruction of
the Locarno treaties; and he refused to take part in any other multilateral
engagements except those he initiated himself.[5]

But independence in policy, as soon as it is successful, attracts associates and scavengers, and raises the obverse problem of how these are to be
best handled. From 1936 onwards, when Germany formed separately
both the Axis entente with Italy[6] and the Anti-Comintern Pact with Japan,[7]
this was a concern of her policy. Italy was the closest associate, but Hitler
acted independently of her whenever it suited him. On 25 September
1937, during a visit to Berlin, Ciano proposed the fusion of the German-
Japanese pact with a similar treaty for which the Italians were at that time
in negotiation with Tokyo. Neurath replied that tripartite arrangements
were unnecessary and it was preferable to keep to bilateral agreements with
Japan.[8] A month later Germany had changed her policy, and the initiative

[1] Niccolò Machiavelli: *Il Principe*, chapter xxi, ed. L. A. Burd (Oxford, Clarendon Press, 1891),
pp. 343–4.
[2] Cf. H. Butterfield: *The Peace Tactics of Napoleon, 1806–1808* (Cambridge University Press,
1929), pp. 56, 74, 82–83, 170, 207; and the same author's *Napoleon* (London, Duckworth, 1939),
pp. 78–79.
[3] Conversation between Hitler and Halifax, 19 November 1937 (*D.Ger.F.P.*, series D, i. 63–64).
[4] See *Survey* for 1933, pp. 305–6; Heiden: *Der Fuehrer*, p. 535. The threat of withdrawal had
been contained in the *Friedensrede* of 17 May 1933: 'Any attempt to do violence to Germany by
means of a simple majority vote . . . could only be dictated by the intention of excluding us from
the conferences [i.e. the Disarmament Conference]. The German people, however, today possesses sufficient character in such a case not to impose its co-operation on other nations but,
though with a heavy heart, to draw the only possible consequence. It would be difficult for us as
a constantly defamed nation to continue to belong to the League of Nations' (Hitler: *Speeches*
(Baynes), ii. 1057).
[5] For the use of unilateral denunciation to revise the Versailles régime for the German waterways see *Survey* for 1937, i. 371–3; Kordt: *Wahn und Wirklichkeit*, p. 79, note 2; Namier: *Europe in
Decay*, p. 233.
[6] *Survey* for 1936, pp. 581–2.   [7] Ibid. p. 384.
[8] Compte rendu de l'entretien de Neurath avec Ciano [25 September 1937] (*Documents secrets*
(Eristov), vol. iii (*Espagne*), no. 2, p. 21). For Mussolini's visit to Germany of 25–29 September
1937, see the *Survey* for 1937, i. 334–5, and 339, note 1.

came from her. Considering his mission to London a failure, and that
England could not be attracted into the anti-Communist orbit, Ribbentrop now arrived in Rome to press for Italy's adhesion to the Anti-
Comintern Pact.[1] But in Hitler's plan for aggression of 5 November 1937,
recorded in the Hossbach Memorandum, there was no question of co-
operation with Italy.

The time for our attack on the Czechs and Austria must be made dependent
on the course of the Anglo-French-Italian war. . . . Nor had the Führer in mind
military agreements with Italy, but wanted, while retaining his own independence of action, to exploit this favorable situation, which would not occur
again, to begin and carry through the campaign against the Czechs.[2]

Germania farà da se. It was the first of the principles upon which the conquest of Czechoslovakia was planned the following summer.

Germany has not committed herself to any military alliance which would
automatically draw Germany into a warlike conflict between foreign powers.
The settlement of the Czech question by my own free decision stands as the
immediate aim in the forefront of my political intentions.[3]

The independence of its stronger partner was a basic characteristic of the
Axis system, and was never so brutally displayed as in the crisis of March
1939. 'The Axis functions only in favour of one of its parts, which tends
to preponderate, and acts entirely on its own initiative with little regard
for us'.[4]

The same principles governed Hitler's handling of his minor jackals.[5]
Poland was skilfully flattered with this role until the time came to trans-
form her into prey. Hungary was controlled more adroitly than Italy.
She was Germany's traditional ally as the subordinate *Herrenvolk* of
Eastern Europe; a weaker Power than Italy, she was less embarrassing
to Germany either as an associate or in an independent part. Hitler

[1] Ciano: *Europa*, pp. 214–16; Eng. version, pp. 139–41; see further below, pp. 360–1.
[2] *I.M.T. Nuremberg*, xxv. 412 (386–PS); *D.Ger.F.P.*, series D, i. 37–38; *Documents* (R.I.I.A.)
for 1939–46, i. 24; cf. *N.C.A.* i. 386 and iii. 304.
[3] Draft for the new directive, 18 June 1938 (*I.M.T. Nuremberg*, xxv. 446 (388–PS, item 14);
D.Ger.F.P., series D, ii. 473; *Documents* (R.I.I.A.) for 1939–46, i. 34; cf. *N.C.A.* iii. 324).
[4] Ciano: *Diario (1939–43)*, 14 March 1939. Again, in the speech to his commanders of 23
May 1939, Hitler laid down the principle: 'Secrecy is the decisive requirement for success. Our
object must be kept secret even from Italy or Japan' (*I.M.T. Nuremberg*, xxxvii. 556 (079–L);
Documents (R.I.I.A.) for 1939–46, i. 277; cf. *N.C.A.* vii. 854). Thus Japan was not informed beforehand of the Soviet-German Pact of 23 August 1939 (see De Witt C. Poole: 'Light on Nazi
Foreign Policy', *Foreign Affairs*, October 1946, pp. 187–8).
[5] They are suggested by an obscure sentence in the draft directive of 18 June 1938, following
Hitler's assertion that he meant to solve the Czech problem by his own free decision, and to
exploit every favourable political opportunity to realize this aim: 'Friends, interested parties, and
enemies could thereby be brought in and other powers remain indifferent, although they could
not be included with absolute certainty in any one of these categories beforehand' (*I.M.T.
Nuremberg*, xxv. 446 (388–PS, item 14); *D.Ger.F.P.*, series D, ii. 473; *Documents* (R.I.I.A.) for
1939–46, i. 34; cf. *N.C.A.* iii. 324)—on its face value a remarkable forecast of Munich.

could always inform her that he did not require her co-operation, but that unless she co-operated she would get none of the pickings. When Imrédy visited Hitler on 23 August 1938 to discuss the attack on Czechoslovakia, he

was most relieved when the Führer stated to him that, in this particular case, he required nothing of Hungary. He himself did not know the precise moment. He who wanted to sit at table must at least help in the kitchen. If Hungary desired General Staff conversations, he had no objections.[1]

Five months later, talking to Csáky, Hitler compared Germany and her associates to a football team.[2] The figure was true of Munich, when Hitler unleashed a plurality of appetites and presided over their concatenation, suffering no disadvantage from those that escaped his immediate control. By March 1939 the system had changed a little; Hungary was bound more closely into the German orbit,[3] but Poland had spun out into the neutral and impotent condition between collaboration and enmity.[4]

The most important and characteristic feature of Hitler's diplomacy was the political penetration and psychological paralysis of other states, and the promotion of revolutionary unrest. In previous ages of European history the dividing-line between war and peace had become blurred and indistinct; it had been especially so during the ascendancy of Philip II, in the Wars of Religion, another period of fanaticism and mass passions. Hitler's policy assumed and exploited this diplomatic twilight. It was a further legacy from the Bolsheviks, who in the infancy of the Soviet Republic had declared 'No war, no peace' against the capitalist world.[5] Undeclared war, 'that brilliant totalitarian German campaign in which propaganda is intertwined with politico-military threats—war is only the continuation of policy—with economic pressure, and the fullest exploitation of the presence of a German minority',[6] was the condition of Europe from the Nazi Revolution onwards, and culminated in the tremendous achievements of 1938–9. Nor was military war, when it succeeded propaganda war, to be announced by the formalities of declaration.[7]

---

[1] German Foreign Ministry minute on conversations between Hitler, Ribbentrop, Imrédy, and Kánya, 23 August 1938 (*I.M.T. Nuremberg*, xxxi. 137 (2796–PS); *D.Ger.F.P.*, series D, ii. 611). The repetition of clichés and figures of speech was a feature of Nazi diplomacy: Hitler saw Imrédy in the afternoon; the same morning Ribbentrop told Kánya that 'he who does not assist departs with empty hands' (ibid. pp. 136 and 610 respectively).

[2] Compte rendu de l'entretien de Hitler avec Czaky, 16 janvier 1939 (*Documents secrets* (Eristov), vol. ii (*Hongrie*), no. 25, p. 79).

[3] See above, pp. 284–5.   [4] See above, pp. 281–2.

[5] Trotsky's declaration of 10 February 1918 at Brest-Litovsk (see J. W. Wheeler-Bennett: *Brest-Litovsk: The Forgotten Peace* (London, Macmillan, 1938), pp. 185–6, 226–7).

[6] Wiskemann: *Undeclared War*, p. 7.

[7] On declaration of war in general see Oppenheim: *International Law*, ii. 234–41. None of Hitler's invasions of other countries was preceded by a declaration of war. He declared war on the United States on 11 December 1941, however, since he was unable to invade her. It may be added that the Soviet invasion of Finland on 30 November 1939 was unaccompanied by a declara-

I well remember one conversation I had with Goebbels in the earliest period of the Nazi Government [said George S. Messersmith in his affidavit for the Nuremberg Tribunal], in which I expressed the opinion that they could never get away with their program in Europe. His reply was 'But you don't know what we can do by creating dissension—without anything being done specifically on our part or which can be laid to our door, we will get these people to fight among themselves and so weaken themselves that they will be an easy prey for us'. I can still recall the cynical manner in which he specifically indicated the 'sore spots' in Austria and in Czechoslovakia and in other countries and on which by insidious means German agents could arouse dissension and get the peoples in the countries themselves disunited.[1]

The creation of revolutionary unrest was Hitler's master technique, the 'new weapon' on which he prided himself. It was the adaptation of propaganda, gangsterism, and insurrection to the conduct of international relations. In 1932 he said: 'How to achieve the moral break-down of the enemy before the war has started—that is the problem that interests me.'[2] The task was facilitated in Eastern Europe by the presence of national and above all German minorities. .

Propaganda warfare must on the one hand intimidate the Czechs by means of threats and wear down their power of resistance; on the other hand it must give the national minorities indications as to how to support our military operations and influence the neutrals in our favor. Economic warfare has the task of employing all available economic resources to hasten the final collapse of the Czechs. The opening of the propaganda and economic campaign may precede military operations in point of time.[3]

Yet it was not in the states of Eastern Europe, with their insecure political and social structures and their German fifth columns, but in France, the greatest state of Western Europe, that Hitler's technique of producing

---

tion of war, though Soviet diplomacy showed a greater degree of formality than German by denouncing the non-aggression treaty with Finland of 1932 on 28 November and severing diplomatic relations with Finland on 29 November 1939.

In Nazi diplomacy the advantages of a surprise attack were not to be marred by the slightest preliminary intimations. Cf. memorandum on 'Timing of the X-Order', 24 August 1938 (*I.M.T. Nuremberg*, xxv. 461 (388–PS, item 17); *N.C.A.* iii. 333): 'Also, the question raised by the Foreign Office as to whether all Germans should be called back in time from prospective enemy territories must in no way lead to the conspicuous departure from Czechoslovakia of any German subjects before the incident. Even a warning of the diplomatic representatives in Prague is impossible before the first air attack, although the consequences could be very grave in the event of their becoming victims of such an attack (e.g. death of representatives of friendly or confirmed neutral powers)'.

[1] Affidavit by George S. Messersmith for the Nuremberg Tribunal (*I.M.T. Nuremberg*, xxx. 298–9 (2385–PS); *N.C.A.* v. 26). Messersmith was United States Consul-General in Berlin from 1930 to 1934, and United States Minister to Austria from 1934 to 1937.

[2] Rauschning: *Hitler Speaks*, p. 19.

[3] Revised draft directive for Operation 'Green' of 20 May 1938 (*I.M.T. Nuremberg*, xxv. 423–4 (388–PS, item 5); *D.Ger.F.P.*, series D, ii. 301; *Documents* (R.I.I.A.) for 1939–46, i. 29; cf. *N.C.A.* iii. 312).

moral breakdown prior to the armed clash produced its most remarkable
result.

There is a note in the first sketch of the plan for the attack on Czechoslovakia which tersely sums up the principal elements in Nazi diplomacy:
'Basic Principle: Create Accomplished Facts so that (*a*) help comes too
late—other powers do not intervene, (*b*) Allies take part (like wolves also
want something out of it), (*c*) State collapse from within. Propaganda:
Directions to Germans. Threats to others.'[1]

Hitler's policy showed the same personal philosophy that is characteristic of the great political adventurers, of Napoleon and Frederick, Wallen-
stein and Cesare Borgia. It was a threefold belief, fusing opposite extremes
—fatalism, the sense of co-operation with destiny; an extreme assertion of
the personal will, the *mystique* of brutal decisions; and a cult of chance, of
those surprise turns to affairs that give the leader the moment for his
inspired interventions, which Cromwell knew as 'providences' or 'dispensa-
tions'.[2] These elements constantly reappear at the basis of Hitler's policy.
He said: 'I go with the assurance of a sleepwalker on the way which
Providence dictates',[3] perhaps the most terrifying sentence he ever uttered,
expressing the menace of a resistless revolutionary tread that was itself
one of the causes of demoralization in his adversaries. But sometimes he
seemed not to embody or follow destiny, but to wrestle with it, as Cromwell
wrestled with God. 'Only he who struggles with destiny can have a good
intuition. In the last years I have experienced many examples of intuition.'[4]
His intuition showed him those critical moments in which the course of
destiny could be seized and diverted. 'Providence has had the last word
and brought me success. On top of that, I had a clear recognition of the
probable course of historical events, and the firm will to make brutal
decisions.'[5] The making of brutal decisions could become intoxicating,

---

[1] 'Bases of the dissertation on "Gruen",' 22 April 1938 (*I.M.T. Nuremberg*, xxv. 418 (388–PS, item 2); *N.C.A.* iii. 308).

[2] Cf. Butterfield: *Napoleon*, pp. 78, 80; also his 'Napoleon and the Study of History', *Time and Tide*, 22 January 1949, pp. 80–82; C. H. Firth: *Oliver Cromwell* (London, Putnam, Heroes of the Nations, 1924), pp. 477–82, and the same author's *The Parallel between the English and American Civil Wars* (Cambridge University Press, 1910), pp. 36–37.

[3] Speech at Munich, 15 March 1936 (Hitler: *Speeches* (Baynes), ii. 1307). Cf. a conversation between Germans in 1934 quoted in Nora Waln's *Reaching for the Stars* (London, Cresset Press, 1939), p. 85: ' "We are all Germans—Germans in trouble—Germans caught in an *Alpdruck*". (An *Alpdruck* is a nightmare in which the dreamer is pressed as with the weight of the Alps). . . "*Wir sind ein schlafwandelndes Volk.*" '

[4] Hitler's speech to his commanders, 23 November 1939 (*I.M.T. Nuremberg*, xxvi. 336 (789–PS); *N.C.A.* iii. 580). Cf. *Mein Kampf*, p. 20; tr. Murphy, p. 31: 'Indem mich die Göttin der Not in ihre Arme nahm und mich oft zu zerbrechen drohte, wuchs der Wille zum Wider-stand, und endlich blieb der Wille Sieger.'

[5] *I.M.T. Nuremberg*, xxvi. 328 (789–PS); *N.C.A.* iii. 572–3. The assertion of the leader's personal will is connected with Hitler's doctrine of the leader's 'responsibility', that is to say, his irresponsibility (his responsibility to nothing except his own intuitions). In the German demo-cracy 'the leader is freely chosen and is obliged to accept full responsibility for all his actions and

almost an end in itself. In the last crisis before the outbreak of general war he said to Henderson that he was 'a man of great decisions. . . . The Führer repeats that he is a man of *ad infinitum* decisions by which he himself is bound':[1] an infinite series of tactical decisions disguised each one at the moment as infinitely binding, the perfect expression of opportunism. It was part of the leader's decisive role that his decisions were satisfying and self-justifying not only as 'brutal' but also as 'irrevocable'. 'The Führer said that his decision was irrevocable. Everyone knew what a decision by the Führer meant.'[2] That one irrevocable decision, like the *rapprochement* with Russia in 1939, could be cancelled by another, like the invasion of Russia in 1941, did not invalidate their irrevocability. Each was tactically justified and emotionally satisfying at the moment. To irrevocable decisions, as to treaties of eternal friendship, the clause *rebus sic stantibus* was always tacitly attached; and Hitler's policy differed from that of Bolshevism only in being too little sophisticated to justify inconsistencies and tergiversations by a theory of dialectics.

Virtù and *fortuna* are opposite sides of the Machiavellian coin. Hitler's policy, having no principle except the extension of German power, was in practice completely opportunist. Heiden describes as the secret of Hitler's political method 'that the vaster the politician's field of action, the more he can expect one difficulty to be superseded and thus solved by another'.[3] It was not until al-'Alamain and Stalingrad that the secret lost its efficacy, the increase of the field of action began to produce diminishing returns, and difficulties, instead of being successive and self-cancelling, became cumulative.[4]

Power becomes opportunist in expression the more it is emancipated from morality; it becomes destructive in character in proportion as it has no purpose save its own expansion. Thus opportunism passes over into nihilism. Hitler's opportunism was carried to an extent that probably was without parallel in previous Western history. Since his aims were limitless, and his methods unqualified by conformity to any exterior standard, his power tended, when checked in its operation, to destroy both itself and the field in which it was exercised. Neither in the war he declared on the

omissions. The problems to be dealt with are not put to the vote of the majority; but they are decided upon by the individual and as a guarantee of responsibility for those decisions he pledges all he has in the world and even his life' (*Mein Kampf*, p. 99; tr. Murphy, p. 88). In other words he is a tyrant who can only be removed by assassination or defeat in war. Cf. ibid. pp. 378–9, 501–2 and 289, 375–7 respectively.

[1] Interview between Hitler and Sir Nevile Henderson, 25 August 1939 (Cmd. 6106, no. 68).
[2] Conference between Hitler and Hácha, 15–16 March 1939 (*I.M.T. Nuremberg*, xxxi. 145 (2798–PS); *Documents* (R.I.I.A.) for 1939–46, i. 55; cf. *N.C.A.* v. 439).
[3] Heiden: *Der Fuehrer*, p. 592; cf. p. 293.
[4] Probably the most dramatic example in Hitler's life of waiting upon chance was in April 1945 when the death of Roosevelt was expected to reverse the fortunes of Germany as the death of the Tsarina Elizabeth reversed Prussian fortunes in 1762. Here the bankrupt gambler's worship of luck reached its nadir of futility. See Trevor-Roper: *Last Days of Hitler*, pp. 109–12.

Weimar Republic nor in that he later declared on Western society was there any possibility of a drawn battle or a compromise peace. 'Every hope of compromise is childish: Victory or defeat! The question is not the fate of a national-socialistic Germany, but who is to dominate Europe in the future.'[1] This determination was enshrined in the myth of the capitulation which, by definition, would never be repeated,[2] whose alternative was conflict continued beyond the bounds of purpose, towards self-destruction and universal destruction. Here was the authentic nihilism of the Third Reich. *Weltmacht oder Niedergang* was its fundamental issue,[3] and its deepest logic drove it to the experience of first one and then the other.

(e) The Combinations of Hitler's Foreign Policy

Hitler divided the international community into three classes—Powers which were the object of conquest for the purpose of acquiring German *Lebensraum*; Powers whose hostility to German expansion would make them inevitable enemies; and Powers which could be cast for the role of temporary allies. The type of the first was Russia; of the second, France; and contrasted types of the third were Italy and Britain. But as German expansion was successively achieved, these three classes would be reduced to two —Powers that would be destroyed altogether and Powers that would be allowed to retain a limited existence as vassals.[4]

When Hitler speaks about Russia in *Mein Kampf* or in his private discourses, a distinction can be observed between Russia considered as a geographical area of potential living-space and Russia considered as a Great Power. He repeatedly asserted that the first must be conquered, but nowhere did he explicitly state that the second must be declared war upon, invaded, and defeated. His basic attitude, perhaps, was that of the German marcher prince of the twelfth century, for whom all the illimitable land to the east was unorganized and stateless, inhabited by primitive and heathen tribes who were beyond the confines of the international community. 'Once again the new German Empire should have set out on

---

[1] Hitler's speech to his commanders, 23 November 1939 (*I.M.T. Nuremberg*, xxvi. 334 (789–PS); *N.C.A.* iii. 578).

[2] 'But even if we could not conquer . . . we should drag half the world into destruction with us, and leave no one to triumph over Germany. There will not be another 1918. We shall not surrender', Hitler in early 1934 (Rauschning: *Hitler Speaks*, p. 125). 'I would, therefore, like to assure all the world that a November 1918 will never be repeated in German history', Hitler's Reichstag speech, 1 September 1939 (Cmd. 6106, no. 106, p. 165; *Documents* (R.I.I.A.) for 1939–46, i. 511). 'I shall stand or fall in this struggle. I shall never survive the defeat of my people. No capitulation to the outside forces, no revolution from the interior forces', Hitler's speech to his commanders, 23 November 1939, *ad fin.* (*I.M.T. Nuremberg*, xxvi. 336 (789–PS); *N.C.A.* iii. 580).

[3] See Trevor-Roper: *Last Days of Hitler*, p. 5. The formula does not appear in *Mein Kampf*; the phrase there is 'Deutschland wird entweder Weltmacht oder überhaupt nicht sein' (p. 742, tr. Murphy, p. 533).   [4] Cf. Rauschning: *Hitler Speaks*, p. 128.

its march along the same road as was formerly trodden by the Teutonic Knights.'[1] But superimposed upon this basic conception was a provisional acknowledgement of the existing international community and of the Soviet Union as a member of it. And on this second level there was the possibility, with regard to Soviet Russia, of an *Interimsethik*.

Hostility to the Soviet Union was, on the face of it, the most marked feature of the new German foreign policy inaugurated by the Third Reich. Within eighteen months it had brought about a diplomatic revolution; the German–Russian entente first concluded at Rapallo in 1922[2] was broken; and Russia was driven into the camp of the Western Powers, into the seat on the Council of the League that Germany herself vacated, and into alliance with France.[3] There was a German council of Ministers on 4 September 1936 to discuss intensification of rearmament; Göring, who was in the chair, declared it to be 'of greater importance than all previous meetings', and based his authority on a memorandum from the Führer which 'starts from the basic thought that the showdown with Russia is inevitable'.[4] There are not many references to aggression against Russia in the Nuremberg documents; this is perhaps the earliest. But the river had eddies and undercurrents beneath its main course, and those which were for a little while to become uppermost in August 1939 were already present.[5] The anti-Communist propaganda and policy of the Third Reich was a double bluff, designed at this time more for the edification of Western opinion than to cover the fulfilment of the basic plans of Nazi expansion. 'The parade of anti-Bolshevik sentiments proved the most potent instrument in sterilising anti-Nazi reactions in the democratic countries of Europe and America.'[6] With the conclusion of the German–Soviet Pact Hitler ascended to the level of the single bluff, and in June 1941 the hour arrived when, all bluff abandoned, he could speak openly.[7]

Russia was the positive pole of Nazi hostility, France the negative.

The future goal of our foreign policy ought not to involve an orientation to the East or the West: but it ought to be an Eastern policy which will have in view the acquisition of such territory as is necessary for our German people. To carry out this policy we need that force which the mortal enemy of our nation, France, now deprives us of by holding us in her grip and pitilessly

---

[1] *Mein Kampf*, p. 154; tr. Murphy, p. 128.

[2] *Survey* for 1920–3, pp. 30–31; cf. the review of German–Russian relations in the *Survey* for 1930, pp. 125–7.

[3] See above, pp. 258 seqq.; *Survey* for 1934, pp. 388–404; *Survey* for 1935, i. 77–82.

[4] Minutes of Cabinet meeting of 4 September 1936 (*I.M.T. Nuremberg*, xxxvi. 489–90 (416-EC); *N.C.A.* vii. 471–2).

[5] See Beloff, i. 94–100, and Heiden: *Der Fuehrer*, pp. 481–2; cf. Rauschning: *Germany's Revolution*, pp. 271–5.   [6] Beloff, i. 94.

[7] 'German people, National-Socialists! oppressed by grave cares, condemned for months to silence, the hour has now arrived when I can speak openly', Hitler's proclamation to the German people on the invasion of Russia, 22 June 1941 (*The Times*, 23 June 1941).

robbing us of our strength. Therefore we must stop at no sacrifice in our effort to destroy the French striving towards hegemony over Europe.[1]

Hitler came to political maturity, and formulated his views on Germany's foreign relations, at a time when France was the preponderant European Power. In January 1923 the French occupied the Ruhr;[2] in November of the same year Hitler made the Munich *putsch*; from April to December 1924 he was in fortress detention in Landsberg, and wrote the first part of *Mein Kampf*. In both its volumes that book reflects the French occupation of the Ruhr.[3]

When the French put their threats into effect [he wrote], and penetrated, at first hesitatingly and cautiously, into the coal-basin of Lower Germany the hour of destiny had struck for Germany. It was a great and decisive moment. If at that moment our people had changed not only their frame of mind but also their conduct the German Ruhr District could have been made for France what Moscow turned out to be for Napoleon.[4]

Hitler's attitude towards France was the converse of the ambiguous mood of defeat in victory with which the French themselves had come out of the First World War.[5] It had three elements: (1) From the defeat of Germany in 1918 until the rearmament of Germany after the National Socialist Revolution, France was the strongest military Power in Europe.[6] She was once again the *Grande Nation* before whom the German experienced traditional inferiority.[7] (2) Nevertheless this renewed ascendancy was temporary, accidental, and in a sense fictitious.[8] Her population and social strength was declining. Dependent for military man-power upon colonial troops, she was 'becoming more and more obsessed with negroid ideas'.[9] (3) Nevertheless France had encircled Germany by her system of eastern

[1] *Mein Kampf*, p. 757; tr. Murphy, p. 542.
[2] *Survey* for 1920–3, pp. 201–2; *Survey* for 1924, pp. 268 seqq.
[3] The French evacuated the Ruhr in July–August 1925 (*Survey* for 1925, ii. 47; supplement, p. 134).   [4] *Mein Kampf*, p. 769; tr. Murphy, pp. 550–1.
[5] See *Survey* for 1920–3, pp. 60–64.
[6] *Mein Kampf*, pp. 695–6; tr. Murphy, p. 503.
[7] Ibid. pp. 705 and 509 respectively. Cf. Ciano's description of Laval at Hitler's headquarters in the Forest of Görlitz on the eastern front in December 1942: 'Laval is a filthy Frenchman—the filthiest of all Frenchmen. To get into the good graces of the German bosses he doesn't hesitate to betray his own compatriots and to defame his own unhappy country. . . . Still, how the Germans respond to the charm of the French! Even of this Frenchman. Except for Hitler, all the others were crowding around trying to talk to him . . . it looked like the entrance of an erstwhile great lord into a circle of new-rich parvenus. Ribbentrop also did his best, but he ended with a gaffe. He reminded Laval that his "eminent compatriot" Napoleon had once been in that same forest. If I am not mistaken, Napoleon was there under entirely different conditions' (Ciano: *Diario (1939–43)*, 19 December 1942).
[8] 'Hitler well understood this: "Today [1923] the disproportion between outward power and inner strength in France is greater than ever. France has only the momentary weakness of Germany to thank for her present position of power"—again the profound insight into the weakness of the enemy to which he has owed so many of his successes' (Heiden: *Der Fuehrer*, p. 135—giving, as always, no source for the quotation from Hitler).
[9] *Mein Kampf*, p. 704; tr. Murphy, p. 508.

alliances, and would in the interests of self-preservation be implacably hostile to German expansion in Eastern Europe. The remark ascribed to Clemenceau, that the trouble with the Germans was that there were twenty millions too many of them, illustrated the anxieties of the French; Nazi propaganda appropriated it to prove their cruelty.[1] The greatness of France depended upon the weakness of Germany, and to keep Germany weak was therefore the main object of French policy. The destruction of France was consequently no less an object of German policy.

As long as the eternal conflict between France and Germany is waged only in the form of a German defence against the French attack, that conflict can never be decided and from century to century Germany will lose one position after another. . . . Only when the Germans have taken all this fully into account will they cease from allowing the national will-to-life to wear itself out in merely passive defence; but they will rally together for a last decisive contest with France. And in this contest the essential objective of the German nation will be fought for. Only then will it be possible to put an end to the eternal Franco-German conflict which has hitherto proved so sterile.

But although this objective is essential in German policy it is still only secondary. 'Of course it is here presumed that Germany sees in the *annihilation* of France nothing more than a means which will make it possible for our people finally to expand in another quarter.'[2]

With the resurgence of Germany the second of these elements in Franco-German relationship overshadowed the first and the third. Hitler's judgement was in nothing more penetrating than in his estimate of French weakness. As early as 1932 he remarked that France would be crushed 'because of the Maginot Line'.[3] In October 1936 he spoke of France to Ciano, 'as do the other Germans—only superficially and with slight contempt. Some abuse of the Jews who govern her and nothing further. In their opinion France has ceased—at least for the moment—to be an active factor in foreign policy.'[4] Perhaps the last official reflection of the old view of an implacably dangerous and hostile France was in the Blomberg directive of 24 June 1937, which considered, as the first of its *Kriegsfälle*, a war on two fronts with the main struggle in the west: 'Presumably hostilities will open with a surprise attack on Germany by the French army and air force and with concerted operations by the French fleet.'[5]

---

[1] See Hitler: *Speeches* (Baynes), ii. 1381, 1592–3.

[2] *Mein Kampf*, pp. 766–7; tr. Murphy, p. 549, where, however, the phrase *die Vernichtung Frankreichs* is flaccidly given as 'the suppression of France'. Cf. *eine Vernichtung der französischen Hegemoniebestrebung in Europa* (*Mein Kampf*, p. 757; tr. Murphy, p. 542; quoted above, p. 350).

[3] F. A. Voigt: 'December in Europe', *The Nineteenth Century*, January 1942, p. 2. Cf. Rauschning: *Hitler Speaks*, p. 124.

[4] Conversation between Hitler and Ciano at Berchtesgaden, 24 October 1936 (Ciano: *Europa*, pp. 98–99; Eng. version, p. 60; *Documents* (R.I.I.A.) for 1939–46, i. 4).

[5] *I.M.T. Nuremberg*, xxxiv. 738 (175–C); *Documents* (R.I.I.A.) for 1939–46, i. 10. The passage is omitted from *N.C.A.* (see vi. 1009).

But in the conference of 5 November 1937 Hitler stated as one of the principal contingencies which German policy must reckon with, that social tensions might bring France to the verge of civil war, making her impotent to aid Czechoslovakia.[1] Though he regarded French proximity to the Ruhr as a matter of particular danger for Germany,[2] in his conferences of 1938 and subsequently Hitler treated France as no longer the chief enemy, but as ancillary to Britain.

Russia and France were the original and lasting objects of Hitler's hostility. Britain and Italy were the original objects of his collaboration. The argument on foreign policy in the second volume of *Mein Kampf* led to the conclusion that 'for a long time yet to come there will be only two Powers in Europe with which it may be possible for Germany to conclude an alliance. These Powers are Great Britain and Italy.'[3] Now, as in antiquity, the penultimate stage in the unification of the world was to be a triumvirate, a triumvirate not of political leaders within an already existing world-state, but of revolutionary Powers.[4] Hitler's British and Italian policies were entwined with one another and must be considered together.

The change in his British policy which occurred about 1937 was the turning-point in the development of National Socialist foreign relations, more important than the sinuosities of his Russian policy, because there the general direction and the ultimate objective were always the same, while with Britain he was compelled, perhaps not without reluctance, to abandon a plan of collaboration and adopt the assumption of enmity. Originally he admired Britain as a ruthless and successful state, showing 'brutality and tenacity in its government', which had built a world-empire and proved its will to survival in the First World War.[5] Expan-

---

[1] Hossbach Memorandum (*I.M.T. Nuremberg*, xxv. 409, 411 (386–PS); *D.Ger.F.P.*, series D, i. 35, 36; *Documents* (R.I.I.A.) for 1939–46, i. 21,23; cf. *N.C.A.* iii. 301 and 303). Cf. minutes of conference between Hitler and Ciano on 12 August 1939: 'Moreover, the Duce was convinced that the present enthusiasm in England and France could not last very long. Soon, particularly in France, the *union sacrée* would once more be replaced by party discord, provided the Axis kept quiet for a time' (*I.M.T. Nuremberg*, xxix. 49 (1871–PS); *Documents* (R.I.I.A.) for 1939–46, i. 178; cf. *N.C.A.* iv. 514).

[2] 'It is imperative for England that the war should be brought as near to the Ruhr basin as possible. French blood will not be spared (West Wall). The possession of the Ruhr basin will determine the duration of our resistance', conference of 23 May 1939 (*I.M.T. Nuremberg*, xxxvii. 550 (079–L); *Documents* (R.I.I.A.) for 1939–46, i. 273; cf. *N.C.A.* vii. 850). Cf. conference of 23 November 1939 (*I.M.T. Nuremberg*, xxvi. 334 (789–PS); *N.C.A.* iii. 578).

[3] *Mein Kampf*, p. 705; tr. Murphy, p. 509.

[4] Cf. Rauschning: *Germany's Revolution*, pp. 237–9.

[5] *Mein Kampf*, p. 366; cf. pp. 158, 746–7; tr. Murphy, pp. 279, 131, 536. There is little evidence that Hitler attached importance, as the politicians and propagandists of the Second Reich sometimes did, to England's claims to be an Aryan or Nordic Power. In the conference of 23 May 1939, when speaking of the tenacity of British opposition to Germany, he said: 'They have the love of adventure and bravery of the Nordic race' (*I.M.T. Nuremberg*, xxxvii. 552 (079–L); *Documents* (R.I.I.A.) for 1939–46, i. 274; cf. *N.C.A.* vii. 851), but this was *en passant* and not an habitual interpretation. Indeed the puritanism and commercial greatness of Britain made her a

sion in Eastern Europe implied association with Britain just as expansion on the oceans had implied conflict with Britain: 'Only by alliance with England was it possible to safeguard the rear of the new German crusade.'[1] Hitler's attitude towards Britain was confirmed by the international situation at the time when he entered politics. He contrasted the British and French attitudes towards defeated Germany: 'England did not want Germany to be a World Power. France desired that there should be no Power called Germany.'[2] Britain was alarmed by the new French military predominance in Europe which culminated in the occupation of the Ruhr,[3] and her policy leaned correspondingly towards Germany.

It was the same with Italy. But Hitler's choice of Italy as a partner had older and more personal roots than his British policy. In his Vienna days before the First World War Italy, like himself, had been 'deutschfreundlich, österreichfeindlich'.[4] She was the natural ally for a *grossdeutsch* policy whose first aim was the partition of Austria-Hungary. The Triple Alliance had been built on the fallacy that the hereditary enemies Italy and Austria could ever fight side by side.[5] The failure of German diplomacy in the First World War had confirmed Hitler's prejudices. He hated the Habsburg Empire, where German interests were increasingly subordinated to those of the Slavs;[6] Germany had fought the war in alliance with the Habsburgs and in support of their interests; Italy had deserted the German alliance in order to fight the Habsburgs; the Habsburg Empire had perished, and Germany had been defeated. 'It was the fantastic idea of a Nibelungen alliance with the decomposed body of the Habsburg State that brought about Germany's ruin.'[7] After the war Italy, like Britain, became a potential ally, alarmed by French preponderance and hostile to the French occupation of the Ruhr.[8] An alliance with Britain and Italy

supreme exponent of the Jewish spirit (cf. Rauschning: *Germany's Revolution*, p. 205). But neither Italy nor Japan was Aryan except in the occult sense of the word. Hitler's political combinations were untouched by racial ideology.

[1] *Mein Kampf*, p. 154; cf. p. 157; tr. Murphy, pp. 128, 130. 'Little German ambitions were directed against England and France, and, being anti-Polish, were by implication friendly to Russia; Greater German ambitions, directed against the Slavs and the Ukraine, were anti-Russian and, indifferent to colonies, were by implication friendly to the western powers' (Taylor: *Course of German History*, p. 218).

[2] *Mein Kampf*, p. 699; tr. Murphy, p. 505.

[3] There is a passage in *Mein Kampf* describing the danger to Britain of French military and air establishments (pp. 699–700; tr. Murphy, p. 505) which echoes Ramsay MacDonald's celebrated letter to Poincaré of 21 February 1924 and was perhaps based upon it (see *The Times*, 3 March 1924; cf. *Survey* for 1924, p. 360).

[4] *Mein Kampf*, p. 162; tr. Murphy, p. 134.

[5] Ibid. pp. 142–3 and 120 respectively; cf. Hitler: *Speeches* (Baynes), i. 55.

[6] *Mein Kampf*, p. 142; tr. Murphy, pp. 119–20.

[7] Ibid. p. 712 and 513 respectively; cf. Hitler: *Speeches* (Baynes), i. 46.

[8] *Mein Kampf*, p. 768; tr. Murphy, p. 550. Hitler exaggerated the Italian reaction to the French occupation of the Ruhr: see *Survey* for 1924, p. 268, and Maxwell H. H. Macartney and Paul Cremona: *Italy's Foreign and Colonial Policy, 1914–37* (London, Oxford University Press, 1938), pp. 145, 154.

would free Germany from the threat of French invasion, and transfer the political initiative out of French hands.[1] Italy, moreover, was the country of the first Fascist state, the first European country to be redeemed from the Jewish world-hydra of freemasonry, Marxism, and internationalism.[2] In 1923 Hitler tried to imitate Mussolini: the Munich *putsch* was to be the beginning of a National Socialist March on Berlin, and it was the failure of the *putsch* that taught him that every national revolutionary movement must adopt its own methods for gaining power.[3]

The Italian alliance was the original illustration of Hitler's doctrine of selectivity in foreign policy, the sacrifice of a lesser objective in order to gain an ally for a greater.[4] Between Italy and Germany lay the Italian annexation of the South Tyrol, and the Italian prohibition of the Anschluss. Hitler contemptuously repudiated a German interest in the South Tyrol; the liberation of 200,000 Germans was not important when 7 million Germans elsewhere were under foreign rule.[5] This renunciation at the beginning of his political career was one of his most striking acts of state-craft. The Austrian problem took fifteen years longer to settle, and when, misjudging its ripeness, he had Dollfuss murdered in July 1934, Mussolini concentrated four army divisions on the Brenner, the only military reply to Hitler's aggressions by any Great Power before the Munich crisis.[6] Göring said in a conversation with Mussolini in January 1937, coming to the Austrian question as the last and most important subject in their political survey: 'In Germany, there is the impression that Austria is being deliberately held in reserve by as yet unidentified forces like a sort of hand grenade which, at the opportune moment, would serve to blow up the Italo-German front'.[7] Nevertheless Hitler remained confident that the destinies of Italy and Germany would ultimately converge. He had hailed Mussolini as the inaugurator of revisionism in Europe;[8] he had perceived that Italy and Germany had the same enemies.[9] In 1938 the renunciation of the South Tyrol brought in its returns, and Hitler fixed the Brenner as the definitive frontier between Italy and Greater Germany.[10]

---

[1] *Mein Kampf*, p. 755; tr. Murphy, p. 541.

[2] Ibid. pp. 521, 721, 774 and 388, 519, 554 respectively.

[3] See G. Ward Price: *I Know these Dictators* (London, Harrap, 1937), p. 79, quoting a remark of Hitler's in 1935. Cf. Hitler: *Speeches* (Baynes), i. 159–60.

[4] *Mein Kampf*, pp. 711, 718–19; tr. Murphy, pp. 512, 517. See above, p. 338.

[5] *Mein Kampf*, pp. 707–11; tr. Murphy, pp. 510–12; Rauschning: *Hitler Speaks*, p. 47; Heiden: *Der Fuehrer*, p. 133.   [6] *Survey* for 1934, p. 475. Cf. above, p. 339, note 3.

[7] Conversation between Mussolini and Göring, 23 January 1937 (Ciano: *Europa*, p. 140; Eng. version, p. 89). In the next sentence Göring went on to identify the unidentified forces: 'In France, in England and in Russia they were probably of the opinion that the Italo-German agreement is not dangerous so long as there exists the possibility of blowing it up by means of Austria.'

[8] Hitler: *Speeches* (Baynes), ii. 1000.   [9] Ibid. p. 1001.

[10] Hitler's letter to Mussolini of 11 March 1938 (*Survey* for 1938, i. 218). In his speech at the banquet in the Palazzo Venezia on 7 May 1938 Hitler defined the inviolable German–Italian frontier more vaguely as the Alps (Wiskemann: *Rome–Berlin Axis*, pp. 108–9).

It was only after the surrender of Italy to the Allies in 1943 and the consequent German occupation of half the peninsula that Germany at last annexed the South Tyrol: a perfidy which more than most of Hitler's perfidies could be defended by the argument *rebus sic stantibus*.[1]

The consistency with which Hitler pursued the Italian alliance was one of the most remarkable features of his political career.[2] Of Italy's military value as an ally he never entertained any opinion, though his conversation lacked the biting animadversions upon Italian prowess that enlivened Bismarck's; for indeed Hitler's conversation lacked wit or pungency of any kind.[3] His opinion of Mussolini is difficult to assess. He would describe Italy as 'driven by necessity and led by a genius',[4] and his attitude seems to have combined a general vindication of the dictatorial status with a degree of patronage for the individual.[5] It was a regard for the forerunner who had become the auxiliary and dependant, a regard therefore that was not endangered by jealousy, and which only in the last years turned into disillusionment about one who showed, in a desperate struggle, that he lacked 'the broad qualities of a world-wide revolutionary and insurrectionist'.[6] In June 1934 when Hitler made his first journey beyond the frontiers of Germany and German Austria in order to meet Mussolini at Venice, the Duce treated him with studied discourtesy.[7] Mussolini was

---

[1] The South Tyrol was incorporated in the Reich on 5 October 1943 (Wiskemann: *Rome–Berlin Axis*, p. 313). [2] Cf. Rauschning: *Germany's Revolution*, p. 226.

[3] For Hitler's opinion of the Italians as soldiers see Rauschning: *Hitler Speaks*, pp. 37, 57. It may be thought that if he had been in the habit of commenting freely upon Italian military qualities, Ciano would have recorded it in his *Diary*, for use in swaying Mussolini against the German alliance.

[4] Hossbach Memorandum (*I.M.T. Nuremberg*, xxv. 407 (386–PS); *D.Ger.F.P.*, series D, i. 33; *Documents* (R.I.I.A.) for 1939–46, i. 20; cf. *N.C.A.* iii. 299).

[5] Cf. Hitler's speech to his commanders on 22 August 1939 (*I.M.T. Nuremberg*, xxvi. 339 (798–PS); *Documents* (R.I.I.A.) for 1939–46, i. 443; cf. *N.C.A.* iii. 582). Some time in 1934 Hitler's opinion of Mussolini was that 'he lacked breadth and boldness of outlook. He could never get beyond the completely misleading prototype of the *Imperium Romanum*' (Rauschning: *Hitler Speaks*, p. 276). When Ciano went to Berchtesgaden for the first time in October 1936 and gave Hitler a special greeting from the Duce, Hitler expressed gratitude to 'the leading statesman in the world, to whom none may even remotely compare himself' (Ciano: *Europa*, p. 93; Eng. version, p. 56). Three years later Hitler had acquired this right, and declared himself 'personally fortunate to live at a time in which, apart from himself, there was one other statesman who would stand out great and unique in history; that he could be this man's friend was for him a matter of great personal satisfaction' (memorandum of conversation between Hitler and Ciano at Obersalzberg, 13 August 1939 (*N.C.A.* viii. 529 (077–TC); *Documents* (R.I.I.A.) for 1939–46, i. 184).

[6] *The Goebbels Diaries*, p. 378. Cf. Wiskemann: *Rome–Berlin Axis*, pp. 312–14.

[7] *Survey* for 1934, p. 468. The most detailed description of Mussolini's behaviour on that occasion is probably in Vernon Bartlett: *This Is My Life* (London, Chatto & Windus, 1937), pp. 269–72. There was another side to the meeting: 'Hitler did not make a good impression on Mussolini; he talked without stopping for an hour, repeating in different words all the arguments from *Mein Kampf*, and only allowing Mussolini a few minutes in which to reply. Mussolini himself told me, when he got back to Rome, that Hitler was simply a gramophone with seven records, and that when he had played them all he began again at the beginning. He said the same thing to everyone who had accompanied him to the interview and the catchword was repeated with

then at the summit of his power, Hitler a beginner entangled in the difficulties he solved in blood at the end of the same month. Hitler never repaid the humiliation.[1] Once Germany had gained the ascendancy, Mussolini's authority in Italy was the pledge of Italian loyalty to the alliance.[2] But already, before that first meeting between them in 1934, Hitler's revolution had trodden out paths of destruction and negation beyond the range of Mussolini's, and at the beginning of that year Hitler had spoken of Fascism

with almost hostile contempt, as a half-measure. 'The Italians can never be trained to become a warlike people, nor has Fascism ever understood the real meaning of the great upheaval of our era. Of course we can make temporary alliances with Italy; but ultimately we National Socialists stand alone, as the only ones who know the secret of these gigantic changes, and therefore as those chosen to set their seal on the coming age.'[3]

In the end what committed Nazi Germany to Fascist Italy was neither their common origins nor their common creed, but Italy's usefulness as an ally too weak to limit Hitler's independence, or to require anything but second place.

Towards Britain Hitler's policy was much more ambivalent. Here, perhaps more than in any other question of his foreign policy, it is difficult to strike the balance between his aims and his tactics, his public statements and his private talk, and to allow for the infinite flexibility which made him ready to experiment with every combination, perceiving the weakness of desirable allies and the strength of potential enemies, and weighing a Power one day as a partner and the next as an object of attack. There is much in the conversations of 1932–4 recorded by Rauschning to show that Hitler emphasized and built upon the quiescence, the pacifism, the arrogance, the degeneration of Britain, planning to dismember her Empire and

admiration all over Rome by his "incense-bearers" ' (Pietro Badoglio: *Italy in the Second World War*, trans. by Muriel Currey (London, Oxford University Press, 1948), p. 2).

[1] The slights subsequently put upon Mussolini by Hitler have the appearance of being not calculated, but due to Hitler's natural lack of breeding. See, for instance, the account of Mussolini's visit to Hitler's headquarters in the Ukraine in August 1941, when Mussolini was treated with neglect and discourtesy, and recouped his injured vanity by asking permission to pilot the Führer's plane, a request which could not be refused (Dino Alfieri: *Due dittatori di fronte* (Milan, Rizzoli, 1948), pp. 220–1).

[2] See Hitler's speeches to his commanders on 22 August 1939 (*I.M.T. Nuremberg*, xxvi. 339 (798-PS); *Documents* (R.I.I.A.) for 1939-46, i. 443; cf. *N.C.A.* iii. 582), and 23 November 1939 (*I.M.T. Nuremberg*, xxvi. 331 (789-PS); *N.C.A.* iii. 575-6).

[3] Rauschning: *Hitler Speaks*, p. 130; cf. p. 276. On the failure of Fascism to extirpate the traditional institutions and ruling classes of Italy see Franz Borkenau: *Totalitarian Enemy* (London, Faber, 1940), pp. 41, 152-3, 229-30. It made a contrast to which Hitler and Mussolini both frequently referred. 'On the whole, there are only three great statesmen in the world: Stalin, myself, and Mussolini. Mussolini, the weakest, has not been able to break either the power of the crown or of the church', the unauthenticated minute of Hitler's speech to his commanders on 22 August 1939 (*N.C.A.* vii. 753 (3-L); cf. Mussolini's own remarks recorded in Ciano: *Diario* (*1939-43*), 27 March 1939 and 25 May 1939.

invade her shores.[1] But the Nazi leaders, and especially Ribbentrop, who survived the Second World War to be interrogated by their captors, said that they and their leader always hoped for an ultimate accommodation with England.[2]

Hitler appeared never to have found it possible to understand why the elephant, Germany, and the whale, England, should not develop their respective realms in mutual understanding and peace. He came back to that idea in the confusion of the very end.[3]

Hitler's rearmament of Germany avoided a great naval programme like that launched by Tirpitz and Bülow a generation earlier, and the extreme of Anglo-German *rapprochement* was marked by the naval agreement of June 1935.[4] This showed, said Doenitz later, that Hitler's policy aimed solely 'to secure Germany's land frontiers against hostile neighbours: his chief potential enemy was Russia, and none of the great naval powers was considered to be among the future opponents of Germany'.[5] Göring took a less limiting view.

The Nazis esteemed the Naval Agreement which Ribbentrop signed with Great Britain in 1935 a splendid achievement, and Ribbentrop's reputation came to a high point. Goering said the Nazis would have settled for less than 35 per cent.; the important thing was that the shackles of Versailles had now been broken and the armament situation could be remade.[6]

But when the Italo-Ethiopian War broke out in the autumn of 1935, Hitler was placed in a dilemma by the conflicting interests of his two prospective allies. Speer had the impression that he was hesitating

whether to side with the Italians or the English. He considered this a fundamental decision. Even then, he emphasised, as he frequently repeated later on, that he was ready to place the Reich with its Wehrmacht at the disposal of the British Empire as a 'guarantee', if England would give him a 'free hand' in the East. He was much preoccupied with this question at the time, especially since he realised the inadequacy of Italy as an ally. He said that it was part of the political testament which Hindenburg had left him . . . that Germany should never again join forces with Italy. In the days of the Abyssinian conflict, therefore, he was distressed by the fact that the situation as he saw it called for Italian co-operation against England.[7]

---

[1] Rauschning: *Hitler Speaks*, pp. 34, 71–72, 82, 123–4, 127–9.

[2] See De Witt C. Poole: 'Light on Nazi Foreign Policy', *Foreign Affairs*, October 1946, pp. 132–3, 145–6, 154.

[3] Ibid. p. 146. Cf. Ribbentrop's letter to Churchill and Eden, undated but after Hitler's death (*N.C.A.* vii. 839–47). [4] *Survey* for 1935, i. 178–93.

[5] Doenitz: 'Essay on the Conduct of the War at Sea', from an official but unpublished source.

[6] De Witt C. Poole, op. cit. p. 133. 'Indeed, Ribbentrop looked good at first to the whole Nazi crowd; they had yet to find out, Göring sneered, that he knew France only through champagne and England through whiskey'.

[7] Examination of Albert Speer, June–July 1945, from an official but unpublished source dated 28 August 1945; cf. *Survey* for 1935, pp. 90–92. Speer's evidence on this point, and at this date,

But at that juncture the next step in securing Germany's position was to remilitarize the Rhineland, a blow at Anglo-French interests, and not the conquest of Austria, a blow at Italian. So having waited through the winter without committing himself, Hitler was able in his own time to seize the Rhineland, which incidentally supplied Mussolini with a welcome diversion for his enemies.[1] Afterwards Hitler drew heavily upon Italian gratitude for having 'stood by Italy when she fought her heroic struggle for her vital rights in Abyssinia'.[2] From then on the policies of Germany and Italy ran parallel; the least that Germany now expected of Italy was benevolent neutrality;[3] and military agreement slowly developed out of political association. The last obstacle was Italian opposition to the An-schluss. When in 1938 Mussolini did not again send divisions to the Bren-ner to protect the independence of Austria, did not stab Germany in the back, Hitler overloaded him with thanks. 'I will never forget it, whatever will happen. If he should ever need any help or be in any danger, he can be convinced that I shall stick to him whatever might happen, even if the whole world were against him.'[4] It was a promise which, five years after-wards, it suited Hitler dramatically to keep.

After 1935 [said Göring in captivity] the decline towards war set in. Ribben-trop made a mess of things in London, and Hitler himself remained unable to understand the English and their way of political thinking. He was tremend-ously surprised by the English reaction to the Rhineland occupation, which on the whole was severe, even though a few in England concurred in what Germany had done.[5]

Ribbentrop was appointed Ambassador in London on 11 August 1936, though he did not take up his post until October. Hans Frank[6] told Mussolini during a visit to Rome in September that 'the despatch of Ribbentrop to London represents the final attempt to make Great Britain understand the needs and position of Germany'.[7] For Germany was already looking to Japan for an alternative third partner in the trium-

is perhaps thin: Hitler does not seem to have been in the habit of discussing policy in terms of 'Hindenburg's political testament' with his intimates.

[1] See *Survey* for 1936, pp. 259–60. For the rumours that Hitler was considering the invasion of Austria as an alternative, see ibid. pp. 261, note, and 402, note 4.

[2] Reichstag speech, 30 January 1939 (Hitler: *Speeches* (Baynes), ii. 1576).

[3] Blomberg directive of 24 June 1937 (*I.M.T. Nuremberg*, xxxiv. 738 (175–C); *Documents* (R.I.I.A.) for 1939–46, i. 10). The passage is omitted from *N.C.A.* (see vi. 1008).

[4] Transcript of telephone conversation between Hitler and Prince Philip of Hesse, 11 March 1938 (*I.M.T. Nuremberg*, xxxi. 369 (2949–PS); *N.C.A.* v. 642; see also Mendelssohn: *Nuremberg Documents*, pp. 161–2). For Hitler's letter to Mussolini of 11 March 1938, see *Survey* for 1938, i. 217–18; for his telegram to Mussolini of 12 March 1938, see ibid. pp. 211, 218.

[5] De Witt C. Poole, loc. cit.

[6] At that time Reichsminister without Portfolio.

[7] Ciano: *Europa*, p. 75; Eng. version, p. 44. For similar German optimism about Britain's attitude at this time, see Ciano's conversation with the German Ambassador Hassell on 30 July 1936 (ibid. pp. 45–46 and 22 respectively).

virate of revolutionary and renovating Powers. Hitler himself expounded his policy in a long talk with Ciano at Berchtesgaden on 24 October 1936.

In his opinion there is no doubt that England will attack Italy or Germany, or both, if she feels that she can do so with impunity or with ease. . . . But—and this is the active part of the policy proposed by the Fuehrer—if England sees the gradual formation of a group of Powers which are willing to make common front with Germany and Italy under the banner of anti-Bolshevism, if England has the feeling that we have a common organised force [in Europe] in the East, the Far East and also in South America, not only will she refrain from fighting against us, but she will seek means of agreement and common ground with this new political system.[1]

But if Britain remained aloof from the Anti-Comintern front, which was about to be inaugurated by the German-Japanese Pact of 25 November 1936,[2] Germany and Italy were rearming much more rapidly than Britain and could check her offensive plans. Ciano concluded that Hitler was still influenced by Ribbentrop's Anglophil optimism, but that Neurath, who detested Ribbentrop, would use any means to wreck the mission to London.[3]

When Göring saw Mussolini in Rome in January 1937 he was not hopeful about an agreement with England: Germany was not interested in the characteristic English offers of economic advantages in return for political concessions,[4] and in Britain the fear of Germany was apparently becoming as strong as the fear of Bolshevism.[5] In May, Neurath told Mussolini that 'English policy is being revealed with increasing clarity—to strike Italy first and then Germany, or even both countries together. British insistence on collective pacts aims at tying the hands of both authoritarian States.'[6] In the Blomberg directive of 24 June 1937, which laid the plans for the annexation of Austria and Czechoslovakia, British neutrality was regarded as likely and of extreme importance to Germany.[7] But from June onwards Anglo-German relations deteriorated rapidly; the speed of British rearmament was accelerating, and the conflict of policies between Britain and France on the one side and Germany and Italy on the other over non-intervention in Spain was acute. Even the sanguine Ribbentrop now confessed failure. On 21 October he arrived in Rome to

---

[1] Ciano: *Europa*, pp. 95–96; Eng. version, p. 58; *Documents* (R.I.I.A.) for 1939–46, i. 2.

[2] *Survey* for 1936, p. 384.

[3] Ciano: *Europa*, p. 98; Eng. version, pp. 59–60; *Documents* (R.I.I.A.) for 1939–46, i. 4. For Neurath's opinion of Ribbentrop's illusions see also Ciano's conversation with Neurath in Berlin, 21 October 1936 (Ciano: *Europa*, p. 88; Eng. version, p. 53).

[4] Ibid. pp. 129 and 82 respectively.

[5] Ibid. pp. 137 and 87 respectively.

[6] Conversation between Mussolini and Neurath, 3 May 1937 (ibid. pp. 177 and 116 respectively).

[7] *I.M.T. Nuremberg*, xxxiv. 744 (175–C); *Documents* (R.I.I.A.) for 1939–46, i. 13; cf. *N.C.A.* vi. 1010.

urge Italy's adherence to the Anti-Comintern Pact, only four weeks after Germany had rejected a similar suggestion from the Italian side.[1] He told Mussolini

how he had wished to learn by means of his mission to London how far England would be willing to go towards meeting Germany's wishes, and towards recognising her vital interests. Today he must frankly admit that his mission failed. Several recent British gestures—among them the Conservative Party vote against the cession of Colonies to Germany—have proved that the interests of the two countries are irreconcilable. At one point he had even thought of attracting England into the sphere of the anti-Communist countries. That has been impossible, since in England the Communist peril is neither felt nor fully understood.[2]

A month later the irreconcilability of German and British interests was confirmed by Halifax's visit to Hitler, when Halifax behaved with firmness.[3] Hitler said that 'means of solving international problems would be very difficult to find until either the political parties became reasonable or methods of government were introduced which gave these parties no longer so much influence on the governments'; Halifax replied that Britain did not propose to change her form of government.[4] Halifax said that the colonial question could only be considered as part of a general settlement, including other interested countries; Hitler replied that he was 'a fanatical enemy of conferences'.[5] No agreement was reached. But already on 6 November 1937, between Ribbentrop's visit to Rome and Halifax's visit to Germany, Italy had signed the protocol by which she acceded to the Anti-Comintern Pact with the status of an original signatory. The Axis and the Anti-Comintern Pact were thus amalgamated; the triumvirate was now formally completed, with Japan in the place of Britain; and at the same moment the Anti-Comintern Pact became a coalition not only against Russia but also against the Western Powers.[6]

[1] See Compte rendu de l'entretien de Neurath avec Ciano [25 September 1937] (*Documents secrets* (Eristov) vol. iii (*Espagne*), no. 2, p. 21); conversations between Ciano and Ribbentrop's Chief Counsellor, Raumer, 20 October 1937, and between Ciano and Ribbentrop, 22 October 1937 (Ciano: *Europa*, pp. 214–15; Eng. version, pp. 139–40; *Documents* (R.I.I.A.) for 1939–46, i. 14). See above, pp. 343–4.

[2] Conversation between Mussolini and Ribbentrop, 22 October 1937 (Ciano: *Europa*, p. 216; Eng. version, pp. 140–1; *Documents* (R.I.I.A.) for 1939–46, i. 15).

[3] *D.Ger.F.P.*, series D, i. 55–71; *Survey* for 1937, i. 337–40. 'When Lord Halifax met Hitler at Berchtesgaden shortly before the Runciman mission to Czechoslovakia, he spoke as a churchgoer —according to the interpreter, Paul Schmidt—and Hitler as a racial propagandist. The meeting broke up in a strained atmosphere' (De Witt C. Poole: 'Light on Nazi Foreign Policy', *Foreign Affairs*, October 1946, p. 140).

[4] *D.Ger.F.P.*, series D, i. 60.   [5] Ibid. pp. 61, 63.

[6] *Survey* for 1937, i. 42–46. In the course of their conference in the Kremlin on the night of 23–24 August 1939 Ribbentrop observed 'that the Anti-Comintern Pact was basically directed not against the Soviet Union but against the Western democracies', and Stalin replied that it 'had in fact frightened principally the City of London and the small British merchants' (*Nazi-Soviet Relations*, p. 75; *Documents* (R.I.I.A.) for 1939–46, i. 406–7). Cf. the opinion of the Irish Foreign

In June 1937 Blomberg had signed his directive on the combined preparations for war of the Wehrmacht;[1] in November 1937 Hitler had expounded to his Commanders-in-Chief his fundamental ideas on German expansion, which were to be looked upon if he died as his last will and testament.[2]

When we asked von Neurath when Hitler definitely decided on war [says Poole] he simply answered, '1937'. We were unsuccessful in obtaining any real enlargement of the answer. The old man, who seemed that day a bit senile but gave this answer very firmly, may have been enunciating a general or intuitive impression. Perhaps he remembered that in 1937 Hitler remarked to a high official in the Ministry of Agriculture (as we had already heard from others) that he would have to have 'a little war in the west and a big war in the east'.[3]

1937 was the watershed of Hitler's plans for war, and it also marked the point at which he finally assumed British hostility and bracketed Britain with France. This already appeared at the conference of 5 November 1937: 'German policy had to reckon with two hate-inspired antagonists, Britain and France, to whom a German colossus in the center of Europe was a thorn in the flesh.'[4] On 2 January 1938 Ribbentrop addressed a highly confidential memorandum to Hitler in which he raised 'the fateful question'—'Will Germany and England eventually be forced to drift into separate camps and will they march against each other one day?'[5] Ribbentrop now tended to think so, and proposed therefore the formation of a militarily superior coalition with Italy and Japan. The British plan for a colonial settlement, put forward by Henderson in March 1938, awoke no response in Hitler; he said that he simply wanted the restoration of Germany's former colonies, that he was in no hurry, and that 'one could wait quietly for 4, 6, 8, or 10 years'.[6] The British offer came three years

Ministry as given in the despatch from the German Minister in Dublin of 17 November 1937 (*D.Ger.F.P.*, series D, i. 50–52).

[1] *I.M.T.* Nuremberg, xxxiv. 732 seqq. (175–C); *Documents* (R.I.I.A.) for 1939–46, i. 7 seqq.; cf. *N.C.A.* vi. 1006 seqq.

[2] Hossbach Memorandum (*I.M.T.* Nuremberg, xxv. 402 seqq. (386–PS); *D.Ger.F.P.*, series D, i. 29 seqq.; *Documents* (R.I.I.A.) for 1939–46, i. 16 seqq.; cf. *N.C.A.* iii. 295 seqq.).

[3] De Witt C. Poole, op. cit. pp. 138–9. The *Kriegsfälle* considered in the Blomberg directive were 'war on two fronts with the emphasis in the west (Operation "Red")' and 'war on two fronts with the emphasis in the south-east (Operation "Green")' (*I.M.T.* Nuremberg, xxxiv. 736 (175–C); *Documents* (R.I.I.A.) for 1939–46, i. 9; cf. *N.C.A.* vi. 1008).

[4] Hossbach Memorandum (*I.M.T.* Nuremberg, xxv. 406 (386–PS); *D.Ger.F.P.*, series D, i. 32; *Documents* (R.I.I.A.) for 1939–46, i. 19; cf. *N.C.A.* iii. 298).

[5] *I.M.T.* Nuremberg, xxxix. 91–92 (075–TC); *N.C.A.* viii. 513.

[6] Conversation between Hitler and Henderson, 3 March 1938 (*D.Ger.F.P.*, series D, i. 247; Kordt; *Wahn und Wirklichkeit*, pp. 88–89; see also above, pp. 164–5). Hitler, intending eastern continental conquests, used the colonial issue as a diversion; this does not mean that he would not have been prepared to accept overseas colonies in order to increase the diversion. The possibility is seen in his statement at the conference of 5 November 1937 that Britain and France 'saw in the establishment of German military bases overseas a threat to their own communications, a safe-

too late. It was an irony of the policy of appeasement that it was inaugurated after Hitler had abandoned hope of an alliance with Britain and had
transferred her to his list of potential objects of war.[1]

Hitler's conquests of 1938 were calculatedly made in the interval of
Anglo-French weakness when Anglo-French intervention was improbable.
It was after Munich that German plans shifted from a defensive war in the
west, resistance against intervention, to an offensive war against the west,
the forestalling of future intervention. Munich itself had been an example
of intervention and Hitler resented it. He had been balked of a local war
against the Czechs; the glory, even for Germans, had gone less to him who
had conquered than to Chamberlain who had surrendered; and a few
days later Schacht overheard him saying to his SS entourage: 'That fellow
has spoiled my entry into Prague'.[2] Moreover, Chamberlain had returned from Munich not to slacken Britain's warlike preparations but to
intensify them, and Hitler's anger at the undependability of appeasement
was seen in his public attacks on the British Opposition.[3]

Germany's action in Czechoslovakia [said Raeder in his history of German
naval policy] certainly caused a deterioration in English opinion and the
Führer began to feel English political resistance everywhere, and believed he
could see in England the soul of resistance to Germany throughout the world. . . .
In the six-month period commencing with the winter of 1938 the Führer considered the abrogation of the Naval Treaty of 1935. The behaviour of England

guarding of German commerce, and, as a consequence, a strengthening of Germany's position in
Europe' (Hossbach Memorandum: *I.M.T. Nuremberg*, xxv. 406 (386–PS); *D.Ger.F.P.*, series D,
i. 32; *Documents* (R.I.I.A.) for 1939–46, i. 19; cf. *N.C.A.* iii. 298).

[1] Chamberlain succeeded Baldwin as Prime Minister on 28 May 1937; Eden resigned the
Foreign Secretaryship on 20 February 1938.

[2] *I.M.T. Nuremberg*, xii. 531: Wheeler-Bennett: *Munich*, pp. 331–2 (inaccurately stating that
the remark was made by Hitler to Schacht); Keith Feiling: *The Life of Neville Chamberlain* [referred
to hereafter as Feiling: *Chamberlain*] (London, Macmillan, 1947), p. 390. Hitler's resentment
about Munich was shown a year later in the first speech to his commanders on 22 August 1939,
when, according to the more colourful but less reliable account, he said: 'The occasion is favourable now as it has never been. I have only one fear and that is that Chamberlain or such another
dirty swine [*Schweinhund*] comes to me with propositions or a change of mind. He will be thrown
downstairs. And even if I must personally kick him in the belly before the eyes of all the photographers' (*N.A.C.* vii. 754; cf. *I.M.T. Nuremberg*, xxvi. 343 (798–PS); *Documents* (R.I.I.A.)
for 1939–46, i. 446; *N.C.A.* iii. 585). In his Reichstag speech of 28 April 1939 Hitler imputed his
own disappointment to the democracies: 'If the cry of "*Never another Munich*" is raised in the
world to-day, this simply confirms the fact that the peaceful solution of the problem appeared to
be the most fatal thing that ever happened in the eyes of those warmongers. They are sorry no
blood was shed—not their blood, of course: for these agitators are, of course, never to be found
where shots are being fired, but only where money is being made! No, it is the blood of many
nameless soldiers' (Hitler: *Speeches* (Baynes), ii. 1617; cf. *Documents* (R.I.I.A.) for 1939–46, i.
214, where the full text of the speech is given): another example of the projection discussed above,
pp. 321–2.

[3] 'It only needs that in England, instead of Chamberlain, Mr. Duff Cooper or Mr. Eden or
Mr. Churchill should come to power, and then we know quite well that it would be the aim of
these men immediately to begin a new World War', Hitler, speech at Saarbrücken, 9 October
1938 (Speeches (*Baynes*), ii. 1535. Cf. ibid. 1532, 1546–9, 1555–9).

in the autumn crisis of 1938 had made a strong impression upon him, and he was firmly convinced that England at that time was prevented from seriously considering war only because of the weak position of its aerial preparedness and as a consequence was forced to seek an agreement.[1]

When Ribbentrop went to Rome in October 1938 to press for the tripartite military pact, he told Mussolini that Hitler was convinced that they must count on inevitable war with the Western democracies within a few years.[2] Japan was now in full control of China, and 'the immediate objective of the Japanese is not Russia but Great Britain'.[3] Germany's military position was excellent; Czechoslovakia was liquidated; with Poland Germany intended to continue a policy of friendship;[4] Yugoslavia, Rumania, and Hungary wanted to tighten their links with the Axis; Russia was weak and would remain so many years; 'all our energies can be directed against the Western Democracies'.[5] On 16 December Weizsäcker gave his friend Hassell a gloomy account of the 'Ribbentrop or Hitler policy', which he said was clearly heading for war:

They only hesitate whether to turn directly against England, while securing Poland's neutrality, or first against the East in order to liquidate the German-Polish and the Ukrainian question—and naturally the Memel business, though in Hitler's opinion this calls for no armed force but merely a registered letter to Kaunas.[6]

Thus already before 15 March 1939 German policy was becoming pre-occupied with the great question, East or West, which was to be its central theme in the month following the fall of Prague: the choice of initiative that rests with a Power possessing interior lines, the obverse of encirclement.

The annexation of Bohemia and Moravia was a clearing-up operation, completing the work of Munich, and leaving Hitler poised above Europe, able to turn this way or that at will.[7] Some in Germany saw that this last stroke differed in kind from its predecessors and would rally foreign opinion

[1] Erich Raeder: 'The Development of German Naval Policy, 1933–1939' (*N.C.A.* viii. 688, 700, with the writer's emendations).

[2] Conversation between Mussolini and Ribbentrop, 28 October 1938 (Ciano: *Europa*, p. 373; Eng. version, p. 242; *Documents* (R.I.I.A.) for 1939–46, i. 146).

[3] Ciano: *Europa*, p. 374; Eng. version, p. 243. Ribbentrop must have known this was false: the Japanese War Office at this stage conceived of the tripartite alliance as directed primarily against Russia (Records of the Proceedings of the International Military Tribunal for the Far East (in mimeograph), pp. 33718–19, and pp. 34116–19).

[4] Four days earlier in a conversation with Lipski at Berchtesgaden Ribbentrop had opened the Polish question by proposing a general settlement of the issues between Poland and Germany, including the incorporation of Danzig in the Reich (see above, p. 281).

[5] Ciano: *Europa*, p. 375; Eng. version, p. 244; *Documents* (R.I.I.A.) for 1939–46, i. 148.

[6] Ulrich von Hassell: *Vom andern Deutschland* (Zürich, Atlantis, 1946), p. 37.

[7] 'Then followed the establishment of the Protectorate and therewith the basis for the conquest of Poland was laid, but I was not clear at that time whether I should advance first against the east and then against the west or vice versa', Hitler's speech to his commanders, 23 November 1939 (*I.M.T. Nuremberg*, xxvi. 329 (789–PS); *Documents* for 1939–46, i. 529; cf. *N.C.A.* iii. 573).

against the Reich; Weizsäcker said to Hassell on 28 March: 'It is clear that with the Czech affair the *Niedergang* has begun.'[1] But, as always, the Germans of this kind were scattered and impotent. On his triumphant entry into the Hradčany Hitler turned to Dietrich, the Reich Press Chief, and asked: 'Have you news of military movements in France, in the Soviet Union or of a mobilisation of the English fleet?' The answer was no. Hitler turned exultantly to his entourage and said: 'I knew it! In a fortnight nobody will speak of it any more.'[2] Formal protests he had anticipated and meant to ignore. A day or two later an official of the Propaganda Ministry in Berlin declared to a Frenchman: 'We have before us so many open doors, so many possibilities, that we no longer know which way to turn or what direction to take.'[3]

[1] Hassell, op. cit. p. 55. On 22 March Hassell wrote in his diary: 'This is the first case of blatant hybris, of the overstepping of all bounds and all decency' (ibid. p. 52).

[2] Kordt: *Wahn und Wirklichkeit*, p. 146.

[3] Despatch from Coulondre, 19 March 1939 (*Livre jaune français*, no. 80).

PART II

COMPARATIVE STRENGTH OF THE GREAT POWERS

By H. C. Hillmann

(i) Introduction

THE central problem of world politics during the inter-war years was to bridge the gap between the interests of the world as a whole and the ambitions and interests of individual states. This cleavage between the requirements of international co-operation and the willingness of nations to meet them was widening in the 1930s. In the political sphere the League of Nations, newly formed after the First World War, provided the institutional framework for such co-operation. But the League itself lacked the whole-hearted support of many powerful states. The United States refused to join it. The U.S.S.R. was deliberately excluded and by 1934, when she came in, international relations had already gravely deteriorated with the beginning of Japanese aggression in China and with the rise to power of 'revisionist' National Socialists in Germany. In the sphere of international economic relations the great depression of 1930 destroyed the multilateral framework for world-wide currency and trade co-operation, a framework which was never rebuilt. It was inevitable that, in this atmosphere of political and economic nationalism, each government should have aimed at strengthening, or at least at preserving, the relative power and position of its own state in the world.

As power in international relations meant, in the last instance, the ability of a state to wage war, attention will in this section be focused on economic strength as one of the major determinants of national power. The components of economic strength are manifold, ranging from the reserves of man-power, the food and raw material resources, and the industrial capacities within a country, to its ability to assure the supply of vast quantities of goods and materials from sources scattered throughout the world. But, like any other kind of potential strength, it would count only if it were exerted. Whether the resources at the disposal of a country represented actual strength depended largely upon their effective mobilization and upon the particular use to which they were put. Thus countries which managed to maintain a vigorous and fully employed economy tended to command more influence in external relations than those which possessed potential strength but were unable to exploit it. On the other hand, the general economic strength of countries, turned to account for raising the living standards of their people, did not necessarily mean the type of strength which was effective in foreign relations. Indeed, in the short run, general economic strength was almost irrelevant. What mattered in diplomacy was the immediately available supply of arms and munitions and of men trained to use them. However, in the long run the division between peace industries and war industries had little meaning. Given the time for transferring resources, all industry could be utilized in the production of things essential for the prosecution of war, so that the proposition that general economic strength was in the long run the equivalent of war potential[1] was so near to the whole truth as to justify a broad comparative analysis of the economic strength of the Great Powers in the years preceding the rape of Czechoslovakia by Germany in March 1939.

(ii) Geopolitical Position of the Great Powers

No wholly satisfactory definition of a Great Power has yet been found.[2] There are, however, certain essential prerequisites for that status: these are that a country should possess a well developed manufacturing industry, a relatively large, educated, and skilled population, an efficient transport organization, and a people with a strong sense of national unity combined with a military or naval tradition. Seven countries fell within this definition. They were the United States, the U.S.S.R., Greater Germany (including Austria and the Sudeten territories), the United Kingdom, France, Japan, and Italy. These nation-states each had before 1939 a larger manufacturing capacity than any country outside their ranks. The closest 'runner-up' to Italy, the least industrialized of the seven Great Powers, was Canada.[3] On the wider criterion of a country's total production of goods (including agriculture, construction, and mining) and of services, the finding was, as before, that each of the above seven countries

---

[1] C. J. Hitch: *America's Economic Strength* (London, Oxford University Press, 1941), p. 60.

[2] 'A Great Power may be defined as a political force exerting an effect co-extensive with the widest range of the society in which it operates' (Toynbee: *World after the Peace Conference*, p. 4); or '. . . the states which accounted themselves to be Great Powers and which tacitly gave notice, in assuming this status, that they believed themselves to be capable of holding their own, even in a lawless world, by the strength of their own right arm' (*Survey* for 1935, ii. 79); or, distinguishing between various shades of Powers, 'a Great Power is a Power with general interests, and with such strength that it can attempt to advance or protect those interests in every sphere. . . . A Great Power is one that can afford to take on any other Power whatever in single combat; and a Dominant Power is one that can take on a combination of any other Powers' (Martin Wight: *Power Politics* (London, Royal Institute of International Affairs, 1946), p. 19). See also below, p. 508, note 1.

[3] League of Nations: Economic, Financial and Transit Department: *Industrialization and Foreign Trade* (League of Nations [printed at Princeton, U.S.A.], 1945), p. 13.

had a higher real national income than any other country in the world with two exceptions, China and British India.[1] But neither China nor British India possessed manufacturing capacity equal to that of Japan or Italy; nor had they a comparable transport organization or system of education. These characteristic features of a Great Power were, however, in the making in many backward nations. It was, indeed, one of the basic purposes of Japan's aggression to hinder the modernization and industrialization in China which seemed such a potential threat to the power of Japan. Her war aimed at destroying China's newly won political unity; in short, at preventing China from becoming a Great Power;[2] or, to put it more mildly, at creating conditions under which Japan herself would enjoy the advantages of developing China's resources.

(a) THE GEOGRAPHICAL BASE AND ITS RESOURCES

In the world as it was in 1939, the geographical location of a country not only conditioned its suitability for different kinds of economic activity but also determined that country's closeness to other centres of national power and to international lines of communication. This was the base from which a country moved towards Great Power status and by which its foreign policy was permanently influenced. Other factors governing foreign policy were the ever changing aspirations, beliefs, and fears of governments and peoples. Germans and Italians used the real or imaginary threat of Bolshevism to seek favour for their own régimes, and at the same time derided 'decadent capitalism in the pluto-democracies' in order to undermine confidence and unity among peoples with a view to furthering their own aggressive policies. On the other hand, the Russians skilfully invoked the ideological weapon of world revolution whenever they deemed it necessary to strengthen their basically defensive strategy. Moreover, these ideological taps could be turned off as quickly as they were turned on. Political and ideological warfare thus accentuated potential conflicts. But it was stark material power, based on the geopolitical position and strength of a country, which ultimately determined whether that country could risk war to achieve its aspirations. What were the conditions that accounted for the Great Power status of the seven countries? In what relationship did they stand to each other and to the rest of the world?

Of the globe's surface only 29 per cent. consists of land masses, two-thirds of which are concentrated in the northern hemisphere: in the latitudes 60 to 70 degrees north of the Equator the globe is nearly encircled

[1] See Colin Clark: *The Conditions of Economic Progress* (London, Macmillan, 1940), pp. 40–56. Of course, aggregate real income was only partially an index of economic strength. More significant was real income per head and in particular its distribution between consumption, investment, and military expenditure. These questions will be considered below, pp. 455 seqq.

[2] See 'Two Years of War in China', *Economist*, 8 July 1939, p. 58.

by land, while in the latitudes 40 to 70 degrees to the south it is almost completely encircled by sea.[1] The location of a state in latitude broadly determines its climate; but the uneven distribution of land and its topography influence winds and ocean currents and thus modify both temperatures and seasons within the tropical, temperate, and polar zones. Climate together with soil sets limits to the range of permissible vegetation, while geological structures serve to indicate at what levels resources of water, coal, petroleum, and metals may be found.[2]

The metropolitan territories of the seven Great Powers were all located on the two continents of the northern hemisphere, six of them in Eurasia and one in North America. The Eurasian continent covered 40 per cent. of the globe's land masses and was inhabited by nearly 80 per cent. of the world's population.[3] It was two and a half times the area of the North American continent and contained nearly ten times the latter's population. The western and eastern outposts of Eurasia were the British Isles and the Japanese Isles. The European part of this continent, within boundaries marked in the north by the polar cap, in the west by the Atlantic Ocean, and in the east by the Ural and the Caucasus Mountains, was about $8\frac{1}{2}$ per cent. of the total land surface and contained one-quarter of the world's population. The territories of four of the Great Powers were situated within Europe; a fifth, the U.S.S.R., was partly within it, and her population was almost wholly included. The very concentration of highly developed industrial states in Europe, and the fact that this small region was shared by more states than any other continent in the world, had continually made Europe the centre of world affairs, and the area where recorded conflicts had most often originated. The extraordinary multiplicity of states in Europe,[4] and the consequent territorial insecurity of each, formed the political framework which had both stimulated European economic development and set limits to its maximum expansion.

In the past the United Kingdom, because of her insular position and her predominance in world sea-power, had enjoyed greater territorial security and more freedom of movement on the oceans of the world than any other European state. This security had enabled her to encourage commercial, financial, and manufacturing developments and to reduce the

---

[1] R. P. Beckinsale: *Land, Air, and Ocean* (London, Duckworth, 1943), p. 29.

[2] See W. Gordon East: *The Geography Behind History* (London, Macmillan, 1938), p. 17.

[3] The total land masses were estimated at 132·7 million square kilometres, which in 1939 were inhabited by 2,170 million persons (League of Nations: *Statistical Year Book, 1941/42* (Geneva, 1943), pp. 12–20).

[4] 'Although it occupies only about one-twelfth of the inhabited land surface of the earth, Europe contained in 1938 rather more than two-fifths of its independent states' (W. Gordon East: *The Political Division of Europe*, an inaugural lecture, Birkbeck College, University of London, 18 May 1948, p. 14).

relative importance of agriculture as a field of employment to an extent unequalled by any other nation.[1]

France was no less well placed for development as a sea-power; but being flanked on her eastern frontiers by Germany, a country with a skilled and disciplined population larger than her own, and on the west by the United Kingdom, in a strong competitive position, she was neither willing nor able to make herself so extensively dependent on foreign sources of food supply as was the United Kingdom.

Greater Germany, though but slightly larger in area, had nearly twice the population of France. Wholly surrounded by smaller continental states, none of which in isolation could threaten her effectively, she was none the less unwilling to push industrialization to a point which would deprive her of a safe basis for food production within her own territory.[2] Being a latecomer as a Great Power, and less favourably placed than the United Kingdom for access to the sea routes of the world, she had to weigh up the advantages and disadvantages of seeking conflict with the United Kingdom in an attempt to establish sea-power parity or of strengthening her position as a continental Power.

Italy's weakness in relation to the other three European Powers was, on the one hand, her extreme shortage of coal resources, which were essential for the smooth operation of an industrial system, and, on the other, her situation in the Mediterranean Sea, of which she controlled none of the entrance gates.

The U.S.S.R. was the largest state in the world. Her territory in Europe and Asia was four times the area of the whole of Europe (without the U.S.S.R.), but her access to ocean routes was severely limited. Within her territory, however, all climatic zones and geological structures were to be found, indicative of food and mineral resources which would suffice to sustain the most rapid and extensive industrialization.[3]

Japan's status as a Great Power was of recent origin. It was only after the First World War that she began to surpass countries like Belgium, Canada, and even Italy in manufacturing capacity. In common with the United Kingdom, she reaped certain advantages for a relatively undisturbed political development from her insular position. But even more important for her industrial development was her remoteness from the

---

[1] A. J. Brown: *Industrialization and Trade* (London, Royal Institute of International Affairs, 1943), p. 12.

[2] In a statement to the Reichstag on 10 December 1891 the German Chancellor Caprivi said: 'I regard it as the better policy that Germany should rely upon its own agriculture than that it should trust to the uncertain calculation of help from a third party in the event of war. It is my unshakable conviction that in a future war the feeding of the army and the country may play an absolutely decisive part' (W. H. Dawson: *The Evolution of Modern Germany*, revised edition (London, T. Fisher Unwin, 1919), p. 249.

[3] Alfred Osterheld: *Wirtschaftsraum Europa* (Oldenburg/Berlin, Gerhard Stalling Verlagsbuchhandlung, 1943), pp. 99–106.

great centres of power in Europe. Although she had reason to expect conflicts with more mature European and American Powers, whose commercial and political spheres of interest extended to the Far East, direct clashes with potential Powers like China were more imminent in the phase of her industrial growth. Apart from her vast timber resources and some coal and copper, Japan possessed few basic industrial resources, but in South-East Asia and particularly China these resources were available, and Japan feared, rightly or wrongly, that her accelerated industrial expansion might be impaired should the awakened national movements in the Asiatic continent, covering more than half the world's population, mould the peoples into strong nation-states which would then perhaps lay prior claim to the resources found within their frontiers.

The geopolitical position of the United States was remarkable in more than one respect. Located in North America, the United States was of continental dimensions, with all that this involved as regards variety and wealth of natural resources. In the north the United States bordered on Canada, a country which, though larger in territory, had only one-tenth of her population, and in the south on Mexico with about one-seventh of her population. With oceans to the east and west, the United States enjoyed greater territorial security than any of the European Powers and had direct access to the main trading arteries of the world. Moreover, in analogy to the division of the globe into the Northern and Southern Hemispheres by the Equator, an arbitrary political division had been drawn which divided the world vertically into unequal halves.[1] The Western Hemisphere, between 180 degrees and 30 degrees western longitude, included both the continents of North America and of South America. Since South America contained many states, each—and in the aggregate—numerically and materially weaker than the United States, there was little prospect that they would threaten the territorial security of the 'colossus of the north' except, possibly, by becoming tools of some other Power outside the limits of their hemisphere. Moreover, while acquiescing in the political spheres of interest which European Powers (i.e. Britain, France, Holland, and Denmark) had established in the New World, the United States as early as 1823 (the year in which the Monroe Doctrine was formulated) had indicated to them that she would not tolerate the use of these possessions as bases for further territorial expansion in the Western Hemisphere, and in 1898 took forcible steps to destroy what remained of the old Spanish Empire.

The two remaining continents of Oceania (i.e. Australia, New Zealand, and the South Sea Islands) and of Africa were large in area but weak in population. Lying in the Southern Hemisphere, Oceania, the last continent to be discovered, was twice as far from Western Europe as from Eastern Asia or Western America. It was situated at the earth's farthest periphery

[1] Rudolf Westermann: 'Zankapfel Island', *Zeitschrift für Geopolitik*, 1944, no. 2.

as seen from Europe—indeed for a long time right off the main trade routes; its development was very slow until it had become of sufficient importance in itself to be the terminus of regular trade routes to and from the Old and New Worlds. In relation to its potential natural resources, Oceania was very thinly populated.

The continent of Africa, which in 1938 supported a population roughly equal to that of the United States, and occupied an area four times as great, was largely situated within the tropical zone. In prevailing technological conditions it had been less suited for settlement for white men, and therefore economic development and the growth of states had been impeded. In its extreme southern and north-eastern regions, where water and mineral resources were to be found, where the soil was tolerably productive, and climatic conditions were more moderate, states had developed. But their growth was originally due to the key positions which they occupied on the main trade arteries of the world rather than to their inherent suitability for development. In general, however, the political weakness of this continent and, above all, its close proximity to the densely populated states of Europe had made Africa a colonizing area for the expansionist nation-states of Europe.

In Table I (which appears opposite) are summarized some of the basic industrial and agricultural resources potentially available in the metropolitan territories of the Great Powers in relation to their population. It illustrates (columns 8 to 12) the relative weakness in 1939 of Italy and Japan, as compared with the U.S.S.R. and the United States, in their endowment with exploitable resources. Moreover, during the last three decades the pressure of a rapidly growing population (column 2) on these resources greatly increased in Italy and in Japan. This pressure was bound to prove disastrous to human standards of life unless it could be relieved through industrialization not requiring these particular kinds of basic resources, through large-scale emigration, or through the acquisition of resources in foreign territories. After the middle of the 1920s the second outlet was largely blocked, and both Japan and Italy, encouraging industrial developments within the limits open to them, became, in concert with Germany, the most outspoken exponents of territorial expansion.

The fact that, next to Japan, the United States had the largest average annual growth of population in these three decades was due to a number of factors. The average rate of growth in each of the seven countries under consideration reflected not only natural fertility and gains from immigration, but also the offsetting of losses incurred in the First World War and in the famines of the post-war period. The United States had not suffered loss of life through war and famines comparable to that suffered by the U.S.S.R., Germany, and France, and, at least until the middle 1920s, she had bolstered up the high rate of births by accepting great numbers

TABLE I. *Demographic and Raw Material Resources in 1939*

	(a) Population data							(b) Natural resources per head				
	Population							Reserves of				
Country	Total in millions	Average annual growth 1910/40 in %	Under 15 years of age	Over 59/64 years of age	Potential working population Age 15 to 59/64 (in millions)	Military man-power males Age 20 to 34 (in millions)	Number of persons per square kilometre	Coal/Lignite (coal equivalent)	Iron-ore (metal content)	Arable land	Pasture	Timber-producing area
			in % of 1					tons per head		acres per head		
	1	2	3	4	5	6	7	8	9	10	11	12
U.S.S.R. . .	170	0·48	36·2	5·4	100·0	21·6	8	6,300	94	2·35	5·70	6·65
United States .	132	1·18	25·0	8·6	87·4	16·2	17	17,000	48	2·66	4·40	(3·98)
Greater Germany .	80	0·51	24·1	10·3	52·1	9·4	136	3,810	14	0·68	0·30	0·44
Japan . .	73	1·30	36·7	6·1	41·8	8·3	191	227	0·4	0·23	0·11	(0·79)
United Kingdom .	47	0·43	22·4	10·8	31·6	5·7	195	3,700	38	0·28	0·40	(0·07)
Italy . .	44	0·71	30·0	9·2	26·7	5·2	143	4	0·4	0·85	0·34	(0·33)
France . .	42	0·04	23·7	12·5	26·8	4·3	76	207	77	1·62	0·65	(0·63)

NOTE: Unless otherwise stated statistics are based on data given by the League of Nations: *Statistical Year-Book, 1941/42,* pp. 13 to 30; Column 3 gives the percentage to total population of all boys and girls under 15 years of age, that is, inclusive age groups 0 to 14; Column 4 gives the percentage to total population of all women over 59, that is, inclusive of those aged 60, plus all men over 64, that is, inclusive of those aged 65; Column 5 gives the number of persons arbitrarily defined as the potential working population, consisting of women aged 15–59 inclusive, and of men aged 15–64 inclusive; Column 6 gives the number of men only aged 20 to 34 inclusive, arbitrarily defined as the military man-power; Column 7 was arrived at by dividing the number of persons in the total population by the square kilometres of the geographical base.

All data for the U.S.S.R. refer to January 1939; as regards Columns 3 to 6, see Frank Lorimer: *The Population of the Soviet Union: History and Prospects* (Geneva, League of Nations, 1946), p. 143; all United States data refer to April 1940; all data for Greater Germany refer to May 1939; as the published figures for Column 3 include age-groups under 14 only, the writer estimates the number of persons in the missing age-group 14 to consist of 2·5 per cent. of the total German population; all data for Japan refer to October 1940 and are based on official data accumulated by the United States Strategic Bombing Survey in *The Japanese Wartime Standard of Living and Utilization of Manpower* (Washington, U.S.G.P.O., 1947); Column 4 for that country is the writer's estimate based on Bombing Survey and on League data, while Column 6 is based on Bombing Survey Table RR plus the item of 'armed forces' from Table PP; all data for the United Kingdom refer to estimates for England and Wales of June 1937, for Scotland of June 1938, and for Northern Ireland of February 1937; all data for Italy refer to December 1939; all data for France refer to January 1940; Column 2, which relates average annual growth to average 'mean' population, is taken from *Statistisches Jahrbuch für das Deutsche Reich, 1941/42* (Berlin, Statistisches Reichsamt, 1942), p. 174; Columns 8 to 11 are, with some adjustments, taken from A. J. Brown: *Industrialization and Trade,* pp. 18–21; bracketed figures in Column 12 mean total timber produced and others mean timber produced for use'.

of immigrants. But in the 1930s immigration had ceased and births had declined, with the result that the average annual growth over the three decades tended to fall. In the U.S.S.R., on the other hand, the average annual growth tended to increase because the high rate of natural fertility year after year began to outweigh the devastating losses incurred in the First World War and in the post-war famines.

This reversal of the relative rate of growth of population as between the United States and the U.S.S.R. during the 1930s was reflected in the corresponding changes in the demographic composition of their populations (Table I, column 3).

The United States in 1939 belonged, like Germany, France, and the United Kingdom, to the group of countries with a small proportion of very young people in their total population, while the U.S.S.R. ranked, like Japan and Italy, among countries with a young and vigorous population. The Malthusian devil of a growing population pressing on limited potential resources, as in Italy and Japan, was no problem in the U.S.S.R. Indeed, the development of her vast internal resources was hampered, despite the rapid rate of increase in population, by (among other handicaps) a shortage of man-power.[1]

The Malthusian devil was tightly chained up in France. France was the only Great Power whose population had been almost stationary for three decades. She had never recovered from the enormous blood-letting which she had suffered in the First World War.[2] But, though France was freed from the menace of a rapidly increasing population, which in relation to her potential resources would have made itself felt sooner than in the United States or the U.S.S.R. though later than in Italy or Japan, she was exposed to other dangers which, under certain conditions of economic policy, would arise from the stagnation of the population.[3] One consequence was that France was saddled with a larger quota of old people in her total population than her contemporaries had to carry (Table I, column 4) and that she occupied, among the Great Powers, the lowest

[1] This shortage of man-power was evident from the fact that in the U.S.S.R. married women were expected to engage in full-time employment. As Colin Clark has rightly observed, the familiar piece of Soviet propaganda about mothers being given a short rest from their employment immediately before and after the birth of a child had served to divert attention from the much more significant fact that the employment of mothers of families in factories was regarded as the normal thing in the U.S.S.R. (Colin Clark: 'Soviet Military Potential', *Soundings*, No. 6, September 1947, p. 40).

[2] See also above, pp. 166–9.

[3] As the late Lord Keynes pointed out, unless, under conditions of stationary population, policies were pursued to increase consumption by a more equal distribution of incomes or to stimulate changes in technique which would involve a much larger use of capital in relation to output, by forcing down the rate of interest, there was a great danger of a chronic tendency towards under-employment of resources which must in the end sap and destroy that form of society (J. M. Keynes: 'Some Economic Consequences of a Declining Population', *Eugenics Review*, April 1937, p. 13).

place in total population (column 1), in potential working population (column 5) and, above all, in military man-power (column 6).

Ignoring, for the time being, other factors to be discussed later, it was roughly true, therefore, that the unequal endowment of the seven Powers with natural resources did set different limits to their industrialization. In relation to the discrepancies of the growth of population in recent decades, a position had been reached by 1939 where, under the abnormal post-war conditions, the material resources of metropolitan Japan in the Far East, of Italy, and, to a very much smaller extent, of Germany in Europe, would not in the long run sustain as progressive a development as would those of the United States or the U.S.S.R. But the very liability of population pressure, which the rulers of Japan, Italy, and Germany deliberately increased, became an asset in the shape of a vigorous and youthful population, comprising a reservoir of men of military age, which might prove immensely useful in the carrying-out of ambitious policies of territorial aggression.

(b) ECONOMIC TRANSFORMATION THROUGH WORLD TRADE

The world economic structure of 1939 and the relationship between nations in different continents were largely forged by the development of world trade. It was the function of external trade to support the process of industrialization which had been initiated in the countries of Western Europe and Eastern America. Under the initiative of private enterprise, the growth of capitalist manufacturing centres gradually transformed the economic structures of the countries facing the North Atlantic. Agriculture declined relatively as a field of employment, and, as agricultural activity was pushed back, the demand for agricultural produce and for industrial raw materials from outlying areas increased.[1] The farther the West European and East American manufacturing centres pushed their industrialization and the smaller their agricultural and mineral resources within their own national territories came to be, the greater became their dependence upon more distant areas. In the course of this internal development and of the consequent external trade expansion, more and more 'open frontiers' were crossed and the densely populated areas of Asia, as well as the thinly populated territories on the American

---

[1] The over-all import gap for each of the seven Powers in the 1930s was roughly as follows: (a) the size of the agricultural sector in each country can be illustrated by the percentage of the total occupied population engaged in agriculture (see *Statistisches Jahrbuch, 1941/42*, pp. 39–40). For the U.S.S.R. the estimate is based on the relation of all persons dependent on agriculture to total population (see League of Nations: Economic, Financial and Transit Department: *Industrialization and Foreign Trade*, p. 28); (b) efficiency in agriculture, depending on differences in soil fertility, livestock quality, and mechanization, can be illustrated by rough estimates of the 'net output per male person in agriculture' (see Clark: *Conditions of Economic Progress*, table facing p. 244); (c) the volume of home-produced supplies is determined by the number of persons in agriculture and by the net output per head. And the level of consumption of food and agricultural

continent and in Oceania, were opened up.[1] The world economic pyramid broadened its base as it increased its height. But this centrifugal expansion of trade from the original manufacturing countries created favourable conditions for the establishment of new industrial centres on the periphery of the Europocentric world. Thus the expansion and intensification of world trade gave impetus to industrialization and to changes in the economic structures of more distant lands. As more countries were drawn into the network of international trade and were industrialized, they began to specialize in those lines of production in which their comparative cost advantages were greatest. Broadly speaking the existence of comparative differences in efficiency meant that each country benefited from international trade, and under this system of free international exchange the economic interests of the world as a whole and of the individual states participating in it tended to move in the same direction.

There were, however, forces at work which caused distribution of the benefits to be derived from the system to be unequal. Only some of these forces can be mentioned here. Countries which had been drawn into the system of world trade at a late phase and were relying only on the initiative of private enterprise did not find it easy to establish those industries in which they seemed to possess certain 'natural advantages'. The perfection of transport, credit, and marketing organizations by the older countries in the course of their development enabled them to attract newer industries for which their 'natural advantages' were by no means the greatest. As Pigou has observed, in a free-trade system an old-established industrial Power had a thousand advantages over new competitors, and if things were allowed to take their 'natural' course the development of the 'potential' powers of younger states might be delayed for an indefinite period.[2]

raw materials in relation to home-produced supplies determines the over-all import gap (see ibid. p. 249). This threefold relationship was roughly as follows:

Countries	(a) Total occupied population in agriculture (1934–5)	(b) Net output per employed male in agriculture (1934–5) in dollars	(c) Import gap (−) Export surplus (+) in per cent. of current consumption
	%	$	%
United Kingdom . .	7	500	−66
United States . . .	20	696	−7
Germany (Old Reich). .	27	516	−16
France	35	415	−17
Italy	48	?	?
Japan	50	120	−7
U.S.S.R.	54	112	+3

[1] See Frank H. Knight: *Economic Theory and Nationalism*, in *The Ethics of Competition and other Essays* (London, Allen & Unwin, 1936), p. 290.

[2] A. C. Pigou: *Protective and Preferential Import Duties* (London, Macmillan, 1906, reprinted 1935), p. 13.

In these circumstances a strong case could be made out for protection in the interests of national economies.

In some young countries, where private enterprise was unable, owing to lack of capital, to develop potentially productive resources, the state, instead of merely keeping order for private enterprise, took upon itself entrepreneurial functions. Japan was a case in point. It has been said of the Japanese spinning industry in the late nineteenth century that 'the Government was the tireless innovator in this industry. . . . In providing capital, the state dominated the scene; directly or indirectly it financed practically all the conspicuous expansion at the time.'[1] In general, if larger production, stimulated by the state, led ultimately to higher efficiency, then no harm was done to international specialization and co-operation. But it was difficult to distinguish whether production for productivity's sake or for mere prestige and military purposes was the dominating motive. In many European countries industries were developed during the inter-war period which could not have stood the test of open international competition. Both the United States and Japan were able in the 1930s to produce automobiles, typewriters, and chemicals, and in the lower price ranges these were of comparable quality. But, despite the very much lower wage-rates in Japan, it required a high degree of protection to keep the corresponding American products from completely dominating the Japanese market.[2]

Here was a dilemma. Infant industries had a habit, even when they had grown in size, of relying upon supports which had assisted them at birth. But why should such protection have been continued, and why should older countries, in turn, also have resorted to protection, since surely it was not in their interests to maintain inefficiency?

The explanation must be sought in terms of changes in the economic and social climate within each of these countries. As industries developed, the individual firms of which they consisted were exposed, in a competitive struggle, to grave risks. There was no security for a man owning and running a plant, save that of using his wits. To stay in the market, and not be pushed out of business, he had to keep abreast of the latest technical developments. He had to keep up his firm's efficiency by keeping down its costs. Only those could stay the course who constantly created new conditions for survival; those who fell behind were destroyed. This process of 'creative destruction' was the essential fact about capitalism.[3] Business

[1] Shigeto Tsuru: 'Economic Fluctuations in Japan 1868–1893', *Review of Economic Statistics*, November 1941, p. 179.

[2] Jacob Viner: *The Prospects for Foreign Trade in the Post-war World*, an address before the Manchester Statistical Society, 19 June 1946 (*Transactions of the Manchester Statistical Society, session 1945–46*).

[3] For a most penetrating analysis of economic progress under a régime of private enterprise, see Joseph A. Schumpeter: *Capitalism, Socialism and Democracy* (London, Allen & Unwin, 1943), especially chapters vii and viii.

first and foremost was a doctrine from which no one could escape. In a hard world, weakness was out of place. A cool assessment of realities and a striving for efficiency, no matter how and at what cost of human effort it was achieved, were the only road to survival. In the course of this struggle all social cohesion was undermined and the reward of those who did survive was the accumulation of wealth.

Both the rewards and the risks of business increased as markets widened. As more countries were drawn into the network of world trade, great fortunes were made in the old industrial countries in the beginning; but the emphasis shifted from profit to risk as soon as the 'industrializing' countries had advanced far enough themselves in some branches of activity to challenge the older industrial countries in their home markets. As competition in the more mature industrial countries grew fiercer, the desire for security and for keeping the risks down to a minimum became more intense in the minds of entrepreneurs who saw no hope of expanding their business to the size of a single monopoly. This led to the formation of trade associations and cartels among business men with a view to regulating and controlling competition sectionally, i.e. industry by industry.

Vested interests became organized, where such organizations had not existed from the very outset. These monopolistic combinations did not necessarily preserve obsolescent plants indefinitely nor, for that matter, did they freeze the *status quo* and prevent progress; their purpose was rather to achieve 'orderly retreat' and 'orderly advance' respectively. It was one thing to attain sectional social cohesion within a country, and quite another to eliminate all adverse repercussions on internal stability where these originated in external competition. Provided, however, that these monopolistic combinations were powerful enough, it was not very difficult for them to convince governments that protection for the purpose of securing orderly adjustments and progress in a world of rapid change was socially desirable.

This transformation of social climate which accompanied industrialization, the growth of monopolistic organizations, and protection, varied from country to country. It was symptomatic of this change that, while during the greater part of the nineteenth century world trade had increased *pari passu* with the expansion of world industrial production, the rate of increase of trade fell behind that of production in the first three decades of the twentieth century, and stagnated or even declined in the fourth.[1]

It was most disconcerting, however, that, although the volume of world trade in 1938 exceeded that of 1913 by about 13 per cent., the trade of the mature industrial countries had decreased absolutely. For instance, the volume of British and German exports had fallen by two-fifths, that of French exports by one-fifth, while that of United States exports had

[1] The volume of industrial production and the volume of world trade (in both cases values are

risen by one-fifth.[1] But even the United States experienced, in the period between 1929 and 1936–8, a contraction in the volume of her exports by one-quarter. More startling still, the whole fall in the volume of Britain's exports could be accounted for by the halving of her trade with the industrialized and industrializing countries of the world, i.e. the industrialized parts of Europe, the United States, Japan, the U.S.S.R., and India. Her exports to three rapidly industrializing countries, i.e. India, Japan, and the U.S.S.R., had actually fallen by two-thirds.[2] Another way of expressing the change in the position of the older Powers in world trade would be to register the fact that Europe's share had declined from 66 per cent. in 1900 to 52 per cent. in 1937.

Was it not true, then, that the export of machinery by the older industrial countries to the rest of the world was damaging the exporting countries' own long-term interests? Was there not some justification for Spengler's indictment that, by communicating their techniques to the Asiatics, the Western peoples were betraying their own culture and paving the way for an inevitable decline of the Western World?

On balance, the evidence was insufficient to sustain these charges; nevertheless, the experience of the mature industrial countries was not reassuring. It is doubtful whether they could have stemmed the tide, for in the past they had derived great benefits from international specialization and they had no means of protecting their original technical monopoly.

Some contemporary observers commented that, with the elimination of the open frontiers towards the Western World's periphery, and with the filling-up of the open spaces, man's struggle with physical nature was bound to be superseded by a political struggle between competing human communities.[3] This conclusion was unduly pessimistic. What became apparent, however, was that the industrially old-established countries,

expressed in 1913 prices) and the ratio of trade to production developed in per cent. (1913 = 100) as follows:

Year	(a) Industrial production	(b) World trade	Ratio (b) to (a)
1900	60·0*	62·0	103·3
1913	100·0	100·0	100·0
1929	139·0	129·9	93·5
1937	152·0	122·7	80·9
1938	144·0	112·8	78·3

Source: Hardy & Co., GmbH., *Wirtschaftsausblick und Kapitalanlage* (Berlin, April 1939), p. 8.
* Rolf Wagenführ: 'Die Industriewirtschaft — Entwicklungstendenzen der deutschen und internationalen Industrieproduktion 1860 bis 1932' [referred to hereafter as Wagenführ: *Industriewirtschaft*] in *Institut für Konjunkturforschung: Vierteljahrsheft 1933, Sonderheft 31*, p. 69.
[1] Based on quantum indices quoted by W. Arthur Lewis: *Economic Survey 1919/1939* (London, Allen & Unwin, 1949), p. 122. For Germany see Hardy & Co., GmbH., loc. cit.
[2] G. D. A. Macdougall: 'Britain's Foreign Trade Problem', *Economic Journal*, March 1947, p. 81.   [3] See Knight: *Ethics of Competition*, p. 291.

confronted, as they now were, by a cessation of the once continual opening of new markets, by a slowing-down or stagnation of the growth of population at home, and by the threat of an intensification of foreign competition in their internal and external markets, would be forced to submit to very painful adjustments in their industries. One of their expedients for easing these adjustments was protection.

As it turned out, however, the tariffs imposed with a view to facilitating orderly adjustment often deteriorated, like those created with a view to protecting infant industries, into instruments for the protection of inefficiency. In some countries the political purpose of promoting economic nationalism was frankly proclaimed. Long before the complete collapse of international codes of behaviour in 1930, Germany, as well as certain other industrial countries, attempted to preserve a broad agricultural base for her economy by taking a number of deliberate measures, ranging from tariffs to subsidies. In conjunction with the rise in productivity in many areas of primary production, this policy of the industrial countries led to over-production and to a severe slump in agricultural prices. Although between 1927 and 1933 the terms of trade moved violently in favour of Britain, Germany, the United States, and France, only Britain, the country with the smallest agricultural sector in her economy, reaped the full benefit of this advantage. Where vested interests were strong, as they were in Germany, no attempt was made to dismantle in any orderly fashion the artificial supports by which agriculture was shored up. On the contrary, for political reasons, agriculture received more aid, despite the fact that the favourable trend of the terms of trade in these industrial countries was partially maintained until 1937.[1] Obviously economic nationalism of this kind had a depressing effect on world trade.

The terms of trade in the 1930s had moved against countries producing primary products, including the U.S.S.R., Italy, and Japan, so that they now had every possible incentive to foster the industrialization of their own countries. In the U.S.S.R., but not in Japan, industrialization was accompanied by a fall in the volume of imports. In this case again, because of the deliberate planning of industrialization for self-sufficiency, it was inevitable that the gap between world production and world trade should widen.

Apart, however, from the political roots of economic nationalism, there were genuine technological roots as well. This is to say that, although much of the blame for the relative decline of world trade must be attributed to the influence of monopolistic 'pressure groups' on statesmen, it was too simple a judgement to dismiss economic nationalism as being based solely on irrational delusions.[2] The argument in favour of world-wide

[1] Clark: *Conditions of Economic Progress*, p. 456.
[2] Adolph Lowe: *The Study of World Affairs*, an address delivered at the Institute of World Affairs 17 November 1943 (New York, Oxford University Press, 1944), pp. 12–13.

specialization and exchange rested on the fact that physical resources, human skill, and reserves of capital had been very unevenly distributed. But, in the course of technical progress and industrialization just these conditions, which had been the making of advantageous trade, were changing. For instance, technical knowledge that had been acquired in the United States or Germany soon became available in the U.S.S.R. or Japan. The discrepancies in the skill of workers as between different countries tended to be ironed out *pari passu* with the spread of industrialization and education. Moreover, as a result of modern electro-technical and chemical processes, some of the natural raw materials, in the shape of either living or fossilized products of organic life, that were scarce or were only to be found in a few localities, came to be more or less successfully replaced by new synthetic materials artificially produced out of more abundant and more accessible inorganic substances, and this again reduced the dependence of one region upon another. Taking all these factors together, we can diagnose a general tendency for the range of comparative differences in costs of manufacture to narrow, and for the economic gain obtainable from international specialization and exchange to decrease.

In so far as this bona fide technological factor in economic nationalism was operative, it would partly explain the stagnation of world trade in the 1930s, but two other considerations were of greater significance. On the one hand, there was a desire in most countries, but especially in Germany and the U.S.S.R., to achieve a high degree of economic self-sufficiency for political reasons, and, on the other, it was a fact that such Great Powers as the United States and France were in this decade quite unable to achieve and to maintain a high level of internal activity. This inability reduced their customary demand for imports and consequently had a depressing effect on the volume of world trade.

It is impossible, therefore, to assess in precise terms the relative strength of the various forces making for economic nationalism. It is clear, however, that the breakdown in 1930 of international relations in the domains of trade and currency aggravated the traditional method of national protection through tariffs by adding new impediments to trade of a much more restrictive kind, such as quotas and exchange control, and that from then onwards there was no longer any semblance of a harmony between the economic interests of the world as a whole and those of individual states.

(c) Spheres of Interest and Communications

One result of the collapse of multilateralism and of the ensuing unilateral actions by individual states in the 1930s was to accentuate the importance of the geopolitical position of the Great Powers and of their political and commercial spheres of interest. The political spheres, constituted by territories which politically were linked to, or controlled by, Great Powers, were very unevenly divided among them.

Indeed, of the seven Powers, neither the U.S.S.R. nor Greater Germany —after the *de facto* recognition by others of the forced incorporation in the Reich of Austria and the Sudetenland—possessed direct political control over territories outside their national frontiers. In essence the United States also fell within the same category, since the economic resources of her dependencies in Asia and in Oceania were small in relation to those found in the continental United States.

The political dependencies of Italy had one thing in common with those of Japan, namely, that they lay in close proximity to their base, the metropolitan country. But there the similarity ended. The large Italian possessions in Africa were relatively poor in resources and had a population which was only one-fifth of that of Italy.[1] In contrast the bulk of Japan's possessions and occupied territories in Asia—ignoring her economically insignificant mandates in Oceania—were very rich in resources, with a population as large as that of the metropolitan country.

The territorial possessions of France, like the British Commonwealth and Empire, stretched over all the continents. The aggregate population of the French dependencies equalled that of the Japanese, and both in French-controlled Africa and Asia rare resources were to be found complementary to those located in France itself. But despite the world-wide diffusion of French political spheres of interest, the French Empire was a much more compact geographical unit than was the British Commonwealth in virtue of the concentration in Africa of France's largest and economically most important possessions.

With nearly a quarter of the globe's territory and population belonging to it, the British Commonwealth and Empire was the world's most extensive political unit. Excluding from it the five Dominions and India, the population of the British colonies and mandated territories was larger than that of the Japanese dependencies, and its distribution between the continents was very much like that of the French colonial populations. In variety of material resources the British colonies surpassed the French Empire. These resources were greatly enhanced through the attachment of India to the Empire. Yet the real strength lay neither in the colonies nor in India but in the five Dominions. Their aggregate population was less than two-thirds that of the United Kingdom, but the potential, and in many respects actual, resources exceeded those found in the British Isles. Moreover, the Dominions, like India, possessed considerable manufacturing capacity and, as long as these juridically independent states decided to act in unison with the mother country, the British Commonwealth and

[1] Even reckoning in Albania, which was virtually an Italian dependency, and the Dodecanese, the position remained much the same.

Empire had at its disposal greater real resources than Germany or the U.S.S.R.

In contrast with the inequality of political spheres of interest, each Great Power was engaged in foreign trade and therefore each had spheres of commercial interest. The political and commercial spheres did not necessarily coincide, but the political allegiance of one country to another would tend to strengthen their mutual commercial exchange and, vice versa, commercial penetration of one country by another might be a first step in the direction of its political conquest. Both these tendencies were particularly pronounced in the 1930s, since the collapse of international trade and currency relations meant, in effect, freedom of action for each government. The Great Powers were now enabled, as they had never been before, to influence directly the geographical distribution of trade. Consequently Italy, Japan, France, and the United Kingdom intensified their commercial relations with countries included in their spheres of direct political control, while Germany strengthened her commodity exchange with, and thus her indirect political influence over, small countries contiguous to herself.[1]

Probably the most compelling force behind this widespread endeavour to make commercial and political spheres conterminous was the desire to increase the security of urgently needed external supplies and the safety of the routes of communication. Nobody could ignore the vital importance of communications, upon whose safety rested the value to a Great Power of its external spheres of interest. Since considerations of security and safety were meaningless without the anticipation of war, it was indeed inevitable that the commercial and transport policies pursued by most Powers in the 1930s should have been a faithful reflection of the shadow that war casts before it.

In view of the close interdependence between trade and communications, what were the size and the character of the transport tasks that confronted the Great Powers? Both were directly determined by the total weight of goods entering into the external trade of each, by their geographical distribution, and by their composition (i.e. bulkiness, &c.). This may be illustrated from the position in 1938. In that year the weight of goods in world trade, passing from countries of origin to countries of ultimate destination, was estimated at about 420 million metric tons.[2] The seven

---

[1] See also below, pp. 481-8.

[2] In contrast with value data, which are available but completely misleading for the assessment of the transport requirements of world trade, statistics of weights are not readily available. Fortunately a fairly reliable estimate of world trade by weight is possible for 1938. According to an analysis by weight of 52 basic foods and raw materials, their aggregate amounted to about 354 million tons (see League of Nations: Economic Intelligence Service: *The Network of World Trade* (Geneva [printed at Princeton, U.S.A.], 1942), p. 71). Not covered were rye, barley, oats, potatoes, cocoa, cheese, eggs, and wine. These weighed 9 million metric tons (see *Statistisches Jahrbuch, 1939-40*, International Section, pp. 185-9). Add 13·5 million cubic metres of timber for mining, wood for pulp, and railway sleepers, as well as 31·7 million cubic metres for all round and sawn woods (see League of Nations: Economic Intelligence Service: *International Trade in Certain Raw Materials and Foodstuff by Countries of Origin and Consumption, 1938* (Geneva,

Powers imported for their own use (i.e. excluding mere transit) about 250 million tons or 59 per cent. of the world total by weight,[1] as compared with 49 per cent. by value. Germany and the United Kingdom together absorbed more than one-quarter of the world's physical quantities of imports. The quite extraordinary dependence of the United Kingdom on external supplies was brought out by the fact that per hundred of population she imported 123 tons, the United States 28 tons, and the U.S.S.R. less than 1 ton.[2]

But the Great Powers were not only exporters of valuable finished manufactures, comparatively light in weight, but also suppliers of substantial quantities of foodstuffs and industrial raw materials. Indeed, they exported 210 million tons, or 50 per cent., of the world total by weight as compared with 48 per cent. by value. The United States was the world's largest exporter.[3] Apart from grain, fruits, vegetables, cotton, and tobacco, all accounting for much weight, there were in particular two industrial materials, namely, petrol products and coal, which together furnished more than half the tonnage of American exports. Just as four-fifths of the exports of the United Kingdom consisted of coal, so, too, the largest share of the

1939), p. 125). Cubic metres were converted into metric tons at the ratio of 1 cubic metre = 0·6 tons. Thus total timber trade amounted to 28 million tons. Other materials and finished manufactures entering into world trade were estimated at about 30 million tons. The latter estimate is approximate only and was based on the ratio by weight of finished manufactures to raw materials for countries which published such data.

[1] These aggregates are based on estimated weights of imports and exports, excluding transit, for each Power. General data for all countries are to be found in League of Nations: *International Trade Statistics 1938* (Geneva, 1939), and also in *Statistisches Jahrbuch, 1939/40*, pp. 121–5. These have been supplemented by specific data for the United Kingdom, see Board of Trade: *Accounts Relating to the Import Trade and the Re-export Trade of the United Kingdom for each of the years 1938 to 1944* (London, H.M.S.O., 1945); for the United States, see U.S. Department of Commerce: *Statistical Abstract of the United States, 1940* (Washington, U.S.G.P.O., 1941), pp. 458 and 482; for Germany, excluding Austria and Sudetenland, see *Statistisches Jahrbuch, 1939/40*, p. 266; for France, see Institut National de la Statistique: *Annuaire statistique 1940–45* (Paris, Imprimerie Nationale, 1946), pp. 215 and 224; for Italy, see Istituto Centrale di Statistica del Regno d'Italia: *Annuario statistico italiano, anno 1938–XVI* (Rome, Istituto Poligrafico dello Stato G.C., 1938), pp. 104 and 119; for Japan, see The Yokohama Chamber of Commerce and Industry: *The Annual Statistical Report 1940* (Yokohama, 1940), pp. 130 seqq., and also United States Tariff Commission: *Japanese Trade Studies* (Washington, U.S.G.P.O., September 1945).

[2] American cargo tons, Japanese kokus, piculs, &c., have been converted into metric tons. Hence the imports by weight are comparable; see (a) below. These total imports have been divided by population figures as given in Table 1 on page 373 in order to determine imported tons per hundred of population; see (b) below. There is one exception: Germany here means the Old Reich only, with a population of 69 millions:

	United Kingdom	Germany	France	U.S.A.	Italy	Japan	U.S.S.R.	Seven Powers
(a) Imports in million tons	58	62	47	37	25	19·5	1·3	250
(b) Imports per 100 persons in tons	123	90	112	28	57	27	0·8	43

[3] Exports in 1938 in million metric tons were: for the United States about 61, for Germany 52·5, for the United Kingdom 47, for France 27, for the U.S.S.R. 13, for Italy 5·6, and for Japan 4, giving a total for the seven Great Powers of about 210 million tons.

export weights of Germany and France represented coal and iron ore respectively. The U.S.S.R.'s share in the weight of world exports, consisting mainly of timber and grain, was more than that of Italy and Japan taken together, although her share in the value was only 1 per cent. as compared with Italy's and Japan's aggregate share of 8 per cent.

There were marked differences between the Powers not only in regard to the weight of their external trade, but also in regard to the geographical distribution. With the one exception of the United Kingdom, the predominant commercial sphere of interest of each Power lay within the continental region of which it was a part. Thus distinguishing between a threefold regional grouping of (1) Europe–Africa, (2) the Western Hemisphere, and (3) Asia–Oceania, it was of significance both for politics and communications that in 1938 Germany, France, and Italy each took more than 85 per cent. of her physical supplies from the Europe–Africa group. Similarly the United States took 70 per cent. from countries of the Western Hemisphere.[1] Again Japan imported by weight about 60 per cent. of her supplies from countries in Asia–Oceania. The United Kingdom alone fell completely out of this setting. She imported more from countries of the Western Hemisphere (46 per cent.) than from those of the Europe–Africa group (42 per cent.).

This regional distribution of trade in relation to the geopolitical position of each Power had a very direct bearing on both the size and the character of their respective transport tasks. Owing to the insular position of the United Kingdom and of Japan on the western and eastern flanks of the Eurasian continent their trade was wholly sea-borne. The trade of other Powers was partly sea-borne and partly land-borne (i.e. carried by rail, road, canal, and to a small extent by air). The share of land-borne trade was highest for Germany, followed by France and Italy.[2]

[1] As compared with only about 33 per cent. by value.

[2] In 1938 the sea-borne and land-borne share of total trade, including transit goods, was distributed for each country as follows:

	Imports		Exports	
	Land-borne	Sea-borne	Land-borne	Sea-borne
	(in million metric tons)			
United Kingdom . .	..	61·0	..	50·0
Germany . . .	39·9	33·4	45·4	15·7
France	17·3	33·5	23·4	7·4
Italy	5·0	20·0	1·8	3·8
U.S.S.R. . . .	0·2	1·1	1·7	11·3
United States . . .	4·0	33·4	5·0	56·4
Japan	..	19·5	..	4·0
Seven Powers . .	66·4	202·0	77·3	149·0

(*Note*: The United States distribution has been estimated on the basis of the distribution by value, data for which were published down to 1935.)

The transport task arising out of the land-borne share of external trade of Germany, France, Italy, and the U.S.S.R. merged directly with the internal transport task;[1] that is to say, imports from contiguous countries were normally taken over at the national frontiers by the various transport agencies operating within each national territory. These four countries— especially Germany and the U.S.S.R.—made considerable progress in perfecting their internal rail, road, and canal systems during the inter-war period. But, despite these improvements, the railways in the U.S.S.R., for instance, were more overburdened in 1938 than they had been in 1928. The extension in railway lines and the addition to the stock of locomotives and goods wagons failed to keep pace with the enormous increase of goods traffic during this decade. It was still the most overburdened railway system in the world. In 1938 the density of goods movement in ton-kilometres per kilometre of line in the U.S.S.R. was nearly three times as high as in Germany and more than four times as high as in France or Italy. In other words a Russian goods train of about the same size as a German goods train had to carry a similar volume of goods about four times as far as had its German counterpart.[2]

While there were these differences in efficiency between each of the national transport systems the general improvement in land mobility had opened up possibilities for more land-borne commercial exchange and— in the long run—for the unification of the trans-continental Eurasian

[1] The fact that the U.S.S.R., which in geopolitical terms was generally regarded as the most land-locked of the Great Powers, imported and exported only a small proportion by land must be explained with reference (a) to her small external trade in general, (b) to the supplementary character of the directly contiguous economies, and (c) to the sparse international lines of communication in Eastern as compared with Western Europe.

[2] The relative strength of the railway systems of the Great Powers is roughly indicated by the following data:

In 1937/8	Goods carried (million tons) (1)	(1) multiplied by average haul (milliard ton-km.) (2)	Length of line (1,000 km.) (3)	Density of movement (ton-km. per km. of line) (4)	Number of	
					Locomotives (1,000) (5)	Goods trucks (1,000) (6)
U.S.S.R.	517	355	85	4,160	23·7	646
Germany	520	89	58	1,535	21·9	590
France	245	37	43	900	18·7	485
Italy	58	12	17	700	5·6	126
U.K.	269	27	32	844	19·7	663
Japan	119	16	24	700	5·0	80
U.S.A.	818	487	376	1,300	42·5	1,677

See *Statistisches Jahrbuch, 1939/40*, p. 108, and also Birmingham Bureau of Research on Russian Economic Conditions: *Results of the Second Five-Year Plan and the Project of the Third Five-Year Plan*, Memorandum no. 12, July 1939. [This will be referred to hereafter as Birmingham Bureau: Memorandum no. 12.]

spaces. But these possibilities were still remote. A closely knit transport network across national frontiers was only to be found in Western Europe. It was embryonic in Eastern Europe, and such communications as existed were less continuous (i.e. because of differences in the width of Western and Russian railway gauges, &c.). Neither were the rivers Vistula and Oder in the east of the same importance as channels for international transport routes as was the Rhine in the west.[1] Thus Germany, located in the very heart of Europe, and having an eye, as Hitler admitted, on an empire to be won in the east,[2] was confronted, in such land-borne ventures, by one serious limitation. She could not normally force the pace of transport developments in the east; nor could she in peace-time operate her own rail and road vehicles in the territories of her sovereign neighbours. It was for precisely this reason that Germany paid great attention in her armament drive from 1933 onwards to strengthening her internal transport system beyond immediate needs, to devising strategic roads and canals linking the Ruhr with Berlin and her eastern provinces, and to accumulating rail and road vehicles suitable to support military operations in foreign territories.

Sea-borne trade was different. On the free oceans of the world any Power had a choice between chartering the services of a foreign fleet or building up its own fleet. Many considerations influenced this choice. But the argument most commonly advanced to justify the operation of a national fleet was the transport task arising out of the sea-borne trade of a Power. Essentially two factors determined the size of the transport task. The first determinant was the weight of sea-borne trade. On the criterion of the weight of imports no other country in the world had so huge a carrying task as had the United Kingdom. In 1938 she imported 61 million tons (including goods in transit). Next came the United States, Germany, and France, each of whom imported by sea about 33 million tons, notwithstanding the fact that the land-borne imports of the two last-mentioned countries were very considerable. Finally, Italy and Japan imported each about 20 million tons. The second determinant was the distance of haulage. For instance, the average haul per ton of imports for the United

---

[1] In fact, within the framework of land-borne West European commodity exchange, Rhine and canal traffic surpassed in significance both rail and road traffic. For instance, of Germany's land-borne imports (including transit goods) of 40 million tons and of her land-borne exports of 45 million tons in 1938, 27 million tons and 30 million tons respectively were carried on barges. Of France's land-borne imports of 17 million tons and of her exports of 23 million tons more than 90 per cent. were received from and supplied to her contiguous or near distant neighbours, namely, Germany, Holland, Belgium, Luxembourg, Switzerland, Italy, and Spain. The largest proportion of this trade also was carried on barges.

[2] Indeed, at a Cabinet meeting on 4 September 1936 Göring announced that Hitler had issued instructions to the Minister for War, declaring 'that the show-down with Russia is inevitable' and that 'all measures have to be taken just as if we were actually in . . . imminent danger' (*I.M.T. Nuremberg*, xxxvi. 490–1 (416–EC); *N.C.A.* vii. 472–3). See also above, pp. 349–50.

Kingdom was more than twice as far as it was for France. Thus the real transport problem which confronted each of the Great Powers was reflected in the ton-mileage of their imports; that is, the total weight of sea-borne imports multiplied by the length of haul.[1] The carrying task for each Power in 1938 was as follows:

Import Carrying Task (1938)
(in milliard ton-miles)

United Kingdom	United States	Germany	Japan	France	Italy	Six Powers
223	97	95	70	54	41	580

In what relation did the carrying capacity, i.e. the mercantile fleet owned by each Power in 1938, stand to its carrying task? The world's mercantile fleet (i.e. taking steam and motor vessels of 100 gross tons and upwards only) increased from 43·3 million gross tons in 1913 to 66·9 million gross tons in 1938. This increase of over 50 per cent. in world mercantile tonnage corresponded to an increase of only about 22 per cent. in the volume of world sea-borne trade,[2] so that in the inter-war period shipping facilities exceeded requirements. The disparity was even greater when account was taken of the larger average size and the higher average speeds of vessels in 1938.

The whole increase of 23·6 million gross tons in world shipping was largely a result of the First World War. In 1922 the world's carrying

---

[1] These ton-mile estimates are approximate. It is extremely difficult to determine whether United Kingdom imports from the United States, for instance, were dispatched from American Atlantic or Pacific ports, and whether they were dispatched to Glasgow, Southampton, or Hull. This affected the length of haul with which the imported weight had to be multiplied. The same difficulty is present in the case of each country. For instance, were French imports unloaded in Atlantic ports or in Mediterranean ports, and were German imports unloaded in Bremerhaven or in Königsberg? A glance at the port statistics of each Power gives some indication of the relative weight imported and exported to and from different ports in each country. In calculating distances these relative weights have been taken into account. When countries (e.g. Japan) did not specify imported weights for some essential commodities, the exported weights of other countries to these countries have been used. And where the main loading and unloading ports remain a mystery, the shortest distance between the trading partners has been assumed to be correct for these calculations.

[2] In 1938 the volume (i.e. values corrected for price changes) of aggregate land-borne and sea-borne world trade was about 13 per cent. higher than in 1913 (see above, pp. 378–9, note 1). It was estimated that the sea-borne share of world trade had increased from 75 per cent. in 1913 to 81 per cent. in 1936 (see H. Leak: 'The Carrying Trade of British Shipping', in *Journal of the Royal Statistical Society*, vol. cii, part ii, 1939, p. 260). As the volume of total trade was only slightly higher in 1938 than in 1936, it might be assumed that in 1938 the volume of sea-borne trade was about 22 per cent. (113 × 81 ÷ 75) higher than in 1913. In 1938 this corresponded to aggregate world sea-borne trade by weight of 328 million tons for imports and 316 million tons for exports. These figures have been estimated by adding to the land-borne trade of the seven Great Powers roughly another 35 million for that of the rest of the world and by deducting total land-borne imports and exports from the aggregate weight of world trade of 420 million tons in 1938.

capacity was already 61·5 million gross tons. The pace for this increase was set by the five war-time allies, Britain, the United States, France, Italy, and Japan. They commanded 27·3 million tons in 1913. The most important shipping nation among them was Britain. As the allies of Britain were deprived during the war of her shipping, on which they had been relying heavily before it, they took steps to increase considerably their own carrying capacity. Indeed, jointly, the five war-time allies commanded in 1922 about 45·6 million gross tons of shipping. On the other hand, the mercantile shipping tonnage of Germany and Russia, which amounted to 5·4 million tons in 1913, had dropped to 2 million tons in 1922.

The structural change in the relative shipping strength of the Great Powers resulting from the First World War did not right itself afterwards. Naturally enough, Germany and the U.S.S.R. made a determined effort to make good their war-time losses, but Italy and Japan did not relinquish their war-time gains; on the contrary, they continued to expand their carrying capacity. Thus between 1922 and 1938 these four Powers, namely Italy, Japan, Germany, and the U.S.S.R., jointly increased their carrying capacity by 5·5 million tons; while, in the same period, the United Kingdom, France, and the United States decreased their capacity by 7·2 million tons. The growth and the distribution of mercantile shipping among the Powers had developed as follows:[1]

Carrying Capacity

(in million gross tons)

Year	United Kingdom	United States	Germany	Japan	France	Italy	U.S.S.R.	Seven Powers	Total World
1913	18·3	4·4	4·7	1·5	1·8	1·3	0·7	32·7	43·3
1922	19·1	16·5	1·7	3·6	3·7	2·7	0·3	47·6	61·5
1938	17·7	11·5	4·2	5·0	2·9	3·3	1·3	45·9	66·9

In 1938 the United States mercantile fleet was the second largest and accounted for 17·2 per cent. of the world's gross shipping tonnage. In the same year her imports by weight amounted to only about 10 per cent. of world sea-borne imports. Obviously, the capacity of the United States should have been more than sufficient to carry her own trade. The United States Tariff Commission, however, pointed out that of the total cargo of United States imports about one-third was carried in American vessels and of her exports less than a quarter, and that 'no matter how efficiently the United States uses its merchant marine in war-time, a serious shortage of vessels of foreign ownership would inevitably affect the ability of the United States to obtain transportation not only for its exports but for its

[1] See Chamber of Shipping of the United Kingdom: *Annual Report, 1937–38* (London, Witherby & Co., 1938), pp. 57–59, and *Statistisches Jahrbuch 1939/40*, p. 110.

imports'.[1] Was it possible then that the United States had a larger percentage of ships which could not cross the oceans than any other Power? That, however, was not the case. On the contrary, taking ships of 3,000 gross tons and upwards, the United States still disposed of more than 10 million tons and, indeed, her relative position in the world in this class of ships was even stronger.[2]

The explanation of this disparity was that, owing to her two ocean coast-lines, nearly 70 per cent. of the United States mercantile fleet was engaged in coastal shipping. Deducting harbour craft, fishing, and coastal vessels from the mercantile fleets of each Power, both the absolute and relative carrying capacity available in foreign trade for each of the Great Powers was radically altered. Leaving the U.S.S.R. out of account, the carrying capacity of the other six Powers might be estimated at about 31 million gross tons, of which the United Kingdom alone commanded about 15 million tons.[3] Second to the United Kingdom was Japan with 4·1 million tons[4] followed by the United States with 3·6 million tons,[5] Germany with 3·3 million tons,[6] Italy and France with 2·6 million and 2·4 million tons respectively.[7] By comparing the share of 'merchant shipping engaged in foreign trade' and owned by each Power (i.e. 31 million gross tons = 100) with the share of their transport tasks (i.e. 580 milliards ton-mileage of imports = 100) the best possible answer was obtained to the leading question in this analysis. For these figures illustrated the relationship in 1938 between the carrying capacity nationally owned by each Power and its sea-borne carrying task.[8] The position was as follows:

---

[1] United States Tariff Commission: *The European War and United States Imports* (Washington, November 1939), p. iii. This refers to cargoes in 1936, but the position in 1938 was not substantially different.

[2] Chamber of Shipping of the United Kingdom: *Annual Report, 1937–38*, p. 63.

[3] L. Isserlis: 'Tramp Shipping, Cargoes, and Freights', *Journal of the Royal Statistical Society*, vol. ci, part i, 1938, p. 103.

[4] Total mercantile tonnage minus about 900,000 gross tons to handle normal peace-time coastal trade (see Clayton D. Carus and Charles L. McNichols: *Japan: Its Resources and Industries* (New York, Harper & Brothers, 1944), p. 93).

[5] Officially registered in 'foreign trade' as distinct from 10·9 million gross tons, including all kinds and sizes of ships, enrolled and licensed in coastwise and internal trade (see *Statistical Abstract of the United States, 1940*, p. 463).

[6] Of the total mercantile fleet 3·9 million tons were registered for trading purposes (see *Statistisches Jahrbuch, 1939/40*, p. 227). From this must be deducted about 700,000 tons for coastal trade. This estimate has been based on figures contained in a privately circulated memorandum of the German Shipowners' Association: *German Sea Shipping in the Peace Treaty* (Hamburg, January 1947), p. 12.

[7] Estimates based on shipping classifications given in *Annuario statistico italiano anno 1937-XV*, p. 101, and in *Annuaire statistique 1938*, p. 132.

[8] It must be emphasized that these are over-all shipping figures, including passenger and cargo liners, tramp ships, oil tankers, and refrigerator boats. It is quite possible that according to the specific character of imported goods a country may be short of the suitable types of ships required for their transport, although its over-all shipping position may be strong. The detailed analysis, however, cannot here be carried any farther.

Relative Carrying Capacities and Carrying Tasks (1938)

(Percentage distribution)

	United Kingdom	United States	Germany	Japan	France	Italy	Six Powers
Foreign trade shipping .	48·4	11·6	10·7	13·2	7·7	8·4	100·0
Ton-mileage imports .	38·4	16·7	16·4	12·1	9·3	7·1	100·0

The conclusion to be drawn from these ratios was that in 1938 Germany, France, and the United States were confronted by a much tighter shipping position than were the United Kingdom, Italy, and Japan. Indeed, it would seem that among the Great Powers Germany was the least able to carry her own trade. But her shipping deficit was exaggerated, while that of France and the United States was understated, for, in 1938, the last two countries were not working at full capacity and their imports were relatively depressed, in contrast with the position of Germany whose internal activity and imports were booming. In addition, Germany's sea-borne imports from South America, involving long hauls, were particularly high, and this exaggerated her carrying task in ton-mileage as well as the apparent tightness of her shipping position.[1] Apart, however, from these differences, the really remarkable feature in the situation of 1938, and the striking contrast to the situation in 1913, was that all the Great Powers were better equipped to carry their own trade than they had been before the First World War.

The reasons for this were political and strategic rather than economic. On purely economic grounds there was no justification for the doctrine that a country should carry its own trade. Great Britain had been the world's principal carrier of goods throughout the greater part of the nineteenth century. Owing to her geopolitical position, her long maritime tradition, and her wealth in skilled seamanship, she was probably better suited for this task than were other countries. Her comparative cost advantage was partly based on the fact that she also used to be the world's main supplier of coal. The cost of carrying staple cargoes from all over the world to Europe was, therefore, cheaper in British than in foreign ships because coal exports from Britain reduced the necessity for British ships to make outward voyages in ballast. These favourable circumstances did not last. British coal exports declined sharply after the First World War, and British seamen's wages, an important item in shipping costs, came to be higher than in many other countries. To the extent that these changes

[1] For instance, Germany's imports from the countries of the Western Hemisphere in 1938 represented only 25 per cent. of her total sea-borne imports by weight. But these 25 per cent. accounted for half her carrying task as measured by ton-mileage.

narrowed Britain's comparative cost advantage, there was an economic reason for the shift in the world's carrying trade from British to foreign ships. Yet, superimposed on this and probably more effective, were two further considerations.

First, countries which were in need of imports had to pay for them by the direct sale of goods (i.e. visible exports), by the receipts from past investments abroad, or by the offer of services, &c. (i.e. invisible exports). In the inter-war period, and especially in the 1930s, when tariffs and to a greater extent quota arrangements limited the sale of goods, many governments were anxious, by the provision of services, to secure for themselves the income needed to bridge the gap between receipts from direct exports and the cost of desired imports. Although total exports by volume, and especially by value, were exposed to fluctuations, there was a hard core of goods of which the sale was more or less assured. The transport of these goods could be undertaken by the seller or the buyer. Frequently some governments induced their own exporters to let their goods be carried by national fleets, in order to reap the benefit of receipts accruing from invisible exports in the form of shipping services. This consideration played a part in the growth of the German and Japanese fleets, in defiance of the fact that the national resources tied up in shipping would not under normal conditions represent their most economical use.

Secondly, questions of national prestige played a vital part. 'Germany's reputation in the world was dependent on her being a powerful shipping nation', wrote Karl Lindemann, president of the board of directors of the Norddeutsche Lloyd; 'without it, German foreign policy would be impotent.'[1]

Naturally the growth of national fleets, for whatever reason, was regarded by the old-established, traditional maritime Powers as a threat to their commercial position and interests. In this respect the 'most serious menace to British shipping came from Japan'.[2] Refuting the British charge that by 1937 Japan was already capable of carrying her trade twice over, the Japanese representative of the Nippon Shipowners' Association, T. Saito, retorted that 'it is not usually considered in Great Britain that nations should possess only such ocean-going tonnage as is sufficient to carry their own trade'.[3] But, remarked Lord Lloyd, although

---

[1] Karl Lindemann: *Die deutsche Seeschiffahrt im Wandel der Nachkriegsjahre bis 1936*, an essay in *Probleme des deutschen Wirtschaftslebens* (Berlin/Leipzig, Walter De Gruyter, 1937), p. 420.

[2] In drawing the attention of the British Government to the Japanese shipping activities in a note presented at the Imperial Conference of 1937, Sir F. Vernon Thomson, the president of the British Chamber of Shipping, argued that 'whilst the proportion of British Empire shipping to world shipping corresponded to the proportion of Empire trade to world trade, Japan's proportion of shipping to world shipping was twice her proportion of international trade'. It might be noted that the argument was overstated because it was based on values rather than on 'ton-mileage', which alone was relevant in assessing carrying tasks.

[3] Letter to *The Times*, 27 January 1937. Saito also maintained that, up to that date, subsidies

no exception could be taken to the principle of a country owning more tonnage than was required to carry its own trade, 'there must be limits in its application', and 'when it results in threatening the communications of the British Empire, it is time we made it clear that the maintenance of Empire shipping is of paramount strategic and commercial interest to the Empire as a whole'.[1] The core of the matter was that Japan, like Germany, was determined on expansion, and, because of the imperialist aims of these two Powers, of which state-sponsored and state-subsidized shipping expansion was only a symptom, it was inevitable that their policies should encroach on the political and commercial spheres of Powers who essentially desired to maintain the *status quo*.

In the inter-war period the desire to be independent of foreign tonnage for the carriage of national trade was widespread. The possession of national merchant fleets did not, however, necessarily mean that security of supplies, or for that matter the safety of the routes of communications, was assured. What was required in addition was military and naval strength.

Naval strength was not a matter merely of numbers of warships. Their armour, speed, range of fire, and so on, as well as the composition of the fleet, were of crucial importance.[2] The last-mentioned factor was governed by a consideration of the defensive or offensive tasks that were imposed upon a Power by its geopolitical location in relation both to its own political and commercial spheres of interest and to the points of their intersection with those of other (potentially hostile) Powers. In the present context we need do no more than compare the relative naval strengths of the Powers, measured in thousands of tons of the aggregate displacement of their battleships, aircraft-carriers, cruisers, destroyers, and submarines,[3] with their relative mercantile strength, measured in thousands of gross tons of shipping engaged in foreign trade. In 1938–9, the position was roughly as shown in the table at the top of the next page.

In terms of naval strength, Britain's superiority over Germany alone was sufficient to enable her to protect her main lines of communication with

paid by the Japanese Government to Japan's shipping interests were lower than those paid by the government of any other Great Power to their shipping companies.

[1] Ibid. 29 January 1937. Lord Lloyd was particularly concerned not about past subsidies, but about officially planned increases for a further huge expansion of the Japanese merchant fleet in the next five years. Or as, in another letter to *The Times* of 1 February 1937, Sir F. Vernon Thomson put it: 'If this [Japanese] policy [of long-term state assistance] is extended unchecked, it can only be a question of time before the British flag is driven out of these trades [with, and often within, the British Empire]. Thus Imperial communications and the marketing of Empire production in such trades would be dependent mainly upon foreign tonnage, a possibility which must give cause for deep concern.'

[2] This subject will be dealt with more fully in Part v of volume iii of the *Survey* for 1938.

[3] A comparison, in this form, was published by the League of Nations: see *Armaments Year Book 1939/40* (Geneva, June 1940).

Naval and Mercantile Capacities

	United Kingdom	United States	Japan	France	Italy	U.S.S.R.	Germany
Naval strength (in ooo's of displacement tons)	1,280	1,277	906	547	481	287	197
Mercantile strength (in ooo's of gross tons) .	15,000	3,600	4,100	2,400	2,600	(999)	3,300

the exception of those passing to and from countries bordering on the Baltic Sea. Germany, on the other hand, could not hope to be able to safeguard any of her sea-borne trade with the important exception of her vital trade with Northern Europe, which was Germany's principal commercial sphere of interest on a reckoning by weight, and not by value.

The Italian naval forces were strong enough, particularly in view of their submarine and destroyer contingents, to threaten British communications through the Eastern Mediterranean and to force upon British merchant ships longer hauls round the Cape. But while Italian naval strength might divert British merchant ships to alternative routes, British naval strength could effectively prevent Italian ships from passing via Gibraltar into the Atlantic and also even from entering the Suez Canal so long as the British had bases at Alexandria and Haifa. Thus by blocking the exits of the Mediterranean, the British navy would not merely divert Italian ships to alternative routes, but completely stop Italy's communications with her main sea-borne trading centres outside the Mediterranean.

The relative naval strength of the Great Powers in the Pacific Ocean was a very different matter. Japan's navy was sufficiently strong to safeguard the routes to her major sources of supply on the Far Eastern mainland and in countries of the Western Hemisphere against British intervention; but it was at least doubtful whether the British navy could prevent Japanese attacks on British trade with Oceania. The defence of that trade depended above all on the safety of British naval stations in Oceania, Hongkong, and especially in Singapore. If Britain had to face Japan as a sole adversary, she had a fighting chance of being able to reduce to a minimum the possible damage of Japanese raids on British commerce. Similarly, if she had to face Germany and Italy singly, the British navy was probably strong enough to protect British merchant ships against German and/or Italian intervention. British naval strength was, however, inferior to that of Germany, Italy, and Japan taken together. Even if France sided with Britain, their joint naval strength would be only slightly greater than that of Germany, Italy, and Japan, the partners in the Anti-Comintern Pact. Therefore, unless the tremendous naval power of the United States were thrown in on the side of Britain and France, the joint naval strength of these two countries imposed upon their diplomacy in 1938-9 an obligation to prevent the Anti-Comintern Powers from entering into an open naval alliance against them.

This diplomatic necessity was even more pressing in view of the relative strength of the Great Powers in military aircraft. The perfection of mobility in the air was one of the greatest achievements of technological and industrial progress in the period following the First World War. The operational range of aircraft was not, however, unlimited. While planes could hardly be used to safeguard the ocean lanes from a terminal base on one continent to that on another, they had been sufficiently perfected to put under attack in Europe the terminal bases themselves. The offensive value of bombing planes varied (i.e. because of variations in size, speed, and armour) and their effectiveness depended on the defensive strength of fighter planes, anti-aircraft gunfire, &c., which they might encounter.

At the beginning of 1939 Germany alone possessed more first-line military aircraft ready for action than France and Britain together. In her total of about 2,400 first-line planes, the bombers were about equal in numbers to the fighters, while in the combined French and British total of about 2,000 planes the contingent of bombers was less conspicuous. If we add Italy's first-line planes, numbering less than 1,000, to Germany's, the combined superiority of the Axis Powers in the air over the combined strength of Britain and France works out at a ratio of rather less than two to one. If Japan, with her 1,000 planes and more, were to be reckoned as being in the camp of the Axis Powers, the Axis's margin of superiority in the air over the Anglo-French combined strength would then be correspondingly greater.[1] Thus calculations of relative air strength, like those of relative naval strength, bring out the inferiority of a Franco-British alliance to an alliance between Germany, Italy, and Japan, unless either the U.S.S.R. or the United States could be brought in instantaneously on the side of Britain and France. Early in 1939 well-informed experts were agreed that numerically there was not a single Power in the world stronger than the U.S.S.R. in military aircraft. Its sheer weight in numbers (3,000 to 4,000), together with the Anglo-French air forces, would have restored a balance with the combined air forces of the Anti-Comintern

---

[1] The above-mentioned over-all figures are based on: (for *Germany*) U.S. Strategic Bombing Survey: *The Effects of Strategic Bombing on the German War Economy* (Washington, U.S.G.P.O., 1945), p. 149, in conjunction with the closing address of the U.S. Chief Prosecutor, Mr. Justice Jackson, at the Nuremberg Trial on 26 July 1946 (*I.M.T. Nuremberg*, xix. 397); (for *Britain*) *League of Nations Armaments Year-Book 1938* and *1939/40*, pp. 155 and 63 respectively, together with: *Great Britain: Statistics relating to the War Effort of the United Kingdom*, Cmd. 6564 (London, H.M.S.O., 1944), p. 14; (for *France*) Bonnet: *De Washington au Quai d'Orsay*, p. 372, and also Pertinax [André Géraud]: *Les Fossoyeurs* (New York, Éditions de la Maison Française, 1943), i. 39–40 and 163; (for *Italy*) Ciano: *Diario (1939–43)*, 29 April 1939; (for *Japan*) U.S. Strategic Bombing Survey: *Summary Report (Pacific War)*, (Washington, U.S.G.P.O., 1946), pp. 2–3.

A detailed analysis of developments in air power during the 1930s will be given in Part v of volume iii of the *Survey* for 1938.

Powers. The United States, on the other hand, possessing about 1,500 combat planes[1]—however useful she might have been as a close military ally of Britain and France—could not, unless herself provoked, be drawn into such an alliance.

Since the Anti-Comintern Powers had, by 1939, accumulated a mighty navy, numerically nearly equal to that of France and Britain, and a superior air force—not to mention the disparity in land forces—the two Western European Powers were bound to consider the possibility of redressing this perilously adverse balance by negotiating an alliance with the Soviet Union, who, like the Western European Powers and unlike the United States, was already well aware that she was in danger of being attacked by the Axis. The hesitancy of the British and French Governments about making overtures to the Soviet Government, and the failure of their eventual belated and unenthusiastic attempt, will be recorded elsewhere.[2] The three main deterrent considerations in French and British minds seem to have been (1) that, especially since the large-scale purge of her armed forces in 1937, the U.S.S.R.'s military value was doubtful, (2) that on ideological grounds an association with her was undesirable, and (3) that she herself had territorial ambitions which it was unwise to encourage. There is no evidence that the French and British Governments' policy on this crucial question of the pros and cons of coming to an understanding with the U.S.S.R. was influenced by any comparative review of the respective internal economic structures and of the external trading structures of the Great Powers—pertinent though these considerations would have been to any realistic appraisal and handling of the international situation.

The Soviet Union's situation was, as a matter of fact, different from that of the other six Great Powers. The industrial strength of these other Powers was bound up with the security of their supply lines and their communications between the different parts of their empires, while the U.S.S.R. was unique in depending less on the security of her external lines of communication than on the safety of her own metropolitan territory. Indicative of this, although not conclusive, was her relatively low volume of imports, both in the aggregate and per hundred of population.[3] Not only was the U.S.S.R.'s actual dependence on the outer world at a low ebb in

---

[1] This estimate is based on figures given in *Foreign Policy Reports*, 1 May 1939, pp. 38 and 45, and in Hanson W. Baldwin's *Defence of the Western World* (London, Hutchinson, 1941), pp. 161–2; also on estimates by Colonel Frederick Palmer, *Congressional Record*, 26 January 1939, p. 1188.

[2] In a later volume of the *Survey* for 1939–46.

[3] Not conclusive, because this generalization depends on the composition of imports. Even imports that were low in terms of value or weight, might, if cut off altogether, bring to a standstill large and important industries, provided that they consisted of key materials such as certain machine tools, magnetos, dyes, optical glass, &c., which are indispensable to the operation of many industries. It might, however, be inferred from the particular attention which the Second Five-Year Plan paid to key industries that—after a fashion—such imports were replaceable by home-produced products in 1938–9.

1938–9, but also the outer world could not regard the U.S.S.R. as an indispensable trading sphere. Without powerful friends, and having become the focus of the expanionist Powers' hostility in the Anti-Comintern grouping, the U.S.S.R. appeared to be the most likely prey of their aggression. For, just as Japan's military successes in China had given her the advantage of broader bases from which to operate against Soviet territory, so had Germany's bloodless victory at Munich opened the gate for German attacks on the U.S.S.R. by breaking the most essential link in the chain of buffer states which separated the two largest continental Powers of the Old World.[1]

On the other hand, for France and Britain it was a matter of life and death that their supply lines and imperial communications should be safeguarded against any interference. Their imports per hundred of population exceeded those of any other Power, and the distribution of Britain's trade, in particular, was quite unique in its dispersal over all the continents of the world. It is true that Britain and France had very efficient navies, and—owing to their world-wide territorial possessions— they had the advantage of naval bases from which to protect many ocean lanes. But, in 1939, naval dominance in the Atlantic meant no longer, as in the greater part of the nineteenth century, *ipso facto* command in the waters of the Far East. In view of Japan's powerful navy, strengthened in operational range by her bases in the South Seas (i.e. her Mandatory possessions), Britain's trade routes to Oceania were extremely vulnerable. Thus the Western European Powers would find a formidable adversary in Japan if they were to be attacked by her; but there is no evidence that a fear of provoking a Japanese attack was one of the considerations that made the British and French Governments hesitate to seek an alliance with Japan's *bête-noire*, the Soviet Union; for—apart from the fact that the Soviet Union was also an object of suspicion to conservative statesmen in Britain and France—it would appear that the British Chiefs of Staff were making their calculations on the assumption that an attack by Japan, as well as by Germany and Italy, was to be expected in any case.[2]

Neither Japan nor Italy but Germany was the focus of anxiety after Munich. But all these three Powers had, at different stages in the 1930s, taken steps to alter unilaterally the political boundaries of their territories and had met no effective resistance. Indeed, as Göring boasted to a foreign diplomat: 'You have only to bang your fist on the table. Then the demo-cratic countries make a few speeches in Parliament, and nothing happens'.[3] Success was cumulative; it was accompanied by ever newer claims for more living space. How was it possible that, twenty years after the First World War, the erstwhile vanquished Power, together with Italy and

---

[1] See above, pp. 280–1, 293.   [2] See Churchill: *Second World War*, i. 196.
[3] R. M. Bruce Lockhart: *Guns or Butter* (London, Putnam, 1938), p. 228.

Japan, was not only ready to put forward revisionist and imperialist claims, but also prepared and willing to enforce them? The answer must be sought in her newly acquired industrial and military strength in relation to that of other Powers; it must be sought, above all, in the fact that in the 1930s her broad industrial potential had been increasingly geared to producing weapons of war. Two questions require elucidation; first, what were the changes which had altered the relative industrial strength of the Great Powers in the two vital decades preceding 1938–9; second, how can these changes be explained?

(iii) Comparative Industrial Strength of the Great Powers

(a) RECONSTRUCTION AND INDUSTRIAL DEVELOPMENT IN THE 1920s

Some years after the First World War, when the major industrial dislocations had been adjusted, when in continental Europe the most unprecedented currency confusion of all times had been replaced by more orderly monetary conditions, and when the industries of both vanquished and victors had been geared to the new territorial settlements, a number of Powers, though not all, quickly regained their pre-war volume of industrial output. Taking as the main gauge for measuring the industrial strength of a country the indices of its physical volume of industrial output,[1] the world as a whole produced more industrial goods in 1923 than in 1913; Italy and the United States produced more in 1922, France in 1924, the U.S.S.R. in 1926, and Germany in 1927. Japan was the only country whose output had never fallen below its pre-war volume. Great Britain, on the other hand, was the last among the Great Powers to reach—and then imperfectly—her pre-war output in 1929. The index of the physical volume of industrial production in each country and in the world as a whole moved after 1913 (referring to post-First World War territory) as shown in Table II on the opposite page.

(1) Italy and Japan

In the period ending in 1929 the greatest industrial advance was made by Japan, who nearly trebled her output of 1913, and by Italy and the United States, who nearly doubled theirs. The war itself had been the greatest boon for Japan. Deprived, as she was, during the war of many industrial goods formerly imported, and confronted by a very active foreign demand for her goods, she found conditions extremely favourable

[1] 'Industrial' activity is conceived to range from the mining of coal, ores, and mineral oils, to the transformation of basic industrial and agricultural materials into products at different stages of manufacture, and to electricity generation and building construction. 'Manufacture' proper excludes mining, electricity generation, and building.

TABLE II. *Industrial Production**

(1928 = 100)

Year	Japan	U.S.A.	Italy	France	U.S.S.R.	Germany	Britain	World
1913	37	63	63	79	70	89	107	73
1921	65	61	61	43	13	65	73	60
1922	68	77	67	61	17	70	87	73
1923	71	92	72	69	26	46	95	79
1924	76	86	82	85	30	69	98	82
1925	82	95	92	84	50	81	93	88
1926	92	98	102	98	70	78	72	90
1927	93	96	95	86	82	98	103	96
1929	110	107	111	109	118†	101	106	106†

Notes: * Wagenführ: *Industriewirtschaft*, pp. 38 and 64–67.
  † Official index figures of 124 for the U.S.S.R. and of 107 for the world have been adjusted downward to allow for estimated inflationary bias in the Russian figure. For basis of estimate see below, p. 432, note to Table III.

for a rapid growth of her own industries, especially mining, metallurgy, and shipbuilding. Much of the industrial capacity which the war had brought into being was only in part rendered superfluous afterwards. Thus, starting from a greatly improved situation at the end of the war, industrial production in Japan expanded at a rate similar to the rate of growth in Italy during the 1920s.

What were the factors influencing the rate of expansion? The volume of output was determined by at least one of three factors: (*a*) by industrial capacity, that is by plant and especially capital equipment; (*b*) by raw material supplies within the country or within its trading sphere: and (*c*) by the volume of available man-power (including hours of work) and by its productivity.

In Japan and Italy, where more than half of the labour force was occupied in agriculture, where, as compared with the more mature industrial Powers, the real income of the whole population was low, and where, consequently, almost all incomes were spent on goods for immediate consumption, the purchase and hence the production of investment goods or of capital goods was very closely restricted. But before industrial production as a whole, including the provision of more consumer goods, could be increased, investment in machinery and in the building-up of industrial capacity was absolutely essential. Here was a real dilemma. Aggregate output and real income were low because there were not enough industries, but, on the other hand, industries could only be built up slowly because the prevailing poverty, which tended to be intensified by the very high average annual increase of population in Japan and Italy, made it increasingly difficult for people to abstain from consumption and to save.

In contrast with Italy, however, recorded savings in Japan apparently amounted to between 10 and 20 per cent. of national income.[1] This extraordinarily high proportion emphasized the significance of yet another feature. For saving was determined not only by the level of income, but also by its distribution; and of all the Great Powers, Japan had the most unequal distribution of incomes. As, in the immediate post-war period, the state-controlled banks pursued an expansionist monetary policy, both the Japanese Government, and especially business men, availed themselves of easy credits for spending on the development of domestic resources. The very spending created new incomes and, consequently, under conditions of income inequality, the savings to replace the credits by which the domestic investment projects had initially been financed.

However, internal output expansion was to some extent conditioned by the availability of foreign machinery and equipment, and, although exports rose to pay in part for necessary imports, a strain on the foreign balance could not be avoided altogether. Fortunately for her, Japan, unlike Italy, was able in the immediate post-war period to spend gold and foreign exchange balances which had accumulated to her credit during the war. When these balances were exhausted, she had, like Italy, to draw on the resources of the outer world, that is, to borrow the savings of foreigners. By 1929 private American investments in Italy had risen to $121 million, of which half was invested in public utilities, while in Japan it had risen to $61 million, of which four-fifths were held by American citizens in Japanese manufacturing enterprises.[2] Apart from American investments in tangible properties, securities were sold in the United States on behalf of the Italian and Japanese Governments, and these yielded, as far as Japan was concerned, sums eight to ten times the amount of direct private American investments.[3] The growing significance to the Japanese economy of external loans was also illustrated by the fact that, over the period from 1923 to 1929, payments to foreigners of interest and dividends on Japanese securities and net income of foreign undertakings in Japan almost doubled.[4] Some part of these loans was dissipated on imports of additional consumer goods, which did nothing to raise productive capacity; but other parts were indeed used on imports of investment goods, especially on machine tools, that is on machines which make machines.[5] The initiative for Japanese industrialization in the post-war period rested primarily, although not exclusively, with private business men. It has been observed that in the

[1] Japan, Ministry of Finance and Bank of Japan: *Statistical Year-Book of Finance and Economy of Japan, 1948* (Tokyo, 1948), pp. 622–3.

[2] Charles A. Beard: *The Idea of National Interest* (New York, Macmillan, 1934), pp. 222 and 230.

[3] Beard, op. cit. pp. 235 and 560.

[4] See E. B. Schumpeter, G. C. Allen, M. S. Gordon, E. F. Penrose: *The Industrialization of Japan and Manchukuo 1930–1940* (New York, Macmillan, 1940), table 1B: Balance of Payments of All Japan (in pocket at end).

[5] Carus and McNichols: *Japan: Its Resources and Industries*, p. 158.

1880s it was the Government who 'financed practically all the conspicuous expansion'.[1] They started spinning-mills and nationalized the railways before the First World War, for the express purpose of encouraging the economic development of the isolated regions of the country. The state owned the largest iron and steel works at Yawata; it owned munitions plant, yards for warship construction, textile and clothing establishments, a very large tonnage of merchant ships; and, in conjunction with private business groups, the state owned electric power companies, wireless companies, colonial development companies, and banks.[2] Here, then, many opportunities existed for direct government investment; it could be used to install machinery and equipment with borrowed foreign capital and to draw into employment 'additional' men from the great masses of the under-employed agricultural surplus population by means of 'government spending in excess of tax revenue'. The real danger of expansionist policies of this kind was that the incomes earned by additional persons drawn into employment tended to compete with existing incomes for food and consumer goods of all kinds, the supply of which was not, in the short run, increased *pari passu* with the establishment of a new steel plant, a new railway, &c.[3]

Temporary bottle-necks to the expansion of output, caused by limited industrial capacity, differed only in degree from those caused by scarcity of raw materials. Both Italy and Japan were extremely short of a great number of industrial raw materials. Hence, in the period of industrial expansion (1922–9) the volume of imports into Italy increased by more than 50 per cent.[4] and into Japan by nearly 100 per cent.[5] The volume of exports, of which in Japan about 60 per cent., and in Italy 25 per cent., were silk and cotton goods, rose by a slightly higher percentage. Yet in both countries the deficits on the trade balances remained very considerable and were not offset by receipts from invisible exports.[6] In Japan

[1] Shigeto Isuru: 'Economic Fluctuations in Japan 1868–1893', *Review of Economic Statistics*, November 1941, p. 179.

[2] Schumpeter and others: *Industrialization of Japan*, p. 729.

[3] The dangers of financing development projects through deficits are very real, but the point here is, as has been rightly observed, that 'the government's expansionist policy had probably raised the productive powers of the nation to a level which they could not have attained in the same space of time under a *laisser-faire* regime' (G. C. Allen: 'The Last Decade in Japan', *Economic History—A Supplement to the Economic Journal*—vol. ii (1930–33), pp. 631–2).

[4] Index of import values divided by Ciani's index of prices: see *UNRRA*: Italian Mission, *Survey of Italy's Economy* (Rome, UNRRA, 1947), p. 400.

[5] Index of import values divided by index of Japanese wholesale prices: see Schumpeter and others: *Industrialization of Japan*, table iv (in pocket at end).

[6] Invisible exports include receipts from different sources, the most important of which are emigrants' remittances, tourist expenditure, freight and shipping services, insurance premiums, transit traffic, copyrights, and returns from investments abroad. Before the First World War such receipts in Italy completely offset the deficits on her trade balance (merchandise only). In Japan, the balance of payments was unfavourable both before and after the war; during the period of the war itself it was favourable.

attempts were made to check the deterioration in the foreign balance by forcing up exports, and by limiting imports both through tariffs and more directly through the restriction of import credits for transactions which were regarded as unnecessary to the economic life of the country. But none of these measures was wholly effective. Throughout the 1920s the foreign balances of Italy and Japan were unfavourable and there was constant pressure on their exchange rates. These were prevented from collapsing and from jeopardizing the internal industrial expansion by the fact that the outer world was prepared to divert savings into both countries.

As long as the outer world was prepared to finance the deficits on Italy's and Japan's balances of payments, the factor which really limited industrial expansion was neither industrial capacity nor raw material, but manpower. There was, of course, no absolute shortage of men, but there was a severe shortage of labour of the right kind, with intelligence, drive, and skill. Industrial employment presupposed a certain level of education and training on the part of those to be absorbed in industry; moreover, it was an essential condition that the various services surrounding industrial activity should operate smoothly. Inefficiency in the organization of transport, slackness and corruption in the police and in local and national administration—all turning on men rather than on equipment and materials—had to be overcome before real industrial advance could be made. In this sphere Italy, Japan, and other industrializing countries were moving forward; but it was a significant defect in their people that organizing ability, skill, and adaptability were less widespread among them than among those of the more mature industrial countries of Western Europe and of the United States. This defect contributed to keeping in check the rate of growth of industrial output and the improvement in the productivity of labour in Italy and Japan.[1]

(2) *The United States*

The United States, like Japan, had escaped being adversely affected by the First World War, and, as in Japan and Italy, the annual growth of

---

[1] The order of magnitude of improvement in the efficiency of labour may be indicated in the broadest of terms. In the decade ending in 1930 the occupied population in industry in Italy rose by 11 per cent. from 4·6 million to 5·11 million persons (*Statistisches Jahrbuch, 1935,* p. 35*) and industrial output rose by 52 per cent. (Wagenführ: *Industriewirtschaft*, p. 67). Comparable data of changes in unemployment and working hours are unobtainable. All that can therefore be said is that productivity per Italian occupied person rose by 37 per cent. in a decade. In Japan industrial output rose by 77 per cent. between 1920 and 1930, and the occupied population rose by 7 per cent. from 5·72 million to 6·13 million (Schumpeter and others: *Industrialization of Japan*, p. 480). There was practically full employment in Japan in 1919 and in 1929. Assuming that the fall of industrial production by 17 per cent. from 1919 to 1920 and by 7 per cent. from 1929 to 1930 was accompanied by a proportional increase in unemployment, it follows that employment must have risen by about 20 per cent. and productivity per employed person in Japanese industry by about 47 per cent. over the decade.

population there, although declining, was still very high indeed in the 1920s. But there the similarity ended. The United States in the past had built up great industries, she was richly endowed with natural resources, and she possessed a highly skilled working class and a vigorous and enterprising business and managerial community, which was prepared to take risks and to experiment in technological application of scientific knowledge and discoveries. Yet expansion of output in the United States would, in the long run, have also been conditioned by available capacity, raw materials, and labour of the right kind; in the short run, however, these limits were much less closely drawn than in the less developed countries. The immediate post-war boom facilitated the adjustment of her industries from war to peace. This boom was followed by a depression in 1920-1, which, though severe, was short-lived, for, once deflation had reduced the price level, American entrepreneurs' confidence in the profitability of business was soon restored. Too many tasks, both at home and abroad, still awaited completion. Industrialists began to replace obsolete machines by better ones, and to put in orders for the extension of existing plant, especially in the electro-technical, the motor-car, and the chemical industries, all of which seemed to offer particularly profitable opportunities for investment. Powerfully supported by outlets for investment in building construction and housing caused by population growth and by a high rate of migration from rural into urban areas, industrial production recovered and surged ahead in the United States. Moreover, the huge tasks of reconstruction in the war-devastated areas of Europe and of industrialization in many parts of the world offered opportunities for investment abroad. Private American investments abroad supported the foreign demand for American machinery which, in turn, contributed to an increase in the volume of industrial output in the United States.

However—and this was the great contrast between the United States and the poorer industrializing nations—at each level of output and employment there accrued, in the United States, sufficient savings to cover not only the replacement of machinery and the extension of industrial capacity at home, but also reconstruction and industrial developments abroad. The extraordinary productive power of the United States could be gauged from the fact that, on the average, over the years from 1925 to 1930, the American share of the savings accruing in the world as a whole was about 42 per cent., as compared with 31 to 35 per cent. of the world total before the First World War.[1] The acceleration of the productive power of American manufacturing industries could be gauged from the continuous rise of productivity per man-hour in the course of the investment boom during

---

[1] 'Before the First World War' is taken to cover the period 1909-14. Savings are estimated at 1925-30 prices. The data are derived from a study on savings and investments by J. Marschak & W. Lederer: *Kapitalbildung* (London, Hodge, 1936), pp. 121-4.

the 1920s.[1] Even in 1929, when the United States had reached her highest peak of industrial output, it could not be said that bottle-necks in the availability of industrial plant rendered further output expansion generally impossible,[2] nor could it be said that bottle-necks in the supply of labour were widespread.[3]

(3) *France*

In France, as in Italy, certain areas had been completely devastated by trench warfare, and the immediate post-war problem was to rebuild industrial plant and equipment, houses, railways, &c. It was an enormous task in view of France's greatly depleted man-power resources.[4] To overcome the shortage of men, France became, in the 1920s, the main recipient of immigrants, especially from Poland, Italy, and Spain. By 1929, the dreadful gap caused by the war had been filled, thanks to the great predominance of young males among the immigrants. Yet, despite immigration, a shortage of labour rather than of raw materials limited the rate of reconstruction; by the return of German Lorraine, France received iron-ore deposits nearly equal to those of French Lorraine; by the temporary acquisition of the Saar, together with an important coalfield found in German Lorraine, France's pre-war import requirements of coal were reduced; by the incorporation of Alsace, she gained an important potash field. Apart from broadening the raw material basis of the French economy, the newly incorporated territories provided steel mills, textile spinning-mills, &c., all of which, though partly destroyed, increased the potential industrial strength of France. The country made a determined and successful effort, initiated by private business men, to solve her

[1] Employment in American manufacturing industries increased from 9·62 million in 1923 to 9·8 million in 1929. But it had risen by 1·9 million between 1921 and 1923: see U.S. Bureau of the Census: *Sixteenth Census of the U.S. 1940. Manufactures 1939* (Washington, U.S.G.P.O., 1942), i. 20. Taking 1929 = 100, manufacturing output indices rose from 77 in 1923, the index of the number of persons employed rose very little from 98, while the index of hours per worker declined from 104, so that the output per man-hour, being 76 in 1923, rose by more than 25 per cent. in 1929 (Arthur F. Burns: *Economic Research and the Keynesian Thinking of Our Times*, in *National Bureau of Economic Research: Twenty-sixth Annual Report* (New York, National Bureau of Economic Research, 1946), p. 14, table i).

[2] While the flour-milling industry was only employed to 44 per cent. of capacity, the pig-iron and electrolytic copper industries utilized 93 and 97 per cent. of capacity respectively. For industry as a whole, capacity utilization was estimated at 83 per cent. (Edwin G. Nourse and others: *America's Capacity to Produce* (Washington, Brookings Institution, 1934), p. 118).

[3] The labour force in the whole American economy was estimated at about 48 million in 1928 (Arthur F. Burns, op. cit. p. 30). No reliable data of unemployment existed, but it might be estimated at about 5 per cent. of the above labour force in 1928 (Alvin H. Hansen: 'Defence Financing and Inflation Potentialities—Some Additional Comments on the Inflation Symposium', *Review of Economic Statistics*, May 1941, p. 91).

[4] 'French casualties during the First World War stood at: officially killed 1,357,000; wounded 4,266,000; missing 537,000 (of whom over 200,000 were in fact dead)' (Pierre Maillaud: *France* (London, Oxford University Press, 1942), p. 68, quoting the official records of the U.S. War Department; cf. above, p. 166 and note 2).

reconstruction task. The French labour force was from the outset fully employed, and, during the whole decade, but for a brief recession in 1921, unemployment was practically unknown. Under a régime of full employment the acceleration of reconstruction was dependent on: (a) an excess of imports over exports, on (b) a reduction of internal consumption, or on (c) a rise in labour productivity. Only in the first three years did France rely for help on the outer world;[1] after 1921 the French balance of payments showed a surplus each year.[2] Reconstruction and industrial expansion were, therefore, primarily carried through by a reduction of internal consumption and by an increase in labour productivity. Labour, materials, and capacity were released from the consumer goods industries for purposes of reconstruction by voluntary savings and by greatly enhanced tax rates on incomes and on goods for mass consumption. Savings were sufficient to finance not only private investment, but also the large budget deficits of the Government,[3] at least until 1924. In that year the Poincaré Government suffered a crushing defeat at the elections, partly because of discontent among the people over the unjust distribution of the tax burden, and partly because of disillusionment over the Ruhr occupation, which had been started with the intention of enforcing payments of reparations by Germany, but which had resulted in a stoppage of all production in the Ruhr, and, consequently, in the complete collapse of the German currency. The new Government, by playing with the idea of a capital levy and increased taxation on the highest incomes, caused the 'rich' to transfer their capital abroad instead of buying government bonds, which up to that time had financed the budget deficit. This deplorable flight of capital had two consequences: first, it forced the Government, which was incapable of increasing tax revenue or of substantially decreasing expenditure, to finance its budget deficit by bank borrowing (i.e. in effect by creating additional money), and second, the outflow of goods (i.e. the form in which the flight of capital took place) reduced the volume of goods available at home. Both measures led to a rise in prices.[4] Price inflation in the period

---

[1] It is not certain whether this surplus of imports was wholly financed by the outer world, i.e. by foreign borrowing. It is possible that it was partly financed by the sale to foreigners of French gold, real estate, and other assets.

[2] League of Nations: Economic, Financial and Transit Department: *The Course and Control of Inflation: a Review of Monetary Experience in Europe after World War I* (League of Nations [printed at Princeton, U.S.A.], 1946), p. 52.

[3] The high, though decreasing, government expenditure, which was the cause of the budget deficit, did not mean that the Government themselves bought large amounts of goods and services as, for instance, in Japan. What it did mean was that the Government, in anticipation of German reparations, made payments in compensation for war damage to private persons, who actually invested them in the production of equipment or saved them by buying new government bonds (ibid., pp. 33–35).

[4] 'In 1924 the budget deficit was 9,000 million francs, or less than the surplus on the current balance of payments; in 1925 it was 4,700 million, or much less than the surplus on the current balance of payments. In those years, therefore, the foreign balance which resulted

from 1924 to 1926 fulfilled the same function as voluntary saving and taxation, since it, too, reduced consumption and released factors of production for purposes of reconstruction. The reduction in consumption by inflation took place, however, in a haphazard and inequitable manner. In 1926, a Government of the 'Right' assumed office; all plans for soaking the rich were abandoned; confidence having been restored, capital returned from abroad, and the currency was stabilized *de facto* at one-fifth of its pre-war gold value. Meanwhile, reconstruction had been completed. It had provided every one of the major French industries (except silk) with the most modern plant. 'The woollen and cotton factories of the Nord, the steel mills of Lorraine and the main coal-mines were now on a technical level with any industries in the world.'[1]

French industrial production continued to expand, mainly because of substantial increases in the productivity of labour.[2] Moreover, since French export surpluses were considerable, neither shortages of materials nor lack of equipment could be thought to impose a check upon industrial expansion. The only limit was set by man-power, and this limit could have been removed by further immigration, or even by more vigorous transfer of population away from agriculture. In the circumstances of the time, the French industrial recovery was quite remarkable. Indeed, 'it would have been excessively optimistic in 1919 to have foreseen that, less than ten years later, France would have recovered so completely from her ordeal and have recovered almost entirely by her own efforts'.[3] Like the United States, she was industrially much more powerful in 1929 than in 1913.

(4) *The United Kingdom*

The United Kingdom at no time during the 1920s surpassed her pre-war volume of industrial production, a fact which was in striking contrast with the experience of all the other Great Powers. It was surprising because the conditions for recovery at first sight appeared to be very favourable to Great Britain. Her man-power losses during the First World War, although severe,[4] had been smaller than those of France; her industrial capacity had been enlarged and was undamaged; and her prospects of

mainly or wholly from the flight of capital abroad appears to have been quantitatively a more important inflationary factor than the Government's deficit expenditure at home' (ibid. p. 53).

[1] D. W. Brogan: *The Development of Modern France (1870–1939)* (London, Hamish Hamilton, 1940), p. 603.

[2] The occupied population in industry can be estimated to have increased by 6 per cent. between 1924 and 1929 (*Statistisches Jahrbuch 1935*, p. 35*) and industrial output by 28 per cent. (see Table II on p. 399 above), so that in this period productivity per occupied person rose by about 20 per cent. or 4 per cent. per annum.   [3] Brogan, op. cit. pp. 609–10.

[4] About 800,000 persons were killed in the war. This figure is based on David Lloyd George: *The Truth about the Peace Treaties* (London, Gollancz, 1938), i. 87, where the figure of 900,000 is quoted for the British Empire losses.

obtaining raw materials by exports were brighter than ever before because her main export competitors, namely Germany and Belgium, had been temporarily eliminated.

As in nearly all the belligerent countries, so in Britain much leeway had to be made up in the replacement of stock and the repair of plant and equipment. Britain's additional requirements in reconstruction turned primarily on restoring her mercantile fleet to its pre-war size.[1] Her task, in this respect, was similar in character, but certainly not in extent, to that of countries where, as a result of military operations on their soil, whole areas had been completely devastated. Reconstruction was taken in hand with vigour; within three years, the repairs and losses had been made good, the British mercantile fleet had been restored, and, indeed, in 1922 world tonnage of shipping was nearly 50 per cent. higher than in 1913. This saturation of immediate demand for purposes of reconstruction broke the post-war boom and, as a contributory cause, the rise of interest rates to 7 per cent. ushered in the depression of 1920–1.

In the subsequent slow recovery British business men's opportunities and incentives to invest were more limited than were those confronting American business men. If private investment was prevented from taking up the slack of unused capacity and unemployed man-power, the Government might have intervened in the creation of effective demand. Yet, in fact, fiscal policy detracted from, rather than added to, effective demand. Throughout the 1920s the consolidated budget of central, local, and social insurance authorities showed a slight surplus.[2]

In these conditions, high hopes were placed on a revival of foreign demand. But, after 1922, when output and employment increased in the rest of the world, the recovery of British exports was not what had been expected. It was insufficiently realized that the world pattern into which British industries now had to be fitted was radically different from that which had existed before the First World War. The reasons for the insufficient recovery of exports were manifold. First, the development of the internal combustion engine had narrowed the demand for coal, since it meant that oil, instead of coal, was used by road vehicles (which to some extent had replaced railways as a means of transport) and also by an ever-increasing proportion of the world's fleet. The development of electricity, based on lignite and on falling water, still further decreased the

---

[1] In October 1918 the tonnage of the British mercantile fleet was about 18 per cent. less than it had been at the beginning of the war (A. C. Pigou: *Aspects of British Economic History, 1918–1925* (London, Macmillan, 1947), p. 78.

[2] Although Central Government accounts showed deficits in 1925, 1926, and 1929 (see Great Britain, Board of Trade: *Statistical Abstract for the United Kingdom for each of the fifteen years 1913 and 1922 to 1935*, Cmd. 5353 (London, H.M.S.O., 1937), p. 153), the consolidated accounts of all authorities revealed a surplus in each of the years under consideration (Colin Clark: *National Income and Outlay* (London, Macmillan, 1937), p. 140).

demand for coal. Secondly, industrialization in many parts of the world had been carried through in lines of manufacture in whose sale Britain had previously possessed a dominant share. The new industries, often artificially protected, forced the onus of adjustment upon the older industrial countries. Thirdly, when the war-devastated agricultural areas in Europe had been brought back into full production, without causing a corresponding contraction in regions that had expanded their production during the war, agricultural prices fell. Great Britain, as the world's largest food importer, benefited by this fall in prices. But foreigners, receiving less for their produce, had less to spend, so that the foreign demand for British industrial products never fully revived. Moreover, British overseas investments fell below pre-war investments and hence did not support foreign demand for British products as they had done in the past.[1] In so far as the difficulties which confronted British export industries were due to technical changes and to industrialization abroad, nothing could alter their plight, except readjustment to new conditions. In so far as they were due to high costs in Britain, the only means of reviving export industries—in the absence of a very substantial reduction in costs[2]—was to devalue the pound; but, having gone off the gold standard in 1919, the British Government firmly intended to re-establish[3] and, in fact, did re-establish the currency on a gold basis at the old parity in 1925.

The reasons for this decision were complex. The main motive no doubt was the desire to restore foreign confidence in the pound, to reassert, in the face of New York's increasing competition, the position of London as a centre in the world of international finance. The fact remained that, after the establishment of the old parity, and in view of the movement of British prices and costs in relation to those abroad, the pound continued to be overvalued. Moreover, the increase in the productivity of labour in Britain was apparently lower than that in other leading countries,[4] and there was reason to believe that the rapid recovery of efficiency in the

[1] Overseas investments were estimated to have fallen from £138 million in 1907 to £72 million in 1924 and to have risen to £103 million in 1929 (Clark: *National Income and Outlay*, p. 185).

[2] It was pointed out that the export industries had 'in fact made substantial reductions in cost of production; indeed wage rates are low in comparison with other occupations. But the export industries require the services of transport and other occupations in which wage rates have been substantially improved as compared with the pre-war level and must therefore carry in their costs of production some part of the increase in the more sheltered industries. In these circumstances the export industries are driven, if they are to be successful in competition, to force their own costs yet lower in so far as the position is not met by increased efficiency in the transport and other occupations above mentioned' (Great Britain, Treasury: *Committee on Finance and Industry: Report*, Cmd. 3897 [usually known, and hereafter referred to, as the *Macmillan Report*] (London, H.M.S.O., 1931), p. 55).

[3] See Pigou: *Aspects of British Economic History, 1918–1925*, p. 148 and also Lionel Robbins: *The Great Depression* (London, Macmillan, 1934), p. 78.

[4] Productivity per employed worker was estimated to have increased by 11 per cent. between 1924 and 1929 or by just over 2 per cent. per annum (*Macmillan Report*, p. 310).

industries of other countries strained the British parity more than did the original overvaluation.

As more than one-quarter of Britain's aggregate industrial and agricultural output was destined for export, and as this sector employed an even higher proportion of persons in terms of the total occupied population,[1] the weakness of British competitive power in world markets had serious internal consequences. It accounted for the persistence of unemployment in Britain. By 1929, the volume of British exports was 20 per cent. lower than in 1913 while the volume of imports was about 20 per cent. higher.[2] The wide gap in the trade balance was, however, more than offset by receipts from invisible exports, so that, from 1924 onwards at least, there was a surplus on the balance of payment which was an indication of, though not a wholly accurate guide to, the volume of British investments abroad during this period.[3]

Thus, although Britain's international financial standing was sound, and although her position as a creditor remained immensely strong, the country's industrial activity was more or less becalmed throughout the 1920s. Industrial output as a whole uneasily reached its pre-war volume of production in 1929, but the margin of unemployed man-power remained high in almost all branches of industry. The number of insured workpeople recorded as unemployed never fell below 10 per cent. of the total in any year after 1923.[4] What was true of man-power was equally true of industrial capacity. Indeed, unlike Italy, Japan, the United States, or France, Great Britain never came near to the point of utilizing to the full her potential productive resources.

(5) *Germany*

Reconstruction in Germany and Russia began later than in the above-mentioned five countries, and the conditions under which it had to be carried through were more complex.

Germany, as a defeated nation, had to pay the price of war. By the Treaty of Versailles she lost about 10 per cent. of her pre-war population, about 14·6 per cent. of her arable area, and 10 per cent. of her industrial capacity.[5] She lost her capital investments abroad, the greater part of her

[1] See Pigou: *Aspects of British Economic History, 1918–1925*, p. 64 and *Macmillan Report*, p. 308.

[2] See G. D. A. Macdougall: 'Britain's Foreign Trade Problem', *Economic Journal*, March 1947, p. 79.

[3] *Macmillan Report*, pp. 305 and 82. It was pointed out that Britain made long-term investments abroad in excess of the current balance available and that the difference was met by attracting short-term funds to London. This lack of balance between long-term and short-term investment was, of course, 'latent with dangers of extensive catastrophe, should anything occur to disturb the insecure prosperity elsewhere' (Robbins, op. cit. p. 9; cf. also W. A. Lewis: *Economic Survey 1919–1939*, p. 43).

[4] See *Statistical Abstract for the United Kingdom*, Cmd. 5353, pp. 122–7.

[5] It was estimated that the value of gross industrial output in the ceded territories was 10 per cent. of the gross output of the pre-war Imperial Reich (Wagenführ: *Industriewirtschaft*, p. 24).

merchant fleet, and substantial portions of her railway rolling-stock, fishing vessels, &c. There was, however, in the new Reich of the Weimar Republic no shortage either of man-power or of industrial capacity. Germany's very heavy casualties during the First World War[1] had been offset by some transfer of population from the ceded territories, and by natural growth; and, unlike France or Italy, she had not suffered physical destruction of industrial capacity. She remained the largest political unit in Europe, and her demographic and industrial strength was regarded by some of the victors, especially France, as a potential threat which had to be held in check.

This fundamental fact of Germany's demographic and industrial strength (63·2 million inhabitants in 1925 as compared with France's 40 million) governed the policy of France towards Germany from the Armistice onwards.

Those men who were responsible for French policy did not consider the German threat on its present merits but on its future potentialities.... Germany's ambitions might be assuaged in the future. But the fate of France could not be entrusted to such a hypothetical process. Mathematically, a nation of less than forty million inhabitants cannot, other things being equal, fight on even terms a country of nearly seventy millions whose industrial output is vastly superior to her own. French policy at the end of the last war was based on this fundamental truth.[2]

Instead of vague assurances the French wanted certainty. The 'Carthaginian Peace' desired by Clemenceau was a peace which would make France safe by destroying the economic power which Germany had attained; 'by loss of territory and other measures her population was to be curtailed; but chiefly the economic system, upon which she depended for her new strength, the vast fabric built upon iron, coal, and transport, must be destroyed'.[3] French statesmen, to quote the belated reflections of Lloyd George,

were bent on taking the fullest advantage of this opportunity [in framing the Treaty] to reduce the potential strength of Germany. Any conceivable peace would leave that terrible foe with a substantially larger population than that of France. . . . The possibility that Germany and France could ever become friends never entered into the calculation of any French statesman I ever met.[4]

This determination to curb Germany's industrial strength, a French policy that was a consequence of the immense blood-letting and destruction suffered, above all, by France, found its expression in the reparations clauses

[1] About 1·9 million of her men were killed during the war (see Germany, Statistisches Reichsamt: *Deutsche Wirtschaftskunde* (Berlin, Reimar Hobbing, 1930), p. 2).

[2] Maillaud: *France*, pp. 68–69.

[3] J. M. Keynes: *The Economic Consequences of the Peace* (London, Macmillan, 1919), p. 32.

[4] Lloyd George: *The Truth about the Peace Treaties*, ii. 990–1.

of the Treaty. Well-informed critics of those clauses, however, held at the time that (*a*) the transfer of such immense amounts in reparations was impracticable and that (*b*) the burden was so excessive as to prevent German recovery and with it European prosperity, views which later on led to a considerable modification of the reparations obligations.[1] But before these changes were introduced, both the actual payments made and the methods applied in collecting them contributed to bring about the utter collapse of the German currency with lasting social and political consequences. It was because of the modifications of Germany's obligations under the Dawes Settlement—that is, it was 'for want of a Carthaginian Peace'—that German industrial strength not only recovered its pre-war level by 1929 but considerably exceeded it. How did the Weimar economy adjust itself to the post-war conditions?

Broadly speaking, Germany's task of reconstruction was similar to that confronting other belligerents; she had to make good the wear and tear of equipment, the depletion of stocks and the loss, under the Armistice, of ships, rolling-stock, &c. These reconstruction demands competed not only with consumer demands but also with reparations demands from abroad. The fulfilment of reparations demands, without any assistance in the form of foreign loans, would, however, have necessitated the curtailment or postponement of both physical reconstruction and consumption, either in an orderly manner through taxation and saving, or in a disorderly manner through inflation. But inflation could only curtail consumption as long as prices continued to rise faster than incomes. Once people had begun to fear and expect inflation, its effectiveness as a deterrent to consumption would become less and less. This situation was, in fact, reached in Germany between the autumn of 1922 and the end of 1923.

Before the advent of hyper-inflation, Germany's industrial revival was quite remarkable. By the end of 1922 she had reached 80 per cent. of her pre-war level of industrial production (taking the area of the Weimar Reich as the basis for comparison of the situation at these two dates). The production of capital goods had doubled since 1919; iron and steel production had more than doubled; cement-manufacture and building had nearly trebled, and the construction of ships had more than trebled.[2] Reports submitted by experts to the Dawes Reparations Committee pointed out[3] that Germany's harbours and canals had been considerably extended since 1919, that the railway network had been enlarged, that the telephone and telegraph system had been equipped with the most modern appliances, and that in many branches of industry, thanks to the erection

[1] It was not until the end of the Second World War that the late Étienne Mantoux challenged controversy when he published his book with the brilliant title: '*The Carthaginian Peace, or the Economic Consequences of Mr. Keynes*' (London, Oxford University Press 1946).

[2] Wagenführ: *Industriewirtschaft*, p. 26.

[3] Ibid. p. 28.

of new plant and the installation of the latest equipment, more could be produced than before the war. This reconstruction and investment boom was initiated above all by government spending. Until the middle of 1921 government expenditure was very high indeed and the budget deficit alone exceeded total revenue.[1] Deficit spending led to the re-employment of demobilized soldiers in projects designed partly to alleviate the desperate shortage of all kinds of materials (i.e. opening of new lignite, coal, and inferior ore mines) and partly to remedy the dislocation in the system of transport and of communications. Bottle-necks in the available supply of many materials and, in particular, absolute shortages of food and consumer goods led to a rise in domestic prices which, although moderate, stimulated production; but at the same time, through the effect that this had on the redistribution of incomes in favour of profits, real consumption was kept low and the rate of reconstruction was accelerated. In this first phase reparations had consisted of payments mainly in kind, particularly coal,[2] and, although Germany had an adverse balance of payments, there was no perceptible deterioration in the external value of the mark.[3]

The second phase, leading to the period of hyper-inflation, opened with the demand for the first large cash payment in reparations by August 1921.[4] Even without this, Germany, in the opening months of the second phase, was running a deficit on her foreign balance at the rate of more than 1 milliard gold marks per annum. As a result of the transfer of an additional milliard gold marks in reparations, the depreciation of the exchange value of the mark, unaccompanied by a corresponding rise of exports or curtailment of imports, was bound to be considerable. The need to fulfil this reparations obligation was followed, a few months later, by the decision of the Council of the League of Nations to partition Silesia, with the result that 'in the Berlin foreign exchange market there was a panic of overwhelming violence'.[5] During the second phase, the Government were able to reduce the budget deficits considerably, so that the fall in the exchange value of the mark,[6] rather than deficit spending, became a leading factor in the mechanism of inflation. This drove up the cost of living,[7]

---

[1] See Costantino Bresciani-Turroni: *The Economics of Inflation* (London, Allen & Unwin, 1937), pp. 437–8.

[2] Up to May 1921, the cash receipts of the Reparations Commission amounted to no more than 124 million gold marks (J. M. Keynes: *A Revision of the Treaty* (London, Macmillan, 1922), p. 40).

[3] The monthly average dollar quotation was 64·8 marks in January 1920, improved to 39·5 marks in July 1920, and deteriorated to 76·6 marks in July 1921 (Gustav Stolper: *German Economy, 1870–1940* (London, Allen & Unwin, 1940), p. 151).

[4] One milliard gold marks were to be transferred between May and August 1921 (R. G. Hawtrey: *Currency and Credit* (London, Longmans, Green, 1928), pp. 420–1).

[5] Bresciani-Turroni, op. cit. p. 96.

[6] The dollar quotation rose from 76·7 marks in July 1921 to 191·8 marks in January 1922, and to 493·2 marks in July 1922 (Stolper, op. cit. p. 151).

[7] The cost of living index was stationary at 10 in 1920 (1913 = 1); it rose from 12 in June 1921 to 42 in June 1922 and to 133 in September 1922 (Bresciani-Turroni, op. cit. p. 444).

brought with it an irresistible pressure for higher wages,[1] and called forth an additional demand for money. Indeed, from the middle of 1922, reduced public deficit spending was offset by a considerable increase of private spending.[2] Although reparations in cash were suspended in July, confidence in the currency had been seriously shaken and there was a general flight into 'real values' (*Sachwerte*). For the great industrialists and speculators it became 'one of the rules of good management to contract as many debts as possible: debts which were repaid later with depreciated currency.'[3] Large-scale and indiscriminate expenditure, dominated by wholly abnormal incentives, signified this flight into real values. It was unaccompanied in the latter part of 1922 by any corresponding rise—partly because of foreign resistance[4]—in exports. This movement in the volume of foreign trade directly contributed to a worsening of the foreign balance[5] and to the continued depreciation of the mark.

When, in this desperate situation, Germany defaulted on her reparations deliveries in kind, the French and Belgians occupied the Ruhr. The result of this occupation was passive resistance, with two consequences: 'aggregate German output of goods and services' was catastrophically reduced by, first, the cessation of production in the Ruhr, together with its very important secondary effects on production in the rest of the Reich (i.e. curtailment of activity because of the non-delivery of Ruhr coal, steel, and chemicals, and because of the non-marketability of products of the Reich in the Ruhr); second, the financing of passive resistance by the Government of the Reich greatly increased the budget deficit. Hyper-inflation and the complete collapse of the mark were inevitable. Once all faith was lost in the currency, hyper-inflation on the foreign exchange market, as on the domestic market, no longer restricted consumption but actually stimulated it. In 1923 aggregate industrial production fell back to its level at the end of 1919 and mass unemployment was widespread.

[1] The index of coal-hewers' wages was stationary at 10 in the first six months of 1921; it rose to 18 in December 1921; to 55 in August 1922; and to 452 in December 1922 (ibid. p. 450).

[2] It was from the middle of 1922 that the share of commercial bills held by the Reichsbank in relation to its total bill holdings continuously increased (League of Nations: Economic, Financial and Transit Dept.: *Course and Control of Inflation*, p. 30).

[3] Bresciani-Turroni, op. cit. p. 294.

[4] e.g. 'there had been assigned to France for 1922 goods in kind worth 950 million gold marks. Actually in that year France received only 179 million marks' worth of goods, almost exclusively coal and coke, and that was because certain French industrial groups used their influence to stop the supply of goods which would have competed with their products.' Moreover the French Government were forced to renounce an order for motor-cars worth 117 million francs 'because of the opposition of the French manufacturers' (ibid. p. 99).

[5] In the four years 1919–22 the deficit on the foreign balance amounted to 11 milliard gold marks (ibid. p. 86). Others estimated it at 10 milliards (H. G. Moulton and C. E. McGuire: *Germany's Capacity to Pay* (New York, McGraw-Hill Book Co., 1923), p. 55). However, since the foreign deficit in 1920 was 0·5 milliard marks, in 1921 about 1 milliard marks, and hardly considerable in 1919, it follows that the widening of this gap was almost entirely due to the flight into real values in 1922.

Two decisive measures brought hyper-inflation to an end and preceded the stabilization of the new currency in November 1923: the first was the valorization of taxes, and the second was the cessation of passive resistance. But fiscal reform and preliminary stabilization were accompanied by foreign aid. This foreign aid, which involved some external control over German fiscal and monetary policy, guaranteed final and lasting stabilization. Had such aid been given earlier and perhaps been accompanied by some form of control, as was adopted under the Dawes Settlement, the political consequences for the new Republic of an impoverished and hostile middle class could probably have been avoided.

The Dawes Plan, as a provisional solution of the reparations problem, reduced Germany's annual liabilities and gave her a breathing-space for real recovery. It was in the period between 1924 and 1928 that private investment activity, supplemented only in the last three years by public investment, initiated recovery. Of the gross investment of about Rm. 40 milliard, both private and public, one-third was absorbed in the building-up of stocks which had been depleted by war and inflation, and two-thirds were devoted to the extension of plant, of transport, of housing, and of public utilities, and to the rationalization and mechanization of processes of production in German industry.[1] In this period German industry was basing its technological policy on American patterns, which, by raising substantially the productivity of labour,[2] increased aggregate output and partially reduced the volume of employment.[3]

The real bottle-neck to further expansion of output was neither a shortage of man-power nor a lack of available capacity,[4] but a shortage of materials. Throughout this period Germany was unable to earn the foreign exchange required both to pay for imports and to transfer money to meet reparations demands which she was fulfilling with admirable precision. Germany never reached her pre-war volume of exports, and, confronted by a permanent deficit on her foreign balance, she could maintain the existing level of internal activity only by borrowing abroad. In fact it was by means of increasing her net foreign indebtedness that Germany financed her reparations obligations as well as part of the modernization and extension of her industrial capacity.[5] It is a matter for

[1] G. Keiser: 'Kapitalbildung und Investition in Deutschland', *Bankwissenschaft*, 20 July 1931, p. 272.

[2] Indeed in 1929, productivity per man-hour was 25 per cent. higher in industry than in 1925 (see Wagenführ: *Industriewirtschaft*, p. 30).

[3] The effect of rationalization was clearly shown by the increase in unemployment, which was not seasonal, from the autumn of 1927 onwards (see Germany, Statistisches Reichsamt: *Deutsche Wirtschaftskunde*, p. 284).

[4] At the peak of the boom in 1928, German industry in general was utilized to only 77 per cent. of capacity (Institut für Konjunkturforschung: *Wochenbericht*, 18 September 1935, p. 152).

[5] In the six years 1924–9 Germany's net foreign indebtedness increased by about Rm. 16 milliard, which financed foreign investments in German industry of about Rm. 5 milliard and

conjecture whether Germany could substantially have reduced the deficit of her foreign balance by a direct restriction of imports and a curtailment of consumption. Such measures certainly would have presupposed a greater degree of control over foreign trade than democratic governments were likely to achieve in the circumstances, and the Allies had no means, short of assuming absolute control over the sovereign Republic by an Allied Military Government, of imposing fiscal policies designed to curtail consumption. It was not sufficient to argue, as Frenchmen have argued, that in the Dawes period German net investments were three to five times as high as actual reparations deliveries, and that therefore there was considerable scope for a much higher reparations burden.[1] What would have to be shown was how reduction of German investment or consumption could have been enforced without the strictest foreign control over German economic life. A Carthaginian peace by way of extracting reparations to an extent which would not have allowed capital growth in Germany would have been 'economically possible', provided, first, that foreign control could have been enforced, and second, that the rest of the world would have been prepared to accept huge export surpluses and the necessary adjustment in their own economies and foreign trade structures. Failing this, Germany's alternative, in the short run, was to raise, by means of foreign aid, the productive power of the country to such a pitch of efficiency as would enable her to achieve a real export surplus in the long run out of which she could repay reparations, foreign debt and interest on it. This was the intention of those governments which, although not wholeheartedly, had honestly supported a policy of treaty fulfilment.[2] But before this could be tested in reality, the house of cards had collapsed. Germany's industrial and economic strength, which by 1928–9 was greater than before the war, was built on unstable financial foundations. What ultimately undermined German finance and wrecked the system of international payments lay outside the sphere of reparations and of inter-Allied debts and was primarily due to causes which checked the outflow of capital from countries which had hitherto financed their own export surpluses.

German payments of reparations of about Rm. 11 milliard (see the writer's 'Analysis of Germany's Foreign Trade and the War', *Economica*, February 1940, p. 69).

[1] See Mantoux: *The Carthaginian Peace*, pp. 116–23.

[2] The supporters of the policy of fulfilment closely corresponded to the genuine supporters of Weimar democracy. Those of the Right who disliked the new internal régime were, broadly speaking, also the fiercest opponents of the Versailles Settlement. The Right exaggerated the burden that reparations imposed upon Germany. One branch of it demanded outright repudiation; another agitated for a refusal of the acceptance of certain foreign loans in order to illustrate Germany's inability to pay reparations. These revisionist and counter-revolutionary groups had to bide their time until a marked deterioration in general economic and political conditions should have induced a substantial section of the population to tolerate both internally and externally the application of more radical solutions.

(6) *The U.S.S.R.*

Reconstruction in the U.S.S.R. could not be seriously undertaken before civil war had been brought to an end in October 1920. With more than 85 per cent. of her population employed in agriculture, pre-war Russia was the least industrialized of the Great Powers.[1] Moreover, her industry relied largely upon imports of foreign materials, upon foreign technical personnel, and, above all, upon foreign capital for its development. It was too weak to withstand the strain of modern war. Completely exhausted by the privations and miseries of the First World War—during which her man-power losses had been greater than those of the United States, the United Kingdom, Italy, and France combined[2]—Russian farm and industrial workers accepted the Bolsheviks' usurpation of political power as a step in the direction of achieving peace. In order to consolidate their power, the Communists divided the big estates among the poorer sections of the farm population and equalized the holdings of peasants. This inevitably meant civil war; and when, in the course of revolutionary fighting, all industry was nationalized, the former Russian ruling classes received, in their desperate struggle for existence, the active support of foreigners, whose material interests were directly threatened and who, on ideological grounds, had reason intensely to dislike the Bolshevik régime.

The economic consequences of war and civil war were disastrous for Russia. Completely cut off from external supplies, and, in the course of the war of foreign intervention, losing control over the areas which contained the country's basic coal, steel, and industrial production centres, the Soviet Government could only secure command over real resources by inflationary deficit spending. When, however, by 1918–19, hyper-inflation had reduced the purchasing power of money to near zero, the Government had to resort to compulsory requisitioning. The replacement of the free market by a system based on the requisitioning of agricultural products and on a central allocation of supplies for nationalized industry, the consumer, and the armed forces alike, aggravated the economic plight of the country. The administration was over-staffed with inexperienced men and was inefficient; central controls were unsystematic; and the whole system, known as 'War Communism', carried within itself the germs of ultimate collapse. During this tumultuous period of civil war, when destruction of

---

[1] In 1913 some 82·3 per cent. of the total population of 139·3 million persons lived in rural areas: see U.S.S.R., State Planning Commission of the U.S.S.R.: *Summary of the Fulfilment of the First Five-Year Plan* (Moscow, 1933), p. 269. But less than 10 per cent. of the population derived their livelihood from industry: see Maurice Dobb: *Soviet Economic Development since 1917* (London, Routledge & Kegan Paul, 1948), p. 36.

[2] Russia's total losses in man-power during the First World War were estimated at 5·3 million persons (i.e. 2·8 million killed and 2·5 million missing) as compared with the combined losses of the other four Powers of 3·3 million (i.e. 2·8 million killed and 0·5 million missing). See W. P. and Zelda K. Coates: *Armed Intervention in Russia 1918–1922* (London, Gollancz, 1935), p. 17.

property, dislocation of transport, and administrative chaos became wide-spread, both the workers and the small peasants, the very sections of the population on which the Bolsheviks depended for support, grew increas-ingly hostile towards the 'new Communist slavery'.[1] In industry producti-vity per man fell to one-third of the pre-war figure, and in agriculture the peasants reacted to compulsory requisitioning not merely by withholding agricultural supplies, but—what was worse—by reducing the area under cultivation. The net result was that, when civil war came to an end and when the Soviet Government again achieved control over their territory, aggregate industrial output was only 14·5 per cent. of the pre-war output, while the agricultural land under cultivation was one-half of the pre-war area and the value of the rouble was only 1 per cent. of what it had been in October 1917.[2]

The task of reconstruction was immense. The Government's first aim was to regain the confidence of the workers and of the peasants. Towards this end, Lenin outlined, shortly after the conclusion of peace with Poland, a new economic policy (NEP). This consisted in abandoning many of the emergency measures of the civil war period. Compulsory requisitioning was replaced by a tax in kind on peasants' surpluses. The central alloca-tion of materials was abolished, except for heavy industry, and was replaced by a system whereby socialized enterprises could make their own con-tracts for the acquisition and disposal of goods and services. Moreover, the partial reintroduction of a denationalized private sector in trade and handicraft as between socialized industry and private peasant agriculture greatly assisted in speeding up the restoration of normal market contacts between town and country. Although the Soviet Government regarded the 'State Capitalism' of NEP as no more than a transitional system, it lasted until 1928-9.

No doubt, NEP provided incentives for recovery. The pace of revival was, however, limited by shortages of some specific materials, and by other factors. At first, agricultural tax yields were smaller than they had previously been under compulsory requisitioning. Since long-term foreign loans were unobtainable and tax revenue and voluntary savings were quite inadequate to acquire the real resources necessary for the recon-struction of transport and of the major part of the heavy industries, the Soviet Government continued to finance this by printing new money. Indeed, until the introduction of a new stable currency in 1924, currency and prices increased more rapidly than ever before; but, in contrast with the civil war period, the increase in currency exceeded the rise in prices, so that the real value of the currency gradually rose. With the accomplishment

---

[1] See Dobb: *Soviet Economic Development*, p. 120.
[2] But by 1917 prices were already eight times higher than in 1913: see Alexander Baykov: *The Development of the Soviet Economic System* (Cambridge University Press, 1946), p. 31.

of monetary reform, budget deficits fell to negligible proportions and ceased to be financed by new issues; taxes in kind were transformed into progressive income-property taxes payable in money, and taxation and profits from state property and enterprises, rather than voluntary savings, became the primary source for financing public expenditure.[1] By 1926–7 reconstruction had been completed and by 1928 industrial output and the real wages of industrial workers were one-third higher than before the war, while the cultivated area and gross yields in agriculture had been restored to pre-war levels.

The economic situation was, however, by no means satisfactory. First, throughout the 1920s the population had been growing above pre-war level,[2] while agricultural output had only just been restored. Since it was estimated that food consumption per head had reached pre-war levels, the result was that the quantity of food available for export had fallen,[3] and since, in the absence of foreign aid, exports decisively determined the volume of the imports which the U.S.S.R. was able to acquire, it was a matter of great concern that the volume of exports amounted in 1928 to only about 40 per cent. of the pre-war figure.[4] Thus, although the Government did control the composition of imports by virtue of their complete foreign trade monopoly, they were aware that the shortage of imports put a brake on further rapid internal industrial advance. But such an advance was required if, in view of the growing population pressure, they desired to prevent a gradual deterioration in the people's still meagre standard of living. Secondly, quite apart from the existence of agrarian over-population and the threat of its further increase,[5] industrial unemployment was also rising, as a result of insufficient industrial equipment. Although shorter working hours and double shifts had been introduced between 1926 and 1928, industrial plant and equipment were inadequate to prevent the emergence of a relatively higher level of industrial unemployment in the U.S.S.R. than existed anywhere under the capitalist system of the other Great Powers. Unemployment among trade union members had been rising to the figure of about 2 million in the middle of 1928. The total number of wage and salary earners had risen from 8 million in 1924 to less than 9 million in 1928, and of these just under 4 million were occupied in large-scale industry and building. Over 12 per cent. of the unemployed were unemployed for more than one year, receiving

[1] Baykov, op. cit. table 10, p. 95.

[2] The population increased from 139·3 million persons in 1913 to 154·2 million in 1928 (see U.S.S.R., State Planning Commission of the U.S.S.R.; *Summary of the Fulfilment of the First Five-Year Plan*, p. 269).

[3] Colin Clark: *A Critique of Russian Statistics* (London, Macmillan, 1939), p. 17.

[4] S. N. Prokopovicz: *Russlands Volkswirtschaft unter den Sowjets* (Zürich, Europa Verlag, 1944), p. 329.

[5] In 1927–8 the agrarian over-population was estimated at 8 to 9 million. See Dobb: *Soviet Economic Development*, p. 189, quoting Russian sources.

benefits amounting to between one-fifth and one-third of the normal wage.[1]

How could these difficulties be resolved? To absorb the unemployed masses and to counter the threat of a deterioration in standards of living as the population increased, productivity all round had to be raised substantially. The immediate bottle-necks were a shortage of steel, industrial equipment, and farming tools, and an inefficient organization of agriculture. At the existing low level of productivity and real income there were narrow limits within which to redirect resources from the production of consumer goods to the production of industrial and agricultural equipment, and, since foreign loans were difficult to obtain, the whole weight of creating a real surplus fell upon the improvement in the organization of farming. Throughout the NEP period, and as a result of the division of the big estates during the Revolution, agricultural produce coming on to the market never exceeded one-half of the marketable surplus of the pre-war years. To increase this surplus was a key objective; and the replacement of small-scale private farming by large-scale collective farming was the means chosen to achieve this end. With all the ruthlessness at the disposal of a one-party government, this greatest of all social revolutions was carried through from 1928 onwards. This decision in favour of collectivization also constituted the turning-point in the transformation of the U.S.S.R. from the transitional State Capitalism of NEP towards Socialism. In the execution of this second revolution a marketable surplus was indeed achieved; this surplus was increased by other methods of restricting consumption. In part the resources set free in consumption were invested in the construction of investment goods, and in part the surplus was exported to finance the import of a larger volume of industrial equipment. These revolutionary measures created the conditions for the rapid industrialization of the country under the First Five-Year Plan (1928–32),[2] which was expected to solve the problem of agrarian over-population and poverty.

(7) *Summary*

Five main features characterized the industrial development of the seven Great Powers in the 1920s.

First, the tasks of reconstruction confronting each Power were of unequal weight owing to the wide differences between them in respect of destruction suffered and disinvestments incurred during the First World War. To the extent that demands on available resources, whether for reconstruction or for reparations, were pushed beyond those released from consumption (by voluntary saving or taxation), absolute shortages and bottle-necks in the supply of specific equipment, materials, and labour were encountered, and

---

[1] Ibid. pp. 190, 417.
[2] See also above, pp. 56–58.

the inevitable outcome was inflation. However, inflation itself, as long as it did not pass from its moderate phase into a run-away phase, was favourable to expansion of output, and it released, by means of changes in the distribution of income, the resources required for reconstruction.

Secondly, when war-time destruction and disinvestments had been made good, and when the currencies of the Powers, temporarily exposed to inflation, had been stabilized, new investment was directed towards expansion or rationalization. The new investment became the basis upon which were built subsequent improvements in productivity, or output per man-hour. By 1929 productivity and efficiency, the real source of all progress, had, in each of the seven countries, surpassed all levels ever previously attained.

Thirdly, full employment and the rise in industrial output per man-hour which accompanied it led jointly to the attainment of unprecedented levels of production in France and in the United States. In the United Kingdom, on the other hand, such improvements in productivity were prevented from leading to an expansion of output beyond the pre-war volume by fundamental changes in foreign demand and by the pursuit of monetary and fiscal policies which caused the country to remain in the doldrums of perpetually under-employed resources. However, at their divergent levels of activity and employment, these three Powers were enabled, in consequence of the prevailing structures of income and consumption, to make loans abroad and, by means of an active foreign balance, to sustain their respective volumes of production.

Fourthly, the volume of investment which Japan and Italy required for industrialization was in excess of the resources that they were prepared to release through the reduction of an already very low level of consumption. In this situation they borrowed from abroad. In so far as these loans were not dissipated on raising the current level of home consumption, the resultant net imports of materials and equipment permitted a broadening of the industrial sector of the body economic and the absorption into it of some part of the growing surplus population. Moreover, in so far as imports of machinery supplemented domestic resources that were in short supply, industrial productivity per man-hour rose, and this, in association with a high and rising volume of employment, carried forward in the post-war decade the conspicuous war-time trend of an ever expanding volume of production. Like Japan and Italy, Germany, too, availed herself extensively of foreign loans for the purpose of meeting her reparations obligations and of modernizing and rationalizing her industries. In contrast with Japan, the consequent improvement in productivity per man-hour was accompanied in Germany, from 1927 onwards, by a growth in the number of unemployed men.

Fifthly, the long-drawn-out and turbulent domestic events in the

U.S.S.R. adversely affected her immediate post-war level of industrial output. Recovery, however, was rapid here when it began. Productivity per man-hour improved, causing an increase of industrial unemployment, however, when once existing capacity had been fully utilized. Since the U.S.S.R. could not rely to any extent on foreign aid, she depended largely upon the stimulation of her own exports to pay for imports of urgently required equipment and materials. This necessitated above all the realization of a marketable surplus of agricultural produce. Small-scale farming, however, being itself the outcome of the Revolution from below (1917), set limits to such surpluses. It was one of the purposes of the Revolution from above (1928) to increase these surpluses and thus to provide the prerequisites for accelerating industrialization. The collectivization of farming was the very essence of that second Revolution.

If, as has been shown, each of the Great Powers attained or exceeded its pre-war industrial output during the 1920s, what then was their relative strength when reconversion and reconstruction had been completed?

(b) Relative Industrial Strength and the Great Depression

In 1928, which was a relatively prosperous year, the value of world industrial production was estimated at about £18 milliard sterling.[1] The seven Great Powers produced in this year about four-fifths of the world's industrial goods, a figure which clearly indicated their combined supremacy in the industrial world.[2] But their individual contributions to this total were extremely unequal, for the comparative share of each Power in the world output of industrial and of manufactured goods or their relative strength was approximately as follows:

Relative Strength in 1928

(World output = 100)

	U.S.A.	Germany	Great Britain	France	U.S.S.R.	Italy	Japan	Seven Powers
Industrial output	44·8	11·6	9·3	7·0	4·6	3·2	2·4	82·9
Manufacturing output	40·8	12·4	9·3	6·6	4·8	3·3	2·6	79·8

The most striking feature of this comparison is that the United States was, both in industrial and in manufacturing strength, the leading Power

---

[1] i.e. 'net output' or 'value added'. It has been estimated at Rm. 350 milliard (Wagenführ, *Industriewirtschaft*, p. 38) and converted into pounds sterling at a rate of Rm. 20 to the pound.

[2] Their combined strength was not very different if building construction, electricity generation, and mining were excluded from 'industry' in order to arrive at 'manufacture proper' (League of Nations: Economic, Financial, and Transit Dept.: *Industrialization and Foreign Trade*, p. 13).

in the world. In the late 1920s she occupied an unrivalled position, producing alone a larger output than that of the other six Great Powers taken together. Her overwhelming productive strength was further underlined by the fact that the gross value of manufactures produced per head of population in the United States was nearly twice as high as in Great Britain or Germany, and more than ten to eleven times as high as in the U.S.S.R. or Italy.[1] And even at that level of output the United States was not utilizing to the full either her existing industrial capacity or her available human resources.

Yet the United States' political influence in the world was in no respect commensurate with her extraordinary industrial strength. In Europe, at least, it was the United Kingdom and, above all, France rather than the United States who wielded significant political influence. There was, however, no close correlation between political and economic power. Broadly speaking, naked power politics were at a discount in the world of the 1920s. It was the heyday of the League of Nations. Since the United States and the U.S.S.R. were not members of the League and since the original pledge to protect France, given by Great Britain and the United States, was repudiated by both those countries, France felt compelled to use her influence in the League to play power politics against Germany; but her policy was based on her military strength rather than on her broad industrial strength. Although the Great Powers potentially possessed the industrial means to assert their will if they had wished to do so, two considerations narrowly limited their political ambitions in the circumstances. First, in view of the close mutual dependence between industrial and primary (i.e. food and raw material) producing areas, between fellow industrial nations, and between various primary producing countries, each Power was in need of certain foreign sources of vital supplies. Its industrial strength would be undermined if it were unable to procure them. Therefore, any country intent on practising naked power politics was forced to develop, even at a cost, effective substitutes in its own territory, to redirect its imports to countries nearer to itself, and to accumulate stocks of irreplaceable imports. Secondly, such measures presupposed that governments could control economic activity within their countries and could alter the geographical distribution of their imports by deliberate, and skilfully conducted, commercial policies. They had in fact assumed a greater degree of control over internal and external

---

[1] For the period 1926–9, the average annual gross value of manufactures, divided by the average annual total population, was, estimated in dollars per head, approximately:

U.S.A.	U.K.	Germany	France	Italy	Japan	U.S.S.R.
350	190	180	160	80	40	30

(League of Nations: Economic, Financial, and Transit Dept.: *Industrialization and Foreign Trade*, p. 84).

economic affairs than before the First World War, but in none of the seven countries, with the exception perhaps of the U.S.S.R., was economic activity directly subjected to central directives.

Indeed, in their external economic relations most countries adhered to an internationally agreed code of rules. Under the currency code of the gold standard different national currencies were interchangeable at a fixed rate, and this made it possible to settle multilaterally the numerous payment balances arising for any single country from the fact that its import and export markets were not identical. But as gold was also the basis for the credit operations of the Central Banks, the various national economies were closely linked to each other. This world-wide inter-dependence had immense advantages, as it enabled each country to reap by trade the benefits from specialization in the production of the goods and services for which each was best suited. Its disadvantage was that any considerable disturbances in any part of the world tended to spread over wide areas. As long as this system worked it was, to say the least, difficult for any country to pursue a far-reaching independent power policy. If any country kept out of step with the rest of the world, if, for instance, in view of a declining world demand, it tried to keep its own resources fully employed, its external balance of payments would be adversely affected. Unless it possessed large international reserves of gold and foreign exchange it would be unable to sustain a prolonged period of trade deficits and would be compelled to restore equilibrium in its external balance by means of restriction of internal credit, curtailment of output, and unemployment.

As foreign trade in all countries, with the exception of the U.S.S.R., was primarily conducted by a great number of individual traders, it was unlikely that, for a country as a whole, all current transactions (i.e. payments and receipts from merchandise, trade, shipping, insurance services, tourist traffic, foreign investments, &c.) would balance completely. It was more probable that some countries would have deficits and others surpluses. However, the necessary internal processes of adjustment were normally kept within limits by the fact that countries with a surplus were prepared to lend capital to countries with a deficit. Thus international lending and borrowing were as important a condition for the smooth operation of the multilateral system as were the uniform valuation of currencies and the existence of a world market to which all countries were admitted on equal terms.[1]

The germs of a potential crisis, which led to the abandonment of the gold standard in 1931, were present in the world economic situation of the 1920s. Great structural maladjustments had arisen in the relation of the world's industries to one another as a result of the First World War and of technical

[1] League of Nations: Economic Intelligence Service: *Network of World Trade*, pp. 73 seqq.

and economic progress. The development of hydro-electric power and oil, the expansion of cotton-spinning mills in India and Japan, and the post-war protection of industries which had been built up in many non-belligerent countries during the war, had created problems of adjustment in the older countries which they were not willing to face squarely. Moreover, the great increase in agricultural productivity, and the refusal of countries that had expanded their agriculture during the war to reduce it afterwards, led to over-production. Similarly, with the rise of industrial output in the 1920s, the export of raw materials rose considerably; but the world's production of raw materials rose still faster, so that the 'export quota' in 1929 was only 88 per cent. of pre-1914 volume.[1] The pressure on the prices of all countries producing primary goods caused strains in their external balances. And difficulties over the balance of payment confronted even some of the larger Powers, which were indebted to the United States for goods and services rendered to them during the war, in very much the same way as Germany was indebted to the Allies on account of reparations obligations. The need for adjustment was postponed because the countries commanding a surplus were willing to lend capital, and the countries labouring under a deficit were willing to borrow it.

All these potential dangers to international co-operation were of less significance than those emanating from violent fluctuations in the internal economic activity of countries which not only had a large share in world trade but were also important exporters of capital. In this respect the Great Powers, and especially the United States, were in a position to draw the world into a depression, just as they could lift it into flourishing boom conditions. For they not only jointly held the largest share in the world's aggregate income and industrial output, but they also accounted for half of the world's volume of trade, for nearly two-thirds of the world's merchant fleet,[2] and for more than two-thirds of the world's liquid gold reserves.[3] Three of them, the United States, France, and the United Kingdom, were the world's main lending and creditor nations. Clearly, a large-scale recession in business activity in some of these countries, preceded, or accompanied, by a cessation of international lending, would inevitably be transmitted to the rest of the world.

In view of the importance of international lending and borrowing for the smooth operation of the multilateral system, reference must be made to the changes in the composition of the two groups of creditor and debtor nations. In 1914 the main creditor countries among the Great Powers were the United Kingdom, with foreign investments amounting to about

[1] Germany: Enquete-Ausschuss: *Der deutsche Aussenhandel unter der Einwirkung weltwirtschaftlicher Strukturwandlungen* (Berlin, E. S. Mittler, 1932), p. 273. (In *Veröffentlichungen des Enquete-Ausschusses*, i, 5. Arbeitsgruppe, 20. Band, 1. Halbband).

[2] *Statistisches Jahrbuch, 1935*, p. 101.*

[3] *Federal Reserve Bulletin* (Washington), September 1940, pp. 925–34.

$20 milliard, France with 9 milliard, and Germany with 6·2 milliard.[1] From being net debtors before the war, both the United States and Japan became creditors after it, and Germany, having lost the war, became a debtor country. The post-war period saw Japan waging a losing battle to sustain her creditor position and to maintain her gold and exchange reserves.[2] On the other hand, the United Kingdom and France, whose foreign assets had been depleted by the war, realized in the 1920s, like the United States, a surplus of visible and invisible exports over their imports and this was added to their investments abroad. In the period from 1923 to 1929 net exports of long-term and short-term capital from the United Kingdom and the United States amounted to about $3 milliard[3] and $5 milliard[4] respectively—amounts that were far in excess of the lending of countries like France, Canada, or Belgium. The strengthening in the position of the creditor countries was accompanied by a rising indebtedness of the borrowing countries. Germany, in particular, was the largest net importer of capital in this period, to the amount of about $4·2 milliard, followed by Australia, Argentina, and Japan. In 1928 aggregate American net investments abroad totalled $8·5 milliard. British foreign assets were very much higher, and probably approached the pre-war level, while French foreign assets were estimated at 60 per cent. of their pre-war figure.

It was immaterial that in the post-war period the United States had replaced Germany in the group of creditor nations. But, since the functioning of the international system depended on lending and borrowing arrangements, it was of the utmost significance that the creditor countries' willingness to lend should not cease abruptly. Indeed, the wreck of this system of international payments was attributable not primarily to 'unsound' borrowing,[5] or to reparations and inter-Ally debt arrangements, but to complex causes operative within each of the seven countries which weakened their willingness to lend. Since American loans had been so powerful a means of aiding the economic development and expansion of

---

[1] Royal Institute of International Affairs: *The Problem of International Investment*: Study Group Report (London, Oxford University Press for Royal Institute of International Affairs, 1937), pp. 113–31.   [2] Schumpeter and others: *Industrialization of Japan*, p. 866.

[3] League of Nations: Economic Intelligence Service: *The Course and Phases of the World Economic Depression*, revised edition (Geneva, League of Nations, 1931), p. 31. Moreover, Great Britain's surplus on all current transactions was estimated by G. D. A. Macdougall at 7 per cent. between 1923 and 1929 as compared with 30 per cent. in 1913 (see 'Britain's Foreign Trade Problem', *Economic Journal*, March 1947, p. 79).

[4] The United States' surplus on current accounts was estimated at $5·2 milliard, the net inflow of gold at $0·18 milliard, and the 'recorded' net capital outflow at $3·6 milliard (U.S. Bureau of Foreign and Domestic Commerce: *The United States in the World Economy* (Washington, U.S.G.P.O., 1943), table i).

[5] By which is meant the absorption and use of loans for purposes not always designed to raise the productive efficiency of the borrowing countries' industries, which alone would have enabled them to have export surpluses in the longer run and to repay the loans.

many parts of the world in the 1920s, internal American events, in so far as they affected American foreign purchases and external lending, became significant for the whole world.

The great prosperity of the American economy in the 1920s was based above all on vigorous internal investment activity. In considering the factors which brought the investment boom to an end, real causes, in the sense of a saturation of the most urgent requirements of plant, business equipment, &c., were closely interlinked with monetary and fiscal causes. There were signs of a real recession in 1927, but it was not until 1929 that the aggregate demand for investment goods began to slacken.[1] New investment during the five years previous to 1929 had been on so enormous a scale in the aggregate that the prospective yield of further additions was, coolly considered, falling rapidly. The boom could not have continued on a sound basis except with a very low long-term rate of interest. 'In fact, the rate of interest was high enough to deter new investment except in those particular directions which were under the influence of speculative excitement and, therefore, in special danger of being over-exploited'.[2] Indeed, American speculative stock values kept on rising even although in 1928 rediscount rates were increased, and government securities were sold in an effort to check the rise. Speculators were not discouraged, because profits made from the speculative sale of securities were far greater than the charges for borrowed money.[3]

However, this stock-market boom, which could not go on for ever, had the effect of checking the export of capital from the United States. American long-term lending was halved between 1928 and 1929 and net capital exports were very much below the American surplus on current account.[4] For different reasons, although with the same adverse effects on the system of international payments, French short-term capital was in these years also repatriated. As a result, many countries got into difficulties over their balance of payments, and these were much intensified when, in September 1929, the speculative boom collapsed in the United States and when, in the subsequent depression, the flow of American lending stopped completely and abruptly.

The causes of the stock exchange crash were complex. The disclosure of the Hatry fraud in London led to a withdrawal of funds from the United States. Big speculators forseeing trouble began to liquidate their security holdings.[5] It is possible also that further increases in interest rates

---

[1] Alvin H. Hansen: *Fiscal Policy and Business Cycles* (London, Allen & Unwin, 1941), p. 57.
[2] J. M. Keynes: *The General Theory of Employment Interest and Money* (London, Macmillan, 1936), p. 323.
[3] George Soule: *Prosperity Decade. A Chapter from American Economic History, 1917–1929* (London, Pilot Press, 1947), p. 280.
[4] U.S. Bureau of Foreign and Domestic Commerce: *United States in the World Economy*, p. 156.
[5] Soule, op. cit. p. 306.

cooled the speculative excitement. In so far as monetary policy was influential in checking that excitement, it belonged to the species of remedy which cured the disease by killing the patient.[1] With reference to the depression in general Professor R. G. Hawtrey wrote:

Even if there were non-monetary causes at work in 1929 and 1930, which were tending to produce a violent compression of consumers' income and collapse of demand, it remains true that the action of the great central banks at that time was independently tending to produce precisely that result. For the curtailment of the flow of money, the central banks, as the sole sources of money, must bear the responsibility.[2]

A falling-off in real investment activity had taken place before the stock exchange crash occurred, not only in the United States but also in Germany, where aggregate public and private investments had continuously declined since 1927.[3] For a short time Germany, not unlike Britain, benefited on foreign account from the catastrophic fall in the prices of raw materials and food. This temporary improvement of Germany's external balance vanished in 1930 with the withdrawal of short-term funds. Even in the United Kingdom, former surpluses on external account turned into a deficit for the first time in 1931.

When once the recession had started in the main industrial centres, the process of contraction became cumulative. The reduction in these countries' demand for imports brought about a further fall in the world prices of primary products. Since, however, countries like the United States and Germany had great agricultural interests of their own, it was an irresistible temptation for them to protect these interests by raising tariffs. As a result of the increase in 1930 of the American tariff to the highest level in its whole history, the American surplus on current transactions remained in that year as high as in 1927 or in 1929. It was not offset by lending. Hence the countries with deficits, joined in 1931 by the United Kingdom, saw their liquid international resources being drained away into France and especially into the United States, where, however, the inflowing gold was not used for an expansion of credit but was 'sterilized' in the vaults of Fort Knox. The loss of liquidity resulting from external deficits, or, as in the case of Germany, from the withdrawal of short-term capital, necessarily produced internal deflation, restriction of output, and increases in unemployment.

In a depressed world with idle productive capacity and severe unemployment each country tended to exclude imports and to foster exports. Imports were regarded as a threat to domestic employment, while exports

---

[1] Keynes, op. cit. p. 323.

[2] R. G. Hawtrey: *The Gold Standard*, 4th edition (London, Longmans, Green, 1939), p. 163.

[3] From Rm. 11·3 milliard in 1927 to Rm. 9·9 milliard in 1928 and to less than Rm. 7 milliard in 1929 (G. Keiser and B. Benning: 'Kapitalbildung und Investitionen in der deutschen Volkswirtschaft 1924 bis 1928', in *Institut für Konjunkturforschung: Vierteljahrsheft 1931, Sonderheft 22*).

were considered as a means of increasing domestic employment, not only by reason of the number of workers engaged in the production of net exports, but also through the additional employment created by the effective demand of the workers producing the export surplus. But it was difficult for any single country to foster exports if other countries refused to take more. What could be done, however, was to reduce imports by tariffs, licences, import quotas, currency depreciation, &c. To a varying degree all countries relied on these measures. They were weapons of defence; but, in so far as they produced export surpluses, they turned out to be the best weapons of attack. For, by the same amount as the depression in the country with a surplus was mitigated, depression in the country with a deficit was intensified. Indeed, in a depressed world, export surpluses meant the export of unemployment; it was a game of beggar-my-neighbour[1] and might with justice be called a policy of economic aggression. As Cordell Hull observed in a later reflection on the crisis: 'Our people are not likely to forget the contribution which the enactment of the 1930 tariff made to the intensification of economic warfare among nations.'[2]

It was an inevitable consequence of this mad struggle for export surpluses that the channels for multilateral trading should narrow. And when in 1931 the United Kingdom went off the gold standard and depreciated her currency, in order to halt the loss of liquidity, the movement towards unilateral monetary and commercial measures by individual states all over the world became a landslide. The abandonment of international trade and currency codes opened up possibilities for action on the part of individual states which might serve to mitigate the depression for them individually,[3] but which might also serve to promote a national practice of power politics. The challenge of the time to conquer the depression was a challenge, above all, to the Great Powers which had drawn the world into it. But they did not even try to find a common basis for joint action, and so left the distortions produced by the crisis to be rectified through measures for economic recovery undertaken by each country in isolation. Economic nationalism was one answer to that challenge; but with it, power politics in international relations came right to the fore.

What had happened to the relative industrial strength of the Great Powers in the course of the Great Depression? The impact of the depression on industrial output had been more severe in some countries than in others. In fact it left almost completely unaffected the output of the

---

[1] See Joan Robinson: *Essays in the Theory of Employment*, 2nd edition (Oxford, Blackwell, 1947), p. 156.

[2] Statement made before the Finance Committee of the Senate on 26 February 1940 (U.S. Congress, Senate Committee on Finance: *Extension of Reciprocal Trade Agreements Act, Hearings . . . 76th Cong. 3rd session on H.J.Res. 407, February 26–March 6, 1940* (Washington, U.S.G.P.O., 1940)).

[3] League of Nations: Economic Intelligence Service: *Course and Phases of the World Economic Depression*, p. 315.

U.S.S.R. and of Japan. In a period of cumulative contraction of output elsewhere, the U.S.S.R. completed her First Five-Year Plan, and in 1932 her volume of industrial production was about 85 per cent. higher than in 1928.[1] The initial downward pressure on output was also quickly overcome in Japan and her material requirements for war in China caused industrial production in 1932 to be about 14 per cent. above the 1928 level. Output within the other five countries continued to fall. It contracted by 11 per cent. in Great Britain, by 22 per cent. in Italy, by 26 per cent. in France, and by 43 per cent. in both Germany and the United States.

Owing to these divergences in rates of expansion and contraction, the relative industrial strength of the Great Powers altered completely. The share in world industrial output of each Power, in 1932, at the bottom of the depression, as compared with 1928, was as follows:

Relative Strength in 1928 and 1932

(World output = 100)

	U.S.A.	Germany	Great Britain	France	U.S.S.R.	Italy	Japan	Seven Powers
Industrial output in *1928* .	44·8	11·6	9·3	7·0	4·6	3·2	2·4	82·9
Industrial output in *1932* .	35·1	8·9	11·3	7·0	12·4	3·4	3·7	81·8

[1] The question has been raised repeatedly: can Russian figures be trusted? Few would say that they were wilfully distorted. But all would admit that, in a period when a society was undergoing rapid changes, it could be no easy matter to calculate indices correctly owing to variations in the relative importance of items entering into them. The official Russian index rose from 100 in 1928 to 232 in 1932 (see Birmingham Bureau: Memorandum no. 12, p. 12). All critics of Soviet statistics pointed out that there was an inflationary bias in the official index, for the index was based on the gross value of industrial output in 1926–7 roubles. Although industry became more efficient in the course of the First Five-Year Plan, commodities brought into the market after 1927 continued to be valued at the prices at which they were first introduced. Hence an inflationary bias was present. The question is: how great was the bias? Colin Clark, who revalued selected Russian commodities both in 1928 and in 1934 at American and at English prices, concluded that for the period 1928–34 the percentage increase was less than half that of the official index (*Critique of Russian Statistics*, p. 46). For a rejoinder to Clark see Maurice Dobb: *Soviet Economy and the War* (London, Routledge, 1931), pp. 30–35. It would seem that Clark's corrections put the real increase too low. More important were the calculations of A. Gerschenkorn: 'The Soviet Indices of Industrial Production', *Review of Economic Statistics*, November 1947, pp. 217–26. He compared the 'increase' of 132 in the official index for large-scale industry and of 140 in that for 'industry as a whole' (always excluding building construction) with the increases in the official indices of physical units of crude oil by 74 per cent., of coal by 80 per cent., of pig-iron by 84 per cent., of electric power by 160 per cent., and of steel by only 40 per cent. in 1932 over 1928. Taking into account (1) the degree of fabrication, (2) foreign trade, and (3) the increased efficiency in the utilization of basic materials, he concluded that the 'true' index of industrial output would lie somewhere between the official index and the series of physical indices of materials. Gerschenkorn's conclusions seemed to be confirmed by an investigation independently reached by the Institut für Konjunkturforschung: see *Wochenbericht*, 21 March 1940, nos. 10–11, pp. 41–46. In the following pages the writer will assume that the official index of 232 for 1932 should more correctly read 185, that is an 'increase' of 85 instead of 132 since 1928.

The most startling consequences of the depression were the rise in the relative strength of the U.S.S.R., and, to a lesser extent, the improvement in the relative positions of Great Britain, Japan, and Italy. Although the United States still held first place in the hierarchy of economic power, her relative position had been immensely weakened. And Germany, who had formerly held the second place, was relegated to the fourth.

But this change in relative strength between the Great Powers was incidental to the depression. Of more immediate consequence was the great and avoidable waste of idle productive capacities and of unemployed man-power. It was estimated that the loss of goods and services which could have been, but which were not, produced or rendered during the depression was at least as high as the cost to all the belligerents of the First World War.[1] In all countries the body politic as well as the body economic had been thrown into a state of violent tension. These internal convulsions led in Germany to a political combination of all the counter-revolutionary forces, which attributed the pitiful state of affairs, including the 6 million unemployed and the ruin of large sections of the middle class, to inefficient and weak governments, to reparations, to the loss of territory and of *Lebensraum*; and their cry that radical solutions, both internal and external, were required to relieve current distress proved effective. The emergence of a totalitarian régime in Germany within four months of the accession to power of the Hugenberg–Hitler coalition in January 1933 meant above all that German revisionist claims would henceforth be pressed with iron determination.

The realization of such external ambitions, however, seemed still a long way off for Germany. Although potentially capable of great strength, she was in fact weak. Not only had her relative industrial strength severely declined in relation to that of the U.S.S.R., it had also deteriorated almost without interruption since the First World War as compared with that of France and Italy. These two Powers, which, in 1913, had jointly produced about three-quarters of Germany's output,[2] nearly equalled her output at the top of the boom and surpassed it by about one-fifth in the middle of 1932. Moreover, Great Britain's industrial output exceeded Germany's in

---

[1] The estimate of loss of goods not produced during the depression at £22 milliard was made by Colin Clark and quoted in the P.E.P. publication *Planning*, 11 May 1943. The direct costs of the First World War in terms of money were estimated at $186 milliard and all indirect costs at $152 milliard (Ernest L. Bogart: *Direct and Indirect Costs of the Great World War* (Carnegie Endowment for International Peace: *Preliminary Economic Studies of the War*, no. 24: New York, Oxford University Press, 1919), p. 299). Apart from the virtually meaningless assessment of indirect costs, i.e. the capitalized value of loss of life, &c., it should be pointed out that the direct costs (converted) at £39 milliard does not represent real costs. Allowance must be made for price changes, which (i.e. monthly wholesale prices)—to take Germany as an example—were 2·5 times higher in December 1918 and 8 times higher in December 1919 than in 1913 (see Bresciani-Turroni: *Economics of Inflation*, p. 442).

[2] Based on Germany's 1919 frontiers.

1932, and, if account were taken of the industrial output of the Dominions and India, the British Commonwealth alone produced twice as much as Germany. To make these comparisons of output might be to understate Germany's effective strength in terms of military preparedness,[1] but watchful observers were convinced that until 1932, at least, substantial rearmament in Germany had not taken place.

All this time [i.e. 1919–32, wrote Churchill] the Allies possessed the strength, and the right, to prevent any visible or tangible German rearmament, and Germany must have obeyed a strong united demand from Britain, France and Italy to bring her actions into conformity with what the Peace Treaties had prescribed. . . . Up till 1934 at least, German rearmament could have been prevented without the loss of a single life.[2]

(iv) Economic Preparation for War

(a) Productivity and Shift in Relative Manufacturing Strength during the 1930s

In the course of the six years running from 1932 Germany became the most formidable military Power in Europe. This was a direct result of the accession to office of the National Socialists, whose determination to create a strong state was unbounded. International conditions were favourable to them; for, with the complete collapse of international codes of behaviour during the depression, self-preservation called for national solutions to be applied to the problem of economic recovery. The special character which recovery assumed in Germany and in Japan was clearly seen by the governments of the other Great Powers, but they were too much engrossed in their own internal problems to be willing to interfere with, or effectively to prevent, such infringements of international law and treaty obligations as inevitably occurred. Even more important, they were unwilling and, for internal reasons, in part unable to keep pace with German expenditure on armaments. Consequently, in less than a decade the whole pattern of relations between the Great Powers was radically transformed; the essential cause of this change was Germany's huge gain in relative military strength under a political leadership which was prepared sooner or later to use that strength in war.

Military strength was not synonymous with economic strength, although the latter was one of the necessary conditions for the achievement of the former. Economic strength was reflected in the volume of manufacturing output, whether or not it corresponded to the full utilization of a country's

[1] Brigadier-General J. H. Morgan quotes a mass of information showing the infringement by Germany of the spirit of the Peace Treaties before Hitler's accession to power in *Assize of Arms; being the Story of the Disarmament of Germany and her Rearmament (1919–1939)* (London, Methuen, 1945).

[2] Churchill: *Second World War*, i. 40.

available resources, while military strength bore a much closer relation to the distribution of that output between consumer goods and capital goods. With regard to the state of economic strength in 1938 it is pertinent to ask: how successful was the recovery of each country and of the world as a whole from the depression? And did the revival restore the relative position of the Powers as it had been in 1929 or did it perpetuate their relative position of 1932?

The recovery of manufacturing output from the depression level showed no semblance of uniformity such as characterized the revival in the decade after the First World War. There were wide disparities in the timing and in the extent of recovery, and, after uneasily reaching a new high post-depression level of production in 1937, the world was drawn into a renewed recession in 1938 owing to a very severe slump in the United States and to a less severe contraction of output in the United Kingdom and

TABLE III. *Manufacturing Production**

	U.S.S.R.	Japan	U.K.	Germany	Italy	U.S.A.	France	World
				(a) 1932 = 100				
1929	62	104	122	166	145	195	135	142
1932	100	100	100	100	100	100	100	100
1933	110	117	108	112	108	121	113	113
1934	130	134	122	145	109	131	105	126
1935	159	148	131	165	131	152	104	143
1936	206	156	144	180	136	184	110	165
1937	230	171	156	195	157	200	117	181
1938	258	179	143	211	158	153	108	169
				(b) 1929 = 100				
1929	100	100	100	100	100	100	100	100
1932	162	96	82	60	69	51	74	71
1937	373	164	127	118	107	103	87	128
1938	417	171	117	127	108	79	80	119

Note: *Industrial production exclusive of mining, construction, and electricity generation. Indices, except those for the U.S.S.R., are based on League of Nations: Economic, Financial, and Transit Dept.: *Industrialization and Foreign Trade*, p. 139. The inflationary bias (see footnote 1 on p. 429), being 47 points between 1928 and 1932, has been eliminated from the figures given in *Industrialization and Foreign Trade* for the U.S.S.R. Assuming an equal distribution of the bias, the official index of 126 for 1929 (with 1928 as base) should be 114 for manufacturing output (and 118 for industrial output). Taking 1929 as a base, the index for 1932 would be 162. Most critics concede that the inflationary bias during the Second Five-Year plan was small, so the official percentage increases have been applied to the corrected 1932 figure in order to determine the index figure with 1929 as base for subsequent years. It might be added that the writer's corrected index figure of 373 for 1937 is still substantially higher than Colin Clark's figure of 240—see *Conditions of Economic Progress*, p. 66.

France. The most conspicuous feature of these developments of output after both 1932 and 1929 was the extraordinary gain of economic strength in the U.S.S.R. and in Japan and the absolute loss of strength in France.

While from the peak of the boom in the 1920s (1929) to that in the 1930s (1937) production had expanded by leaps and bounds in the U.S.S.R. and in Japan, it had risen by only a fair margin in the United Kingdom, Germany, and Italy. And, as far as developments in the United States were concerned, output had only just surpassed its previous boom level when the severe slump in 1938 produced a state of economic weakness comparable only to that which had persisted in France throughout the 1930s.

In the broad setting of the general trends of international production, Germany's achievement was by no means startling. As compared with the boom level of production in 1929, the net expansion of output in the United Kingdom, not to mention Japan or the U.S.S.R., was in 1937 more marked than it was in Germany; and as compared with the depression level of production, the United States' rate of recovery was at least as fast as was Germany's.[1] What, however, lent significance to Germany's economic strength was, above all, her relative gains *vis-à-vis* France. For while Germany expanded her production, there was in France virtual stagnation of production at a level little above that of the depression, and, while in 1938 Germany maintained a high rate of expansion of output, in the United States, the United Kingdom, and France there took place an absolute contraction of production.

These developments in output were closely related to the level of employment and to gains in productivity per man-hour in each of the seven countries. With some reservations to be noted below, the latter concept measured roughly the improvement in the efficiency of each country's employed population. Broadly speaking, productivity per man-hour in 1937 as compared with 1929 was higher by about 9 to 10 per cent. in Italy and Germany, by 20 per cent. in the United States and in the United Kingdom, by 21 per cent. in Japan, by 33 per cent. in France, and by about 70 per cent. in the U.S.S.R.[2] Again, there was nothing to suggest that the real productive power or efficiency of labour had developed in Germany more favourably than in other countries. It would appear that the reverse was the case, that the gains in efficiency of labour in the

---

[1] In the five years between 1932 and 1937 the average annual rate of expansion of output was 26 per cent. in the U.S.S.R., 20 per cent. in the United States, 19 per cent. in Germany, 14·2 per cent. in Japan, 11·4 per cent. in Italy, 11·2 per cent. in the United Kingdom, and only 3·4 per cent. in France.

[2] It has been assumed that indices based on manufacturing industries for the United States, the United Kingdom, and Germany (see L. Rostas: 'Industrial Production, Productivity and Distribution in Britain, Germany and the United States, 1935–7', *Economic Journal*, April 1943, pp. 40–54) were comparable with those based on industrial production for Italy, Japan, and France (League of Nations: Economic Intelligence Service: *World Production and Prices 1938/39* (Geneva, League of Nations, 1939), p. 34). Productivity indices have been arrived at by dividing output indices by employment indices, making allowance in the latter for changes in hours of work. For U.S.S.R. see below, p. 434, note 2.

democratic countries and in a Communist Soviet Union were greater than were those in Germany under the Nazi régime.

Among the many factors which influenced efficiency only a few need be mentioned. The most important was the extent to which existing industrial capacity was utilized. In so far as under-utilization of capacity would make it possible for activity to be concentrated in the most efficient plants, productivity per man-hour was likely to be higher in these circumstances than at full utilization of capacity. It was estimated that, in 1935, about 60 per cent. of industrial capacity was utilized in France, 66 per cent. in the United States, 76 per cent. in Germany, 80 per cent. in the United Kingdom, about 80 per cent. in Italy, and between 95 and 100 per cent. in Japan and the U.S.S.R.[1] Apart from the question of the utilization of capacity, a shortening of working hours might have increased individual effort and hence output per man-hour. Similarly output per man-hour might have risen as a result of improvement in the skill of labour through education and technical training; it might have risen owing to an increase of tools and equipment through net investment or owing to the provision of workers with better tools by the mere reinvestment of accumulated depreciation allowances. How significant each of these divergent influences had been in the enhancement of productivity could hardly be ascertained. Therefore, in interpreting the meaning and the causes of these gains in each of the seven countries, only the most dominant factors need be considered.

In the period covering the First and Second Five-Year Plans, the U.S.S.R. was reaping the fruits of her very active outlays in investment. It was noted that, before 1928, unemployment was higher in the U.S.S.R. than in any other of the seven countries, by comparison with the numbers of hands employed in industry. The unemployed could not be absorbed because there were insufficient plant and equipment. But in the course of the two Five-Year Plans outlays in investment created the industrial capacities, so that from about 1930 onward the main bottle-neck checking expansion of output was a shortage of the right kind of labour rather than a shortage of capacity. The fact that the ever increasing industrial labour force, whose technical skill rose with the simultaneous expansion of education, was being employed on the most up-to-date industrial plants accounted for the tremendous gains in the productivity of Russian labour.[2]

---

[1] Institut für Konjunkturforschung (Berlin): *Industrielle Mobilmachung: statistische Untersuchungen* (Hamburg, Hanseatische Verlagsanstalt, 1936), p. 76.

[2] The writer's estimate of an increase of about 70 per cent. in Russian productivity per man-hour compares with an increase of 49 per cent. in productivity per man between 1929 and 1937. It was arrived at as follows: In 1937 there were 8·3 million persons employed in large-scale industry, excluding construction (Baykov: *Development of the Soviet Economic System*, p. 348) as compared with 3·37 million in 1929 (Birmingham Bureau: Memorandum no. 12, p. 5). Thus the employment index rose from 100 in 1929 to 246 in 1937. These figures include employment in mining and electricity generation. Knowing the physical units of iron-ore, coal, brown coal,

This increase in the productive power of Russian labour became the main source of the increase in industrial production. And, since 80 per cent. of the entire industrial output in 1937 was produced by newly built or by completely reconstructed plants,[1] it might be assumed that the improvement in the efficiency of labour was primarily based on net investment in more and better tools and equipment.

In Japan also until 1935 net expansion and modernization of plant accounted for gains in efficiency of labour. But after that year new investment did not keep pace with the further transfer of agricultural surplus population into industry, and consequently a utilization of the full capacity of existing plant ensued. As the upkeep of machines was rendered difficult by continuous working of plant at full capacity, and as at the same time bottle-necks were encountered in the supply of labour of the right kind (necessitating a slight increase in working hours), productivity per man-hour began to fall after 1935. Nevertheless, the gain in productivity in Japan, as in the U.S.S.R., was a vital factor in the great expansion of output between 1929 and 1937. But the very fact that these two Powers were utilizing their available productive resources to the full implied that, in the short run at least, their realized economic strength could not be greatly increased.

High productivity per man-hour in France and in the United States was caused by a completely different set of circumstances and had a meaning very different from what it had in Japan or the U.S.S.R. A stagnation in the growth of population and a low utilization of capacity set narrow limits in France to the incentive to increase existing industrial plant. In the

---

lead-, zinc-, copper-, manganese-ores and mineral oil output in 1937 for the U.S.S.R., and also similar output and employment figures for Germany, Russian employment in mining was estimated at about 800,000. In physical units most output indices trebled since 1929. Allowing for increases in physical productivity per man, employment in mining was estimated at about 370,000 in 1929. Thus employment in manufacturing increased from about 3 million to 7·5 million and the employment index rose from 100 in 1929 to 250 in 1937. As the manufacturing index rose to 373 in 1937 (see Table III on p. 432 above), productivity per man must have risen by 49 per cent. Estimating that Russian working hours were reduced from about 2,336 per man-year in 1929 to 2,044 in 1937 (based on L. E. Hubbard: *Soviet Labour and Industry* (London, Macmillan, 1942), pp. 47 and 98), Russian productivity per man-hour must have risen by about 70 per cent. between 1929 and 1937. Incidentally, the increase of productivity per man by about 49 per cent. as here estimated would compare with a decrease by about 3 per cent. on the basis of Colin Clark's figures and with an increase of 157 per cent. on the basis of official Soviet pronouncements. The latter increase refers to 1928 as a base. According to Dobb the Russians expected a doubling of labour productivity during the First Five-Year Plan, but the actual increase by the end of 1932 was, in fact, no more than 41 per cent. (see Dobb: *Soviet Economic Development*, p. 239). On the other hand, 'the Second Five-Year Plan provided for a 63 per cent. increase in the productivity of labour in industry. Actually it increased by 82 per cent.' (V. M. Molotov: *The Third Five-Year Plan* . . . speech of 14 March 1939 reprinted in *The Land of Socialism Today and Tomorrow: Report and Speeches at the Eighteenth Congress of the Communist Party of the Soviet Union (Bolsheviks), March 10–21, 1939* (Moscow, Foreign Languages Publishing House, 1939), p. 140).

[1] Molotov, op. cit. p. 105, and Baykov: *Development of the Soviet Economic System*, p. 286.

absence of new investment the rise in the efficiency of labour was due mainly to the very heavy depletion of the industrial labour force. In 1937 man-power employed in industry was 21 per cent. less than in 1929;[1] many of the immigrants who had entered France in the 1920s had returned in the 1930s to their countries of birth and many Frenchmen had left the towns for the country, so that those remaining in industrial employment were most probably the more skilled and efficient men. Other factors which contributed to raising the efficiency of labour included some re-organization of plant, and the concentration of activity in the most efficient plants. And while the reduction by 16 per cent. in the normal working week was probably accompanied by some increase in individual effort, it is likely that this beneficial effect on productivity from shorter hours of work was offset by the spread of employment over available capacity. The enormous gain in productivity per man-hour in France remained potential in the sense that, instead of being reflected in higher aggregate output, it was absorbed in an increase of leisure-time for employed French workers.[2] In terms of aggregate output France, in the 1930s, never came near her realized economic strength of 1929. Therefore unlike Japan and the U.S.S.R., she possessed potential reserves which should have enabled her to increase output considerably in the short run.

The 20 per cent. increase of productivity per man-hour in the United States[3] was not due to the provision of more capital per employed person, for net investment in business plant and equipment rose by only about $1 milliard in the eight years ending in 1937, as compared with an increase by about $25 milliard during the previous eight years ending in 1929.[4] On the other hand, the qualitative composition of industrial capacity was greatly improved in the 1930s by the reinvestment of large amortization and depreciation funds.[5] The introduction, by these means, of conveyer belts in large-scale American factories and, above all, the installation of more efficient prime movers, such as electrical motors in place of steam engines, were very significant causes of gains in productivity during this period. As a knowledgeable observer of the American scene pointed out, 'the most important factors [in gains in productivity] have undoubtedly

---

[1] League of Nations: *Statistical Year Book, 1937/38*, p. 61.

[2] The small rise in aggregate output in 1936 and 1937 was completely lost when French industry was drawn into a renewed recession in 1938. In 1938 the French motor-car industry was utilized to only 60 per cent. of capacity. For criticism of some official French statistics relating to the period under consideration see T. Balogh: 'French Reconstruction and the Franco-U.S. Loan Agreement', *Bulletin of the Oxford University Institute of Statistics*, vol. viii, August 1946, p. 266.

[3] Solomon Fabricant: *Labor Savings in American Industry, 1899–1939* (National Bureau of Economic Research, Occasional paper no. 23: New York, 1945), p. 46.

[4] In 1929 prices (Clark: *Conditions of Economic Progress*, p. 419).

[5] Gross capital formation, as reflected in 'producer durable goods' and 'private non-residential construction', might serve to illustrate the point. It rose in the eight-year period of the 1930s by $49 milliard as compared with that of the 1920s of $75 milliard (Arthur Burns: *Economic Research and the Keynesian Thinking of Our Times*, p. 31).

been the increased use of mechanical energy . . . the improvements in machines, and the technique of using them.'[1] This increase in productivity remained potential; it was not reflected in higher aggregate output but was wholly absorbed by a reduction, by 15 per cent., of man-hours worked.[2] Consequently the United States, like France, at the top of the boom in the 1930s possessed greater productive reserves, both in the form of under-utilized capacity and in the form of under-employed man-power, than at the top of the boom in the 1920s.

High gains in productivity in the United Kingdom were mainly due to internal reorganization of plant and to net investment.[3] By 1937 the level of employment exceeded that of 1929; but hours of work had neither increased, as in Japan, nor had they decreased, as in France, the United States, or the U.S.S.R., so that the gain in productivity was fully reflected in a considerable increase in aggregate output.

Of all the Great Powers, Italy and Germany recorded the lowest gains in productivity. In both countries employment had been pushed beyond the peak level of the 1920s, so that shortages of labour of the right kind as well as bottle-necks in the supply of materials adversely affected labour efficiency. In Italy it decreased from 1935, but was prevented from falling below its 1929 level by a reduction of working hours which apparently was accompanied by an increase of effort on the part of individual Italian workers. However, the result of spreading employment in this way was the aggravation of the existing shortages of skilled labour and materials by scarcities of specific equipment resulting from the fuller utilization of plant. In Germany, on the other hand, working hours remained unchanged and new investment was directly controlled. Indeed—and this is a most significant point for the interpretation of the economic revival in Nazi Germany—gross investment in plant and equipment until the beginning of 1937 was not sufficient to maintain industrial capacity, so that the comparatively small gains in productivity per man-hour after 1929 resulted primarily from the reinvestment of depreciation allowances. Although net investment in industry amounted to Rm. 2·2 milliard in the three years 1937–9, this was inadequate to make good industrial disinvestments

---

[1] Hitch: *America's Economic Strength*, p. 56.

[2] Fabricant, op. cit. p. 46.

[3] No accurate information about investment in industrial plant and equipment is available. But net accumulation of capital at home, that is net total investment, exclusive of foreign investment, investment in dwellings and in public works, was considerably higher in the 1930s than in the 1920s. Net home investment amounted to £101 million and £28 million in 1924 and in 1929 respectively, as compared with £120 million in 1935 and £163 million in 1937. A considerable part of this no doubt represented net investment in industry (see Clark: *Conditions of Economic Progress*, p. 397). As regards the 20 per cent. gain in productivity per man-hour, estimated above, there is this further confirmation from census data. Apparently, physical output per man rose by 7 per cent. between 1924 and 1930 and by 15 to 25 per cent. between 1930 and 1935 (see G. L. Schwartz: *Output, Employment and Wages in the United Kingdom, 1924, 1930, 1935* (London and Cambridge Economic Service, Special Memorandum, no. 47: London, 1938).

amounting to Rm. 2·6 milliard during the eight years 1929–36, and it certainly could not immediately have benefited the productivity of labour.[1] Thus the delays in new investment meant that existing capacity was utilized beyond the usual working level.[2] 'Machines which had in the past normally been worked one or two shifts are now [in 1938] frequently being worked in three shifts, with only brief pauses, if any, for current repairs and the necessary maintenance works.'[3]

However questionable some of the statistical data may be, the main conclusions based thereon would continue to be valid, even if further statistical refinement were attempted. Broadly speaking, as compared with 1929, industrial capacity increased slightly during the 1930s in Britain, and greatly in Japan and the U.S.S.R. It did not increase in the other four countries. As employment was pushed nearly to the limit of potentialities of production, as set by existing capacity, productivity per man-hour improved more conspicuously in countries where net investment in plant and equipment had been considerable (U.S.S.R. and Japan) than in those where that was not the case (Germany and Italy). Full utilization of capacity together with gains in productivity per man-hour accounted for the rise in manufacturing output between 1929 and 1937 in the U.S.S.R., Japan, Germany, and Italy. In these four countries 'potential' economic strength, as limited by capacity, was more or less 'realized'. This was in stark contrast with the situation in France and in the United States, where the gains in productivity were wholly absorbed in increases of leisure-time for their people and where, in 1937, there was a gap between 'realized' and 'potential' strength, which was further widened in 1938 as a result of a renewed contraction of output.

These divergent developments of production completely altered the pattern of the relative manufacturing strength of the Great Powers. In 1937–8 as compared with 1929 or with the depression year of 1932, the share of each Power in world manufacturing output had changed as shown in Table IV on the opposite page.

Germany's relative strength, which had greatly increased since 1932, was further enhanced by the incorporation of Austria and the Sudetenland in the Reich, so that in 1938 Greater Germany, with a share of 14·3 per cent. of the world's manufacturing output,[4] produced more than France and the United Kingdom combined. The superior strength which these

---

[1] *Statistisches Jahrbuch, 1941/2*, pp. 610–12.

[2] German data, adjusted by Colin Clark, showed that over-all industrial capacity was utilized in the second half of 1928 to 77 per cent., in 1929 to 75 per cent., and in November 1937 to 85 per cent. (*Conditions of Economic Progress*, p. 65).

[3] Reichs-Kredit-Gesellschaft A. G., Berlin: *Economic Conditions in Germany in the middle of . . . 1939* (Berlin, 1939), p. 4.

[4] The joint share of Austria and the Sudetenland was about 1·1 per cent. of the world's manufacturing output in 1938 (League of Nations: Economic, Financial, and Transit Dept.: *Industrialization and Foreign Trade*, p. 128).

two countries had together enjoyed over Germany in the late 1920s had gone.

TABLE IV. *Relative Manufacturing Strength*

(World output = 100)

Year	U.S.A.	U.S.S.R.	Germany	United Kingdom	France	Japan	Italy	Seven Powers
1929	43·3	5·0	11·1	9·4	6·6	2·5	3·3	81·2
1932	31·8	11·5	10·6	10·9	6·9	3·5	3·1	78·3
1937	35·1	14·1	11·4	9·4	4·5	3·5	2·7	80·7
1938	28·7	17·6	13·2	9·2	4·5	3·8	2·9	79·9

Note: The weights for 1925–9 given in League of Nations: Economic, Financial, and Transit Dept.: *Industrialization and Foreign Trade*, p. 128, have been applied to corrected output indices (Table III above, p. 432). 1937 weights, corrected by using data of net output for the United Kingdom, Germany, and United States, have been derived from Rostas's data ('Industrial Production . . .', *Economic Journal*, April 1943, p. 41). If the weights given in *Industrialization and Foreign Trade* had been applied to the uncorrected production index, the U.S.S.R.'s share in world output would have been 14·7 per cent. for 1932, 18·9 per cent. for 1937, and 22·2 per cent. for 1938; i.e. shares which surely must be highly improbable.

Even more significant was the U.S.S.R.'s forward surge to second place in the manufacturing hierarchy among the Great Powers in the course of the Great Depression, which had left her unaffected. From this position, once attained, there was no return to her pre-depression status. Although she produced at the time of the completion of her Second Five-Year Plan (1937) only two-fifths of the output of the United States, her output exceeded Germany's by a quarter. There were many specific indications to attest the reality of her great achievements. For instance, in 1937, the U.S.S.R. manufactured the same number of motor-cars, twice as much cotton yarn, twice as many leather shoes and cigarettes, and six times as many tractors as did Germany.[1] Perhaps the most astonishing feature of her progress was, so far as can be ascertained, that the productivity per employed Russian worker was as high as, or even higher than, that of a British or German worker.[2]

But neither the Germans nor anyone else were unduly worried about

[1] *Statistisches Jahrbuch, 1941/2*, pp. 90*, 83*, 215 and 260, 94*, and Birmingham Bureau: Memorandum no. 12, p. 5.

[2] This statement, which cannot be more than approximately true, was based on the following considerations: By applying production indices to the 1935 (British) and 1936 (German) net output census data, the 1937 net output values were determined at £1,366 million for Britain and at £1,669 million for Germany, comparable to that of £5,096 million for the U.S.A. Since Britain's values represented 9·4 per cent. of world output (see Table IV above, this page) the U.S.S.R.'s share of 14·1 per cent. must have represented £2,049 million. Dividing the values by employment figures, i.e. 5·8 million for Britain, 6·6 million for Germany, 7·5 million for the U.S.S.R., and 9·8 million for the U.S.A. (based on Rostas, loc. cit.), it follows that productivity per employed person in 1937, taking the United Kingdom = 100, was 108 in Germany, 116 in the U.S.S.R., and 220 in the United States.

Russian strength. They shared Stalin's view (which showed that the Russians themselves had no illusions about their strength) that

the economic power of a country's industry is not expressed by the volume of industrial production in general, irrespective of the size of population, but by the volume of industrial output taken in direct reference to the amount consumed per head of population.[1]

In respect of units of manufactures produced per head of total population the U.S.S.R. fell far behind the more mature industrial Powers.[2]

Comparative Output of Manufactures per Head of Population

	U.S.A.	United Kingdom	Germany	France	U.S.S.R.	Italy	Japan
1937	268	198	165	108	83	63	48
1938	219	194	180	108	104	67	52

These ratios suggest that it might have been much harder for the U.S.S.R., France, Italy, and Japan to spare industrial resources for the building-up of military strength than it would have been for the United States, the United Kingdom, and Germany. Indeed because, in 1938, Greater Germany, next only to the United States, actually produced more manufactured goods per head of population than the United Kingdom and her four Dominions combined, or than the United Kingdom and France combined,[3] she was entitled to regard herself as the second strongest industrial Power in the world and as one possessing a vast military potential.

(b) HEAVY INDUSTRIES AND WAR POTENTIAL

In the assessment of war potential the division of manufacturing output between capital goods and consumer goods was more revealing than its mere volume. For capital goods industries which turned out industrial, agricultural, trade, and transport equipment could with some adjustment just as easily produce military equipment and vehicles. Therefore the size of the capital goods sector within the economy of each of the Great Powers reflected their war potential more accurately than did their aggregate manufacturing output. Because of this it is relevant to inquire, first, what were the conditions and the foundations upon which rested a well de-

[1] J. Stalin: *Report on the Work of the Central Committee* . . . speech of 10 March 1939 reprinted in *The Land of Socialism Today and Tomorrow*, p. 22.

[2] Table IV (p. 439 above) divided by Table I, col. 1 (p. 373 above), except Germany for 1937 = 69 million population. See also E. Lokshin: *Industry in the U.S.S.R.* (Moscow, Foreign Languages Publishing House, 1948), p. 83.

[3] In 1938 the addition of Canada, Australia, South Africa, and New Zealand would have increased the British share in world output to 13·4 per cent., giving an output per head of population of 173 for the British Commonwealth, as compared with per capita output of 154 for the United Kingdom and France combined.

veloped capital goods sector and, second, how large it was within each country and in relation to the output for the whole world.

Under conditions of spontaneous industrialization, such as characterized the growth of the older industrial Powers, capital goods industries[1] were established after consumer goods industries had reached a certain size. It became profitable to produce machines when the demand for machines emanating from the consumer goods industries was sufficiently large. But this was not the only pattern of development. For instance, under conditions of state-directed, deliberately planned industrialization, such as was characteristic of the U.S.S.R. during the 1930s, the growth of capital goods industries preceded rather than followed the development of consumer goods industries.

Forming the core of a well-developed capital goods sector were the steel and pig-iron industries, which, in turn, depended primarily on coal and iron-ore. The pig-iron industry tended to be located at points where coal and iron-ore could be most conveniently assembled, either close to coal-fields or to iron-ore deposits, or on intermediate water and rail routes of communication between these two centres of raw material. Broadly speaking, the combination of effective demand, whether spontaneous or state-directed, and of available coal and ore resources accounted for the concentration of the world's iron industry: (a) based on coal: in the Ruhr, in the Belgian South Basin, in the English Midlands, in the Donetz and Kuznets areas and in Western Pennsylvania (round Pittsburgh); (b) based on iron-ore: in French Lorraine, in Alabama (round Birmingham) and in the Russian Krivoi Rog and Ural areas; and (c) based on water and rail routes between coal and iron-ore centres: in the Rhineland, on the American east coast and in the Middle West (round Chicago), on the Russian Sea of Azov (near Mariopol) and in the Yokohama–Tokyo, Yawata, and Kobe-Osaka areas.

The United States and the U.S.S.R., being of continental dimensions, had been endowed by nature with great coal and iron-ore reserves. Germany and the United Kingdom also happened to possess huge coal deposits, and France owned rich iron-ore resources. An essential condition, therefore, for the development of a pig-iron industry was fulfilled in these five countries. But even in Italy, which was extremely weak in both coal and ore, and in Japan which had some coal but hardly any ore

[1] The difficulties inherent in any classification of industries into capital and consumer goods are great. Capital goods have generally been taken to include durable goods of the engineering, ship-building, construction, and other industries which do not satisfy consumers' demand directly; they also include semi-manufactures of the iron and steel, metallurgical, cement, and other industries intended for ultimate transformation into capital goods. Mining and similar primary stages of production are either wholly included or divided. Obviously, any classification must be arbitrary; provided, however, that the same principles of grouping are followed, intra-national comparisons should bring to the fore certain essential differences between the industrial structures of the various Great Powers.

(before the acquisition of Manchuria), pig-iron production was fostered on a small scale.[1]

Although the German and British pig-iron industries depended on imported ores, and that of France on imported coal, it was not from France that Germany and Britain covered their ore requirements. In the late 1930s more than one-half of Germany's ore imports came from Sweden and less than one-third from France and Luxembourg; while just under one-half of Britain's ore imports came from Spain and about one-fifth each from Scandinavia and North Africa. Nor was that all, for such ores as Germany imported from France went primarily to the iron works in the Saar region, which had been reincorporated in the Reich in 1935, while Swedish ores fed the iron works in the Ruhr, Rhine, and Silesian districts. From the military standpoint it was an important fact that the great German iron industry in the Ruhr was less dependent on French ore than was the French industry on Ruhr coal and coke.

The location of steel production was roughly determined by the location of the pig-iron industry, except in cases of steel works which primarily consumed scrap. This exception was of importance in Japan and Italy, where the manufacture of steel was largely based on the utilization of imported scrap. Although in Germany (as in Britain but not in France) the normal constituents of steel were about 65 per cent. pig-iron and 35 per cent. scrap, the locational attraction exercised by scrap upon the location of steel was small; first, because pig-iron continued to predominate in the production of steel; second, because scrap accrued in the German steel centres; and third, because to the extent that scrap was imported, it came normally from the United States, Belgium, and Holland and reached the German pig-iron centres by river and canal. Since transport was cheaper by water than by rail, imported scrap could not appreciably alter the location of the steel works, which tended to be closest to the pig-iron centres.

In view of the importance of these heavy industries, which include coal, iron-ore, pig-iron, and steel, for a well founded capital goods sector in the economy of any country, it was significant that, during the 1930s, all the Great Powers, except the United States and France, increased their shares in the world's output of heavy materials (see Table V opposite).[2]

Clearly, it was the U.S.S.R. who showed the most conspicuous improvement in her relative strength in the production of heavy materials. Occupying fourth or fifth place in the hierarchy of heavy material producers in the late 1920s, she had advanced in the 1930s to second place

[1] It has been stated that 85 to 90 per cent. of Japan's iron-ore requirement came from very distant Asiatic regions and was 'transported most of the way over water at costs lower than the costs incurred in some Western countries, where ores had to be moved shorter distances by land' (Schumpeter and others: *The Industrialization of Japan*, p. 233).

[2] Recovering from the trough of the Great Depression, the world's output of heavy materials,

TABLE V: *Relative Strength in Heavy Materials*

(World output = 100)

	Coal		Iron-ore		Pig-iron		Crude Steel		
	1929	*1938*	*1929*	*1938*	*1929*	*1938*	*1929*	*1937*	*1938*
	(Percentage distribution)								
U.S.S.R. . . .	2·8	9·3	4·5	18·5	4·4	17·7	4·1	13·1	16·5
Greater Germany . .	13·4	15·5	3·0	6·0	16·0	22·6	15·4	14·9	20·7
Italy	0·0	0·1	0·4	0·7	0·7	1·0	1·8	1·5	2·1
Greater Japan . .	2·6	4·2	0·3	1·4	1·4	4·3	1·9	4·4	6·0
Great Britain . .	19·8	19·1	4·5	5·0	7·8	8·3	8·3	10·0	9·8
France . . .	4·1	3·9	20·6	14·2	10·5	7·4	8·0	5·8	5·6
United States . . .	41·6	29·6	42·4	20·0	43·7	23·7	47·0	38·0	26·4
Seven Powers . . .	84·3	81·7	75·7	65·8	84·5	85·0	86·5	87·7	87·1

Note: In 1938, as well as in 1929 and 1937, Greater Germany includes the Saar, Austria, and Sudetenland, and Greater Japan includes Manchuria.

in the mining of iron-ore and to third place in the production of pig-iron and crude steel. This tremendous expansion of her heavy industries was accompanied by an eastward shift of her producing centres. Obviously military considerations played some part in the deliberate encouragement given to the development of centres in Siberia and the Urals. These two areas accounted for nearly one-third of Russian steel production in 1938, while the traditional centres of production in the Ukraine accounted for about one-half.[1] Next to the U.S.S.R., steel production had increased most rapidly in Greater Japan, largely because of the exploitation of Manchuria.

With a production of 22 million tons of steel, Greater Germany in 1938 surpassed the combined British and French total by one-quarter; and in actual output, although not in steel capacity, she came near to that of the United States.[2] Production per head of population was higher in Germany than anywhere else in the world. Two additional features characterized Germany's steel strength: first, steel output had risen while exports had

except coal, was higher in 1937 than in 1929 but again fell below the 1937 peak level of production in 1938. In million metric tons, world output fluctuated as follows:

	1929	*1932*	*1937*	*1938*
Coal	1,329	957	1,295	1,208
Iron-ore (iron content) . .	90	52	97	72
Pig-iron	98	39	104	82
Crude steel . . .	122	51	135	109

(Cf. *Statistisches Jahrbuch, 1935* and *1941/42*.)

[1] Baykov: *Development of the Soviet Economic System*, p. 308.

[2] In 1938 about two-thirds of the capacity of American steel plants were estimated by the American Iron and Steel Institute to have stood idle, in contrast with Germany, the U.S.S.R., and Japan, where existing capacity was being fully utilized (*New York Times*, 11 December 1941).

fallen, so that steel available for domestic use increased from 10·2 million tons in 1929 to the remarkable total of 18·8 million tons in 1938. Thus the domestic use of steel almost doubled under the Nazi régime. Second, Germany, like the U.S.S.R., aimed at a geographical redistribution of her industry. She planned to thin out the two centres of heavy industry in the Ruhr and in Silesia, situated on the western and eastern frontiers of the Reich, and to develop a strategically more secure centre based on the low-grade ore resources in the Hanover–Brunswick area of Central Germany: work on the construction of the Reichswerke Hermann Göring was begun in that area in 1937. It was expected that 'the new blast furnaces would represent a transfer of 33 per cent. of the present or of 25 per cent. of the future production of pig-iron and that with this geographical redistribution of the German iron industry important military-political requirements would be fulfilled'.[1]

Thus the systematic re-location of the heavy industries in the U.S.S.R. and in Germany reflected the importance which these two countries attached to the safety of the raw material base of the capital goods industries. But how large was the capital goods sector in the industrial structure of each of the seven countries? All evidence suggested that it was greatest in Germany. Counting as capital goods industries the metal goods, optical, engineering, shipbuilding, vehicles, and chemical industries, and part of the heavy industries (namely, pig-iron and crude steel), the share of the capital goods sector in total manufacturing output in 1937 was about 51 per cent. for Germany, 48 per cent. for the United States, 44 per cent. for the United Kingdom, 40 per cent. for Japan, 39 per cent. for the U.S.S.R., and 37 per cent. for France and Italy.[2]

Germany's outstanding lead with the largest capital goods sector in her manufacturing structure implied that in the late 1930s she, more than any other Power, had geared her industrial economy to yielding a maximum of war potential. For it was the products of these industries that were most easily convertible into armaments. On this basis of comparison, however, the United States stood not far behind Germany. Indeed, taking into account the fact that the United States had not reached the same degree of utilization of capacity as had Germany and that her volume of manufacturing output was three times as high as was Germany's, the absolute and relative superiority of the United States in war potential was unquestionable. But there was one great difference between the United States and the United Kingdom, on the one hand, and the U.S.S.R. and Germany on the other, which lent special significance to Germany's position. While the share of capital goods in the flow of aggregate manu-

---

[1] Paul Rheinländer: 'Die deutsche Eisen- und Stahlwirtschaft' (Der Vierjahresplan, Zeitschrift für Nationalsozialistische Wirtschaftspolitik, Berlin, January 1939, p. 19).

[2] See Appendix I, p. 491 below.

factures had hardly changed between the late 1920s and the late 1930s in the United States and in the United Kingdom, it had considerably increased in both the U.S.S.R. and Germany. In the U.S.S.R., where war potential constituted 20 per cent. of total output in 1928, it had risen to 39 per cent. in 1937, while in Germany it had risen during the same period from about 41 per cent. to 51 per cent. It was this shift towards capital goods which, in an economy as fully matured already as that of Germany in 1928, clearly reflected the impact of National Socialist policy on German industry.

Normally a large part of the flow of capital goods, especially of engineering products, is required to replace plant and equipment, or to extend the capacity, not only of war-potential industries, but also of consumer goods industries. Thus, in an industrializing country like the U.S.S.R., the increasing flow of capital goods was needed in order to create more capacity, and the expansion of capacity was an essential prerequisite for a broader flow of capital goods. The situation in Nazi Germany was very different. There the greatly enhanced flow of capital goods was not used for the building-up and extension of existing productive capacity, but rather—among other things—for the accumulation of armaments. This fact was of the utmost importance in that it reflected the kind of war which German leaders hoped to wage, and it can be illustrated very roughly as follows.

The flow of capital goods rose by Rm. 6 milliard, from Rm. 11·7 milliard in 1928 to Rm. 17·6 milliard in 1937. In the same period gross investment in all German industries rose only by Rm. 0·2 milliard to Rm. 2·8 milliard in 1937. Since gross investment in the capital goods industries rose by Rm. 0·5 milliard to Rm. 2·2 milliard, it follows that the slight expansion in the capacity of the war-potential industries was largely financed by disinvestment, amounting to about Rm. 0·3 milliard, of the consumer goods industries.[1] The significant fact, to use the words of General Thomas, who was in supreme charge of industrial rearmament in Germany, was that until 1937 there had been very little 'armament in depth' in the sense of creating armaments 'capacity', but rather a maximum concentration on finished weapons ready for use, that is an 'armament in width'.[2]

The realization, however, in Germany that the flow of armaments, and more especially their ultimate use, might be hampered because of insufficient domestic supplies of iron-ore, oil, rubber, and non-ferrous metals led to some 'rearmament in depth'. This was initiated under the German Four-Year Plan in 1936 and was begun in earnest in 1937 with an acceleration in the development of the use of light metals and their alloys as substitutes

[1] *Statistisches Jahrbuch, 1941/42*, pp. 610–12 and *1935*, p. 318.
[2] U.S. Strategic Bombing Survey: *The Effects of Strategic Bombing on the German War Economy*, p. 20.

for copper and its alloys, of the hydrogenation of coal as a substitute for mineral oil, and of the synthetic production of Buna as a substitute for rubber. Gross investment in war-potential industries was stepped up from Rm. 2·2 milliard in 1937 to Rm. 2·9 milliard in 1938 and to Rm. 3·6 milliard in 1939,[1] suggesting the beginnings of a departure from the fundamental character of Germany's rearmament drive in its concentration hitherto on armaments rather than on armaments capacity.

But how did Germany's war potential compare with that of the other Great Powers in 1937? What was her relative strength in the distribution of the production of capital goods among the Great Powers? The joint share of the seven Powers was about 90·5 per cent.[2] of the world output of capital goods, and the relative share[3] of each was as follows:

Relative War Potential
(percentage distribution)

	U.S.A.	Germany	U.S.S.R.	United Kingdom	France	Japan	Italy	Seven Powers
1937	41·7	14·4	14·0	10·2	4·2	3·5	2·5	90·5

Not only did Germany's output in 1937 equal that of France and Britain combined, but it exceeded that of the U.S.S.R. Indeed, in 1938, when the total output of the two Western European Powers slightly contracted, Greater Germany's advantage over them was further increased and, on the test of output per head of population, she held, next to the United States, an undisputed lead in war potential.

(c) Machine Tools, the Key to Rearmament

The extent to which existing war potential had been or could be converted into arms depended on the size of existing munition and gun factories and even more on the speed with which motor-car, sewing-machine and tractor manufacturing plants, &c., could be adapted to producing tanks and military lorries. The rate of adaptation depended on the balance within the capital goods sector itself; that is, on the size of the precision instrument and machine-tool industries. Indeed, the latter was the keystone in the structure of all industrial production, for it ensured the manufacture of tools which formed the equipment with which engineering firms were enabled to produce engines, equipment, &c.

Because machine tools occupied a strategic position in the industrial

---

[1] *Statistisches Jahrbuch, 1941/42*, p. 612.

[2] This figure is based on estimates for 1935 (Institut für Konjunkturforschung: *Industrielle Mobilmachung*, p. 79).

[3] Shares of capital goods in total manufacturing in each country are here applied to relative manufacturing output for 1937 (see Table IV on p. 439 above), and the total for the seven Great Powers is assumed to be equal to 90·5 per cent. of world capital goods production in 1937.

system of any country, easy access to the supply of tools or possession of a machine-tools industry was of considerable importance to all the Great Powers. For instance, if the demand for engineering products changed— say, from one type of car to another, from car engines to aero engines, from tractors to tanks—the speed with which engineering firms could satisfy this change of demand would be dependent on the speed with which their equipment could be retooled. Similarly if, as a result of instantaneous, or forced, industrialization, or as a result of rearmament being superimposed on peace-time production, the demand for engineering products increased, the speed with which this demand could be satisfied would again be determined largely by the supply of tools. A full awareness of the crucial importance of lathes, drill presses, grinders, planers, and milling, boring, and other metal-cutting machinery, both for industrialization and for rearmament, was reflected in strenuous efforts on the part of nearly all the Great Powers in the 1930s to increase the capacity of their own national machine-tool industries.

Traditionally, the world's largest producers were the United States and Germany. Their tool import requirements were negligible, and between them they accounted for about 70 to 80 per cent. of the world's tool exports.[1] The next three leading exporters were the United Kingdom, France, and Switzerland; but their import requirements were considerable in contrast with those of either Germany or the United States. The relative position of these five Powers as the world's machine-tool suppliers had changed little in 1938 as compared with 1928; but the world's machine-tool 'capacity' had been greatly extended in response to Russian and Japanese industrialization, to Japanese war requirements, and to German, and subsequently to French and British, rearmament.

The difficulties involved in setting up a machine-tool industry (i.e. in Japan and the U.S.S.R.) or of enlarging one already in existence (i.e. in Germany and the United Kingdom) were enormous, for in no other single branch of engineering were the requirements of highly skilled labour so great. But if lack of skill constituted the main bottle-neck in the development of tool capacity, it was shortages in the supply of tools which put a brake on the rate of industrialization, and of industrial reconversion for armament purposes. Another difficulty inherent in the possession of a tool industry was its extreme sensitiveness in normal times to trade cycle

[1] German and U.S. shares in world exports of tools:

	1929	1932	1936	1937	1938
World exports, in Rm. million	526	357	342	469	583
of which, in per cent. German share	40	60	43	45	35
,, U.S. ,,	20	10	38	35	42

(See *Statistisches Jahrbuch*, International Section, for the respective years.)

fluctuations. It was one of the trickiest and most ill-starred branches of engineering; it was what the Americans called a 'feast or famine' industry, because the demand for tools depended on the demand for capital goods, and this fluctuated more violently with the trade cycle than did the demand for consumer goods. But the 1930s were not normal times; trade cycle considerations could be ignored by countries which had embarked on planning their economic life and which were conscious of the requirements of war.

Tool production severely declined during the Great Depression in Germany, Great Britain, and the United States.[1] This fall in output would have been much greater but for the huge machine-tool purchases of the U.S.S.R. In the event, contrary to the development of all other economic indices, that of exports of tools from Germany and from the United Kingdom actually increased during the depression.[2] It was only with the aid of these vital supplies, especially from Germany, that the 'revolution from above' in the U.S.S.R., as symbolized in the First Five-Year Plan, could have been carried out at all. But, having been supplied with the most up-to-date engineering equipment, the Russians lost no time in analysing these Western wonders of technical ingenuity and in setting themselves the task in the Second Five-Year Plan of 'forcing the speed of production of those machines, tools, etc., which had to be imported during the First Five-Year Plan period' and of placing the machine-tool industry in a position 'where maximum development is possible, so that the machine-tool requirements of national economy can be met and the Soviet Union made technically and economically independent in this field as well'.[3] The Russian State Planning Commission aimed at a reduction of imports of tools, which was achieved after 1933, and at an annual production for 1937 of 40,000 metal-cutting machines.[4] Despite this great achievement,

---

[1] Selling value (i.e. gross output) of machine tools, metal-working machinery and parts thereof in millions of local currency:

$$\text{U.S.A.} \quad (\$) \quad 1929 = 240 \cdot 0; \; 1933 = \quad 40 \cdot 0;$$
$$\text{Germany (Rm.)} \quad 1928 = 363 \cdot 0; \; 1933 = 165 \cdot 0;$$
$$\text{U.K.} \quad (\pounds) \quad 1930 = \quad 6 \cdot 2; \; 1933 = \quad 3 \cdot 7 \text{ (roughly).}$$

(See *Statistical Abstract of the United States, Statistisches Jahrbuch*, and *Statistical Abstract for the United Kingdom*, Cmd. 5353, for the respective years.)

[2] Exports of tools in millions of local currency from

$$\text{U.K.} \quad (\pounds) \quad 1928 = \quad 1 \cdot 8; \; 1932 = \quad 3 \cdot 1;$$
$$\text{Germany} \quad (\text{Rm.}) \quad 1929 = 210 \cdot 0; \; 1932 = 214 \cdot 0;$$
$$\text{of which to U.S.S.R. } 1929 = \quad 22 \cdot 0; \; 1932 = 160 \cdot 0.$$

(See *Statistical Abstract for the United Kingdom*, Cmd. 5353, and *Statistisches Jahrbuch* for the respective years.)

[3] U.S.S.R., State Planning Commission of the U.S.S.R.: *The Second Five-Year Plan* (Moscow, Co-operative Publishing Society of Foreign Workers in the U.S.S.R., 1936), pp. 129 and 131.

[4] This would be 2·7 times the quantity and 5 times the value of those produced in 1932. Moreover, it was intended in the Second Five-Year Plan to invest about 300 million roubles in fixed capital in the specialized tool industry, representing a threefold increase in such investments made under the First Five-Year Plan (ibid. p. 132).

however, Russia's total production fell far behind that of Germany who, in 1938, produced about 180,000 tools.[1]

The increase in machine-tool capacity in the U.S.S.R. was matched by a similar rise in Japan. Until 1932 Japan imported the greater part of her requirements from the United States and Germany. But in subsequent years the number of persons employed in the tool industry might be estimated to have risen from 7,500 persons in 1929 to about 30,000 persons in 1938. In the latter year the value of the output of machine tools was about £4·7 million,[2] as compared with a value of £8·2 million in 1935 in the United Kingdom—which, however, was produced with a labour force of only 21,000 persons.[3] As a result of this expansion of tool capacity, the ratio of Japanese production to tool requirements increased, but, unlike the U.S.S.R.'s, Japan's imports of tools continued to rise.[4] This simply meant that the rate of requirement, based on industrialization and war needs, was rising even faster than the rate of increase in domestic tool production.

In the decade before 1938, machine-tool capacity was expanded not only in the U.S.S.R. and in Japan, but also in the more mature industrial communities of Germany and Great Britain. In Germany the value of gross output doubled between 1928 and 1936;[5] in the United Kingdom the selling value of finished tools was at least 30 per cent. higher in 1935 than in any previous year;[6] and in both these countries machine-tool capacity was considerably expanded after 1935–6. Its expansion was limited

---

[1] See N. Kaldor: 'The German War Economy', in *The Manchester School of Economic and Social Studies*, September 1946, p. 24. In 1941 German tool production had risen to 198,000. In the third quarter of 1941 the U.S.S.R. had called for an output of 22,000 tools (i.e. 88,000 per annum), of which 14,000 were allocated to enterprises of the Ministries of Ammunition, Armaments, and Aviation Industry (Nikolai A. Voznesensky: *The Economy of the U.S.S.R. during World War II* (Washington, Public Affairs Press, 1948), p. 22).

[2] In 1935 the Japanese machine-tool industry employed about 16,000 persons. Between 1936 and 1938, the factory value of 'total engineering' more than doubled, while that of employment nearly doubled. Assuming that the ratio of tool production to total engineering was about the same in 1938 as in 1936, that would mean that employment in the tool industry was about 30,000 persons and the value of tool output about 80 million yen in 1938, at the conversion rate of 17·2 yen = £1 (Schumpeter and others: *Industrialization of Japan*, pp. 610, 797, 812, 813).

[3] 'Fifth Census of Production (1935) Preliminary Report no. 7' (Supplement to *Board of Trade Journal*, 22 April 1937, p. yi).

[4] See Schumpeter and others, op. cit. p. 814.

[5] It rose from Rm. 363 million in 1928 (*Statistisches Jahrbuch, 1935*, p. 146) to Rm. 657 million in 1936 and in the latter year there were 90,000 employed persons. See Germany, Reichsamt für Wehrwirtschaftliche Planung: *Die deutsche Industrie* (Berlin, P. Schmidt, 1939), p. 46.

[6] United Kingdom production of finished tools:

	1924	1930	1933	1934	1935
Value (£1,000) . .	2·951	4·563	2·894	4·348	6·030
Quantities (1,000 tons)	29·2	35·3	25·9	41·0	52·4

(See *Board of Trade Journal*, 22 April 1937 and *Statistical Abstract for the United Kingdom*, Cmd. 5353, for the respective years.)

primarily by the lack of skilled workers.[1] But while Germany's tool capacity increased and her output more than doubled, her tool exports were about the same in 1932–9 as in 1929,[2] so that the enormous increase in tool production was completely absorbed by Germany's own engineering industries. This rise of 'tools available for use' within the Reich, like the increased output of steel, facilitated the rapid rearmament which was taking place in Germany and enhanced her ability to gear large sections of her capital goods industries to the purpose of war quickly should that need arise.

In strong contrast with Germany the other great net exporter of tools, namely, the United States, supplied the rest of the world with an increasing volume of tools, partly at least because the domestic market was unable to absorb current output. In the United States both employment and the value of gross output in the tool-producing industry was the same in 1937 as in 1929. If machine-tool accessories were added, aggregate output increased at most by about 10 per cent.[3] But the United States' exports rose by 50 per cent. Indeed, in 1939 her exports of tools were nearly 300 per cent. higher than in 1929,[4] which meant that, with an unchanged volume of tool production, the United States was equipping the engineering industries of the United Kingdom and France (which together took

[1] This is fully borne out by a sample inquiry into engineering labour in the London area in 1936 under the auspices of the Economic Research Division of the London School of Economics (see R. G. D. Allen and Brinley Thomas: 'The Supply of Engineering Labour under Boom Conditions', *Economic Journal*, June 1939, pp. 259–75). In Germany energetic steps were taken 'to provide for an increase in the supply of skilled workers' under a Four-Year Plan Law of 7 November 1936, which required machine-tool firms to furnish evidence that the number of apprentices that they employed was an adequate proportion of their total force of skilled work-people. The Ministry of Labour decided what was an 'adequate proportion' (*Deutscher Reichs- und Preussischer Staatsanzeiger*, no. 262, 9 November 1936).

[2] German machine-tool exports developed as follows:

	1929	1936	1938	1939
Value (Rm. million) .	210	148	204	238
Quantities (1,000 tons) .	107	90	101	113

(See *Statistisches Jahrbuch, 1941/42*, p. 316.)

[3] Output and employment in the United States tool industry was:

	Number of persons in employment		Gross output in $ million	
	1929	1937	1929	1937
Machine Tools .	47,391	47,266	245	260
Accessories .	26,682	32,893	144	162
Total	74,073	80,159	389	422

(See U.S. Bureau of the Census: *Census of Manufactures*, 1937, vol. ii, part 2, p. 413, and *Statistical Abstract of the United States, 1931*, pp. 835–6.)

[4] United States exports of tools and accessories rose from $41 million in 1929 to $64 million in 1937, to $102 million in 1938, and to $118 million in 1939 (*Statistical Abstract of the United States, 1940*, pp. 558–9).

more than half of the United States exports),[1] and also the industry of Japan, instead of her own.

The machine-tool industry did not occupy so predominant a position in the industrial structure of the United Kingdom as it did in that of Germany and the United States; nor did British tools count for so much in the world as did the products of other branches of British engineering. Thus in 1935–6, when in terms of employment and output the British tool industry was only one-quarter the size of that of Germany and when general economic activity was rapidly improving, some specialized branches of British engineering experienced acute shortages of tools. Many British tool-producers could not offer deliveries within a year;[2] and, in giving a first account of his stewardship as Minister for Co-ordination of Defence to the House of Commons in May 1936, Sir Thomas Inskip confessed to an anxiety regarding the development of bottle-necks in the gauge and tool industry which had necessarily to be eased before bulk production of shells could be put in hand.[3] Meanwhile the volume of British machine tools available for export had decreased[4] and the volume of imports had considerably increased. Indeed, the United Kingdom imported from Germany alone more tools in 1938 than she had imported in previous years from all her foreign suppliers taken together.[5] The United Kingdom's engineering trades were, like those of Japan and of the U.S.S.R., to a very appreciable extent dependent on Germany and on the United States for all the more advanced types of machine tools, as was clearly evident from British trade statistics, which showed that the average value per ton of imported tools was higher than that of exported tools.[6] The extraordinary superiority of the German over the British tool industry in the aggregate might best be summed up in this one fact that, in every single year during

---

[1] In 1939 United States exports of tools to Great Britain and France amounted to $65 million (Hitch: *America's Economic Strength*, p. 70).

[2] Engineering Supplement to *The Economist*, 14 November 1936, p. 2.

[3] The Minister was at that time about to allocate contracts for the supply of tools and gauges to be used for the manufacture of shells. For gauges he was unable to anticipate a substantial supply in under four to five months. To obtain the required machine tools might take even longer (21 May 1936, H.C.Deb. 5th ser., vol. 312, col. 1403).

[4] United Kingdom exports of machine tools developed as follows:

	1929	1934	1935	1936	1937	1938
Value (£1,000)	2·153	1·610	2·243	2·014	2·152	4·473
Quantities (1,000 tons)	16·2	12·2	16·4	13·9	11·9	24·1

The quite exceptional increase in British exports in 1938 must on no account be interpreted as meaning that the capacity of the tool industry had by then reached such a size as to supply fully both the home and foreign markets. What it did reflect was that recession in general economic activity that afflicted Britain as well as the United States, and the persistence of a high foreign demand for the specific types of British tools.

[5] Aggregate imports of tools weighed 11,000 tons in 1929 and 7,700 tons in 1935. In 1938 British imports from Germany alone weighed 12,600 tons.

[6] As looked at from the point of view of the two great net exporters, it was a reflection of closer political alinements that, in the late 1930s, the United States became the arsenal supplying

the decade before 1938, German machine-tool exports exceeded by quantity British tool production.

Moreover in 1938–9 Germany produced not only more than twice the number of comparable machine tools produced in the United Kingdom, but she also possessed a stock of about 1·3 million tools in her whole economy, which was at least twice the stock available to British industries. The stock of tools in existence in the economy of the United States was slightly smaller than Germany's stock,[1] and in the U.S.S.R. it was about one-third of Germany's.[2] But since, in Germany, quite apart from her numerical superiority in stock and in current production of tools, by far the largest proportion of available tools were of the multiple-purpose type, Germany was better equipped to convert and adapt her peace-time industry, and was less likely to experience bottle-necks, owing to a shortage of tools, in her rearmament drive, than any other country in the world.

(d) COMPARATIVE EFFORTS FOR MILITARY PURPOSES

Until 1932 Germany's rearmament had been kept well in check; but by 1938 she possessed a large and well-equipped army and she commanded more first-line planes than Britain and France together. This achievement was the reward of a broader flow of capital goods originating in factories whose capacity had not greatly changed since the late 1920s. This implied that the National Socialists were reaping the benefit from the drives for the modernization and rationalization of industries that had been carried through in Germany before the Great Depression. Thus the basic armaments potential existed already in 1929. It was at that time prevented from yielding a large flow of arms: first, because treaty obligations restricted the production of certain categories of weapons; secondly,

machine tools to France and the United Kingdom, and Germany the arsenal for her Axis partners, Italy and Japan. Distribution of German exports in Rm. million:

	1929	1932	1934	1936	1938	1939
France	25·6	13·4	5·4	7·4	10·0	7·6
U.K.	16·8	7·4	7·8	16·9	20·6	15·4
Japan	4·1	2·7	8·0	6·0	25·1	29·6
Italy	11·5	5·2	6·0	13·4	21·0	27·3
U.S.S.R.	22·2	160·0	23·8	45·2	7·4	15·7
Total Exports	210·1	214·1	87·0	148·2	203·5	238·1

(See *Statistisches Jahrbuch* for the respective years.)

[1] The figure for Germany's stock was derived from an official census carried through in May 1938. Early in 1943 stocks of tools in the United Kingdom numbered 740,000 and stocks in the United States about 1·6 million (N. Kaldor, loc. cit.). The pre-war stock in the United States was lower than the 1943 figure but higher than a Russian estimate of 1 million tools for 1940 (E. Lokshin: *Industry in the U.S.S.R.*, p. 156).

[2] Based on the statement that the planned annual production for 1937 would represent between 12 and 15 per cent. of all metal-working machine tools in existence (U.S.S.R., State Planning Commission: *Second Five-Year Plan*, p. 132).

because under the Weimar régime successive German governments genuinely believed in peaceful solutions of existing conflicts; and, thirdly, because the reparations 'burden' precluded any light-hearted attempt, which some German parties were always willing to support, to impose upon the people any additional burden in the shape of rearmament.

These three limiting conditions disappeared when the National Socialists came into power. Preparations for conflict were begun immediately. Expenditure for military purposes, which included expenditure on weapons, on the erection of war plants, on fortifications, on the building of military barracks, on soldiers' pay and rations, rose from Rm. 720 million in 1932 to Rm. 1·9 milliard in 1933 and to Rm. 3 milliard in 1934. In the latter year this sum was about the same as that spent in 1929 for military purposes and on reparations together. But while in 1929 this expenditure represented about 3·5 per cent. of the German net national product or income, in 1934 it represented about 5 per cent. By comparison, France in 1934 devoted to military purposes approximately 4 per cent. of her net national product and Britain in 1934 less than 3 per cent.[1]

Spending for military purposes forged ahead in Germany; as in Italy and Japan it more than doubled between 1934 and 1935. The other Powers, except the U.S.S.R., were slow in stepping up their efforts in the military sphere. Neither Japan's successes in China, nor Germany's and Japan's withdrawals from the League, nor Italy's attack on Ethiopia, nor the occupation of the Rhineland in March 1936 by the German army and its subsequent remilitarization, nor the vast expansion of Japanese spending for military purposes in 1937, nor even the dissolution of the Conference on the Far East at Brussels in November 1937, gave Britain and France shocks severe enough to induce them to reach the rate of increase in military expenditure which had taken place in Germany between 1935 and 1936 and between 1936 and 1937. It required the annexation of Austria in March 1938, and the surrender to Germany of the Sudetenland in September 1938, to bring about a rate of increase in military spending between 1937 and 1938 which was higher in Britain and France than anywhere else in the world, except Japan. The United States, who was three times as strong as Germany in manufacturing output and war

---

[1] The figures for the German net national product are based on Professor A. J. Brown's studies. He made the 'official' figures comparable with those in Britain in a series of articles in the *Bulletin of International News* (R.I.I.A.) for 1941 (nos. 12, 13, 15). He later restated his conclusions and added estimates made by the United States Bombing Survey for certain pre-war years, on the basis of fuller data which had since become available (A. J. Brown: *Applied Economics* (London, Allen & Unwin, 1947), p. 14, col. 5, and p. 15). French income data are based on Duge de Bernonville: 'Revenus privés et consommations', *Revue d'Économie Politique*, May–August 1939, and raised proportionately to correspond with the official estimates for 1938, given in France, Commissariat Général du Plan de Modernisation et d'Équipement: *Estimation du revenu national français* (Paris, 1947), p. 18, items 11 and 15. For details of Germany's expenditure for military purposes, see Appendix II, p. 492 below.

potential, held aloof from this uneven armaments race throughout the 1930s. Indeed, her isolationism, in spirit and in fact, gave German leaders a convincing reason for virtually leaving out of their calculations the possibility of American intervention in any conflict in the Old World.

While the course of military spending was roughly known to most governments, such aggregate expenditures were only imperfectly relevant to the assessment of real preparedness for war. For without specific information on the proportions of aggregate spending on Maginot and Siegfried Lines, on aerodromes, on bombers and fighters, on soldiers' uniforms, rations, and pay, comparisons of real military strength as between one country and another were nearly impossible. Apart from these handicaps, it was no less difficult to arrive at rates of exchange which would reflect the real purchasing power of different currencies, in terms of one currency, in respect of each specific object of expenditure. For this reason, the following table, VI, in which total military expenditures for 1938 and for the six years from 1933 to 1938 have been converted into pounds sterling, can provide no more than a tentative and approximate answer to the question; 'Which of the Great Powers held the lead in the armaments race in 1938 in terms of quantitative superiority?'

TABLE VI. *Military Expenditures**

(At market prices)

Year	Japan	Italy	Germany	U.S.S.R.	U.K.	France	U.S.A.
	Yen	*Lire*	*Rm.*	*Roubles*	£	*Francs*	$

A (in millions of local currency)

Year	Japan	Italy	Germany	U.S.S.R.	U.K.	France	U.S.A.
1933	873	4,824	1,900	1,547	108	12,324	792
1934	942	5,590	2,800	5,000	114	11,200	708
1935	2,206	12,624	6,200	8,200	137	13,000	933
1936	1,078	16,357	10,000	14,816	186	15,000	1,119
1937	3,972	13,270	14,600	17,500	262	19,000	1,079
1938	6,097	15,030	16,000	23,100	391	29,000	1,130
1933–8	15,200	67,700	51,600	70,200	1,200	100,000	5,761

B (in £ million purchasing power)†

	(a)	(b)	(c)	(d)	(e)	(f)	(g)
1938	508	167	1,170	924	391	207	231
1933–8	1,266	930	3,540	2,808	1,200	1,088	1,175

Notes: * For data for Germany, see Appendix II (p. 492 below); for data for other countries, see League of Nations: *Armaments Year Book* for the respective years, also sources quoted for the item 'Expenditures for military purposes' in Appendix III (pp. 493–503 below).

† Conversion rate to pound: (a) 12 yen; (b) 64 lire from 1933 to 1936; 90 lire in 1937–8; (c) Rm. 13·5 for 1938; Rm. 15 assumed for average of previous years; (d) 25 roubles; (f) 75 francs for 1933–6; 108 francs for 1937; 140 francs for 1938; (g) $4·9. These conversion rates are based on *London and Cambridge Economic Service*: Bulletin I, vol. xviii, January 1940, p. 21, and on A. J. Brown's *Applied Economics*.

It will be seen that Germany's military expenditure in the six years before 1939 had been nearly three times as high as that of Britain. The United Kingdom's actual state of preparedness began to look still more inadequate when in 1937 the British Cabinet 'felt obliged to instruct the Service ministries to include Italy alongside Germany and Japan in the list of possible aggressors, and to plan their defensive preparations accordingly'.[1] For the superiority, in quantitative military preparedness, of the three aggressive-minded Powers even over Britain and France combined was in a ratio of about two to one. It was greater than the disparity in strength between these two groups of Powers in terms of either manufacturing output or war potential. Next to Germany, the most massive arming had been carried through in the U.S.S.R.[2] Since the U.S.S.R. had to build munition and armaments factories, while existing plants in the more mature industrial countries had in the main only to be converted, it seemed probable that Germany's effective military strength exceeded that of the U.S.S.R. by far more than the proportion of one-third that was suggested by mere comparisons of aggregate military expenditure.

But how great was the armaments effort in each of these seven countries? To what extent had the total economic resources available within each country been mobilized for defence or aggression in 1938? Clearly, spending for military purposes had to be expressed as a proportion of total spending on all available goods and services. The concept of 'net national product' expresses the total amount of goods produced by the manufacturing and building industries, and the total amount of services rendered by transport, administration, &c., within a year, always on the assumption that in the process of producing those goods and services the stock of domestic capital, such as plant and equipment, is being kept intact. In so far as more goods and services are available within a country than were nationally produced in a year there has to be added to the net national product the excess of imports over exports (i.e. external disinvestment or foreign borrowing) as well as the depletion of domestic capital (i.e. internal disinvestment) in order to arrive at the net product nationally available. Moreover, for purposes of international comparisons account will have to be taken also of the valuation of the net available products. Since in some countries the valuation was made at the prices at which goods and services were bought in the market, and since those market prices grossly overstated a country's real net available product—especially where, as in the U.S.S.R., indirect taxation was the main source of government income— it was necessary for international comparisons to value the net available

---

[1] W. H. Hancock and M. M. Gowing: *British War Economy* (London, H.M.S.O., 1949), p. 64.

[2] Aggregate Russian military expenditure would still have amounted to £2,400 million, if (as suggested for 1937 by Colin Clark) a rate of 30 roubles to the £ had been taken as the correct purchasing power parity instead of 25 roubles to the £ as suggested by A. J. Brown (*Applied Economics*, p. 29).

product at factor costs by the exclusion of all indirect taxes, which merely raised the prices of the current product without increasing it in real terms.

The following Table, VII, represents a careful attempt to contrast the composition of the net available products in 1938. Since in that year, as compared with 1937, manufacturing output had fallen in the United States, France, and the United Kingdom, it was obvious that their short-term, potential reserves were larger than were those in the full employment economies of the other four Powers, and that, by the mere re-employment of unemployed and idle resources, their net products could be greatly expanded. Keeping in mind this significant difference in employable reserves of man-power and industrial capacities as between the United States, France, and the United Kingdom on the one hand, and the U.S.S.R., Germany, Italy, and Japan on the other, attention here is simply focused upon the composition of the net products actually available in each of the seven Powers in 1938:

TABLE VII. *Structure of the Net Available Products at Factor Costs in 1938*[1]

Expenditure for:	Japan	Germany	Italy	U.S.S.R.	U.K.	France	U.S.A.
A. Expenditure in milliards of local currency							
1. Military purposes	5·8	14·5	14·0	20·0	0·380	28·0	1·03
2. Goods and services by public authorities	} 1·1	16·1	} 15·0	31·0	0·328	27·0	8·67
3. Net investment } (a) Public				38·0	0·132	16·2	1·72
(b) Private	1·8	1·7	1·0	..	0·176	2·8	−1·36
4. Personal consumption	14·1	55·1	80·0	127·0	3·725	282·0	55·03
Net available product	22·8	87·4	110·0	216·0	4·741	356·0	65·09
B. Expenditure in per cent. of net available product							
1. Military purposes	25·4	16·6	12·7	9·3	7·9	7·9	1·5
2. Goods and services by public authorities	} 4·8	18·4	} 13·7	14·6	7·0	7·6	13·3
3. Net investment } (a) Public				17·1	2·8	4·6	2·7
(b) Private	7·9	2·0	0·9	..	3·7	0·7	−2·1
4. Personal consumption	61·9	63·0	72·7	59·0	78·6	79·2	84·6
Net available product	100·0	100·0	100·0	100·0	100·0	100·0	100·0

Table VII b shows clearly that expenditures for recorded military purposes absorbed the highest proportion of the net available product in Japan, Germany, and Italy. Their economies in 1938, therefore, were more extensively geared to aggression than were those of the other four Powers. Japan's lead in military effort was undisputed. Being at war with China, she was already using in 1938 one-quarter of her total resources for that purpose. The world's attention was, however, diverted from the Far East and focused on Europe, where the pace of development was

[1] For details of calculation, see Appendix III, p. 493 below.

decisively determined by Germany. She, like Italy, was applying to military purposes about one-sixth of her available resources.

Formally, at least, the Soviet military effort did not claim more than one-eleventh of her available resources. But while six of the Great Powers treated investment expenditure for the construction of armament plants and fortifications as spending for military purposes, it is uncertain that the U.S.S.R. followed the same procedure. In view of the abnormally high level of expenditure on investment in the U.S.S.R., it was at least a possibility that some of it might have been potential military expenditure. For example, it was possible that plants under construction for the production of tractors might have been designed with small adjustments in plans to produce tanks.

What, however, the U.S.S.R. had in common with Japan, Germany, and Italy was that the share of the net product available for personal consumption by civilians was very much lower there than in the United States, France, or the United Kingdom. This low level of consumption was perfectly consistent with high military and investment expenditure. It will also be noticed that the expenditure on goods and services bought by public authorities was high in the U.S.S.R., Germany, Italy, and, surprisingly, at first also in the United States. But whereas in the United States it reflected the attempts made to combat the depression of 1938, in Germany it reflected largely the costs of maintaining and accommodating the huge Party and semi-military organizations by public funds. Indeed the high share of this item in Germany revealed that her specific military effort had not as yet reached its optimum. That is to say, public authorities were in 1938 still putting exceedingly large claims upon real resources and were thus preventing the attainment of a possible maximum of military effort.

Moreover, public expenditure was high in the collectivist society of the U.S.S.R. simply because a great number of services were provided directly to civilian consumers by the state. In part that was true also of Germany, where some civilians benefited directly from the state-sponsored *Kraft durch Freude* organizations. It may be presumed that these state-provided additions to civilian consumption would have raised the extremely low level of consumption substantially in the U.S.S.R. and slightly in Germany; but it was unlikely that in these two countries it would have been raised to anywhere near the level prevailing in either of the three Western democracies.

There cannot be a shadow of doubt that Germany, like Japan and Italy, devoted more of her available resources to strengthening her military preparedness than did the democracies. It was, however, one thing to say that because Germany's military effort was large in 1938, her resources left for consumption were small; and quite another thing to say that the steady increase in her military effort over a period of time had been accomplished only through a gradual reduction in the standard of living of her people. Careful investigations have shown that, although military expenditure rose from less than 2 per cent. of her net available product in 1929 to over 16 per cent. in 1938, aggregate real consumption increased slightly in Germany during this period and real consumption per head of population was only insignificantly lower in 1938 than in 1929.[1] Net investment in real terms had not changed either. It follows that the great increase in Germany's military strength, accompanied by an increase in purchases of goods and services by her public authorities, was not the result of a deterioration in real civilian consumption; it was instead the result of an expansion by about 20 per cent. in Germany's real net national product or income between 1929 and 1938.[2] This expansion of Germany's real national product, closely conforming to that of her manufacturing output (cf. Table III on p. 432), was above all the result of economic and commercial policies which ensured the attainment and the maintenance of a full employment of her resources in the late 1930s.

(e) Economic and Commercial Policies

(1) *Internal Position*

There was clearly some connexion between economic strength and military strength. The four countries whose output had risen since 1929, and had been maintained at a high level in 1938, were also the countries which devoted relatively the largest proportion of their available resources to war or to preparations for it. It had become painfully obvious that the four Powers which, since the First World War and in consequence of the Great Depression, had adopted a totalitarian form of government had been able to infuse a higher degree of stability into their economies than had either of the three Western democracies. Indeed, France never, and the United States only once, attained, in any year after the depression, the level of output and prosperity which had been reached in those two countries in 1929; and they, like the United Kingdom, were in 1938 once again drawn into a new recession.

If economic performance was the test of strength, what were the reasons for the economic strength of the totalitarian Powers and the apparent weakness of the democracies? Totalitarianism, as a political system, meant the imposition of the will and aims of one single party upon the rest of the

---

[1] U.S. Strategic Bombing Survey: *The Effects of Strategic Bombing on the German War Economy*, p. 19.

[2] Based on Ferdinand Grünig: 'Probleme der Zusammensetzung und Verteilung des Sozialprodukts', *Vierteljahrshefte zur Wirtschaftsforschung* (Berlin, Deutsches Institut für Wirtschaftsforschung, 1949), part i, pp. 15–16. See also Burton Klein: 'Germany's Preparation for War: A Re-Examination', *American Economic Review*, March 1948, p. 63.

community.[1] Whatever the merits of the faith which inspired the members of the Communist Party in the U.S.S.R., of the Fascist Party in Italy, of the National Socialist Party in Germany, and of the Militarists in Japan, these groups would not tolerate open opposition to the aims of their régimes.[2] This intolerance, this repression and persecution of opinions which ran counter to those of the party in power, were precisely the kind of 'evils that democracy came into being to prevent'.[3]

The great advantage, therefore, which totalitarian governments enjoyed over democratic governments was that they could impose upon their people clear-cut objectives for national policy. Democratic governments, in formulating such objectives, had constantly to take into account the opposition. The totalitarian governments could gear existing institutions and social forces to the one purpose of realizing their set plans, and in the economic life of their community they had the power to enforce a totalitarian discipline. Democratic governments had to rely on discipline by consent for the execution of their policy, and, while such consent was possible, it certainly was never assured.

Yet the many political features which the totalitarian Powers had in common should not obscure the wide differences between them in other spheres. There was a deep gulf between the economic and social systems of the U.S.S.R. on the one hand and of Germany, Italy, and Japan on the other. In successive stages the U.S.S.R. completely abolished private ownership of land and of all means of production and thus rid herself of one of the principal forms of inequality in human society. In the other three totalitarian states this inequality continued. Indeed, it was greater in Japan than in the United States or in the United Kingdom. Moreover, in Germany and in Italy industrialists, although subjected to controls, remained in executive command of their enterprises.[4] In this respect, totalitarian capitalism had much more in common with democratic capitalism than with totalitarian collectivism of the Russian brand. This meant that it was not a similarity in their economic and social systems that accounted for the greater industrial stability in the totalitarian states; it was a similarity in the political power which their governments could wield.

---

[1] R. G. Hawtrey: *Economic Destiny* (London, Longmans, Green, 1944), p. 18.

[2] What distinguished the Japanese governmental system from the British, French, and American systems was that the armed forces were not subordinated to the civil authorities. In questions relating to armaments and military operations, the Emperor was advised not by his Cabinet, but by the military and naval officers who held the posts of Minister of War and of Minister of the Navy in the Cabinet. An increase in armaments, for example, might be recommended by the Supreme Command. Such an increase required money, and it was the Cabinet's responsibility to get this money voted by parliament. It might have to urge expenditure which it did not approve. In this sense the will of the military authorities could override that of any other element; this is the reason for numbering Japan among the totalitarian instead of among the democratic Powers (see W. B. Munro: *Governments of Europe* (New York, Macmillan, 1938), p. 807).

[3] Hawtrey: *Economic Destiny*, p. 56.   [4] Ibid., p. 186.

But what was the bearing of the economic and commercial policy of all these Powers during the 1930s on their relative strength or weakness?

The situation of the U.S.S.R. was quite unique. Subject to the ultimate paramountcy of the Communist Party, the Government assumed exclusive responsibility for the destiny of the Soviet Union's economy. Taking as their main target the conversion of a primarily agricultural society into an industrial society, the Government through their various agencies planned all production, industry by industry, and in the light of available resources determined beforehand the amounts to be allocated respectively to consumption and to the building-up of its industrial equipment. When once the plans had been decided, all means were used to assure their execution. As Stalin said at the Fifteenth Party Congress:

Admittedly they [i.e. under the capitalistic system] too have something akin to plans. But those plans are prognosis, guess-plans which bind nobody, and on the basis of which it is impossible to direct a country's economy. Things are different with us. Our plans are not prognosis, guess-plans, but *instructions* which are *compulsory* for all managements and which determine the future course of the economic development of our *entire* country. You see that this implies a difference of principle.[1]

While such a planned economy was capable of eliminating the violent fluctuations which had been observed hitherto in the individualist and capitalist world, there always were, of course, even in the U.S.S.R., some factors that could never be completely foreseen (i.e. weather, harvest, human stupidity) and that were bound to throw out of joint the most wisely conceived plan. Indeed, any error of judgement on the part of Soviet planners—as to what should be produced and on what scale— might create losses of welfare far greater than the costs of trial and error under private enterprise. What costly errors were, in fact, committed in the course of planned industrialization nobody will ever know. However, there was no reason why in the planned economy of the U.S.S.R. there should be depressions and unemployment resulting from a lack of effective demand.

Nor could fluctuations of foreign demand greatly affect internal stability in the U.S.S.R., since in 1937 exports constituted less than 1 per cent. of the Soviet Union's net national product. In the course of execution of the two Five-Year Plans, manufacturing production more than trebled (see Table III above, p. 432), and until 1931 this expansion was accompanied by a considerable increase in the physical volume of imports. Thereafter, imports fell owing to the development of the manifold potential resources to be found in this state of continental dimensions.[2] The success of the Soviet Government's vigorous pursuit of a policy of import substitu-

---

[1] Quoted in Baykov: *Development of the Soviet Economic System*, p. 424.
[2] Ibid. p. 265.

tion was reflected in the decline of imports by 47 per cent. between 1929 and 1937 and in the claim that the U.S.S.R. had been the first country where the practical problems involved in manufacturing synthetic rubber had been solved.[1] This most striking tendency towards autarky, inspired in part by considerations of political power and strategy (for the Russian public were never allowed to forget that they were surrounded by a hostile capitalist world), implied that the pressing need of exports to pay for imports was coming to an end. And, as the Government possessed a complete monopoly in foreign trade, Soviet commercial policy ensured (by the application of rigorous exchange control, and of import and export licensing) that the internal production plan could not be jeopardized by external influences.

The production plan was translated into a financial plan by price fixing. State trading companies concluded with state factories or trusts delivery contracts for specified quantities and qualities of goods, the prices of which were determined not by the factories but by the planning authorities. Since the planned prices were fixed on the basis of estimated production costs, including wages, the monetary authorities had to put the total credits[2] required to finance the production programme at the disposal of the trusts. Thus, in principle, these credit arrangements were entirely contingent upon the production plan, and the state banks could not by their credit policy cause variations in effective demand, output, or employment.

It was the function of Soviet fiscal or budgetary policy to see that financial transactions did not upset the economic plan. In order to obtain the means with which to finance their huge investment or industrialization programme, the Soviet authorities relied almost exclusively on one single indirect tax, i.e. the turnover tax. This tax was so devised as to establish equilibrium between the demand for consumer goods (as determined by earned incomes) and their supply (as planned in the production programme).[3] The retail price at which goods were sold exceeded the factory price by the amount of this tax. To the extent to which the planning authorities decided upon the speeding-up of industrialization (i.e. upon the increase in the rate of investment) fiscal policy had to follow suit and the turnover tax had to be raised.

Obviously the very speed of industrialization had initially to be paid for with great sacrifices by the Russian people. During the First Five-Year Plan, when compulsory collectivization was carried through, total agricultural output fell and livestock was slaughtered of which the products

[1] A. G. B. Fisher: *Economic Self-Sufficiency* (London, Oxford University Press Pamphlets, 1939), p. 21.

[2] Georg Kieser: *Warum ist Russland so stark?* (Biel, Chasseral-Verlag, 1945), p. 111.

[3] E. M. Chassudowsky: 'The Soviet Conception of Economic Equilibrium', *Review of Economic Studies*, vol. vi, 1938–9, p. 143.

certainly did not reach the town markets. Of this smaller total of agricultural produce a larger volume had to be exported, in order to pay for a larger volume of imports of equipment and machine tools and to compensate for the unfavourable terms of trade which confronted the U.S.S.R. during the Great Depression in the rest of the world. But at the same time as the agricultural product available for domestic consumption declined, incomes available for spending increased with the doubling of the industrial labour force. In this acute 'famine of goods' prices were raised, and rationing was introduced of the greater part of all essential commodities, leaving a smaller part to find its own price-level on a legalized black market. The official rations discriminated in favour of the industrial worker, and, although his incentive to earn a money income was kept alive by the temptation to supplement his rations on the black market, the very multiple prices robbed the money wage differentials, required in order to reward efficient workers and to induce mobility, of their uniform significance. There was no doubt that this situation and the deliberate discrimination in the distribution of scarce goods contained dangers which might have resulted in the collapse of all effective planning. These obvious dangers to planning decreased when, in the course of the Second Five-Year Plan, the supply position improved, and when in 1935 multiple prices and rationing could be abandoned and human suffering could at least not get worse. Judged by the data illustrative of the fulfilment of the plan, it cannot be said that the achievements in different sections of the economy were unrelated or chaotic.[1]

In this collectivist society in which the decisions for the development of the economy were firmly concentrated in the hands of the Government and in which economic planning, monetary regulations, and fiscal and commercial policies were intended to be closely co-ordinated, the maintenance of economic stability and the achievement of a tremendous rise in national production presented no insoluble problems.

In individualist countries which had reached an advanced stage of industrial maturity, it was much more difficult to sustain a high or rising level of output. A master plan, consciously formulated by a single authority and imposed upon all, was alien to capitalist societies. What and how much was to be produced depended on effective demand for various kinds of goods and services at existing market prices. In contrast with the planned allocation of resources in the U.S.S.R., the capitalist or market economies relied on responses to price changes for the direction of resources to the points where there was the greatest demand.

[1] There would certainly have been disruptive consequences if powerful critics of the Soviet system had been right in their judgement that it was not conscious economic planning, but inflation, produced by an incautious monetary policy, which had assured full employment and brought about the required restriction of consumption in the U.S.S.R. See Michael Polanyi: *Full Employment and Free Trade* (Cambridge University Press, 1945).

But why was the revival of effective demand since 1932 completely lacking in France and very imperfect in the United States, and why was it not sustained in the United Kingdom? No simple answer which would be valid for all three countries alike can be given to this question. What was required in all of them was an increase of expenditure by one (or a combination) of four broad groups of agents, i.e. by consumers, by business men, by the Government, or by foreigners. The masses of ordinary people, and particularly the unemployed, wanted to buy more, but they had no means to finance even essential purchases. Without assets capable of serving as securities on the strength of which the banks would lend them money, this great majority of the population was precluded from increasing effective demand. Foreign demand, although extremely helpful in stimulating production, was hampered in the 1930s by direct controls and currency restrictions. Consequently increased demand, employment, and output depended primarily on increased spending by governments and by business men.

As long as public expenditure (i.e. expenditure by the Government and by local authorities) was financed by tax revenue, so that—without any significant change in the structure of tax rates—the budget was balanced, governments neither detracted from, nor added to, aggregate demand. They could only increase it through incurring budget deficits, by way either of reductions of taxes or of increases in expenditures on goods and services. But deficit spending (financed by the creation of credit) was, for a variety of reasons, opposed by business men, and in the United Kingdom in 1931 this element in the community contributed to bringing about the downfall of the Labour Government when the May Committee on National Expenditure[1] reported that the budget would show a deficit of £120 million in the next financial year. The demand for a balanced budget was a contributory cause also in the eventual discomfiture of the Blum Government in France. And the financing of considerable 'Federal' deficits incurred by Roosevelt's New Deal certainly aggravated an already existing hostility between American business and the Administration. Business leaders held that it was not the function of government to aim at balancing the national accounts in the widest sense; and if, in the name of 'sound finance', governments acted in accordance with this doctrine and limited themselves to balancing the budget account, the only channel through which effective demand could be increased would be private enterprise.

In deciding whether to spend more, in order to expand production and employment, leaders of business were moved—although not exclusively— by expectations of profit. These expectations were in turn influenced by

[1] Great Britain: *Committee on National Expenditure: Report July 1931*, Cmd. 3920 (London, H.M.S.O., 1931).

changes in costs, by technical inventions, by variations in the structure of taxation, &c., and, above all, by the monetary policy of the banking system, that is, in the last instance, by that of the semi-autonomous Central Banks.

In all mature economies, the Central Banks controlled the supply of money. So long as the public preferred to hold money rather than part with it (at given rates of interest), the Central Banks could lower the level of interest rates by increasing the supply of money.[1] And even if for various reasons the public preferred to hold more money, the Central Banks could keep interest rates at a desired level by satisfying them through changes in the supply of money. Bank operations would in the first instance affect the short-term rate of interest; but, by influencing the short-term rates, the Central Banks would indirectly affect the long-term rate. They could also directly affect the latter by appropriate 'open-market operations', that is by the purchase and sale of bonds and of long-term securities. If the Central Banks bought securities, they would drive up their prices and thereby reduce the long-term rate. The lower this rate, the greater would be the range of profitable investment opportunities for business men. If, therefore, the revival of effective demand depended on the investment policy of private enterprise only (as it would where for political reasons governments were debarred from incurring budget deficits), the monetary policy of the banks would be of decisive importance in creating suitable conditions for investment.

Balanced budgets, low rates of interest, and the prevalence of international prices for raw materials that were low by comparison with the prices of manufactures were the major single factors which, in conditions of idle capacity and unemployment, were apt to restore the confidence of entrepreneurs in the profitability of investment in the United Kingdom. When in 1931 the Labour Party split, the new National Government raised taxes, reduced benefits, brought about considerable savings through the conversion of the huge public debt to a lower scale of interest, and obtained higher revenues from the imposition in 1932 of tariffs on imports. By these means the national accounts were, until 1936, quite adequately balanced year by year with the sole exception of 1931.[2]

Having promised to 'save the pound', the new Government, within a month of coming to power, abandoned the gold standard. By this action it severed the British from the world price level—a severance that was necessary if deflation and rising unemployment in Britain were to be brought to a halt. Moreover, the depreciation of the pound was calculated to stimulate exports so long as competitors, such as the United States,

---

[1] Provided, of course, that they could satisfy any external drain of gold or that external gold payments were suspended (cf. R. G. Hawtrey: *The Art of Central Banking* (London, Longmans, Green, 1932), p. 135).

[2] Cf. Ursula K. Hicks: *The Finance of British Government, 1920–1936* (London, Oxford University Press, 1938), p. 287.

France, Germany, Belgium, Holland, and Switzerland, adhered to gold, while Britain's main suppliers and customers, namely, the Empire and some Scandinavian countries, also depreciated and kept their currencies at a fixed ratio to sterling. In this respect Britain's fortunes were quite unique: she continued to obtain her food and raw materials cheaply, while procuring an export advantage over her competitors.[1] Not counting gold and silver, the British balance of payments on income account was in equilibrium in 1933 and in 1934 and showed a surplus in 1935.[2]

Another result of depreciation was the easing of money rates. By open market operations the Central Bank increased the cash basis of the whole banking system. But, despite lower money rates, 'advances to industry' in the 1930s never approached the volume that they had reached in the 1920s. Consequently the banks, possessing more cash but being unable to find customers for 'advances', purchased bills and securities, thereby helping firms to become liquid and enabling them to finance expansion without recourse to the banks.

These monetary, fiscal, and commercial measures engendered optimism among employers, an optimism which, however, by itself hardly sufficed to foster recovery. What was decisive was that, throughout the 1920s, Britain alone of all the Great Powers had remained in the doldrums. She had been starved of investment; her industries had not undergone rationalization and modernization as had those of Germany or of the United States; moreover, there was a large backlog of unsatisfied demand for housing. Thus, given favourable commercial, fiscal, and monetary conditions, there were quite considerable opportunities for investment.

At first the increase of exports was greater than the increase of industrial production.[3] Currency depreciations and the tariff stimulated investment in protected industries, especially in iron and steel (see Table V on p. 443 above), where it took the form of labour-saving devices and helped to increase productivity per man-hour. Moreover, the terms of trade, after having moved heavily in Britain's favour, continued throughout the 1930s to provide the country with cheap food and materials. The prices of these basic materials remained low, partly because of protection in Germany, Italy, and France. As the cost of living fell by more than the extent of the reduction of fixed incomes or of wage-rates of employees, there arose additional demand for houses[4] and for other durable consumer goods

[1] Bank for International Settlements: *Twelfth Annual Report, 1st April 1941—31st March 1942* (Basle, 1942), p. 103.

[2] Colin Clark: 'National Income at its Climax', *Economic Journal*, June 1937, p. 313.

[3] League of Nations: Economic, Financial, and Transit Dept.: *International Currency Experience* (League of Nations [printed at Princeton, U.S.A.], 1944) p. 127.

[4] In the eleven years, 1920–30, about 1·5 million houses were built in England and Wales, of which nearly two-thirds were state-assisted, but slightly more were built in the five years 1934–8, of which less than one-quarter was state-assisted (F. Benham: *Great Britain under Protection* (New York, Macmillan, 1941), p. 223).

(i.e. motor-cars). Thus recovery was well under way at home when the British export advantage was lost owing to the subsequent depreciation of the currencies of the gold bloc countries, and particularly owing to the intensification abroad of quantitative restrictions on imports.

In conformity with the increase of manufacturing output (see Table III on p. 432 above), the volume of British imports rose, and it was about 4 per cent. higher in 1937 than in 1929. On the other hand, the volume of exports remained 20 per cent. lower.[1] Excluding gold and silver, the external balance on income account showed deficits which increased from £20 million in 1936 to £66 million in 1938.[2] These external deficits might have been corrected by making the exchange rates fluctuate, but this would have had obvious disadvantages for a large trading nation. By the institution of an Exchange Equalization Fund, external deficits, and particularly short-term capital movements, were prevented from affecting the exchange rates. But this kind of exchange control was fundamentally different from that practised in the totalitarian countries.[3] Since the adverse external balance was not allowed to put a brake on internal recovery, British foreign assets were sold to meet the small but persistent deficits.

Clearly, a number of favourable circumstances combined to revive British activity in the 1930s. The Government prepared the ground for recovery, but they did not initiate it by any deficit spending. When once effective demand had risen it became cumulative, and in the middle of 1937 employment and output were higher than in 1929.[4] A number of factors contributed towards bringing about a rise in the long-term rate of interest in 1937. It followed upon the Government announcement, in February, that they intended to spend £1·5 milliard on rearmament in the course of five years and to finance £900 million of this sum by means of borrowing. The remainder was to be financed by a special tax on the growth of company profits. Both the rise in the rate of interest and the anticipated taxation of profits adversely affected private investment. Aggregate demand and employment declined, and this decline was not sufficiently checked by the sharp increase of budget deficits in 1937 and

[1] Colin Clark: 'Determination of Multiplier from National Income Statistics', Economic Journal, September 1938, p. 444.

[2] Benham, op. cit. p. 253, also G. D. A. MacDougall: 'Britain's Foreign Trade Problem', Economic Journal, March 1947, pp. 69–113.

[3] It did not prevent a British importer from obtaining the currency that he required for the purchase of foreign goods (Benham, op. cit. pp. 47 seqq.).

[4] Nevertheless, the rise in employment had not fully caught up with the increase in the working population, so that unemployment in 1937 remained slightly above the 1929 level (Ministry of Labour Gazette, January 1938). Moreover, in the so-called special areas of England and Wales 27 per cent. remained unemployed even in March 1937, and this ratio of unemployment presented social and political problems in these areas which the private enterprise system did not solve and could not solve without vigorous government action (Great Britain, Commissioner for Special Areas in England and Wales: Report for the year ended September 30, 1937, Cmd. 5595 (London, H.M.S.O., 1937).

1938. Thus in the United Kingdom the recovery (which was remarkable, though only temporary) was brought about by business men. All that the Government did was to prepare the way for them, to restore their confidence, and to wait for their response.

In the United States internal recovery was less successful, despite the fact that she, unlike any other Great Power except the U.S.S.R., doubled her output of manufactures between 1932 and 1937 (see Table III, p. 432 above). But in her case the depression had been more severe. National income, which in Britain had fallen by only 15 per cent. between 1929 and 1932, had fallen by 44 per cent. in the United States. During the subsequent recovery manufacturing output and real national income were only just restored to their pre-depression levels; and the implication was that, in the period from 1929 to 1938, the American economy was stagnating. This generalization meant little, however, when proper account was taken of the great variety of experience in different sectors of the economy. Here only some of the apparently significant features can be stressed.

When Roosevelt's New Dealers took power, the monetary authority, i.e. the Federal Reserve Bank, had already reduced the rate of interest and attempted to expand the basis of credit in the United States by open market operations. But these attempts were completely neutralized by the loss of gold. Since the British Exchange Equalization Fund had been acquiring gold in order, so the Administration feared, to keep the sterling bloc currencies deliberately undervalued, an embargo was placed on the American export of gold, and the dollar was devalued in 1933.[1] The gold embargo made internal credit operations effective and, in 1934, exports increased quite considerably.[2]

But, apart from the short-lived revival of foreign demand, cheap money in the United States did not of itself generate effective internal demand. Considering the vigour of the investment boom in the United States in the 1920s, it was unlikely that the depression there, which largely reflected a saturation of the demand for plant, equipment, and housing, could be easily overcome. Indeed, the New Dealers considered that revival was hampered (a) by a temporary decline of opportunities for private investment, and (b) by the extreme concentration of economic power in a few hands. It was on this latter aspect that, rightly or wrongly, they focused their attention.

However, the concentration of economic power was not, at first, attacked

[1] In July 1933 the dollar was 28 per cent. below gold par, and had thus nearly caught up, in the race to depreciate, with the pound sterling which was then 31½ per cent. below gold par (Hawtrey: *Gold Standard*, p. 191).
[2] There was an increase in the merchandise export surplus of $250 million over 1933, and the surplus on all current transactions increased to $341 million. The deflationary pressure on the other gold bloc countries was thereby greatly intensified (U.S. Bureau of Foreign and Domestic Commerce: *The United States in the World Economy* p. 181).

directly by means of enforcing the existing anti-trust laws, but indirectly by measures designed to protect and to strengthen labour and the farmer. The Government helped farmers by keeping up prices; they supported the formation of trade unions, recognized collective bargaining, reorganized the system of labour exchanges, &c. Big business resented the innovations. How was 'factory discipline' to be maintained if the labour exchanges could refuse to refer workers to a plant where a strike was in progress or to permit an employer to express a preference for non-union workers, or if they could refuse to refer applicants to openings for employment on terms that were below standard?[1] The position of the 'boss', as master in his own house, would be weakened if he could not dismiss a troublesome trade unionist, or if the 'sack', i.e. the threat of unemployment, could no longer be used to enforce discipline. The political and social implications of the new American labour legislation, far from restoring, shook rather the employers' confidence in the profitability of business.

Since private gross domestic investment, which between 1925 and 1929 had averaged $14 milliard per annum, or $16 milliard in 1929, had fallen to $1 milliard in 1932, the New Dealers were unwilling to wait upon the revival of business men's effective demand for the restoration of pre-depression levels of activity. Since consolidated Federal, state, and local budgets between 1925 and 1929 had yielded a small surplus, they attempted to increase aggregate effective demand by increasing the budget deficit which had emerged in 1930.

In the eight years 1931–8, the annual average budget deficit averaged $1·7 milliard, having reached its maximum of $2·9 milliard in 1936. In the same period average private gross domestic investment averaged $5·3 milliard, having reached a new very high level of $11·4 milliard in 1937.[2] Thus over this period both private investment and government deficit combined equalled only half the amount of private investment in the later 1920s. This fact, if nothing else, would explain the American stagnation. But why did private investment recover so slowly?

The salient feature no doubt was that, because of the large investments in the 1920s, quite extraordinary incentives were required in the early 1930s to stimulate private investment. Such incentives were lacking. The confidence of business men,[3] having already been shaken by labour legislation, was in no way raised by public deficit spending. Since these deficits,

---

[1] Harold W. Metz: *Labor Policy of the Federal Government* (Washington, Brookings Institution, 1945), p. 136.

[2] All data are based on U.S. Bureau of Foreign and Domestic Commerce: *National Income and Product Statistics of the United States, 1929–46* (Supplement to *Survey of Current Business*, July 1947), table 5.

[3] For a detailed analysis of the factors influencing the confidence of United States big business, see Joseph A. Schumpeter: *Business Cycles* (New York, McGraw-Hill Book Co., 1939), iii. 983–1011.

financed by borrowing, did not increase either the short- or long-term rates of interest, it might have been expected that business men would have welcomed deficit spending. For deficit spending was almost entirely due to relief payments which neither challenged the business man's position nor involved the Government in embarking on any sort of 'enterprise'. Nevertheless, because relief might weaken the willingness to work, and might encroach upon the employer's bargaining strength, it encountered a hostility from business men not less intense than that caused by the New Deal's labour and social legislation.[1]

Finally, the opposition of big business to direct Government intervention in matters of employment, i.e. by spending on public works, was most outspoken. For, when once the Government learnt to influence employment, the leaders of business feared that their social and economic power would be threatened and that the widening of the public enterprise sector would mean the end of private enterprise. In fact, aggregate government expenditure (Federal, state, and local) on public works amounted to about half a milliard dollars less per annum in the period from 1931 to 1938 than in 1930, so that, in contrast with expenditure on relief, the net contribution to recovery made by expenditure on public works was nil.[2] But, whereas Federal expenditure on public works alone accounted for only 10 per cent. of all public construction in 1930, it constituted about 58 per cent. per annum in 1931–8.[3] It was the dramatic expansion of Federal expenditure, financed by Federal funds, which attracted attention. Indeed, 'some of the individual projects like those connected with the Tennessee Valley Authority were of such vast size and unusual kind as to create an exaggerated popular idea of the ambitious character of the total public works program being undertaken'.[4] This Federal expenditure on public works was subjected to severe criticism for being competitive with private enterprise and for weakening confidence among business men. It was held that in an individualist society of the American type a state of confidence which would lead to vigorous investment, employment, and prosperity could be awakened among business men only if the Government remained in the background.

The New Dealers' measures, which caused deficits to be maintained, ignored the doctrine that it was the social function of 'sound finance' and of balanced budgets to make employment dependent on private investment. Nevertheless, to judge by the spending habits in the 1920s, a budget

[1] See M. Kalecki: 'Political Aspects of Full Employment', *Political Quarterly*, October–December 1943, pp. 322–30; also Sidney S. Alexander: 'Opposition to Deficit Spending for the Prevention of Unemployment', in *Income, Employment and Public Policy, Essays in Honor of Alvin H. Hansen* (New York, W. W. Norton, 1948).

[2] Hansen: *Fiscal Policy and Business Cycles*, p. 87.

[3] Emile Benoit-Smullyan: 'Public Works in the Depression', *American Economic Review*, March 1948, p. 136 (table ii).   [4] Ibid. p. 137.

deficit at least three times the size of that actually incurred would have been required—without private investment on a substantial scale—to restore activity to boom levels.[1] Whether or not rugged American individualism counteracted the effects of substantial, although inadequate, deficit spending over a number of years, as some commentators implied, it was obvious that the Government had appeared in a new role and that the deep-seated antagonism between the Administration and big business, reinforced by government-sponsored labour, cost and price legislation, undermined in turn the very confidence upon which private investment depended. Within six months of August 1937 the United States had tumbled into a depression as severe,[2] if not as lasting, as the one which had started in September 1929.

There were many reasons for the new recession. In the first six months of 1937 hourly wages rose and stood at 20 per cent. above the 1929 level. This increase in costs was not compensated for by higher prices; hence profit margins were squeezed. At the same time employers were faced with new taxes under the social security legislation. Moreover, the sterilization of gold imports and the raising of the reserve requirements of the member banks by the Federal Reserve Board in March and May 1937 led to an appreciable rise in the long-term rate of interest. These factors, together with the threatened enforcement of the anti-trust legislation, weakened considerably all hope of further revival of private investment. But the most important causes of the actual recession were the reduction in government expenditure in and after June 1936 and the increase in taxes: the latter discouraged private consumption and investment and the former reduced net aggregate demand in so far as it had been generated previously by budget deficits.

The volume of imports, which in 1937 had been 2 per cent. higher (and that of exports 21 per cent. lower) than in 1929, fell catastrophically in the new recession. This fall in imports produced a huge surplus in the external balance which more than wiped out the external deficits on current account during the previous three years. On balance the United States had still in the 1930s a small external surplus, and since, by the Johnson Act of 1934, American lending of capital was virtually prohibited,[3] the rest of the world had to pay the balance in gold.[4] But the flow of gold

---

[1] Hitch: *America's Economic Strength*, p. 92.

[2] 'In November 1937, an unemployment census suggested that there were 10,870,000 wholly unemployed persons, after making allowance for the incompleteness of the census; and, in February 1938, President Roosevelt estimated that a further 3 million persons had lost their occupations during the preceding three months' (League of Nations: Economic Intelligence Service: *World Economic Survey . . . 1937/38* (Geneva, League of Nations, 1938), p. 13).

[3] Bank for International Settlements: *Twelfth Annual Report* (1941–2), p. 103.

[4] In contrast with what had happened in the late 1920s, the withdrawal of gold could not jeopardize business activity, as in most countries national credit policies no longer rested primarily on a gold base.

into the United States exceeded by ten times the amount of the surplus on her foreign balance, reflecting (a) the repayment of American loans abroad and (b) the flight of capital from Europe[1] as a result of political unrest and of the shadow that war casts before it. By the end of 1938 the United States 'net' holding of foreign assets plus gold amounted to nearly $18 milliard, as compared with the United Kingdom's 'gross' holding of international reserves of $20 milliard.[2] The United States' strength in international reserves was unsurpassed, but economic conditions within the United States were as deeply depressed as they had been when Roosevelt assumed office.

The salient features of France's economic weakness throughout the 1930s were the persistence of an adverse foreign balance, of a high long-term rate of interest, and of inflexible wage rates. Prices, on the other hand, had been falling until 1936. Under these conditions business men had no expectations of profits, and so it could not be expected that an increase of effective demand would be generated by private investment. But the other possible way out of the depression, namely, by large-scale deficit financing, was equally unrealistic in France as long as interest rates were high and equilibrium was not restored in France's foreign account. Therefore the key to unlock the gates that barred the way to French revival was, in the first instance, in the hands of the Regents of the Bank of France, who controlled the rate of interest and who could influence the balance of the foreign account by the attitude that they took on the question of what should be the gold value of the currency.

France was in a strong financial position at the time when she was drawn into the depression. Next to the United States, she held the largest gold stocks in the world. But, when the franc became over-valued as a result of shifts in relative international price levels and as a result of currency devaluations in other countries, the balance of the foreign account deteriorated and gold flowed out of the country. The Bank of France and, in the last instance, the Government were confronted by a choice between two alternative policies. They could attempt to restore the balance of the foreign account either by forcing down internal prices in order to justify the existing exchange rate (i.e. by deflation) or by altering the exchange value of the currency (i.e. by devaluation). The Regents of the Bank of France decided against devaluation and, by forcing deflation[3] upon the country, they caused the whole social fabric to disintegrate under the shock of the bitter class struggle that was unleashed.

[1] Lord Keynes: 'The Balance of Payments of the United States', *Economic Journal*, June 1946, pp. 172–87.

[2] Bank for International Settlements: op. cit. p. 102 (exchange rate £1 = $4).

[3] Coupled with an imperfect system of import licences and quotas (League of Nations: Economic, Financial, and Transit Dept.: *Quantitative Trade Controls* (Geneva, League of Nations [printed in Princeton, U.S.A.], 1943), p. 11).

No brief analysis could do full justice to the complex origins of this most tragic social strife in France. The alinement of social forces, however, appears to have been as follows: Until the coalition of the Front Populaire parties took office in 1936 under Blum's auspices, French governments received their main backing from the farmers, business men, and financiers, i.e. from those sections of the population which also represented the bulk of the so-called 'rentiers'. A policy of depressing prices directly benefited the rentiers, but it was not in the interest of individual business men, especially if it proved less easy to reduce wages. But if, as business men, they might have desired a reversal of the deflationary policy, they did not desire this as rentiers, among whom they formed only one of many groups. Moreover, for them it was a political question: should they antagonize the groups whose support was indispensable to them if a government of the Left was to be prevented from coming into power?

The answer was in the negative for other reasons also. French labour was fighting for the recognition of the principle of collective bargaining and for better wages. French employers resented the attempt to prevent them from regulating wages and conditions of work in their own way. They were obstinate, and so were the workers, who resisted wage cuts by strikes. In these circumstances unemployment increased; and employers, no doubt, hoped that a state of poverty and privation would teach the workers a lesson and make them more amenable. While this intensive struggle between capital and labour was proceeding in the factories, there was direct pressure on French governments not to embark on policies which might run counter to the interests of the social groups which they represented (e.g. by the offer of employment to workers through the initiation of public works programmes). In France perhaps the greatest pressure that was exerted on the duly elected Government came from the Regents of the Bank, who encouraged the rentiers to resist every proposal for devaluation and thus forced the Government to remain in the background even though the economic strength of the country and the social peace of the whole nation was at stake.[1]

This struggle was fought out to the bitter end. The financiers hoped that they would have the greater staying power. But, as the conflicts grew

---

[1] The extent of the power wielded by the French financial oligarchy, supposed to consist of 200 families, was clearly illustrated 'in a semi-official communiqué issued by the Bank of France in 1935: "M. Flandin's Government has some praiseworthy actions to its credit. The Budget was voted in good time. By opposing the abolition of the economy decrees, it has shown a sound instinct. Its economic measures—though a little less certain—still deserve a good mark, in view of the difficulties of the situation. This good mark has been given to M. Flandin in the form of credit facilities. These credit facilities may not prove sufficient. He will ask for more credit. Our reply will then depend on whether we are satisfied with the actions of the Government during the first respite we have given it as a reward for its present determination to defend the currency" ' (David Thomson: *Democracy in France* (London, Oxford University Press for Royal Institute of International Affairs 1946), pp. 70–71).

fiercer, the state of confidence in the country was so shaken that speculators carried gold out of the country. These speculative withdrawals of
gold, rather than those resulting from the adverse balance, ultimately
undermined the basis from which the Regents of the Bank could exert their
influence. When, during the early months of 1936, the forces of the Left
gathered strength, and speculative withdrawals of gold mounted in anticipation of devaluation, France's external financial position became desperate
and economic depression reached its bottom level.[1]

Two months after Hitler's march into the Rhineland the Front Populaire coalition under Blum's leadership came into power. Blum, like
Roosevelt, introduced far-reaching policies designed to combine recovery
measures with social reform. The Bank was brought more directly under
Government control, but at the same time wage rates were increased, and
holidays with pay and the forty-hour week were introduced.[2] And when,
as a result of the further deterioration of the external balance, the Bank
asked for the suspension of gold sales, Blum devalued the franc by 25 per
cent. and concluded with the United Kingdom and the United States
a Tripartite Agreement which prohibited any further devaluation without, not mutual consent, but mutual consultation. In 1937 employment increased slightly, but the total number of hours worked fell. The
volume of imports was 20 per cent., and that of exports over 30 per cent.,
lower than in 1929. The increase in wages and in costs of raw material
was wholly absorbed by proportional increases of prices,[3] which caused
further deterioration in the foreign balance. This deterioration would
have made its influence felt to a distressing degree on the internal level of
employment had it not been for increased Government deficit spending
on public works and on rearmament.[4]

Blum's short-lived coalition aggravated the class conflict and completely
killed the private incentive to invest. But, as long as the external balance

[1] At this time Hitler announced his intention of occupying the Rhineland. At first the French
favoured resistance, but, when Sarraut learned from Gamelin that mobilization would cost
6 milliard francs, he feared that this additional strain on the budget would make devaluation
inevitable, and decided against resistance. As Dr. Einzig said at the time, Sarraut had to choose
between defending the franc and defending France. He chose that which was dearest to him,
and by so doing, ultimately lost both. See G. R. Taylor: *Economics for the Exasperated* (London,
John Lane, 1947), p. 332.

[2] Whatever the social justification of this last measure, it was fatal in view of the fact that, in
Germany, hours of work were being increased in many branches of industry. Moreover, the
resulting rise in prices put a further strain on the external balance and fostered the flight of
capital (H. W. Arndt: *The Economic Lessons of the Nineteen-Thirties* (London, Oxford University
Press for Royal Institute of International Affairs, 1944), p. 142).

[3] For a penetrating analysis of the economic situation under the original Front Populaire
coalition, lasting from mid-1936 to mid-1937, see M. Kalecki: 'The Lesson of the Blum Experiment', *Economic Journal*, March 1938, pp. 26–41.

[4] Ordinary and extraordinary budget deficits increased from 10·4 milliard francs in 1935 to
16·9 milliard in 1936, to 21·2 milliard in 1937, and 27·7 milliard in 1938 (see France, Ministère
des Finances: *Bulletin statistique*, no. 1, 1er trimestre, 1947, p. 215).

remained uncontrolled—and this in turn was one of the main reasons for the relative stringency of credit—economic revival even by deficit spending could never be more in France than a fortuitous product of circumstances. In the prevailing cost and price conditions there, the real basis for recovery, i.e. exchange control, was lacking. It was not before the end of 1938 that rises in costs and prices were stopped, that the forty-hour week was abrogated, that the currency was stabilized at a level which corrected all over-valuation, and that—temporarily—some of the truant French capital was in fact repatriated.

Thus France, without producing so much as a spark of real economic revival, remained weak throughout the 1930s while Germany and the other totalitarian Powers were gaining in strength. There was not the slightest doubt that, during this decade, economic forces played a critical part in the fateful reorientation of leadership in Europe and in the shift of the balance of power in the whole world.

What were the reasons which accounted for the attainment and maintenance of economic strength in the totalitarian capitalist[1] countries? Italy, Japan, and Germany, like the democracies, were largely dependent on foreign trade. But their governments made sure that the adverse effects on the internal economy, resulting from fluctuations of their foreign balance, were reduced to a minimum. Japan, like the United Kingdom and (for different reasons) like the United States, had chosen devaluation as a means of improving her foreign balance. But she also introduced exchange controls over capital movements during the depression, which were retained and extended to cover commodity payments when the second China campaign started. Germany, and (at first) Italy, like France, rejected uniform currency depreciation. Instead, Italy introduced exchange control in 1934 and Germany, within two years of Hitler's access to power, extended exchange control, which had been used since 1931 to regulate capital movements, to all current transactions. In this way the Government could indeed prevent total external payments from exceeding total receipts.

What relief, however, could this foreign trade technique bring to an expanding economy? If world demand was slow to revive, did exchange control guarantee that Germany would receive the imports that she required? Certainly not. If export receipts did not expand, imports would have to be limited, and this, in turn, would put a brake on any internal recovery programme. To prevent this from happening, the Germans went two steps farther: (1) they coupled exchange control with import licensing and quotas, which enabled them to discriminate between essential and unessential imports; and (2) possessing, as they did, complete information on the state and structure of Germany's foreign trade, the German Government

[1] 'Capitalist' denoting no more than individual property-ownership.

fostered the development of domestic resources and substitutes to replace former imports. Thus half the battle was won. For, if external influences were not allowed to jeopardize internal revival, the latter was a matter of stimulating home demand by means of monetary and fiscal policies.

In all three totalitarian countries the monetary authorities co-operated with their governments. In all of them the long-term rate of interest was kept well below the pre-depression level. Although in Germany its stabilization at 4·5 to 5 per cent. only began in 1935, steps had already been taken in 1933 to reduce the short-term rate of interest considerably and to restore liquidity to business, the banks, and the whole economy. It was the halting of deflation and the easing of the tight financial position of all enterprises and public institutions through the issue of tax remission certificates and special rediscountable employment bills[1] which contributed forcefully towards a revival of optimism among members of the business community.

More significant perhaps than favourable monetary conditions for the restoration of confidence among business men were internal political stability and social peace. Since powerful financial and industrial leaders had contributed more than their share in helping the Nazis into office, Hitler redeemed his promises to them.[2] As in Italy, so in Germany, these problems were solved by political force. The complete suppression of all free trade unions and the threat of concentration camps were more powerful and direct weapons for assuring 'factory discipline' than were the more indirect weapons of dismissal and unemployment which employers in the democracies could wield, if necessary, to enforce discipline. Krupp, the steel magnate of the Ruhr, noted that, 'by the legal appointment of the employer as leader of his employees, a much wider, more pleasant and more promising field of activity than before was assigned to him'[3] just as

---

[1] See C. W. Guillebaud: *The Economic Recovery of Germany from 1933 to March 1938* (London, Macmillan, 1939), especially chapter ii; and also Thomas Balogh: 'The National Economy of Germany', *Economic Journal*, September 1938, p. 484.

[2] Invited as early as January 1932 to address members of the famous or infamous Herrenklub in Düsseldorf, consisting of leading business men of the Ruhr, Hitler convinced them of the desirability of a totalitarian state, founded on internal strength and political stability, and freed externally from the shackles of the Versailles *Diktat* and powerful enough to be respected once again in the world (see Hitler: *Speeches* (Baynes), i. 777–829). The ambitious Schacht felt compelled to write to Hitler after the elections of November 1932: 'I have no doubt that the present development of things can only lead to your becoming Chancellor. It seems as if our attempt to collect a number of signatures from business circles for this purpose was not altogether in vain' (*I.M.T. Nuremberg*, xxxvi. 535 (456–EC); *N.C.A.* vii. 512–13). And speaking a fortnight before the March election of 1933 before some twenty leading industrialists in Berlin, Hitler's prediction that 'private enterprise cannot be maintained in the age of democracy' and his demand that the parliamentary system must be abolished, all opposition crushed by force, and the power of the Wehrmacht restored, were enthusiastically applauded, whereupon Schacht was induced to propose the collection of Rm. 3 million from the members of the audience (see *I.M.T. Nuremberg*, xxxvi. 521 (439–EC); *N.C.A.* vi. 1080).

[3] Speech written by Krupp (but not delivered) on the occasion of an invitation to the University of Berlin during January 1944 (*I.M.T. Nuremberg*, xxxv. 70 (317–D); cf. *N.C.A.* vii. 23).

he praised on another occasion 'the labour peace in our enterprises'[1] as among the great accomplishments of the new régime. In this respect, as in many others, conditions in Japan differed from the totalitarian pattern. Trade unions there remained in existence; there were even strikes there as late as 1937. But they were weaker than in the more mature industrial societies. Japan was still in process of industrializing; Japanese employers could draw on a huge pool of surplus labour, and the worker, drawn into industrial employment out of his agricultural surroundings, was better paid than in agriculture; he was only just beginning to acquire political consciousness and he did not yet seriously endanger 'social and political stability'.

Next to the assurance of 'labour peace in enterprises', leaders of big business were strengthened in their confidence in the new régime by legislation which enacted 'compulsory cartellization' for a large number of industries in Japan in 1931, in Italy in 1932, and in Germany in 1933.[2] Clearly compulsory cartels afforded protection against 'ruinous' competition, which had been so conspicuous during the depression, and thus became a significant condition for a revival of business men's willingness to invest.

These monetary and institutional measures, accompanied by fiscal policies which were designed to encourage private investment, brought about in Germany a complete psychological change among employers; and yet an expansion of effective demand was not primarily initiated by business men. For as the Government had decided not to devalue the currency, they had to prevent any strain upon the foreign balance arising from imports in excess of exports. Exchange control, it is true, formally enabled the authorities to maintain the equilibrium of the foreign balance. But German prices were higher than foreign prices. To lower them would have nipped the revival of confidence in the bud; in these circumstances the maintenance of the existing level of exports presupposed that German prices should not rise. The imposition of the wage- and price-stop, as far as German action was concerned, froze German exports at the prevailing level. The level of exports, however, limited the scope for imports. Care had to be taken that investments, both private and public, were concentrated upon industries whose raw material requirements could be supplied from domestic rather than foreign sources. The building and certain heavy industries could obviously be given maximum scope for expansion. Investment in other industries had to be selective. This power of selection, indirectly exercised by the authorities concerned with allocating raw materials, was reinforced by a strict control over private issues in the capital market amounting to a virtual ban. In these circumstances the expansion

---

[1] Speech by Krupp on 1 May 1936 (*N.C.A.* vii. 8 (291–D)).
[2] Neumann: *Behemoth*, p. 218.

of demand through credit-financed investment in building and similar industries was primarily dependent upon action by public authorities rather than by business men.

From the very beginning of the Nazi régime, public expenditure by central, state, and local authorities greatly increased. It rose from Rm. 14 milliard in 1932 to about Rm. 40 milliard in 1938, and in the latter year was about twice as high as in 1929. The deficits rose from 4 per cent. of public expenditure in 1933 to about 22 per cent. in 1935, decreased in the two subsequent years, but exceeded 25 per cent. of expenditure in 1938.[1] In so far as these deficits were credit-financed, effective demand was continuously expanded. The economic revival which was induced by this spending occurred in the shape of an investment boom, unprecedented in German history.

Aggregate gross investment, both public and private, during the six years ending in 1938 (amounting in monetary terms to Rm. 73·2 milliard) exceeded that of the six years ending in 1929 (Rm. 67·7 milliard in monetary terms) by nearly 6 milliard; but, allowing for price changes, the increase in real terms was about 29 per cent. Moreover, although public investment (which determined the speed of revival) had doubled in 1938 as compared with 1929, private investment, too, had reached the 1928 level and exceeded the 1929 level by 10 per cent.[2] More revealing still, the investment boom was in the first instance concerned with a vast expansion in construction and building. Public construction (i.e. the building of Party houses, stadia, roads, canals, aerodromes, and fortifications) had in real terms nearly quadrupled between 1929 and 1938, while private construction, both residential and industrial, was as high in 1938 as in 1929.

The really striking feature in the totalitarian experiment was that business responded to large governmental spending. How did the totalitarian states dispose of the myth of sound finance, which was used by business men in democratic countries to prevent governments from off-setting a crisis of confidence by public spending? For while in the United States public expenditure increased by only 60 per cent. between 1933 and 1938, in Germany it increased by 170 per cent., and while over these six years 11 per cent. of expenditure was deficit-financed in the United States, in Germany the percentage was about 19. And if, in the United States and France, public spending shook the confidence of business men, why did not deficit spending by governments evoke a similar hostility in the business community in totalitarian countries? There were many reasons.

In the first place, the objections of the business community to public spending were overcome because the machinery of government, including the 'Self-governing Estates' (of agriculture, industry, labour, and culture),

---

[1] For details see Appendix IV, A, p. 504 below.
[2] For details see Appendix IV, B, p. 506 below.

was under the direct control of a partnership between leaders of industry and leaders of the totalitarian party. There were frictions and jealousies between these leaders, but the one could not function without the collaboration of the other. The Estate of Industry and Commerce, with its territorial and functional groups, was deliberately developed so that, in the field of industry, the primacy of politics over economics could be assured, and the community's interest safeguarded against self-interest. In fact, however, the cartels, which were led by the firms with the largest production or sales quota, were infinitely more significant bodies, though less in the public eye, than were the Estate and its subsidiary groups. Indeed, as the best-informed organ of the German press used to complain, 'the known identity of the personnel of groups and cartels has, in practice, resulted in the use of the influence and power of the Estate, which should not regulate the market, to strengthen the private power of the cartels'.[1] Thus the institutional pattern of totalitarian organization happened to be so designed as to permit big business to exercise considerable influence in the state, and this helped to reduce the opposition of the business community to government spending. If, under democracy, a government was in power which had the backing of industry, business men's objections to government spending were maintained because they could not know what the next government would be like. Under totalitarianism there was no next government.[2]

Furthermore business men's objections to public spending were overcome when the objects of such spending did not impair the profitability of the private sector of the economy. The vast, and entirely new, investment projects, such as roads, Party houses, and sports stadia upon which public spending was initially directed, fell completely outside the range of investment objects 'normally' developed by private enterprise. Thus German industrialists welcomed these projects for public works for their own sake and because of the derivative benefits, accruing from them, to many industries and especially the steel industry. Japanese industrialists were glad of the development of public utilities which were a basic condition for the successful furtherance of industrialization, and Italian industrialists welcomed the land reclamation schemes carried through by public authorities. As long as there were unemployed resources, they all approved armament expenditures. In democracies also, business men could have no objection to these kinds of non-competing public investments. Never-

---

[1] *Frankfurter Zeitung*, 18 November 1938.

[2] M. Kalecki: 'Political Aspects of Full Employment', *Political Quarterly*, October–December 1943, p. 327. It might be added that in Japan, where at least democratic forms were retained, industry could do little to prevent deficit spending if the Militarists had, with the approval of the Emperor, decided on such a course of action. It was sound sense to keep on tolerably good terms with the Militarists, for there was nothing to prevent them, because of their special position in the state, from seeking support among the more radical sections of the population.

theless, in the United States, they opposed the Tennessee Valley project because they saw in it a means by which the Roosevelt administration, which they did not trust, might more effectively enforce its anti-trust legislation. Moreover, in democracies business men feared that the scope for government spending on projects for public works was narrow and that the temptation for governments of the Left to nationalize industries in order to create spheres for public investment was great. They found justification for their anxieties in the party programmes of the labour movements in France and in the United Kingdom. If, as in Germany and Italy, there was no free labour movement, business men had reason to believe that the private sector of the economy would be respected.[1]

As long as there were unemployed resources, business men did not object to ever increasing public expenditure. Since it was not devoted primarily to relief, as in the United States, but to public works and armaments, its effect in reducing unemployment was instantaneous. Given the wage-stop, production costs fell owing to the better utilization of plant, and consequently industrial profits increased more than did other incomes.[2] Because the distribution of dividends was limited, and because, in contrast with the position in France, the export of capital was impossible, liquidity (in spite of heavy taxation) increased to such an extent that business men were able to buy, in the money market, short-term government bills (*Metallforschungs GmbH* bills, known as 'Mefo' bills) by which public deficit spending was secretly financed.

Schacht and Schwerin von Krosigk who, being in charge of monetary and fiscal policy, were best able to appreciate the economic effects likely to arise from the accelerated public spending on armaments from about 1935, began to urge caution upon the Government in respect of expenditure by state and Party on projects other than armaments.[3] Broadly speaking, their attitude was that the Government should be no more than a midwife in the creation of full employment and that, when this phase was reached, credit financing should cease and public expenditure should be fully covered out of taxation and long-term borrowing.

For all practical purposes the full employment level of activity had been passed in the autumn of 1937,[4] but public expenditure continued to

[1] They were confirmed in this belief by the transfer to private investors of assets acquired by the Reich during the depression and from the confiscation of Jewish property. Moreover, they had initially been invited to become the owners of the obviously risky Hermann Göring enterprises; only when they hesitated did the Government themselves proceed with this venture.

[2] Otto Donner: 'Die Grenzen der Staatsverschuldung', *Weltwirtschaftliches Archiv*, September 1942, p. 217.

[3] Memorandum by Schacht to the Cabinet, dated 3 May 1935 (*I.M.T. Nuremberg*, xxvii. 50–52 (1168–PS); *N.C.A.* iii. 287–30.

[4] When the number of unemployed represented no more than 2·5 per cent. of the total active labour force (see Oxford Institute of Statistics: *The Economics of Full Employment* (Oxford, Blackwell, 1944), p. 182.

increase unabated throughout 1938 and until the outbreak of war. Secret credit financing of armament expenditure by means of 'Mefo' bills[1] ceased in March 1938, but Schwerin von Krosigk found it impossible, despite higher tax rates, to cover expenditure out of increasing tax revenues and long-term borrowing, and thus was forced to close the gap by openly borrowing in the short-term money market.

But meanwhile the concentration of public spending on armaments had led to working to capacity in the capital goods industries—i.e. armaments and heavy industries. In order to fulfil these armament orders, plant and equipment had to be increased. Thus private gross investment in these industries, having already in 1936 reached the level of 1929, almost doubled between 1936 and 1938.[2] The fact that this private investment boom took place in conditions of full employment meant that business men were bidding against one another in order to attract workers and obtain scarce materials. The consequence was that, in obvious defiance of the wage-stop, costs rose to the disadvantage of the business community, and since these additional costs could only be passed on partially in higher prices, industrial profits tended to fall. These profits were, however, sub-jected to higher tax rates, and this meant that the reduction of liquidity not only prevented business men from lending cash to the money market, but actually forced them to replenish it by discounting such 'Mefo' bills as they held with the Reichsbank.

The discounting of bills caused the currency in circulation to increase by Rm. 3 milliard during the last ten months of 1938; that is to say, far in excess of the increase of currency by Rm. 1·7 milliard during the preceding five years.[3] This rapid rise gave cause for anxiety. Was not inflation just round the corner? To be sure, 'when Schacht saw that the risky situation which [through previous "Mefo" financing] he had sponsored was becom-ing insoluble he was more and more anxious to get out. This . . . was for a long time the leitmotif of Schacht's conversation with the directors of the bank.'[4] He had the courage, however, to warn Hitler of the dangers which lay ahead, and of their causes, and to suggest the remedies required to prevent disaster. The basic cause was the increase of effective demand, through currency-financed public deficit spending, without a correspond-ing increase in the real national product under conditions of full employ-ment. To make matters worse, the dams which should have stemmed the

[1] In about three and a half years ending in March 1938 secret armament financing—'secret' because it was not reflected in the published public debt accounts—totalled Rm. 12 milliard. Rm. 6 milliard each of 'Mefo' bills were carried by the Reichsbank and by the money market respectively (*I.M.T. Nuremberg*, xxxvi. 367 (369–EC); *N.C.A.* vii. 428).

[2] See Appendix IV, B, item 5 (pp. 506–7 below).

[3] See letter to Hitler of 7 January 1939 signed by Schacht and other directors of the Reichs-bank (*I.M.T. Nuremberg*, xxxvi. 371 (369–EC); *N.C.A.* vii. 431).

[4] According to an affidavit made on 8 November 1945 by Emil Puhl, a director of the Reichs-bank from 1933 to 1939 (*I.M.T. Nuremberg*, xxxvi. 520 (438–EC); *N.C.A.* vii. 500).

waves of additional purchasing power, all the controls so elaborately developed, seemed to be wholly ineffective. For 'the parties placing the orders force the manufacturers to corner material and labor', and this in turn was causing 'an excessive price- and wage-racket'.[1] The effects of the policy pursued during the past ten months could still be mended provided that public expenditure was covered by taxes and through 'loans without disturbing the long-term investment market' and that controls were 'rendered effective'.[2] Schacht was dismissed; but—because presumably his recommendations were heeded—Funk, who had taken his place, could on 25 August 1939 state in a letter to Hitler: 'Through the suggestions I have worked out to keep down ruthlessly any non-vital consumption and any public expenses and tasks of no importance to the war, we will be in a position to satisfy all demand to be made on the finances and economy without any serious shocks.'[3]

The internal stresses and strains, which were a direct consequence of the continuation of deficit spending, financed by currency creation, under conditions of full employment, no doubt produced waste and an inefficient use of resources. But the waste was of a very different kind and less serious than that associated with unemployment and idleness of real resources. It was inevitable, therefore, that the relative industrial strength of the totalitarian Powers increased during the 1930s, for in those countries full employment had been achieved and maintained, while the democratic Powers had never achieved full employment and certainly were unable to avert the renewed set-back of activity in 1938. However, the fact that armaments became the backbone of totalitarian economic policies had a profound influence on the character and structure of these economies.

Large-scale armaments are inseparable from the expansion of the armed forces and the preparation of plans for a war of conquest. They also induce competitive rearmament of other countries. This causes the main aim of the spending to shift gradually from full employment to securing the maximum effect of rearmament.[4]

(2) *External Position*

The character and methods of economic policy pursued internally by the various Powers had a decisive influence on their external relations

---

[1] *I.M.T. Nuremberg*, xxxvi. 369 (369–EC); *N.C.A.* vii. 429.

[2] *I.M.T. Nuremberg*, xxxvi. 372 (369–EC); *N.C.A.* vii. 432. Four months earlier, on 1 September 1938, Schwerin von Krosigk had written to Hitler in similar terms, emphasizing more specifically that the long-term investment market would yield more funds for financing armaments if it were 'made unavailable for all other purposes, especially the building of homes' (*I.M.T. Nuremberg*, xxxvi. 493–4 (419–EC); *N.C.A.* vii. 475).

[3] *I.M.T. Nuremberg*, xxvi. 257–8 (699–PS); *N.C.A.* iii. 509.

[4] M. Kalecki: 'Political Aspects of Full Employment', *Political Quarterly*, October–December 1943, p. 327.

with other Powers. In the democracies imports fluctuated with fluctuations of industrial activity. This was not the case in the totalitarian countries, with the single exception of Japan. Thus while the volume of imports
between 1929 and 1937 declined in the U.S.S.R. by 43 per cent., in Germany by 24 per cent., and in Italy by 31 per cent., it rose in Japan by over
30 per cent. But the rate of industrialization and of war preparation was
so great in Japan, where there were few exploitable internal resources
as compared with those possessed by either the U.S.S.R. or Germany, that
the scope for autarkic projects was limited.

There was no doubt that in Germany the reduction in the volume of
imports, accompanied by a rise in the domestic output of materials and
substitutes, meant, as in the U.S.S.R., a lessening of the country's dependence on foreign economies. While from the standpoint of military power
this was eminently desirable, the Germans maintained that it was beneficial within limits even from an economic point of view. They admitted
that domestic ores, synthetic petrol, and synthetic rubber (Buna) were
more costly than imported materials.[1] What, however, did it signify for
Germany, they argued, that natural rubber cost £4 while synthetic rubber
produced at home cost £10, if it was impossible to increase exports sufficiently to earn the £4 with which to purchase imports of natural rubber?[2]
This stock argument was hammered into the Germans on every occasion;
to them the so-called peace of the 1930s was based on a closure of frontiers.
The American tariff, the British tariff (in combination with the preferential
arrangements for interchange within the Commonwealth), and the French
quantitative restrictions on imports were alleged to have made it impossible for Germany to earn the means of paying for the purchase of foreign
goods. Was it really certain, in view of the elasticities of foreign demand—
as foreigners had asserted—that the volume of exports could be increased
considerably by a reduction (through devaluation) of export prices? If
indeed, as a result of a 10 per cent. devaluation, exports were to rise by
20 per cent. in volume—drawing here on the famous Keynesian example
relating to the reparations transfer problem of the 1920s[3]—the marginal
productivity for the nation as a whole of 20 additional real units of exports would consequently be only 8 additional real units of imports (i.e.
$1·2 \times 0·9 = 1·08$). On these assumptions it would surely pay the economy
as a whole to abstain from importing certain commodities, provided that
they could be produced at home at a real cost of less than two-and-a-half

---

[1] R. Regul ('Zollschutz, Preisschutz und Subventionen als Mittel der staatlichen Wirtschaftspolitik', in *Institut für Konjunkturforschung: Vierteljahrshefte zur Wirtschaftsforschung 1938/9*, part i,
p. 84) stated that it cost about Rm. 260 to produce 100 kg. of Buna, as compared with
imported rubber c.i.f. Hamburg at Rm. 100.

[2] Constantin von Dietze: *Volkswirtschaft und Weltwirtschaft 1936*, an essay in *Probleme des Deutschen
Wirtschaftslebens*, p. 658.

[3] J. M. Keynes: 'The German Transfer Problem', *Economic Journal*, March 1929, p. 4.

times the world market price.[1] Thus, on purely economic grounds, it paid Germany—as long as unemployment existed—to invest her real resources in additional autarkic projects rather than in additional exports,[2] and to maintain the external value of the Reichsmark at pre-depression parity. However, economic arguments receded into the background as Germany approached full employment, and her insistence on a high degree of autarky was prompted increasingly by military and political motives. Addressing the International Chamber of Commerce in Berlin in July 1937, Göring emphatically asserted that it was intolerable for a self-conscious people with a desire to live to linger in a state of dependence upon the greater or lesser goodwill of foreign Powers.[3]

In the 1930s Germany, as well as Italy or the U.S.S.R., did everything to make that dependence more 'tolerable'. Even so, in 1937 both Germany's degree of external dependence (measured by the value of her imports of merchandise shown as a percentage of national income), and also her weight and significance in world trade (measured by the value of these imports shown as a percentage of world imports) continued to be high in relation to those of the other Great Powers:

TABLE VIII. *Great Powers' Dependence on and Significance in World Trade in 1937*

	Japan	U.K.	Italy	France	Germany	U.S.A.	U.S.S.R.
Import dependence on trade . . .	29·3	14·8	14·5	11·9	7·8	4·2	0·9
Significance in world trade . . .	5·0	17·3	3·7	6·3	8·1	11·2	1·0

The relevance of these ratios was twofold. Broadly speaking, in order to sustain a high national product or income, Germany's dependence on imports was more pronounced than that of either the United States or the U.S.S.R. On the other hand, occupying, as she did, the third place after the United Kingdom and the United States, Germany, because of her weight and significance in world trade, could so manipulate her commercial policy as to turn her dependence on other countries, which might be a serious weakness in time of war, into a source of strength in time of peace. She had an opportunity, so long as she remained one of the world's foremost trading nations, to influence the level and character of economic activity within the boundaries of her main commercial partners. In

[1] von Dietze, loc. cit. and Regul, loc. cit.
[2] It is to be noted, however, that the economic argument in favour of autarky no longer holds when a country approaches full employment of her resources, and from about 1937 many of Germany's autarkic projects implied a wasteful and costly maldistribution of real resources.
[3] Cf. *Deutsche Volkswirt*, August 1937.

totalitarian Germany foreign trade itself became a means towards the preparation for aggression. By contrast the U.S.S.R., owing to her small dependence on trade and her insignificance in world trade, had little scope for the pursuit of an aggressive commercial policy.

Germany endeavoured with success from the middle 1930s onwards to gain by trade the political influence over her next-door neighbours which the United Kingdom and France wielded in their dependent territories.[1] Having in 1934 extended exchange control to all 'current' transactions, Germany could adjust her imports to correspond to the fluctuations in her exports, but she could not determine the volume of her exports. Her exports depended on fluctuations of foreign demand which were outside her control. Therefore, in spite of exchange control and of autarkic projects to supply vital needs, fluctuations in the amount of Germany's exports continued to present a problem for her in her efforts to maintain full employment. In order to escape from this dilemma, Germany made provision for obtaining vital supplies by means of long-term contracts of a compensatory kind with countries whose natural resources were complementary to her own.

Most territories contiguous to the Reich had, however, similar geological and climatic conditions and consequently afforded similar, instead of complementary, opportunities for production. The agricultural and mining resources of tropical Asia, South America, and Africa were far more complementary to German manufactures than were the resources of most parts of Europe. But the possibility of long-term contracts with African countries to obtain substantial supplies was limited, because more than four-fifths of the trade of the African continent came from territories included in the empires of Germany's European rivals.[2]

During the 1930s the European countries possessing colonial empires increased their imports from their African colonies and dominions and from their Asiatic possessions. The situation was different in South America which, unlike Africa, consisted of politically independent states. Because the imperfect recovery in the United States was accompanied by a reduction in imports from Latin America, and because the European Powers with colonial empires concentrated the locus of their purchases in self-governing and dependent territories under their own flag, Latin America was free to conclude compensatory trade deals with Germany and also with Japan. Such arrangements could give Germany the 'certainty' of supplies from some complementary South American states in peace-time, but these supplies from this source would not be assured in time of war. It was for that political reason that Germany also concen-

[1] Albert O. Hirschman: *National Power and the Structure of Foreign Trade* (Berkeley, University of California Press, 1945), pp. 34–40.
[2] League of Nations: Economic Intelligence Service: *Network of World Trade*, pp. 42–48.

trated her trade drive on economically less complementary countries in Europe and, in particular, on South-Eastern European countries. However, the political conception of a combination of states forming a militarily secure geographical unit was at loggerheads with the economic conception of a combination of countries with complementary resources. To get over this difficulty Germany sought, with some success, to induce the South-Eastern European countries to concentrate on the production of materials which she required.

In the past, governments had had little influence on the geographical pattern of trade, because trade had been conducted on the principle of the most-favoured-nation clause, non-discrimination, and the convertibility of currencies, and had been regulated almost exclusively by tariffs. But all this changed with the breakdown of internationally agreed monetary and trade codes. The fragmentation of the world into more or less lasting parochial currency blocs—the Central and South-Eastern European 'exchange control' group, the Western European 'gold bloc' group, the North European and British Commonwealth 'sterling group', and Japan's East Asian 'yen bloc'—tended to encourage trade inside each of these currency blocs because there was exchange stability inside each of them.[1] Discriminatory commercial policy in the 1930s changed the geographical pattern of world trade. Bilateral clearing as a means of commercial policy inevitably implied discrimination against other countries, but so did policies based on quotas or on tariff preferences. When, in 1931, the United Kingdom abandoned the principle of free trade, she discriminated against the rest of the world by incorporating in the Ottawa Agreements of 1932 the principle of special preferences within the British Commonwealth. While France relied primarily on quotas and on preferential arrangements as means of regulating imports, the United States, on the whole, used straightforward tariffs and abstained from commercial discrimination, with the exception of such preferences as those given to sugar imports from the Philippines. On a small scale the United Kingdom also made use of quotas and of bilateral clearing. Indeed, it was not Germany who first introduced the bilateral device into the Western Hemisphere, but the United Kingdom who, having successfully applied it to the Dominions at Ottawa, used it (to the annoyance of the United States) in a payments convention concluded with Argentina in 1932.[2] Nevertheless, the bilateral principle as applied by the Nazis became the most potent weapon in their armoury of a deliberately discriminating commercial policy. They realized that 'national economic and political power *necessarily inheres* not only in the magnitude of a country's international trade

---

[1] League of Nations: Economic, Financial and Transit Dept.: *International Currency Experience*, p. 198.

[2] N. J. Spykman: *America's Strategy in World Politics* (New York, Harcourt Brace, 1942), p. 267.

but also in the division of a country's exports and imports among its trading partners'.[1]

Some rough indication of the disintegration of world trade can be obtained by a comparison of the trade between each Great Power and the other members of its economic bloc in 1929 and in 1938:

TABLE IX. *Trade Blocs*

(As per cent. of the Great Powers' trade)

	Imports from Bloc		Exports to Bloc	
	1929	1938	1929	1938
U.K.: Empire	30	42	44	50
„ : Other sterling blocs	12	13	7	12
France: Empire	12	27	19	27
Italy: colonies and Ethiopia . . .	0·5	2	2	23
Japan: Korea, Formosa, Kwantung, Man-churia	20	41	24	55
Germany: Balkans	4·5	12	5	13
„ : Latin America	12	16	8	11·5

Although Germany's next-door neighbours in South-Eastern Europe, whom she had made her economic partners, provided a smaller share of her requirements than the share covered by the blocs of states grouped round the other Great Powers, Germany was anxious for political and strategic reasons to develop this South-Eastern European sphere of her commercial interests. Since she was dealing with independent states, she could not proceed in the same direct way in making the South-Eastern European countries complementary to her own, as could Japan or Italy within their empires. The subtler methods which Germany applied[2] were, first of all, to make very large purchases; second, to pay prices higher than those prevailing in the world market for specific materials which she wished these countries to produce in increasing quantities, leaving the countries in question to finance the deal until such time as it was paid off by German exports; and third, to supply these countries with goods which they could not easily obtain from other countries. Germany succeeded in diverting to herself between 40 and 60 per cent. of the volume of trade of these South-Eastern European countries. In this way she created vested interests which could make their voices heard in their internal political life. As their dependence on Germany grew, on account of their having specialized in the production of a number of materials which were to be obtained in the world market at lower prices, it became increasingly difficult for them to divert their exports from Germany to some other quarter. And

[1] Howard S. Ellis: *Removal of Restrictions on Trade and Capital*, in *Post-War Economic Problems* ed. S. E. Harris (New York, McGraw-Hill Book Co., 1943), p. 355.
[2] See *Survey* for 1938, i. 43–62.

under conditions of bilateralism, a real impossibility of switching exports induces a *technical* impossibility of switching imports. In this way the device of bilateralism is seen to be an important link in the policies by which the aim of maximum power through foreign trade may be attained.[1]

Since Germany was interested in 'certainty' and continuity of supply, the very high level of German economic activity was tantamount to the guarantee of a market for the South-Eastern European countries. By this policy Germany certainly made it difficult for these independent states to be their own masters in external relations. And there was the danger that, as a large country confronting a number of smaller ones, she might take advantage of her superior bargaining strength to turn the terms of trade in her favour.[2] But there is no evidence that she did this until March 1939.[3]

The formation of economic blocs, based on rigid bilateralism as in the German case or on increasing bilateral transfers as within the 'imperial' blocs, implied a short-circuiting of transfer routes. This reduced the means at the disposal of countries like Germany for financing the purchase of those raw materials with which she could not dispense because she was unable to produce them herself or to procure them within the bloc. It was for this reason that the problem of 'commercial access to raw materials' arose. From the very beginning of their rule the National Socialists had emphasized their demand for the return of their former colonies. But the problem of raw materials became even more urgent when the German economy was running at the level of full employment, as it was from 1937 onwards. The heavy demands on the part of the German armed forces for products of the capital goods industries reduced the margin of such goods available for exports. The German claims for colonies were intensified. And when a special committee of the League of Nations was set up in 1937 to investigate the question of the commercial access to raw materials, the German Finance Minister, von Krosigk, insisted that the

colonial problem of Germany cannot be got rid of with the argument that a sufficient supply of raw materials can be assured to her by the policy of the 'open door'. Only the possibility of buying a sufficient quantity in our own currency can produce a proper balance of Devisen for Germany.[4]

To Germany's mind, the rest of the world must choose between giving Germany colonies or accepting Reichsmarks in exchange for which Germany would not be able to supply such capital goods as the world would demand. When the League Committee presented its findings in draft, the Soviet member insisted, with clear reference to Germany, on the

---

[1] Hirschman: *National Power and the Structure of Foreign Trade*, p. 33.

[2] Gh. N. Leon: 'Die wirtschaftlichen Grundlagen eines dauerhaften Friedens', *Weltwirtschaftliches Archiv*, January 1942, pp. 34–52.

[3] See Royal Institute of International Affairs: *South-Eastern Europe*, p. 196.

[4] League of Nations: Economic, Financial and Transit Dept.: *Raw-Material Problems and Policies* (Geneva, League of Nations [printed in New York], 1946), p. 57.

insertion of a rider to show 'that the obstacles, especially of a financial nature, in the way of access to raw materials, of which certain industrial states complained, were due in the first place to their armaments policy, their ambitions and aggressive acts'.[1]

(v) Conclusion

Customary economic and social relationships within countries and between them had been deeply shaken by the First World War. Even victorious countries, rich in colonial territory and in raw materials, suffered from grave social tensions which originated, partly at least, in economic distress. This distress was much worse in the defeated countries and in those others that were relatively poor in resources and were industrially undeveloped. It facilitated revolutionary changes in government within the U.S.S.R., Germany, and Italy; and in the U.S.S.R. this revolution inaugurated an economic and social transformation of society which was still more significant than the change in Russia's form of government. In this uneasy post-war atmosphere a new framework for the regulation of international relations was slow in coming into being and, even then, it was short-lived; for all semblance of orderly international relations completely collapsed with the onset of the Great Depression.

Once again economic hardships in countries drawn into the slump aggravated the existing social and political tensions. In nations, both vanquished and victorious, which had been dissatisfied with the Versailles Settlement, certain vested interests which were outspoken in their criticism of the treaties defeated the more moderate social and political forces. The most fateful outcome was the addition of Germany to the group of totalitarian Powers.

With the sharpening of ideological differences between nations, and in the absence of international codes of behaviour, it was impossible to find a basis for joint action between the Great Powers in order to combat the Great Depression. Consequently measures for economic recovery had to be undertaken by each country in isolation. Economic nationalism was their answer to the challenge of the time; but, with it, the practice of power politics in international relations came right to the fore.

In the later 1930s the totalitarian Powers, in contrast with the democracies, not only achieved recovery, but sustained it in 1938. As a result there was a marked shift in 'relative' manufacturing strength from the three democracies of Western Europe and of Northern America in favour of the four totalitarian Powers in the central and eastern quarters of the Old World.[2]

---

[1] League of Nations: *Raw-Material Problems and Policies*, p. 63.
[2] The joint share of the United States, the United Kingdom, and France in the world output

Upon the achievement, through government expenditure on arma-ments and on non-military goods, of full employment in Germany (whose industrial economy was the most mature of the four economies in question), the economic régime was converted into one of scarcities. Under these con-ditions the piling-up of armaments could only be continued by a reduction of private or public non-military investment and consumption. For such reduction there was considerable scope. The alternative to it was the acquisition of potential resources to be found abroad.

Where, as in Germany, the political objective of economic policy was military strength, war would inevitably be the result, first, because the production and accumulation of arms served a purpose other than that of merely creating employment, and second, because the strain to which the economy was subjected by further arms production (in the absence of corresponding reductions in non-military investments and consumption) increased the temptation to seek relief in the acquisition of foreign territory by means of aggression.

But where could complementary resources be found? Those who partici-pated in the drawing-up of Germany's plans for expansion testified that her

principal strategic aim . . . was the acquisition of Southern Russia. The wheat fields of the Ukraine, the coal and iron-ore deposits of the Donets, and the oil wells of Baku were . . . coveted parts of the German 'living space' and essential to Germany's further development.[1]

In 1938 Greater Germany alone, without the resources of her partners in the Anti-Comintern alliance, surpassed the U.S.S.R. in military strength. Her military expenditure (her capital goods and steel strength) was still higher than that of the U.S.S.R., and it was twice as high as that of Britain and France combined. Thus, for the kind of war which Germany hoped to fight in the east, her military preparations appeared to be fully adequate. But the volume of her armaments production was not sufficient to enable her to fight a war involving the U.S.S.R., France, and Britain, together—not to mention the possible inclusion of the United States on their side.

This inadequacy of German armaments sprang directly from Hitlerian strategy, for Hitler never expected to fight a group of Great Powers nor did he expect to fight a prolonged war.[2] He expected to gain his limited objectives in the short run by diplomatic threats or by *blitzkrieg*. It was for this reason that the volume of German armament production was not determined by available resources, but was set at the much lower level called for by the estimates of requirements to carry out this kind of

of manufactures fell from 59 per cent. in 1929 to 42 per cent. in 1938; while that of the U.S.S.R., Germany, Italy, and Japan rose from 22 per cent. to 38 per cent.; see Table IV on p. 439 above.
  [1] U.S. Strategic Bombing Survey: *Effects of Strategic Bombing on the German War Economy*, p. 16.
  [2] Ibid. pp. 19 and 6.

strategy. Moreover, concentration on the production of weapons for immediate use, i.e. on 'armament in width', was precisely the kind of policy that suited a *blitzkrieg* strategy.

But General Thomas, who was in charge of German war mobilization, and many of his colleagues on the German General Staff, never underwrote Hitler's strategy. They wanted 'armament in depth', that is a solidly prepared, expertly organized, and conscientiously conducted war; 'they wanted to be capable of fighting a prolonged war against a combination of Great Powers'.[1] In addition to arms in hand they wanted large stocks of equipment and heavy industries for replacing these stocks in the mass. Although Germany's output of coal, iron-ore, pig-iron, and crude steel had increased considerably, and although a large part thereof had been allocated to war industry in the 1930s, an increase in her coal and steel output from 'existing' plants was not tantamount to armament in depth, nor was the allocation of resources to war industry in any sense a maximum allocation. There was quite a gap between resources going into civilian consumption and those going into armaments. Public expenditure on non-military goods, such as equipment for Party buildings, stadia, &c., which constituted a part of this gap, directly used up resources which had not in fact been directed towards armament in width. The failure to create synthetic fuel and rubber plants on an even more massive scale sprang directly from the fundamental weakness of Hitler's strategy.

But if the strategic conception of the generals responsible for supply differed from that of Hitler, there was sufficient evidence that Thomas invariably over-estimated Germany's requirements in raw materials and labour. To his mind an adequately developed war economy was one in which basic resources were so abundant in relation to any conceivable military requirements that no problem of scarcity could ever arise. In any case Hitler instructed the generals, and not they him. All the same, much more could have been done in the way of economic mobilization for war, if German planners had relied less on *blitzkrieg* strategy. If that strategy was to succeed, it was absolutely essential that the U.S.S.R. should not be able to receive immediate military support from the Anglo-French alliance.

In view of the fact that, throughout the critical periods of the late 1930s, the British and French Governments treated the U.S.S.R. with disdain, German expectations of a free hand for ventures in the east did not appear entirely unfounded. Whatever may have been the ultimate cause of the extreme hesitancy on the part of Britain and France to work for such an alliance with the U.S.S.R., there is no doubt that they needed time when once they had allowed Germany to surpass them in military strength.

[1] N. Kaldor: 'The German War Economy', *The Manchester School of Social and Economic Studies*, September 1946, p. 44.

Moreover, Britain's strategy was based on the assumption that she might have to fight Germany, Japan, and Italy together. For the execution of military preparations on such a scale, time was essential, and playing for time became the main purpose of the policy of appeasement.

During 1938 British and French efforts to arm had been stepped up considerably. Germany's superiority in armaments was bound to be reduced if the intensification of British and French war-production was allowed to bring into play the immensely greater war potential in men and materials within the empires of these two Western European Powers. But with the liquidation of the remainder of Czechoslovakia in March 1939, and with the incorporation of one of the world's largest armaments plants, the Skoda works, in the Reich, Germany—as her press boasted—relegated to a 'cloudy uncertainty the day, hoped for by London and Paris, when parity or superiority in armaments could be attained by them'.[1] When, notwithstanding this new act of aggression, Britain and France committed themselves to supporting Poland in the defence of her rights, the U.S.S.R. distrusted their sincerity and began to feel her way towards neutrality, while Germany, on her side, was bound to do everything in her power to make certain of Russian neutrality, in order that Hitler's *blitzkrieg* strategy might be given a chance to succeed.

APPENDIX I

SHARE OF CAPITAL GOODS IN THE TOTAL MANUFACTURING OUTPUT OF THE GREAT POWERS

CAPITAL goods industries are taken to mean the optical, engineering, metal goods, shipbuilding, vehicles, chemical, and part of the heavy industries (i.e. pig-iron and crude steel).

On the basis of data for net output, the share of these industries in total manufacturing was 40·8 per cent. in the United Kingdom in 1935, 47·8 per cent. in the United States in 1937, and 50·2 per cent. in Germany in 1936.[2] Using manufacturing indices to bring all data to a 1937 base, the share of capital goods increased to 44 per cent. in Britain and to 51 per cent. in Germany.

Employment figures which are given for years other than 1937 can be estimated for 1937 by applying employment indices to the original data. On the basis of these estimated employment figures for 1937, it is found that the number of persons employed in capital goods to total manufacturing employment was 29 per cent. in Italy,[3] 31 per cent. in Japan,[4] and 34 per cent. in France.[5]

---

[1] *Hamburger Fremdenblatt*, 16 March 1939.

[2] L. Rostas: 'Industrial Production, Productivity and Distribution in Britain, Germany, and the United States, 1935–37', *Economic Journal*, April 1943, table iv, p. 44.

[3] Muriel Grindrod: *The New Italy* (London, Royal Institute of International Affairs, 1947), p. 69.

[4] Schumpeter and others: *Industrialization of Japan*, p. 480.

[5] *Annuaire statistique 1940–45*, pp. 148–51.

Making allowance for the higher productivity per employed person in the capital goods industries, the share of the capital goods industries by output in 1937 has been estimated to have been approximately 40 per cent. for Japan and 37 per cent. for France and Italy.

In 1937 the U.S.S.R.'s gross output of 'means of production' amounted to 55 milliard roubles in 1926–7 prices, or to 57·6 per cent. of gross industrial output.[1] But capital goods in the sense of the definition given above (i.e. machine working, metal, and chemicals) amounted to 33·5 milliard roubles or to 35 per cent. of gross industrial output. This share is still too low, because gross industrial output includes mining and electric power, and it is impossible to say what was the gross value of output of these two industries. Since in the Soviet Union in 1937 about 800,000 workers out of a labour force of 8·3 million workers in large-scale industry were employed in these two industries, it has been assumed that the ratio of output was roughly proportional to the ratio of employment. Thus, deducting about 9.2 milliard roubles from the gross output of 95·5 milliard roubles for large-scale industry, the share of capital goods industries in total manufacturing output was about 39 per cent. in 1937 and by a similar calculation about 20 per cent. in 1928.

APPENDIX II

GERMAN EXPENDITURE ON ARMAMENTS

THE following evidence is available for the determination of German expenditure for military purposes. In the first two years of Nazi rule armament expenditure from the budget amounted to Rm. 0·75 milliard and Rm. 1·1 milliard. Secret armament expenditure outside the budget, financed from loans and note issue, amounted to Rm. 2.9 milliard.[2] If the latter sum is spread over the two years in the same proportion as budget expenditure, total expenditure for armaments purposes must have amounted to about Rm. 1.9 milliard in 1933–4 (fiscal year beginning in April), and to Rm. 2.8 milliard in 1934–5. In the following year budget expenditure on armaments was Rm. 2·5 milliard.[2] By raising the 1935–6 budget figure in the same proportion as that for 1934–5 was raised, total expenditure on armaments amounted to about Rm. 6·2 milliard in 1935–6. Thus, in the first three years 1933–4 to 1935–6, total expenditure (open and secret) on armaments was about Rm. 11·0 milliard. According to Schacht, a similar amount was raised for extra-budgetary expenditure on rearmament and re-employment,[3] so that, by implication, expenditure for purposes of non-armament re-employment during the first three years of Nazi rule amounted to about Rm. 4·35 milliard.

According to the Supreme Commander of the Armed Forces, the allocation of Rm. 10 milliard for armaments in 1936–7 was insufficient, and he estimated the additional requirements at Rm. 3·6 milliard.[4] Since presumably these

---

[1] *Land of Socialism Today and Tomorrow*, pp. 122–3.
[2] See *I.M.T. Nuremberg*, xxvii. 122–3 (1301–PS); *N.C.A.* iii. 869.
[3] See *I.M.T. Nuremberg*, xxvii. 136 (1301–PS); *N.C.A.* iii. 879.
[4] See *I.M.T. Nuremberg*, xxvii. 151 (1301–PS); *N.C.A.* iii. 892–3.

additional requirements were paid for in 1937–8, the total expenditure on armaments for that year (Rm. 11 milliard according to the Minister of Finance)[1] must in fact have been Rm. 14·6 milliard. This figure corresponded closely to the estimate of expenditure requirements of Rm. 14·2 milliard for 1937–8 made by the Supreme Commander of the Armed Forces in the previous year.[2]

Provision was made in 1937 to spend about Rm. 14 milliard on armaments in 1938–9.[3] But, according to Keitel, the army alone was given permission to spend up to Rm. 8·6 milliard in 1938–9.[4] Since the navy and air force requirements in 1937–8 were estimated at Rm. 1·2 milliard and Rm. 6 milliard respectively,[5] it has been assumed that amounts not less than these were spent by these two services in 1938–9, bringing the total expenditure on armaments for all armed forces to Rm. 16 milliard.

The development of expenditure on armaments would, therefore, appear to have been as follows:

Total in six years	1933–4	1934–5	1935–6	1936–7	1937–8	1938–9
			(in milliard Rm.)			
51·5	1·9	2·8	6·2	10·0	14·6	16·0

A broadly similar conclusion is reached by Dr. Klein,[6] who gives the following figures:

Total in six years	1933–5	1935–6	1936–7	1937–8	1938–9
51·0	5·0	6·0	10·0	14·0	16·0

APPENDIX III

COMPOSITION OF THE NET PRODUCTS NATIONALLY AVAILABLE AT FACTOR COSTS

THE apparent precision of the figures in Table VII on p. 456 above should not lead the reader to suppose that the margins of error which they contain are negligible. British authorities who, next to the Americans, have collected by far the most reliable information on these figures, insisted on inserting a warning rider to their annual White Papers on National Income and Expenditure.

It cannot be too strongly emphasised [they say] that the estimates in this paper are not based on exact information collected by census enumerators or obtained by scientifically designed sample enquiries. They are, in almost every case, estimates based on incomplete information collected by Government

---

[1] I.M.T. Nuremberg, xxxvi. 493 (419–EC); N.C.A. vii. 474.
[2] I.M.T. Nuremberg, xxvii. 152 (1301–PS); N.C.A. iii. 893.
[3] I.M.T. Nuremberg, xxxvi. 493 (419–EC); N.C.A. vii. 475.
[4] I.M.T. Nuremberg, xxvii. 167–8 (1301–PS); N.C.A. iii. 907.
[5] I.M.T. Nuremberg, xxvii. 152 (1301–PS); N.C.A. iii. 893.
[6] Klein uses the same sources but does not specify how he arrived at the annual totals. See Burton Klein: 'Germany's Preparation for War: A Re-examination', American Economic Review, March 1948, p. 68.

Departments in a form designed to suit needs other than those of the national income investigator. In some cases the information available is exiguous in the extreme.[1]

If such a warning was deemed necessary with regard to the British figures, there is good reason to suppose that it was all the more relevant with regard to Italian, French, or Russian figures. Clearly then the answers which we have sought to our problem in Table VII cannot possibly claim greater accuracy than is warranted by the existing official data for each country.

For international comparisons of the 'net available products', as defined in the text, an attempt has been made to include in, or to exclude from, the varying concepts in different countries items which are or are not included in the British concept. For instance, some countries unlike Britain count interest on government debt and contributions of employers to social insurance funds as part of the national income.

After these preliminary adjustments of the data, the 'net national product' at factor costs has been subdivided into five categories: expenditure (i) by civilians on personal consumption, (ii) on private investment, (iii) on public investment, (iv) for military purposes, and (v) on goods and services purchased by public authorities (that is, central, state, local authorities, and other public bodies). Category (v), public expenditure on 'goods and services', unless specifically stated in this form in official publications, has been derived by deducting from the aggregate expenditures of public authorities all so-called 'transfer payments', such as pensions, benefits, &c. For although these transfers have to be provided for out of current production, they do not arise from productive activity and are not therefore part of the national income. The significance of public expenditure on goods and services derives from the fact that it involves a direct call upon the real resources of the country for use by public authorities.

The basic data have been assembled for each country in the following notes:

The United Kingdom

The first official estimate of the national income of the United Kingdom for 1938 was published in 1941 by the newly established Central Statistical Office in Churchill's war administration. This estimate amounted to £4,638 million.[2] In order to arrive at the 'net available product' at market prices, it was necessary to add to the national income £70 million of resources borrowed from, or acquired through the sale of assets to, foreigners,[3] and £640 million of net indirect taxation, that is 'indirect taxes minus subsidies'.[4]

How was this net available product, amounting to £5,348 million, distributed between its various component categories? At market prices, expenditure by civilians on personal consumption (i), amounting to £4,304 million, was the

---

[1] Great Britain, Treasury: *National Income and Expenditure of the United Kingdom, 1946 to 1948*, Cmd. 7649 (London, H.M.S.O., 1949), p. 2.

[2] Great Britain, Treasury: *National Income and Expenditure of the United Kingdom 1946 to 1949*, Cmd. 7933 [referred to hereafter as Cmd. 7933] (London, H.M.S.O., 1950), p. 9, table 5, item 12.

[3] Ibid. p. 27, table 20, item 54.

[4] Ibid. p. 24, table 18, items 30 minus 37.

largest item.[1] Net domestic capital formation was divided into net private investment (ii), amounting to £183 million, and into net public investment (iii), amounting to £137 million.[2] Expenditure for military purposes (iv) amounted to about £391 million,[3] thus leaving for public expenditure on goods and services (v), excluding defence, an amount of £333 million.[4]

For purposes of international comparisons, net indirect taxes have had to be deducted from the net available product and its component categories in order to arrive at factor costs. The adjusted total of net indirect taxes, amounting to £607 million,[5] has been allocated among the five component categories of the net available product as follows:

Expenditure in the United Kingdom in 1938 on	Market prices	Net indirect taxes	Factor costs
	(in £ million)		
(i) Personal consumption	4,304	579	3,725
(ii) Net private investment	183	7	176
(iii) Net public investment	137	5	132
(iv) Military purposes	391	11	380
(v) Goods and services by public bodies	333	5	328
Net available product	5,348	607	4,741

The United States

Previous official estimates of the national income of the United States were severely revised in the *Survey of Current Business* for July 1947. In its new form the official American concept of national income corresponds very closely to that held in the United Kingdom, with, apparently, the one exception of continuing to regard employers' contributions to social insurance as an ingredient part of the national income.[6] These contributions will be treated here as indirect taxes and deducted in order to arrive at the net available product at factor costs.

In 1938 the net national product at market prices amounted to $76,691 million.[7] Deducting from this total $1,109 million for net foreign investment,[8] the net product nationally available for use amounted to $75,582 million.

[1] Ibid. p. 25, table 17, items 22 plus 23.

[2] Ibid. p. 27, table 19, items 48 minus 43 = £320 million minus p. 37, table 26, items 72 minus 38 plus p. 39, table 28, items 19 minus 14 = £137 million leaves £183 million for net private investment.

[3] League of Nations: *Armaments Year Book, 1939/40* (Geneva, 1940), p. 74.

[4] Cmd. 7933 (p. 25, table 18, items 33 to 36) gives a total of public expenditure on goods and services, including that for military purposes, amounting to £724 million.

[5] A quoted total of £640 million of net indirect taxes (ibid. p. 46) has been adjusted so as to relate to net available product by the deduction of £22 million which is paid by foreigners, and by the deduction of an additional £11 million which is borne by depreciation. The exclusion of the £11 million can be justified by comparing table 34 of Cmd. 7933 with table 34 of Cmd. 7099 (*National Income and Expenditure of the United Kingdom, 1938 to 1946* (London, H.M.S.O., 1947)).

[6] U.S. Bureau of Foreign and Domestic Commerce: *National Income and Product Statistics of the United States, 1929–46* (Supplement to *Survey of Current Business*, July 1947), p. 19, table 1.

[7] Ibid. p. 20, table 4.   [8] Ibid. p. 19, table 2.

The values of component categories of the net available product at market prices were as follows: Expenditure by civilians on personal consumption (i) amounted to $64,513 million.[1] In the depression year of 1938 in the United States there was no net private investment (ii); indeed, the stock of private enterprise capital was actually depleted by about $1,497 million.[2] On the other hand, spending on net public investment (iii) might be estimated at about $1,893 million,[3] and expenditure for military purposes (iv) amounted to $1,130 million.[4] Since government purchases of goods and services[5] included both public investment and military expenditures, it follows that public expenditure on goods and services (v), excluding investment and defence, must have amounted to about $9,543 million.

In order to reduce the net available product and its component categories from market prices to factor costs, net indirect taxes, amounting to $9,316 million,[6] plus employers' contributions to social insurance, amounting to $1,276 million,[7] had to be deducted, giving a total of $10,592 million. For the allocation of this total to the different categories, a calculation by Richard Stone has been used. He estimated that in 1941 spending by Americans on civilian consumption constituted 69·5 per cent. of the net national product

Expenditure in the United States in 1938 on	Market prices	Net indirect taxes	Factor costs
	(in $ million)		
(i) Personal consumption	64,513	9,479	55,034
(ii) Net private investment	−1,497	−137	−1,360
(iii) Net public investment	1,893	173	1,720
(iv) Military purposes	1,130	103	1,027
(v) Goods and services by public bodies	9,543	873	8,670
Net available product	75,582	10,491	65,091
Add: Net foreign investment	1,109	101	1,008
Net national product	76,691	10,592	66,099

at market prices and that it carried about 74 per cent. of the total number of indirect taxes and employers' social insurance contributions.[8] Since in

[1] U.S. Bureau of Foreign and Domestic Commerce: *National Income and Product Statistics of the United States, 1929–46*, p. 19, table 2.

[2] i.e. gross private domestic investment (ibid.) minus capital consumption allowances (ibid. p. 21, table 7).

[3] i.e. new public construction activity (ibid. p. 44, table 31) minus capital consumption allowances (ibid. p. 20, table 4) plus business capital consumption allowances (ibid. p. 21, table 7).

[4] League of Nations: *Armaments Year Book, 1939/40*, p. 366.

[5] Amounting to $12,750 million (U.S. Bureau of Foreign and Domestic Commerce, op. cit. p. 19, table 2) minus an allowance of $184 million for public capital consumption (ibid. p. 20, table 4, minus p. 21, table 7).

[6] Ibid. p. 20, table 4.

[7] Ibid. p. 23, table 10.

[8] Richard Stone: 'The National Income, Output and Expenditure of the U.S.A., 1929–41' (*Economic Journal*, June–September 1942, pp. 159 and 165, table 1, item 38) in conjunction with an article by the same author: 'Two Studies on Income and Expenditure in the United States (ibid. April 1943, pp. 66–67).

1938 expenditure on civilian consumption was 84 per cent. of the net national product at market prices, and since between 1938 and 1941 subsidies to the cost of living had not appreciably changed, the writer has used Mr. Stone's relation between the two percentages and has applied it to the 1938 civilian consumption figure in order to determine the proportion of total net indirect taxes which should be allocated to it. This proportion was 89·5 per cent. Thus deducting from the total amount of $10,592 million of net indirect taxation 89·5 per cent. or $9,479 million, the residue of $1,113 million has been distributed proportionately between the categories of the net national product, excluding civilian consumption, as shown in table on p. 496 opposite.

France

According to the most reliable post-war estimate, the French net national product at factor costs amounted to fr. 348 milliard in 1938.[1] Adding to this sum net imports of fr. 8 milliard,[2] and net indirect taxes of fr. 27 milliard,[3] the French net available product at market prices must have amounted to about fr. 383 milliard.

In the distribution of this product between its component categories, expenditure for military purposes (iv) accounted for fr. 29·4 milliard,[4] net private investment (ii) for fr. 3 milliard, and net public investment (iii) for fr. 17 milliard.[5] Since aggregate public expenditure amounted to fr. 116 milliard, it follows that after the deduction of about fr. 42 milliard of 'transfer payments',[6] public expenditure on goods and services (v), excluding expenditures for military purposes and public investment, must have amounted to fr. 27·6 milliard. Expenditure on civilian consumption(i), amounting to fr. 306 milliard, has been calculated by the subtraction from the total net available product of the sum of categories (ii) to (v).

In order to arrive at factor costs values, net indirect taxes have been allocated and deducted from the component categories of the net available product at market prices as follows:

Expenditure in France in 1938 on	*Market prices*	*Net indirect taxes*	*Factor costs*
	(in fr. milliard)		
(i) Personal consumption	306·0	24·0	282·0
(ii) Net private investment	3·0	0·2	2·8
(iii) Net public investment	17·0	0·8	16·2
(iv) Military purposes	29·4	1·4	28·0
(v) Goods and services by public bodies . .	27·6	0·6	27·0
Net available product	383·0	27·0	356·0

[1] Commissariat Général du Plan de Modernisation et d'Équipement: *Estimation du revenu national français*, p. 18, items 11 and 15.

[2] Ibid. p. 32, items B minus C.   [3] Ibid. p. 18, items 12 and 13.

[4] *Bulletin statistique du Ministère des Finances*, no. 1, 1er trimestre (Paris, 1947), p. 220.

[5] *Estimation du revenu national français*, p. 40.

[6] Ibid. p. 46.

Japan

In 1938 the net national product of Japan, estimated at factor costs, amounted to yen 22·5 milliard.[1] Adding to this sum external disinvestment amounting to about yen 0·3 milliard,[2] the net available product amounted at factor costs to about yen 22·8 milliard. Adding about yen 0·9 milliard for indirect taxation,[3] and deducting about yen 0·1 milliard for subsidies,[4] the net available product at market prices amounted to about yen 23·6 milliard.

Distributed between its component categories, net private investment (ii) has been assumed to be about yen 1·8 milliard.[5] Since total public expenditure of about yen 7·8 milliard[6] included 'transfer payments' (that is interest on the national debt and pensions) of yen 0·7 milliard,[7] public expenditure on goods and services, including that on public investment and defence, amounted to about yen 7·1 milliard. But as expenditure for military purposes (iv) was yen 6 milliard,[8] there was left for public expenditure on goods and services (v) and for public investment (iii) combined no more than yen 1·1 milliard. Having for four of our five categories some estimated values and knowing the total, it follows that expenditure by civilians on personal consumption (i) must have been about yen 14·7 milliard.

Net indirect taxes have been distributed between the categories of the net national product at market prices (as shown below) in order to determine the respective values at factor costs:

Expenditure in Japan in 1938 on	Market prices	Net indirect taxes	Factor costs
	(in milliard yen)		
(i) Personal consumption	14·7	0·6	14·1
(ii) Net private investment	1·8	0·0	1·8
(iv) Military purposes	6·0	0·2	5·8
(iii and v) Public investment and goods and services by public bodies . . .	1·1	0·0	1·1
Net available product	23·6	0·8	22·8

Italy

The value of Italy's net national product at factor costs for 1938 was estimated at lire 110 milliard.[9] Since in that year the foreign balance was most probably

[1] Japanese Economic Federation: 'National Income of Japan, 1930/39', in *East Asia Economic Intelligence Series*, Tokyo, October 1939, no. 1.

[2] League of Nations: *Statistical Year Book, 1938/39*, p. 239.

[3] Estimates based on *Statistisches Jahrbuch, 1941/42*, pp. 296 and 304.

[4] Schumpeter and others: *Industrialization of Japan*, p. 734.

[5] Planned capital investments for 1938 were put at yen 4·1 milliard, of which yen 2·0 milliard were planned for manufacturing industry. How much of this was private or public investment must be conjectural (*Statistical Year Book of Finance and Economy of Japan, 1948*, pp. 276–7).

[6] Bank for International Settlements: *Twelfth Annual Report* (1941–2), p. 179.

[7] *Statistisches Jahrbuch, 1939/40*, pp. 301–19.

[8] Bank for International Settlements, loc. cit.

[9] United Nations, Department of Economic Affairs: *Survey of Current Inflationary Tendencies* (Lake Success, New York, September 1947), p. 47.

in equilibrium, the net national product might be taken to reflect the net available product. Including about lire 16 milliard[1] of indirect taxes, the net available product at market prices amounted to about lire 126 milliard.

Aggregate public expenditure amounted to lire 39·2[2] milliard. This included transfer payments, i.e. interest on public debt and pensions, amounting to about lire 7·2 milliard,[3] so that public expenditure on goods and services, including military expenditure and public investment, must have amounted to about lire 32 milliard, leaving for civilian consumption and private investment lire 94 milliard. Since net private investment (ii) was certainly higher than the lire 1 milliard which can be traced,[4] expenditure by civilians on personal consumption (i) must have been less than lire 93 milliard. On the other hand, as expenditure for military purposes (iv) amounted to lire 15 milliard,[5] public expenditure on goods and services (v) including public investment (iii), must have amounted to lire 17 milliard.

Net indirect taxes have been allocated between the component categories of the net available product at market prices in order to arrive at their values at factor costs as follows:

Expenditure in Italy in 1938 on	Market prices	Net indirect taxes	Factor costs
	(in milliard lire)		
(i) Personal consumption	93·0	13·0	80·0
(ii) Net private investment	1·0	0·0	1·0
(iv) Military purposes	15·0	1·0	14·0
(iii and v) Public investment and goods and services by public bodies	17·0	2·0	15·0
Net available product	126·0	16·0	110·0

Germany

The official German definition of national income differs widely from the British.[6] Drawing attention to the discrepancies between the concepts used in Germany and in Britain, Professor A. J. Brown[7] as early as 1941 adjusted the income data for Germany so as to make them conform to the British definition. But at the same time German statisticians had begun, for specific purposes of their own, to adjust official data in a manner which brought the revised German

---

[1] *Statistisches Jahrbuch, 1941/42*, pp. 296 and 304.

[2] UNRRA: Italian Mission: *Survey of Italy's Economy*, p. 7, table 1.

[3] United Nations, Department of Economic Affairs: *Public Debt, 1914–1946* (Lake Success, New York, 1948), p. 89, and also *Compendio statistico italiano*, vol. i, August 1946, pp. 134 seqq.

[4] Ibid. p. 134.

[5] UNRRA: Italian Mission: *Survey of Italy's Economy*, p. 7, table 1.

[6] Germany, Statistisches Reichsamt: *Das deutsche Volkseinkommen vor und nach dem Kriege* (Berlin, Reimar Hobbing, 1932).

[7] See Royal Institute of International Affairs: *Bulletin of International News*, especially issues of 14 June and 28 June 1941; moreover, for a comparison of his estimates with German income estimates which became available after the war see A. J. Brown: *Applied Economics*, chapter i, p. 1.

figures more closely into line with those based on British and American defi-
nitions.[1] Even now, however, the values attached to the components of the pre-
war German national income, adjusted to Western concepts, are, to say the
least, no more than broad approximations.

According to the widely quoted semi-official estimate of Dr. Grünig, the net
national income amounted in 1938 to Rm. 90 milliard.[2] Deducting Rm. 1
milliard of interest on the public debt,[3] which, together with an estimated
amount of Rm. 1·6 milliard of employers' contributions to social insurance,[4] is
included in the income figure, the net national product at factor cost (American
definition) amounted to Rm. 89 milliard. Since the foreign balance was
roughly in equilibrium, the net national product was assumed to be the net
available product at factor costs. Adding to this figure an amount of Rm. 7·6
milliard of indirect taxes,[5] the net available product at market prices amounted
to Rm. 96·6 milliard.[6]

Aggregate public expenditure amounted to Rm. 41·8 milliard[7] of which
transfer payments (including interest on the debt, pensions, and taxes transferred
from the Reich which are included in the expenditure figures of the Länder, &c.)
can be estimated at about Rm. 8 milliard for 1938,[8] so that public expenditure
on goods and services, including expenditure for military purposes and for
public investment, must have amounted to about Rm. 33·8 milliard. Deducting
this sum from the net available product at market prices, Rm. 62·8 milliard is
left for personal consumption plus net private investment. Expenditure on net
private investment (ii) has been estimated at Rm. 1.8 milliard, leaving about
Rm. 61 milliard for expenditure by civilians on personal consumption (i).
Since total net investment (both public and private), excluding stocks, can be
estimated at Rm. 5 milliard, public net investment (iii) in plant and equipment
must have amounted to Rm. 3·2 milliard. But as expenditure for military purposes (iv), amounting to Rm. 16 milliard, included investment expenditure, it is
impossible to say more than that net public investment (iii) and public expenditure on goods and services (v) together, excluding what has been counted as
expenditure for military purposes, amounted to Rm. 17·8 milliard.

[1] See Ferdinand Grünig: 'Probleme der Zusammensetzung und Verteilung des Sozialprodukts', *Vierteljahreshefte zur Wirtschaftsforschung*, part i, 1948; Otto Donner: 'Die Grenzen der
Staatsverschuldung', *Weltwirtschaftliches Archiv*, September 1942, part 2.

[2] Grünig, op. cit. p. 12, Übersicht 4.

[3] United Nations, Department of Economic Affairs: *Public Debt, 1914–1946*, p. 67 (estimated).

[4] *Statistisches Jahrbuch, 1941/42*, p. 529, table 8.

[5] Ibid. p. 598, table 20 (*Reichsverbrauchsteuern und Zölle*), p. 547, table 4 B (*Landes- und
Gemeindesteuern vom Verbrauch*), and p. 593, table 7 (*Umsatzsteuer*).

[6] Rm. 95 milliard according to Donner, op. cit. p. 201, table 3.

[7] Reich expenditure was Rm. 31·8 milliard according to 'Die Kriegsfinanzierung im Reichs-
haushalt' in *Statistische Praxis*, 1946, part 1, Kartelblatt F 7112; and expenditure of *Länder* and
Gemeinden was Rm. 10 milliard according to *Statistisches Jahrbuch, 1941/42*, p. 543. It will be
noticed that the figure for aggregate public expenditure used here (Rm. 41·8 milliard) is higher
than the one (Rm. 40·1 milliard) quoted for 1938 in Appendix IV, A, items I + II (see p. 504
below). The former includes some transfer payments from the Reich to the Länder which are
not included in the latter, while the latter is composed of a number of items, some of which are
estimates which must be subject to some margin of error.

[8] Cf. Reichs-Kredit-Gesellschaft A.G., Berlin: *Deutschlands wirtschaftliche Lage an der Jahreswende
1938/39* (Berlin, 1939), p. 58; also Donner, op. cit. p. 201, table 2.

To arrive at factor cost values, indirect taxes plus employers' contributions to social insurance have been distributed as follows:

Expenditure in Germany in 1938 on	Market prices	Net indirect taxes	Factor costs
	(in Rm. milliard)		
(i) Personal consumption	61·0	5·9	55·1
(ii) Private net investment	1·8	0·1	1·7
(iv) Military purposes	16·0	1·5	14·5
(iii and v) Public investment and goods and services by public bodies . . .	17·8	1·7	16·1
Net available product	96·6	9·2	87·4

U.S.S.R.

The Soviet concept of national income covers material production only. The official Soviet definition is, for purposes of international comparisons, too narrow because of the exclusion of nearly all forms of services—governmental, professional, passenger transport, &c. An even more serious weakness is the fact that current output is valued and published in 1926–7 prices, while budget expenditure is expressed in current prices. Thus the official national income figure at 1926–7 prices was given as 105 milliard roubles for 1938, while the combined budget expenditure amounted to 124 milliard roubles at current prices.[1] Since price indices have not been published, it is impossible to translate the values at 1926–7 roubles into current roubles.

Several extremely useful estimates of Soviet national income have been made by revaluing the published Soviet production data at current English and/or American prices,[2] and by directly estimating the value of services.[3]

By far the most penetrating analysis of U.S.S.R. income figures—based on Russian sources which are quoted in great detail—was made by a group of statisticians which included Paul Baran, Abram Bergson, Colin Clark, and others.[4] The methods used by these writers to arrive at the gross national product at market prices for 1940 have been used with some minor modifications to arrive at the net national income at factor costs for 1938.

In estimating total income payments, including those in kind, several items have to be taken into account. According to the Central Accounting (Statistical) Administration of Soviet Economy (Tsunkhu), the volume of retail (other than collective farm market) trade in 1938 was 138·6 milliard roubles,[5] and of collective farm trade 24·4 milliard roubles, giving a total of 163 milliard roubles. Of this total, 18·4 milliard roubles represented sales to institutional buyers, which

---

[1] Baykov: *Development of the Soviet Economic System*, pp. 397–400.

[2] See State Planning Commission of the U.S.S.R.: *Second Five-Year Plan.*

[3] See Colin Clark: *Critique of Russian Statistics*, and Julius Wyler: 'The National Income of Soviet Russia', *Social Research*, vol. 13, no. 4, December 1946.

[4] In the *Review of Economic Statistics*, November 1947, no. 4.

[5] Baykov, op. cit. p. 260.

means that 144·6 milliard roubles represented retail sales (including collective farm market sales) to households in 1938.

According to a Gosplan monograph on money income and expenditure for 1938 by Margolin,[1] these sales constituted 79·6 per cent. of all money outlays of the population. Hence the total money income paid out to the population was 181·7 milliard roubles.

To this must be added (a) collective income of the agricultural population, (b) agricultural produce consumed on farms, and (c) net profits of enterprises.

With regard to (a), Margolin's study shows that the total money income of the agricultural population (received for work performed on collective farms and for output sold on the free market) represented 12·3 per cent. of total money income paid out, or 22·3 milliard roubles. But this was only 75 per cent. of all agricultural money incomes, the latter being $\frac{22·3 \times 100}{75} = 29·7$ milliard roubles. The difference, 7·4 milliard roubles, was retained in the form of a collective fund for payment of teachers, &c.

With regard to (b), the agricultural produce consumed on farms, it has been pointed out that the 'marketed value of 29·7 milliard roubles of agricultural produce represented 42 per cent. of gross agricultural output'. The latter amounted, therefore, to 70·7 milliard roubles. As the relation between the value of net output to gross output was about 70 per cent. in 1938, the value of agricultural net output must have been 49·5 milliard roubles. By deducting the marketed value of 29·7 milliard roubles from the value of net output, the value of agricultural produce consumed on farms must have been 19·8 milliard roubles.

With regard to (c), the net profits of enterprises can be estimated at about 15 milliard roubles for 1938.[2]

To arrive at the national income at factor cost, certain 'transfer incomes' included in the above, of about 8 milliard roubles (i.e. social insurance benefits and interest on debts), will have to be excluded.[3] It follows:

		Milliard roubles
I. *Net Income and Gross Product*		
1. Total money income paid out to population		181·7
2. Collective income of farms		7·4
3. Agricultural produce consumed on farms		19·8
4. Net profits of enterprises		15·0
5. *Minus*: transfer payments		−8·0
A. NET NATIONAL INCOME AT FACTOR COSTS		216·0
6. Indirect taxes[4]		80·0
B. NET NATIONAL INCOME AT MARKET PRICES		296·0
7. Depreciation[5]		12·0
C. GROSS PRODUCT AT MARKET PRICES		308·0

---

[1] Quoted by the writers in *Review of Economic Statistics*, loc. cit.
[2] Colin Clark: *Critique of Russian Statistics*, p. 75.
[3] Baykov, op. cit. pp. 387 and 394.
[4] Ibid. p. 397.
[5] See V below, and *Review of Economic Statistics*, loc. cit.

Milliard
roubles

II. *Distribution of Gross Product*

  8. Total public expenditure (Combined budgets)[1] . . . . 124·0
  9. Gross investment outside the budget,[2] about . . . . 5·0
10. *Minus*: transfer payments (I. 5) . . . . . . −8·0

D. GOVERNMENT EXPENDITURE ON GOODS AND SERVICES . . . . 121·0
E_1. CONSUMPTION (C–D)[3] . . . . 187·0
  6. GROSS PRODUCT AT MARKET PRICES . . . . . . 308·0

III. *Check on Consumption Estimates*

11. Retail sales to households (see above, p. 502) . . . . 144·0
12. Farmers' self supply and retained income . . . . 27·2
13. Travel, entertainment[4] . . . . 18·0
E_2. CONSUMPTION[3] . . . . 189·2

IV. *Composition of Government Expenditure on Goods and Services*

14. Gross investment through the budget[5] . . . . . 52·0
15. Gross investment outside the budget . . . . . 5·0
16. Aggregate gross investment . . . . . . 57·0
17. Defence expenditure[6] . . . . 23·0
18. Other government expenditure [D−(16+17)] . . . 41·0
D. GOVERNMENT EXPENDITURE ON GOODS AND SERVICES . . . 121·0

V. *Depreciation and Net Investment*

19. Planned capital in industry in 1937[7] . . . . . 195·0
20. Depreciation in all branches of Soviet economy[8] . . . 12·0
21. Gross investment (IV. 16) . . . . 57·0
22. Net investment in 1938 . . . . 45·0

Since in 1938 the foreign balance of the U.S.S.R. was in equilibrium, the net national product at market prices reflects the net product nationally available. In order to reduce the net available product and its component categories to factor costs, indirect taxes have been allocated and deducted as follows:

Expenditure in the U.S.S.R. in 1938 on	*Market prices*	*Net indirect taxes*	*Factor costs*
	(in milliard roubles)		
(i) Personal consumption	187	60	127
(ii) Net public investment	45	7	38
(iv) Military purposes	23	3	20
(v) Goods and services by public bodies . .	41	10	31
Net available product	296	80	216

[1] See Baykov, op. cit. p. 397.   [2] Ibid. pp. 386 and 395.
[3] The difference between E_1 and E_2 is small and inevitable since none of the estimated items can be precise.
[4] According to Margolin, this item was 10 per cent. of I (1), the total money income paid out to the population.   [5] Baykov, op. cit. p. 397.   [6] Ibid.
[7] State Planning Commission of the U.S.S.R.: *Second Five-Year Plan*, p. 561.
[8] *Review of Economic Statistics*, loc. cit., and Colin Clark: *Critique of Russian Statistics*.

APPENDIX IV

A. EXPENDITURES OF GERMAN PUBLIC AUTHORITIES

(in Rm. milliard)

	1929	1932	1933	1934	1935	1936	1937	1938	Last six years
				(fiscal years beginning 1 April)					
1. Tax, receipts of Reich, states, communes .	13·5	10·2	10·6	11·9	13·3	15·5	18·6	22·7	92·6
2. Administrative receipts, net profits of public enterprises . .	3·5	2·9	2·7	2·9	3·0	3·2	3·5	3·6	18·9
3. Surplus of insurance funds, levies and contributions . .	..	..	0·8	1·4	2·5	2·7	2·8	3·1	13·3
I. Items 1–3: Total taxes and levies . . .	..	..	14·1	16·2	18·8	21·4	24·9	29·4	124·8
4. Increase of published debt of Reich, states, communes . .	3·3	0·5	0·5	0·8	1·6	1·0	2·3	10·7	16·9
5. Allocation of increase of secret debt .	..	..	..	1·0	3·6	4·4	3·0	..	12·0
II. Items 4+5: Total public borrowing .	3·3	0·5	0·5	1·8	5·2	5·4	5·3	10·7	28·9
Items I+II: AGGREGATE PUBLIC EXPENDITURES .	20·3	13·6	14·6	18·0	24·0	26·8	30·2	40·1	153·7
of which 6. Military expenditure .	..	..	1·9	3·0	6·0	10·0	14·0	16·0	51·0

Sources: Item 1 is based on *Statistisches Jahrbuch, 1941/42*, p. 547; ibid. *1935*, pp. 431–9; *Reichs-Kredit-Gesellschaft* report 1939, p. 58 and report 1938/9, p. 101.

Item 2 is based on *Statistisches Jahrbuch, 1941/42*, p. 544; ibid. *1935*, p. 433; (for net profits from public property) *Wirtschaft und Statistik*, 1939, p. 706; *Statistisches Jahrbuch, 1935*, p. 431.

Item 3 is based on Otto Nathan: *Nazi War Finance and Banking* (New York, National Bureau of Economic Research, 1944), p. 94. His figures for Unemployment Insurance Fund have been reduced by about three-fifths for 1938 in order to take into account only what is stated to be the 'surplus' plus an amount of expenditure by the Fund to the Reich used for children's allowances. In this sense the surplus rose from about Rm. 172 million in 1934 to about Rm. 700 million in 1938 (*Statistisches Jahrbuch, 1935*, p. 413 and ibid. *1941/42*, p. 529).

Item 4 is based on *Statistisches Jahrbuch, 1941/42*, p. 555; ibid. *1935*, p. 455; *Reichs-Kredit-Gesellschaft* report 1939, p. 60.

Item 5. The allocation of the secret debt has been arrived at as follows: When secret debt financing ceased at the end of the fiscal year 1937–8, the total amount was Rm. 12 milliard (*N.C.A.* vii. 428). Of this amount about Rm. 3 milliard were issued in 1937 (*N.C.A.*

vii. 500). The 'Reich' budget deficit was about Rm. 5·5 milliard in 1935 (*N.C.A.* iii. 869) and since the published Reich debt rose by Rm. 1·9 milliard, about Rm. 3·6 milliard of secret debt must be allocated to this year. Of the remaining secret debt of Rm. 5·4 milliard, it has been assumed that Rm. 1 milliard fell into 1934. For, although Schacht pointed out that some Rm. 3 milliard of 'Mefo' bills would have to be redeemed in 1939, five years after the date of issuance—thus suggesting that Rm. 3 milliard should be allocated to the year 1934 (*N.C.A.* vii. 430)—another Reichsbank director pointed out that 'Mefo' bill-financing of armaments started in early 1935 and that the total life of the bills only in some instances exceeded 'four' years (*N.C.A.* vii. 494). It is therefore unlikely that more than Rm. 1 milliard were issued in the first three months of 1935 which belong to the fiscal year 1934. The remaining sum of Rm. 4·4 milliard must have been issued in 1936.

Item 6. For details see Appendix II, p. 492 above.

Note: It cannot be too strongly emphasized that, despite the apparent precision suggested by these figures, some series (e.g. 3 and the allocation of 5) are estimates, and may make a great difference to the determination of, say, the size of the budget deficit or of aggregate public expenditures during specific years.

B. GROSS INVESTMENT IN GERMANY

(in Rm. milliard)

Spheres of Investments	1929	1932	1933	1934	1935	1936	1937	1938
1. Agriculture . . .	0·9	0·5	0·6	0·7	0·8	0·9	1·0	1·1
2. Handicraft, retail, wholesale trade	1·4	0·5	0·6	0·7	0·8	0·9	1·0	1·1
3. Residential construction .	2·9	0·8	0·9	1·5	1·6	2·2	2·1	2·2
4. Ships, buses, taxis, lorries .	0·3	..	0·1	0·1	0·2	0·3	0·3	0·5
5. Industry, classified:								
Armaments . . .	0·7	0·1	0·2	0·4	0·6	0·9	1·2	1·6
Heavy	0·6	0·1	0·1	0·3	0·6	0·7	1·0	1·3
Other	0·7	0·2	0·3	0·3	0·4	0·5	0·6	0·8
A. Items 1–5: Private sector of the economy . .	7·5	2·3	2·8	4·1	5·0	6·4	7·3	8·5
6. Public utilities . . .	1·1	0·2	0·2	0·3	0·4	0·5	0·6	0·7
7. Roads, waterways, harbours .	0·7	0·2	0·5	0·8	1·1	1·3	1·4	2·0
8. Railways, tramways, airways, post	1·5	0·6	0·7	0·9	0·8	0·9	1·0	1·3
9. Government:								
Military facilities . .	..	..	..	..	1·3	2·4	3·1	3·7
Other projects . .	2·0	0·9	0·8	2·1	3·0	2·3	2·6	2·3
B. Items 6–9: Public sector of the economy . .	5·3	1·9	2·2	4·1	6·6	7·4	8·7	10·0
I. Items A+B: AGGREGATE GROSS INVESTMENT . .	12·8	4·2	5·1	8·2	11·6	13·8	16·0	18·5

of which: (a) Building Construction

	1929	1932	1933	1934	1935	1936	1937	1938
10. Building Construction:								
Private	2·9	..	0·9	1·4	1·6	2·2	2·1	2·0
Industrial . . .	2·7	..	0·6	3·8	1·0	1·4	1·8	2·1
Private sector . . .	5·6	..	1·5	2·2	2·6	3·6	3·9	4·1
11. Building Construction: Public sector . . .	2·7	..	1·7	3·5	4·9	5·4	6·1	7·9
II. Items 10+11: AGGREGATE BUILDING CONSTRUCTION .	8·3	..	3·2	5·7	7·5	9·0	10·0	12·0

(b) Non-Building Investments

	1929	1932	1933	1934	1935	1936	1937	1938
12. Items A–10: Private sector non-building investments .	1·9	..	1·3	1·9	2·4	2·8	3·4	4·4
13. Items B–11: Public sector non-building investments .	2·6	..	0·5	0·6	1·7	2·0	2·6	2·1
III. Items I–II: AGGREGATE NON-BUILDING INVESTMENTS. . . .	4·5	..	1·8	2·5	4·1	4·8	6·0	6·5

Sources: Items 1 to 9 are based on *Statistisches Jahrbuch, 1941/42*, pp. 609–13; ibid. *1935*, p. 493; also on *Reichs-Kredit-Gesellschaft* report 1937/8, p. 6.

Item 5 for the three years 1936 to 1938 is based on *Statistisches Jahrbuch, 1941/42*, p. 612. *Armament Industry* includes the electro-technical, machinery building, vehicles, locomotive, shipbuilding, iron-, steel- and metal-goods, chemical, optical and precision instrument industries. *Heavy Industries* include the coal, steel, metal ore, and foundry construction material, and rubber industries. *Other Industry* includes everything else from the textile and clothing, food and drink, paper and printing industries, &c. Figures for the years up to and including 1935 are based on Burton Klein: 'Germany's Preparation for War: A Re-examination', *American Economic Review*, March 1948, p. 66.

Item 9 is a residual item after the deduction of traceable items 1–8 in the *Statistisches Jahrbuch* from the aggregate gross investment data (item I) quoted in the *Reichs-Kredit-Gesellschaft* report 1939, p. 5. The estimate of military facilities which includes barracks, airfields, fortifications, &c., is taken from Klein, loc. cit.

Items 10 and 11 are based on *Reichs-Kredit-Gesellschaft* report 1939, p. 6.

Items 12 and 13 are derived directly from the preceding items. The aggregate non-building investment (amounting to Rm. 6·5 milliard in 1938) consisted to a large extent of installations of machinery (home engineering sales totalled about Rm. 4·7 milliard in 1938), the purchase of motor-cars, electrical installations, &c. (ibid. p. 5).

PART III

THE BALANCE OF POWER

By Martin Wight

HITLER's entry into Prague on the evening of 15 March 1939 was the climax of German territorial aggression in time of formal peace. For five years Germany had dominated and terrorized Europe, in widening circles, without beginning a war. For the past year Hitler's chalet at Obersalzberg had been the centre of European diplomacy, as once were the convent of the Escurial and the palace of Versailles. Like Philip II's occupation of Portugal in 1580, and Louis XIV's seizure of Strasbourg in 1681, the German annexation of Bohemia and Moravia in March 1939 was the last expansionist triumph of an overmighty state before the tardy revival of a concern to preserve the balance of power produced a grand alliance in counterpoise and led to general hostilities.

After the First World War it was possible to believe that the Great Powers had lost something of their former primacy in the international system, because of the multiplication of small states on the principle of nationality and the new attempt to constitutionalize international politics through the League of Nations. In the course of the 1930s the Great Powers reasserted their predominance, and by 15 March 1939 the ultimate decisions of peace and war were seen to lie once more with them and not with the majority of states.[1] Since the final territorial resettlement after the First World War there had been several clashes between the Small Powers, but only two had been on a scale amounting to war, the Bolivian-Paraguayan conflict of 1932–5 and the Sa'ūdī–Yamani War of 1934, and these happened to be in regions of the world remote from Great Power rivalries.[2] But the acts of international violence that suc-

---

[1] See Toynbee: *World after the Peace Conference*, pp. 24–35; *Survey* for 1936, pp. 30–31. Of the many attempts to define a Great Power (cf. p. 367 above, note 2) perhaps the best is Treitschke's: 'A State may be defined as a Great Power if its total destruction would require a coalition of other States to accomplish' (Heinrich von Treitschke: *Politics*, translated from the German by Blanche Dugdale and Torben de Bille (London, Constable, 1916), ii. 607; cf. *Survey* for 1937, i. 1–2). A Small Power may be defined as any state that is not a Great Power—a negative quality that outweighs in importance all variations of size, population, and resources. Seldom since the system of independent sovereign states first appeared in the sixteenth century has the number of Great Powers approached as much as one-quarter of the whole. This highest proportion of Great to Small Powers was probably attained between 1870 and 1914, when the number of Great Powers rose to eight, and the principle of nationality had not yet run its length in multiplying the small (Toynbee: *World after the Peace Conference*, pp. 7–8, 12).

[2] *Survey* for 1933, pp. 393–438 and *Survey* for 1936, pp. 837–72; *Survey* for 1934, pp. 310–21. The Bolivian-Paraguayan conflict had produced the first declaration of war since the end of the

ceeded one another in an unbroken chain of causation and with increasing
momentum up to Hitler's seizure of Prague had all been done by Great
Powers—the Japanese conquest of Manchuria in 1931–2,[1] the Italian
conquest of Ethiopia in 1935–6,[2] the Japanese invasion of China in 1937,[3]
and the series of aggressions by Germany herself that culminated in the
conquest of Bohemia and Moravia on 15 March 1939; and it was through
the intervention of the Great Powers that the Spanish Civil War, which
came to an end in the same month, had been magnified into an international danger.[4] It had always rested with the Great Powers whether
a local conflict should develop into a general war, for a general war is to
be defined as one in which all the Great Powers take part.[5] By 1939 the
psychological ascendancy of the Great Powers was so marked that it rested
with them whether there should be any local conflict at all.

An attempt had been made in 1919 to restrain the collective authority
of the Great Powers within the forms of permanent membership of the
Council of the League of Nations. The Great Powers soon threw off these
constitutional trappings. Some did not join the League, some resigned
from it, and those which retained their membership found a greater
common interest with the Great Powers outside than with the other members of the League. As early as the Corfù dispute of 1923 the tendency
reappeared for the Great Powers to act as a supreme junta, directing
international relations if necessary at the expense of the Small Powers as
the Concert of Europe had done in the nineteenth century.[6] This habitual
trend ran on through the Four-Power Pact of 1933,[7] the Laval–Hoare
Plan of 1935,[8] and the British policy of appeasement, to culminate in the
Munich Conference of 1938. None the less, the solidarity of the Great
Powers was never more than the thin casing of an explosive bomb. Their
consciousness of a common interest became most acute in international
crises as a symptom of rising conflict between their private interests, a
spasm of contraction before the flight from unity. 15 March 1939 marked
the point at which the pretence of common interest between the two
coalitions of Great Powers was finally abandoned and the conflict of
private interests was recognized as insuperable.[9]

The Great Powers now fell into three divisions: the Western Powers,

First World War (*Survey* for 1933, pp. 398, 417. It was also to be the last declaration of war before
the British declaration of war on Germany on 3 September 1939). The Anatolian War of 1919–
23 (*H.P.C.* vi. 25–26, 31–39, 44–48, 104–6), the Russo-Polish War of 1920 (ibid. vi. 318–22),
and the Najdī-Hijāzī War of 1924–5 (*Survey* for 1925, i. 271–308) may be regarded as parts of the
territorial resettlement immediately consequent on the First World War.

[1] *Survey* for 1931, pp. 438 seqq.; *Survey* for 1932, pp. 432–70.
[2] *Survey* for 1935, vol. ii.   [3] *Survey* for 1937, i. 145 seqq.
[4] Ibid. ii. 126 seqq.; *Survey* for 1938, i. 307 seqq.
[5] See Toynbee: *World after the Peace Conference*, p. 4.
[6] *Survey* for 1920–3, pp. 348–56.   [7] *Survey* for 1933, pp. 206–24.
[8] *Survey* for 1935, ii. 280–311.   [9] Cf. *Survey* for 1937, i. 6–8.

the Anti-Comintern Powers, and Soviet Russia. The Western Powers were the rump of the victorious alliance of the First World War; the phrase meant primarily Britain and France. These were the two senior nation-states of Western Christendom, whose rivalry had long determined European politics, until both alike were threatened in the nineteenth century by the ascendancy of newcomers to the Western power-system, Russia and Prussia, who lacked or rejected the traditions of Western Civilization.[1] The United States of America was grouped with them by a more tenuous historical association and by a community of political ideals.[2] But their common ideals had not precluded mutual conflicts in the past,[3] and it could not be said that if the three Western Powers had been the only Great Powers in the world the danger of war would have been abolished. What made the Western Powers conscious of their common ideals in 1939 was consciousness of their common interests. The principal victors of the First World War, they supported, with whatever varieties of emphasis and

[1] The rivalry of the French and English Crowns dated from the accession to the English throne in 1154 of a French feudatory who was Duke of Normandy, Count of Anjou, and husband to the heiress of Aquitaine. In the Hundred Years War of 1337–1451 dynastic rivalry became confirmed by the formation of national consciousness on either side, and the Anglo-French conflict replaced the Papal-Imperial conflict as the central issue of Western politics. In the sixteenth and seventeenth centuries the Anglo-French conflict was interrupted by the ascendancy of the Spanish Power, between approximately the Treaty of Amiens of 1527, which was the first Anglo-French alliance against Spain, and the Treaty of Dover of 1670, which was the last English alliance with a France that had already replaced Spain as dominant European Power. The traditional Anglo-French hostility was resumed with the adhesion of England to the Grand Alliance against Louis XIV by the Treaty of Vienna in 1689, and lasted down to the final defeat of Napoleon in 1815. From then on France and Britain found themselves increasingly drawn into co-operation—in the nineteenth century against the preponderance of Russia, so that they became allies for the first time since the Franco-Anglo-Dutch War of 1670–4 in the Crimean War of 1854–6, and in the twentieth century against the preponderance of Germany.

[2] In American history Britain was the traditional enemy. The American states fought Britain for their independence in the War of 1775–83; as the United States they fought her again in 1812; and on at least three subsequent occasions war between the two Powers was possible— during the Oregon controversy of 1845–6, during the American Civil War in the Mason and Slidell dispute of 1861 and the Laird rams dispute of 1863, and in the Venezuela dispute of 1895. The unbroken tradition of diplomatic co-operation between Britain and the United States dated only from Britain's tacit support of American interests in the Spanish-American War of 1898. With France, however, the American states formed in 1778 the one 'entangling alliance' of their history; and though there was a breach of diplomatic relations and a *de facto* state of war between the two Powers from 1798 to 1800, and France violated the Monroe Doctrine by intervening in Mexico in 1862–6, nevertheless the United States and France continued to regard one another as traditional friends. The sentiment was symbolized by the Statue of Liberty in New York harbour, which was presented to the United States in 1884 by the French people, and whose new flood-lighting system, consisting of ninety-six 1,000-watt lamps flashing upwards on the monument and fourteen 1,000-watt lamps in the torch of the Statue itself, was inaugurated on 26 October 1931 by Mademoiselle José Laval, daughter and companion of the French Premier on his visit to President Hoover (*Survey* for 1931, pp. 124–5), by pressing a button on the top of the Empire State Building.

[3] And their mutual conflicts had modified their common ideals, as when in the nineteenth century Britain built her second empire in accordance with the lessons of the American Revolution, and adapted her political system to the democracy of the French Revolution.

irresponsibility between themselves, the division of international power that had resulted from the war and the international system based thereon. This, in the last analysis, separated them from the Powers which rejected those international arrangements.

Nevertheless, there were serious divergences of opinion both within and between the Western Powers, whether or not their vital interests were indeed the same. There was a very uneven distribution of power between the three states, and it was characteristic of democratic politics in that period that power varied inversely with acceptance of responsibility for maintaining the international system from which all three benefited. France probably had the clearest understanding of enlightened self-interest in foreign relations, but she was the weakest in resources and geographically the most vulnerable, with the least chance among the three of taking a lead. Britain was the middle term. She had greater resources of strength than France, though she had now yielded the world-predominance of the past two centuries to the United States; she was a member of the League like France, but was trying as far as possible to limit her commitments on the European continent. But since the German remilitarization of the Rhineland France and Britain had walked in step, and the British guarantee of assistance to France of 9 March 1936 was final explicit recognition that the European vital interests of the two Powers were identical.[1] The United States was incomparably the strongest and most impregnable of the Western Powers, but after the First World War she had dissociated herself from them and withdrawn into isolation, repudiating all political commitments outside the American continent and its Pacific outliers. This made it impossible for Britain and France to count upon her support, and easy for their less percipient enemies to suppose that they would not enjoy it.[2] British statesmen assumed after the First World War that henceforward British policy was conditioned by American policy, at least in issues of peace and war,[3] but they could not assume that American statesmen were

[1] *Survey* for 1936, p. 275. The evasion by France of her treaty obligations to Czechoslovakia in September 1938 showed that in defining Anglo-French vital interests in Europe the stronger partner would have a preponderant voice, and that the definition would be in minimum rather than maximum terms.

[2] For Hitler's belief in the decadence and imminent collapse of the United States, and in the impossibility of a new American intervention in Europe, see Rauschning: *Hitler Speaks*, pp. 14, 34, 72, 78–79. As late as 23 November 1939 Hitler could write off the United States as a potential factor in the anti-German coalition: 'America is still not dangerous to us because of its neutrality laws. The strengthening of our opponents by America is still not important', conference with his supreme commanders, 23 November 1939 (*I.M.T. Nuremberg*, xxvi. 331–2 (789–PS); *N.C.A.* iii. 576). The Italian Government had a clearer understanding of American politics, and Mussolini saw that the coming war would mean a third term for Roosevelt (conference between Hitler and Ciano, 12 August 1939 (*I.M.T. Nuremberg*, xxix. 49 (1871–PS); *N.C.A.* iv. 514–15; *Documents* (R.I.I.A.) for 1939–46, i. 178. Cf. *N.C.A.* viii. 523 (077–TC)).

[3] The dependence of British upon American policy was illustrated by Baldwin's declaration on 23 November 1935 that 'so long as I have any responsibility in a Government for deciding whether or not this country shall join in a collective peace system, I will say this: never as an

making the same assumption on their side. A Power may conclude that its policy is dependent on the policy of a friendly Power with which it possesses no alliance, but it cannot infer that the other Power's policy is based on the reciprocal principle, least of all when the other Power is the stronger and has the greater apparent freedom of action. In the spring of 1939 there was perhaps, among the politicians of the Western Powers, only a single man who could see that the safety of the Rhine frontier was a vital interest of the United States as well as of Britain and France—Franklin Roosevelt. And he was certainly the only man who, for all the limitations imposed by the public opinion of his countrymen, was in a position to say it.[1]

In opposition to the Western Powers stood the three Powers of the Anti-Comintern Pact.[2] Germany was the loser of the First World War. Italy and Japan, the weakest and least satisfied of the victors, had gone over to the malcontents' camp. Banded together by dissatisfaction and greed, the three might appear in Western eyes to be a fortuitous confederacy of aggressor states. But their partnership, no less than that of the Western Powers, was an expression of historical forces. Germany and Italy had much in common. They were the newest and most politically retarded of the European Great Powers.[3] The recentness of their national

individual will I sanction the British Navy being used for an armed blockade of any country in the world until I know what the United States of America is going to do' (quoted in the *Survey* for 1935, ii. 50). The limits to that dependence were illustrated by Chamberlain's rejection of Roosevelt's offer in January 1938 to initiate conversations with the European Powers with the purpose of finding a general settlement (Churchill: *Second World War*, i. 196–9). Cf. above, pp. 38–40.

[1] He said it in his conference with the Senate Military Affairs Committee on 31 January 1939 (*Survey* for 1938, i. 632–3, and Joseph Alsop and Robert Kintner: *American White Paper* (London, Joseph, 1940), pp. 46–48).

[2] The various treaty engagements between the Anti-Comintern Powers were as follows: (1) *The Axis.* A limited German-Italian agreement was announced on 25 October 1936, and followed by Mussolini's speech at Milan on 1 November 1936 proclaiming the existence of the Axis (*Survey* for 1936, pp. 581–2). The German-Italian military alliance known as the Pact of Steel was signed in Berlin on 22 May 1939: this was a general offensive alliance (*Documents* (R.I.I.A.) for 1939–46, i. 68). (2) *The Anti-Comintern Pact.* The German-Japanese Agreement against the Third International was signed in Berlin on 25 November 1936 (*Survey* for 1936, p. 384). Italy adhered, with the status of an original signatory, on 6 November 1937 (*Survey* for 1937, i. 43). Manchukuo adhered on 16 January 1939, Hungary on 24 February 1939, Spain on 27 March 1939. At the Anti-Comintern Conference in Berlin on 25 November 1941, those Powers renewed their adherence, and the following adhered for the first time: Bulgaria, Croatia, Denmark, Finland, Nanking (Wang Ching-wei), Rumania, Slovakia. (3) *The Tripartite Pact.* This was a ten-year pact of mutual assistance signed by Germany, Italy, and Japan at Berlin on 27 September 1940: it provided for mutual co-operation in establishing a new world order (*I.M.T. Nuremberg*, xxxi. 55–57; *N.C.A.* v. 355–7). Hungary adhered on 20 November 1940, Rumania on 23 November 1940, Slovakia on 24 November 1940, Bulgaria on 1 March 1941, Yugoslavia on 25 March 1941, Croatia on 15 June 1941. The Tripartite Pact as between Germany, Italy, and Japan was automatically transformed into a full military alliance on the United States' entry into the Second World War.

[3] Prussia became a Great Power with the conquest of Silesia in 1740 and its successful retention through the ensuing War of the Austrian Succession, though she did not enlarge herself into

unity, moreover, and the mutual dislike and contempt of Italians and Germans, might tend to obscure the antiquity of a German-Italian association, which went back for twelve centuries to a period before an English or French state existed.[1] It was appropriate that the Nazi appeal to the traditions of the Ottonian Empire should be accompanied by an alliance between Germany and the country whose possession first gave the German kings the imperial title.[2] And as Germany and Italy were the newest of the European Great Powers, Japan was the newest of all the Great Powers, and the only non-Western state (apart from Russia) that had yet attained that diplomatic rank.[3] The envy and admiration felt by Germany and Italy for their more mature, wealthy, successful, and civilized fellow members of Western Civilization was felt by Japan towards Western Civilization as a whole. The community which Germany and Italy resented from within, as its most backward and unfortunate children, Japan resented from without as its most precocious apprentice. Thus the three

a national German Great Power until the establishment of the North German Confederation in 1866. United Italy was formally recognized as a Great Power by her invitation to the London Conference on the Luxembourg question in 1867.

[1] The political dependence of Italy upon a transalpine Germanic Power began when the Frankish King Pepin III was recognized as overlord of the Lombard kingdom in 755. In 774 his son Charlemagne annexed the Lombard kingdom and assumed its crown, which proved a prelude to his assumption of the imperial title; in 780 he set up a subordinate *Regnum Italicum*, rather larger than the old Lombard kingdom, on behalf of a son. Otto the Great, king of the Germans, conquered Italy in 951 and assumed the title of king of Italy as a step towards reviving the imperial title. His successors down to the thirteenth century ruled Germany, Burgundy, and Italy, and the title 'the Empire' became the official designation for this complex of lands (see G. Barraclough: *The Mediaeval Empire: Idea and Reality* (London, Philip, Historical Association publications, General Series G17, 1950), p. 16); the kingship of Italy was thus merged in the imperial dignity. The last Emperor to wield effective authority in either sphere was Frederick II Hohenstaufen, and Italy became separated from Germany when Charles IV in 1346 agreed to the virtual abandonment of imperial claims in Italy as the price of papal support for his election. The Italian ascendancy of Charles V (who was the last Emperor, except for Napoleon, to receive the iron crown of the Lombards) was the expression not of German but of Spanish power. But with the partition of the Spanish Monarchy at the Peace of Utrecht in 1713 Italy passed under the domination of the Austrian Habsburgs; and against the Austrian Habsburgs the common interest of national unification brought Prussia and United Italy into alliance in 1866. 'Italy has often revolted against German rule; and Germany has often resented Italy's cultural leadership. The Habsburg monarchy was for long the hyphen between the two; and in the perspective of history the Axis appears as the partition of the Habsburg monarchy by the two revolutionary nations of 1848' (A. J. P. Taylor in *Manchester Guardian*, 3 May 1949).

[2] It reflected the difference in strength and vigour between the two régimes that Nazi political archaism was in terms of the early history of Western Civilization; Fascist political archaism was in terms of a dead civilization, of a balance of historical forces that was remote and irrecoverable. Mussolini's Roman imperialism was the most vapid and pretentious of the political ghosts that have haunted Italian history in medieval and modern times, the successor to the Roman senate of Arnold of Brescia and the tribunate of Rienzi. It could not be logical and claim the Rhine and Danube frontier; but the German front in Italy in 1943–4 was a transient reappearance of the wavering and contracting frontier of the medieval *Regnum Italicum*.

[3] Japan became recognized as a Great Power through her defeat of Russia in the Russo-Japanese War of 1904–5.

Powers found an ideological affinity in repudiating the Western tradition and embracing a fanatical authoritarian nationalism.

But between the Powers of the Anti-Comintern Pact, as between the Western Powers, it was common international interests that provided the essential link. They were the proletarian nations.[1] Their declared aim was to renovate the world: 'to establish and maintain a new order of things'.[2] This meant territorial redistribution. 'We must not make a purely defensive alliance. There would be no need of one, since no one is thinking of attacking the totalitarian States. Instead we wish to make an alliance in order to change the map of the world.'[3] But the partnership of the Anti-Comintern Powers was inherently limited to a combine of aggression. Their common interest was purely predatory, their common ideology was the assertion of incompatible national egoisms.[4] They had no loyalty to a common tradition, and rejected the conceptions of political morality which mitigated the unequal distribution of strength between the Western Powers. The mutual relations of the Anti-Comintern Powers were implicitly those of naked force. The alliance between Germany and Italy was only possible because there was no question which was lion and which was jackal, and while it sometimes seemed that the co-operation of Germany and Japan was hampered by their geographical remoteness, it was in fact the condition of their effective partnership that they were separated by the whole length of the Soviet Union and of the British sphere of influence in the Indian Ocean.[5]

The seventh Great Power, the Soviet Union, stood apart from these groups. It was the greatest victim of the First World War. The peace that had been imposed upon it by Germany at Brest-Litovsk was incomparably more severe than the peace subsequently imposed upon Germany by the

[1] For Mussolini's use of this expression as early as 1919 see below, p. 517, note 1. Cf. his speech in the Italian Chamber of 3 June 1925: 'We who, without rhetoric, are a nation eminently proletarian' (quoted in the *Survey* for 1927, p. 296, note 5), and his speech at Pontinia on 18 December 1935: 'That war which we have begun on African soil . . . is the war of the poor, of the disinherited, of the proletariat. Against us is ranged the front of conservatism, of selfishness, of hypocrisy' (quoted in the *Survey* for 1935, ii. 312).

[2] Preamble to the Tripartite Pact of 27 September 1940 (*I.M.T. Nuremberg*, xxxi. 56; *N.C.A.* v. 356).

[3] Mussolini to Ribbentrop in Rome, 28 October 1938 (Ciano: *Europa*, p. 378; Eng. version, pp. 245–6).

[4] Cf. *Survey* for 1937, i. 46–47.

[5] See Mussolini's remarks on being told that a German had described him as 'our Gauleiter of Italy', in Ciano: *Diario (1939–43)*, 13 October 1941; cf. affidavit by Halder, 22 November 1945 (*N.C.A.* viii. 644); Rauschning: *Hitler Speaks*, p. 128. 'The aim of our struggle must be to create a unified Europe. The Germans alone can really organize Europe. There is practically no other leading power left. In this connection the Fuehrer re-emphasized how happy we can be that there are no Japanese on the European continent. Even though the Italians today give us many a headache and create difficulties, we must nevertheless consider ourselves lucky that they cannot be serious competitors in the future organization of Europe. If the Japanese were settled on the European continent the situation would be quite different. Today we are practically the only power on the European mainland with a capacity for leadership' (*Goebbels Diaries*, pp. 279–80).

Western Powers, and in the final settlement after the war Russia lost a greater proportion of her territory than any other European state except Hungary. Russia was the first revolutionary nation, repudiating all the traditions of the West, since the French Revolution;[1] and she was the original proletarian nation, feared, despoiled, and segregated by other Powers. Thus there were affinities between Russia and the Anti-Comintern Powers, and it was not inconsistent that as soon as the Anti-Comintern Powers bound themselves together in the Tripartite Pact of 1940 there should be negotiations for the adhesion to that Pact of the Soviet Union.[2] Like the Anti-Comintern Powers, Russia had an ambivalent attitude towards Western Civilization whose earliest convert she was, having entered the comity of nations as a Great Power two centuries before Japan, and a generation before Prussia rose to that rank. Like Italy, Russia had a tradition of political and cultural dependence upon Germany: the Russo-German partnership had always been an uneasy one, but it had been the principal theme of Eastern European history since the passing of the Ottoman ascendancy at the end of the seventeenth century.[3] Heir to the Byzantine tradition, Russian possessed a sense of messianic vocation as world-leader and supplanter of the decadent West; but it was the Western doctrine of Marxism that inspired her political and economic revolution in the twentieth century, paradoxically cutting her off from the West at the same time as it illustrated her involvement in it.

Nevertheless, there were also deep divisions between Russia and the Anti-Comintern Powers. United in their sense of international proletarianism and in their adoption of totalitarian government, they professed

---

[1] '. . . it is permissible to suggest that the deepest significance of the bolshevik revolution will in future be found, not in the changes which it introduced in Russia and elsewhere, but in its successful repudiation of the rule of law among the nations' (H. A. Smith: 'The Anarchy of Power', *Cambridge Journal*, January 1948, p. 215).

[2] See draft agreement between the Powers of the Tripartite Pact and the Soviet Union, prepared during Molotov's visit to Berlin in November 1940 (*Nazi-Soviet Relations*, pp. 255-8). During his conference with Stalin in the Kremlin on the night of 23-24 August 1939, Ribbentrop 'remarked jokingly that Herr Stalin was surely less frightened by the Anti-Comintern Pact than the City of London and the small British merchants. What the German people thought of this matter is evident from a joke which had originated with the Berliners, well known for their wit and humor, and which had been going the rounds for several months, namely, "Stalin will yet join the Anti-Comintern Pact" ' (ibid. p. 75).

[3] 'While in literature, the arts, and fashion France became, until the close of the eighteenth century, the predominant influence or the main intermediary, in other fields German influence was, and remained, more important. This was due to four reasons: the proximity of the German lands, the original partiality of Peter to German ways, the long series of Romanov marriages with the German courts, beginning with Peter's children, and above all the consequences of his acquisition of Livonia and Estonia and his virtual protectorate of Courland, with their predominant German upper class' (Sumner: *Survey of Russian History*, pp. 340-1). Russia and Austria had a common interest in the dismemberment of the Ottoman Empire, though this later developed into rivalry in the Balkans; Russia and Prussia had a common interest in the partitioning of Poland. The earliest Russo-Austrian alliance was in 1697; the earliest Russo-Prussian alliance was in 1762, and this inaugurated an *entente* that lasted virtually unbroken to 1914.

hostile ideologies. The renovation of the world desired by Russia was incomparably more profound than that desired by the Anti-Comintern Powers. They aimed primarily at horizontal conquest, the redistribution of territories that had often been redistributed before; she aimed primarily at vertical conquest, at the extension of her power through an irrevocable social transformation.[1] Besides, their territorial interests conflicted. The inclusion of Russia in the Tripartite Pact was to prove impossible because there cannot be co-operation between expanding Powers of similar strength when their spheres of aggression overlap.[2] The Nazi programme of conquest, moreover, was ultimately directed against Russia. In the modern balance of power Russia and Britain had a certain tradition of co-operation against the strongest Power on the Continent; and since the end of the nineteenth century Russia, France, and Britain had shown a tendency to co-operate against Germany.

The public argument between these three groupings of Great Powers, in the press, over the wireless, and on the platform, giving contradictory interpretations of the crisis in which they were involved, had gone on ever since the Russian Revolution in 1917 and the German defeat in 1918, and with heightened intensity since 1933. The essential affirmations of the controversy might be presented in the form of a conventional three-cornered dialogue, in which the Western Powers sought to justify the maintenance of the existing international system, the Axis Powers asserted the necessity of a redistribution of the world, and the Soviet Union contradicted both by declaring the inevitability and desirability of world revolution.[3]

Western Powers. 'It is true that the present arrangement of the world has some of the characteristics of a hegemony of the Anglo-Saxon and French nations. It is also true that the establishment of their great empires and spheres of interest in the extra-European world was largely brought about by aggressions which, on the whole, few people now seek to defend morally. However, we have now embarked on the endeavour to turn the former anarchy of international relations into a reign of law and order and a reasonable measure of justice, such as has already been achieved on

---

[1] Borkenau has pointed out that Mussolini claimed that the twentieth century would be the century of Fascism, and Hitler claimed that the Third Reich would last a thousand years; but that these claims imply the idea of an end. 'Communism admits of no such idea of an end. It is in no need of statements about duration' (Borkenau: *The Totalitarian Enemy*, p. 233).

[2] *Nazi-Soviet Relations*, pp. 217–59; Beloff, ii. 348–54.

[3] The spokesmen for the Western Powers were Anglo-Saxon rather than French, not only because of the Anglo-Saxon preponderance among the Western Powers, but also because the Anglo-Saxons possessed the combination of moral self-analysis verging upon guilty conscience and of moral self-justification verging upon hypocrisy which carried the Western argument to its deepest levels. Similarly the spokesmen for the Anti-Comintern Powers were the Axis Powers strictly speaking, since it was they rather than Japan who elaborated the Fascist case. Though the controversy was in principle world-wide, in fact it was still a European debate.

the whole in the national life of the more advanced countries of the world today. The League of Nations provides a basis for approximating towards a higher concept of civilization and an unprecedented degree of world co-operation.'

Axis Powers. 'Is it difficult for you to understand that for us the League of Nations is simply part of the Versailles Treaty? that it is an expression of the predominance you achieved at the end of the World War? We suspected from the outset that the League was to be only a coalition of the rich nations against the proletarian nations.[1] And our suspicion has been confirmed by the consistent neglect of that part of the League Covenant which provides for revision of treaties, and the employment of those parts that are concerned with the maintenance of the established order, as in the attempt to strangle Italy by sanctions.'

Western Powers. 'It is true that the League is part of the Versailles Settlement. But we believe that the Versailles Settlement is far from being unjust. You yourselves pay lip-service to the principle of national self-determination. The Versailles Settlement has reorganized Europe on that principle with a much higher degree of honesty, reasonableness, disinterestedness, and success than might have been expected, and certainly in a manner never before attempted by any general European treaty.'[2]

Axis Powers. 'A treaty brutally dictated to the defeated Powers; which severed or excluded more than 10 million Germans from their fatherland; which partitioned Hungary so that a third of the Hungarian nation passed under alien rule. A treaty which ignored or violated the promises made to Italy during the war. A treaty, anyway, which is obsolete. Have you sufficiently recognized the fact that two of us were your allies in the war, but have long ago ceased to accept the authority of the Versailles Settlement? Twenty years have passed since 1919, and you seek, by appealing to age-yellowed archives, to arrest the outward march, the dynamic growth of the young and virile nations. What solution have you to offer

---

[1] This interpretation of the League was put forward by Mussolini in the speech of 23 March 1919 at Milan which marked the birth of Fascism: 'If the League of Nations is to be a solemn "put-up job" in the interests of the rich nations against the proletarian nations for fixing and perpetuating as far as possible the existing balance of world power, let us keep a good eye on it' (*Scritti e discorsi*, i. 374–5). The word here translated as 'put-up job' is *fregata*, which echoes the motto of the Fascist Squadristi *Me ne frego*—an expression of defiance that, conversely, Mussolini commended in his *Enciclopedia* article of 1932 (Oakeshott: *Social and Political Doctrines of Contemporary Europe*, p. 171). For other references by Mussolini to Italy as a proletarian nation, see above, p. 514, note 1.

[2] 'Cannot we recognize that the settlement of 1919 was an immense advance on any similar settlement made in Europe in the past? In broad outline, it represents a peace of reason and justice, and the whole fabric of the continent depends on its maintenance' (Sir James Headlam-Morley: *Studies in Diplomatic History*, p. 185). 'It was a very remarkable treaty. It fulfilled our acknowledged war aims with a degree of perfection that no other European settlement to which we had ever set our hand could equal' (R. B. McCallum: *Public Opinion and the last Peace* (London, Oxford University Press, 1944), p. 22).

to these practical and imperative problems—the desire for reunion of 80 million Germans and their demand for the return of their stolen colonies, the need for expansion of Italy and Japan with their soaring birth-rates and their inadequate resources?'

Soviet Union. 'Neither the Western Powers nor yourselves have the answer to that question, nor the solutions for those problems. They are economic problems which cannot be solved within the limits of the system of production which you all alike exist to maintain. The most important thing about the First World War was not that it produced a new division of the world between the imperialist Powers, for that division (as your argument itself shows) was inherently unstable, and is now being challenged by the Fascist states for the sake of a new division of the world that would not be less unstable. Such is the predatory nature, such is the inner contradiction of imperialism. But during the First World War the imperialist crust was broken at its weakest point by the international revolutionary working-class movement, and there was established in Russia the first proletarian state. From then on there were two camps in the world, a capitalist camp originally led by Britain and America and a socialist camp led by the Soviet Union.[1] If the rise of Fascism has since seemed to confuse this alinement, it is only the supreme example of the conflicts and antagonisms that are generated by capitalism in extreme decay. Fascism is the open terrorist dictatorship established against the rising revolt of the working class by the most aggressive, chauvinist, and reactionary elements of finance-capitalism; and it is at the same time the highest expression of the preparation for a new imperialist war to redivide the spoils of the world. Thus it is that the hopes of all progressive mankind are fixed on the Soviet Union, where Socialism holds power, and the economic system which produces this anarchy of possessors and pursuers has over one-sixth of the earth been for ever transcended.'

Axis Powers. 'We who have had practical experience of the revolutions,

---

[1] 'Two dominant and mutually antagonist poles of attraction have come into existence, so that, the world over, sympathies are diverging towards one pole or the other: the sympathies of the bourgeois governments tending towards the British-American pole, and the sympathies of the workers of the West and of the revolutionists of the East tending towards the Soviet Union pole. Britain-America is attractive in virtue of its wealth, for in this quarter loans are obtainable. The Soviet Union is attractive in virtue of its revolutionary experience, in virtue of the experience gained in the struggle for the liberation of the workers from the yoke of capitalism and for the liberation of the oppressed nations from imperialist oppression. You see why there is a trend of the sympathies of the workers of Europe and of the revolutionists of the East towards our country. You know what a stay in Russia means to a worker from central or western Europe, or to a revolutionist from one of the oppressed countries; you know how such pilgrims come to us in crowds, and you know how keen is the sympathy towards our country felt by trusty revolutionists all over the world' (J. Stalin: Political report of the Central Committee to the Fourteenth Congress of the Communist Party of the Soviet Union, 18 December 1925, in *Leninism* (London, Allen & Unwin, 1938), pp. 369–70, where, however, the date is wrongly given as May 1925).

disturbances, and bloody uprisings produced by Bolshevism in our own countries, and who have successfully undertaken the duty of stamping it out, know best how to answer the pretensions of international Marxism. Whatever its philosophical claims, Bolshevism breeds anarchy. Soviet Russia is the exponent of an international political system which promotes world unrest with the declared aim of world revolution. For the natural and living solidarity of the nation and of the state, Marxism tries to substitute an international solidarity of the proletariat, and pursues that end by disseminating strife, bloodshed, and violence. For spiritual and cultural values, for heroism and leadership, for the creative work of great men and gifted races, it offers the negative and inhuman doctrine of historical materialism, by which men would be only the by-products of economic forces. Thus Marxism is a solvent of all the beliefs and ties we hold most sacred, of our whole human order in state and society. Far from being a higher stage of social development, Communism is the starting-point, the most primitive form of existence: it means a retrogression in every aspect of culture and the subversion of our faith, our morals, and our whole conception of civilization.[1] We who understand this are the bulwark of European discipline and civilization against the enemy of mankind, and by taking upon ourselves the struggle against Bolshevism we are undertaking a truly European mission, which sooner or later the Western Powers will be compelled to recognize.'

Western Powers. 'We must say that your talk of the menace of Bolshevism and your crusade against it seem to us to be disingenuous. We were ready to believe in the danger of Communism until your immoderate insistence on it (together with your other activities) made us begin to think that we might be faced by more immediate dangers. We suspect that the Anti-Comintern Pact may be a good piece of propaganda, serving to conceal your designs against us. From our point of view the similarities between yourselves and Russia are not less striking than the contrasts. You and she are all alike totalitarian states, copying one another's methods and profiting from one another's existence in a dialectic of interdependent hostility. You are all equally far from democracy as we understand it and value it; and this indeed underlies the lack of confidence we have generally felt about the possibility of successful co-operation with Russia.[2] But, how-

---

[1] 'That a British leader-writer refuses to recognize this signifies about as much as if in the fifteenth century a humanist in Vienna should have refused to admit the intention of Mohammedanism to extend its influence in Europe and should have objected that this would be to tear the world asunder—to divide it into East and West', Hitler, speech at Nuremberg, 14 September 1936 (*Speeches* (Baynes), i. 675–6).

[2] 'I must confess to the most profound distrust of Russia. I have no belief whatever in her ability to maintain an effective offensive, even if she wanted to. And I distrust her motives, which seem to me to have little connection with our ideas of liberty, and to be concerned only with getting every one else by the ears. Moreover, she is both hated and suspected by many of the smaller States, notably by Poland, Roumania, and Finland', Chamberlain, letter to his sister of

ever that may be, we do not think it useful to enter into argument about the ideological interpretation of our international tensions.[1] Our approach is empirical, and we have been hoping to build a law-abiding society in which we could all make our contribution to the common good of mankind according to our several lights. That is why our immediate controversy is with you, the Axis Powers. We are ready to admit considerable truth in what you have said about your economic problems, and latterly in particular we have gone far to meet you. We are ready to discuss the revision of treaties and the redistribution of the resources of the globe —or at least, the question of your easier access to them. But it is impossible to start discussions unless you honestly accept the principle of negotiation and repudiate the principle of force. So long as we live in expectation of acts of aggression and *faits accomplis* from you there can be no confidence between us, and it is impossible for the normal machinery of diplomatic intercourse to be effective. It is our view that the system of international law and order which we now possess, based on the Versailles Settlement and inadequate in many respects as it is, is as precious as it is fragile, and that to respect it and seek its gradual modification is a much surer road towards justice than are acts of violence which endanger our common interests and destroy the foundations of orderliness upon which alone justice can be built.'[2]

Axis Powers. 'But it has been our experience that we have never obtained what we believe to be justice by the normal machinery of diplomatic intercourse, as you call it, by conferences, in a word by waiting for you. We have obtained it by the process of being strong enough to take it for ourselves. (Sometimes you have then called conferences to pronounce a verbal condemnation of our act, which has satisfied you without bothering us; of recent years, however, as we have grown stronger, you have shown greater readiness to excuse and condone our acts—a development that we welcome.) And we believe that this procedure, of relying upon our own strength to defend our interests, is as a matter of fact far more normal than what you call "the normal machinery of diplomatic intercourse".

26 March 1939 (Feiling: *Chamberlain*, p. 403). 'I can't believe that she had the same aims and objects as we have, or any sympathy with democracy as such. She is afraid of Germany and Japan, and would be delighted to see other people fight them' (ibid. p. 408).

[1] 'Let us . . . win an ever larger body of opinion to reject those dangerous doctrines which would have us divide the world into dictatorship of the Right and Left. This country will have none of either. Nor will it align its foreign policy with any group of states because they support the one or the other', Eden, speech at Bradford, 14 December 1936 (quoted in the *Survey* for 1937, ii. 159).

[2] 'The first task of government is to create order by preponderant power. The second task is to create justice' (Reinhold Niebuhr: *Discerning the Signs of the Times* (London, S.C.M., 1946), p. 46. Cf. the same author's *The Children of Light and the Children of Darkness* (London, Nisbet, 1945), p. 123; J. L. Brierly: *The Outlook for International Law* (Oxford, Clarendon Press, 1944), pp. 73–74; Sir Alfred Zimmern: *Spiritual Values and World Affairs* (Oxford, Clarendon Press, 1939), pp. 112–13).

Indeed we have the feeling that throughout this argument we are talking about *facts*, about the forces that govern history and make the real stuff of politics, while you are talking about *theories*, about legal abstractions and moral utopias. We are realists, and perhaps we understand the nature of international relations more clearly than you do.[1] Man's existence is subject to the law of eternal struggle; men, by a natural law, always rule where they are stronger. We have not made this law, nor are we the first to act on it;[2] we see it existing, and you yourselves have supplied the precedent. You cannot expect to arrest the process of history at the point at which you happen to be on top; at least you cannot expect less favoured nations to share your hope. It is plain to us that liberal democracy is exhausted and decadent, and that all the vital movements of the present century are anti-liberal.[3] We believe that the process by which you— English, French, and Americans alike—built your empires at the expense of the Spanish world-empire or of the Habsburg Monarchy in Europe is likely to be repeated in the present century in favour of new and dynamic Powers like ourselves. The only question that remains is whether you are ready to co-operate with the onward march of history, in which case we shall be ready to give consideration to your legitimate interests, or whether, by a selfish and useless obstruction, you will bring about a head-on collision between us which we should be glad to avoid.'

Soviet Union. 'When you identify "the process of history" with the sterile struggles of imperialism, it becomes necessary once again to assert a secure and scientific interpretation of that process. It is true that

---

[1] This was a theme of Mussolini's first speech in the Chamber on foreign policy, on 16 February 1923: 'I see the world as it actually is: that is, a world of unchained egoisms. If the world was a shining Arcadia, it would perhaps be nice to frisk among nymphs and shepherds; but I see nothing of that sort, and moreover when the great banners of the great principles are raised, I see, behind these more or less venerable trappings, interests that are seeking to assert themselves in the world' (*Scritti e discorsi*, iii. 61). For a sophisticated version of this critique of international politics see E. H. Carr: *The Twenty Years' Crisis, 1919–1939* (London, Macmillan, 1939); cf. also 2nd revised edition of 1946.

[2] Thuc. v. 105. It may be noted that this famous phrase which Thucydides puts in the mouth of the Athenian envoys to Melos is probably *more* than the Athenians actually said, an inspired evocation of their principles rather than a record of their words (cf. Werner Jaeger: *Paideia: The Ideals of Greek Culture*, translated from the second German edition by Gilbert Highet, vol. i (Oxford, Blackwell, 1939), pp. 388, 398–9). When attributed to the Axis Powers, on the other hand, it appears a good deal *less*—that is to say much more temperate and more restrained— than the statements which Axis leaders were accustomed to make. The *loci classici* in Fascist writings for the doctrine that politics is nothing but a struggle for power are in Mussolini's *Enciclopedia* article (Oakeshott: *Social and Political Doctrines of Contemporary Europe*, pp. 170–1), and in *Mein Kampf*, pp. 148–9, 267, 317, 386, 571, 769, 773.

[3] '. . . all the political experiences of the contemporary world are anti-Liberal, and it is supremely ridiculous to wish on that account to class them outside of history; as if history were a hunting ground reserved to Liberalism and its professors, as if Liberalism were the definitive and no longer surpassable message of civilisation . . . It is to be expected that this century may be that of authority, a century of the "Right", a Fascist century', Mussolini's *Enciclopedia* article (Oakeshott, op. cit. pp. 174–5).

the hegemony of the Western Powers is not the culmination of history: it represents only the highest stage capable of being reached by the bourgeois order. The disruption of that order is historically inevitable, because it breaks on its own contradictions and because out of those very contradictions the forces of the future grow in strength. But Fascism, aggressive socially as well as internationally, and seeking to reduce the working class, above all in Russia, once again to slavery, follows a policy which can divert the path to the ultimate world socialist organization through an epoch of immense destruction and human suffering. That is why the Soviet Union, which came into existence in the struggle of the working class against the First World War, and whose earliest action was the famous decree calling for immediate peace without annexations and without indemnities,[1] has consistently fought to avert the menace of a new imperialist war. That is why, in these last years, the Soviet Union has entered the League of Nations and put itself at the head of those elements within imperialism which are against immediate war, and thus carries on its historic role in actively leading the struggle for peace of the peoples of all countries.'

Western Powers. 'Though we naturally do not agree with the terms in which you state your case, we acknowledge some degree of force in what you say. Indeed we confess that, in certain moods, the Marxist analysis of recent history has seemed cogent to us, and made us wish to believe that what divides us from you is a disagreement about means rather than an incompatibility of ends.[2] But more important for our immediate purpose, we are happy to recognize that you, like us, are anxious above all for peace. This leads us to hope that, if the Axis Powers insist on pursuing their objectives by other than peaceful means, it may be possible to co-operate with you in the preservation of our common security. For we must make

[1] Decree of Peace, 8 November 1917 (*Soviet Documents on Foreign Policy*, selected and edited by Jane Degras (London, Oxford University Press for Royal Institute of International Affairs, 1951), i. 1–3).

[2] 'Ma conviction d'aujourd'hui n'est-elle pas du reste comparable à la *foi* . . . Simplement mon être est tendu vers un souhait, vers un but. Toutes mes pensées, même involontairement, s'y ramènent. Dans l'abominable détresse du monde actuel, le plan de la nouvelle Russie me paraît aujourd'hui le salut. Il n'est rien qui ne m'en persuade! Les arguments misérables de ses ennemis, loin de me convaincre, m'indignent. Et, s'il fallait ma vie pour assurer le succès de l'U.R.S.S., je la donnerais aussitôt . . . comme ont fait, comme feront tant d'autres, et me confondant avec eux' (André Gide: *Journal*, 23 avril 1932 (Paris, N.R.F., Bibliothèque de la Pléiade, 1940), p. 1126). 'I am not a Communist, though perhaps I might be one if I was a younger and braver man, for in Communism I can see hope. It does many things which I think evil, but I know that it intends good' (E. M. Forster: address delivered at the Congrès International des Écrivains at Paris, 21 June 1935, in *Abinger Harvest* (London, Arnold, pocket edition, 1940), p. 63; cf. pp. 73–74). 'I speak as one who came slowly, even painfully, to Marxism from the Fabian tradition. I accepted Marx as the central clue because without his methods the events of the post-war years, especially since 1933, became a maze without a central clue. With Marx, especially as seen through the eyes of Lenin, that maze becomes an intelligible pattern. More; with Marx, one gains the power of prediction which it is essential for the socialist to have if he is to be able to control the destiny of the movement' (H. J. Laski's review of John Strachey's *Theory and Practice of Socialism* in *Left Book News*, November 1936).

one thing clear to the Axis Powers without more ado: that if their final appeal is to force, we shall meet them with force. It is true that, since 1914, aversion to war as a means of policy has become one of our accepted principles; and so great indeed is our reluctance to consider it that sometimes optimism may have swayed our judgement, and encouraged us to speak as if we did not think war possible.[1] If this be an illusion (and that will be shown by what you, the Axis Powers, decide to do) it may be creditable to our hearts rather than our heads, but we cannot think it dishonourable. Nevertheless, do not be mistaken. In the last analysis you will find us

---

[1] See speech by Sir Samuel Hoare (then Home Secretary) at the annual meeting of the Chelsea Conservative Association, 10 March 1939: 'Since the beginning of the year, he said, there had been a notable change in public opinion. Confidence, almost suffocated in the late autumn by defeatism, had returned, hope had taken the place of fear, moral and physical robustness had overcome hysteria and hesitation. . . . Suppose that political confidence could be restored to Europe, suppose that there was a five-year plan, immensely greater than any five-year plan that this or that particular country had attempted in recent times, and that for a space of five years there were neither wars nor rumours of wars; suppose that the peoples of Europe were able to free themselves from a nightmare that haunted them and from an expenditure upon armaments that beggared them, could they not then devote the almost incredible inventions and discoveries of the time to the creation of a golden age in which poverty could be reduced to insignificance and the standard of living raised to heights never before attained? "Here, indeed, is the greatest opportunity that has ever been offered to the leaders of the world. Five men in Europe, the three dictators and the Prime Ministers of England and France, if they worked with a singleness of purpose and a unity of action to this end, might in an incredibly short space of time transform the whole history of the world. These five men working together in Europe, and blessed in their efforts by the President of the U.S.A., might make themselves the eternal benefactors of the human race. Our own Prime Minister has shown his determination to work heart and soul to such an end. I cannot believe that the other leaders of Europe will not join him in the high endeavour upon which he is engaged"' (The Times, 11 March 1939; cf. Wheeler-Bennett: Munich, pp. 328–30).

' "No one can foretell what may happen", Borah said, interrupting Hull. "But my feeling and belief is that we are not going to have a war. Germany isn't ready for it." "I wish the Senator would come down to my office and read the cables", Hull answered, with a sort of sad patience. "I'm sure he would come to the conclusion that there's far more danger of war than he thinks." "So far as the reports in your Department are concerned, I wouldn't be bound by them", countered Borah firmly. "I have my own sources of information which I have provided for myself, and on several occasions I've found them more reliable than the State Department" ' (Alsop and Kintner: American White Paper, pp. 63–64, relating the conference on the revision of the Neutrality Law between Roosevelt, Hull, and leaders of the Senate on 18 July 1939; cf. New York Times, 20 July 1939).

The London newspaper which congratulated itself on the world's largest daily sale had on 19 October 1938 carried the following headline on its front page: 'The Daily Express declares that Britain will not be involved in a European war this year or next year either' (cf. the issues for 14 and 17 October). On 2 January 1939 it contained a New Year's article by George Malcolm Thomson, beginning thus: 'There will be no great war in Europe in 1939. There is nothing in our present situation which affords any ground to suppose that an upheaval will, or must, come. Nothing is here today that we have not experienced over and over again in our history—at moments when we stood on the threshold of an era of peace.' After the German seizure of Prague, the oracle became more mysterious. On 20 March 1939 there was a box on the front page declaring: 'No War Now', and the leading article said: 'We believe that there will not be any further manœuvres in Europe likely to involve us in an armed conflict.' On 23 March there was a front-page box saying: 'Peace through Strength. The Daily Express declares that there will be no European war now.' This was inexplicit enough to be proved correct.

defending our interests and fulfilling our obligations as stubbornly as yourselves. We feel it necessary to say this so that you may make no mistake
about it.'

Axis Powers. 'We are glad to have an admission from your own mouths
of your Marxist foible. We have always thought that the decadence of
liberal democracy was in nothing more clearly shown than in its inherent
drift towards Communism. As for your declarations of contingent defiance,
they are the common form of diplomacy, and we shall know what value
to give them. We have noted that as our power has increased your resolution appears to have faltered; and it has been natural for us to entertain
the idea that you may after all be prepared to acquiesce in the establishment of a more just order in the world.'

Western Powers. 'You are making another mistake, more far-reaching
than the first, if you assume that our readiness in recent years to go to such
lengths to seek an accommodation with you has been altogether inspired
by material weakness. It is at this point, thanks to the frankness with
which you have been speaking, that our fundamental differences are laid
bare. You spoke just now as if the forces which you claim to represent
are the only "facts" in history; but we believe that morality and the conscience of mankind are equally facts that must be taken into account. We
believe that civilization consists, not in the mere assertion of vitality,
impulse, and will, but in their control; not in the exhibition and accumulation of force, but in disciplining it to serve settled habits of persuasion
and law, and so reducing as far as possible the need for its use.[1] Thus our
dealings with you in these two decades have been grounded upon the
premiss that another war would be an immeasurable disaster for all of us,
and that the test of civilization is its ability to avert such a catastrophe.'[2]

Soviet Union. 'The point at which you say "your fundamental differences are laid bare" appears, in an objective view, to be the point at which

---

[1] 'Civilisation is nothing else than the attempt to reduce force to being the *ultima ratio*' (Ortega
y Gasset: *The Revolt of the Masses*, p. 82). 'Anyone can be a barbarian; it requires a terrible
effort to be or remain a civilized man. Civilization, in one of its most important aspects, is
a method of regulating the relations between the individual and his fellow-men, between individuals and the community. The control or sublimation of instincts is always an essential part
of it, and the more complicated the life of a community or the more "advanced" the civilization,
the more complicated, incessant and severe becomes the control of instincts which is demanded
from the individual. The immediate satisfaction of the simple and primitive instincts is characteristic of those forms of society which are the antithesis of civilization and which we may call
barbarism' (Leonard Woolf: *Barbarians at the Gate* (London, Gollancz, 1939), p. 83). These
quotations echo the famous definition of Baudelaire, 'Théorie de la vraie civilisation. Elle n'est
pas dans le gaz, ni dans le vapeur, ni dans les tables tournantes. Elle est dans la diminution des
traces du péché originel' (*Journaux intimes*, lxxxi).

[2] 'It is a true saying that to keep this country at peace is a great contribution to the peace of
Europe, and whatever may be said about "Peace at any price", if the right honourable gentleman
[Lloyd George] puts it "Peace at almost any price", I shall scarcely quarrel with him', Eden in
the House of Commons, 25 June 1937, H.C.Deb. 5th ser., vol. 325, col. 1614 (quoted in the
Survey for 1937, i. 50 and ii. 152, note 2).

your fundamental similarities to the Fascist states are revealed. Your sentiments are formally irreproachable; it is when they are compared with your practice that their value becomes apparent. Your readiness to seek an accommodation with the Fascist Powers, your efforts to avoid another war, have been entirely at the expense of other states, not of your own interests. Your policy of non-intervention has sacrificed to the aggressors successively China, Abyssinia, Spain, Austria, and now Czechoslovakia. The Soviet Union has reason to know this, since it alone has striven to enforce the policy of collective security on which you congratulate yourselves. During the Italo-Ethiopian War it was only the Soviet Union who took a firm and honest stand against imperialist aggression; since then only the Soviet Union has striven to obtain collective action against German aggressions. You have abandoned the policy of collective security for a policy of non-intervention, whereby you seek only to defend yourselves, and make no discrimination between the aggressors and their victims. It is not for the Soviet Union to moralize upon this, for the policy of non-intervention simply shows that in practice bourgeois politicians acknowledge no human morality at all. It is only necessary to point out that such a policy of cynical self-interest, while it is all that can be expected from bourgeois states, is based upon a fundamental miscalculation and will inevitably accelerate the imperialist war which it pretends to avert.'

Axis Powers. 'We have no concern with this quarrel between the supporters of the Geneva institution, except that it confirms our belief in the Geneva institution's futility. But we decisively repudiate the assumption which underlies the arguments of the Western Powers, that they are still as ever the guardians and interpreters of civilization. This conscious assumption of effortless superiority is all the more offensive in that it has become obsolete and hypocritical.[1] You who remind us of the sanctity of international obligations broke your assurances to Germany after the Armistice of 1918. You who exhort us to settle international problems by peaceful discussion have solved no decisive international problem in that way through the League of Nations, and the greatest of you has refused to join the League. You who condemn our struggle for living space (a struggle which in the European field has been successfully carried on without resort to arms) possess vast empty territories, with illimitable fertility and mineral resources, and a density of population that is inconsiderable

---

[1] 'There is only one thing that we want and that applies particularly to our relations with England. It would be a good thing if in Great Britain people would gradually drop certain airs which they have inherited from the Versailles epoch. We cannot tolerate any longer the tutelage of governesses!', Hitler, speech at Saarbrücken, 9 October 1938 (*Speeches* (Baynes), ii. 1536). 'The Western Democracies were dominated by the desire to rule the world and would not regard Germany and Italy as in their class. This psychological element of contempt was perhaps the worst thing about the whole business', conversation between Hitler and Ciano, 13 August 1939 (*I.M.T. Nuremberg*, iii. 230; cf. *N.C.A.* viii. 527 (077–TC); *Documents* (R.I.I.A.) 1939–46, i. 183).

compared with ours. You who attribute all the unrest in the world to us ignore your own continuing record of violence, bloodshed, and oppression in Ireland, Egypt, Palestine, Syria, India, and Latin America.'

Western Powers. 'It is the weakness of open diplomacy, which we invented and you have perverted,[1] that it reduces diplomatic intercourse to a competition of simultaneous gramophone programmes in unrelated languages. We have honestly sought to give weight to your views and to meet your reasonable demands, but our divided conscience about the lengths to which we have gone is likely in the long run to be forgotten and overlaid by anger at the realization that you have made no attempt to meet us.'

Soviet Union. 'You are wrong: open diplomacy was inaugurated not by Wilson but by the Soviet Government, with the publication of the imperialist secret treaties immediately after the October Revolution.[2] But the forms of diplomacy are less important than the forces of politics, and understanding is to be inferred from facts rather than from arguments. Why have the Western Powers abandoned their professions of collective security and adopted a policy of non-intervention? Because in the last resort all capitalist states, whether aggressive or non-aggressive, have a common fear of the working-class movement throughout the world, and a common hostility to the U.S.S.R. From the first establishment of Mussolini in Italy and of Hitler in Germany the governments of the Western states have consistently courted Fascism, for the governments of the Western states represent the same social forces which in Italy and Germany brought Fascism into being. Thus the first diplomatic repercussion of the Nazi Revolution in Germany was the project for a Four-Power Pact of Italy, Germany, France, and England, which by excluding the Soviet Union was implicitly directed against her. Since then the Western policy of non-intervention has in fact been a policy of conniving at and encouraging aggression. Behind the readiness of the Western Powers to sacrifice

---

[1] 'I certainly believe that it is not feasible to make such a statement to the head of any foreign State, but rather that such statements should preferably be made to the whole world, in accordance with the demand made at the time by President Wilson for the abolition of secret diplomacy. Hitherto I was not only always prepared to do this, but, as I have already said, I have done it only too often', Hitler, Reichstag speech of 28 April 1939 (*Speeches* (Baynes), ii. 1646; cf. p. 1316).

[2] 'The Government abolishes secret diplomacy and on its part expresses the firm intention to conduct all negotiations absolutely openly before the entire people; it will at once begin to publish in full the secret treaties concluded or confirmed by the Government of landowners and capitalists from February to 25 October [7 November] 1917', Decree of Peace, 8 November 1917 (Degras: *Soviet Documents on Foreign Policy*, i. 2). 'The Russian representatives [at Brest-Litovsk] have insisted very justly, very wisely, and in the true spirit of modern democracy, that the conferences they have been holding with Teutonic and Turkish statesmen should be held within open, not closed, doors, and all the world has been audience, as was desired', Wilson, Fourteen Points speech of 8 January 1918 (*H.P.C.* i. 432). Cf. Potemkin: *Histoire de la diplomatie*, ii. 326, 391.

small and weak states to the greed of the Fascist Powers lies the hope of
directing the Fascist Powers against the U.S.S.R. The policy of the Four-
Power Pact and the policy of non-intervention together culminated in the
Munich Conference, when the four European capitalist Powers met together, to arrange the partition of Czechoslovakia and again deliberately
excluded the Soviet Union.[1] The lesson of these facts is inescapable. The
Soviet Union is well able to draw the lesson and to defend its own interests,
which are the interests of humanity at large, by every means that the
current diplomatic and political situation may offer.'[2]

This was the state of the argument between the Great Powers on
15 March 1939. At that time the balance of power appeared extremely
fluid owing to the imbecility of Western policy, the arbitrariness and
caprice of German, the inscrutability of Russian. Great Power relation-

[1] 'The plans for a Western grouping against the U.S.S.R. had perhaps never been nearer
fruition than they were at Munich. And in the ten or eleven months which followed Munich
Mr. Chamberlain and his immediate entourage must have regarded both the aggressive activities
of Hitler and the pressure of his own public opinion, which forced him into the negotiations
with the U.S.S.R. . . . right up to the signature of the non-aggression pact in August between
Germany and the U.S.S.R. as something quite temporary, and must have believed that once
these difficulties that had arisen between the Munich Allies were smoothed out there would be
the full possibility of armed advance, that is of Hitler's expected advance, into the U.S.S.R.
This would have been an admirable spectacle for Britain and France, a fight between the
capitalist friend they feared and the Socialist enemy they hated' (D. N. Pritt: *Must the War
Spread?* (Harmondsworth, Penguin Books, 1940), p. 61; cf. the same author's *Light on Moscow*
(Harmondsworth, Penguin Books, 1939), pp. 52–53).
'If we see that Germany is winning we ought to help Russia and if Russia is winning we ought
to help Germany and that way let them kill as many as possible, although I don't want to see
Hitler victorious under any circumstances. Neither of them think anything of their pledged word',
Senator Harry Truman of Missouri on 23 June 1941 (*New York Times*, 24 June 1941). 'There
are people in high places who declare that they hope the Russian and German armies will
exterminate each other, and while this is taking place we, the British Commonwealth of Nations,
will so develop our Air Force and other armed forces that, if Russia and Germany do destroy
each other, we shall have the dominating power in Europe. That point of view has been expressed
quite recently by a Cabinet Minister—a member of the present Government—a gentleman who
holds a very important position—none other than the Minister for Aircraft Production,
Colonel Moore-Brabazon' (Jack Tanner, president of the Amalgamated Engineering Union,
at a meeting of the Trades Union Congress at Edinburgh on 2 September 1941 (*The Times*,
3 September 1941); referring to an extempore speech by Moore-Brabazon at a private meeting
in Manchester on 31 July 1941). These two utterances were quoted by Molotov in his speech
at Moscow on the thirtieth anniversary of the October Revolution, 6 November 1947 (*Moscow
News*, 7 November 1947).
[2] 'We never had any orientation towards Germany, nor have we any orientation towards
Poland and France. Our orientation in the past and our orientation at the present time is
towards the U.S.S.R., and towards the U.S.S.R. alone. And if the interests of the U.S.S.R.
demand *rapprochement* with one country or another which is not interested in disturbing peace,
we take this step without hesitation' (J. Stalin, report to the Seventeenth Congress of the
C.P.S.U.(B), 26 January 1934 in *Problems of Leninism*, p. 467); *Survey* for 1934, p. 384. 'It is our
duty to think of the interests of the Soviet people, the interests of the Union of Soviet Socialist
Republics—all the more because we are firmly convinced that the interests of the U.S.S.R.
coincide with the fundamental interests of the peoples of other countries', Molotov, speech to
the Supreme Soviet, 31 August 1939 (*Soviet Peace Policy*, four speeches by V. Molotov (London,
Lawrence & Wishart, 1941), p. 14).

ships fell into an equilateral triangle; and it was possible for different observers to convince themselves that destiny would be fulfilled by the alliance of the Western Powers with Russia to encircle Germany, or of Russia with Germany to overbalance the Western Powers, or of the Western Powers with the Fascist Powers against the interests of Russia. Each of these combinations had its historical precedents, so that the Germans could point to the Franco-Soviet Pact[1] and to Russian policy as a member of the League of Nations; the Western Powers could point to the German-Soviet alliance originating with the Treaty of Rapallo;[2] the Russians could point to the programme of *Mein Kampf*,[3] the Munich Conference, the Four-Power Pact,[4] the Allied intervention in Russia of 1918–20, and the Allied use of German troops under the armistice of 1918 to prevent a Bolshevik invasion of the Baltic States.[5] Each of these combinations had its arguments from interest. And two of them were to be dramatically fulfilled before three years had passed.

The third combination—the possibility of an alinement of the Western Powers with the Axis at the expense of Russia—was never so substantial as the other two, for its main foundation was Marxist doctrine. There were two determining factors in any calculation of the balance of power. Firstly, the Axis was setting the pace. The Axis alone was expansionist and aggressive; the Western Powers and Russia alike were on the defensive. The most extreme Soviet interpretations of the common purpose of the capitalist imperialist Powers recognized the distinction between the non-aggressive democratic states and the Fascist states,[6] and official Soviet policy, represented by Litvinov at Geneva and Maisky in London, had for five years been based on the assumption of a common interest between the Soviet Union and the non-aggressive democratic states in the preservation of peace.[7] Conversely, the most hostile Western interpretation of Russian policy saw a danger of Communist expansion and the promotion of unrest abroad rather than of Russian territorial aggrandizement.[8] Indeed, it was at that time the characteristic mistake of those who most

[1] *Survey* for 1935, i. 84 seqq.

[2] *Survey* for 1920–3, pp. 30–31; *Survey* for 1927, pp. 301–15; *Survey* for 1930, pp. 125–7.

[3] See above, p. 337.   [4] Beloff, ii. 164, note; i. 90–91.

[5] Armistice Convention of 11 November 1918, article xii (*H.P.C.* i. 463–4 and 345–6).

[6] Cf. Stalin, op. cit. pp. 601–2.

[7] Cf. Maisky's speech in London of 15 March 1939, quoted in Beloff, ii. 229.

[8] Cf. F. A. Voigt: *Unto Caesar* (London, Constable, 1938), pp. 259–62. The process of Western enlightenment about Russian territorial ambitions was yet to come. Like the process of enlightenment about German policy it passed through two stages. The Russian share in the partition of Poland in September 1939 corresponded to the German annexations of Austria and the Sudetenland, causing disquiet which might still be met by the specious arguments of irredentism. The Russian attack on Finland in November 1939 corresponded to the German occupation of Prague on 15 March 1939, finally dispelling illusions (though there was only a partial comparison between the two events, since the Russian motive was primarily one of strategic defence; cf. Beloff, ii. 304–5). It was the latent Russian tendency towards aggrandizement, more clearly

feared Russia as a revolutionary Power most to exaggerate her military weakness.

Secondly, the principal conflict of interests between the Great Powers on 15 March 1939 was the conflict between the Western Powers and the Axis. The German conquest of Czechoslovakia was a defeat primarily for France, for it was France and not Russia that had been predominant in Eastern Europe since 1919. It put the Great Power status of France, not of Russia, in immediate danger.[1] The conflicts of interest between the Western Powers or the Axis Powers on the one side and Russia on the other side were as yet potential. The conflict between Germany and Russia was at one remove from the existing situation, the conflict between the Western Powers and Russia was at several removes.

But if the main conflict was between the Axis and the Western Powers, it followed that the third party, Russia, held the balance of power. From September 1938 to August 1939 the central question of world politics was which way Russia would go, and thus in the six months after the German seizure of Prague the Anglo-Russian negotiations became 'the tragic core of diplomatic history'.[2] And since the immediate bearing of German aggression was against Western rather than Russian interests, Germany had an immediate advantage to offer Russia which the Western Powers lacked—exclusion from the coming war. The Western Powers were soliciting a defensive alliance, Germany asked only neutrality. 'What could England offer Russia?' said the German Foreign Ministry official Schnurre to the chief of the Soviet trade mission in Berlin in July 1939.

At best, participation in a European war and the hostility of Germany, but not a single desirable end for Russia. What could we offer, on the other hand? Neutrality and staying out of a possible European conflict and, if Moscow

seen by the Western governments than by their peoples, that underlay the failure of the Western Powers and Russia to come to an agreement in the summer of 1939 about assistance to the states bordering Russia in the event of German aggression.

[1] See above, pp. 276–7. Churchill, with his clear vision of the balance of power, saw that Britain's position also as a Great Power was at stake after Munich. 'The question which we have to vote upon, in my opinion, is little less than this: Are we going to make a supreme additional effort to remain a great Power, or are we going to slide away into what seem to be easier, softer, less strenuous, less harassing courses, with all the tremendous renunciations which that decision implies?', speech in House of Commons, 17 November 1938 (H.C.Deb. 5th ser., vol. 341, col. 1145). Cf. his speech in the Munich debate of 5 October 1938: '. . . few things could be more fatal to our remaining chances of survival as a great Power than that this country should be torn in twain upon this deadly issue of foreign policy at a moment when, whoever the Ministers may be, united effort can alone make us safe' (ibid. vol. 339, coll. 371–2).

[2] Namier: *Diplomatic Prelude*, p. 143. 'If ever there was a chance of avoiding a second world war, that chance lay in a defensive alliance between the Western Powers and Soviet Russia' (Namier: 'The Russo-German Treaty of 1939', *The Listener*, 1 September 1949, p. 355; cf. '1939: How War Came', by the same author in ibid., 11 March 1948, p. 429). 'But how improvidently foolish we should be when dangers are so great, to put needless barriers in the way of the general association of the great Russian mass with the resistance to an act of Nazi aggression', Churchill, speech at Manchester, 9 May 1938 (*The Times*, 10 May 1938); cf. speech in the House of Commons, 13 April 1939 (H.C.Deb. 5th ser., vol. 346, coll. 34–35).

wished, a German-Russian understanding on mutual interests which, just as in former times, would work out to the advantage of both countries.[1]

Here the various factors were summed up: that Germany was setting the pace, that her immediate conflict of interests was with the Western Powers, that Russia held the balance, and that Germany could offer her the supreme advantage of exemption from immediate war. The Western Powers could not outbid Germany unless they could convince Russia that the defensive alliance with them would prevent war altogether. This was the old theory of collective security; the record of the Western Powers had made it improbable that Russia should any longer accept it.

The Russian disengagement from the Western Powers and withdrawal into a position of diplomatic freedom had begun immediately after Munich.[2] On 10 March 1939 Stalin addressed the Eighteenth Congress of the Communist Party of the Soviet Union. He declared that the Munich period of appeasement was already ended. (It was the day after the Czech Cabinet had dismissed Tiso from the government of Slovakia, the day before Bürckel and Seyss-Inquart intervened at Bratislava to order Sidor to proclaim Slovak independence.)[3] He described the Fascist Powers as a military bloc of aggressors, but interpreted German designs on the Ukraine as a 'hullabaloo raised by the British, French and American press', and said that the Soviet Union wanted to strengthen business relations with all countries. (This might be a gesture towards Germany.) He described the Western Powers as non-aggressive and democratic, but denounced their policy of non-intervention, and said that the Soviet Union would not be drawn into conflicts by warmongers who were accustomed to have others pull the chestnuts out of the fire for them. (This might be a warning to the Western Powers.)[4] The speech was closely studied in Germany at the time and considered as encouraging;[5] and five months later, when the German-Russian Pact had been signed and Ribbentrop was drinking toasts with the Soviet chiefs in the Kremlin, Molotov 'raised his glass to Stalin, remarking that it had been Stalin who—through his

---

[1] Memorandum by Schnurre of 27 July 1939 (*Nazi-Soviet Relations*, p. 34).

[2] 'The earliest definite sign of a reconciliation between Germany and Soviet Russia, following the estrangement of 1932 and subsequently, occurred in the autumn of 1938, when the two Governments formally agreed to reduce to tolerable proportions the attacks against each current in the public press of the other' (De Witt C. Poole: 'Light on Nazi Foreign Policy', *Foreign Affairs*, October 1946, p. 141).

[3] See *Survey* for 1938, iii, part I, sections x (*b*) and xi (*a*).

[4] Stalin, op. cit. pp. 603, 605–6.

[5] *New York Times*, 12 March 1939; *Temps*, 15 March 1939; Beloff, ii. 226–7. 'The Germans saw a second and clearer sign when, in the spring of 1939, Stalin in a public address asserted that even violent contradiction in outlook and governmental forms need not constitute an obstacle to practical co-operation between two states having common interest in concrete matters, and Moscow let Britain know informally (the Germans said) that this utterance was spoken with Germany particularly in mind' (De Witt C. Poole, loc. cit.). But the version of Stalin's speech in the translation of the eleventh edition of *Problems of Leninism* contains no such passage.

speech of March of this year, which had been well understood in Germany
—had brought about the reversal in political relations'.[1] This became the
official legend about the speech for Soviet politicians praising the German-
Soviet Pact and for discredited German politicians trying to exculpate
themselves by inculpating Russia.[2] But it was an *ex post facto* interpretation
which exaggerated Stalin's gesture towards Germany, for the speech could
equally well have been cited to prove his statesmanship if events had gone
the other way and Russia had alined herself with the Western Powers.
In fact the speech was cautious and non-committal; it emphasized Russia's
detachment, and said that she was prepared to negotiate with either side.[3]
On 15 March 1939 the positive movement towards Germany can scarcely
be said to have begun; in so far as these things can be estimated, the
pendulum was at the middle point of its swing; and, just as Germany then
possessed her maximum freedom of action as aggressor, so Russia enjoyed
perhaps her maximum freedom as holder of the balance of power.

This fluid threefold arrangement of power not only made it uncertain
on what alinements the coming war would be fought. It also showed,
though few saw it at the time, that those alinements would be temporary
and precarious. The victors in the war, whoever they were, would be only
an incongruous *ad hoc* combination of Powers. If the Axis were to defeat
the Western Powers with the co-operation or the benevolent neutrality of
Russia, the Axis and Russia would not be likely thereafter to set up an
international organization for the harmonious future ordering of the world.
Alternatively if Germany with the tacit encouragement of the Western
Powers were to conquer Russia, the turn of the Western Powers would
follow. Even if the Axis Powers by their unaided strength were to defeat
successively both the Western Powers and Russia, partitioning the world
between themselves, it would soon become clear that the Axis was a fortuitous coalition for predatory purposes, and Germany and Japan would
probably proceed to a further struggle for ultimate mastery. And if the
Western Powers in alliance with Russia were to defeat the Axis, the future
co-operation of such ill-assorted and suspicious partners could only be
assumed by those who ignored the gulf between the Byzantino-Marxist
ideology of the Soviet Union and the liberalism of the West.

[1] *Nazi-Soviet Relations*, p. 76. When Ribbentrop on the same occasion remarked that Hitler
had interpreted the speech as expressing a wish for better relations with Germany, Stalin replied
briefly: 'That was the intention' (Gaus's affidavit, *I.M.T. Nuremberg*, xl. 297).
[2] Cf. Molotov's speech to the Supreme Soviet, 31 August 1939 (*Soviet Peace Policy*, p. 16); cf.
Documents (R.I.I.A.) for 1939–46, i. 437; see also Ribbentrop's evidence (*I.M.T. Nuremberg*
x. 267) and Seidl's plea for the defence (ibid. xix. 366).
[3] See I. Deutscher: *Stalin: A Political Biography* (London, Oxford University Press, 1949),
pp. 429–30. Namier (*Diplomatic Prelude*, pp. 286–7; *Europe in Decay*, p. 260) minimizes the significance of the speech; cf. Max Beloff: 'Professor Namier and the Prelude to War', *Fortnightly*,
April 1950, p. 237. A. Rossi (*Deux ans d'alliance germano-soviétique* (Paris, Fayard, 1949), pp.
19–21) exaggerates it.

INDEX